Challenging Immigration and Ethnic Relations Politics

Challenging Immigration and Ethnic Relations Politics

Comparative European Perspectives

Edited by

RUUD KOOPMANS

and

PAUL STATHAM

OXFORD
UNIVERSITY PRESS

*This book has been printed digitally and produced in a standard specification
in order to ensure its continuing availability*

OXFORD
UNIVERSITY PRESS

Great Clarendon Street, Oxford OX2 6DP

Oxford University Press is a department of the University of Oxford.
It furthers the University's objective of excellence in research, scholarship,
and education by publishing worldwide in

Oxford New York

Auckland Bangkok Buenos Aires Cape Town Chennai
Dar es Salaam Delhi Hong Kong Istanbul Karachi Kolkata
Kuala Lumpur Madrid Melbourne Mexico City Mumbai Nairobi
São Paulo Shanghai Taipei Tokyo Toronto

Oxford is a registered trade mark of Oxford University Press
in the UK and in certain other countries

Published in the United States
by Oxford University Press Inc., New York

ISBN 0-19- 829561-8

Preface

The idea for this volume dates from a Conference that was held at the Department of Public Sphere and Social Movements at the Wissenschaftszentrum Berlin WZB (Science Centre), in November 1997. At that time we were setting out rather blindly having launched ourselves into a comparative research project on migration and ethnic relations politics. The Conference event was enormously helpful in providing an opportunity to learn new approaches to the subject matter and meet a new 'tribe' from the academic community, after years of frequenting the circles of social movements scholars. Although it has its origins in the Conference, the present volume is a project in its own right. Most of the chapters from contributors who attended the Conference have changed beyond recognition from the presented papers. In addition, the volume draws on contributors whom we met along the road from then until now, and whose research fitted well with our stated objectives. We take this opportunity to thank the many friends and colleagues who contributed to the Conference, this volume and our understanding of the topic. We would also like to thank the generous support of the WZB for the Conference event, and Dominic Byatt and Amanda Watkins at OUP for their professional help in bringing the idea to fruition. Finally, Claudia Daheim at the WZB, deserves a mention for taking on the onerous task of formatting the various parts into a whole document. We hope that you find the end-product worthwhile!

Ruud Koopmans and Paul Statham

Berlin and Leeds, April 2000

Contents

List of Figures

List of Tables

List of Contributors

Tore Björgo, Senior Research Fellow at the Norwegian Institute of International Affairs, and affiliated researcher at the Norwegian Police Academy and the University of Leiden.

Roger Eatwell, Professor of Politics, University of Bath, UK.

Han Entzinger, Professor of Social Sciences, Utrecht University, The Netherlands. Academic Director of the interuniversity Netherlands School for Social and Economic Policy Research (AWSB). President of the Research Committee on Migration of the International Sociological Association.

Adrian Favell, Lecturer, Sussex Centre for Migration Research, School of European Studies, University of Sussex, UK.

Meindert Fennema, Associate Professor of Political Theory, University of Amsterdam, The Netherlands.

Romain Garbaye, Doctoral Student in Politics Worcester College, University of Oxford, UK.

Andrew Geddes, Senior Lecturer, School of Politics and Communication Studies, University of Liverpool, UK.

Patrick Ireland, Associate Professor, Sam Nunn School of International Affairs, Georgia Institute of Technology, Atlanta, GA, USA; and Co-Director, EU Center of the University System of Georgia.

Christian Joppke, Professor of Sociology, European University Institute, Florence, Italy.

Roger Karapin, Associate Professor, Dept. of Political Science, Hunter College, New York, USA.

Ruud Koopmans, Senior Researcher, Wissenschaftszentrum (Science Centre) Berlin, Germany.

Cathie Lloyd, Director, Centre for Cross Cultural Research on Women, International Development Centre, University of Oxford, UK.

John Rex, Professor Emeritus, Centre for Research in Ethnic Relations, University of Warwick, UK.

Liza K. Schuster, Research Fellow, Faculty of Humanities and Social Science, South Bank University, London, UK.

John Solomos, Professor of Sociology, Faculty of Humanities and Social Science, South Bank University, London, UK.

Paul Statham, Senior Research Fellow and Director of the Centre for European Political Communications (Eur Pol Com), Institute of Communications Studies, University of Leeds, UK.

Dietrich Thränhardt, Faculty of Political Science, Wilhelm University Westfalia, Munster, Germany.

1

Introduction

RUUD KOOPMANS and PAUL STATHAM

Over the last decade migration and ethnic relations have emerged as contentious political issues across Europe. Manifest in public divisions between political elites over asylum, urban riots by youths of migrant descent against perceived police discrimination, and the emergence of extreme-right political parties, to name but a few examples, conflicts over such issues have left their imprint on the politics of all European nations, as well as becoming subject to the emergent transnational levels of authority such as the European Union. Previously a rather benign and marginal policy field, migration and ethnic relations politics are now seen as central problems to the working of liberal democracies by policy-makers and academics alike.

New migration and, in particular, waves of asylum seekers in the 1990s have provided the lighted touch-paper for explosive public conflicts and deep rifts among political elites over the important questions of national identity and citizenship. This occurred at a time when the sovereign state powers of European countries already felt themselves under threat from globalization and the emergence of transnational governance in the European Union. In addition, a new political assertiveness has been evident among migrants and minorities in their societies of settlement. Their demands for rights as groups organized along ethnic, national, or religious lines, have provoked reactions, both xenophobic and supportive, from groups of the majority population in the public domain. Challenged by threats of globalization from without and pluralization from within, the public discourses of liberal democratic nation-states have been characterized by waves of political controversies over migration and ethnic relations issues, where elite responses have sometimes been more likely to provoke a further escalation in public disputes than rational policy 'solutions'. It appears that within Europe at least, such political controversies over immigration and ethnic relations are set to run and run. The objective behind bringing together the contributions for this volume was to give a timely academic intervention into the debates over the nature of migration and ethnic relations politics in contemporary Europe.

After a slow start, academic research has started to address the challenge of this new politicized and public dimension of migration and ethnic relations politics. This collected volume explicitly aims to carry this research agenda forward by promoting a more systematic and integrated approach to the variety of theoretical and methodological frameworks that have addressed this problematic. More specifically, we felt that the field of research could benefit, firstly, from more systematic cross-national comparison, secondly, from the linkage of policy-centric analyses with collective action, and thirdly, from a greater cross-thematic conceptualization, so that the clearly related topics of ethnic relations and xenophobia are no longer dealt with as largely distinct fields of research.

Although a plurality of different perspectives are present in the volume, the contributions have been organized within a framework that makes a concerted effort to adhere to the goals of a more integrated research agenda that is based on cross-national comparative insights. The volume is divided into four sections. In the first, authors offer conceptual approaches to migration and ethnic relations politics drawing strongly on cross-national observations; whereas the substantive contributions on the more institutionalized aspects of migrations and ethnic relations politics in section two, and the more public contentious dimensions in section three, are all empirical analyses based on a method of systematic cross-national comparison. Lastly, in light of the important claims that nation-states are no longer the significant framework of reference for political actors in migration and ethnic relations, the contributions to section four address aspects of the emergence of the transnational level of political authority, and its implications for political approaches at national and subnational levels, and challenges by social movements.

After briefly tracing the shortcomings and advances of the study of migration and ethnic relations politics, particularly in the 1990s, in the first part of Chapter 2 we outline our reasons for advocating steps towards a more systematic, comparative, and theoretically and thematically integrated research agenda. The benefits of comparative cross-national research in this field have been widely recognized for some time, though strict comparison has often been eschewed for edited volumes consisting of largely unrelated and descriptive single-country cases. Similarly, advocating a greater acknowledgement of the importance of political mobilization by both migrant/minority and xenophobic actors in migration and ethnic relations politics is a rather obvious step in the wake of the undoubted politicization of the field, but one which has been relatively neglected. After fulfilling the task of a conventional introduction and setting the scene, we set our sights directly on the more partisan objective of outlining our own conceptual approach to the topic.

Our substantive aim in chapter 2 is to propose a set of conceptual tools that is better equipped for a more systematic, comparative, and better-integrated type of analysis. Drawing inspiration from recent debates on citizenship, we distinguish between formal rights and the cultural obligations which are placed by countries on access to citizenship. These axes define the conceptual political space for the migrations and ethnic relations approaches of different countries. Lest this approach appear too schematic or static, we advocate the utility of a political opportunity structure perspective, that has been successfully applied in cross-national and longitudinal studies of social movements since the mid-1980s, but seldom to the topic of migrations and ethnic relations politics. This approach allows us to account for the institutional and discursive dimensions of politics that explain how conflicts over migration and ethnic relations differ cross-nationally, and which determine to what extent specific countries may be open to challenges 'from below' by xenophobic or migrant/minority actors. Lastly, in a volume dedicated to cross-national comparison, we challenge the recent theoretical assumptions of transnational and postnational citizenship that, in our opinion, have called time somewhat prematurely on the political authority of the nation-state.

Chapters 3 and 4 in the first section are less directly concerned with approaches to research, and focus more on the substance of the migration and ethnic relations topic. Both the contributions of John Rex and John Solomos/Liza Schuster give general accounts of the ways in which political conflicts and dilemmas over migration and ethnic relations have become manifest in liberal democratic states. Drawing on a lifetime's experience and path-breaking research in the field, Rex strongly argues in Chapter 3, that it is necessary to look at the structural relation between societies and the policies which they develop with regard to the collective mobilization by migrant communities themselves. Starting from a discussion of different national approaches to migrant minorities, he outlines the potential and pitfalls of the different policy approaches which come under the label of 'multiculturalism'. Rex advocates—as he has done consistently—the benefits of a 'limited multiculturalism', which he argues can strengthen democracy by stimulating the participation of ethnic minority groups, in part through their collective action in democratic institutions. For Rex, 'limited multiculturalism' makes it easier for liberal anti-racist allies to back minorities, whereas more radical forms of multicultural policies would pose a threat to the integrity of society, potentially provoking racist reactions, and possibly contributing to the institutionalization of the inferiority of ethnic minority communities. Clearly, with a critical eye on the contribution by Solomos and Schuster, Rex argues that the assault on racism requires a focus on social structures as well as on bodies of ideas. In Chapter 4, John Solomos and Liza Schuster focus on conflicts over meanings of citizenship, identity, and cultural difference that resonate in public debates on multiculturalism as a form of 'identity politics'. Building on the current trend within academia for seeing the political expression of cultural diversity by minority groups as a central feature of contemporary societies, they argue that such conflicts are indicative of the new modes of social, economic, and cultural exclusion facing minorities, and increasingly complex forms of ethnic and racial identities. Seeing political struggle by minorities as manifest in discourses about identity and belonging, Solomos and Schuster make a plea for new concepts and political strategies that will transcend the existing notions of racism and multiculturalism, both of which have a tendency toward essentializing cultural difference when translated out into the social world.

In the second section of the volume, authors focus on the political institutional strategies that have been used by different countries for responding to the dilemmas thrown up by conflicts over immigration, the presence of migrants and minorities, and xenophobic reactions by members of the majority population.

Han Entzinger sets the scene in Chapter 5, by defining a typology for policy approaches that different European states have applied with the aim of integrating migrants and minorities into their national societies. For Entzinger the holy grail of a successful integration policy will ultimately remain elusive, as the different variables that make up an approach are founded on conceptions of nation, state, and market that are by necessity in tension. His six-fold typology distinguishes between the legal-political, cultural, and socio-economic dimensions of integration—derived from this nation, state, and market distinction—and argues that incorporation can be designed for either groups (communitarianism) or individuals (liberalism). Entzinger argues that this typology of incorporation approaches is preferable to typologies of countries, which he sees as prone to reification and caricatures. Countries which apply similar policies in one domain may diverge importantly in others. In addition, the consequences of policies are not experienced evenly by different types of migrants and minorities within a single country. In general, he argues for a pragmatic and sensitive domain-specific comparison of policy approaches, that will facilitate cross-national learning processes.

In Chapter 6, Meindert Fennema switches our attention to the development of policies by which liberal democratic states seek to repress racial discrimination and xenophobia by politically mobilized sections of the majority population against minorities and migrants. Fennema traces how liberal democracies in post-war Europe used the trauma of the Nazi period, and in many cases occupation, as the basis for legitimating the repression of neo-fascist political sentiments and expressions. 'Militant democracy' had no political space for the fascist propaganda which had so recently threatened to overthrow its liberal values. When anti-immigrant political sentiment emerged in response to large scale immigration to Europe, however, liberal democratic states' attempts to legitimate 'anti-racist' principles by referring to a 'human equality' principle were less consensual. Outlawing freedom of expression—even of what the majority may consider harmful racist sentiments—presents a challenge to the self-legitimating basis of liberal democracies, and a dilemma that is not easily resolved. Indeed Fennema shows how this has led to ongoing conflicts between different political factions and between intellectuals, especially in countries such as France, Belgium, and Austria, where the ideological cleavages manifest in the Fascist era remain a basis for political division. More generally, Western

European liberal democracies have experienced difficulties in finding a philosophical basis for justifying 'anti-racism' that fits easily within their cultural tradition, without provoking reactions from liberals and xenophobes alike.

Cultural traditions and their relationship to formal citizenship rights are also a focus for Chapter 7, where Christian Joppke offers up the latest instalment from his impressive cross-national comparative research. Joppke's contribution argues that Rogers Brubaker's influential concept of national citizenship as a form of symbolic closure is incomplete, as it is unable to account for fundamental changes from one type of citizenship model to another. Departing from Brubaker, and to some extent from his own previous work, Joppke describes what he sees as the defeat of ethnicity-based citizenship traditions in Germany, by looking at the counter-cultural norms that were available to elites for mobilizing opposition, regardless of public opinion. His contrast to the United States, where the dominant inclusive citizenship approach proves resistant to counter-cultural challenges, is used to make the claim that there is a general normative tendency within all liberal democracies for a more inclusive citizenship, which is upheld and preciously guarded by legal elites. However, if Germany was inevitably bound to shed itself of the historical anomaly of denying political rights to migrants, then we might plausibly ask, what are the factors which caused it to take this step when it did?

Dietrich Thränhardt, in Chapter 8, takes up the dimensions of the political process which may account for such contingencies. Germany is again compared to a country that has a more inclusive political approach toward integrating migrants and minorities, this time a European country, The Netherlands. Thränhardt's study, like Joppke's, goes some way to exploding the cliché that Germany's longstanding tradition for ethnic exclusionist citizenship is uni-dimensionally 'bad' when compared to the more inclusionist Netherlands. Presumably, Entzinger would also approve of the way Thränhardt compares the different political and social dimensions of approaches in relation to their outcomes. First, Thränhardt sets about explaining how such close neighbours came up with such radically different approaches for dealing with migrants and their descendants. Of key importance was the role of political elite responses to migration, and the relationship of immigrants to the host society. Elite consensus in The Netherlands confined the issue to policy experimentation behind closed doors. In Germany, by contrast, open party-political competition raged, leading to trenchant public 'left-right' cleavages over immigration that were highly resistant to the formation of an elite consensus. When judged by social outcomes for migrant populations, however, the lack of political rights for Germany's 'Ausländer' has not prevented them from achieving significantly higher levels of employment and experiencing less segregation in schools than their Dutch minority counterparts. These advances for German migrants have been made in part through collective action and participation in trade unions, which has offset their formal exclusion from the most visible part of the political arena. Moreover, the Dutch case shows that political approaches based on inclusive formal citizenship and cultural pluralism are no guarantees of minority/migrant integration within the society of settlement. Indeed they may simply reinforce national myths of presumed 'tolerance' among the majority population, leading to complacency about the reality of minority and migrant participation in society.

Moving on from the national policy approaches supported by elite strategies, the third section of the book focuses directly on the political process in the field of migration and ethnic relations, by looking at the challenges that are mobilized by minority and migrants in the public domain, and the reactions by their xenophobic opponents among sections of the majority population.

The first three contributions to this section focus on different aspects of ethnic mobilization and their political outcomes. In Chapter 9, our own contribution compares political claims-making by minorities in Britain and Germany. Drawing from an original data source on collective claims-making, the central objective is to test whether the claims made in postnational and multicultural citizenship theories—namely, that political mobilization by minorities is fundamentally challenging the authority of the nation-state— are supported by empirical evidence. On the contrary, our findings show that far from being symbolic leftovers from a bygone era, the nation-state continues to be the overriding dominant frame of reference for the identities, organizations, and claims of minorities and migrants, and that national authorities are the almost exclusive addressee of their political demands. Moreover the striking differences in minority claims-making between the two countries closely mirror the ways in which the nation-state defines the relationship between minorities and the political community. This leads us to conclude that national institutions and discourses of citizenship continue to shape minority and migrant mobilization today, despite the fashion within academia for focusing—largely in the absence of evidence—on the global and plural characteristics of migrant mobilization as the sweeping winds of fundamental change.

In a similar vein, the contribution by Patrick Ireland in Chapter 10 takes the different national institutional approaches to minorities and migrants as 'political opportunity structures' that have shaped minority and migrant patterns of political participation in their societies of settlement. Building on his earlier influential perspective, Ireland's five-country comparison finds that the persistent differences in policy approaches, institutional contexts, and migrant participatory patterns across France, The Netherlands, Belgium, Germany, and Switzerland show that top-down institutional factors provide better explanations for the paths taken by migrant participation than bottom-up group characteristics of 'class' or 'ethnicity'. According to Ireland, however, processes of decentralization across Europe mean that we should increasingly address our attention to the local level of political institutional arrangements that structure the opportunities for migrant participation, as in some cases local-level differences are becoming greater than national differences.

Romain Garbaye's city-level comparison between the management strategies for dealing with ethnic diversity in Birmingham in Britain and Lille in France, presented in Chapter 11, would presumably meet with Ireland's approval. Garbaye's analysis is locally focused and emphasizes that the differences between minority political activism in the two cities are the result of the different institutional strategies which are pursued. Importantly, however, his study also shows that city-level politics is located within a national profile for politics. Thus the relationship between central and local politics in the two countries determines the autonomy which cities have to act and implement policies designed to their local needs. In addition, differences in party systems and styles of government—'parliamentary' British versus 'presidential' French politics—at the city level, have an important impact in structuring the way that politics opens or closes the door to minority and migrant populations. In this view, the city-level analysis constitutes a refined extension and not a replacement of the analysis of national differences.

Turning to the opponents of migrants and minorities, Roger Karapin in Chapter 12 examines the causal relationships between anti-immigrant political campaigns and anti-immigrant riots, by comparing periods of mobilization in Britain and Germany. Echoing the thoughts of Fennema, he concludes that liberal immigration policies are vulnerable to reactions from racist and xenophobic mobilization, and that these tend to develop rapidly and have the greatest political impact when combining routine and violent forms of collective action. At such peaks of mobilization, the escalation of issues is carried by anti-immigrant political campaigns and violent public reactions that are mutually reinforcing, at least in the short term. In the long-term, the cultural cleavages which provide the spark for hostile reactions to new migrants are likely to die down, as strategies for mediating conflicts between majority and minority publics become commonplace, routine, and institutionalized. Anti-immigrant rioting is thus likely to have a limited shelf-life within the repertoire of xenophobic political movements, though when cultural cleavages re-emerge, such as in the aftermath of German reunification at a time of massive inflows of asylum-seeking migrants, such features may be more than an unsavoury anecdote in the history of contemporary liberal democratic societies.

Whereas Karapin looks at the political impact of the most extreme forms of public reaction to the presence of migrants, and their relation to more conventional forms of political expression by referring to social movements, Roger Eatwell in Chapter 13 aims to explain the electoral breakthroughs of political parties that express ethnocentric and xenophobic sentiments into mainstream party politics. Arguing against narrow rational-choice theories of voting for ethnocentric political parties, Eatwell's discussion of instances of extreme-right

electoral successes in the local and national politics of several European countries emphasizes the importance of explanations that link voter self-perceptions
to political, institutional, and systemic contexts. Right-wing voting is thus more
than an expression of blind protest, it is most likely under conditions where,
firstly, an ethnocentric party acquires legitimacy often through elite or mass
media sponsorship, and secondly, in which a general decline in political trust
coincides with an increase in the perceived efficacy of certain individuals and
groups. These factors can become rapidly reinforcing and dynamic, which in
part explains why ethnocentric party mobilization often emerges as a sudden
'breakthrough' on the public and political stage.

In Chapter 14, Tore Björgo draws from the Scandinavian experience of
ethnic conflicts at the local level. Away from the realm of conventional politics,
Björgo argues that youth violence ought not be reduced simply to specific
ideological or political motives. His 'hands on' study of instances of violent
youth conflict between different ethnic groups sees competition over territory
and women as important causal factors, reminiscent in part of the cultural
cleavages that Karapin also sees as an initial stimulus for violent reaction. In
addition, Björgo argues that youths often use racist forms of expression strategically, due to their effective way of challenging existing social and interper-
sonal relations. Of course, this does not make racism any less real, in an
objective sense, in the way it is perceived by the victim and its damaging effect
on society as a whole. But according to Björgo, it is the task of politics to both
control and repress the contexts which lead to violent behaviour, and at the
same time provide channels, outlets, and alternatives for youth expression that
are less damaging to society.

In the final section of the volume, the contributors focus on the transnational level of politics. In the light of theories of globalization and postnational
citizenship that have risen to prominence in the field through the work of
authors such as Saskia Sassen and Yasemin Soysal, the two chapters in this
section assess to what extent national forms of political action are being transformed by the emergence of the EU level of governance.

In Chapter 15, Cathie Lloyd points out the severe limitations and barriers
to transnational mobilization faced by anti-racist movements in Europe. Not
least of these is that they come from different national contexts and face different country-specific problems, often from a resource-weak organizational
position. Thus, defining the common European ground for an agenda for
bottom-up transnational anti-racist mobilization is seldom a self-apparent
immediate concern of most anti-racist movements. Moreover, the European
Union offers little in the way of a transnational civil society and subsequent
political opportunities for anti-racism beyond shallow symbolic gestures. In as
far as European initiatives and funding provide opportunities for anti-racist
organizations, there is a real danger of co-optation and detachment from grass
roots support.

The Europeanization of migration and ethnic relations politics is discussed systematically in Chapter 16 by Adrian Favell and Andrew Geddes. In a fitting finale to this volume, and pointing to an important direction for future research, Favell and Geddes argue that Europeanization and globalization are far from co-terminous processes. Cutting through the theoretical literature that starts from such a premise, Favell and Geddes argue that it only makes sense to look for a European 'transnational opportunity structure' as an empirical phenomenon, in those spheres where EU political power has actually taken on institutional forms. Contrary to recent academic mythology, these are as yet highly limited, uneven across policy domains, and open principally to organized technocratic and judicial elites, and thus hardly welcoming to a transnational social movement of migrants. In fact, the emergent European conceptions of citizenship are nation-state derivatives, and the EU should be seen as a region-ally located co-operation of nations that in some respects prevents globaliza-tion as well as being a cause, source, and symptom of it. From this ambivalent starting point, the EU is hardly likely to be a source of inspiration for the kinds of universalistic global values at the basis of visions of postnational member-ship. In fact, what is needed is more empirical research on the links between the transnational and nation-state levels of authority, and the outcome this has on mobilization by migrants and minorities at the local, national, or transna-tional level.

I

Conceptual Approaches

2

Migration and Ethnic Relations as a Field of Political Contention: An Opportunity Structure Approach

RUUD KOOPMANS and PAUL STATHAM

Introduction

Immigration politics, that is, a state's capacity to regulate immigration, is intimately related to the field of ethnic relations politics, the contentious politics where a state's policies deal with resident migrants and minorities, and where influential political actors such as parties and interest groups, and majority and minority publics, dispute the criteria for entry to the national community. Since countries in Europe put up restrictive policy barriers to new immigration in the early 1970s (Baldwin-Edwards and Schain 1994), conflicts over ethnic relations have become explicitly politicized issues focused on the social, political, and cultural integration of resident migrants, minorities, and their offspring into the nation state. Meanwhile debates over new immigration have been framed predominantly through the issue of political asylum. This emergence of ethnic relations and immigration as a central issue within European polities was especially apparent in the 1990s, due in no small part to the emergence of migrants and minorities themselves as influential political actors making demands within the framework of national politics. In many cases these demands provoked reactions, both xenophobic and supportive, from mobilized sections of the majority public, and political responses, both liberal and restrictive, from the state. In addition, the multi-levelled nature of political responses, where supranational EU policies, and national and local policies compete for sovereignty to make decisions and implement measures, has arguably made ethnic relations politics and immigration a challenge to the nation-state (Joppke 1998).

Starting from a position where European countries implemented starkly contrasting policy approaches for the migrant populations who stayed on to become permanent residents, ethnic relations politics would appear to be a prima-facie case for testing the degree of convergence or divergence in Europe, brought by the globalizing pressures of increasing supranational political influence, and especially EU governance. At the same time, since national approaches to migration and ethnic relations are closely tied up with issues of national identity and belonging, resonant political conflicts over whether or not states should acknowledge cultural diversity as a legitimate basis for giving special rights of recognition or redress to groups from migrant populations, have been apparent across the continent, often framed explicitly around the issue of Islam in Western societies. The ethnic pluralization of European countries, a product of past immigration and contemporary flows of asylum seekers, refugees, and illegal immigrants, plus the increased assertiveness of resident minorities within national and local politics, is a disputed issue in many national polities often heated up by the dynamics of public confrontation and street violence. Trapped within this pressure cooker of globalizing and pluralizing strains, national variants for ethnic relations and migration policies seem increasingly incapable of fulfilling the political demands that different actors make on the nation-state. This gap between the delivery capacity of states' policies and the increasingly acute and conflicting political aspirations—often diametrically opposed—of actors entering the field, has transformed ethnic relations and migration into a central field of political contention across Western Europe.

Following the agenda set in the introduction, the primary objective of this chapter is not to provide an exhaustive literature review of research on migration, ethnic relations, and xenophobia. Instead we aim to specify the important developments that have contributed to the emergence of a more comparative and politics-focused paradigm for research in the 1990s, and to identify persistent gaps and missing links, before proposing an integrative theoretical framework that draws on social movement and collective action approaches, and links national citizenship to a political opportunity perspective.

Prior to the recent resurgence of academic interest in migration and ethnic relations in response to the politicization of the issue in the 1990s, much of the literature can be categorized by three main research topics: migration studies and integration policy approaches, minority/migrant associations and collective action, and extreme-right politics and xenophobic mobilization. Surprisingly, given their overlapping concerns, these approaches have remained largely distinct from one another.

Much research in the migration studies tradition tends to focus rather apolitically on social structural, socio-economic, and demographic aspects of migrations flows (for a criticism, see Miller 1981, 1982).[1] To the extent that it considers political processes at all, this approach is dominated by policy-centric accounts focusing on élite concerns. Often based on statistics drawn from official sources or designed to collect information for state bodies, such approaches see migrants themselves primarily as passive 'objects' of policies for incorporation into the national host society, with the patterns of their presence strongly determined by economic and demographic trends and cycles, for example, in the labour market, housing, or education (e.g., Vermeulen and Penninx 1994; Münz, Seifert, and Ulrich 1997). The dominant focus is on social and economic integration of migrants in a welfare-state perspective. Little consideration is given in this context to non-elite actors, or the political process in general.

Among the research which addresses such criticisms by focusing on the relationship between minorities/migrants, their collective action, and the host society, two main approaches prevail: those operating within a class paradigm, and those within a race or ethnicity paradigm (see Ireland 1994, and Chapter 10 in this volume). Class theory provides a suitable framework for extending the underprivileged structural and socio-economic position of migrants in the host society into a theory that refers to political participation and migrant action (e.g., Castles and Kosack 1974, 1985; Miles 1982; Miles and Phizacklea 1977, 1984). Here economic divisions within the working classes are seen as racialized under the structural crises of advanced industrial capitalism. Thus shared ethnicity or race is primarily a 'class' identity and all forms of political participation by migrant and minority populations are seen as evidence for an emergent class consciousness of migrant workers. When migrant activism includes political co-operation with indigenous workers—for example, through trade union activities, and labour and communist political parties—then it becomes seen as evidence for a common class consciousness transcending the false consciousness of ethnic and racial identity. Although they at least focused on the migrants themselves and offer a relational theory that links them to the host society, these neo-marxist approaches often remain overly deterministic, tending to explain the associational activities of migrants as a condition of processes of industrial modernization in the capitalist economy, rather than as responses to the political environment. The relationship between migrants/minorities and the political institutions facing them remains undertheorized, with references to political processes limited to largely descriptive case-studies, with class basis as the dominant explanation for collective action.

The ethnicity/race paradigm is in fact, in many formulations, largely similar to the class paradigm (see e.g., Rex and Tomlinson 1979; Miller 1981, 1982). The important difference is, however, that in contrast to neo-marxist approaches the ethnic and racial collective identities of minorities and migrants are not seen simply as 'false consciousness' waiting to be unveiled by the forces of history and class warfare. On the contrary, many authors point out that the ethnic and racial identities of minorities will continue to form the basis for collective action independently from class, not least because of shared experiences of racism and discrimination in their societies of settlement. Although importantly seeing ethnic differences as a basis for societal cleavages, such approaches have a tendency to replace the socio-economic determinism of class by the cultural characteristics of the group itself—that is, 'ethnic' or 'homeland' identities—as the determinant of behaviour (e.g., Fijalkowski 1994; Schoeneberg

1985). Once more the relationship of minorities and migrants to the political institutional framework is relatively neglected in explaining levels and types of activism.

Besides theories of class and ethnicity/race, which at least focus on migrants and their collective action, even if they do not fully and systematically relate this to the political process, there is another research tradition which makes a more direct link between social structure and collective behaviour. Taking a cue from Durkheimian sociological traditions, this research uses models of socioeconomic change and ethnic competition between migrants and majority populations for taking phenomena such as xenophobic violence and urban riots as indicators of social disintegration. Through this lens, the consequences of migration on the economy create pressures that translate into psychological frustrations and anomie among the 'losers of the modernization process' (Heitmeyer et al. 1992) who respond to increasing social inequalities by violent mobilization. Riots over ethnic difference—explained by perceptions of relative deprivation held by different ethnic groups—are routinely taken as evidence for a breakdown in the 'social order'.

As well as being a popular explanation in media and public discourses for riots by minorities or violent reactions against them, this approach has a strong salience in academic and policy responses to periods of race riots and ethnic urban violence. The Scarman Report, a response to the inner urban ethnic riots of the 1980s in Britain, is an example which defines policy solutions within a social integration paradigm. In addition, it has been particularly pervasive in research on extremist behaviour, shaping much of the work on xenophobic mobilization and extreme-right voting, not least because it is drawn from classical approaches for explaining the rise of pre-war fascism. More recently, this approach has been present in several guises. In research on xenophobia and support for extreme-right political parties, perpetrators of racist violence or holders of right-wing values are seen as reacting to a loss of prestige and status that is caused by structural modernization processes, such as industrialization and individualization. For a recent example of the modernization thesis, see Betz (1994). In addition, Islamic extremism in Germany has been explained by the disaffection of Turkish youth in response to a lack of social integration (Heitmeyer, Schröder, and Müller 1997). And the same logic also underpins the 'ethnic competition' approach that explains inner-urban ethnic conflict by perceptions of relative deprivation among 'white' lower classes forced to compete with migrant labour (e.g., Husbands 1993; Olzak 1992; Esser 1999).

In short then, much traditional work in the migration, ethnic relations, and xenophobia field, has not taken the political process systematically into its explanatory approach. Moreover, although they clearly relate to similar topics and have overlapping concerns, migration, ethnic relations, and xenophobia have tended to remain separate and distinct research fields. In addition, approaches drawn either from class, ethnic, or modernization theories, are strongly influenced by the dominant national integration paradigms in different countries. This insularity militates against cross-national learning processes. The specific national integration paradigms that are evident in the different ways in which European countries label migrants and minorities—as 'racial minorities' in Britain, 'immigrés' (immigrants) in France, or 'Ausländer' (foreigners) in Germany—are so strongly entrenched in the perceptions of actors and reproduced in social relationships, that this leads to a myopia toward alternative scenarios by politicians and social scientists alike. In reviewing the development of the ethnic relations fields in Britain and France, Adrian Favell (1998) has recently argued this point strongly, describing how British scholars defining everything as 'race', could find little to learn from their French colleagues' 'colour-blind' republicanism, and vice versa.

Nation-bound, inward-looking, and overly descriptive, the migration, ethnic relations, and xenophobia field remained thematically fragmented and seriously lagged behind the political and transnational developments that had carried the subject matter to the centre stage of politics by the start of the 1990s. A particular weakness was the lack of systematic cross-national research, or even cross-national references when explaining specific national cases (Bovenkerk, Miles, and Verbunt 1990). With increasing trans-European academic exchanges, in part unleashed by EU sponsorship, the 1990s witnessed an upsurge in cross-national volumes. Initially, this produced a wave of largely descriptive edited volumes in the distinct extreme-right/xenophobia and migration/ethnic relations fields, where authors from different countries offered their expertise in single-country case-studies (on ethnic relations see: Wrench and Solomos 1993; Baldwin-Edwards and Schain 1994; Rex and Drury 1994; Fassman and Münz 1996; in relation to Europe Thränhardt and Miles 1995; on extreme-right see Husbands 1993, Hainsworth 1992; and Witte 1996).

Helpful in allowing strangers to meet and talk with one other for the first time, this batch of single-country studies was seriously hamstrung in the attempt to develop common theoretical approaches, even within the two distinct disciplines. Although marked sometimes by excellent individual single-country studies, there was a generic unevenness in the substantive scope, not least because authors largely remained committed to their national interpretation of the problematic. As a result, the end product seldom measured up as a collective project. Cross-national reflection, the most telling and potentially important contribution of such projects, was often limited to either introductory or concluding essays, although some of these did develop emergent general theoretical observations (e.g., Rex and Drury 1994; Cornelius, Martin, and Hollifield 1994) that were to stimulate the group of researchers who took up a more systematic comparative research agenda. This emergent agenda for research has crystallized around three perspectives, which we want to discuss and develop in more detail in the following sections: studies of citizenship and conceptions of nationhood, neo-institutionalist and political opportunity perspectives, and finally studies that emphasize postnational and European developments transcending the nation-state.

Citizenship and Conceptions of Nationhood

One important way in which the theoretical deficit and the lack of genuinely comparative studies in the migration and ethnic relations literature has recently been addressed is through the emergence of citizenship—the set of rights, duties, and identities linking citizens to the nation-state—as a central analytic category. This interest in citizenship is rooted in the reinvigoration of the concept in wider political-philosophical debates on civil society, social cohesion, and communitarianism (e.g., Walzer 1983; Schlesinger 1992; van Steenbergen 1994; Young 1998). Particularly in the United States, there has been a strong preoccupation in these debates with the position of ethnic minorities and the beneficial or harmful effects of 'multiculturalism', the extension of cultural group recognition and rights to ethnic minorities (e.g., Taylor 1994; Kymlicka 1995; Glazer 1997; Shapiro and Kymlicka 1997). While these philosophical debates have remained largely normative and prescriptive, they have inspired a number of studies with a more empirical focus in Europe (e.g., Ålund and Schierup 1991; Rex 1996; Modood and Werbner 1997; Martiniello 1998; Parekh 1998). Faced by several *causes celèbres* across Europe, such as the Rushdie affair in Britain and the *foulard* affair in France, where fierce political controversies developed over the position of Islam in relation to the nation state, these authors took the nationally specific problems of policy approaches to cultural diversity in different European states as a starting point for revisiting the concept of citizenship. This work contributed to a greater sensitivity to the increased processes of cultural differentiation and pluralization brought by migration to European societies as both normative and policy relevant issues. However, these more empirically-oriented studies often have the disadvantage of using 'multiculturalism' in a very loose way—more or less as a fashionable alternative for 'ethnic relations' or 'minority integration'—that has sometimes little to do with the more precise meaning of a form of citizenship based on cultural recognition and group rights. Moreover, empirically, many of these studies tend to draw thinly and descriptively from a few well-known and sup- posedly representative examples.

At the same time, interest in citizenship has been revived in a somewhat dif- ferent and more focused way by the rise of nationalist and xenophobic move- ments throughout the world, and the resultant boom in academic studies addressing these phenomena (e.g., Hobsbawm 1990; Greenfield 1992; Canovan 1996; Jenkins and Sofos 1996; Calhoun 1997). Taking up the distinction between 'ethnic' and 'civic' forms of nationalism that is common in this literature, Rogers Brubaker's (1992) comparative historical work on citizenship and traditions of nationhood in France and Germany provided an important catalyst for an increase in comparative work in ethnic relations in the 1990s. Brubaker explains the divergent ways in which France and Germany have dealt with post-war migrants by the different 'cultural idioms' of citizenship—based on ethno-cultural belonging in Germany, and on civic culture and political institutions in France—that have historically guided institutional practices and legal traditions in the two nation-states. Citizenship is seen not only as a form of membership, but also as a specific cultural imprint of nationhood, which functions as a form of symbolic closure restricting, albeit to different extents and under nationally specific conditions, the ability of migrants to join the national community. Thus, Brubaker explains the persistently higher naturalization rates in France compared to Germany, by contrasting the *jus soli* acquisition of citizenship—where access is either automatic by birth on the national territory or easily available through naturalization—dominant in the French tradition of nationhood, to the *jus sanguinis* basis of citizenship—where access is difficult for those who do not have ethno-cultural ties to the nation—which is the dominant tradition in Germany. Brubaker's distinction between ethno-cultural and civic-cultural forms of citizenship largely ignores, however, the cultural rights dimension that has been central to the multiculturalism debate. Particularly, this leads him to overstate the 'openness' of the French citizenship regime, which may provide for easy formal access to citizenship, but couples this with the expectation that new citizens of migrant origin will assimilate to a unitary, national political culture.

It therefore seems fruitful to combine the cultural rights dimension of the multiculturalism debate with the formal criteria for access to citizenship central in Brubaker's analysis. This is what many scholars in the migration and ethnic relations field have done in distinguishing different citizenship models or regimes (e.g., Castles and Miller 1993; Castles 1995; Kleger and D'Amato 1995; Smith and Blanc 1996; Safran 1997). Generally, these authors have come up with three types of citizenship regimes, which each define a particular institutional and discursive setting for political contention over migration and ethnic relations. The first regime, labelled 'ethnic' or 'exclusive' denies migrants and their descendants access to the political community, or at least makes such access very difficult by way of high institutional and cultural barriers to naturalization. Germany is usually the typical example for this model, other examples given include Austria, Switzerland, and Israel. The second type of regime, labelled 'assimilationist' or 'republican' and exemplified by France or the old 'melting pot' approach in the United States, provides for easy access to citizenship, among other things through *jus soli* acquisition at birth, but requires from migrants a high degree of assimilation in the public sphere and gives little or no recognition to their cultural difference. Thirdly, 'multicultural' or 'pluralist' regimes, usually including the present-day USA, Canada, Australia, and in Europe, Britain, and The Netherlands, provide both for easy formal access to citizenship, and recognition of the right of ethnic minorities to maintain their cultural difference.

This three-fold typology has two drawbacks. First, it does not exhaust the logical possibilities. If indeed there are two dimensions to citizenship, one—ethnic versus civic—defining the formal criteria of access, and another—multicultural versus assimilationist—defining the cultural obligations which such citizenship entails, we end up with four, not three models (see Koopmans and Kriesi 1997; Koopmans and Statham 1999, 2000). Second, the 'typology' approach to citizenship has rightly been criticized for its tendency to obscure both the dynamic aspects of the process of migrant integration, and the important differences within states, both among the integration approaches advocated by different political actors, and among those applied to different categories of migrants (Joppke 1996; see also Entzinger in Chapter 5 of this volume). We propose to address these two problems by conceiving of citizenship not in the static categories of typological 'models' or 'regimes', but as a conceptual and political space, in which different actors and policies can be situated, and developments can be traced over time. The contours of this conceptual space are defined by the formal and cultural dimensions of citizenship.[2] Thus conceptualized, the stability of citizenship regimes, and the uniformity with which they cover different political actors, policies, and immigrant groups become issues for empirical investigation, not implicit assumptions tied to the rigidity of a conceptual typology.

On the vertical axis, the continuum runs from conceptions of citizenship which favour ethno-cultural bonds as the basis for the constitution of the political community, to those which emphasize a universalist civic-political culture and attribute citizenship on the basis of the territorial principle. It is easily argued that these extremes hardly occur in reality. Few nation-states completely exclude the possibility of naturalization for those who do not belong to the own ethno-cultural group,[3] and every civic nation attributes citizenship on the basis of descent or cultural belonging in addition to the territorial principle. It has even become somewhat fashionable in the migration and ethnic relatons literature to give up the distinction between ethnic and civic nationhood altogether.[4] However, in view of the important cross-national differences that can be found along this dimension, we must consider this rejection as an overreaction to the rigidity of some of the earlier formulations of this distinction, including Brubaker's.

Partly, the problems with national citizenship models such as Brubaker's derive from the fact that they are unidimensionally based on the ethnic-civic distinction and confound it with the second, cultural dimension of citizenship, which in fact largely crosscuts it. Here, the continuum runs, on the horizontal axis in the Fig. 2.1, from conceptions of citizenship that insist on conformity to a single cultural model that is to be shared by all citizens, to culturally pluralist conceptions, which seek to retain, or even stimulate cultural heterogen-

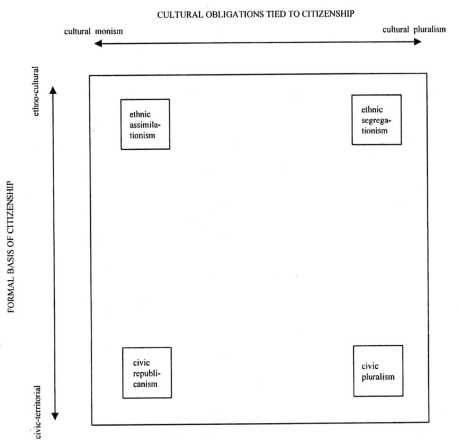

FIG. 2.1. A two-dimensional space for situating conceptions of citizenship

eity and allow their subjects to follow a variety of cultural patterns. Again, it hardly needs to be pointed out that these ideal-typical conceptions do not empirically occur in their purest form. In liberal democracies, controversy mainly focuses on cultural conformity outside the strictly private sphere, for example in the sphere of law, the education system, or the media. There are clear boundaries to cultural pluralism, too, which in Western societies are usually related to the respect of individual human rights or notions of equality. For instance, no Western democracy has legalized female circumcision, although some advocates of multiculturalism have gone as far as proposing to tolerate it in a 'limited' form so as to respect cultural pluralism. Nevertheless, here too, differences among Western democracies remain large enough to make the distinction a fruitful one for analytical purposes. For instance, no one with any knowledge of French and Dutch integration policies could fail to notice the difference regarding the degree of cultural pluralism that is tolerated and facilitated. Muslim and Hindu schools, migrant organization on the basis of ethnicity, television and radio channels catering specifically to migrants, including a Dutch Muslim Broadcasting Corporation, and all this publicly funded in The Netherlands—French policy-makers would not even think about such extravagances in their wildest dreams.

In Fig. 2.1, we have put small named boxes in the outer corners of the conceptual space which indicate the four ideal-typical configurations of citizenship and migrant incorporation that arise from the combination of the vertical and horizontal axes. We are well aware that most countries, actors, or policies will be situated, or on the move somewhere in the space between these boxes. Nevertheless, we think they are usually closer to some ideal-types than to others, and even if they are in the process of moving from one point to another we need a conceptual system of coordinates in order to tell where they are going and where they come from.

The logical starting point for a discussion of these basic models of citizenship is ethnic segregationism, because this is often the point of departure in the process from migration to settlement. Ethnic segregationism is defined by exclusion from the political community of migrant newcomers who do not share the ethno-cultural background of the majority society. At the same time migrants are not forced to give up their own cultures, and the state may even actively promote such cultures and disencourage assimilation to the majority culture. This comes close to the typical 'guestworker' approach, which did not give migrant workers any political rights, nor much prospect to attain them through naturalization, but did not make any cultural demands on them, either. On the contrary, countries with guestworker programmes often put some considerable effort and financial resources into stimulating migrants to retain their cultural heritage and ties to their homelands, which were seen as facilitating their eventual repatriation. Even in the early twenty-first century, countries such as Germany and Switzerland still offer 'education in own language and culture' to children of migrants.[5] In Switzerland and some of the German federal states, such education is often still given in close co-operation with embassies and other homeland authorities. It is interesting to note that in other cases—The Netherlands and some of the more liberal German states—such educational programmes still exist, too, but are now legitimated with reference to 'multiculturalism' instead of as a way to facilitate migrants' eventual return. This example may serve to demonstrate that in spite of the ideological rifts that separate the two, it is in actual practice not always such a long way from the ethnic segregationist guestworker philosophy to the civic-pluralist, multicultural approach. This, of course, is due to the fact that, as Fig. 2.1 illustrates, both share the idea of retaining cultural boundaries between ethnic groups and of preventing assimilation. As a consequence, the educational approach in conservative Bavaria has a surprisingly cultural-pluralist touch. Bavaria was the first and is still one of very few German states to have instituted Islamic education for pupils from Turkey in public schools: in separate classes, of course, in Turkish, and given by religious teachers appointed by the Turkish Ministry of Religious Affairs.

Ethnic segregationist approaches have not disappeared with the formal end of the guestworker programmes. As indicated above, conservative regions and parties in Switzerland and Germany still adhere to them. Moreover, in almost all European countries similar policies are now applied with regard to asylum seekers and refugees, who are usually physically separated from the rest of society, have no or a very restricted right to work, and are generally not stimulated in any other way to assimilate, since that would only make it more difficult to send them back if their asylum requests were denied. In addition, ethnic segregationism is the leading ideology of the so-called 'New Right' (*Nouvelle Droite, Neue Rechte*), whose ideologues such as Alain de Benoist advocate the notion of 'ethnopluralism' (Gessenharter and Fröchling 1998). Departing, at least publicly, from blatantly racist ideas of cultural superiority, this notion entails the claim that all cultures are equal, but should be kept separate and 'intact' in order to prevent a loss of identity and social cohesion that would benefit neither the majority society, nor minority cultures. No wonder then, that extreme-right parties such as the *Front National* or the *Vlaams Blok* sometimes have warm relations with right-wing organizations from migrant homelands, such as the Turkish Grey Wolves or the Maghrebian *Amicales*, which share the same objective.

The latter examples indicate that ethnic segregationism even has its advocates among minority representatives. First and foremost this includes those organizations closely linked to homeland governments, which have often little interest in too much integration of migrants into the host society. For instance, when migrants were first allowed to vote in the Dutch local elections of 1986, the Moroccan authorities officially prohibited Moroccan nationals in The Netherlands to use their right to vote. Non-governmental organizations based in migrant homelands may also have reasons to promote ethnic segregationism. This includes movements for regional independence such as the Kurdish PKK, which has not much to gain and much to lose from Kurdish ethnics in Germany obtaining the German nationality or assimilating to German culture. For another variant of ethnic segregationism promoted by minority organizations we may look beyond Europe at the United States, where radical black organizations such as the Nation of Islam go as far as condemning mixed marriages and demanding an independent black state.

Although ethnic segregationism still has its defenders, most of the guestworker countries have meanwhile moved at least partly away from it. In view of the—slowly and in some circles still not realized—fact that former guestworkers have become permanent settlers, this seems to be an inevitable development. No democratic state can uphold for very long a situation in which a significant percentage of the permanently resident population is excluded from political rights. From Fig. 2.1 it becomes clear that two basic options present themselves: either the idea of distinct and separate cultures is retained, but ethnicity is given up as the formal basis of citizenship, which can then be extended through easier naturalization and the introduction of *jus soli* elements to include migrants from a different ethnic and cultural background. This constitutes a move in the direction of the multicultural, civic-pluralist model. In this case, allowing dual nationality may offer itself as an additional instrument to include migrants as citizens, for in the civic-pluralist view the fact that retaining the nationality of the homeland might constitute a barrier to adaptation to the majority culture is not seen as a problem, but as a fundamental right or even a virtue.

The other option, which is philosphically close to the communitarian position (Cohen 1999: 263), is to retain the formal ethno-cultural basis of citizenship in its essence, but to make it easier for migrants to obtain citizenship through naturalization on the condition that they fulfill certain criteria of assimilation to the majority culture.[6] In this case, conditional naturalization remains the single option for becoming a member of the community and unconditional attribution of citizenship through *jus soli* is not considered. Dual citizenship cannot be tolerated from this perspective, since it would mean to extend citizenship without demanding that the candidate give up her or his original ties to the homeland culture. In other words, it would imply a move towards civic-pluralist multiculturalism, which in the eyes of ethnic assimilationists can lead to nothing but dangerous 'parallel societies' (Laurence 1999).

The debate in the late 1990s in Germany on the reform of citizenship law was to an important extent about which of these two options should be chosen. While most politicians—except perhaps the Bavarian CSU Christian Social Union—agreed that something had to be done to make it easier for migrants to become citizens, they disagreed strongly on how this should be achieved and about the kind of Germany that this should lead to. For conservative adherents of the ethnic assimilationist view, to become a 'German' in the formal sense of nationality requires that one first has to become a German in the cultural sense. This idea is expressed in the Christian Democrats' maxim that 'naturalization should be the crowning of the integration process, it cannot be a means towards integration'. Not surprisingly, the controversy with the Red-Green government focused on the latter's proposal to introduce *jus soli* and to generally tolerate dual nationality, which would have put Germany firmly in the civic-pluralist camp. After the Christian Democrats had staged the most successful signature campaign in German history, with five million signatures, and had won the Hesse elections, a compromise was passed by Parliament, which is considerably less radical than the original proposal. Instead of a bold move to multiculturalism, Germany now moves more carefully along a path somewhere between ethnic assimilationism and civic pluralism.

While the story so far captures the experience of countries such as Germany or Switzerland, it does not describe the typical pattern for countries which already had some civic-territorial notion of citizenship in place when post-war immigrants began to arrive on a massive scale. Civic-territorial as against ethno-cultural notions of citizenship have been facilitated in those countries which used to be colonial powers and have in the post-war period become the target of large flows of postcolonial migration, such as Britain, France, and The Netherlands. In an effort to continue their domination over their colonies, all these colonial powers, albeit to varying extents, transformed the relation with the colonies from one of pure domination and patronage to an at least formally more equal partnership such as the British idea of the 'Commonwealth' between the 'mother country' and the 'overseas territories'. This also implied certain rights to settlement and citizenship in the mother country for the inhabitants of the colonies (Thränhardt and Miles 1995: 6). For instance, according to the new statute for the Kingdom of The Netherlands of 1954, the inhabitants of Surinam and the Dutch Antilles obtained full citizenship rights and unlimited rights of settlement in the European part of the Kingdom. Moreover, already before such changes, conceptions of nationhood based on a notion of ethnic purity had become untenable as a result of the colonial experience. Thus, after Indonesian independence, more than 300,000 people who could claim Dutch citizenship came to The Netherlands, many of whom were people of mixed Dutch-Indonesian descent, or ethnic Indonesians who had co-operated with the colonial regime.

However, there were important differences among the imperialist philosophies and practices of the colonial powers, some of which are still important for understanding these countries' migrant incorporation regimes today. Although the colonial experience strengthened civic-territorial notions of nationhood in all colonialist countries, its impact on the second, cultural dimension of citizenship was not uniform. Here the contrast is greatest between Britain and France, with The Netherlands less clear-cut, but closer to Britain. Britain ruled its colonies and particularly its 'crown jewel' India through a system of 'indirect rule', in which local structures of authority were left largely intact as semi-autonomous intermediary structures between the colonial administration and the native population. By contrast, France's system of colonial rule reflected the centralized, uniform structures prescribed by Jacobinism which also characterize metropolitan France's own polity. Parts of the colonial empire, such as French Guyana, Réunion, or Algeria before independence, were even fully assimilated into the French polity as *départements outre mer* as if there was nothing distinguishing them from, say, Valle de Marne. These different traditions of colonial rule served, consciously or unconsciously, as important models when former colonial subjects started to arrive on a massive scale in the imperial centre. To an important extent, the British multiculturalist and the French assimilationist approaches to incorporating post-war migrants were not invented in the London or Paris of the 1960s, but long before in Delhi and Algiers.

Partly, the problems the former colonial powers have had in the field of migration and ethnic relations derive from the fact that what worked well as a recipe for colonial rule has not always been the optimal solution towards the integration of post-war migrants. France's main problem has been that while, in the colonial situation, conformism to the French republican political culture could simply be imposed, post-war migrants, particularly those of Muslim belief, have not been so easily assimilated and have sometimes demanded a *droit à la différence*: a right to be different, not just inconspicuously in the private sphere—a form of cultural pluralism that does not conflict with republican standards—but publicly and officially recognized. Moreover, the French approach has difficulty in dealing with the fact that the cultural group differences that are denied as legitimate policy categories, do form the basis of discrimination and racism from the side of the majority population, most clearly voiced by the *Front National*'s polemic against 'unassimilable' immigrants. Insisting on the equal treatment of all and loathing group-specific approaches, France does not have the policy instruments to combat forms of social exclusion that are rooted in ethnic and cultural difference (see also Fennema in Chapter 6 of this volume).

As a result, France has been confronted with two countervailing pressures for change. The Socialists in the 1980s, supported by some migrant organizations tried to steer France in the direction of a more culturally pluralist approach, offering limited recognition to the right to be different. One important policy change in this context was the Socialist-led government's 1981 liberalization of association law, which for the first time allowed migrant organization on the basis of nationality or ethnicity. However, the cautious moves in this direction seem to have come to a complete halt afterwards, especially after the notorious headscarf affair, which demonstrated the strong resistance among important sections of the French political and intellectual élite against making even the slightest concession to unitary citizenship.

To the extent that the republican model fails to eradicate ethnicity and cultural difference as publicly visible and contested categories—as it obviously has—this also opens up opportunities for a challenge from the right, which proposes to resolve the dillema by moving in another direction, namely towards an ethnic assimilationist model.[7] Thus, one of the most important and successful demands of the *Front National*—partly implemented in the *Loi Pasqua* of the Chirac government[8]—has been the abolition of the *jus soli* attribution of citizenship and making naturalization dependent on assimilation to French culture. In the eyes of the extreme-right, and judging by its success in those of many French voters, easy access to French citizenship has created increasing numbers of *faux français*, 'false Frenchmen', who are French by nationality, but not by culture—culture understood, of course, not in the 'thin' sense of adherence to republican values such as democracy, liberty, and equality, but in the 'thick' sense of folk traditions, Catholicism, and sometimes plainly race.

Britain and The Netherlands' 'multicultural' approaches to migrant incorporation have had their own problems. Here the problem has not been a lack of policy instruments to tackle disadvantage based on ethnic, cultural, or racial difference, but rather that these instruments have sometimes reinforced and solidified the very disadvantages they were supposed to combat. Taking ethnic and racial criteria as a basis for policy-making geared to ending disadvantage and discrimination on the basis of ethnic and racial criteria has often been much like trying to drive the Devil out with Beelzebub. As Miles (1982) has argued for Britain, and Rath (1991) for The Netherlands, the labelling of migrant groups as disadvantaged minorities has led to a process of 'racialization' or 'minorization', which has tended to reproduce race and ethnicity as bases for social disadvantage and discrimination.

This problem seems to have been aggravated by the particular mixture of paternalism and guilt that describes these countries' postcolonial hangover. On the one hand, there has often been a tendency on the side of the authorities to see migrants as incapable of ameliorating their own position and thus in need of benevolent assistance to overcome their *achterstand*, or 'lagging behind' as the prevalent Dutch policy term puts it, in a language reminiscent of that used in relation to Third World countries. This tendency has been reinforced by the sense of postcolonial guilt and the ever-present fear among authorities of being accused of racism, which has led to a rather 'soft' handling of problems which disproportionally affect minorities such as social welfare dependence and crime; and a great wariness in using the state's sanctioning powers to push migrants to also make a contribution to alleviating their own disadvantage by, for example, learning the language of the host country in order to improve employment opportunities.

Particularly in the Netherlands, the combination of these factors has led to a vicious circle in which state policies have reinforced the image of migrants as a problematic, disadvantaged category in need of constant state assistance— not only in the eyes of the majority population, but also in those of many migrants and their representative organizations.[9] To the majority population, migrants thus appear as a group deserving help, respect, tolerance, and solidarity, but not the kind of people that anyone in his or her right mind would want to employ or would want one's child to be in school with. As a result, in spite of the liberal rhetoric, the much better legal position, and the much higher level of tolerance for cultural diversity in the public sphere and in political debate, levels of ethnic segregation in the school system as well as levels of unemployment, relative to the majority population, are much higher in The Netherlands than in Germany (see Thränhardt in Chapter 8 of this volume).

More recently, this tendency of civic pluralism in a postcolonial context to slide in practice into a form of ethnic segregationism has inspired a reappreciation of the civic republican model, especially in The Netherlands—Britain has always been closer to that model anyway. Instead of policies geared to specific ethnic groups, the central authorities as well as many local ones now prefer general policies for socio-economically disadvantaged groups, that include not only minorities, but also the 'native' underclass. Moreover, the authorities have become more demanding with regard to migrants. For instance, newly arriving migrants are now obliged to follow an *inburgeringstraject*, a sort of 'integration program', which entails intensive Dutch language courses and courses offering basic information about Dutch politics and culture.

What this extensive discussion of configurations of citizenship and the many shades in between them shows, is that unlike the more rigid typologies, our model of a two-dimensional conceptual space in Fig. 2.1 assumes neither fixed, nor uniform national coordinates. Each of the countries we have discussed has been almost continuously shifting position since the 1970s. This reflects that all over Western Europe, the incorporation of large numbers of culturally different migrants—after all a hitherto unknown challenge—has been much of a trial and error process. However, it is equally clear that the elements these countries used, combined, and varied during this learning process, were to an important extent drawn from pre-existing institutional and cultural repertoires of citizenship and nationhood. For all its changes back and forth in the direction of more civic republicanism, ethnic assimilationism, or civic pluralism, France has always remained somewhere in the lower left corner of the conceptual space. The Netherlands, in spite of the recent reappreciation of republican policy instruments, remains much closer to the civic pluralist corner than France, with Britain somewhere in between. Until very recently, Germany's policies, despite some minor shifts, remained close to the ethnic segregationist corner of the conceptual space. However, with its new citizenship legislation that went into force on January 1, 2000, Germany may be about to engage in the most radical process of change of the countries discussed here, although for the moment it is still unclear where it will end up.

Although it is sometimes necessary and useful to talk about national configurations of citizenship in this generalizing way, we should not let this obscure the important differences that exist among policy areas as well as those among actors within countries. Regarding policy areas, we have noted that asylum seekers everywhere tend to be subjected to a segregationist regime. In countries such as France and The Netherlands, which have both had guestworker programmes and have experienced massive postcolonial migration, there have been important differences, at least initially, between the respective incorporation regimes. The contrast was perhaps largest in The Netherlands, where guestworker (non-)incorporation initially proceeded along much the same ethnic segregationist lines as in Germany and Switzerland, while the regime for postcolonial migrants was much more inclusive. Germany's incorporation of Aussiedler[10] is an interesting and rather pure case of an ethnic assimilationist approach. Despite their often important cultural and linguistic differences from the German majority society, the inclusion of Aussiedler is based on the presumption that they are ethno-culturally Germans. As a result, Aussiedler are in fact confronted with strong assimilation pressures. They have to become what they were already unambiguously supposed to be on entry, that is, Germans, and have to give up what they supposedly never had, that is, the Russian, Polish, or Romanian parts of their cultural identity.

Especially important from the point of view of developing a framework for the analysis of migration and ethnic relations as a field of contention, are the different positions taken by actors within countries. In this context, we may conceive of the conceptual space delineated in Fig. 2.1 as the 'playing field' on which such contention takes place, where actors position themselves relative to one another, and strategic decisions are taken to move in one direction or another. The increased contentiousness of the field means that the positioning of different actors within countries has become increasingly divergent. The massive post-war migration and the settlement of culturally different migrants have challenged traditional conceptions of citizenship and nationhood, and different actors have proposed different answers to these challenges. In the process, consensus around traditional conceptions of citizenship and nationhood has partially eroded, and—as in the case of France where republicanism has never been fully accepted by the Right—latent dissent surrounding them has flared up again. In each country, one may point out actors whose positions correspond most closely to one of the four ideal-typical models. In Germany the variation is relatively large. If we limit ourselves to party actors, the Greens take a civic-pluralist position, the Liberals and less outspokenly the Social Democrats tend towards a republican position, the main Christian Democrat party (CDU) has recently shifted in tbe direction of the ethnic assimilationist corner, while the Bavarian CSU still clings to the ethnic segregationist model, which most other parties—with the exception of the extreme-right parties such as the Republikaner—have now left behind.[11]

Neo-Institutionalism and Political Opportunity Structures

A second and related development in the literature that has contributed to an increased awareness of the political dimensions of migration and ethnic relations has been the increased focus on the role of political institutions. Following the broadly influential 'neo-institutionalist' perspective (e.g., Hall and Taylor 1996; March and Olsen 1984), where institutional configurations are seen to influence the preference formation and strategies of political actors, and thereby specify the contours within which specific political actions are formulated and conducted, several authors have focused on political institutional arrangements for explaining the different national patterns of migration and ethnic relations policies (e.g., Cornelius, Martin, and Hollifield 1994; Freeman 1992, 1995; Ireland 1994; Joppke 1997, 1998; Guiraudon 1998; as well as Soysal 1994 in as far as her analysis deals with national 'incorporation regimes'). These authors share a focus on politics and institutional arrangements, thus avoiding the socio-economic and cultural determinism that was present in the class, race/ethnicity, and modernization approaches discussed above. In this view, migration and ethnic relations are no longer marginal policy fields, but political issues which take centre stage in liberal democracies, and where state control and policy outcomes are defined in the struggles over rights between individuals, groups, and the state in the arena of domestic politics.

With a few exceptions of research that focuses on political institutional frameworks for explaining the success of extreme-right political parties (Kitschelt 1997; Koopmans and Statham 1999; Eatwell, Chapter 13 in this volume), xenophobic violence (Koopmans 1996a, 1997; Karapin, Chapter 12 in this volume), and state responses to racism (van Donselaar 1995; Witte 1996; Fennema, Chapter 6 in this volume), neo-institutionalism has made little impression on the analysis of xenophobic movements. Applications of the institutional perspective to explaining ethnic minority political mobilization and participation have remained scarce, too. An important exception here is Patrick Ireland (1994 and Chapter 10 in this volume; see also Bousetta 1996; Koopmans 1999; Rosenhek 1999; Statham 1999; and Garbaye, Chapter 11 in this volume), who explains the different forms and levels of political participation by similar ethnic groups in France and Switzerland, by referring to the differential legal and political institutions—residence laws, naturalization procedures, political rights, and welfare policies—which shape migrants' involvement in the host polity. His main finding, that similar migrant groups act differently in the two countries, shows that 'institutional channelling' is a better explanation for the patterns of migrant activism than the socio-economic or cultural characteristics of the group itself, that is, 'class', 'ethnic' or 'homeland' identities.[12] If cultural and social background were determinant of political behaviour, one would have predicted, counter to Ireland's findings, similar patterns of participation by the same ethnic groups in different countries.

Most neo-institutionally inspired studies, however, tend to take policies as the dependent variable and focus primarily on the role of political élites. Moreover, they mostly deal with the issue of state control over entry, and rarely with issues concerning the integration of ethnic and racial minorities (exceptions are Joppke 1996, and in Chapter 7 of this volume). Freeman's (1992, 1995, 1998) work on 'immigration regimes', for instance, emphasizes the ability of political élites to control decisions over immigration control away from the public domain. For Freeman this élite monopolization of power relative to the general public produces expansive immigration policies. He argues that politics has an intrinsic 'anti-populist norm'. Although the costs and benefits of immigration are unevenly distributed with the poor sections of the public facing the most costs, the organized pro-immigrant lobbies—the usual suspects listed as powerful economic interests, ethnic kin, the legal establishment, intellectuals, anti-racist movements, and the media (Freeman 1998: 103)—ultimately get their way in the political process as they are better organized and resource-rich in contrast to the marginal sections of the public who have tendencies toward xenophobic sentiments. National similarities and differences in policy approach are therefore best explained by 'client politics'.

Besides its policy and elite biases, another weakness of neo-institutionalist approaches is their often weak appreciation of the role of public discourse and political culture. Discursive approaches have a long tradition in ethnic relations studies, but have long been heavily dominated by the crusade against racism of Teun van Dijk (1993) and his followers. This approach has not been very helpful for the development of comparative work within the field, since it tends to find 'racism' wherever it looks for it—thus turning the concept into a constant feature of Western societies rather than a variable to be explained. Recently, however, there has been a reappreciation of discursive approaches in genuinely comparative work. This is evident in the work of some authors who also draw on neo-institutionalism (e.g., Soysal 1994), but especially in Adrian Favell's (1998) comparison of 'public philosophies of integration' in Britain and France, which he sees as embedded in nationally-specific sets of language and symbols. However, his and similar analyses remain impressionistic and largely fall back on describing a limited number of famous political incidents. The same holds for many attempts to analyze the role of public debates and the media in explaining xenophobia, which in addition tend to present a one-sided, top-down picture of political party and media elites controlling public opinion (e.g., Husbands 1994; Thränhardt 1993; Brosius and Esser 1995).

In spite of the significant insights that the reappreciation of the political in both its institutional and discursive guises has brought, further advances seem to depend on a better theoretical integration of the different approaches. First and foremost, this requires a theoretical linkage among political institutions, public discourses, and the level of actual interaction among the actors involved in migration and ethnic relations politics. Second, we need to move beyond the usual loose and vague references to 'institutions', 'political process', or 'public discourse', and specify much more clearly what these consist of, which dimensions can be distinguished, and which indicators might be used in empirical investigations. Especially for systematic comparative purposes, such specifications seem to be of the utmost importance if one wants to identify explanatory factors and move beyond the reproduction of holistic national clichés. Third, there is an obvious need to include a broad spectrum of actors and actions in the analysis, instead of focusing exclusively on élite actions and discourses. This may help to bridge the gap between institutional and discursive analyses on the one hand, and the many descriptive accounts of ethnic and xenophobic organizations and mobilizations that are produced in a theoretical void, on the other. Last but certainly not least, it is necessary to provide a framework that can connect studies of minority integration and ethnic mobilization to the literature on xenophobia and extreme-right movements. Given the obvious and important links between these phenomena it is almost absurd how the majority of studies on the extreme-right continue to ignore migration and ethnic relations as a decisive political context, and how, on the other side, students of migration and ethnic relations have paid only marginal attention to the extreme-right as an actor shaping political developments in this field.

We propose that such a theoretical integration can be furthered by drawing on theories of social movements and collective action and particularly the concept of 'political opportunity structures'.[13] Following Tarrow's succinct but accurate definition, political opportunity structures consist of 'consistent—but not necessarily formal or permanent—dimensions of the political environment that provide incentives for people to undertake collective action by affecting their expectations for success or failure' (1994: 85). The political opportunity perspective builds on resource mobilization theory's conception of collective action as rationally based on the perceived costs and benefits of different strategies, and its emphasis on the need to mobilize resources as a precondition for mobilization (e.g., Zald and Ash 1966; Oberschall 1973; McCarthy and Zald 1977). However, where resource mobilization theory has a strong internal focus, the opportunity structure perspective places social movements firmly in their political context and emphasizes the importance of drawing resources from that environment, particularly for challenger groups which tend to control few resources of their own (e.g., Eisinger 1973; Tilly 1978; McAdam 1982).

An important cue for the political opportunity approach comes from the seminal historical research of Charles Tilly and his collaborators (e.g., Shorter and Tilly 1972; Tilly, Tilly, and Tilly 1975; Tilly 1978). These authors demonstrated that crises in political authority and especially dissent among political élites are better predictors for widespread periods of popular mobilization and revolution than processes of socio-economic modernization, such as industrialization or urbanization. Popular revolts typically occurred at times of political crisis, for example, after defeat in war, when actors perceived opportunities for challenging the nation-state from below. As for cross-national differences in periods of political revolt, the basic premise to draw from Tilly is that levels of mobilization are not a direct outcome of national differences in patterns of modernization, but are mediated by a country's particular structure of political institutions and its configuration of power relationships. In the intervening years, the concept of 'political opportunity structure' has been applied and further developed in both longitudinal (especially Tarrow 1989) and cross-national studies (especially Kriesi *et al.* 1992, 1995). Akin to the pervasive influence of neo-institutional approaches in other fields, this body of research has set the pace for the development of the social movements field over the 1990s, and now branches increasingly into other fields of political study, for example, by extending the research focus to the policy outcomes of movements, and extending the type of political actors studied beyond the narrow focus on movements (see especially, contributions to Guigni, McAdam, and Tilly 1999).

Partly due to the different needs of diachronic and cross-sectional research designs, different dimensionalizations of political opportunity structure co-exist. Tarrow's four dimensions are typical for the American research tradition, which usually focuses on the opening or closure of 'windows of opportunity' over time within a single polity: 'the opening up of access to participation; shifts in ruling alignments, the availability of influential allies, and cleavages within and among elites' (1994: 86). By contrast, Kriesi *et al.*'s (1995: xiii–xvi) categorization is typical for the European focus on cross-national studies. Thus, three of their four dimensions consist of relatively stable features of political systems, which are extremely important in comparative analyses, but will often be constants in diachronic analysis: 'national cleavage structures', 'formal institutional structures', and 'informal procedures and prevailing strategies'. Their fourth factor, 'alliance structures' summarizes the more volatile aspects of political opportunity emphasized by Tarrow. Thus, the two categorizations can easily be combined, and depending on one's primary interest in diachronic or cross-sectional analysis one may choose the one or the other operationalization as one's frame of reference.

Following Kriesi *et al.*, a particularly important dimension of political opportunities are the national cleavage structures which define the political space which is available for challengers to introduce new conflicts into a polity. Here the chances for challengers to mobilize contentions are shaped by the existing politicized cleavages in society, such as conflicts over national identities, class conflicts, centre–periphery conflicts, or postmaterialist–materialist conflicts. Thus the emergence of a supranational level of governance through the EU and the decline of the East–West bloc conflicts of the Cold War, have once more brought into question in the political domain, issues of national sovereignty and identity that were in previous decades relatively non-contentious. In the face of globalization and pluralization, political demands for regional devolution may appear more legitimate if they can build on old ethnic cleavages. Alternatively, new political demands may emerge that stigmatize non-EU migrants as the threat to social cohesion, using the legitimacy of the supranational political order to make claims. Both these trends are visible in the formation of demands by ethno-regional movements, such as the *Lega Nord* in Italy (Statham 1998).

Formal institutional or legal structures refer to the set of institutional actors in a polity and the legal arrangements which define their relationships and competencies. Specific dimensions of this opportunity variable may include the degree of centralization of political institutions, the type of electoral system, and the separation of powers between the executive, legislative, and judiciary. These institutional dimensions define the available channels of access for challengers to the polity, and may be relatively more open or more closed to specific types of challenges. For example, the 'first-past-the-post' local constituency-based electoral system in Britain provides less opportunities for extreme-right political parties to gain office in national politics than most proportional or majoritarian electoral systems in mainland Europe. This may in part explain why xenophobia in Britain has become more channelled into diffuse violent racist attacks on the political margins than into conventional forms of political electioneering.

Regarding the more informal dimensions of political opportunities, prevailing élite strategies refer to the rules and procedures that have historically emerged within a polity for managing and resolving conflicts and for dealing with political challengers. Here, instead of the cleavage structures, one refers to the more inclusive, consensual, or more exclusive, polarizing political traditions through which conflicts, for example, over class or between church and state, have traditionally been approached by élites, in ways that continue to shape official reactions to new challengers. To give a relevant example, the British official 'race-relations politics' formula for integrating postcolonial minorities through measures to combat racial discrimination through equality of opportunity in the labour market, follows an élite political tradition for pacifying the class conflict by incorporation of the working classes through the establishment of the welfare state (Rex 1994, following the basic tenet of T. H. Marshall). This means that the opportunities available for political participation to British minorities have been strongly defined by class politics which is shown by high levels of involvement through the Labour Party and trade unions. And secondly, political opportunities facing minorities in Britain have been 'racialized', which has the effect of providing greater access to the polity for African Caribbeans who define themselves as a racial group, than it does for Bangladeshi and Pakistani groups who more often use a religious political identity as 'Muslims' (Statham 1999).

The fourth dimension of political opportunity structure is more tied to the specific contingencies of time and place. Alliance structures refer to the specific balance of power relationships between actors at a given time and place, including the composition of the party system, and the relative strengths of political parties and the government. Regarding the opportunities for challenges, a particularly conducive situation for mobilization is when political élites are internally divided, as they are more likely under such conditions to attempt to form strategic alliances with extra-parliamentary actors and thereby shift the balance of power in their favour. Élite divisions can be common over issues such as immigration and may at times be stimulated by the legal constitutional framework. For example, constitutional change in Germany requires the consent of opposition parties. In the 1990s, this facilitated the fact that the Christian Democratic demand to limit the constitutional right to asylum caused intense élite-level political controversies, followed by waves of public protest, collective mobilization and counter-mobilization in the public domain, that contributed to important and substantive changes in the outcomes of the policy process (Koopmans 1996b; and Karapin, Chapter 12 in this volume).

These specifications of the political opportunity approach undoubtedly introduced more theoretical and comparative rigour in the social movement field, but came under criticism for over-focusing on the institutional dimensions of opportunities, and failing to take seriously the cultural basis, that is cultural codes, and collective identities, and discursive contents, or frames and symbols, that carry the message of political contention (Gamson 1988; Melucci 1990; Eder 1993). Whereas these political opportunity approaches emphasized the strategic dimensions and material resources for mobilization, the framing perspective draws on symbolic interactionism (Goffman 1974) and the public construction of social problems (Hilgartner and Bosk 1988). In this view, discontent, resources, and opportunities are not simply 'out there' in the external world, but have to be cognitively perceived, constructed, defined, communicated, and mediated into public discourses, that is 'framed', to become a basis for collective action (see especially, Snow et al. 1986; Snow and Benford 1988; Gamson and Modigliani 1989). This approach underlines that social movement organizers have to define issues as problematic concerns, identify causes, present solutions, and make the political actors and institutions who are considered responsible for implementing policy decisions visible and accountable in the public domain. In addition, they have to convince their potential adherents that collective action is a necessary and a potentially successful means towards these ends—what Klandermans (1988) has called 'consensus mobilization'. Mobilizing public constituencies is difficult, firstly, because of competition from other actors who offer alternative definitions and solutions for the contentious issue, and secondly, because the public sphere has a structure that favours access to élites over movements, and the political discourse will already have a dominant way for defining a contentious issue-field that again is likely to be biased toward established elite views. Facing such constraints, movement organizers have to outflank other actors, such as countermovements, civil society actors, and public authorities, to successfully promote and mediate their own definitions of the situation and policy proposals.

Framing approaches have in turn been criticized for producing many *ad hoc* and descriptive studies, and for lacking clear hypotheses about the effects of framing on levels and forms of collective action (see especially the self-critique by Benford 1997). This is the main point of Koopmans and Duyvendak (1995), whose analysis of anti-nuclear movements in several European countries shows that, although the movements had very similar argumentative strategies, the ones which were more successful in influencing public opinion, were those active in countries such as The Netherlands, where the movement faced favourable institutional opportunities for preventing the construction of nuclear plants. In France, on the other hand, where all the major parties were firmly behind nuclear power and few opportunities for juridical intervention were available, levels for rejecting nuclear energy actually decreased among the public during the 1980s, contrary to the prevalent trend across Europe (see also, Nelkin and Pollak 1981; Kitschelt 1986). This example shows that the success of discursive efforts depends not just on the argumentative 'quality' of the framing strategies used by collective actors, but on their 'fit' with hegemonic discourses, and on the institutional opportunities for inserting challenger frames into the process of policy formation and implementation. The important question is how one can insert this dimension of public discourse within a political opportunity perspective. More recent research in the social movements field has specifically addressed this need for combining and integrating the insights from opportunity and framing perspectives more systematically (see especially McAdam, McCarthy, and Zald 1996; Tarrow 1998; Koopmans and Statham 1999, 2000).

If one takes on board that only perceived realities can affect collective action, then it follows that we should focus on the type of political opportunities that are rendered publicly visible. Such manifest dimensions of political opportunities may be derived directly from the characteristics of political systems. This is clearly the case for the more stable aspects of political culture and institutions, for which the opportunities and constraints have been internalized by the citizenry in a learning process that extends across several generations. Thus French citizens have learnt that they will achieve little if they direct their demands at impotent peripheral authorities instead of at the all-powerful centre in Paris. Similarly, British citizens know that given the country's electoral system, the formation of a new political party is not a very effective means to promote change—an important factor for explaining the national electoral weakness of the British extreme-right. However, in addition to the more stable institutional and cultural dimensions that can be derived from political systems, there are more volatile dimensions of political opportunities, and this is where public discourse dynamics play a crucial role. For example, dissent among a political élite becomes perceived as an opportunity for mobilization only after it becomes public knowledge, instead of remaining limited to the insider-publics of cabinet meetings, parliamentary committees, or other non-public arenas.

When élite dissent enters the public sphere, a process in which the organizational structure of the public sphere and the mass media in particular plays an influential intermediary role, contentious discourses may develop powerful dynamics of amplification, extension, and bridging into broader political issue fields. Such political discourse dynamics have potentially more influence over outcomes, when the dispute is transmitted beyond the conflict between the challenger and the élite, and other collective actors in civil society are drawn into taking up a stance, either as 'third party' mediators, or alternatively as new protagonists. Under certain conditions, political contentions and their discursive contents can have an influential feedback into shaping the configuration of political power relationships and thereby opportunities (Gamson and Meyer 1996). Political discourse dynamics for a contested issue-field may be seen as constituting a set of discursive opportunities that determines which of the strategic political demands that are made by movements are more likely to succeed in the public sphere.

The likelihood of success for challengers who attempt to mobilize their claims in the public sphere is dependent on their ability to achieve three strategic aims: visibility, resonance, and legitimacy. Firstly, a collective actor and her aims must be rendered publicly visible. Many challenges simply fail because they do not cross the first hurdle of being reported by the media, or they are able to mobilize only ephemeral or local-level public attention. Secondly, to have an impact, the mobilized challenge must provoke public reactions from other actors: the claims must resonate and carry the contention to a wider public. Even public claims that are reported in the media remain inconsequential if no one reacts to them, and political business continues as usual. Thirdly, no matter how much visibility and resonance a challenge achieves, it will only achieve a level of success when it becomes a legitimate contention. This means that an actor needs to legitimate herself and her claims in public, by resonating positively in the reactions of a significant number of other actors, who are willing to declare at least partial support by acknowledging that something has to be done about the problem. Including the discursive dimension extends the institutional focus of the traditional concept of political opportunities, and brings the dynamic cultural and discursive elements of issue-fields back into consideration as variables for shaping collective action. By relating the discursive and institutional dimensions of political opportunities in this way, the indeterminacy of the framing approach is redressed, by giving explanations for why some framing efforts succeed in mobilizing a public constituency, whereas others, which are not necessarily less elaborate or consistent in any objective sense, fail to do so.

Conceptualized in this way to include both institutional and discursive aspects, the political opportunity perspective provides a theoretical framework that may be fruitfully applied to link the different perspectives on political contention over migration and ethnic relations which we have discussed above. Importantly, our discussions on citizenship and nationhood in the previous section can be translated into the language of political opportunities and vice versa. One may see conceptions of citizenship and nationhood as a subset, or as a specification of the general dimensions of political opportunity structures, which is particular to the field of contention over migration and ethnic relations.

Conceptions of citizenship and nationhood are first of all part of a nation's cleavage structure. Generally, one may expect greater contestation over issues related to citizenship in countries in which the conception of the nation has historically been a contested issue. This is for instance clearly the case in France, where the dominant republican conception of the nation that emerged from the French Revolution has never been fully accepted by the right. The recent rise of the *Front National* and the success it has had in challenging French citizenship and immigration politics are therefore no mere accident in French history, but are but the latest manifestations of a structural cleavage which earlier produced Poujadism, the Dreyfuss controversy and the Boulanger movement. In Belgium, the success of the Vlaams Blok cannot be understood without referring to its roots in Flemish nationalism, a cleavage in Belgian politics which long precedes the post-war immigration issue. The contentiousness of immigration and citizenship issues in Germany is similarly linked to the contested nature of German nationhood and the linkage of these issues to controversies over *Vergangenheitsbewältigung*, the ways in which Germany should deal with its past and the lessons it should draw from it.

Second, citizenship also has a formal institutional dimension, which especially affects the opportunities of access of migrants to the political system. In countries such as Britain, where citizenship is easily obtained, migrants have the important advantage of electoral leverage, which puts them in a much better position to influence political decisions than in countries such as Germany where politicians stand to gain little from catering to minority interests. Similarly, migrants and minorities have greater access to the political system where they are officially recognized and their organizations facilitated, and where their claims can refer to existing legal frameworks for equal opportunity, anti-discrimination, and cultural rights.

Third, national configurations of citizenship reflect prevailing strategies for dealing with societal cleavages and conflicts. Thus, the Dutch approach to ethnic minority politics has to an important extent been copied from the approach to the resolution of internal religious and political conflicts through 'pillarization' in the early twentieth century. In this model, minority organizations were officially recognized by the state and ethnic élites were given an important role in shaping and implementing policies for 'their' constituencies. Similarly, ethnic minorities have been able to claim cultural rights such as state-financed religious schools or broadcasting time in public television by framing their demands in terms referring to the existing provisions and rights for Protestant and Catholic denominations.

Finally, controversies over citizenship and nationhood are important determinants of the alliance and conflict structures in the politics of migration and ethnic relations. Élite divisions and shifting alignments over these issues will particularly enhance the opportunities for challengers from below if such controversies are not limited to more or less technical discussions of immigration control and minority integration, but become framed in terms of the 'deep' cultural idioms of citizenship and nationhood.

Of course, this does not mean that every relevant aspect of the political opportunity structure for contention over migration and ethnic relations can be viewed in terms of citizenship and nationhood—the electoral system or the composition of government are obviously important but unrelated to citizenship. However, it is probably justified to say that cleavages, institutional and legal frameworks, political cultural idioms, and alliance and conflict structures relating to citizenship and nationhood, are of paramount importance in this particular field.

Globalization, European Union, and the Nation-State

What we have presented so far is a set of conceptual tools for the comparative analysis of political contention over migration and ethnic relations issues. As we have indicated, such comparisons may be cross-national, longitudinal, or among actors or issues differentially located within the field. In all these cases, however, the nation-state remains the central frame of reference, both institutionally and culturally. The external environment of nation-states may well play an important role in such an approach, but it is likely to be viewed in the traditional international relations fashion as a system of nation-states, which defines particular opportunities and constraints for the actions of each of its constituent parts. Likewise, there is no contradiction between using this kind of political opportunity approach and focusing attention on the local level of politics. Indeed, local variation is what a political opportunity approach would lead us to expect. After all, national political opportunities and constraints are just that, not imperatives that impose a uniform pattern on each regional or local subunit of the political system. However, such variation is likely to be conceptualized as variation on a nationally defined theme, its extent defined by the degree of autonomy given to subnational units within the more federalist, or more centralized, national institutional framework.

Recently, a growing number of authors have argued that such nation-state-centred approaches are obsolete. Associated with the buzzword 'globalization', these critiques claim that we have have entered, or are about to enter a new 'postnational' or 'transnational' era characterized on the political level by complex and qualitatively new patterns of 'multi-level governance', in which the nation-state still plays a role, but a drastically reduced one (e.g., Basch *et al.* 1994; Held 1996; Sassen 1998; Cohen 1999). This decline of the nation-state's sovereignty is accompanied by a growing importance of supranational and transnational actors, institutions, legal norms, and discourses, on the one hand, and increased local autonomy from national constraints, on the other.

Given the inherently transnational nature of migration and ethnic relations issues, it is not surprising that this critique of national approaches had been particularly prominent in this field of study—for an overview of current debates, see Portes (1997). A number of authors have seen a new form of 'post-national' citizenship developing, superimposed on national citizenship and rendering it increasingly irrelevant (Soysal 1994; Jacobson 1996). The primary empirical example on which this conclusion is based are the former guest-workers in several Western European countries. Although originally invited on a temporary basis, many of them have stayed after the formal ending of the recruitment programmes in the wake of the 1973 Oil Crisis. Moreover, by way of family reunification and formation, immigration from the sending countries has continued, albeit on a lower level. Finally, the receiving countries have extended most civil and social rights, and in some cases even limited political rights to these immigrants, even though many of them have not been naturalized and are thus not formally citizens of the countries in which they reside.[14] Postnationalists argue that such extensions of residence, immigration, and other rights to immigrants have been forced on nation-states by their commitments to international law and conventions, pressure from homeland governments, and the growing normative force of international human rights discourses.

In another related argument for the relativization of the nation-state, the significant drop in the cost of long-distance international travel and increase in the speed and extent of global communication are seen as undermining nation-states' attempts to assimilate immigrants to national politics and culture. Instead, immigrants now form 'transnational communities' or 'diasporas' retaining their cultural difference and strong ties with their homelands (Lie 1995; Glick-Schiller et al. 1997; Kleger 1997; Shain and Sherman 1998). As a result, the capacity of the nation-state to regulate migration and ethnic relations is significantly reduced. In a radical formulation of this view—offered in the preface to the first issue of the journal Diaspora—nation-states have been reduced to little more than the spatial settings in which global forces materialize: 'This vision of a homogeneous nation is now being replaced by a vision of the world as a "space" continually reshaped by forces—cultural, political, technological, demographic, and above all economic—whose varying intersections in real estate constitute every "place" as a heterogeneous and disequilibriated site of production, appropriation, and consumption, of negotiated identity and affect' (Tölölyan 1996: 6).[15]

More specifically for the European context, the process of European union is often seen as another challenge to the nation-state's sovereignty generally, and in the migration and ethnic relations field in particular (e.g., Meehan 1993; Rosas and Antola 1995; Wiener 1997). The emergence of European-level human rights codes, the enhanced role of the European Court of Justice, and the embryonic European citizenship that has been introduced with the Maastricht Treaty are seen as guaranteeing basic migrant rights and thereby limiting the scope of autonomous action of the member states.

Though resonating with the present popularity of 'globalization' and 'Europeanization' in the scientific community, these perspectives have not gone unchallenged. Criticism has focused both on the actual extent of the alleged decline in the nation-state's sovereignty, and on the degree to which such a shift to a transnational or supranational order actually has the beneficial effects for migrants and ethnic minorities that postnationalists tend to emphasize. To begin with the latter point, it is striking that parallel to the literature emphasizing the empowering effects of postnational and European citizenship, there is an equally resonant literature that comes to the opposite conclusion and sees the process of European union leading to a 'Fortress Europe' (e.g., Miles and Thränhardt 1995; Overbeek 1995; Roche and van Berkel 1997). Pointing to agreements such as those of Schengen and Dublin, the European project is seen here as curtailing migrant and minority rights by strengthening external border controls, promoting internal security co-operation, and devaluating migrant rights to the level of the lowest common denominator of the participating member states. Similar developments can be observed in other contexts of intergovernmental co-operation on migration issues, such as in the case of NAFTA. One has to admire the creativity with which some postnationalists manage to see a subjugation of the nation-state's prerogatives to international human rights codes even in such cases:

Another major effort to come out of the Zacatecas meeting was the facilitation of documented migration and the return of undocumented migrants in full compliance with human rights codes. . . . Finally, both delegations are developing criteria, procedures, and legal conditions consistent with international practices for the safe and orderly repatriation of undocumented Mexican migrants to ports of entry within Mexico without intermediate stops, with full respect for their human rights (Sassen 1998: 68).

Moreover, the high hopes for improving migrant rights that some place in European citizenship seem to lack any foundation at the present moment. According to the provisions of the Maastricht treaty, European citizenship is fully derivative of national citizenship in one of the member states and therefore does not improve the rights of third-country nationals in any way. The same is true for the abolition of most barriers in the way of freedom of movement, settlement, and seeking employment within the EU, which applies only to nationals of member states (Hailbronner 1995: 194–8). European citizenship and the rights it entails have so far, in fact, not improved the rights of migrants from third countries in the slightest sense. On the contrary, while in many national contexts the rights status of permanent residents approximated that of citizens, third-country nationals now find themselves again in a second-class position on the European level (Faist 1995: 192).

Of such improvements in migrant rights that have undeniably taken place since the 1970s, it is debatable whether they are due to the rise of a new, post-national form of citizenship based in international human rights codes, emphasizing personhood instead of citizenship as the basis of rights. First, this perspective cannot explain why such extensions of rights to migrants can only be observed in Western democracies, whereas other countries, such as the Persian Gulf states, extend very few rights, if any at all, to their labour migrants (Joppke 1997). Moreover, more recent labour migration schemes in Western European countries—Germany's import of East European labourers being perhaps the most prominent example—seem to indicate that if they so wish, Western nation-states, too, are well able to restrict the rights of labour migrants to a minimum: 'The rights of these, mostly temporary, workers tend to be inferior to that of the former guestworkers in Germany, for example, the rotational principle is strictly enforced. Thus, not only have immigration policies become more restrictive but the social rights status of labour migrants has also become more precarious' (Faist 1997: 213).

What these examples indicate is that the factors that have led to the extension of rights to immigrants have been domestic rather than postnational in any meaningful sense. First, a commitment to human rights has been a founding principle of Western liberal nation-states, not something imposed on them in the post-war period by supranational institutions, conventions, or discourses—recall that the French revolutionary constitution begins by stating not just the Rights of the Citizen, but the Rights of Man and the Citizen, in that order.[16] While the commitment to such values and rights may partly explain why Western states have not treated their labour migrants like, say, Saudi Arabia or Nigeria, there were also less noble, domestic interests behind the giving up of the rotation model for Western European guestworkers, such as the pressure on governments by employers interested in a stable, committed workforce (Freeman 1995; Lakeman 1999).[17]

Empirical evidence on the mobilization of migrants and ethnic minorities in Europe does not provide much support for a significant erosion of the nation-state as a frame of reference. In our own contribution in Chapter 9 of this volume, we show that only a very small proportion of migrant and ethnic minority claims-making in Britain and Germany in the 1990s involved the supranational level in some way, either in the form of transnational minority organizations, demands directed at supranational institutions, or the legitimation of claims by referring to existing or proposed international legal frameworks, conventions, or treaties. Most of minority claims-making remained firmly within a national framework, either that of the country of residence or that of the country of origin. The latter type of homeland-related demands might be interpreted within the transnational communities or diaspora perspective. However, homeland issues played a significant role only in Germany, not in Britain, which can be plausibly related to differences in these two countries' national citizenship regimes, not to a greater exposure of Germany to transnationalization processes. Moreover, there does not seem to be anything new about such 'transnational' action by political exiles against authoritarian homeland regimes.

The fledgling attempts that have been made to institutionalize something of a migrant and minority representation on the level of the European Union are not indicative of a strong and irresistable postnational thrust, either. As Cathie Lloyd describes in Chapter 15 of this volume, most attempts at organization at the European level have been failures (see also Favell and Geddes in Chapter 16). This has not been because of a lack of co-operativeness from the side of the EU: in fact most of these efforts would not have lived a day without the generous financial assistance of the Commission. Both the European Migrants' Forum and attempts to set up a European anti-racist network failed because of internal controversies along national lines—national lines, it should be emphasized, referring to the participating migrant organizations' countries of residence, not to their ethnic homelands.[18] This is in line with Ireland's (1994) finding from his French–Swiss comparison, in which he demonstrates that the patterns of political participation of Turks in France tend to resemble those of Italians in France more than those of Turks in Switzerland, who in turn resemble Italians in Switzerland.

The EU's weak development as a forum of political contention, not only in the immigration field but more generally, is hardly surprising given the weakness of representative institutions such as the European Parliament and the predominance of intergovernmental forms of decision-making such as the Council of Ministers. In this constellation, nation-states remain the central actors and the principal addressees of demands from civil society organizations. Only nation-state representatives have both the capacity to advance such societal interests, and to be held accountable if they do not adequately do so, regardless of whether this requires state action on the national or EU level. A simple look at the resources at the EU's disposal may serve to further underline its weakness and dependence on the constituting nation-states. In 1991, total EU expenditures amounted to 53 billion ECU: a mere 1 per cent of the total GDP of the member states. Moreover, no less than 64 per cent of these expenditures were on the Common Agricultural Policy, a policy field no one would claim to be at the forefront of a postnational challenge to the nation-state (Maraveyas 1996: 116). In addition, the few resources that the EU has at its disposal do not derive from independent tax revenue, but from contributions of the member states, which are always contestable and never unconditional. In that sense, in as far as the EU resembles a polity, it is one controlled by fifteen extremely rich taxpayers, who pretty much decide amongst themselves how much they want to pay and what they expect in return—an agricultural subsidy here, subvention for an 'underdeveloped' region there.

Although there is, so far even in the European case, little indication of an important shift of the locus of power and political contention from the nation-state to the supranational level, it cannot be maintained either that nothing has changed in the role and influence of the nation-state. In the face of the increased transnationalization and mobility of capital, nation-states have lost much of their regulatory capacity in the economic sphere. This obviously has also affected their capacities to maintain extensive nationally-defined welfare-state programmes. In the cultural sphere, too, the recent exponential increase in world-wide communication and cultural diffusion have made it virtually impossible for nation-states to maintain a distinguishable 'national' politics of culture, information, and communication—the French seemingly fight a rear-guard battle here.

To understand how this fits with the continuing importance of the nation-state as a locus of political contention, we should distinguish between the nation-state's sovereignty and it's capacity for autonomous action:

... the concept of 'sovereignty' is usually taken to mean that a nation state has power and control over its own future: that it has, in other words, the ability to take final decisions and to make and enforce the law in a given community or territory. A loss of sovereignty implies a loss of legal and actual control over the determination of the direction of national policy. Sovereignty must be distinguished from 'autonomy'. The idea of autonomy refers to the capacity of nation states, not to set goals, but to achieve goals and policies once they have been set, because in an interdependent world all instruments of national policy may be less effective. It is a diminution of the capacity to achieve national policies—a loss of national autonomy—which may alone be behind the anxieties about a loss of 'sovereignty'. The question to pose is: has sovereignty remained intact while the autonomy of the state has diminished, or has the modern state actually faced a loss of sovereignty?   (Held 1996: 407)

The answer to Held's question is, we suggest, that in spite of the decline in its autonomous capacity to act, the nation-state still is by far the most important locus of sovereignty. The loss of regulatory capacity of nation-states as a result of processes of globalization has not been compensated at the supranational level. Thus, Streeck and Schmitter describe the process of European union as ' "negative integration" through preemption of national regulatory regimes without a simultaneous supranational restoration of regulatory capacity' (1996: 185). It is important to note that such 'deregulation' is not something imposed on nation-states, but is actively promoted by them in an effort to further economic globalization (Sassen 1998: 54).

This may be the main paradox of our present situation: that the nation-state's capacities are eroding, but that there is nothing that can credibly fill the void, or at least not yet. As a result of the nation state's erosion, many people experience a loss of identity and of control over their destinies. But simultaneously there is nothing beyond the nation-state—except perhaps local communities and identities—that can serve as a new anchor for collective identities and renew the sense of control. However eroded it may already be in an absolute sense, compared to its local and supranational 'competitors', the nation-state is in a relative sense still by far the most important source of sovereignty and collective identity. It is therefore that our age of globalization is also a time of nationalism, of ethnic mobilization, of the rise of xenophobic movements, and of a proliferation of new nation-states with newly invented national histories, anthems, flags, and languages—unfortunately also accompanied by a series of atrocities in the name of the 'national' cause that has few historical precedents.[19] As the single force to give at least some counterplay against the impersonal forces of globalization, many turn to the nation-state and the national community as havens in a heartless world.

In the context of Western countries, issues such as immigration and minority integration are particularly well suited to such attempts to reinvigorate the nation-state. Precisely because it seems futile, and in many respects clearly disadvantageous, to try to stem the tide of economic globalization, those policy fields where the nation-state still has pretty much retained its capacity to act, become the focus of such reinvigoration attempts: 'The control of entry becomes one of the few domains in which states can still be strong—"renationalizing" immigration policies as antidote to the "denationalizing" logic of globalization' (Joppke 1998: 3).[20] The same can be said in the cultural realm of minority integration politics. As a macro force, cultural globalization seems unstoppable, and because of its many advantages also irresistible—after all, who wants to miss Hollywood, ethnic restaurants, and holidays in the sun? However, its manifestations in everyday life in Western cities in the form of women wearing headscarfs, mosques, black people, or 'strange' cooking smells, seem within people's and nation-states' reach of control and have for many people become the focus for everything they dislike about our global age.

We may conclude, then, that so far there is little reason to drop the nation-state as a central unit of analysis in studies of immigration and ethnic relations. Of course, it is possible that the process of European unification will in the future lead to real transfers of sovereignty, accountability, and collective identity from the national to the supranational level, although the increasing heterogeneity of the European Union as a result of the upcoming admission of a series of new members seems to work against this scenario. However, the usefulness of the conceptual framework we have proposed here does not depend on whether or not the nation-state will in the future lose its pivotal role in migration and ethnic relations politics. On the contrary, the conceptual framework of the political opportunity structure approach seems well-equipped to deal with situations of so-called 'multi-level governance', just as it is helpful in analysing the multi-level dynamics of federal states such as Switzerland. Moreover, the dilemmas that nation-states have faced in regulating migration and integrating migrants will not dissolve in the face of the emergence of a European polity. Such a Europe, too, will have to develop rules and discursive legitimation for who gets access to its territory, who can become a member of its political community, and how it will deal with cultural diversity and demands for special group rights. These are fundamental dilemmas any form of political regulation of migration and ethnic relations will have to deal with—they do not arise from specific deficiencies of the nation-state that will magically disappear with the arrival of some form of 'postnationalism'.

Notes

The authors wish to thank Adrian Favell for offering comments on parts of this text.

1. Obviously the time dimension here is different for different countries. In Britain, the migrations field developed earlier than in other European countries, in response to its early definition as a central political problem and also considerable state funding. In countries such as Italy, with a later trajectory of migration and politicization, there is still relatively little research that deals with migration as anything other than a policy issue. Our aim here is to pick out general trends of development.
2. Kriesi et al. (1995: 37) similarly combine formal institutional and political-cultural dimensions in their analysis of new social movements.
3. There are a few examples, though, which come pretty close to this extreme, e.g., Israel, or until recently Estonia.
4. Even Brubaker (1999) now seems to share this view, and in doing so departs radically from his earlier position.
5. In the early stages of the guestworker programmes, migrant children were often even in completely separate school classes. Ironically, multiculturalism sometimes unintentionally leads to a similar outcome: for example, the phenomenon of 'black schools' in The Netherlands discussed by Thränhardt in Chapter 8 of this volume.
6. At first sight, the term 'ethnic assimilationism' may seem contradictory, at least if one sees 'ethnicity' as an objective category based on blood ties into which one can only be born, and not assimilated to. However, ever since Weber (1985), the dominant sociological view of ethnicity has emphasized the constructed, 'imagined' (Gellner 1983; Anderson 1991) character of ethnic community.
7. The ultimate end of the extreme-right may well be ethnic segregationism or even simply throwing immigrants out of the country. However, that is not the kind of discourse with which one can win elections in France. The insistence on cultural assimilation as a precondition to citizenship is much more resonant.
8. The restrictions to the *jus soli* that this law entailed were later mostly reversed by the Socialists.

9. The British case seems less extreme, which is probably related to the much more limited version of multiculturalism that characterizes this country. British 'multiculturalism' is rather superficial in that it refers mainly to an atttitude of tolerance and respect for cultural diversity in the phenotypical—that is, as an extension of 'racial'—sense, and to a much more limited extent than in The Netherlands to special rights for cultural groups. Thus, although representatives of the British race-relations industry like to present Britain as Europe's multicultural example *par excellence*, British Muslims do not have nearly the same rights as their Dutch counterparts, such as their own state-funded schools.

10. *Aussiedler* are immigrants of ethnic German descent, often from Poland, the former Soviet Union, Romania, and other Eastern European countries. In many cases, current flows of *Aussiedler* claim a heritage dating back over a century to the German homeland and do not even speak the language.

11. There are of course many other relevant classes of actors, which we cannot all discuss here. Here we want to at least mention that the conceptual map can also be helpful to place regions or cities relative to each other, or relative to the national level of the polity.

12. The part of Yasemin Soysal's (1994) work that compares different national 'incorporation regimes' uses a very similar approach and makes very much the same point. This part of her work stands in odd contrast to her 'postnational citizenship' thesis in the same book, which claims that the nation-state and national citizenship have become largely irrelevant in defining migrant rights and opportunities for participation (see our discussion in the last part of this chapter).

13. This concept has sometimes been referred to explicitly by neo-institutionalist scholars (e.g., Ireland 1994), but in a vague way to generally point out the importance of the political context.

14. Hammar (1985) has used the term 'denizens' to capture the particular status of these permanently resident non-citizens, when referring to post-war migrant communities in Europe.

15. In a similar vein, Jacobson (1996) argues that '(t)he state is becoming less a sovereign agent and more an institutional forum of a larger international and constitutional order based on human rights.'

16. Saskia Sassen is not convinced by this argument:

Even where rooted in the founding documents of nation-states, as is the case with the United States and France, we need to understand the specific development of these rights over the last few years. Human rights today are a force that can undermine the exclusive authority of the state over its nationals and thereby contribute to transform the interstate system and international legal order . . . Human rights codes can erode some of the legitimacy of the state if it fails to respect such human rights—it is no longer just a question of national self-determination. This is a very significant shift.   (Sassen 1998: 70)

This argument seems to be based on the idea that there was a time when nation-states could do with their citizens and residents whatever they wanted and that this is no longer true. The truth is, of course, that some nation-states have always been limited in what they could or would do with the persons on their territory—that is why we call them 'liberal', 'democratic', or 'states under the rule of law'. Conversely, other states such as China, who are apparently ignorant of the fact that a very significant shift has occured, continue to ignore such principles and are allowed to do pretty much whatever they like with their subjects.

17. As Joppke argues, the differential extent to which notions of human rights have been formally encoded in national constitutional law may also play a role in explaining differences among Western states:

Britain showed how far a state with weak domestic human rights constraints can go in shielding itself from unwanted migrations. Britain is the one case that approximates the picture of a domestic state confronted with international human rights norms. Alas, it is also the case that demonstrates the impotence of such external norms if not backed by a domestic bill of rights and independent courts (Joppke 1997: 294).

18. Streeck and Schmitter make a similar observation regarding the attempts of labour movements to organize at the European level (1996: 175–6).

19. Eric Hobsbawm, reflecting on regionalist movements in Britain in 1977, probably did not realize how close he was to the mark when he wrote that '(t)he United Nations Organization . . . is soon likely to consist of the late 20th century equivalents of Saxe-Coburg-Gotha and Schwarzberg-Sondershausen.' (cited in Nairn 1996: 272).

20. Generally, these are policy fields that do not, like the classical welfare-state related issues, depend heavily on the state's eroded extractive capacity, but that are relatively resource-extensive and symbolically intensive. On the left side of the political spectrum they include issues such as the environment and women's emancipation, as well as ethnic and other identity politics. On the right, they include moral issues such as abortion and the role of the family, as well as crime and immigration control.

References

ÅLUND, ALEXSANDRA, and SCHIERUP, CARL-ULRIK (1991), *Paradoxes of Multiculturalism. Essays on Swedish Society* (Aldershot: Avebury).

ANDERSON, BENEDICT (1991), *Imagined Communities: Reflections on the Origin and Spread of Nationalism* (London: Verso).

BALDWIN-EDWARDS, MARTIN, and SCHAIN, MARTIN (eds.) (1994), *The Politics of Immigration in Western Europe* (London: Sage).

BASCH, LINDA, GLICK-SCHILLER, NINA, and SZANTON-BLANC, CRISTINA (1994), *Nations Unbound: Transnationalized Projects and the Deterritorialized Nation-State* (New York, NY: Gordon & Breach).

BENFORD, ROBERT D. (1997), 'An insider's critique of the social movements framing perspective', *Sociological Inquiry*, 67: 409–30.

BETZ, HANS-GEORG (1994), *Radical Right-Wing Populism in Western Europe* (Basingstoke: Macmillan).

BOVENKERK, FRANK, MILES, ROBERT, and VERBUNT, GILLES (1990), 'Racism, migration and the state in Western Europe: a case for comparative analysis', *International Sociology*, 5/4: 475–90.

BROSIUS, HANS-BERND, and ESSER, FRANK (1995), *Eskalation durch Berichterstattung? Massenmedien und fremdenfeindliche Gewalt* (Opladen: Westdeutscher Verlag).

BRUBAKER, ROGERS (1992), *Citizenship and Nationhood in France and Germany* (Cambridge, MA: Harvard University Press).

——(1999), 'The Manichean Myth: Rethinking the Distinction between "Civic" and "Ethnic" Nationalism' in Hanspeter Kriesi, Klaus Armingeon, Hannes Siegrist, and Andreas Wimmer (eds.), (1999), *Nation and National Identity. The European Experience in Perspective* (Zurich: Rüegger).

BOUSETTA, HASSAN (1996), 'Citizenship and Political Participation in France and the Netherlands: Reflections on two local cases', *New Community* 23/3: 215–31.

CANOVAN, MARGARET (1996), *Nationhood and Political Theory* (Cheltenham: Edward Elgar).

CALHOUN, CRAIG (1997), *Nationalism. Concepts in Social Thought* (Minneapolis, MN: University of Minnesota Press).

CASTLES, STEPHEN (1995), 'How Nation-States Respond to Immigration and Ethnic Diversity', *New Community* 21/3: 293–308.

——and KOSACK, GODULA (1974), 'From Aliens to Citizens: Redefining the Status of Immigrants in Europe. How the Trade Unions Try to Control and Integrate Immigrant Workers in the German Federal Republic', *Race*, 15/4: 497–514.

————(1985), *Immigrant Workers and Class Structure in Western Europe*, 2nd edn. (Oxford: Oxford University Press).

——and MILLER, MARK (1993), *The age of migration. International population movements in the modern world* (London: Macmillan).

COHEN, JEAN L. (1999), 'Changing Paradigms of Citizenship and the Exclusiveness of the Demos', *International Sociology*, 14/3: 245–68.

CORNELIUS, WAYNE, MARTIN, PHILIP, and HOLLIFIELD, JAMES (eds.) (1994), *Controlling Immigration. A Global Perspective* (Stanford, CA: Stanford University Press).

DIJK, TEUN A. VAN (1993), *Elite Discourse and Racism* (Newbury Park, CA: Sage).

DONSELAAR, JAAP VAN (1995), *De staat paraat? De bestrijding van extreem-rechts in West-Europa* (Amsterdam: Babylon-De Geus).

EDER, KLAUS (1993), *The New Politics of Class: Social Movements and Cultural Dynamics in Advanced Societies* (London: Sage).

EISINGER, PETER K. (1973), 'The Conditions of Protest Behavior in American Cities', *American Political Science Review*, 67: 11–28.

ESSER, HARTMUT (1999), 'Die Situationslogik ethnischer Konflikte', *Zeitschrift für Soziologie*, 28/4: 245–62.

FAIST, THOMAS (1995), 'Boundaries of welfare states: immigrants and social rights on the national and supranational level' in Robert Miles and Dietrich Thränhardt (eds.), *Migration and European Integration. The Dynamics of Inclusion and Exclusion* (London: Pinter).

——(1997), 'Immigration, Citizenship and Nationalism. Internal Internationalization in Germay and Europe' in Maurice Roche and Rik van Berkel (eds.), *European Citizenship and Social Exclusion* (Aldershot: Ashgate).

FASSMAN, HEINZ, and MÜNZ, RAINER (1996), *Migration in Europa. Historische Entwicklung, aktuelle Trends, politische Reaktionen* (Frankfurt on Main: Campus).

FAVELL, ADRIAN (1998), *Philosophies of Integration. Immigration and the Idea of Citizenship in France and Britain* (Houndmills, Basingstoke: Macmillan).

FIJALKOWSKI, JÜRGEN (1994), 'Conditions of Ethnic Mobilisation: The German Case' in John Rex and Beatrice Drury (eds.), *Ethnic Mobilisation in a Multi-cultural Europe* (Aldershot: Avebory).

FREEMAN, GARY P. (1992), 'The consequence of immigration policies for immigrant status: a British and French comparison' in Anthony Messina, L. Fraga, L. Rhodebeck, and F. Wright (eds.), *Ethnic and Racial Minorities in Advanced Industrial Democracies* (New York, NY: Greenwood Press).

——(1995), 'Modes of Immigration Politics in Liberal Democratic States', *International Migration Review*, 29/4: 881–902.

——(1998), 'The Decline of Sovereignty? Politics and Immigration Restriction in Liberal States' in Christian Joppke (ed.), *Challenge to the Nation-State. Immigration in Western Europe and the United States* (Oxford: Oxford University Press).

GAMSON, WILLIAM A. (1988), *The Strategy of Social Protest* (Homewood, IL: Dorsey Press).

——and MEYER, DAVID S. (1996), 'Framing political opportunity' in Doug. McAdam, John. D. McCarthy, and Mayer N. Zald (eds.), *Comparative Perspectives on Social Movements* (Cambridge: Cambridge University Press).

——and MODIGLIANI, ANDRE (1989), 'Media Discourse and Public Opinion on Nuclear Power. A Constructionist Approach', *American Journal of Sociology*, 95: 1–38.

GELLNER, ERENST (1983), *Nations and Nationalism* (Ithaca, NY: Cornell University Press).

GESSENHARTER, WOLFGANG, and FRÖCHLING, HELMUT (eds.) (1998), *Rechtsextremismus und Neue Rechte in Deutschland. Neuvermessung eines politisch-ideologischen Raumes?* (Opladen: Leske + Buderich).

GLAZER, NATHAN (1997), *We Are All Multiculturalists Now* (Cambridge, MA: Harvard University Press).

GLICK-SCHILLER, NINA, BASCH, LINDA, and BLANC-SZANTON, CRISTINA (1997), 'Transnationalismus: Ein neuer analytischer Rahmen zum Verständnis von Migration' in Heinz Kleger (ed.), *Transnationale Staatsbürgerschaft* (Frankfurt: Campus).

GOFFMAN, ERVING (1974), *Frame Analysis. An Essay on the Organization of Experience* (Cambridge, MA: Harvard University Press).

GREENFELD, LIAH (1992), *Nationalism. Five Roads to Modernity* (Cambridge, MA: Harvard University Press).

GUIGNI, MARCO, MCADAM, DOUG, and TILLY, CHARLES (eds.) (1999), *How Social Movements Matter* (Minneapolis, MN: University of Minnesota Press).

GUIRAUDON, VIRGINIE (1998), 'Citizenship rights for non-citizens: France, Germany, and the Netherlands' in Christian Joppke (ed.), *Challenge to the Nation-State. Immigration in Western Europe and the United States* (Oxford: Oxford University Press).

GUTMANN, AMY (ed.) (1994), *Multiculturalism* (Princeton, NJ: Princeton University Press).

HAILBRONNER, KAY (1995), 'Third-Country Nationals and EC Law' in Allen Rosas and Esco Antola (eds.), *A Citizens' Europe. In Search of a New Order* (London: Sage).

HAINSWORTH, PAUL (ed.) (1992), *The Extreme Right in Europe and the USA* (London: Pinter).

HALL, PETER, and TAYLOR, ROSEMARY (1996), 'Political science and the three new institutionalisms', *Political Studies*, 44/5: 936–57.

HAMMAR, TOMAS (1985), 'Introduction' in Tomas Hammar (ed.), *European Immigration Policy* (New York, NY: Cambridge University Press).

HEAR, NICHOLAS VAN (1998), *New diasporas. The mass exodus, dispersal and regrouping of migrant communities* (London: UCL Press).

HEITMEYER, WILHELM, BUHSE, HEIKE, LIEBE-FREUND, JOACHIM, MÖLLER, KURT, MÜLLER, JOACHIM, RITZ, HELMUT, SILLER, GERTRUD, and VOSSEN, JOHANNES (1992), *Die Bielefelder Rechtsextremismus-Studie. Erste Langzeituntersuchung zur politischen Sozialisation männlicher Jugendlicher* (Munich: Juventa).

——SCHRÖDER, HELMUT, and MÜLLER, JOACHIM (1997), 'Desintegration und islamischer Fundamentalismus. Über Lebenssituation, Alltagserfahrungen und ihre Verarbeitungsformen bei türkischen Jugendlichen in Deutschland', *Aus Politik und Zeitgeschichte*, 7/8: 17–31.

HELD, DAVID (1996), 'The Decline of the Nation State' in Geoff Eley and Ronald G. Suny (eds.), *Becoming National: A Reader* (Oxford: Oxford University Press).

HILGARTNER, STEPHEN, and BOSK, CHARLES L. (1988), 'The Rise and Fall of Social Problems', *American Journal of Sociology*, 94: 53–78.

HOBSBAWM, ERIC. J. (1990), *Nation and nationalism since 1780. Programme, myth, reality* (Cambridge: Cambridge University Press).

HUSBANDS, CHRISTOPHER T. (1993), 'Racism and Racist Violence: Some Theories and Policy Perspectives', in Tore Björgo and Robwitte, *Racist Violence in Europe* (London: Macmillan).

——(1994), 'Crises of national identity as the "new moral panics": political agenda-setting about definitions of nationhood', *New Community*, 20/2: 191–206.

IRELAND, PATRICK (1994), *The Policy Challenge of Ethnic Diversity. Immigrant Politics in France and Switzerland* (Cambridge, MA: Harvard University Press).

JACOBSON, DAVID (1996), *Rights across Borders. Immigration and the Decline of Citizenship* (Baltimore, MD: Johns Hopkins University Press).

JENKINS, BRIAN, and SOFOS, SPYROS A. (eds.) (1996), *Nation and Identity in Contemporary Europe* (London: Routledge).

JOPPKE, CHRISTIAN (1996), 'Multiculturalism and Immigration: A Comparison of the United States, Germany, and Great Britain', *Theory and Society*, 25: 449–500.

——(1997), 'Asylum and State Sovereignty. A Comparison of the United States, Germany, and Britain', *Comparative Political Studies*, 30/3: 259–98.

——(ed.) (1998), *Challenge to the Nation-State. Immigration in Western Europe and the United States* (Oxford: Oxford University Press).

KITSCHELT, HERBERT (1986), 'Political Opportunity Structures and Political Protest: Anti-nuclear Movements in Four Democracies', *British Journal of Political Science*, 16: 57–85.

——in collaboration with Anthony J. McGann (1997), *The Radical Right in Western Europe. A Comparative Analysis* (Ann Arbor, MI: The University of Michigan Press).

KLANDERMANS, BERT (1988), 'The Formation and Mobilization of Consensus' in Bert Klandermans, Hanspeter Kriesi, and Sidney Tarrow (eds.), *From Structure to Action: Social Movement Participation across Cultures*, International Social Movement Research, Vol. 1 (Greenwich, CT: JAI Press), 173–96.

KLEGER, HEINZ (ed.) (1997), *Transnationale Staatsbürgerschaft* (Frankfurt on Main: Campus).

——and D'AMATO, GIANNI (1995), 'Staatsbürgerschaft und Einbürgerung—oder: Wer ist ein Bürger? Ein Vergleich zwischen Deutschland, Frankreich und der Schweiz', *Journal für Sozialforschung*, 35/3–4: 259–98.

KOOPMANS, RUUD (1996a), 'Explaining the rise of racist and extreme right violence in Western Europe: Grievances or opportunities?', *European Journal of Political Research*, 30: 185–216.

——(1996b), 'Asyl: Die Karriere eines politischen Konflikts' in Wolfgang van der Daele and Friedhelm Neidhardt (eds.), *Kommunikation und Entscheidung. Politische Funktionen öffentlicher Meinungsbildung und diskursiver Verfahren.* (Berlin: Edition Sigma), 167–92.

——(1997), 'Dynamics on Repression and Mobilization: The German Extreme Right in the 1990s', *Mobilization: An International Journal*, 2/2: 149–65.

——(1999), 'Germany and its immigrants: an ambivalent relationship', *Journal of Ethnic and Migration Studies*, 25/4: 627–47.

——and DUYVENDAK, JAN WILLEM (1995), 'The Political Construction of the Nuclear Energy Issue and its Impact on the Mobilization of Anti-Nuclear Movements in Western Europe', *Social Problems*, 42/2: 235–51.

——and KRIESI, HANSPETER (1997), 'Citoyenneté, identité nationale et mobilisation de l'extrême droite. Une comparaison entre la France, l'Allemagne, les Pays-Bas et la Suisse' in Pierre Birnbaum (ed.), *Sociologie des nationalismes* (Paris: PUF), 295–324.

——and STATHAM, PAUL (1999), 'Ethnic and Civic Conceptions of Nationhood and the Differential Success of the Extreme Right in Germany and Italy' in Marco Guigni, Doug McAdam, and Charles Tilly (eds.), *How Social Movements Matter* (Minneapolis, MN: University of Minnesota Press), 225–51.

————(2000), 'Political claims-making against Racism and Discrimination in Britain and Germany', in Jessika Ter Wal and Maykel Verkuten, *Comparative Perspectives on Racism* (Aldershot: Ashgate).

KRIESI, HANSPETER, KOOPMANS, RUUD, DUYVENDAK, JAN WILLEM, and GUIGNI, MARCO (1992), 'New social movements and political opportunities in Western Europe', *European Journal of Political Research*, 22: 219–44.

————————(1995), *New Social Movements in Western Europe. A Comparative Analysis* (Minneapolis, MN: University of Minnesota Press).

——ARMINGEON, KLAUS, SIEGRIST, HANNES, and WIMMER, ANDREAS (eds.) (1999), *Nation and National Identity. The European Experience in Perspective* (Zurich: Rüegger).

KYMLICKA, WILL (1995), *Multicultural Citizenship. A Liberal Theory of Minority Rights* (Oxford: Clarendon).

LAKEMAN, PIETER (1999), *Binnen zonder kloppen. Nederlandse immigratiepolitiek en de economische Gevolgen* (Amsterdam: Meulenhoff).

LAURENCE, JONATHAN (1999), '(Re)constructing Community in Berlin; Of Jews, Turks and German Responsibility', Discussion Paper FS III 99–102. Wissenschaftszentrum Berlin für Sozialforschung.

LIE, JOHN (1995), 'From International Migration to Transnational Diaspora', *Contemporary Sociology*, 24: 303–6.

MANN, MICHAEL (1996), 'Nation-states in Europe and Other Continents: Diversifying, Developing, Not Dying' in Gopal Balakrishnan (ed.), *Mapping the Nation* (London: Verso).

MARAVEYAS, NAPOLEON (1996), 'The Agricultural Strata in The European Union and The Common Agricultural Policy' in George A. Kourvetaris and Andreas Moschonas (eds.), *The Impact of European Integration. Political, Sociological, and Economic Changes* (Westport, CT: Praeger).

MARCH, J., and OLSEN, J. (1984), 'The new institutionalism: organizational factors in political life', *American Political Science Review*, 78/3: 734–49.

MARTINIELLO, MARCO (ed.) (1998), *Multicultural policies and the state: a comparison of two European societies* (Utrecht: ERCOMER).

McADAM, DOUG (1982), *Political Process and the Development of Black Insurgency, 1930–1970* (Chicago, IL: University of Chicago Press).

——McCARTHY, JOHN D., and ZALD, MAYER N. (1996), *Comparative perspectives on social movements* (Cambridge: Cambridge University Press).

McCARTHY, JOHN D., and ZALD, MAYER N. (1977), 'Resource Mobilisation and Social Movements: A Partial Theory', *American Journal of Sociology*, 82: 1212–41.

MEEHAN, ELIZABETH (1993), *Citizenship and the European Community* (London: Sage).

MELUCCI, ALBERTO (1990), *Nomads of the Present: Social Movements and Individual Needs in Contemporary Society* (Philadelphia, PA: Temple University Press).

MILES, ROBERT (1982), *Racism and Migrant Labour* (London: Routledge and Kegan Paul).

——and ANNIE PHIZACKLEA (1977), 'Class, Race, Ethnicity, and Political Action', *Political Studies*, 25: 491–507.

MILES, ROBERT (1984), *White Man's Country* (London: Pluto Press).

——and DIETRICH THRÄNHARDT (eds.) (1995), *Migration and European Integration. The Dynamics of Inclusion and Exclusion* (London: Pinter).

MILLER, MARK J. (1981), *Foreign Workers in Western Europe: An Emerging Political Force?* (New York, NY: Praeger).

——(1982), 'The Political Impact of Foreign Labour', *International Migration Review*, 16/1: 27–60.

MODOOD, TARIQ, and WERBNER, PNINA (eds.) (1997), *The Politics of Multiculturalism in the New Europe: Racism, Identity and Community* (London: Zed Books).

MÜNZ, RAINER, SEIFERT, WOLFGANG, and ULRICH, RALF (1997), *Zuwanderung nach Deutschland. Strukturen, Wirkungen, Perspektiven* (Frankfurt on Main: Campus).

NAIRN, TOM (1996), 'Internationalism and the Second Coming' in Gopal Balakrishnan (ed.), *Mapping the Nation* (London: Verso).

NELKIN, DOROTHY, and POLLAK, MICHAEL (1981), *The Atom Besieged: Extraparliamentary Dissent in France and Germany* (Cambridge, MA: MIT Press).

OBERSCHALL, ANTHONY (1973), *Social Conflict and Social Movements* (Englewood Cliffs, NJ: Prentice-Hall).

OLZAK, SUSAN (1992), *The Dynamics of Ethnic Competition and Conflict* (Stanford, CA: Stanford University Press).

OVERBEEK, HENK (1995), 'Towards a new international migration regime: globalization, migration and the internationalization of the state' in Robert Miles and Dietrich Tränhardt (eds.), *Migration and European Integration. The Dynamics of Inclusion and Exclusion* (London: Pinter).

PAREKH, BHIKHU (1998), 'Integrating minorities' in Tessa Blackstone, Bhikha Parekh, and Peter Sanders (eds.), *Race Relations in Britain: A Developing Agenda* (London: Routledge).

RATH, JAN (1991), 'Minorisering: De Sociale Constructie van Ethnische Minderheden', PhD Thesis, University of Utrecht, The Netherlands.

REX, JOHN (1996), *Ethnic Minorities in the Modern Nation State. Working Papers in the Theory of Multiculturalism and Political Integration* (Houndsmill, Basingstoke: Macmillan).

——and DRURY, BEATRICE (eds.) (1994), *Ethnic Mobilisation in a Multi-cultural Europe* (Aldershot: Avebury).

——and TOMLINSON, SALLY (1979), *Colonial Immigrants in a British City: A Class Analysis* (London: Routledge and Kegan Paul).

ROCHE, MAURICE, and BERKEL, RIK VAN (eds.) (1997), *European Citizenship and Social Exclusion* (Aldershot: Ashgate).

ROSAS, ALLAN, and ANTOLA, ESKO (eds.) (1995), *A Citizens' Europe. In Search of a New Order* (London: Sage).

ROSENHEK, ZEEV (1999), 'The politics of claims-making by labour migrants in Israel', *Journal of Ethnic and Migrations Studies*, 24/4: 575–95.

RUDOLPH, HEDWIG (1996), 'The new *gastarbeiter* system in Germany', *New Community*, 22/2: 287–300.

SAFRAN, WILLIAM (1997), 'Citizenship and Nationality in Democratic Systems: Approaches to Defining and Acquiring Membership in the Political Community', *International Political Science Review*, 18/3: 313–35.

SASSEN, SASKIA (1998), 'The *de facto* Transnationalizing of Immigration Policy' in Christian Joppke (ed.), *Challenge to the Nation-State. Immigration in Western Europe and the United States* (Oxford: Oxford University Press).

SCHLESINGER, ARTHUR D. (1992), *The Disuniting of America: Reflections on a Multicultural Society* (New York, NY: Norton).

SCHOENEBERG, ULRIKE (1985), 'Participation in ethnic associations: the case of immigrants in West Germany', *International Migration Review*, 19/3: 416–35.

SHAIN, YOSSI, and SHERMAN, MARTIN (1998), 'Dynamics of disintegration: Diaspora, secession and the paradox of nation-states', *Nations and Nationalism*, 4/3: 321–46.

SHAPIRO, IAN, and KYMLICKA, WILL (eds.) (1997), *Ethnicity and Group Rights* (New York, NY: New York University Press).

SHORTER, EDWARD, and TILLY, CHARLES (1972), 'Hardships and Collective Violence in France, 1830–1960', *Amercian Sociological Review*, 37: 520–32.

SMITH, DAVID M., and BLANC, MAURICE (1996), 'Citizenship, Nationality and Ethnic Minorities in Three European Nations', *International Journal of Urban and Regional Research*, 20/1: 66–82.

SNOW, DAVID A., and BENFORD, ROBERT D. (1988), 'Ideology, Frame Resonance, and Participant Mobilization' in Bert Klandermans, Hanspeter Kriesi, and Sidney Tarrow (eds.), *From Structure to Action: Social Movement Participation across Cultures*, International Social Movement Research, Vol. 1 (Greenwich, CT: JAI Press).

——ROCHEFORD JR., E. BURKE, WORDEN, STEVEN K., and BENFORD, ROBERT D. (1986), 'Frame Alignment Processes, Micromobilization, and Movement Participation', *American Sociological Review*, 51: 464–81.

SOYSAL, YASEMIN NUHOGLU (1994), *Limits of Citizenship. Migrants and Postnational Membership in Europe* (Chicago, IL: University of Chicago Press).

STATHAM, PAUL (1998), 'The Political Construction of Immigration in Italy: Opportunities, Mobilisation, and Outcomes', Discussion Paper FS III 98-102, Wissenschaftszentrum Berlin.

——(1999), 'Political mobilisation by minorities in Britain: a negative feedback of "race relations"?', *Journal of Ethnic and Migration Studies*, 25/4: 597–626.

STEENBERGEN, BART VAN (ed.) (1994), *The Condition of Citizenship* (London: Sage).

STREECK, WOLFGANG, and SCHMITTER, PHILIPPE C. (1996), 'Organized Interests in the European Union' in George A. Kourvetaris and Andreas Moschonas (eds.), *The Impact of European Integration. Political, Sociological, and Economic Changes* (Westport, CT: Praeger).

TARROW, SIDNEY (1989), *Democracy and Disorder. Protest and Politics in Italy 1965–1975* (Oxford: Clarendon).

——(1994), *Power in movement. Social movements, collective action and politics* (Cambridge, UK: Cambridge University Press).

Taylor, Charles, Appiah, K. Anthony, Habermas, Jürgen, Rockefeller, Steven C., Walzer, Michael, and Wolf, Susan; edited and introduced by Amy Gutmann (1994), *Multiculturalism* (Princeton, NJ: Princeton University Press).

Thränhardt, Dietrich (1993), 'Die Ursprünge von Rassismus und Fremden-feindlichkeit in der Konkurrenzdemokratie. Ein Vergleich der Entwicklungen in England, Frankreich und Deutschland', *Leviathan*, 3: 336–57.

——and Robert Miles (1995), 'Introduction: European integration, migration and processes of inclusion and exclusion' in Robert Miles and Dietrich Thränhardt (eds.), *Migration and European Integration. The Dynamics of Inclusion and Exclusion* (London: Pinter).

Tilly, Charles (1978), *From Mobilization to Revolution* (Reading, MA: Addison-Wesley).

——Tilly, Louise, and Tilly, Richard (1975), *The Rebellious Century, 1830–1930* (Cambridge, MA: Harvard University Press).

Tölölyan, Khachig (1996), 'The Nation-State and Its Others: In Lieu of a Preface' in Geoff Eley and R. Grigor Suny (eds.), *Becoming National: A Reader* (Oxford: Oxford University Press).

Vermeulen, Hans, and Penninx, Rinus (eds.) (1994), *Het democratisch ongeduld. De emancipatie en integratie van zes doelgroepen van het minderhedenbeleid* (Amsterdam: Het Spinhuis).

Walzer, Michael (1983), *Spheres of Justice* (New York, NY: Basic Books).

Weber, Max (1985), *Wirtschaft und Gesellschaft* (Tubingen: Mohr).

Wiener, Antje (1997), 'Making sense of the new geography of citizenship: Fragmented citizenship in the European Union', *Theory and Society*, 26: 529–60.

Witte, Rob (1996), *Racist Violence and the State: a comparative analysis of Britain, France and the Netherlands* (London: Longman).

Wrench, John, and Solomos, John (eds.) (1993), *Racism and Migration in Western Europe* (Oxford: Berg).

Young, Iris Marion (1998), 'Polity and Group Difference: A Critique of the Ideal of Universal Citizenship' in Gershon Shafir (ed.), *The Citizenship Debates. A Reader* (Minneapolis, MN: University of Minnesota Press).

Zald, Mayer N., and Ash, Roberta (1966), 'Social Movement Organizations: Growth, Decay, and Change', *Social Forces*, 44: 327–41.

3

Multiculturalism and Political
Integration in Europe*

JOHN REX

Immigration and Models of the Structure and Dynamics of West European Societies in Ideology and Social Science

Western European countries have become increasingly conscious of multiculturalism as a major structural problem as a result of the presence in these countries of immigrants and of children who in some degree share their parents' culture. Their models of the dynamics of democratic societies had been developed by liberals and social democrats to deal with the question of social class. They had seen society as developing, either in accordance with the needs of free markets in labour as well as other commodities, or as being based upon a plurality of conflicting class interests reconciled through the mechanism of the welfare state. The problem, however, was that of the integration of new collectivities and new political actors whose motivation and forms of organization did not seem to fit easily into this model.

The Size of the Immigrant and Minority Population

The actual numbers of those involved in these new collectivities is actually very unclear from available statistics. What the official statistics (Eurostat 1995) record most easily are simply of those with foreign nationality or foreign birthplaces, but these do not include the number of those naturalized or of the children and grandchildren of immigrant parents who may still identify with their parents' culture and that of their parents' homeland. Attempts to discover the numbers in these categories, however, are resisted in some countries, whose governments see their enumeration as itself a form of discrimination and the denial of citizens' rights. Only the United Kingdom has included an 'ethnic question' in its census. There, an earlier attempt in 1981 to discover the numbers of immigrant children by recording the national origin of the head of household within which an individual lived, was still thought to be unsatisfactory, and, in 1991, subjects were asked to record to which of a number of ethnic groups they felt they belonged, the options offered being based upon categories of colour and nationality.

The objection to the British system was that it reflected the categorization of groups and individuals in a political order in which these groups or individuals suffered discrimination, even if there was some benign intent to rectify the consequential disadvantage from which they suffered. None the less it is the intention of the British system to deal with what is a real structural problem in Europe, because it is the case that there are substantial numbers of individuals born in European countries, or naturalized within them, who still have some feeling of belonging to structurally and culturally distinct minorities. Together with their immigrant parents they may number some twenty million of the population of West European countries. The policy problem for all the West European nation-states has been how to define the political status of these groups whatever their size.

It has been the intention in this volume that the present chapter should deal with structural problems whereas Chapter 4 by John Solomos and Liza Schuster should look at the question in its discursive aspects. I have sought to recognize this distinction but it should be clear from what I say below that I am concerned with spelling out in structural terms what is required for the implementation of certain ideals elaborated in political discourse. In Chapter 4, multicultural discourse is discussed in its general aspects without emphasizing the different structural implications of different versions of this discourse.

National Policies Towards Immigrant Minorities

Four policies have been posited. The first is that represented by a demand for the exclusion of immigrant minorities and for their repatriation to the countries from which the immigrant generation had come. The second is that which refuses to recognize their separate existence, but offers instead rights of citizenship under the *jus soli* to those born in the country of immigrant settlement and to those immigrants who become naturalized. The third is that which regards both the newcomers and their children as temporary residents, who, in principle if not in practice, are expected to return to their countries of origin and are not therefore entitled to political citizenship. The fourth is that of some variant of what is called multiculturalism.

The first of these policies has not yet been openly adopted by any government. It is, however, the case that political parties of the populist right which have adopted possible repatriation as one plank of their platform have been able to gain between 10 and 25 per cent of the vote in several countries—notably in France, Austria, and Belgium—and that, in attempting to win back that vote, mainstream parties have adapted their policies to tighten up immigration procedure, to deny rights to immigrants and their children, and to offer some form of encouragement for voluntary repatriation.

The second assimilationist alternative would prima facie appear to be the alternative most compatible with democracy. It does, however, have the consequence that it might encourage positive hostility towards minority cultures, reinforcing that which is engendered by populist racism.

The third alternative does not necessarily imply the total denial of social rights to immigrant workers and their children, and trades unions, which initially opposed immigration as such, may come to fight for the social rights of immigrants and their children. None the less it does make a distinction between citizens and what Hammar (1990) has called 'denizens', the former being thought of as having unquestionable rights guaranteed by the state, the latter being dependent upon the beneficent paternalistic concern of bodies like trades unions and churches.

The fourth alternative, multiculturalism, may take three very different forms. It may envisage a total transformation of the culture of the society in which, in the public, as well as in the private sphere, a formerly unitary national culture is displaced by a new one which is both more complex and diverse or hybrid; it may be based upon the recognition of minority cultures and communities but involve negotiation with them so that they are brought under the control of the state; finally, however, it may attempt to combine the recognition of cultural diversity with the promotion of individual equality.

In the United Kingdom all four of the political tendencies which I have mentioned and, within the multicultural alternative, all three of the types of multiculturalism, have gained some support. The nationalist and racist repatriation alternative was enunciated by the Conservative Enoch Powell and pursued by various minority parties, as well as influencing mainstream thinking in an anti-immigrant direction. The second alternative was influential in government thinking in the early-and mid-1960s before the full consequences of cultural diversity became evident amongst South Asian immigrants particularly in the schools. The third alternative appeared to be operating in that, although most immigrants from the former Commonwealth had the right of political citizenship *de jure*, they were, in fact, denied many social rights because of racial discrimination.

Types of Multicultural Policy

Turning now to the multicultural alternative, the first form of multiculturalism was thought by some to be inevitable in that a new diversity was evident in cuisine as well as in the arts and literature, and this diversity was set as indicative of an overall cultural transformation. The second form was the one spontaneously adopted by central and local governments as they sought to bring minority communities under control. There was, however, a third alternative, enunciated by some democrats and supported by minority leaders which was best expressed by the Labour Home Secretary, Roy Jenkins, when he defined the term 'integration' as implying 'not a flattening process of uniformity, but cultural diversity coupled with equal opportunity in an atmosphere of mutual tolerance' (Rex and Tomlinson 1979).

It was the possibility of creating a society embodying this third concept of multiculturalism which my colleagues and I sought to explore in 1993 in our discussions with European colleagues (Rex and Drury 1994). It seemed to us that this was the one alternative through which new immigrant groups could become integrated into European societies without threatening national cultures or the established institutions of democracies. What we found it necessary to do, however, was to spell out the meaning of the Jenkins formula in clear structural terms.

There is no suggestion here that British experience is more important than the experience of other countries in Europe, but the formula enunciated by Jenkins does provide an analytically useful tool in looking at policies in all these societies. What matters in all of them is the problem of recognizing cultural diversity without undermining a shared ideal of equality.

The Structural Implications of the Egalitarian Form of Multiculturalism

My own first suggestion was that the formula seemed to imply the existence of two sets of institutions or cultural domains. The first consisted of the institutions of the public political domain which were based upon the promotion of equality of opportunity for all individuals. The second consisted of the institutions of the private or communal sphere centring around different languages, religions, family practices and other customs. I argued that the former had to be unquestionable in a democratic society and could not be altered to accommodate diverse cultures. Sometimes this was what was referred to as the civic culture and support for it seems to be what Habermas refers to as 'constitutional patriotism' (1994). This culture is often thought of as secular, being divorced from the control of religion, but it may be better to refer to it as a shared culture in that it is supported by most of the different religious and value systems to be found in the society.

Of course the institutions of the public sphere involve far more than the affirmation of equality as a principle. They involve, for example, the institutions of the market and of public bureaucracy, the political system and the criminal and civil law. Immigrants have to accept these institutions as part of the structure within which they have chosen to live. What I wished to emphasize, however, was a commitment by the democratic national societies that these institutions should be shaped in accordance with the principle of equality (Rex 1996b).

The discussion of the question of equality has been shaped in Europe by the discussion of citizenship by T. H. Marshall (1951). He invites us to see citizenship as resting firstly upon legal rights, that is, equality before the law; secondly political rights, the right to vote both locally and nationally; and, thirdly, social rights in the form of a guaranteed minimum standard of life for all. Under the third heading it is not required that there should be total equality of outcome but only an assured minimum standard, thus leaving space for market principles to operate. It is the existence of a concept of citizenship of this kind which Marshall believes should lead to citizenship providing a stronger focus of loyalty than any other, such as loyalty to class or to any local regional grouping. Arguably, of course, this kind of social citizenship was undermined in the 1980s by attacks on the welfare state, but it is important to notice that in Britain, at least on the level of rhetoric, the Conservative Party continued to assert its belief in the system of social insurance and even, in the case of John Major, in the 'classless society'. The arguments here are repeated at a European level in the debate about the Social Chapter of the Maastricht Treaty.

If, however, a civic culture of this kind exists, and if the population develops a sense of 'constitutional patriotism', it may be asked whether there is any reason for the preservation of minority cultures. I have suggested two reasons. One is the necessity for all individuals, but particularly for those whose lives have been disrupted by migration, to have some immediate group to turn to for emotional and moral support. Durkheim (1933), it will be remembered, saw it as an essential element of organic solidarity, as opposed to a state of anomie, that such groups standing between the individual family and the state should exist. His own belief was that even for ordinary members of society there would have to be occupational guilds to perform this function. Whatever the merits of this proposal, it does seem that ethnic minority groups and their cultures do play this role.

The second reason for sustaining minority communities and their cultures is that they provide the means for collective political action. Such collective political action is a normal feature of democracy. In the democracies of Europe it has had a basis in social class. In the United States, however, where such class-based politics are less developed, immigrant communities have been the main means through which individuals have acted collectively in politics. With the decline of class-based politics in Europe something like the American alternative becomes important, although usually the immigrant communities do not act totally independently through their own parties, but rather through forming negotiating factions within mainstream, and often class-based, parties.

Having made these points about the desirability of sustaining minority communities as sources of moral and emotional support, and as a means to collective action, it now becomes necessary to consider the main sorts of bonding which exist in these communities. As we have noted they involve the maintenance of minority languages, minority religions, family practices, and other customs.

Looking at these in detail, each presents problems. So far as language is concerned the maintenance of mother tongue has a real although limited role. It is through the mother tongue that primary socialization occurs most naturally. On the other hand survival in the society of settlement requires of immigrants that they should learn the national language, or sometimes one of the national languages, as is the case in Belgium. They therefore have to become bilingual in order to access their rights within these societies, particularly in the spheres of employment and education. This would seem to involve an intrusion of the public into the private and communal sphere. On the other hand it is to be expected that, in order to administer its own services, the national state may well provide these services with the aid of translation of its own documents into immigrant languages, which is what frequently happens in the social services in Britain. In this case the minority culture intrudes into the public sphere.

Similar problems arise in the sphere of religion. Minority religions may provide their own world views but usually there is also a national religion or religions. Living with these national religions is therefore part of the immigrant experience and it is not uncommon in most European countries for the leaders of various minority religions to come together with those of the various Christian sects and denominations to act collectively on some moral issues. This is even true of Muslims, some of whom may insist that Islam is not a private matter but a 'whole way of life'. This does not, however, mean the disappearance of the minority religions which may still serve to underpin communal values.

Further problems arise with regard to family practices and customs. The belief in individual human rights, particularly amongst feminists, seems to be at odds with some of the practices relating to the position of women and marriage in ethnic minority communities. This problem, however, is not understood if it is assumed that women in modern societies have rights, whereas those in minority communities have none. In fact there is often argument *within* the minority communities themselves about these rights. As I shall emphasize later in discussing ethnic mobilization, we should not assume an essentialist view of ethnic minority cultures as traditional and unchanging.

A radical version of the notion of separate minority cultures would be that which suggests that on domestic matters they should be subject to a different legal system. Thus there are Muslims who would wish these matters to be regulated by *Sharia* law. Such an alternative is adopted in some colonial plural societies where the various communities remain territorially and economically segregated. In Europe it has not been seriously discussed, and could hardly be viable when many members of minority communities have ceased to practice their own religions. The most that is suggested, therefore, is that in matters like divorce, for example, the divorces granted by ordinary courts should be supplemented by unofficial courts which give their decisions an additional moral reinforcement (Poulter 1986, 1987, 1989).

Taken all in all, one may say that, despite the difficulties involved, there is still a place for the recognition of minority cultures in modern democratic industrial societies. It has to be acknowledged, however, that this does not mean the recognition of unchanging traditional cultures. I would certainly not advocate such an essentialist position myself. Moreover it also has to be recognized that over several generations the descendants of immigrants may gradually lose their loyalty to their own cultures. Most migrants recognize this and accept that one of the costs of migration is some loss of members.

Social Scientists' Criticism of the Concept of Multiculturalism

My advocacy of some limited recognition of minority cultures was not fully understood and was criticized by many European colleagues. Amongst these I would mention Wieviorka in France, Rath in the Netherlands, Radtke in Germany, and Schierup and Ålund in Sweden (See Rex and Drury 1994; Rath 1991; Ålund and Schierup 1991).

Wieviorka (1994) draws attention to the fact that in normal political discourse in France the very notion of ethnicity and ethnic communities only occurs in the discussion of inferiors. Rath argues that in Dutch multiculturalism the recognition of minorities often means that they are 'minorised' and thereby marked for inferior treatment. Radtke (1994), reflecting on the experience of Frankfurt, suggests that whereas post-war German society has been built upon the notion of the democratic welfare state in which a plurality of conflicting class interests are reconciled, the approach to the problems of Turkish minorities has been to assign them to a special and separate multicultural apparatus, so that the problem of an individual who is exploited or oppressed by a spouse, a landlord, or employer is wrongly seen as arising solely because of cultural difference. Schierup and Ålund see the Swedish policy of dealing and negotiating with traditional leaders, usually elderly men, which is convenient as a form of social control, as failing to recognize the extent to which younger members of these communities are forming alliances with, and becoming acculturated to, new syncretic cultures which are shared across different minority groups and with disadvantaged young Swedes. Finally it should be noted, in this volume Solomos and Schuster treat multiculturalism as possibly a new form of racist discourse.

All of these criticisms are, in my view, valid, and are to be kept in mind in evaluating multicultural programmes and policies. Indeed I would expect that the actual practices of multiculturalism in all European countries to be infected by the tendencies which these critics describe, as they are inclined in fact to deal with minorities as inferiors. If one wishes to put it that way, they reflect racist tendencies in the societies concerned. This, however, makes it all the more necessary to keep alive the notion of a limited multiculturalism which is compatible with, and can actually strengthen democracy. Such a notion, moreover, is supported by the ethnic minority groups and their liberal-minded allies in the anti-racist movement. The support of minority communities and their anti-racist allies is also itself an important structural fact.

It is important to notice here that in assessing what policies operate in practice it is necessary to look not merely at national policies but also at the policies developed by local governments in large cities. It is primarily at this local level in fact that the integration of immigrants takes place, whether that integration rests upon manipulation and control or upon the democratic empowerment of their communities. There is now a considerable amount of evidence on local institutions of this kind (Ireland 1994; Soysal 1994; Rex 1996a).

Some rather more fundamental problems arise, however, when we look at immigrant communities and cultures in a larger and more global context. Here we have to ask two complementary questions. The first is how far these groups retain or develop loyalties beyond those to the nation state. The second is whether the interests of immigrant minority communities are best served through their achievement of normal national citizenship or whether they should seek and be helped to achieve a transnational citizenship.

Talking in structural terms, I conceive of the structure of European society as being the resultant of the pursuit of different ideals by three different groups: immigrant ethnic minority groups seeking equal treatment as well as some kind of recognition of their culture, indigenous groups mobilizing in what is sometimes called a racist and xenophobic way against immigrant groups, and anti-racist mobilization. Each of these is discussed in what follows.

The Nature of Ethnic Minority Mobilization

So far as the first of these questions is concerned, I have suggested (Rex 1996b) that migrant communities have three points of reference. Firstly they may have continuing connections with the homeland; secondly, they are concerned to win a place for their members in their land of present settlement; and, thirdly they may envisage further onward migration.

Two things should be understood about homeland connections. One is that they are likely to remain strong in several important respects and that this will affect the ways in which they intersect with their societies of present settlement; the second, however, is that these links will not prevent that interaction.

The first type of link is that of kinship in some type of extended family. It is within these extended families that migration is planned rather than, as classical economic theories of migration suggest, purely by individuals—for a discussion of some of the issues involved here see the section on 'The new economics of migration' in Massey *et al.* (1993). In consequence, links with those members of the family who remain, will be sustained. Migration of other members of the family will be planned, spouses will be sought in the homeland and the children of migrants are likely to return there for visits.

Secondly, undoubtedly savings made as a result of employment abroad will be sent back in the form of remittances, and one of the motivations for employment will precisely be obtaining the money for remittances. Also the improvement of the status of the kin group in the homeland will be one of the main objectives of the migrants.

A third factor binding the migrants to the homeland will be a continuing interest in homeland politics. There are very few migrant groups in which this is not the case. Such politics involve conflict and these conflicts will serve to divide the migrant community abroad. Some, moreover, will use their base abroad to plan political actions, including violent ones, which are not possible at home. Such acts may also involve conflict with the law in societies of settlement.

All of these things may be true, but this does not imply that migrants are only temporary sojourners who will in due course return home. There is, it is true, usually some sort of myth of return in the minds of all migrants, but it is a myth except amongst purely seasonal migrants, and, after a period of successful employment abroad, most migrants will be reconciled to the fact that they will not in fact return.

I do not think, however, that it is helpful to refer to migrant communities abroad as 'diasporas' if that term is used in a narrow sense. As the term has been applied in the case of the Jews or in that of the descendants of Africans living in the new world, the usual implication is that dispersal has resulted from a traumatic political experience such as genocide and that there will be some kind of desire to return to 'Zion'. In fact the migrant groups to be found in Europe have most commonly come for economic reasons and choose to live away from such Zions. Because it does not seem sensible to use the same term to refer to those who plan a political return and those who plan to continue to live abroad, I think that, unless a better term is suggested, we should simply refer to 'transnational communities'.

Given that it is the intention of migrants to earn their living abroad, the second important point of reference is that of the society of present settlement. In these societies the first goal of migrants will be to have access to the labour market and other economic opportunities. This means that an important part of immigrant culture will be centred around the notion of equality of opportunity and opposition to discrimination through political action, and this will be a powerful modernizing element in immigrant culture pulling away from mere continuing involvement with the homeland. In pursuing this aim they may form alliances with class-based groups in the society of settlement at the same time as recognizing their own ethnic fellows as potential allies regardless of class, this recognition being possible because of the shared language, religion, and family practices to which I have referred. As time goes on it is true these boundary markers may be less significant, but it is interesting to note that even the most acculturated descendants of migrants often continue to deal with the life crises of birth, marriage, and death in their own religious institutions.

The third point of reference for migrants is that of onward migration. The opportunities which are presented in other countries may well be greater than those in the countries of present settlement, and extended families are likely to take advantage of these. This is most obviously true in the case of migrants to Europe who may see greater opportunities across the Atlantic in the United States or Canada, which, being themselves immigration societies, are less likely to discriminate against immigrants to the extent that it is the case in Europe. Migrant communities in Europe, therefore, will often establish bridgeheads in the United States which will facilitate onward migration. These bridgeheads will be based upon the first kin who establish themselves, upon entrepreneurs of immigration, both legal and illegal, and on the help of liberal-minded non-governmental organizations.

In summary, it may be asked how far migrant transnational communities of this kind serve to undermine the integrity of nation-states. To some extent they must do, but if they are contributing to the economy of these societies and filling the demographic deficit caused by falling birth-rates, the governments of the receiving societies will have an interest in winning their loyalty so that they do not seek to return home or emigrate further. It is true, of course, that labour markets fluctuate and that, when they are less buoyant, there may be pressure to force migrants to return home, but the experience of Germany suggests that guestworkers will remain even in times of economic difficulty, and that their children may have little interest in going to their parents' homeland. In these circumstances national governments in Europe may find that they have an interest in eliminating the discrimination against immigrants and their descendants which prevents their becoming a valuable economic resource. To say this is not to argue for total and uncontrolled immigration, but, since it is the case that there are young economically active minorities settled in Europe, it is the development and use of their skills which is at issue.

Economic and Political Migrants

All that has been said so far, of course, refers to the economic migrants of the 1950s and 1960s and to their families who joined them after most European governments acted to prevent further economic immigration in the 1970s. A different set of problems arises in the case of political migrants and asylum seekers. Their relation to their homelands will be very different from that of economic migrants. They may still have kin whom they wish to support, but possibly these kin may have been wiped out, and whether they wish to return will depend upon the changing political circumstances back home. Some will seek only temporary refuge but others will, like economic migrants, seek to take advantage of such economic opportunities as their land of refuge offers. It is sometimes said of this latter group that they have become the new immigrants, and governments, unwilling to accept their responsibilities, may express concern about 'bogus asylum seekers' and seek to return them to their homes as soon as the political situation there makes this possible. On the other hand, if there is a need for labour and professional skills, some political migrants may well be seen as a potentially valuable economic resource.

The Structural Complexity of National Responses

Actual nation-state policies towards both economic and political migrants will be the resultant of conflicting internal political pressures. Employers may have an interest in accepting them although they will be conscious of the fact that the presence of immigrants is likely to be feared and resented. They may therefore accept tight forms of immigration control while relying on the labour of those who have gained entry.

So far as organized labour is concerned, trades unions have often, at first, feared the competition of cheap immigrant labour, but national trades union leaders in a corporate system may be persuaded that the use of immigrant labour is essential to economic growth, and concentrate their attention on ensuring that those who have settled have equal rights and conditions of work, rather than being used as a cheap source of docile labour.

More problematic is the position of those native workers and their children who, lacking education and necessary skills, see themselves as being in competition with immigrants. They may well seek to defend their position by opposing and attacking immigrants in the wrong belief that it is the presence of such immigrants which is the cause of their problems. This will lead to what one might call spontaneous 'skinhead' racism but it may also be expressed in support for racist and neo-fascist parties.

Actual national policies will therefore not be developed by politicians seeking to achieve ideal aims; they are likely to be the resultant of conflicting goals and pressures. It may still be asked, however, what the aims ought to be, of those concerned with the integration of immigrants, in a just democratic society. This leads us to a discussion of the nature of citizenship and to answering the second major question mentioned above.

National and Transnational Citizenship

Two alternative responses to the situation of immigrants have been suggested. One with which I have been associated bases itself upon the work of T. H. Marshall (1951). According to Marshall, in a democratic society all people must first of all gain legal, then political, and, finally, social rights. The assumption here is that the acquisition of political rights is essential because it is only by exercising them that individuals are able to go on to the third stage of winning social rights. An alternative view, however, which has been lucidly defended by Soysal (1994) is that it is quite possible that the acquisition of social rights might take place even where a group lacks political rights.

The crux of the argument here is concerned with the position of guest-workers. The usual argument offered from a Marshallian perspective is that these guestworkers should seek citizenship in a national state, and that to do this they must be able to participate fully in the democratic political process. A society whose population includes some who are denizens rather than citizens will fall short of the ideals of democracy.

Soysal counters this ideal by arguing that denizens do have rights as part of transnational communities, who are protected by an international regime, expressed in the decisions of international courts, and in new forms of political discourse based upon the notion of individual rights. An alternative form of citizenship, she argues is available to them because of this, and they would do well to fight, not for the old national form of citizenship but for a transnational citizenship based upon personhood. Baubock (1994) has also explored the possibility of this new form of transnational citizenship being inserted into the philosophical debate about the requirements of a liberal society.

Any comprehensive political sociology or political theory necessarily has to recognize the legal and moral forces to which Soysal draws attention. What is more arguable is that they are effective means to the attainment of rights. It can surely be argued that access to international courts is a slow and cumbersome process and that, even when international courts support the rights of migrants, nation-states may find ways of complying only formally or even not complying at all. Moreover a less optimistic view of the new moral discourses is that they contain much rhetoric which is at odds with the actual experience of migrants and minorities. The crucial question is not simply whether rights are asserted in the court or in moral discourse, but by whom and how these rights are actually enforced. It does still seem to be the case, even in a globalizing world, that the right to vote in a nation-state offers the most effective form of enforcement.

Social Structure, Racism and Anti-Racism

In this final part of the chapter I should like to address the question of racism and anti-racism. In doing so I shall distinguish between real structural conflicts within societies in which immigration has occurred, and the way in which those conflicts are perceived and misperceived by groups in European societies. I shall then go on to talk about the consequences of certain perceptions for immigrant minority groups and what can be done to prevent those actions which are damaging to these groups and to the structure of democracy. I do this on the assumption that there is a democratic and egalitarian form of multiculturalism under which racism would not occur and that the mere fact of immigration, whether of economic or political migrants, need not lead to racism.

What I have to say in this section can be looked at in another way as supplementing my account of the effect on European societies of ethnic minority mobilization with an account of racist and anti-racist mobilization. With these three aspects of group mobilization set out it is then possible to ask what policies should be pursued by governments seeking to implement an egalitarian democratic and multicultural ideal.

All of the four policy responses which I have discussed may lead to hostile reactions to immigrants and their descendants, or to their unequal treatment as inferiors. Firstly, it does seem to be the case that there is a minority in most societies of perhaps between 10 and 25 per cent which will seek simply to exclude or to repatriate immigrants together with their descendants. Secondly, where a government is committed to a policy of total assimilation, even to an equal citizenship, the persistence of immigrant cultures may be seen as a threat. Thirdly, under the guestworker alternative a society would be divided between full political citizens and denizens without political rights. Fourthly, it is possible that multicultural policies might be of a kind which 'minorises' minority groups and marks them for inferior treatment or for special forms of manipulation and control. The democratic and egalitarian form of multiculturalism which I have outlined seeks to avoid all of these problems and to strengthen democracy.

The first of these alternatives, most clearly advocated by Le Pen, in France, Haider in Austria and the Vlaams Blok in Belgium, can only be resisted if there is a clear and accepted policy on economic and political immigration. The danger is that mainstream parties will seek to win back this populist anti-immigrant vote by adopting anti-immigrant policies. This is a recurrent problem in European politics, as is shown by recent attempts by parties of the centre to recapture the support of those who have defected to racist parties, rather than opposing them with arguments which draw attention to real economic needs of the host societies or to international obligations towards refugees.

The second policy of assimilationism runs the risk of representing minority cultures as a threat to society. Immigrant cultures are conceived of in essentialist terms and represented as fixed, traditional, and unchanging. They are commonly called 'fundamentalist' and this term is used to imply irrationality and a commitment to violence. It seems to me that there is a need, in societies committed to this policy, to consider the possibility that there is at least a limited place for minority cultures which need to be understood as considerably more flexible and adaptive than they are usually thought to be.

In the guestworker alternative I would argue that, as long as there is a distinction between full citizens and denizens, the denizens represent a potential target for attack. I would argue against Soysal that the existence of international courts and of new forms of moral discourse cannot, of itself, prevent this, and that the only way for denizens to be protected is for them to have the means of taking political action themselves through their enfranchisement. What international courts and the new moral discourse can and should do is to reassure members of the receiving societies that the transnational nature of migrant communities does not constitute a threat to the modern democratic order but is compatible with it.

Finally, it is essential in the multicultural alternative that minorities should not be marked for inferior treatment and special control. Rather they should be seen as changing and adapting, and as capable of playing a part through collective action within democratic institutions.

Ordinary people, however, do not derive their perception of social reality from an objective sociology. They derive it from the ideologies offered to them by their political leaders, and these ideologies are themselves a structural fact in West European societies. Nevertheless there are not merely racist ideologies; there are also anti-racist ones and anti-racist movements, and they too constitute a structural fact. Favell (1997) has explored the way in which such movements have developed in the French and British traditions. The task of social science must be to understand the basis of both racist and anti-racist movements.

One important feature of racist movements, however, should be noted. This is that they describe and explain the behaviour of the groups whom they target in a hostile way in terms of some kind of determinism. The characteristic type of explanation offered in earlier times was a biological or genetic one. Such simple explanations, however, were discredited by the experience of fascism in the 1930s and were replaced by other sorts of determinism or essentialism. The groups involved were seen as bound by their structures and their histories to behave in particular ways (Rex 1982). Guiliaumin's analysis is also interesting here because in defining racism, she sees it as not necessarily resting upon biological theories but on a wider category of theories which offer explanations which naturalize the behaviour of groups (Guiliaumin, quoted in Miles 1993).

Attempts to counter these naturalistic, deterministic, and essentialist explanations have often focused upon offering some sort of intellectual correction. This seemed to be the case with the various interventions by UNESCO in the post-war period (Montagu 1981). Such intellectual correction, however, is hardly likely to be effective unless anti-racist movements also look at the structural factors which give rise to the theories. This is why I suggested, after participating in one of the UNESCO meetings, that there were three aspects to any situation which was thought of as a 'race-relations situation'. These were that there was some form of discrimination, exploitation, and oppression occurring which went beyond that ordinarily occurring in markets—especially labour markets; that the discrimination, exploitation, and oppression was not simply that between individuals but between groups, and that it was not possible for an individual to leave one group and join the other; and finally that this system of discrimination, exploitation, and oppression was rationalized in terms of some sort of deterministic theory (Rex 1982). The assault on racism therefore required a focus on social structures as well as on bodies of ideas.

Turning to actual anti-racist political movements in Europe, it should also be noticed that they have often been concerned not simply to deal with intergroup relations as between majorities and minorities. Often, recalling the experience of fascism, they have suggested that the true purpose of racism is to enable extreme right-wing and authoritarian groups to take power in a society. Racism itself is seen as a surface phenomenon only or as a means of obtaining political support from the masses. It is used by political leaders who have quite other political goals. There clearly are problems in European societies of this kind but I would argue that, even though that may be true, there are also other structural factors in modern society which exacerbate racial and ethnic conflict, and that racial discrimination, exploitation, and oppression exists as problem in its own right. A similar type of argument might be put against the view advanced by Baumann in his *Modernity and the Holocaust* (1989) to the effect that the real problem in the holocaust was not that of racist attack and racial prejudice but the very nature of modernity.

A final point needs to be made about racism and anti-racism. This is that, whether it arises from wrong ideas or from oppressive structural situations, it also takes on a life of its own, and racist movements as such, and in their own right, lead to racial discrimination and racial attack which would not have occurred had there not been some form of racial mobilization. Such acts of discrimination and attack are themselves incompatible with democracy and they have to be resisted whether or not their underlying causes are dealt with.

Concluding Remarks

This chapter looks mainly at the structural relation between societies and the policies which they develop on the one hand and the mobilization of transnational migrant communities on the other. Both the national policies and the forms of ethnic mobilization are seen as involving the possibility of conflict, intergroup hostility, and 'racism' of various kinds. On the other hand I have sought to show that there are versions of multicultural policy towards immigrant minorities and aspects of ethnic mobilization which point to the successful integration of minorities without such hostility occurring. Which outcomes occur is to some extent a matter of political choice and any anti-racist movement will be concerned with fighting for the more positive outcome.

It does seem to me that the anti-racist movement too often ignores this structural context, both the context of the encounter between democratic nation-states and immigrant minority groups, and that of internal non-ethnic non-racial contexts within these states. None the less it is the case that these conflicts often become, to use Miles' term 'racialised' (Miles 1993) and this process of racialization has to be studied in its immediate forms. There has to be argument about racist ideas which give a deterministic account of inter-group differences, and all groups in a democracy have to be defended against the consequences of these 'racist' beliefs in the form of racial discrimination, racist hostility, and racist attack. Any overall anti-racist movement must be concerned both with these immediacies and with the structural situations which are conducive to their occurrence.

Note

*Revised version of a paper delivered to a conference of the Forum International des Sciences Humaines on *Cultural Difference, Racism and Democracy*, Paris, 18th to 20th September 1997.

References

BAUBOCK, R. (1994), *Transnational Citizenship* (Aldershot, Edward Elgar).

BAUMANN, Z. (1989), *Modernity and the Holocaust* (Cambridge: Polity Press).

DURKHEIM, E. (1933), *The Division of Labour in Society* (Glencoe, IL: Free Press).

EUROSTAT (1995), Demographic Statistics (1995), Trends in International Migration, OECD (Paris/Brussels: S.O.P.E.M.I).

FAVELL, A. (1997), *Philosophies of Integration: Immigration and the idea of citizenship in France and Britain* (Basingstoke: MacMillan).

HABERMAS, J. (1994), 'Citizenship and National Identity' in B. van Steenbergen, *The Condition of Citizenship* (London: Sage).

HAMMAR, T. (1990), *Democracy and the Nation State* (Aldershot: Avebury).

IRELAND, P. (1994), *The Policy Challenge of Ethnic Diversity* (Cambridge, MA: Harvard University Press).

MARSHALL, T. (1951), *Citizenship and Social Class* (Cambridge: Cambridge University Press).

MASSEY, D. et al., (1993), 'Theories of International Migration—A Review and Appraisal', *Population and Development Review*, 19/1.

MILES, R. (1993), *Racism after 'Race Relations'* (London: Routledge).

MONTAGU, A. (1981), *Statements on Race* (London: Greenwood Press).

POULTER, S. (1986), *English Law and Ethnic Minority Customs* (London: Butterworth).

——(1987), 'Ethnic Minority Customs, English Law and Human Rights', *International and Comparative Law Quarterly*, 36.

——(1989), 'The Claim to a Separate Islamic System of Personal Law for British Muslims' in C. Mallat and J. Connors (eds.), *Islamic Family Law* (London: Graham and Trotman).

RADTKE, F-O. (1994), 'The Formation of Ethnic Minorities; The Transformation of Social into Ethnic Conflicts in the So-Called Multicultural Society—The German Case' in J. Rex and B. Drury, *Ethnic Mobilisation in a Multicultural Europe* (Aldershot: Avebury).

RATH, J. (1991), *Minorisering: De Social Constrtucte van Ethnische Minderheden* (University of Utrecht: Ph.D. Thesis).

REX, J. (1982), *Race Relations in Sociological Theory* (London: Routledge and Kegan Paul).

——(1992), 'Race and Ethnicity in Europe' in J. Bailey (ed.), *Social Europe* (London: Longman).

——(ed.) (1996a), *Multiculturalism and Political Integration in European Cities*, Special Issue of *Innovation*, 9/1 (Abingdon: Carfax).

——(1996b), *Ethnic Minorities in the Modern Nation State* (Basingstoke: MacMillan).

——and DRURY, B. (eds.) (1994), *Ethnic Mobilisation in a Multicultural Europe* (Aldershot: Avebury).

——and TOMLINSON, S. (1979), *Colonial Immigrants in a British City* (London: Routledge and Kegan Paul).

SCHIERUP, C-U., and ÅLUND, A. (1991), *Paradoxes of Multiculturalism* (Aldershot: Gower).

SOYSAL, Y. (1994), *Limits of Citizenship* (Chicago, IL: University of Chicago Press).

WIEVIORKA, M. (1994), 'Ethnicity as Action' in J. Rex and B. Drury, *Ethnic Mobilisation in a Multicultural Europe* (Aldershot: Avebury).

4

Citizenship, Multiculturalism, and the Politics of Identity: Contemporary Dilemmas and Policy Agendas*

JOHN SOLOMOS and LIZA K. SCHUSTER

Introduction

European debates about immigration, race and ethnicity have become increasingly focused on questions about citizenship and multiculturalism. In many ways this is not surprising, given the reality that the patterns of migration and settlement that have shaped many countries in Western Europe since the Second World War have had an important impact on their social, political, and cultural institutions (Wrench and Solomos 1993; Soysal 1994; Freeman 1995; Castles and Davidson forthcoming). In this environment existing notions about the nation-state, national culture, and identity are being questioned, from a variety of perspectives (Giroux 1993; Calhoun 1994). As a consequence we are currently in the throes of intense debates about the changing meanings of citizenship, identity, and cultural difference. These debates are certainly part of academic discourse, but they are also a key issue in everyday political and policy debates in local and national environments. This is most evident in those debates that have focused on the interplay between increasingly complex forms of ethnic and racial diversity and new modes of social, economic, and cultural exclusion and inclusion of minorities.

In this chapter we want to address some aspects of these debates, by focusing specifically on the terms within which accounts of citizenship and multiculturalism have been framed. The chapter is organized around five themes. First, it explores the contested nature of notions of multiculturalism in contemporary debates about citizenship. While it is clear that a much wider debate about the changing nature of citizenship has taken place in recent years (Kymlicka and Norman 1994), the focus of this chapter will be specifically on the relationship between citizenship and multiculturalism. Second, it looks in some detail at the changing language about notions such as race and culture in contemporary societies. Third, it seeks to highlight the ways in which the question of *identity* is at the heart of current debates about multiculturalism. Fourth, it focuses on the debate about what measures can be taken to protect the rights of minorities and tackle patterns of discrimination and exclusion. Finally, the chapter concludes by arguing that we need to go beyond the terms of current debates in order to develop strategies for change that take account of the complex dilemmas that face us at the present time.

This chapter is essentially exploratory, in the sense that we want to open up issues for further analysis and debate rather than claim to resolve all the dilemmas that arise. We shall attempt, in particular, to show that a critical analysis of current debates needs to move beyond the simple binary view of multiculturalism as by definition good or bad, and address the more complex question of the limits and contradictions that arise when ethnic and racial identities are politicized and constructed into a basis for social and political mobilization.

The Boundaries of Citizenship and Multiculturalism

It is useful at the beginning to reflect on the ways in which key terms have been defined and used to analyse contemporary social and political trends. This is all the more important since it is evident that the extensive nature of debates about citizenship and multiculturalism has not led to much agreement about the core concepts. If we take the term *multiculturalism*, for example, it is clear that it remains a hotly debated term within social and political discourses. There is an extensive literature on the notion of multiculturalism and its usage in academic and policy discourses (Takaki 1993; Goldberg 1994; Gutmann 1994; Kymlicka 1995a; Solomos and Back 1995; Gordon and Newfield 1996; Wieviorka 1996). This literature has helped at a certain level to clarify one key point: namely, that multiculturalism is not a fixed notion on which there is agreement about what it means, even within the boundaries of individual societies (McLaren 1993). But beyond that point it is evident that debates and controversies about multiculturalism and citizenship, whether pitched at an abstract philosophical level or concerned with everyday policy issues in relation to employment or housing, provide little evidence of agreement about either terminology or policy objectives.

It has to be noted that, although many of these debates take place within academia, they are conceived as political in a broader sense. They relate in this sense to understandings of social and political power relations. As Charles Taylor has noted, discussions of multiculturalism and of racial inequality are 'undergirded by the premise that the withholding of recognition can be a form of oppression' (Taylor et al. 1994: 36). Debates about these issues are thus inherently politicized and take place in the context of mobilizations that use racial and ethnic symbols as a basis for making demands for social and cultural rights, as well as political representation. Such mobilizations can occur outside the mainstream structures in separate ethnic organizations, or they can mean action within those structures by groups united by particular identifications (Castles and Davidson forthcoming).

In its most general usage, however, the notion of multiculturalism refers to a wide range of forms of interaction in societies that contain a variety of cultures. This is certainly the starting point of Amy Gutmann's insightful account of the politics of multiculturalism, where she argues:

By multiculturalism, I refer to the state of a society or the world containing many cultures that interact in some significant way with each other. A culture is a human community larger than a few families that is associated with ongoing ways of seeing, doing, and thinking about things.   (Gutmann 1993: 171)

Gutmann makes it clear, however, that in a very practical sense questions concerning whether and how the rights of minorities and cultural groups should be recognized in politics are among the most salient and vexing on the political agenda of many societies (Gutmann 1994; Gutmann and Thompson 1996). From this perspective she sees the political controversies about multiculturalism as symbolic of wider uncertainties about the position of racial and ethnic minorities.

On the basis of a comparative analysis of recent trends in the United States, Germany, and Britain, Christian Joppke has argued that contemporary debates about multiculturalism need to be understood against the background of the social movements that demand *equal rights* and *recognition* for a range of social groups:

'Multiculturalism', the seeking of equal rights and recognition for ethnic, racial, religious, or sexually defined groups, is one of the most pervasive and controversial intellectual and political movements in contemporary Western democracies.   (Joppke 1996: 449)

For Joppke, however, it is also clear that multiculturalism is inherently contradictory, both in conceptual and political terms:

Following Charles Taylor, one may characterise multiculturalism as a 'politics of difference' that fuses egalitarian rhetoric with a stress on authenticity and rejection of Western universalism, which is seen as falsely homogenising and a smokescreen for power. Multiculturalism is modern and anti-modern at the same time.   (Joppke 1996: 449)

From this perspective multiculturalism has to be seen as being partly about the struggle for equality by minorities who are excluded from equal inclusion in society, and the affirmation of cultural difference through claims to ethnic and racial authenticity.

Joppke's account certainly captures something of the contradictory nature of the political and cultural agendas that go under the label of multiculturalism. It is also clear, however, that in practice, policies that are labelled 'multi-culturalist' have arisen in particular historical environments and political cultures. Elsewhere, Joppke (1999) characterizes American multiculturalism as a response to the oppression of African Americans, Native Americans, and Hispanics, whereas in Britain and Germany multiculturalism is a response to immigration. Stephen Castles, writing from a comparative perspective, has tried to link the question of multiculturalism to the socio-economic and political realities of the migration process itself. Drawing on his research in Europe and Australasia he argues:

> Immigrants cannot simply be incorporated into society as individuals. In many cases, a large proportion of immigrants and their immediate descendants cluster together, share a common socio-economic position, develop their own community structures, and seek to maintain their languages and cultures. This is partly an issue of cultural affinity, but it is above all a reaction to experiences of racism and marginalisation. Culture and ethnicity are vital resources in the settlement process, which will not just disappear if immigrants are granted full rights as individuals. This means that immigrants cannot become full citizens unless the state and the national community are willing to accept—to some extent at least—the right to cultural difference. (Castles 1996: 54–5)

In reality, of course, the final sentence of the above quotation signals the key issue around which much recent discussion has focused: namely, the extent to which 'the right to cultural difference' is seen as a basis for the formulation of policies and strategies for action.

Race, Culture, Citizenship

It should be evident from the above that debates about citizenship and multiculturalism are fundamentally concerned with the role of racial and ethnic categorization in the construction of social and political identities. Yet it is paradoxically the case that there is still confusion about what it is that we mean by the use of concepts such as race and racism, as evidenced by the range of terminological debates that have tended to dominate much discussion in the 1990s (Miles 1993; Goldberg 1993; Solomos and Back 1996). It is perhaps partly the result of this focus on terminology that much of the academic debate in this field has remained somewhat abstract and unsatisfactory.

We must make clear straight away that we shall not spend much time debating whether or not there are races, or whether or not it represents a scientific error to actually use the term race. This is not because we take notions such as race as given or unproblematic. We, along with the vast majority of researchers in this field, do not regard race as a scientific category. Efforts to divide human beings into groups on the basis of alleged genetic or phenotypical differences have proved to be spurious and misleading, and in some cases politically disastrous (Kohn 1995). It is by now widely accepted that race has been used as a means of representing difference, such that contingent attributes such as skin colour, are transformed into essential bases for identities. But this is not to deny that race remains, at the level of everyday experience and social representation, a potent political and social category around which individuals and groups organize their identity and construct a politics. As such, race is socially constructed, and blackness and whiteness are not categories of essence but defined by historical and political struggles over their meaning.

Research on race and political identities in Birmingham by Solomos and Back has shown how race and ethnicity are essentially political resources, that can be used by both dominant and subordinate groups for the purposes of legitimizing and furthering their own social identities and interests (Solomos and Back 1995). Indeed a key theme running throughout the analysis of race and changing political cultures is that it is precisely through contestation and struggle that identities based on race and ethnicity gain meaning as both political and social categories. In this sense racialized identities are not simply imposed, since they are also often the outcome of resistance and political struggle in which racialized groups play a key and active role. For this reason it is more accurate to speak of a racialized group rather than a racial group since race is a product of racism and not vice versa. For example Joppke argues that the category 'Asian-American' is a product of the anti-racist, not racist, movement (1999: 635).

If race and ethnicity are about the representation of difference, it is also necessary to be aware of the complex ways in which they are structured by relations of power. Sites of difference are also sites of power, a power too whereby the dominated comes to see and experience themselves as 'Other'. Dominant representations of difference may function to exclude and exploit, and to justify unequal access and involvement in specific institutions. Every regime of representation is a regime of power formed, as Foucault reminds us, by the fateful couplet, power/knowledge (Foucault 1980; Stoler 1995). Those in positions of power in a society can validate and impose their own definitions of normality, and define boundaries for the purpose of excluding, enclosing, or exploiting others. These definitions carry with them particular notions of value and entitlement, and so defend privilege either directly or through the operation of codes, norms, and rules that may appeal to universalism, but which actually represent the social interests of dominant groups.

From a historical perspective it is clear that part of the power of racism lies in the way in which racist ideologies operate by constructing impassable symbolic boundaries between racially-constituted, or racialized, categories. A recurrent theme in racist discourses is the attempt to fix and naturalize the difference between belongingness and otherness. A principal means of accomplishing this is to perceive the self as carried in the genes rather than transmitted via culture, as distilled through what appears to us as most 'natural' and immediate: the body. Corporeal properties, and most fetishistically, skin colour, thus come to furnish an epidermal schema not only for anchoring difference but for distinguishing the pure from the impure, the included from the excluded. To the extent that the body comes to signify difference, so too does it become a site and target for strategies of normalization and discipline, a site for an obsessive imperative that aims to expunge any kind of syncretism which questions the authenticity of the truth propositions about these em-bodied polar identities of *black* and *white*. We see this in the constant preoccupation in racist discourses with questions of 'racial purity' and the dangers of hybridity and miscegenation. The concern with policing racial boundaries and ensuring that 'purity' is maintained can, and indeed has, taken many forms. In the United States and in South Africa, albeit in very different forms, there were attempts to control and regulate miscegenation through legislation and state intervention. During the Nazi period in Germany, the attempt to construct racial purity took the form of systematic genocide aimed at Jews and other groups, and programmes of euthanasia aimed at 'undesirable' elements in German society.

The point we are trying to make through these examples is that race and ethnicity are not 'natural' categories, even though both concepts are often represented as if they were (Mosse 1985; Appiah 1989; Wolf 1994). Their boundaries are not fixed, nor is their membership uncontested. Racial and ethnic groups, like nations, are imagined communities. They are ideological entities, made and changed in struggle. They are discursive formations, signalling a language through which differences are accorded social significance, and through which they may be named and explained. But what is of importance for us, as social researchers studying race and ethnicity, is that such ideas also carry with them material consequences for those who are included within, or excluded from, them.

Recent developments in Western and Eastern European societies are a case in point. The rise of extreme-right-wing, and neo-fascist movements and parties has resulted in the development of new forms of racist politics and in the articulation of popular racism and violence against migrant communities. At the same time we have seen a noticeable rise in anti-Semitism in both Western and Eastern Europe, evident in both physical and symbolic threats to Jewish communities. In this environment it is perhaps not surprising that questions about immigration and race have assumed a new importance, both politically and socially, helping to construct an environment in which the future of both settled migrant communities and new groups of migrants and refugees is very much at the heart of public debate (Wrench and Solomos 1993; Habermas 1994; Miles 1994).

Developments such as these show why it is impossible in the present political and social environment to ignore the impact of race and ethnicity on the social and political institutions of most advanced industrial societies. Whereas until the 1980s it was still relatively common to treat questions about racism, ethnicity, and nationalism as relatively marginal to the agenda of both social scientists and policy-makers, it is perhaps no exaggeration to say that in many ways these issues have moved right to the core of public debate. Indeed, what has become evident in the late 1990s is how almost every aspect of social and political relations is deeply inflected with a racial or ethnic dimension. In this context it is vital that we develop a grounded and historically based view of the role that racialized social relations play in contemporary societies and are likely to play in the future.

This is partly because the terms of both official and popular discourses about race and racism are in a constant state of flux. The recent changes we have seen in European societies are perhaps the most clear example of this volatility, represented both by the development of new racist political movements and by intense official debate about what kinds of policies should be pursued to deal with such issues as immigration and the political and social rights of migrants (Ford 1992; Wrench and Solomos 1993). But it is also the case that similar transformations are evident in other parts of the globe. Castles and Miller's (1993) account of the changing politics of migration in various parts of the world illustrates the complex variety of factors that have helped to construct political understandings of the position of migrant communities in quite disparate geographical and social contexts. Numerous other accounts have shown how ideas about race, nation, and ethnicity are constantly changing as a result of both governmental regulation and popular mobilization (Goldberg 1993; Bhatt 1997).

There is by now a wealth of historical research that shows that the social and political impact of ideas about race needs to be seen in the context of the experience of modernity and post-modernity which has shaped our societies over the past two centuries (Habermas 1987, 1994). But if modern racism has its foundations in the period since the late eighteenth century there is little doubt that it has had a major impact on the course of historical development during the twentieth century and seems destined to continue to do so. It seems clear that racist ideas and movements are continuing to have an impact on a range of contemporary societies in a variety of ways, including access to citizenship both legally and politically (Brubaker 1992; Winant 1994). What is more we have seen in recent years the growth and genocidal impact of new forms of racial and ethnically based ideologies in many parts of the globe, including most notably in the 1990s in both West and East Europe and parts of Africa. It is almost impossible to read a newspaper or watch television news coverage without seeing the contemporary expressions of racist ideas and practices, whether in terms of the rise of neo-fascist movements in some societies or the implementation of policies of genocide and what is euphemistically called 'ethnic cleansing'.

Such trends need to be situated within the changing socio-economic environment of contemporary societies. It is also important to situate them within processes of cultural and social change. By this we mean that it is of some importance not to lose sight of the complex social, political, and cultural determinants that shape contemporary racist discourses and movements and other forms of racialized discourse and mobilization. Indeed what is clear from accounts of the growth of new forms of cultural racism in the late twentieth century is that within the language of contemporary racist movements there is both a certain flexibility about what is meant by race as well as an attempt to reconstitute themselves as movements whose concern is with defending their 'nation' rather than attacking others as such. It is perhaps not surprising in this context that within the contemporary languages of race one finds a combination arguments in favour of cultural difference along with negative images of the 'Other' as a threat and as representing an 'impure' culture (Enzensberger 1994; Gilman 1985; Mosse 1985).

It is also quite evident that subordinate groups may use difference to stress their own separateness, to authorize their own representations, and to mobilize support. They may seek to legitimize their definitions of cultural differences, including those against others from within their own collectivity. They may seize the category, claim it for their own and invert it, attaching positive value where before it was negative. This at times can lead, as we shall see later, to a strange convergence in the language of the racist right and of the black or ethnic nationalists, as both infuse categories such as race or ethnicity with essentialist, and supposedly naturally inherited, characteristics.

Identities in Question: Race, Ethnicity, and Difference

The arguments presented above are held together by a notion that we have already hinted at, namely that race and ethnicity are intrinsically political resources, used by both dominant and subordinate groups for the purposes of legitimizing and furthering their own social identities and social interests. In this contest, nothing—not boundaries, criteria for allocating or withholding membership, or the consequences that flow from membership—is unchanging. And it is perhaps because race and ethnicity are intrinsically forms of collective social identity that the subject of identity has been at the heart of both historical and contemporary discussions about these issues. The question of identity is certainly the one that everyone has wanted to talk, debate and write about in the late 1990s (Appiah and Gates 1995; Connolly 1995; Gitlin 1995). As a keyword in contemporary politics it has taken on so many different connotations that sometimes it is obvious that people are not even talking about the same thing. Nevertheless, it is quite evident that contemporary studies of race and ethnicity are centrally concerned with the ways in which constructions of identity and mobilization around identities have an impact on the social and political role of minorities (Kymlicka 1995b; Tomasi 1995; Parekh 1996).

The preoccupation with identity can, at one level, be taken as an outcome of concerns about where racialized minorities in societies such as our own actually belong. At a basic level, after all, identity is about belonging, about what we have in common with some people, and what differentiates us from others. Identity gives one a sense of personal location, and provides a stable core of one's individuality; but it is also about one's social relationships, and one's complex involvement with others, and in the modern world these have become even more complex and confusing. Each of us lives with a variety of potentially contradictory identities, which battle within us for allegiance: as men or women, black or white, straight or gay, able-bodied or disabled. The list is potentially infinite, and so therefore are our possible belongings. Which of them we focus on, bring to the fore, or identify with, depends on a host of factors. At the centre of the citizenship debate, however, are the values we share or wish to share with others.

In exploring questions around the changing dynamics of identity, we therefore need to ask: who is constructing the categories and defining the boundaries? Who is resisting these constructions and definitions? What are the consequences being written into or out of particular categories? What happens when subordinate groups seek to mobilize along boundaries drawn for the purposes of domination? What happens to individuals whose multiple identities may be fragmented and segmented by category politics?

One of the problems with much of the contemporary discussion of identity politics is that the dilemmas and questions outlined above are not adequately addressed. This is largely because much discussion is underpinned by the presumption that one's identity necessarily defines one's politics and that there can be no politics until the subject has discovered or laid claim to his/her identity. Inherent in such positions is the failure to understand the way in which identity grows out of, and is transformed by, action and struggle. This is one of the dangers, as we see it, of the preoccupation of exactly who is covered by the category *black* in contemporary British society. The usage of the notion of black to cover a variety of diverse communities has been rejected by some scholars in favour of other categories such as Asian, Muslim, or African Caribbean. Yet others have sought to argue for a notion of black grounded in 'racial' particularity. But the danger of these approaches is that they present no more than a strategy of simple inversion wherein the old bad black essentialist subject is replaced by a new good black essentialist subject whose identity necessarily guarantees a correct politics: such a strategy ends up validating racist discourses.

Part of the dilemma we have to face is that collective identities are not things we are born with, but are formed and transformed within, and in relation to, representation. That is, we only know what it is to be English or German because of the way Englishness and Germanness have come to be represented, as a set of meanings within a national culture. It follows that a nation is not only a political entity but something that produces meanings—a system of cultural representation. People are not only legal citizens of a nation; they participate in the idea of the nation as represented in national culture. A nation is a symbolic community and it is this that accounts for its power to generate a sense of identity and allegiance.

National cultures then are composed not only of cultural institutions, but of symbols and representations. A national culture is a discourse: a way of constructing meanings which influences and organizes both our actions and our conceptions of our selves. National cultures construct identities by producing meanings about 'the nation' with which we can identify; these are contained in the stories which are told about it, memories which connect its present with its past, and images which are constructed of it. As Benedict Anderson has argued, national identity is an 'imagined community', and differences between nations lie in the different ways in which they are imagined (Anderson 1991).

But how is the modern nation imagined? What representational strategies are deployed to construct our common-sense views of national belonging or identity? What are the representations of, say, England or Germany, which shape the identifications and define the identities of 'English' or 'German' people? These are by no means easy questions to answer, and there is a clear need for more detailed historical and contemporary research about national identities are constructed and reconstructed through time and space. Studies by historians such as Linda Colley have highlighted, above all, the ways in which many of our own taken-for-granted images of 'British' identity are the product of processes centred around a struggle to forge cultural, religious, class, and other boundaries in the period since the eighteenth century (Colley 1992). Brubaker (1992) has illustrated the different ways in which French and German national identities, too, are the result of political and economic processes.

More importantly, perhaps, what such research has shown is that the formation of collective identities is based on selective processes of memory and remembering, so that a given group recognizes itself through an edited recollection of a common past. From this perspective national identity is a specific form of identity based on collective memories about 'the nation', its origins and history. But it is also clear that the defence of a given 'national identity' inherently involves images of 'other nations', and it is for this reason that debates about cultural differences easily slip into the most hackneyed nationalism, or even racism, and the nationalist affirmation of the superiority of one group over another.

Take, for example, the notion of 'national tradition' and the ways in which it shapes many debates about education, religion and related issues. Part of the power of nationalist rhetoric is to be found in the construction of naturalized images of 'national culture', 'tradition' and related notions. Whatever the power of these images, however, it is clear that tradition is not a matter of a fixed and given set of beliefs or practices that are handed down or accepted passively. Rather, as Patrick Wright and others have argued, tradition is very much a matter of present-day politics and the way in which powerful institutions function to select particular values from the past and to mobilize them in contemporary practices (Wright 1985; Dodd 1995). Through such mechanisms of cultural reproduction, a particular version of the collective memory and thus a particular sense of national and cultural identity, is produced.

A key process in play in contemporary British cultural life is one in which a romantically sanitized version of the English/British past is being busily re-created: a quite reactionary vision of pastoral England/Albion. Raphael Samuel describes this as the creation of a 'born-again cultural nationalism', which operates across a number of fields (Samuel 1988). Thus we see the boom in the conservation and heritage movement; the re-evaluation of English landscape painting; educational reforms aimed to returning to 'traditional standards' in English and history as core components of the curriculum. This 'England' is being reconstructed around a tradition that is unproblematically white, a tradition which tends towards a morbid celebration of England and Englishness from which blacks and other minorities are systematically excluded.

A similar process can be seen at work in Germany, not so much in relation to history, which would be problematic, but in the vociferous promotion of the environment and arguments surrounding the threat posed by Islam, as well as the refusal to acknowledge that Germany is a country of immigration (Räthzel 1990). In popular discourse 'Germanness' involves an attachment to the 'land' and to Christianity. As in Britain, attachment to, and responsibility for the land is considered part of the responsibility of citizenship. The notion of 'Heimat' and its historical resonances reflects some of this complexity. Although difficult to translate, it means home, but a particular German home 'connected to a German landscape, a German history, and a feeling of being German' (Peck 1992: 171). Confronted with a housing shortage, protecting the German landscape from exploitation has come to mean controlling population increases, even for some associated with radical parties such as the Greens. Since Germany's birth-rate is negative, any increase in population is due to migration. Protecting Germany's green spaces becomes contingent on keeping out non-Germans. This logic explains the sentiments of Herbert Gruhl, a founder of the Greens—which he subsequently left—who claimed that 'most refugees are essentially biologically or organically incompatible with Germans' (Mattson 1995: 71).

In other words the making of identities is an active process that involves inclusion and exclusion. There is no identity that is without the dialogic relationship to the Other. To be 'us', we need those who are 'not-us'. The imaginary process of creating traditions and of activating collective memories extends through time.

One of the issues that we have become increasingly aware of in recent years is that the history of identity politics is not one that has moved unproblematically from resistance to a broader politics of democratic struggle. While the growth of identity politics has been seen by some as challenging cultural homogeneity and providing spaces for marginal groups to assert the legacy and importance of their respective voices and experiences, it has often failed to move beyond a notion of difference structured in polarizing binarisms and an uncritical appeal to a discourse of authenticity. Identity politics may have allowed many formerly silenced and displaced groups to emerge from the margins and to reassert and reclaim suppressed identities and experiences. In doing so, however, they have often substituted one master narrative for another, invoking a politics of separatism, and suppressed differences within their own 'liberatory' narratives (Giroux 1993; Bhatt 1997).

Stuart Hall's critique of black essentialism (1991) highlights some of the inherent limits of 'identity politics'. Hall argues that essentialist forms of political and cultural discourse naturalize and dehistoricize difference, and therefore mistake what is historical and cultural for what is natural, biological, and genetic. The moment, he argues, we tear the signifier 'black' from its historical, cultural, and political embedding and lodge it in a biologically constituted racial category, we valorize, by inversion, the very ground of the racism we are trying to deconstruct. We fix the signifier outside history, outside of change, outside of political intervention. This is exemplified by the tendency to see the term 'black' as sufficient in itself to guarantee the progressive character of the politics articulated under that banner, when it is evident that we need to analyse precisely the content of these political strategies and how they construct specific 'racial' meanings through politics (Hall 1991; see also Fuss 1989).

We have, Hall argues, arrived at an encounter, the 'end of innocence', or the end of the innocent notion of the essential black subject. What is at issue here is the recognition of the extraordinary diversity of subject positions, social experiences, and cultural identities which compose the category black, that is, the recognition that it is essentially a politically and culturally constructed category, which cannot be grounded in a set of fixed trans-cultural or transcendental racial categories, and which therefore has no guarantees (Hall 1990). What this brings into play is the recognition of the immense diversity and differentiation of the historical and cultural experiences of minority communities in western European societies. This inevitably entails a weakening or fading of the notion that race, or some composite notion of race around the term 'black', will either guarantee the effectivety of any cultural practice or determine in any final sense its aesthetic value.

It is interesting to note in this regard that new right political discourses have also become increasingly preoccupied with defending the importance of ever more fixed notions of culture and nation. They have sought to reconstruct primordial notions of ethnic exclusivity that celebrate national identity and patriotism in the face of criticism from multiculturalists and anti-racists.

Central to such discourses is the attempt to fuse culture within a tidy forma-tion that equates nation, citizenship, and patriotism, with a racially exclusive notion of difference. It is also crucial to recognize that the new right, just as much as ethnic nationalists, have given enormous prominence to waging a cul-tural struggle over the control and use of the popular media and other spheres of representation in order to articulate contemporary racial meanings and iden-tities in new ways, to link race with more comprehensive political and cultural agendas, and to interpret social structural phenomena such as inequality or social policy with regard to 'race' (Smith 1994). It has to be said that for the new right the appeal is by and large no longer to racial supremacy but to cul-tural uniformity parading under the politics of nationalism and patriotism. The emphasis is on heritage, the valorization of an elitist view of self and social development, the view of civilization as synonymous with selected aspects of Western tradition. In this sense, difference in the language of the new right is removed from the language of biologism and firmly established as a cultural construct, but only to be reworked within a language that naturalizes race and nation as essentialized categories.

The question of multiculturalism is a central concern in contemporary debates about states and political institutions. In this paper we want to explore some key strands in recent attempts to produce a clearer theoretical under-standing of the politics of multiculturalism and the impact of these debates on current policy debates. A particular issue we want to explore is the question of what debates about multiculturalism tell us about the changing nature of states, citizenship, and political identity.

Rights, Citizenship, and Minorities

At the heart of contemporary discourses about identity there lie questions about what it means to 'belong' or to be excluded from particular collectivities. It is to this issue that we want to move on now, particularly as regards the ques-tion of 'citizenship rights' in societies that are becoming increasingly multicul-tural (Bauböck 1994, 1996; Bader 1995; Gorham 1995; Kymlicka 1995a). Within both popular and academic discourse there is growing evidence of concern about how questions of citizenship can be reconceptualized in the context of multicultural societies. Indeed in contemporary European societies this can be seen as in some sense the main question which governments of various kinds are trying to come to terms with. Some important elements of this debate are the issue of the political rights of minorities, including the issue of represent-ation in both local and national politics, and the position of minority religious and cultural rights in societies which are becoming more diverse. Underlying all of these concerns is the much more thorny issue of what, if anything, can be done to protect the rights of minorities and to develop extensive notions of citizenship and democracy that include those minorities that are excluded on racial and ethnic criteria (Phillips 1995).

There are clearly quite divergent perspectives in the present political environment about how best to deal with all of these concerns. There is, for example, a wealth of discussion about what kinds of measures are necessary to tackle the inequalities and exclusions that confront minority groups. At the same time there is clear evidence that existing initiatives are severely limited in their impact. A number of commentators have pointed to the limitations of legislation and public policy interventions in bringing about a major improvement in the socio-political position of minorities.

This raises a number of questions. What kind of policies could tackle discrimination and inequality more effectively? What links could be made between policies on immigration and policies on social and economic issues? What kind of positive social policy agenda can be developed to deal with the position of both established communities and new migrants? All of these questions are at the heart of contemporary debates and have given rise to quite divergent policy prescriptions. It is quite clear that in the present political environment it is unlikely that any sort of agreement about how to develop new policy regimes in this field will be easy to achieve. On the contrary, it seems likely that this will remain an area full of controversy and conflict for some time to come.

But it is also the case that some key issues are coming to the fore in public debate. A case in point is the whole question of citizenship in relation to race and ethnicity. Policy debates in Britain, unlike other European societies, have often not looked seriously at the issue of political and citizenship rights of migrants and their descendants. This is partly because it is widely assumed that such issues are not as relevant in this country. But it also clear that ethnic minorities in Britain and elsewhere are questioning whether they are fully included in and represented through political institutions. It is not surprising, therefore, that an important concern in the late 1990s has been with the issue of citizenship and the rights of minorities in British society. This is partly because there is a growing awareness of the gap between formal citizenship and the *de facto* restriction of the economic and social rights of minorities as a result of discrimination, economic restructuring, and the decline of the welfare state.

The relationship between identity, difference, and culture needs to be located within a broader reconceptualization of substantive democracy that can include a place for the 'rights of minorities'. The value of such a politics is that it makes the complicated issue of difference fundamental to addressing the discourse of substantive citizenship; moreover, it favours looking at the conflict over relations of power, identity, and culture as central to a broader struggles to advance the critical imperatives of a democratic society. Primary to such a struggle is rethinking and rewriting difference, in relation to wider questions of membership, community, and social responsibility.

In essence we need to get away from the idea that solidarity can only be forged when we all think alike. Solidarity begins when people have the confidence to disagree over issues because they 'care' about constructing a common ground. Solidarity is not impermeably solid but depends to a certain degree on antagonism and uncertainty. If a radical democracy is to function and provide a point of articulation between and across difference, then a key question must be posed: what kind of society do we want? We need to retain some kind of moral, ethical, and political ground—albeit a provisional one—from which to negotiate among multiple interests. Without a shared vision of democratic community, argues Peter McLaren (1993) we risk endorsing struggles in which the politics of difference collapse into new forms of separatism. We have to be mindful that in trying to avoid the Scylla of the 'tyranny of the whole' that we do not meet up with the Charybdis of the 'dictatorship of the fragment'.

The controversies about the Rushdie Affair, the rights of religious minorities, and a number of other similar issues across Europe have highlighted the increased prominence of these issues in current political debates. The growing public interest about the role of fundamentalism among sections of the Muslim communities in various countries has given a new life to debates about the issue of cultural differences and processes of integration (Asad 1990, 1993). By highlighting some of the most obvious limitations of multiculturalism and anti-racism in shaping policy change in this field, such controversies have done much to bring about a more critical debate about the role and impact of policies which are premised on notions such as multiculturalism. But they have also highlighted the ever-changing terms of political and policy agendas about these issues, and the fact that there is little agreement about what kind of strategies for change should be pursued.

The full impact of current debates on the future of immigration is not as yet clear, but it seems likely that they will have an influence on how such issues as multiculturalism and anti-racism are seen in the future. In the context of national debates about the position of ethnic minority communities the impact is already evident. In Britain, for example, there are already signs that the Rushdie affair has given a new impetus to debates about issues such as immigration, integration, and public order, while in France, the furore over Muslim girls wearing headscarves to school has obliged even the liberal sections of society to re-evaluate questions of integration, assimilation, and religion. The hostile media coverage of the events surrounding the political mobilizations around the Rushdie and Foulard affairs also served to reinforce the view that minorities who do not share the dominant political values of British/French society pose a threat to social stability and cohesion. Some commentators have argued that as a result of the Rushdie affair, more attention needed to be given to the divergent political paths seemingly adopted by sections of the African-Caribbean and Asian communities. Whatever the merit of such arguments, it is clear that in the current environment one cannot develop any analysis of contemporary racial and ethnic relations without accounting for differentiation within both majority and minority communities.

Beyond Multiculturalism?

Finally, we want to take up a question that is at the heart of the issues we have been talking about in this paper: is it possible to create a kind of society that can acknowledge difference, and not simply diversity? In other words is there a capacity to use difference as a resource rather than fear it as a threat? In spite of a liberalization of naturalization procedures introduced since the 1998, German Federal elections, belonging is still predicated on 'blood' rather than 'soil'. Children born in Germany can now conditionally get citizenship, but even this advance has unleashed an outcry from the Conservative opposition parties. In Britain too, recent trends seem to indicate that a mythic longing for cultural homogenization is alive, not just among nationalists and racists who are celebrating Great Britain, but among the minorities and anti-racists as well.

The preoccupation in much of the recent literature in this field with issues of identity, and the assertion of the relevance and importance of understanding the role of new ethnicities, has not resolved the fundamental question of how to balance the quest for ever more specific identities with the need to allow for broader and less fixed cultural identities. Indeed, if anything, this quest for a politics of identity has helped to highlight one of the key dilemmas of liberal political thought (Moon 1993; Squires 1993). Amy Gutmann captures this contradiction well when she argues:

One reasonable reaction to questions about how to recognise the distinct cultural identities of members of a pluralistic society is that the very aim of representing or respecting differences in public institutions is misguided. An important strand in contemporary liberalism lends support to this reaction. It suggests that our lack of identification with institutions that serve public purposes, the impersonality of public institutions, is the price that citizens should be willing to pay for treating us all as equals, regardless of our particular ethnic, religious, racial or sexual identities.   (Gutmann 1992: 4)

Yet what is quite clear is that the quest for ever more specific as opposed to universal identities is becoming more pronounced in the present political environment. The search for national, ethnic, and racial has become a pronounced, if not dominant, feature of political debate within both majority and minority communities in the 'post-modern' societies of the 1990s.

One of the dilemmas we face in the present environment is that there is a clear possibility that new patterns of segregation could establish themselves and limit everyday interaction between racially-defined groups. Hazel Carby, writing of the situation in the United States, argues that many suburban middle-class white Americans are effectively cut off from contact with inner-city blacks.

She contrasts this with the explosion in the number of books published by black women and men who provide narratives of black lives, and which are often read by these same middle-class whites. She makes the poignant point that:

For white suburbia, as well as for white middle-class students in universities, these texts are becoming a way of gaining knowledge of the 'other', a knowledge that appears to satisfy and replace the desire to challenge existing frameworks of segregation. Have we, as a society, successfully eliminated the need for achieving integration through political agitation for civil rights and opted instead for knowing each other through cultural texts?   (Carby 1992: 198)

The growing evidence of a 'crisis of race' and of racialized class inequalities in the United States is a poignant reminder that the Civil Rights Movement and other movements since then have had at best a partial impact on established patterns of racial inequality, and have not stopped the development of new patterns of exclusion and segregation.

The arguments developed by Carby and others have to be situated carefully in the rather specific context of the racial politics that have shaped American society in the post-Civil Rights Movement era. But it is also clear that there is evidence that within contemporary European societies there is the danger of institutionalizing new forms of exclusion as a result of increased racial violence and racist mobilizations by the extreme-right. It is no surprise in the present environment of fear, violence, and physical attacks on foreigners that commentators such as Hans Magnus Enzensberger warns of the danger of violence and 'civil war' becoming an endemic feature of many cities in contemporary Europe unless the conditions which produce racism and xenophobic nationalism are fully understood (Enzensberger 1994). Yet others warn of the dangers faced by liberal democracies in the context of the growth of 'corporate national populism' and 'postmodern racism' (Zizek 1993: 224–6; see also Zizek 1989).

Pronouncements such as these are, of course, intentionally melodramatic and they are meant to be both a warning as well as a description of the present situation. But given our recent experiences in quite diverse local and national political environments who would argue with any real faith that we can ignore them? Can we be sure that the resurgence of racist nationalism does not pose a very real danger for the possibility of civilized coexistence between groups defined as belonging to different racial, ethnic, and national identities.

One of the great ironies of the present situation is that during the second half of the twentieth century transnational economic, social, and political relations have helped to create a multiplicity of migrant networks and communities that transcend received national boundaries. Categories such as migrants and refugees are no longer an adequate way to describe the realities of movement and settlement in many parts of the globe (Huyssen 1995). In many ways the idea of diaspora as an unending sojourn across different lands better captures the reality of transnational networks and communities than the language of immigration and assimilation. Multiple, circular, and return migrations, rather than a single great journey from one sedentary space to another, have helped to transform transnational spaces.

This links up with a question that we need to address directly in the present political environment, namely: what degree of cultural relativism is compatible with democratic principles and the maintenance of a democratic state? In the present environment this is by no means an easy question to answer. But answer it we must, if we are to avoid some of the divisive and destructive aspects of the move towards 'identity politics'. One obvious trend is to conflate culture and ethnicity, and this tends to privilege a form of categorizing that emphasizes ethnic constructs at the expense of other cultural practices, for example, those that generate the embodiment of gender and class relations. This is evident in most discussions of multiculturalism and cultural diversity. This conflation gives rise to unitary categories such as 'black culture' or 'Asian culture' used without further analysis, despite obvious complexities of regional, class, gender, or historical, and social differences within such categories. Even more serious is the tendency to conflate human values such as liberty, freedom, justice, and democracy with particular ethnic communities, and to identify them and celebrate them as the qualities of particular national or ethnic groups.

In searching for an alternative vision of what kind of society can accommodate both cultural diversity, and democracy and justice, there is a need to go beyond the certainties within which much of the debate about immigration, race, and ethnicity is currently framed. If we accept Stuart Hall's assertion that 'the capacity to *live with difference* is, in my view, the coming question of the twenty-first century' [our emphasis] (Hall 1993: 361), then we need to develop the conceptual ideas and political strategies that can allow us to move beyond both racism and multiculturalism.

Note

* This paper is based on research about race and immigration in contemporary Europe that was funded by the Leverhulme Trust.

References

ANDERSON, B. (1991), *Imagined Communities: Reflections on the Origin and Spread of Nationalism*, Revised Edition (London: Verso).

APPIAH, K. A. (1989), 'The Conservation of "Race"', *Black American Literature Forum*, 23/1: 37–60.

——and GATES Jr., H. L. (eds.) (1995), *Identities* (Chicago, IL: University of Chicago Press).

——and GUTMANN, A. (1996), *Color Conscious: The Political Morality of Race*, (Princeton, NJ: Princeton University Press).

ASAD, T. (1990), 'Ethnography, Literature, and Politics: Some Readings and Uses of Salman Rushdie's The Satanic Verses', *Cultural Anthropology*, 5/3: 239–69.

——(1993), *Genealogies of Religion: Discipline and Reasons of Power in Christianity and Islam* (Baltimore, MD: Johns Hopkins University Press).

BADER, V. (1995), 'Citizenship and Exclusion: Radical Democracy, Community, and Justice. Or, What is Wrong with Communitarianism?', *Political Theory*, 23/2: 211–46.

BALIBAR, E., and WALLERSTEIN, I. (1991), *Race, Nation, Class: Ambiguous Identities* (London: Verso).

BAUBÖCK, R. (1994), *Transnational Citizenship: Membership and Rights in International Migration* (Cheltenham: Edward Elgar).

——(1996), 'Cultural Minority Rights for Immigrants', *International Migration Review*, 30/1: 203–50.

BHABHA, H. K. (1994), *The Location of Culture* (London: Routledge).

BHATT, C. (1997), *Liberation and Purity* (London: UCL Press).

BRUBAKER, R. W. (1992), *Citizenship and Nationhood in France and Germany* (London: Harvard University Press).

CALHOUN, C. (ed.) (1994), *Social Theory and the Politics of Identity* (Oxford: Blackwell).

CARBY, H. (1992), 'The Multicultural Wars' in G. Dent (ed.), *Black Popular Culture* (Seattle, WA: Bay Press).

CASTLES, S. (1996), 'Democracy and Multiculturalism in Western Europe', *Journal of Area Studies*, 8: 51–76.

——and DAVIDSON, A. (forthcoming), *The Citizen who Does not Belong: Citizenship in a Global Age* (London: Macmillan).

——and Miller, M. J. (1993), *The Age of Migration* (London: Macmillan).

COLLEY, L. (1992), *Britons: Forging the Nation 1707–1837* (New Haven, CT: Yale University Press).

CONNOLLY, W. E. (1995), *The Ethos of Pluralization* (Minneapolis, MN: University of Minnesota Press).

DODD, P. (1995), *The Battle Over Britain* (London: Demos).

ENZENSBERGER, H. M. (1994), *Civil War* (London: Granta Books).

FORD, G. (1992), *Fascist Europe: The Rise of Racism and Xenophobia* (London: Pluto Press).

FOUCAULT, M. (1980), *Power/Knowledge: Selected Interviews and Other Writings 1972–1977* (Colin Gordon—Editor) (London: Harvester Wheatsheaf).

FREEMAN, G. P. (1995), 'Modes of Immigration Politics in Liberal Democratic States', *International Migration Review*, 29/4: 881–902.

FUSS, D. (1989), *Essentially Speaking: Feminism, Nature & Difference* (New York, NY: Routledge).

GILMAN, S. L. (1985), *Difference and Pathology: Stereotypes of Sexuality, Race and Madness* (Ithaca, NY: Cornell University Press).

GIROUX, H. (1993), 'Living Dangerously. Identity Politics and the New Cultural Racism: Towards a Critical Pedagogy of Representation', *Cultural Studies*, 7/1: 1–27.

GITLIN, T. (1995), *The Twilight of Common Dreams: Why America is Wracked by Culture Wars* (New York, NY: Metropolitan Books).

GOLDBERG, D. T. (1993), *Racist Culture* (Oxford: Blackwell).

——(ed.) (1994), *Multiculturalism: A Critical Reader* (Oxford: Blackwell).

GORDON, A. F., and NEWFIELD, C. (eds.) (1996), *Mapping Multiculturalism* (Minneapolis, MN: University of Minnesota Press).

GORHAM, E. (1995), 'Social Citizenship and its Fetters', *Polity*, 28/1: 25–47.

GUTMANN, A. (1993), 'The Challenge of Multiculturalism in Political Ethics', *Philosophy and Public Affairs*, 22/3: 171–206.

——(1994), 'Introduction', in Taylor, C. *et al.*, *Multiculturalism and The Politics of Recognition* (Princeton, NJ: Princeton University Press).

——and THOMPSON, D. (1996), *Democracy and Disagreement* (Cambridge, MA: Belknap Press).

HABERMAS, J. (1987), *The Philosophical Discourse of Modernity* (Cambridge: Polity Press).

——(1994), *The Past as Future* (Cambridge: Polity Press).

HALL, S. (1990), 'Cultural Identity and Diaspora', in Rutherford, J. (ed.), *Identity: Culture, Community, Difference* (London: Lawrence and Wishart).

——(1991), 'Old and New Identities, Old and New Ethnicities', in King, A. D. (ed.), *Culture, Globalisation and the World System* (London: Macmillan).

——(1993), 'Culture, community, nation', *Cultural Studies*, 7/3: 349–63.

HUYSSEN, A. (1995), *Twilight Memories: Marking Time in a Culture of Amnesia* (New York, NY: Routledge).

JOPPKE, C. (1996), 'Multiculturalism and Immigration: A Comparison of the United States, Germany, and Great Britain', *Theory and Society*, 25/4: 449–500.

——(1999), 'Immigration and Citizenship: A Comparative Perspective', forthcoming in *Ethnic and Racial Studies*.

KOHN, M. (1995), *The Race Gallery: The Return of Racial Science* (London: Jonathan Cape).

KYMLICKA, W. (1995a), *Multicultural Citizenship* (Oxford: Clarendon Press).

——(ed.) (1995b), *The Rights of Minority Cultures* (Oxford: Oxford University Press).

——and NORMAN, W. (1994), 'Return of the Citizen: A Survey of Recent Work on Citizenship Theory', *Ethics*, 104: 352–81.

MATTSON, M. (1995), 'Refugees in Germany: Invasion or Invention?', *New German Critique*, 64: 61–85.

McLAREN, P. (1993), 'Multiculturalism and the postmodern critique: towards a pedagogy of resistance and transformation', *Cultural Studies*, 7/1: 118–46.

MILES, R. (1993), *Racism After 'Race Relations'* (London: Routledge).

——(1994), 'A rise of racism in contemporary Europe?: Some sceptical reflections on its nature and extent', *New Community*, 20/4: 547–62.

MOON, J. D. (1993), *Constructing Community: Moral Pluralism and Tragic Conflicts* (Princeton, NJ: Princeton University Press).

MOSSE, G. (1985), *Toward the Final Solution: A History of European Racism* (Madison, WI: University of Wisconsin Press).

PAREKH, B. (1996), 'Minority Practices and Principles of Toleration', *International Migration Review*, 30/1: 251–84.

PECK, J. (1992), 'Refugees as Foreigners: The Problem of Becoming German and Finding a Home', Paper given at the Conference on Trust and the Refugee Experience, University of Lund.

PHILLIPS, A. (1995), *The Politics of Presence: Democracy and Group Representation* (Oxford: Clarendon Press).

RÄTHZEL, N. (1990), 'Germany: One Race, One Nation', *Race and Class* 32/3: 31–58.

SAMUEL, R. (1988), 'Little England Today', *New Statesman and Society*, 21 October.

SMITH, A. M. (1994), *New Right Discourse on Race and Sexuality: Britain, 1968–1990* (Cambridge: Cambridge University Press).

SOLOMOS, J., and BACK, L. (1995), *Race, Politics and Social Change* (London: Routledge).

——— (1996), *Racism and Society* (Basingstoke: Macmillan).

SOYSAL, Y. N. (1994), *Limits of Citizenship: Migrants and Postnational Membership in Europe* (Chicago, IL: University of Chicago Press).

SQUIRES, J. (ed.) (1993), *Principled Positions: Postmodernism and the Rediscovery of Value* (London: Lawrence and Wishart).

STOLER, A. L. (1995), *Race and the Education of Desire: Foucault's History of Sexuality and the Colonial Order of Things* (Durham, NC: Duke University Press).

TAKAKI, R. (1993), 'Multiculturalism: Battleground or Meeting Ground?' *Annals of the American Academy of Political and Social Science*, 530: 109–21.

TAYLOR, C., APPIAH, K. A., HABERMAS, J., ROCKEFELLER, S. C., WALZER, M., and WOLF, S.; edited and introduced by A. Gutmann (1994), *Multiculturalism* (Princeton, NJ: Princeton University Press).

TOMASI, J. (1995), 'Kymlicka, Liberalism, and Respect for Cultural Minorities', *Ethics*, 105/3: 580–603.

TOURAINE, A. (1995), *Critique of Modernity* (Oxford: Blackwell).

WIEVIORKA, M. (1996), 'Identity and Difference: Reflections on the French Non-Debate on Multiculturalism', *Thesis Eleven*, 47: 49–72.

WINANT, H. (1994), *Racial Conditions: Politics, Theory, Comparisons* (Minneapolis, MN: University of Minnesota Press).

WOLF, E. R. (1994), 'Perilous Ideas: Race, Culture, People', *Current Anthropology*, 35/1: 1–12.

WRIGHT, P. (1985), *On Living in an Old Country: The National Past in Contemporary Britain* (London: Verso).

WRENCH, J., and SOLOMOS, J. (eds.) (1993), *Racism and Migration in Western Europe* (Oxford: Berg).

YOUNG, I. M. (1990), *Justice and the Politics of Difference* (Princeton, NJ: Princeton University Press).

ZIZEK, S. (1989), *The Sublime Object of Ideology* (London: Verso).

—— (1993), *Tarrying With the Negative: Kant, Hegel, and the Critique of Ideology* (Durham: Duke University Press).

II

National Approaches to Migration and Ethnic Relations Politics

5

The Dynamics of Integration Policies: A Multidimensional Model

HAN ENTZINGER

This chapter deals with the situation of immigrants and minority communities in Europe, especially in Western Europe. It analyses different options for their integration, as individuals or as communities. It focuses on the role of the public authorities in the integration process, particularly on the objectives that may be set for an integration policy. These objectives are often relatively one-sided. They tend to emphasize only one aspect of the integration process and they account insufficiently for the complexity of this process as it develops in the modern state. As a consequence, many of the existing integration typologies are inadequate for the explanation of differences between countries and also insufficient for an understanding of changes that occur over time.

Nation, State, and Market

The history of Europe is one of nations and states, and of attempts to come to terms with the relationship between these two. A nation may be defined as a collectivity of people who share a sense of togetherness. A common history, a common language, religion, culture, or ancestry, or any combination of these may serve as a basis (Smith 1991: 43). Members of one nation interact more frequently with each other than with members of other nations. This is facilitated by the fact that those who belong to one nation usually live together in one territory, although this is not an absolute condition. Modern communication facilitates intense contacts among members of one group, even over long distances. At the basis of a state lies a set of laws, rules, and regulations that are binding for the people living in a specific territory (Weber 1985: 815). The state also comprises the institutions set up to implement those laws, rules, and regulations. These institutions are usually referred to as 'public authorities'. They include the arrangements set up to enforce sanctions: the court system, the police, and ultimately, the armed forces. In a liberal democracy, decisions on laws, rules, and regulations, and on the functioning of the state system as such, are taken by the people. The state, therefore, finds its legitimation with the people.

Since the notion of peoplehood plays a role in both 'nation' and 'state' it is no wonder that there is a relationship between these two concepts. In fact, in many parts of Europe 'nation' and 'state' almost coincide in everyday language. Over the past centuries the concept of the 'nation-state' has become a familiar phenomenon in Europe. This concept suggests that all people who live in the territory of one state are members of the same nation. In reality, however, this is rarely the case. Most European states are characterized by one dominant national community and one or more smaller 'nations' or communities. A significant number of countries outside Europe are exclusively built up of minority nations, even though one of these minorities often plays a dominant role in the state system.

The presence of minority communities may result from the fact that inter-state boundaries do not always coincide with boundaries between nations—for example the Spanish state or the Hungarian nation. Minority formation also occurs in situations where members of more than one nation share the same territory, such as in parts of former Yugoslavia. Finally, it may result from immigration. Minority communities may be centuries old, but they may also be relatively new, particularly if they stem from recent immigration. Over the years changes will occur in the cultural orientation of both majority and minority communities. This will affect their relationship and the patterns of identification of individual members. This is particularly true for immigrants, many of whom tend to lose their specific identity after several generations, and to assimilate to dominant cultural patterns. However, there are also examples of immigrant communities who have preserved their cultural or religious identity and who have developed into national minorities within a state system.

The relationship between nation and state has been affected fundamentally by the dramatic increase in state influence on the functioning of society, a historical fact in many European countries. As long as the role of the state was limited to some basic functions, such as protecting the territory from enemies or from floods, there was little need to be concerned about the functioning of multinational states. However, as the role of the state expanded, areas that once had been private, such as education, health care, housing, or social security, now became public. This meant that the public authorities were to decide about the laws, rules, and regulations in these domains and, by implication, about the cultural values and the norms of behaviour that lie at the basis of these laws. We have witnessed this process in Western Europe throughout the twentieth century. The establishment of the welfare state, in particular, has dramatically increased the impact of the public sector on society (Esping-Andersen 1990). This has been welcomed by many as a guarantee for a fairer distribution of scarce resources, and as a democratic asset. But, if democracy implies that the majority decides without taking minority interests and minority values into account, the welfare state may easily produce undesirable forms of cultural uniformity and lead to discrimination. Thus, there can be a tension between 'nation' and 'state'. It is not unsurmountable, but certain skills and some thoughtfulness are required to reconcile the two.

There is also a third factor in the delicate interplay between basic concepts: the market. The expansion of the public sector and the establishment of the welfare state largely found their legitimation in the desire to control the impact of market forces on European societies, and to limit the degree of social and economic inequality that these forces generated. To achieve this, the classical state functions were supplemented by the introduction of large scale education, and of sophisticated mechanisms of redistribution and protection from exploitation. The aim of all this was to ban poverty, to keep the people healthy and happy, and to maintain social order without the use of force. In fact, the establishment of the welfare state—even after the recent trimmings that many European countries have witnessed—has had a lasting impact on the relationship between market and state. The social and economic situation of citizens is no longer determined by market forces alone. Market forces may be redressed through government intervention, for instance in an effort to provide more and better opportunities, and to create more equity for citizens, irrespective of their belongingness to a specific community.

Thus, there is a tension not only between 'state' and 'nation', but also between 'state' and 'market'. Consequently, there is also a tension between 'nation' and 'market'. In principle, the rules of the market are supposed to be 'colour blind'. In reality, however, cultural differences that stem from differences in national origins are often reflected in (labour) market positions. Members of immigrant or national minorities may be faced, for example, with higher access barriers than the majority, not only to employment, but also to housing, education, or health care. These barriers often result from racism, prejudice, or discrimination, or from a cultural bias in mechanisms for recruitment, selection, and attribution of scarce resources. This is why it is relevant to include the role of the market in an analysis of integration policies in multinational and multicultural societies.

Integration Typologies

We now have the three ingredients for an analysis of integration policies: state, nation, and market. These three correspond with the three major dimensions of the integration process: the legal-political, the cultural, and the socio-economic dimensions respectively. Any policy that aims at promoting integration should take account of these three, also in their interrelationship. This is irrespective of the fact whether we analyse integration at the individual or at the group level—a distinction that will be discussed later. Many of the existing typologies and models that explain integration processes and minority–majority relations tend to overlook this complexity and put too much emphasis on only one of the three dimensions. To illustrate this I will now discuss a few examples of such typologies, mainly drawn from relatively recent studies on immigrant integration in Western Europe.

Guestworkers and Immigrants

A substantial part of Europe's recent immigration has been induced by needs of the economy and has been defined as temporary. Under such circumstances there seems to be little need for reflection on complex issues such as integration, multiculturalism, or equal treatment. Temporary residents are citizens of another state and for that reason they are supposed not to require the same degree of protection which a state provides for its own citizens. This model has become widely known as the guestworker model. Quite often, however, temporary migrants may become permanent settlers after some time. This indeed is what happened in Germany and also in countries such as Switzerland, Austria, Belgium, and The Netherlands (Castles 1984). Of these countries, Germany has had the most serious problems in acknowledging this development. This has severely harmed the immigrants' opportunities for integration. Up to the late 1990s the federal government formally maintained that Germany is not an immigration country, even though under the coalition in power in 2000 a change seems imminent. More recently, Greece, Italy, Spain, and Portugal—formerly labour sending countries—have also been faced with labour immigration. Many of the newly arrived workers are not given a formal immigrant status and are accommodated in the informal sector of their economies, particularly at the lower skill levels. This makes it easier for the authorities in those countries to define their stay exclusively in economic terms. From time to time, however, social, cultural, and political tensions that arise from the presence of these irregular immigrants become too strong. Large-scale amnesties then appear to be a welcome relief. Needless to say that such amnesties attract new irregular migrants, who anticipate a repetition of this procedure.

The opposite of the guestworker model is the permanent immigration model. Permanent immigration for economic reasons has hardly taken place in Europe, except in small numbers for specific professions. Large scale permanent immigration is a characteristic of so called classical immigration countries, such as the United States, Canada, or Australia. These countries deliberately define immigration as an element in their policies not only of economic expansion, but also of nation building. In reality, differences between the two models are much smaller than their opposing labels suggest. This is reflected appropriately in the terminology proposed by Kubat (1993). Rather than opposing a guestworker model to a model of permanent immigration, he confronts an in-migration model—most of Europe—with an immigration model—classical countries. Indeed, the problem in Europe has been that labour migration meant as temporary, often became permanent. Paradoxically, permanent immigration in classical immigration countries often turns out to be less permanent than suggested. Although there are significant variations between immigrant communities in this respect, a return rate of 40 per cent within the first ten years is not unusual. Hence there is a gap between public ideologies and the realities of migration. This makes the temporary vs. permanent immigration model less useful for an understanding of integration processes. It focuses too strongly on the economic determinants of migration and it neglects the realities of what happens after the moment of immigration, in the economic domain, but even more so in the political and cultural domains.

Differences in Citizenship

Irrespective of the degree of permanency in their perception of immigration, all immigrant societies sooner or later see themselves faced with growing numbers of non-indigenous residents, mostly non-citizens. Therefore, states must reflect on the legal and political position they wish to grant to these people and their children. Here we may also distinguish two approaches, which tell us something about the nature of the integration process as it is envisaged by the host societies. I am referring here to the classical distinction between *jus soli* and *jus sanguinis*. Under the *jus soli* system all residents who live in one territory have the same rights, irrespective of their ancestry or length of residence. In the case of newly-arrived immigrants there may be a short transition period, during which these rights can be acquired gradually. Under the *jus sanguinis* system, by contrast, full citizenship and all rights related to that status, such as voting rights or access to public service, are passed on from one generation to the next along the 'lines of blood'. Citizenship and political status are acquired by birth. This means that not all residents of one country are treated similarly. Immigrants and those who descend from immigrants, and sometimes also national minorities, may have rights and obligations that differ from those of the dominant population.

Of course, both systems are ideal types; the reality is usually a mixture of the two models, with considerable differences between European states. Traditionally, the United Kingdom is one of the most outspoken examples of *jus soli*: anyone born in that country is a British citizen. Germany, by contrast, has long favoured the *jus sanguinis* system. Access to German citizenship is extremely difficult for anyone who has no German parent, even for the second and subsequent generations born and living in Germany. The other side of this coin is that ethnic Germans (Aussiedler), for instance those who have 'returned' from Russia, are granted German citizenship from the very moment of their settlement in Germany, even after six or more generations. Because of their German descent they are not seen as immigrants, even though in sociological terms their position is highly comparable to that of new arrivals from other countries. The current federal government is planning to introduce more elements of *jus soli* into the German system. French policies in this field oscillate between the two others. When the Right is in power it tends to listen to the nationalists and to favour *jus sanguinis*, whilst the Left tends to give more weight to the interests of the second generation of immigrants.

The distinction between *jus sanguinis* and *jus soli* is fundamental in the analysis of immigration and integration, since it defines ways individuals can accede to membership of a new state system. Several scholars have argued that this distinction reflects deeply rooted differences between nation-states in their cultural traditions and in their self-image (Hammar 1990; Brubaker 1992; Joppke 1999). In its practical implications, however, this distinction limits itself essentially to only one dimension: the relationship between individuals and the state. The effects on the social and economic position of immigrants as well as on their cultural situation are obvious, but in essence these effects are indirect. These are the limitations of the *jus sanguinis* vs. *jus soli* typology.

Minorities and Assimilation

Another typology focuses on the cultural dimension. Again, two basic approaches may be distinguished: the ethnic minorities model, and the assimilation model. More than the two previous ones, this typology can be applied to non-immigrant minorities as well. In the European literature the United Kingdom is usually seen as a prototype for the ethnic minorities model (Rex 1991; Hollifield 1997). Starting from the assumption that immigration is permanent, immigrants are defined as members of their new society, but primarily in terms of their ethnic or national origins. In this approach immigration is seen as having reinforced the multicultural character of society. Facilities should be created for each community to preserve and further develop its cultural identity. A mutual understanding between the communities is a condition for a harmonious multicultural society. If necessary, the public authorities must take measures to promote this. In the ethnic minorities model, migrants are first of all defined in terms of their group membership, which is usually determined by their national origin, for example Greek, or Moroccan, or their religion, such as Muslims, or Jews. The ethnic minority model has been followed by several other countries in the North-West of Europe, in particular by The Netherlands and also, in varying degrees, by the Nordic countries.

The second model is the assimilation model, of which France is usually cited as a prototype. Elements of it, however, can be found in many other countries. In this model, the permanent nature of immigration is not really disputed, but immigrants are expected to assimilate to their hosts. Immigrant communities are not recognized as relevant entities by the public authorities. In the French *jacobin* tradition, the emphasis is on the individual relationship between the citizen and the state, without intermediaries. It is not possible to acknowledge differences in culture or religion in the public sphere—which in France includes education—as the 1989 *affaire du foulard* has illustrated. In that *cause célèbre* Muslim girls were forbidden to wear headscarves at school. These were seen as symbols of their religion, while the school is a public lay institution where such symbols cannot be tolerated (Hargreaves 1995). This model requires from most immigrants a significant degree of cultural adaptation to their new environment. Those who are successful in doing so may have interesting opportunities; those who are not successful risk becoming marginalized. The ethnic minorities vs. assimilation typology has the advantage that it also accounts for the important difference between group and individual approaches. As we shall see later, this difference is essential in the analysis of integration processes. However, it finds its limits in the fact that it tends to overemphasize the relevance of the cultural dimension at the expense of legal and socio-economic aspects.

Other Typologies

The three typologies discussed in the previous sections reflect some of the major dilemmas of immigration and integration. However, since each of these emphasizes one dimension only—market, state, or culture—their explanatory power is limited. Various attempts have been made to develop models that do more justice to the complex dynamics of immigrant integration, and that reconcile its different dimensions (e.g. Bryant 1997; Zolberg 1997). Most model-constructing in Europe, however, is inductive rather than deductive, based as it is on a comparative assessment of the situation in two or more countries. Some interesting, but very diverse examples are: Hammar (1985), Brubaker (1992), Schnapper (1992), Todd (1994), Wihtol de Wenden and De Tinguy (1995), Kastoryano (1996), and Joppke (1998).

Hollifield (1997), for example, distinguishes three models for Europe:

1. The guestworker model, for which Germany is prototypical. Immigration is largely determined by the conjunctural needs of the labour market, and the immigrants' presence is seen as temporary. As a consequence, there is no need neither to reinforce their legal status, nor to reflect on the consequences of increased cultural diversity.

2. The assimilation model, for which France serves as a prototype. Immigration is seen as permanent, immigrants are welcome, and they are given a sound legal status on the condition that they are willing and able to assimilate to the dominant cultural pattern. Immigrants are seen as individuals in the first place; the notion of immigrant or minority communities is alien to this model.

3. The ethnic minorities model, for which the United Kingdom serves as a prototype. Here too immigration is seen as permanent, but immigrants are defined in terms of their ethnic or national origin. They constitute new communities, culturally different from the existing communities, and from

each other. The challenge is to make these communities live together harmoniously.

Another typology that attempts to reconcile different dimensions, has been developed by Castles (1995). He also distinguishes three models, which he calls: (a) the model of differential exclusion, (b) the assimilationist model, and (c) the pluralist model. Differences in terminology do not conceal that his three models combine elements of all previous distinctions. Germany and Southern Europe are examples of model (a), while Britain, France, and The Netherlands of model (b). Model (c) only exists in the classical immigration countries outside Europe—countries that deliberately use immigration in their process of nation building. The weak point of this model is that it lumps Britain, France, and The Netherlands together in one model, whereas many other authors point precisely at the significant differences in the approaches of these countries, particularly between between France on the one hand, and the United Kingdom and The Netherlands on the other (Freeman 1979; Lapeyronnie 1993).

Ideology and Reality

All typologies and all models presented so far are a little unsatisfactory when it comes down to understanding and explaining differences in immigrant integration policies in Europe. Of course, typologies always tends to oversimplify reality. But what is reality here? Is it the official government ideology or is it the actual situation of the immigrants in the different countries and the dynamics of their integration? And which immigrants are we talking about, given the wide variations between and within the different communities? It is interesting to note that despite deep ideological differences between, for example, Germany and France, the actual course of immigrant integration processes in these two countries is quite similar. The same applies to many concrete policy measures taken to facilitate immigrant integration. Thus, one has to be extremely careful in sticking the label of one model or typology on a country without paying further attention to the actual contents of its integration policies (Favell 1998). Forcing countries into the straightjacket of a model does insufficient justice to changes that occur over the years, and to differences in viewpoints that exist within each of the countries, for instance between political parties or between the national and the local authorities.

Therefore, it is my aim in the following sections, to develop a more analytical approach of which some elements have already been introduced. This analytical approach focuses primarily on public policy ideologies, that is on objectives set for integration policies, rather than on the process of integration as such. Obviously, these two are not the same: nicely formulated integration objectives cannot always prevent exclusion. It must be acknowledged that one of the reasons why public policy-making in this domain is often ambiguous, lies in the fact that immigrant integration may not always really be envisaged, at least not for certain categories of immigrants. Policies may sometimes be called integration policies by the authorities, but their 'hidden' objective may be window dressing, or worse.

In this chapter we are not really concerned with such forms of half-heartedness, nor with the analysis of discrepancies between facts and realities. Our primary interest lies in the publicly stated objectives of integration policies and the existing options for the implementation of these policies. What do public authorities claim they wish to achieve with their integration policies and what policy instruments may help them reach this outcome? What conflicting demands may arise in the course of the integration process, and how do public authorities cope with these? The basic assumption, however, is that integration is actively pursued at the level of policy-making, even though the actual outcome of the integration process may not always be a fuller integration.

A Multidimensional Approach

The analytical approach I am advocating takes account of two major dimensions, both of which are highly relevant for an understanding of what actually happens in integration processes. One is that integration is a multidimensional process which becomes manifest in different domains of society. The most important domains are the legal and political domain, the social and economic domain, and the cultural domain (Bauböck 1994a: 9–12; Penninx and Slijper 1999). These domains roughly correspond to the notions of 'state', 'market', and 'nation' respectively, which I discussed earlier.

The second dimension is equally important and needs some further introduction. It refers to the way in which the post-immigration settlement process is perceived by the surrounding society and the public authorities. Are the immigrants defined primarily in terms of their membership of a non-indigenous community, or are they seen as individuals? In essence, this opposition reflects the classical difference between communitarian and liberal views, a difference which has been actively debated in social and political philosophy ever since Rawls published his *Theory of Justice* in 1971. In the communitarian view societies are primarily made up of groups that share certain characteristics which distinguish them from other groups. Immigration has brought different groups together in one territory. In an open and democratic society the public authorities will have to account for this in their integration policies. This should be done not only in the cultural domain—as seems obvious in view of the difference in culture between the established population and the newcomers—but also in the legal, political, social, and economic domains. This will often require the creation of separate institutional arrangements for immigrant communities. In the liberal perception, in contrast, the individual is the primary unit in society. Immigration is primarily understood as the outcome of an individual decision-making process. Immigrants are seen as individual settlers in the first place, whose aim it is to become integrated into the new society. The public authorities have a task in facilitating this. They should do so by creating the best possible conditions for each individual. This is usually understood as enabling immigrants to accede to society's major institutions.

More recently, new dimensions have been added to this debate. Scholars like Taylor (1994) and Kymlicka (1995) have argued that a liberal integration policy may very well account for differences between groups and aim at recognizing such differences. Habermas (1994), in contrast, has argued that a liberal democratic state must require from its immigrants a certain degree of adaptation in their ethical and cultural orientation. This limits the possibilities for preserving their collective identity, as advocated in the communitarian approach. This is not the place to elaborate on this ongoing debate. Whatever the different ideological viewpoints may be, there is a common understanding that the individual vs. group approach in issues of immigrant integration and minority–majority relations reflects a highly relevant distinction, which has important consequences for policy-making (Martiniello 1997: 100). This is why we will include this distinction into our analysis of integration policies.

The two major distinctions outlined here may be combined together to produce six options—see Fig. 5.1. These options reflect six different objectives of an integration policy. The instruments that may be implemented to achieve each of these objectives vary accordingly. We will briefly discuss all six options.

Six Options for Incorporation

The first column in Fig. 5.1 refers to the legal and political domain, in which the relationship between immigrants and the state is defined. Newly-arrived migrants often have fewer rights than the established population, particularly if they are foreign citizens. If this situation persists too long, it will contradict the idea of equality before the law, which is so vital for modern liberal democracies, and it may undermine the legitimacy of political processes. Therefore, sooner or later, public authorities will feel the need to define a policy that aims to reduce legal differences between the various residents of a given country. If preference is given to an approach which emphasizes equal rights for individuals, barriers for naturalization will be removed or the acquisition of citizenship of the new country will be actively encouraged. An alternative route is to grant resident non-citizens all or most rights usually linked to citizenship, without forcing them to opt for naturalization and to cut the formal ties with their country of origin. Another alternative is to allow dual citizenship, an approach often advocated by migrants, but not very popular with most Euro-

	legal and political domain	cultural domain	social and economic domain
individual approach	equal rights	liberal pluralism	equal opportunity
group approach	group rights	multiculturalism	equity

FIG. 5.1. Six options for incorporation policies

pean governments. The latter claim that dual citizenship implies dual loyalty, while in the classical legal and political thinking, an individual can only be loyal to one state at a time (Bauböck 1994b). However, such fundamental objections may be overruled at times by the practical advantages of dual citizenship. It enables immigrants to travel more freely in Europe, while they may continue to own property in the country of origin. It also reduces the number of foreigners living in a territory, an attractive perspective for certain governments wishing to counter racist trends.

In cases where a group approach prevails over an individual one, preference will be given to recognizing immigrant group rights, for instance in family law or in schooling. In its most far-reaching form this implies that different legal systems exist alongside each other within one state: 'separate but equal'. Such forms of legal pluralism are not at all common practice for immigrant communities, even in countries with a tradition of institutionalized pluralism such as The Netherlands or Belgium. Claims that have been put forward occasionally for the recognition of, for example, Muslim family law or criminal law, have been systematically rejected by the authorities in most of Europe. European states are not very keen on introducing forms of pluralism in their legislation, particularly not in the case of immigrants. They fear that this will undermine the unity of the nation-state. This does not exclude, however, that in the practice of their jurisdiction, cultural considerations are often taken into account in cases that involve immigrants. Parallel legal systems are more common, although still within certain limits, in the case of national minorities, who are often more concentrated geographically than immigrants (Sowell 1990). The special regime then applies to a certain territory, rather than to the members of one community, although examples of the latter do exist. A milder and more widespread form of group rights recognition may be found in those cases where legislation has been changed in order to take into account certain religious practices of immigrant communities, for example the manner of burying their dead or slaughtering their animals. This, in fact, has occurred in many European countries.

In processes of political decision-making, the individual approach focuses on providing the usual political rights to immigrants. If immigrants become naturalized these rights will come automatically with the new passport. Active and passive voting rights in elections are generally seen as the most important of these rights. In most West European states there is an ongoing debate on the extension of voting rights to immigrant non-citizens with a certain residence record, for instance five years. The idea is that this will enhance the legitimacy of public decision-making, since it involves more people who are affected by these decisions. As a consequence, this will encourage immigrant integration. In the 1980s and 1990s several European states actually changed their legislation to enable foreign residents to take part in elections, but so far only at the local, and occasionally also at the regional level. This has been the case in the five Nordic countries and in The Netherlands for all foreigners, while several other states have introduced local voting rights for immigrants of selected nationalities, mostly from other EU countries. No country allows foreign residents to vote in national elections.

The classical group approach in political participation implies that, in representative bodies, a certain number of seats is reserved for minority members (Kymlicka 1995: 131). This practice exists in certain European countries, but always for national minorities and never for immigrants. In contrast, most countries in Western Europe have a long experience with consultative arrangements for immigrant communities at all levels of public administration and policy-making (Soysal 1994). The practicalities of such arrangements vary considerably from one country to another, and even from one city to another (Entzinger 1999). Immigrant consultation is usually limited to issues that relate directly to the immigrants' living conditions, and is never binding. The membership of consultative bodies is often a point of debate. Which communities should be represented? Should the members be appointed or elected, and by whom? Should non-immigrants also be involved in the consultation process, since they may also be affected by its outcome?

The second column in Fig. 5.1 refers to culture. The issue here is how to cope with the increased ethnic and cultural diversity that stems from immigration and that may be seen by some as a challenge to the nation's unity. In the individual approach, culture is largely considered a private affair. If the migrants themselves wish to create facilities to preserve and support their cultures, or to cater for specific needs in this domain, they are free to do so. It is not very likely that the state will actively support these facilities nor take any initiative in this respect. It is assumed that a neutral attitude of the state will permit different cultures to coexist in a pluriform society, hence the term liberal pluralism for this option. Public intervention may be limited to promoting a better mutual understanding between members of the population with different ethnic or religious backgrounds, for example through the organization of anti-racism campaigns or the development of anti-discrimination legislation. However, there is strong evidence that under such circumstances liberal pluralism often leads to assimilation to the dominant culture within two or three generations. Certain immigrants, however, may find it difficult to familiarize themselves with the dominant culture, while important elements of their original culture may no longer be functional in the new surroundings. This may lead to anomie and social exclusion.

Advocates of a group approach see this as one argument in favour of acknowledging and even institutionalizing cultural differences in public policy-making. In their view, explicit policies of multiculturalism do more justice to the principle that all individuals should be treated equally, irrespective of their cultural background. A basic assumption is that minority cultures can only survive and develop if embedded in an infrastructure of a more or less permanent nature. In the group approach, the prevailing idea is that the state has to see to the development of this infrastructure as a matter of principle. The state should encourage and protect it whenever necessary. Paradoxical as it may seem to some, advocates of the group approach claim that a policy of multiculturalism that takes explicit account of ethnic diversity and minority interests will eventually produce better opportunities for the participation of minority communities in society as a whole, as well as in the political, social, and economic domains. In the multiculturalist view, the establishment of immigrant organizations should be encouraged and supported. Immigrant communities should be aided to gain public visibility, for example in the media, and to pass on their cultural heritage to subsequent generations. Education in the mother tongue can be a very effective instrument here. In fact, the debate on multiculturalism in many European countries focuses on mother tongue teaching, its position in the school curriculum, and the role of the public authorities in facilitating this.

The underlying question is how far states should go in their recognition and support of cultural pluralism (Struijs 1998). Not all elements in all immigrant and minority cultures are equally acceptable to all members of the surrounding society. The law defines certain limits, but these limits are not always as clear as they may seem. They may also be interpreted differently by different groups. But even if minority behaviour and the expression of minority cultures remain within the law, the majority may find them less socially acceptable or they may impede smooth contacts between members of different communities. One may think here, for example, of the relationship between men and women, between parents and their children, or of attitudes towards homosexuality. School teachers, police officers, social workers, medical doctors, and all those who function in a multicultural setting every day have become familiar with such challenges.

Another potential risk of institutionalizing multiculturalism is that this may develop into an obstacle in the rapid process of change that immigrant cultures often undergo. The 'mother tongue' has a completely different function for a newly arrived immigrant child to that for a young member of the second or third generation, and the role of mother tongue teaching changes accordingly. Institutionalizing multiculturalism, however, requires a certain degree of codification of minority cultures. It may also require decisions on what are essential elements of cultures that are worth being recognized and preserved. All this may produce certain delicate dilemmas in the field of language, national politics, and religion, which in turn may affect the relationship with the country of origin. This problem comes up in immigrant situations, but also in relation to well established national minorities (Entzinger 1999; Rath *et al.* 1999).

Finally, there is the social and economic domain. In this domain market forces prevail, but there is also a role for public authorities in correcting these forces through policy measures. These, of course, may differ in intensity and scope. As in the other domains, there are basically two approaches. The individualist approach, as we have seen, is rooted in the classical liberal view. In this view, immigrants are seen as newcomers who often start at the lower end of the labour market and who will have to work their way up from there. If the public authorities wish to promote integration, their major task is to ensure equal opportunity. Immigrant status or ethnic origin should not be obstacles to equal access to relevant institutions in the field of housing, schooling, or work. Anti-discrimination legislation offers important instruments to achieve this aim. In fact, several European states have reinforced their laws in this area. Occasionally, these instruments have been supplemented by training and language courses for immigrants, particularly for the newcomers among them (Foblets and Hubeau 1997). Such courses may help compensate for certain 'deficits' and ensure more equality in starting positions for everyone.

Equal opportunity is not always easy to achieve since the dominant culture decisively affects the nature of most policy instruments, often unintentionally. As a consequence of their cultural bias these instruments and mechanisms tend to favour members of the original population over people of immigrant origin, to whom certain facilities may be less readily accessible. Firing procedures, for example, are often based on the classical last-in-first-out principle. Since immigrants almost by definition tend to be over-represented among the more recent employees, they will also be over-represented among those dismissed. This explains why, even in the absence of explicit discrimination, immigrants are often more vulnerable than non-immigrants in times of economic downturn. Measures to compensate for this mechanism will be perceived by many as unacceptable forms of positive discrimination.

If a group approach prevails in this domain, policy ambitions usually reach out further. The objective is not equality of opportunity but equality of outcome, or equity, for all groups. There is a certain paradox in this approach. On the one hand it is based on the ideal that differences in race, ethnic origin, or immigrant status should not be reflected in the distribution of scarce resources, nor affect the chances of participation in relevant social or economic institutions. All groups and communities should have a proportional share in goods and services, in particular in areas such as housing, schooling, and work. On the other hand, in order to achieve this situation, compensatory measures should be developed that do take into account race, ethnicity, or immigrant status. Equity will usually be pursued through policies of affirmative action that aim at overcoming social deprivation of particular groups in society, as well as at combating discrimination. It cannot be excluded that equity may also be achieved without public intervention, but this will be a very long process over several generations, if it occurs at all. Moreover, if equity will be achieved only after a very long time, one may wonder if, meanwhile, racial and ethnic differences will not have disappeared. The challenge of active and consistent policies to achieve equity between groups in the social and economic domain is that differences in other domains, or at least the potential for such differences, be respected.

One of the most far-reaching forms of affirmative action is the setting of quotas. Within different institutional settings, such as schools, enterprises, or housing projects, positions are reserved for members of a specific group. These positions are attributed on the basis of group membership rather than merit. In Europe this is not a very customary way of handling immigrant integration. It is more common when achieving equality between men and women is at stake. Classical immigration countries, in contrast, are much more familiar with the setting of quotas. In the United States, for example, quota policies still exist at certain universities and schools, but they are by no means undisputed

(Skrentny 1996). Until the early 1990s such policies were much more widespread not only for African Americans, but also for certain immigrant communities.

Less far-reaching forms of affirmative action tend to be somewhat more acceptable in Europe, particularly in countries such as the United Kingdom and The Netherlands. These countries have long acknowledged the permanent nature of the presence of their immigrants, and indeed tend to define them more clearly than many countries in terms of their community membership. Certain schools and some employers have been making efforts to attract more students or employees with an immigrant background, for example, by adapting the curriculum or by introducing different forms of preferential treatment in recruitment. Such efforts may be actively encouraged or even subsidized by the state. Nevertheless, affirmative action policies continue to be looked upon with suspicion, not only by members of the dominant population but also by certain immigrants themselves who fear their stigmatizing effect.

A Discussion of the Model

All six options just discussed share integration as their common objective. However, they interpret that objective in different ways and, consequently, they also differ in their choice of policy instruments. The most fundamental difference we have distinguished in the model is between the individual and the group approach. A major problem with strategies that focus on individual integration rather than on the group is that these tend to underestimate the impact of the culturally biased mechanisms for selection and attribution within the dominant society. Such biases systematically disadvantage individuals of an immigrant or minority cultural background and may therefore limit their opportunities in all three domains that we have distinguished. For obvious reasons, individuals are seldom in a position to counter this. Group strategies, in contrast, tend to overemphasize differences between the communities within one society. Attempts to acknowledge and preserve such differences require forms of classification that may not only obstruct social and cultural change, but also create a strong dependency on public protection and support. If these are withdrawn, the minority communities may rapidly become marginalized.

Problems may also arise in incorporation policies if the three domains that we have distinguished are not sufficiently in balance. An approach that focuses primarily on the legal and political domain tends to overlook discrepancies between rules and reality. A strong residential status for migrants, active naturalization policies, and the granting of voting rights to foreign residents, as well as the granting of certain specific rights and entitlements to immigrant communities, may facilitate their integration. However, such policy measures do not automatically guarantee a sufficient understanding of cultural differences on the part of the surrounding society, nor will they provide sufficient opportunities for integration into the social and economic life of that society. Thus, a one-sided emphasis on legal and political instruments may create expectations for integration in other domains that cannot be fulfilled without additional measures. Nevertheless, many European states tend to focus their immigrant policies almost exclusively on this legal and political domain (Fassmann and Münz 1994). In the other domains, general policy instruments prevail. Possible reasons for this limitation may be that certain countries are somewhat weary of institutionalized pluralism or lack a strong social policy tradition.

The major problem with approaches that focus on the primacy of the cultural domain is that these tend to define culture in substantialist terms. Seemingly neutral as well as more pluralist approaches take insufficient account of the nature of cultural dynamics, particularly in immigrant situations. Almost by definition a state's policy in the cultural domain concentrates on laying down values and prescribing norms in laws and regulations, which subsequently will have to be enforced. The introduction of mother tongue teaching, a characteristic of the multiculturalist approach, requires a definition of what actually is someone's mother tongue in specific cases. Is Turkish really the mother tongue for a second generation child of Kurdish parents living in Germany, or Arabic for a Moroccan Berber child in France? In many cases it is not so easy to account for cultural change as it occurs over time. Thus, the cultural approach runs the risk of 'fossilizing' cultures or of forcing people into the cultural straightjacket of the receiving society. Policy-making in the cultural domain is hard to reconcile with the view that cultures are living expressions of what people feel and think under rapidly changing circumstances.

Of course, approaches based on the primacy of the social and economic domain also have disadvantages. As we have seen, the major objective of such approaches is to influence distribution and selection mechanisms that provide access to scarce resources so that minorities and newcomers may benefit more from these resources. For members of the original population this is not always acceptable. They may feel that, as a consequence of this, they will not obtain a fair share themselves any longer. Many studies indicate that this is not the case. At a macro-level there is nearly always an 'underconsumption' of social policy benefits by immigrants in comparison to non-immigrants, provided one controls for social and economic status. However, the mere fact that such arguments are regularly put forward has a political significance. It indicates that there are limits to the applicability of incorporation strategies for immigrants in this domain and that these strategies ought to be supplemented by strategies in the other domains. Besides, in a market economy public authorities should always be able to find a sufficient jusitification for attempts to interfere in the interplay of supply and demand.

We may conclude from this rapid overview of the three domains that they are indeed complementary to one another. Integration policies that focus too strongly on one domain and neglect the other two run the risk of being ineffective or even counterproductive. The explanation for this lies in the tension between the concepts of nation, state, and market, discussed at the beginning of this chapter. It is essential, therefore, that approaches in the three domains are interlinked, even though this implies that none of the stated objectives can be fully achieved. In other words, group rights, multiculturalism, and equity can never be achieved in their perfect forms and simultaneously. The same holds for equal rights, liberal pluralism, and equal opportunity. Concessions will have to be made, and this requires implicit or explicit choices in policy-making. An additional complication lies in our earlier distinction between individual and group approaches. This distinction may be perfectly legitimate at an analytical level, but in real policy-making elements of both tend to creep in. Or, for that matter, one approach may be dominant in one of the three domains, and the other approach in the other domains. Quite often this is the result of political compromising, but it is obvious that this will harm the policy's effectiveness.

The question that remains is the one about the determinants of political decision-making in matters of integration. What factors affect the choice for one of the six options in the model or for a combination of these? One factor may be the situation of a country's economy. Immigrant integration tends to be smoother during periods of economic growth. Public investment in integration will be accepted more readily in times of prosperity. Paradoxically, it may be less needed then, as market conditions are more favourable. However, it is safe to assume that integration policies vary in their scope and intensity in accordance with the business cycle. A second factor may be labelled as the 'matureness' of the immigration process. As time goes by, the nature of integration problems changes. Numbers of immigrants increase, the immigrant population diversifies, the situation of children and grandchildren of immigrants differs fundamentally from that of their (grand)parents. From the public authorities this requires a constant reflection on integration objectives and a preparedness to adapt policy instruments.

A third factor is related to the competence of the state and its ability to influence integration in specific domains. If, for example, the state has a strong influence on the school system, it is more likely that education will play a dominant role in integration policies than if the state's influence is weaker, irrespective of the objectives of that policy. If there is a large public housing sector, improving housing conditions for immigrants is more likely to be selected as a policy target. European states differ considerably in their possibilities for public intervention (Van Waarden 1999). This also accounts for differences between countries in their preferences for integration objectives. Understandably, integration policies tend to be more comprehensive and more ambitious in countries with a relatively large public sector.

A fourth factor is less pragmatic and more ideological. It has to do with political preferences. Political parties all over Europe differ in their views on immigrant integration. Some prefer an active interventionist policy, others assume a more liberal *laissez faire* attitude. Some tend to support the development of migrant communities, others prefer to create opportunities for the individual migrant. Some wish to take account of the specific cultural background of migrants, others see them primarily as individuals in a situation of deprivation. Parties with a nationalist outlook tend to expect a higher degree of assimilation from immigrants than parties that adhere to more pluralist or internationalist values. Thus, the preferred option for integration varies in accordance with the ideologies of the incumbent political parties. Parties usually alternate in incumbency or they may form coalitions. Moreover, party preferences may change over the years as a result of changing appreciations of immigration. This is another reason why actual integration policies are less clear cut than the policy options represented in models (Fermin 1997).

Conclusion

In this chapter we have discussed a number of typologies that are commonly used to assess differences between European countries in their integration policies for immigrants. Almost by definition typologies tend to oversimplify reality, but the typologies presented in the first part of this chapter do so too strongly. They account insufficiently for the complexity of integration dynamics and for changes in integration policies as these have taken place over the years in all countries. Therefore it seems more appropriate to develop a typology of approaches rather than a typology of countries. This is what we have done in the second part of this chapter. The primordial distinction in the typology is between individual and group approaches. The former find their roots in liberalism, the latter in communitarianism. The typology also accounts for the fact that integration processes cover a number of domains in society, each of which may require different policy objectives and different policy instruments. We have distinguished the legal and political, the cultural, and the social and economic domains. The two approaches and the three domains combined create six possible options for integration policies. Some of these six can be combined more easily than others, but any combination of options requires concessions in their implementation. However, if only one option is pursued at the time, its effectiveness will also be sub-optimal, because of negative repercussions in other domains. A major reason why it is impossible to achieve 'perfection' is the natural tension between the concepts of nation, state, and market.

The typology of approaches developed in this chapter has several advantages over more traditional typologies of countries. It makes it easier to understand changes in policy objectives and policy instruments that occur over the years in almost every country. It also makes it easier to understand why not all immigrants are treated in the same way. Another advantage is that it enables us to compare countries without caricaturising them. Integration policies certainly differ from one European country to another, but these differences are not always as radical as dichotomies suggest. Finally, and perhaps most importantly, the typology may help to explain why certain policies are more effective than others. As a general rule policies are more effective as they cover more domains and as the number of built-in contradictions is more limited. This conclusion may serve as an agenda for further comparative research.

References

BAUBÖCK, RAINER (1994a), *The integration of immigrants* (Strasbourg: Council of Europe).
—— (1994b), *Transnational Citizenship* (Aldershot: Elgar).
BRUBAKER, ROGERS (1992), *Citizenship and Nationhood in France and Germany* (Cambridge, MA: Harvard University Press).
BRYANT, CHRISTOPHER G. A. (1997), 'Citizenship, national identity and the accommodation of difference: reflections on the German, French, Dutch and British cases', *New Community*, 23/2: 157–72.
CASTLES, STEPHEN (1984), *Here for good: Western Europe's new ethnic minorities* (London: Pluto).
—— (1995), 'How nation-states respond to immigration and ethnic diversity', *New Community*, 21/3: 293–308.
ENTZINGER, HAN (1999), 'Immigrants' political and social participation in the integration process', in *Political and Social Participation of Immigrants through Consultative Bodies* (Strasbourg: Council of Europe), 9–63.
ESPING-ANDERSEN, GÖSTA (1990), *The Three Worlds of Welfare Capitalism* (Princeton, NJ: Princeton University Press).
FASSMANN, HEINZ, and MÜNZ, RAINER (eds.) (1994), *European Migration in the Late Twentieth Century* (Aldershot: Elgar).
FAVELL, ADRIAN (1998), *Philosophies of Integration: Immigration and the Idea of Citizenship in France and Britain* (London: Macmillan).
FERMIN, ALFONS (1997), *Nederlandse politieke partijen over minderhedenbeleid, 1977–1995* (Amsterdam: Thesis).
FREEMAN, GARY P. (1979), *Immigrant Labor and Racial Conflict in Industrial Societies: The French and British Experience, 1945–1975* (Princeton, NJ: Princeton University Press).
FOBLETS, MARIE-CLAIRE, and HUBEAU, BERNARD (eds.) (1997), *Nieuwe burgers is de samenleving? Burgerschap en inburgering in België en Nederland* (Leuven: Acco).
HABERMAS, JÜRGEN (1994), 'Struggles for Recognition in the Democratic Constitutional State', in Charles Taylor *et al. Multiculturalism* (Princeton, NJ: Princeton University Press) 107–48.
HAMMAR, TOMAS (1990), *Democracy and the Nation State* (Aldershot: Avebury).

HARGREAVES, ALEC (1995), *Immigration, 'Race' and Ethnicity in Contemporary France* (London: Routledge).

HOLLIFIELD, JAMES F. (1997), *L'immigration et l'état-nation à la recherche d'un modèle national* (Paris: L'Harmattan).

JOPPKE, CHRISTIAN (ed.) (1998), *Challenge to the Nation-State: Immigration in Western Europe and the United States* (Oxford: Oxford University Press).

——(1999), 'How immigration is changing citizenship: a comparative view', *Ethnic and Racial Studies*, 22/4: 629–52.

KASTORYANO, RIVA (1996), *La France, l'Allemagne et leurs immigrés: négocier l'identité* (Paris: Colin).

KUBAT, DANIEL (ed.) (1993), *The Politics of Migration Policies* (Staten Island, NY: Center for Migration Studies).

KYMLICKA, WILL (1995), *Multicultural Citizenship* (Oxford: Clarendon).

LAPEYRONNIE, DIDIER (1993), *L'individu et les minorités: La France et la Grande-Bretagne face à leurs immigrés* (Paris: Presses Universitaires de France).

MARTINIELLO, MARCO (1997), *Sortir des ghettos culturels* (Paris: Presses de Sciences Politiques).

PENNINX, RINUS, and SLIJPER, BORIS (1999), *Voor elkaar? Integratie, vrijwilligerswerk en organisaties van migranten* (Amsterdam: IMES).

RATH, JAN, PENNINX, RINUS, GROENENDIJK, KEES, and MEYER, ASTRID (1999), 'The politics of recognizing religious diversity in Europe. Social reactions to the institutionalisation of Islam in the Netherlands, Belgium and Great Britain', *Netherlands' Journal of Social Sciences*, 35/1: 53–68.

RAWLS, JOHN (1971), *A Theory of Justice* (Cambridge, MA: Harvard University Press).

REX, JOHN (1991), *Ethnic Identity and Ethnic Mobilisation in Britain* (Coventry: Centre for Research in Ethnic Relations, University of Warwick).

SCHNAPPER, DOMINIQUE (1992), *L'Europe des immigrés* (Paris: Bourin).

SKRENTNY, JOHN D. (1996), *The Ironies of Affirmative Action* (Chicago, IL: University of Chicago Press).

SMITH, ANTHONY D. (1991), *National Identity* (London: Penguin).

SOWELL, THOMAS (1990), *Preferential Policies; An International Perspective* (New York, NY: Morrow).

SOYSAL, YASEMIN (1994), *Limits of Citizenship. Migrants and Postnational Membership in Europe* (Chicago, IL: University of Chicago Press).

STRUIJS, ALIES (1998), *Minderhedenbeleid en moraal* (Assen: Van Gorcum).

TAYLOR, CHARLES, APPIAH, ANTHONY K., HABERMAS, JÜRGEN, ROCKEFELLER, STEVEN, C., WALZER, MICHAEL, and WOLF, SUSAN; edited and introduced by AMY GUTMANN (1994), *Multiculturalism* (Princeton, NJ: Princeton University Press).

TODD, EMMANUEL (1994), *Le destin des immigrés* (Paris: Seuil).

VAN WAARDEN, FRANS (1999), 'Ieder land zijn eigen trant?' in Wieger Bakker and Frans Van Waarden (eds.), *Ruimte rond regels: Stijlen van regulering en beleidsuitvoering vergeleken* (Amsterdam: Boom), 303–39.

WALZER, MICHAEL (1983), *Spheres of Justice* (New York, NY: Basic).

WEBER, MAX (1985), *Wirtschaft und Gesellschaft* (Tubingen: Mohr).

WIHTOL DE WENDEN, CATHERINE, and DE TINGUY, ANNE (eds.) (1995), *L'Europe et toutes ses migrations* (Brussels: Complexe).

ZOLBERG, ARISTIDE (1997), 'Modes of Incorporation: Towards a Comparative Framework', in Veit Bader (ed.), *Citizenship and Exclusion* (Houndmills: Macmillan), 139–54.

6

Legal Repression of Extreme-Right Parties and Racial Discrimination*

MEINDERT FENNEMA

The Origins of Anti-Racist and Anti-Fascist Legislation

Natural rights were formulated for the first time as an authoritative political statement in the Declaration of Independence of the United States of America (1776): 'We hold these truths to be self-evident, that all men are created equal, that they are endowed by their Creator with certain unalienable Rights . . .'. In 1776 these rights still had to be elaborated in positive law. The founding fathers in general regarded slavery as a relic of the past and most of them found it repulsive. Yet some ten years later in Philadelphia, they wrote a Constitution that made it virtually impossible to outlaw it. It forbade Congress to interfere with the slave trade for twenty years to come and required putting down slave rebellions wherever they might occur. It denied slaves the right to sue in federal courts (Lazare 1998: 16). So the United States was slow indeed in the legal implementation of natural rights. It took some 200 years before these rights were fully applied to all African-Americans.

The French Revolution contributed much more, and in shorter notice, to the legal implementation of natural rights. The *Déclaration des droits de l'homme et du citoyen* (1789) had as its first article an already more positive formulation. According to this article no distinctions between citizens can be made under French law but those that develop from their contribution to the common good. According to the *Déclaration* social distinctions based on achievement are acceptable, but social distinctions based on ascription are not. Yet racial discrimination was not explicitly prohibited for obvious reasons: France still possessed colonies and practised slavery. It was not until the successful slave rebellion in Saint Domingue that the issue of black slavery was taken up. In February 1794 the *Assemblée Nationale* declared slavery illegal in the whole of French territory.

No more than eleven years later, racial discrimination was declared unlawful for the first time in a Western constitution. Article 14 of the 1805 Haitian constitution stated that all references to colour should disappear: 'Haitians will only be known under the general term of blacks' (Moïse 1988: 29–33). Not much later the independent Black Republic of Haiti supported the independence movement of Simon Bolivar financially, on the condition that slavery would be abolished in the new republics of Spanish America. During the entire nineteenth century Haiti was a source of inspiration for abolitionists and all those who struggled for racial equality in the Americas.

In Europe, however, it was not until after the Second World War that racial discrimination became a central issue in national constitutions, even though some anti-racist legislation did develop earlier as a reaction to the racist legislation of the Nazi regime. This legislation was, however, less concerned with racial discrimination than with the repression of fascist organizations. Anti-fascist legislation started in most countries with the prohibition to wear uniforms. Although in The Netherlands racial discrimination was explicitly prohibited as early as 1934, in most countries legislation that prohibited racial discrimination was a post-war phenomenon. The French constitution of 1946 added to the sacred and unalienable rights of man the provision that they should be guaranteed 'without distinction of race, religion or belief.' In the 1958 French constitution, the term 'of origin' was added to the list of unconstitutional distinctions among citizens (*Mots* 33: 346).

The post-war legislation was initially aimed at fighting *political* racism and was directed at political caucuses and parties that could be considered as neo-fascist organizations. Racism and anti-Semitism was considered as a proxy for fascism. Its prohibition should be seen in that light.

In the Federal Republic of Germany, the *Grundgesetz* (Basic Law) of 1949 restricted freedom of association by allowing for the possibility of outlawing organizations 'the purpose or activities of which conflict with criminal laws or that are directed against the constitutional order or the concept of international understanding'. Under article 21, even political parties may be declared unconstitutional if their objectives include the obstruction or abolition of the democratic order (Hofmann 1992: 161). The main victims of article 21 have been the *Sozialistische Reichspartei* in 1952, and the *Kommunistische Partei Deutschlands* in 1956. However, a specific law against incitement to racial hatred was not adopted until 1960, after a wave of anti-Semitic violence. The renewed article 130 of the criminal code prohibited 'attacks on human dignity which are likely to breach the public peace, committed in the form of acts of particular gravity against parts of the population' (Hofmann 1992: 63). The same wave of anti-Semitism that led up to article 130 in West-German criminal law prompted the United Nations to formulate, in 1963, a 'Declaration on the Elimination of all Forms of Racial Discrimination' (Lerner 1980: 1); initiating what Michael Banton (1998: 210) describes as the 'second era' in UN action against racial discrimination which was prioritized by new African member states that wanted to act against racist regimes in the southern part of their continent.

The 1963 Declaration was a further elaboration of the Universal Declaration of Human Rights of 1948 that had already an explicit reference to racial discrimination. Article 2.1 stated that 'Everyone is entitled to all rights and freedoms set forth in this Declaration, without distinction of any kind, such as race, colour, sex, language, religion, political or other opinion, national or social origin, property, birth or other status.' This 1948 UN Declaration should be read against the background of the imminent decolonization. Racism and anti-Semitism had shown their ugliest faces in the imperialist atrocities and in the Holocaust. Racial theories had lost their attraction and their legitimacy for some time to come. The United Nations was founded in an anti-colonial spirit. In 1949, UNESCO called upon an international group of anthropologists to provide a scientific response to racist theories. Their 1950 Declaration was the ideological anchor for the post-war anti-racist policies. The Declaration itself did not deny the existence of human races; it was primarily directed at denying the inequality of races. Not only all people but also all races were equal in dignity and worth. This anti-racist discourse was taken over from the rationalist discourse of the eighteenth century. Hence, racism was defined as a system of thought that was fundamentally anti-rational, that is, based on prejudice. (Comas *et al.* 1956: Foreword)

The UNESCO experts denounced scientific racism by turning science against racism. Racist theories, then, were thought to be unscientific. Modern science was said to have demonstrated that inequality among races did not exist. Theories of racial inequality were both scientifically false and morally wrong. They were, according to the Enlightenment tradition, based on ignorance and were only defended by those who had a vested interest in white supremacy. Yet, in the discourse of the UNESCO expert group, 'race' remained a distinct category of human existence. The opening sentence of the book leaves no doubt.

It is a matter of observation that men are not alike in appearance; there are variations in the external physical characteristics transmitted wholly or partially from father to son. It is groups relatively homogeneous in this respect, which constitute what is commonly called 'races'. Not only do races differ in appearance; they are also usually at different levels of development, some of them enjoying all the blessings of an advanced civilisation while others are backward to a greater or lesser extent. This last fact is the true *fons et origo* of racism in all its subsequent developments. (Comas 1956: 11)

Comas went on to affirm that races *can* and *do* mix, which already presupposes that they exist. Nevertheless, interracial amalgamation makes it, according to the UNESCO experts, increasingly difficult to speak of races in terms of physical anthropology. Pure races do not exist any more, hence races have lost their social relevance. However, this notion of amalgamation still upholds the concept of race and even implies the notion of original differences between races. The UNESCO experts were well aware that these differences could easily be interpreted as inequality; they solved that thorny problem by admitting that differences between races exist but at the same time maintaining that similarities of human beings across racial boundaries outweigh these differences (see Taguieff 1992: 222).

In anti-racist legislation, however, the difference between races was not just taken as less important than the similarity of human beings, it went much further: to build policies on the differences between races was squarely prohibited as we will see in the following section. This contradiction in anti-racist discourse between anthropological and political arguments exploded forty-five years later, when Le Pen announced at the Summer School of the *Front National*, on 30 August 1996, that he did not believe in the equality of races (Soudais 1996: 277). Less than one month later, the French government announced the preparation of a new law to prohibit the diffusion of racist and xenophobic messages (*Le Monde* 22/23 September 1996). The proposal provoked some negative reactions amongst legal experts, philosophers, and politicians. They felt that such a '*Lex Lepenia*' would restrict freedom of expression (*Le Monde* 27 September 1996) and that it would turn the political arena into a classroom as the French philosopher Bruno Latour wrote in *Le Monde* (4 October 1996). The polemic that exploded in France also raged in other countries (see for Belgium: Voorhoof 1995; for The Netherlands: Fennema 1997a, b and Van Boven 1997; for Germany: Stein 1987; for the United Kingdom: Leopold 1977).

The International Convention on the Elimination of All Forms of Racial Discrimiation

These polemics not only followed from the contradictions in anti-racist discourse, but also from the ambiguities that had been implicit in the International Convention on the Elimination of all Forms of Racial Discrimination (ICERD or New York Convention), which maintained that all adhering states should fight racism 'both in theory and in practice'. Racial discrimination, then, referred not only to unequal treatment, but also to verbal expressions. This ambiguity was deepened when in 1968 the General Assembly, acting on a proposal from the USSR, designated 1971 as 'International Year for Action to Combat Racism and Racial Discrimination'. Though it did not then, or subsequently, explain how the addition of the word 'racism' extended the meaning of 'racial discrimination', the two have continued to be bracketed together, according to Michael Banton (1998: 210) unnecessarily. Not just racist slurs and incitement to racial hatred, but also formulating racist theories became unlawful in most countries that signed the ICERD.

Indeed, from 1965 onwards, in the legal practice of most Western countries, a certain ambiguity has entered with the term 'racial discrimination'. On the one hand, it refers to the acts of making illegitimate, distinction between citizens by political authorities and social and economic actors. Anti-racist legislation was in that sense designed to prevent racial discrimination by local or national governments and in the institutions and organizations that make up civil society. But because it was assumed that racist theory and racist practice are closely connected, the term 'racial discrimination' also referred to verbal statements with a racist character. This implication soon became a problem for democracy and it is not difficult to see why. In the USA the First Amendment protected the freedom of speech to such an extent that formulation of racist theories and xenophobic policies remained legal. But in Western Europe this was no longer the case. In the fight against racism, freedom of political expression was restricted.

The infraction of the political rights of citizens by anti-racist legislation was furthered by another discursive shift in legal reasoning. Rather than state authorities and institutions—as in the case of South Africa or the Southern states of the USA—in Western Europe it was political movements and individual citizens that came under surveillance. The UN anti-racist declarations were initially expressing that *authorities* should not be racist. In the ICERD, explicit reference was made to the policy of apartheid in South Africa and to racial segregation that was, at that time, still being practised in the Southern states of the USA. As it was applied in Western European countries, however, it came to mean that citizens should not be racist.[1] The prohibition of racist ideas, being only a small part of the ICERD, was not uncontested. Five Latin American States objected to the prohibition of 'dissemination of ideas based on racial superiority', as suggested in article 4, because they did not wish to condemn 'the fact that a scientist might publish a document pointing out differences among races' (Lerner 1980: 46). Their amendment was defeated by a vote of fifty-four against, twenty-five in favour and twenty-three abstentions. Yet, of the Western European countries that signed the New York convention, Austria, Belgium, France, Italy, and Great Britain made reservations to article 4 of the convention, because it would encroach upon the civil liberties (Lerner 1980: 156).

The reservations about article 4 made in 1966 by most West-European governments implicitly or explicitly raised two important questions. Firstly, what and who decide whether a statement about races conforms to the definition of racial discrimination? Secondly, what exactly is the relationship between freedom of expression and the prohibition of racial discrimination, and how should one strike a balance between the two democratic parameters? (Coliver, Boyle, and D'Souza 1992)

The first question brings us back to the anthropological discussion about race. As we have argued, the UNESCO conception of race and racism tended towards the vision that differences between races exist but that they are not absolute or fixed, and that the similarities among human beings across racial boundaries are greater than the differences between races. This 'politically correct' position coincided with the alleged 'scientifically correct' position at the time. However, this assumed coincidence of the 'politically correct' with the 'scientifically correct' still begged the question of who decided whether a statement on race is racist. Should scientific experts judge political statements or should the judge decide on the scientific correctness of a political statement on race? Would this not lead to 'state truths' as Vidal-Naquet feared (*Le Monde* 4 May 1996), or even to a 'thought police' as the *Front National* maintains?

The problem becomes even more knotty if we do not accept the naive epistemology of the UNESCO experts, but assume a more relativist position towards scientific truth. In that case, even a consensus in the scientific community does not guarantee the infallibility of scientific truth (see also Maris 1995). From this perspective there is even less justification to allow the state to be arbitrator in a politico-scientific dispute. Should one not also permit the freedom to express opinions that have been scientifically be proven 'wrong'? In other words, should one not be allowed to state that races exist, even if, according to most modern biologists, this is not the case?

This latter question takes us right into the debate about democracy. From the perspective of liberal democracy, the principle of the intrinsic equality of all citizens is a basic tenet. However this basic tenet of democracy is not that all human beings are created equal, but that democrats 'hold these truths to be self-evident . . .'. In other words, human equality is not a scientific axiom but a democratic creed. From this it follows that those who adhere to a democratic creed do not have to believe that human beings are born equal, they just assume them to be equal before the law on an 'as if' assumption. Liberal democrats start from an individualist assumption that all persons are of equal dignity and worth, regardless of racial and other differences. However, it is my contention that on questions about race in physical anthropology, liberal democrats should be agnostic. From a democratic point of view, the prohibition of racist statements can never be based on its scientific falsity. Furthermore, since in a liberal democracy the state may not require citizens to share the values of democracy, the state has no right to prohibit citizens to express racist statements. But from the conclusion that the state should allow its citizens to express the (racist) opinion that no equality exists between races, one cannot conclude that governments are permitted to do the same, and even less so that they are permitted to draw policy conclusions from such a conviction. In a democracy, equality before the law is a fundamental human right, which should be guaranteed by the state. Thus, not only should the state itself refrain from racial discrimination, it should also prevent unequal treatment based on racial discrimination in civil society.

By making a distinction between what the authorities and institutions are (not) allowed to do and what individual citizens are allowed to express, we assume that there is a fundamental distinction between freedom of expression and racial discrimination. By making such a sharp distinction between what is allowed to be said and what is allowed to be done, we run the risk of under-estimating the connection between words and deeds. In modern discourse analysis, such a rigid distinction is not accepted. Maybe it is true that there *are* 'words that kill'. However true this may be in discourse analysis and in psychology, in legal science this is not acceptable. The statement 'I want to kill my father' should, in court, not be taken as a proxy for patricide. The *passage à l'act* is crucial in the determination of punitive measures. To say that those who do not work should not eat may not be considered as equivalent to starving the unemployed. Why should this legal rule be broken when it comes to racism? There is a positive answer to this question that is based on the following line of reasoning. By stating that a certain racial or ethnic or religious group is infe-rior one actually commits an offence to others, an act of libel which may impede the members of this group to function properly in civil society (see Feinberg 1985). This approach is often presented as an elaboration of the harm principle defended by John Stuart Mill (Maris 1995). However, the pedigree of the offence principle is not uncontested (Fennema 1997b). Mill himself at least thought that restricting freedom of expression would encroach upon the freedom of conscience. This freedom of conscience

comprises, first, the inward domain of consciousness; demanding liberty of conscience, in the most comprehensive sense; liberty of thought and feeling; absolute freedom of opinion and sentiment on all subjects, practical or speculative, scientific, moral or theological. The liberty of expressing and publishing opinions may seem to fall under a different principle, since it belongs to that part of the conduct of an individual which concerns other people; but, being almost of as much importance as the liberty of thought itself, and resting in great part on the same reasons, it is practically insepar-able from it.   (Mill 1989: 15)

Mill himself would, no doubt, have been extremely reluctant to see the offence principle as an extension of the harm principle. But let us assume that we do accept the offence principle in matters of racism and therefore prohibit all statements that express a preference for racial discrimination. We will still not have solved half of the problems, because racism is not always expressed in a preference for racial discrimination. If one states that blacks are less intelligent than whites, this does not necessary lead to the wish to discriminate against blacks. Some racist humanitarians may even want to engage in programmes of affirmative action to make up for biological arrears. On the other hand one may well discriminate against racial groups without assuming that these groups are biologically inferior. The statement 'blacks are less intelligent than whites' may merely be an explanation of the social differ-ences that blacks encounter. It should be clear in advance, then, that for a state-ment on racial inequality to be unlawful it should lead—or be intended to lead—to harm a racially-defined group. In other words, it should be proven first that such a statement would lead to racial discrimination or that it is an incitement to racial hatred—'hate speech' as one would call it in the United States of America.

We have noted already in passing that there is a large difference between the legislation on racial discrimination in the USA and that in most Western European countries. In the USA, political statements are much better protected by the First Amendment than similar statements expressed in civil society. Indeed, racist slurs or racist discrimination are much more likely to be punished by law if they are expressed at the workplace or in places of public resort. If, on the other hand, racist utterance is considered part of political discourse, then they nearly always fall under the protection of the First Amendment. In Western Europe the situation seems to be the other way around. In European civil society, much of what would be considered as racial discrimination in the USA is not brought to court or even to the attention of the authorities; whereas many political statements that express relatively weak forms of racism and ethnicism, have been brought to court. In The Netherlands, for example, one court has declared it against the law for a political party to campaign under the slogan 'our own people first' (Fennema 1997b). In France, it has been prohibited to use the term 'invasion' for the influx of migrants into France (Bonnafous and Fiala 1992: 21). In Germany, an extreme-right youth was convicted for having shouted 'Foreigners out' and 'We don't want to provide housing for asylum seekers' (Velaers 1995: 83). This was considered an 'incitement to hatred'. This amazing difference between the USA and Europe should be understood against the background of the European democratic traditions that have tended towards a more substantial conception of democracy, whereas in the USA a procedural conception of democracy has prevailed. According to a procedural conception of democracy there is no philosophical or moral ground to restrict the freedom of political expression, even though this may hurt other people, and even if directed against democracy itself. Some people say that the First Amendment, which states that 'Congress shall make no law . . . abridging the freedom of speech, or of the press' has been interpreted in an absolutist way.[2]

It is no accident, then, that it was an American scholar, Noam Chomsky, who came to the rescue of Robert Faurisson when the latter was brought to court for denying the Holocaust. Chomsky maintained that 'for those who have learned something of the 18th century (cf. Voltaire) it goes without saying that the defence of freedom of expression should not be restricted to those opinions one approves of. It is precisely in the case of opinions one finds most horrifying that this right should be defended most vigorously.' (Chomsky 1980: xii).

Why is it that such conception of democracy does not have the same vigour in Western Europe? The reason for this lies in historical experience. Western European countries have lived through a series of fascist take-overs in which the possibilities offered by democratic institutions were exploited to arrive at power. This traumatic experience resulted in specific legislation to prevent the enemies of democracy from destroying the democratic institutions from within. The term 'militant democracy' was introduced by a German exile in the United States, Karl Loewenstein (1937), to defend a democratic constitution in which political extremism was curtailed by outlawing anti-democratic groups and parties. The West-German Basic Law of 1949 was the most vivid expression of such a militant democracy. But anti-fascist legislation was introduced in nearly all European countries because they had endured Nazi occupation.

Between 1950 and 1970 anti-fascist laws functioned quite effectively in nearly all European countries to prevent fascist organizations from forming political parties. They were not invoked very often and when they were, they did not meet with substantial opposition. When, after 1970, these laws came to be applied to anti-immigrant parties, however, they proved less effective, partly because the leaders of the anti-immigrant parties could not always be directly linked to pre-war fascism, partly because their political propaganda diverged from the neo-fascist repertoire. Hence, new legislation based on the ICERD was now invoked more often.

The Implementation of the International Convention on the Elimination of all forms of Racial Discrimination

Although there were some reservations about article 4, all European countries soon signed the 1965 ICERD and implemented anti-racist legislature in due time. Within five years most countries had ratified the New York Convention, although it took some of them longer to implement it. Table 6.1 provides the data of the major laws following the ICERD.

TABLE 6.1. Ratification and legal implementation of the ICERD

	Ratification	Implementation
Austria	1972	1975 (Section 283)
Belgium	1975	1981 (Moureau, Art. 1)
Denmark	1971	1971 (Act 288 and 289; Art. 266b)
France	1971	1972; 1981 (Pleven, Gayssot, Art. 23, 24)
FRG	1969	1973 (Art. 130)
Italy	1975	1975 (Act 654 and decree 205)
The Netherlands	1971	1971 (Art. 137)
Sweden	1972	1973; 1977 (Hets mot folkgrupp)
United Kingdom	1969	1970; 1976 (Race Relations Act)

Sources: Lerner (1980), Schuijt and Voorhoof (1995).

In Austria the ICERD was implemented in 1973 and section 283 in the Criminal Code of 1975 was seen as covering part of the obligations imposed by article 6. It prohibited hostile acts against churches and religious societies or against persons belonging to these. It also prohibited (incitement to) hostile acts against persons on the ground of belonging to a race, a people, a tribe or a state (Gallhuber 1994: 643–4).

In Belgium, a law was passed in 1981 against discrimination of persons on the basis of their race, colour, or national or ethnic origins—'the Moureau law'. The law was tightened in 1993 and again in April 1994. It prohibits incitement to discrimination and segregation, to hatred and violence. It also prohibits the publication of the *intention* to practise discrimination. Furthermore, the law punishes membership or support of groups and organizations that practice or preach discrimination and segregation. The Government sponsored 'Centre for equality and the struggle against racism' is mentioned in article 5 as one of the organizations that can initiate a lawsuit against persons and organizations. An attempt to outlaw the distribution of Hitler's *Mein Kampf* failed and the complaints filed against *Vlaams Blok* propaganda also failed to lead to a conviction. Between 1981 and 1992, the Moureau law was applied only fourteen times (Van Donselaar 1995: 144). Yet, in 1993 the *Parti des Forces Nouvelles* was found guilty of publishing an intention to practise racial discrimination. They had campaigned under the slogan 'We will send them back'. The court of Liège on formal grounds, however, dismissed a lawsuit against Karel Dillen of the *Vlaams Blok*. Anti-racist laws in Belgium are quite explicit, but the penalties are not as severe as in France, Germany, or in Austria and the laws have not been applied with the same severity as has been done in France, Germany, or The Netherlands. Furthermore, there is no possibility under Belgian law to prohibit political parties. Yet in December 1998 a law was passed that made it possible to exclude parties from state funding if they advocate racial discrimination. The passing of this law caused a lot of public turmoil. In parliament the *Vlaams Blok* tried to prevent the law from passing by presenting hundreds of amendments. When this was to no avail, the *Vlaams Blok* left the parliament in protest. Whether or not the law will prove effective remains to be seen. Still, it is one more step on the road of legal repression of anti-immigrant parties.

In France, the ICERD was implemented in 1972 by the Pleven law (*loi 72-546*). The law was applied in a number of cases, the most important being the prohibition of the *Ordre Nouveau* in 1973. This organization was directly related to the *Front National*. Also related to the *Front National* was the *Fédération d'Action Nationale et Européenne* (FANE), which was outlawed in 1980 and again in 1985 and 1987. The argument to ban these organizations was not only 'incitement to discrimination, hatred and violence', but also 'racist insults' and 'racist libel'. In 1985, racial discrimination in the housing and the labour market was explicitly forbidden (art. 416–1). In 1990 additions to the 1981 Gayssot press law, prohibiting the circulation of racist messages, made it possible to suspend a person's political rights (*loi 90-615*). The denial of crimes against humanity committed during the Second World War was also prohibited (art. *24 bis*). The culmination point of anti-racist legislation in France came in September 1996. A new law was proposed by Jacques Toubon that would outlaw any message against any person or group '*atteinte à la dignité, l'honneur ou la consideration*' on account of their origins, alleged race, or nationality (*Le Monde* 22/23 October 1996). This proposal was strongly contested as an illegitimate encroachment upon the liberty of opinion. That freedom of expression in France had been severely curtailed already, was showed by the verdict of a court in Dunkerque, 27 September 1996. The leaders of the *Front National* especially, were under close scrutiny. Two representatives of the *Front National* were condemned to six months imprisonment, a fine of 65,000 French Francs, and deprivation of political rights for five years. They were held responsible for publishing a cartoon in which a person held an Algerian ballot paper in his left hand and a French social security card in his right hand. The *legenda* of the cartoon was: 'This is the double nationality'. In the accompanying article they called for sending second generation immigrants back to their country of origin (National-Hebdo 639: 9).

Whereas the legislation against racism and anti-Semitism is very strict and often implemented, the laws against racial discrimination are far less elaborate; they leave much room for dodging the law and are hardly ever implemented. An especially weak point in French law is that racial discrimination has to be proven intentional and persistent, which leaves nearly all discrimination at discos and other public places unpunished. In France, then, *incitement* to racial hatred and discrimination is severely persecuted (between 1984 and 1988 395 persons have been condemned for racist offences), while the *act* of racial discrimination is largely tolerated. It seems that political racism is more severely prosecuted that racial discrimination in civil society (See Costa-Lascoux 1991: 115; also *Le Monde* 26 November 1996).

In Germany the ICERD was implemented in 1973. In fact, the anti-Semitic '*Schmierwellen*' in 1960 were the direct cause for the initiation of this convention. In the German Criminal Code, incitement to racial hatred was included in 1973 as a criminal offence. As a consequence, German courts penalized slogans like 'Foreigners out' and 'Miscegenation is genocide' (Van Donselaar 1995: 87). Furthermore, the *Radikalenerlass* of 1972 denied the position of civil servant to anybody who belonged to a political organization that was hostile to the German constitution. This legislation, however, was not directed against racist parties but against the extreme left.[3] Between 1970 and 1980 not a single racist or extreme-right organization was convicted and it was not until 1992, after the racist arson in Mölln, that racist violence became a priority for German attorneys. In that same year the Government decided, together with the representatives of all the 'Länder' that the Republikaner Party was to be monitored by the *Bundesverfassungsschutz* (Federal Office for the Protection of the Constitution). In Rheinland-Pfaltz and in Berlin, local courts later overturned this decision (*Tageszeitung* 20 January 1998). The Republikaner were also prevented from registering a 'Franz Schönhuber Foundation'. The Republikaner have never been considered as an anti-constitutional organization. Such a label was reserved for those organizations that engaged in political and racist violence or in national socialist propaganda.

Between 1992 and 1999, 1,000 extreme-right organizations have been banned (*Der Spiegel*, 3 August 1998). Individual neo-Nazis have been convicted with heavy penalties. In August 1996, Gary Lauck was sentenced to four years imprisonment because of '*Volksverhetzung*': incitement to racial hatred and national socialist propaganda. This was an interesting case, because Lauck was a US citizen who had launched his propaganda from the US and had been protected there by the First Amendment. This conviction demonstrated the enormous difference between the legal system in the USA and the Federal Republic of Germany. In 1996, 1997, and 1998, the number of racist crimes steadily increased, and this may at least partly have been caused by a greater vigilance of the legal authorities.

Dutch criminal law was adapted in 1971, and in 1983 the Constitution came to include an article against discrimination based on 'religion, philosophy of life, political beliefs, race, gender or on any other ground' (article 1). The leader of the *Nederlandse Volks-Unie* (NVU) was, in 1975 and in 1977, convicted for incitement to racial discrimination and hatred. His party was considered 'a criminal organization' but it was not prohibited because of legal loopholes. A new law on the prohibition of parties presented in 1982 did not survive the parliamentary discussion and was only approved in 1988 after severe changes. Several members of the *Centrum Partij* were convicted but the party itself was never convicted as a 'criminal organization'. The *Centrum Partij* went bankrupt in 1986, partly due to the indemnities it had to pay in a number of lawsuits. Its successor, CP'86, became more and more radical and was eventually convicted as 'a criminal organization' in 1995. On November 18, 1998, the CP'86 was declared illegal and an Amsterdam Court disbanded the party. This was the first time that anti-racist legislation led to the prohibition of a political party.

A lawsuit against Hans Janmaat and his newly founded *Centrumdemocraten* initially failed, but in 1994, and again in 1997, Janmaat was convicted for incitement to racial hatred. New legislation is being prepared according to which parties that have been convicted for incitement to racial hatred or discrimination can lose the entitlement to financial support from the state. In this respect legislative activity in The Netherlands parallels that of Belgium. What has been unique in the legal approach to anti-immigrant parties in The Netherlands is the systematic prohibition of public meetings on the ground that these meetings endangered 'the public peace'. 1996 was the first time that an anti-immigrant party was allowed to organize a public march. Anti-fascist and anti-racist laws have been applied strictly in The Netherlands, though not as strictly as in Germany. A national office to combat racism (LBR), created in 1985 in reaction to the election of an extreme-right representative in parliament, has been quite effective in publicising racist discrimination, and in quite a few instances cases of racial discrimination have been taken to court. In some instances positive discrimination has been practised, but with little effect. In 1994 the Dutch parliament accepted an Employment Equity. Act that was copied from the Canadian legislation. This law, however, has not been very effective and has been revised and softened in 1998. Recently the LBR has become more focused on political racism, at the expense of racial discrimination in the labour market. In 1999 it merged with two subsidized anti-discrimination organizations, thus becoming less focused on legal issues and more on politics and the mass communication media. The situation in Holland has become more like that in France in this respect.

In Sweden the 1933 law against the wearing of political uniforms was adapted in 1947 to include clothes and symbols, but it was not applied until 1995 when a 19-year old man was prosecuted for wearing an armband with a swastika on it. The reason that the law had not been used before, according to a Swedish newspaper editorial, was that the mere existence of the law combined with a common sense of right and wrong made the problem negligible. When it was tested on several occasions in 1995 and 1996, it proved too general and did not result in any convictions. The courts judged the law anti-constitutional and it could therefore not be used (*Gotenborgs-Posten* 28 November 95 and 23 December 95). Racist offences have been successfully prosecuted under the '*Hets mot folkgrupp*' (agitation against an ethnic group) Act that was first written in 1948 and changed many times to cover article 4b of the ICERD. There were eight cases of 'Hets mot folkgrupp' between January 1973 and September 1983, but only three of them led to a verdict. Between 1989 and 1996, 363 cases were reported but no more than nine were taken to court (*Svenska Dagbladet* 4 August 1996). In 1970 a new law was made against unlawful discrimination that was revised in 1987. This law is mainly aimed at landlords, restaurant or pub owners, credit agencies and the like. Again, between 1973 and 1983 there were only eight cases brought to court. In 1995 and 1996 there were 371 reports of unlawful discrimination but only two of them were taken to court. Finally in 1994, a law was passed against ethnic discrimination in the labour market while the sentences for racist crimes were made harsher. All this new legislation has not led to a substantial increase in the number of sentences, and yet it seems to have curbed to amount of racist violence in Sweden.[4]

In the UK, the Public Order Act of 1936 was amended in 1963 to deal with racist and anti-religious utterances. The 1965 Race Relations Act was drawn up to deal with racism and racial discrimination that did not breach the public peace and hence could not be seen as an offence under the Public Order Act. Both laws preceded the ICERD. The Race Relations Act was established in answer to the growing racial conflict and racist violence in the 1960s. It was controversial because it made words and actions punishable without reference to public order. It was a somewhat bitter irony that, after sentencing the leader of the National Socialist Movement to an 18-month imprisonment for incitement to racial hatred, it was Michael Abdul Malik, leader of the Racial Adjustment Action Society, who was found guilty of incitement to racial hatred. He was sentenced to 12-month imprisonment in 1967. This, and another trial of a 'Black Power' leader received a extensive press coverage and hence a lot of free publicity for the Black Power movement. The same happened to a 'White Power' newspaper, Southern News, which was on trial. The important difference was that the white racists were acquitted. In addition to the greater publicity given to the trials of the Black Power spokesmen this led to the impression that most prosecutions under the Race Relations Act were against blacks (Leopold 1977: 398). It also gave some form of respectability to anti-immigrant discourse. In the new Race Relations Act of 1976, incitement to racial hatred also became an offence even if it was not intended, thus tightening the legislation rather than loosening it, as some would have preferred. More importantly, however, the Act has installed a *Commission for Racial Equality* that is to monitor racial discrimination in the fields of employment, education, and leisure. A 1986 amendment to the Public Order Act defines the concept of racial hatred and also the lists the carriers of messages of racial hatred (Costa-Lascoux 1991: 122). Hence the UK claims, with some justice to have the earliest and most elaborate anti-racist legislation. One might conclude that, compared to other European countries, the legislation against racism and hate speech is more liberal in the UK whereas the law against racial discrimination is more elaborate and its application stricter. As in The Netherlands, British law acknowledges the existence of different ethnic groups and has more room for group rights alongside individual rights.

The European Union

Anti-racist legislation was a relatively neglected field in the European Community. It was not until 1986 that a special commission against racism and xenophobia took the initiative for a joint declaration of the European Commission, the European Parliament, and the Council. It stated that they wanted 'to ensure that all acts or forms of discrimination are prevented or curbed' (European Commission 1997: 12). It was a very meek declaration which demanded no specific legal measures. In that same year a Committee of Inquiry into the rise of Fascism and Racism in Europe, installed by the European Parliament (EP), published a first report. This was followed in 1991 by the Ford Report commissioned by the EP and looking into racism and xenophobia in member countries. Both inquiries were triggered off by the electoral successes of the extreme-right in the European elections in 1984 and 1989 respectively. However, in these two reports no specific legal measures were suggested. It was not until 1993 that the EP called upon the Commission 'to strengthen the legal instruments existing in the field in the Member States'. This resolution, and subsequent ones in December 1993, October 1994, January, April, and October 1995, would eventually lead up to a Joint Action adopted by the Council in July 1996 on the basis of article K.3 of the Treaty on the European Union in the framework of the Third Pillar. This Joint Action aimed at further collaboration between the Member States in the prosecution of racial discrimination and 'public incitement to discrimination, violence or racial hatred'. Title I A, b refers to 'public condoning, for a racist or xenophobic purpose, of crimes against humanity and human right violation'. Title I A, c refers to the Holocaust denial while (d) refers to 'public dissemination or distribution of tracts, pictures or other material containing expressions of racism and xenophobia'.

In the prosecution of these crimes judicial co-operation should be improved and it was acknowledged that such crimes 'should not be regarded as political offences justifying refusal to comply with requests for mutual legal assistance' (Title I B, b). It is clear from this text that the Joint Action gave priority to combating racism over the defence of the freedom of speech. This has caused Greece to make a reservation about Title I B, b. The Danish delegation declared that Denmark will apply Title I A only where the relevant behaviour is threatening, insulting, or degrading. At the same time it was decided that 1997 was to be the 'European Year against Racism'.

It looks as if the European Union wanted to make up for its slow start in the judicial approach to the combat of racial discrimination by stretching the articles under A even further than article 4 of the ICERD. The distinction between racism and racial discrimination has disappeared altogether. The concept of racism appeared for the first time in public discourse in 1968 when the General Assembly of the United Nations, acting on a proposal from the USSR, designated 1971 as 'International Year for Action to Combat Racism and Racial Discrimination' (see Banton 1998: 210). By 1997 racism has become as prohibited as if it were equal to racial discrimination.

A second important step that has been taken by the European Union is the foundation of a European Monitoring Centre for Racism and Xenophobia that was eventually established in Vienna. It was meant to provide the Union and its Member States with 'objective, reliable and comparable data at European level on the phenomenon of racism, xenophobia and anti-Semitism in order to help them when they take measures or formulate courses of action'. Furthermore the Center has to set up and co-ordinate a 'European Racism and Xenophobia Information Network' consisting of 'national university research centers, non-governmental organisations and specialist centuries set up by national or international organizations'. The Monitoring Centre should also 'facilitate and encourage the organisation of regular round-table discussions or meetings of other existing, standing advisory bodies within the Member States'.

It is clear from this proposal that the Center was not established to be just a research centre: it was supposed to become the hub of a European network of anti-racist organizations, universities, and (local) authorities. Such a network may easily become, if it is not intended to be, an advocacy coalition in the judicial and educational war on racism. It will, of course, collaborate with national organizations that have been founded to fight racism like the British Commission for Racial Equality (CRE) and the Dutch LBR, but also with grassroot organizations that struggle against racism like the French SOS-racisme, the Dutch *Nederland Bekent Kleur* or the European organization UNITED. The European Union budget for anti-racist activities has increased substantially during the last few years.

Denial of the Holocaust

Immediately after the war, but especially after the Nuremberg trials in 1946, there was opposition to the persecution of war criminals. This opposition argued that the Nuremberg trials could not be fair because they had been organized by the victors. They were an act of revenge rather than an act of justice. Soon, however, the critique took another turn and in its extreme form denied German war crimes and concentration camp atrocities altogether. The particular position of France *vis-à-vis* the memory of the Second World War is illustrated by the fact that the denial of the Holocaust as a form of revisionist historiography was invented in France, rather than in Germany (Lipstadt 1993; Brayard 1996). The fascist writer Maurice Bardèche published in 1948 *Nuremberg and the Promised Land*, in which he denied the existence of the Holocaust. According to Bardèche, Nazi documents that spoke of the 'final solution of the Jewish problem' referred to the proposed transfer of the Jewish population to ghettos in the east. The Jews themselves were to blame for their predicament because they had supported the Treaty of Versailles. The Nuremberg trials were set up to cover up the war crimes of the Allied forces. For his apology of German war crimes, Bardèche was sentenced to one year imprisonment of which he was serve only a few weeks due to a general amnesty (Milza 1987: 279). His book did not have much impact on public debate in post-war France. The books of Paul Rassinier had more impact because the author himself had been an inmate of Buchenwald and Dora. In his first book, *Passage de la ligne, Du vrai à l'humain* (Crossing the line; From the truth to the human, 1949). Rassinier maintained that the survivors of the concentration camps were in general very unreliable witnesses because of an all too human inclination to exaggerate their suffering and to offer rumours and gossip as realities. Secondly, the excesses in the concentration camps were said to be mainly due to the atrocities of the convicts themselves, some of whom were given responsibilities of overseeing the other inmates. As a matter of fact, alleges Rassinier, the SS were in general noble people and humane guards who interfered very little in the daily life of the concentration camp. Rassinier affirmed, correctly, that there were no gas chambers in Buchenwald and Dora—even though there had been crematoria—and that he knew of no eyewitnesses of such gas chambers (Brayard 1996: 97). This argument was to set the trend for a generation of Holocaust deniers to come.

The fact that Rassinier did not come from extreme right-wing circles but had been a resistance fighter and a socialist deputy contributed to his credentials as a revisionist historian. During the 1960s Rassinier's position became more radical. Initially he had not denied the existence of gas chambers but denied, like Bardèche had done, that the Nazi's had a policy of extermination. In *The Drama of the European Jews* (1964) he maintained that the gas chambers were an invention of the 'Zionist establishment' with the purpose to 'make Germany an ever-lasting milk cow for Israel' (Quoted in Lipstadt 1993: 56). Hence the mature and most effective version of the Holocaust denial had been put forward. The Holocaust was an invention of Zionism that used historians for its purposes. Non-Jewish historians were thus bribed into confirming the 'Auschwitz lie'. The fact that many of the Holocaust historians were Jews themselves only strengthened the suspicion that the Holocaust was a hoax. Raul Hilberg and Hannah Arendt especially became the target of revisionist writing. The 'Zionist lobby' must have been very powerful indeed to make so many people believe the Auschwitz lie. For that purpose, the Hollywood film industry had set up the horror scenes and had built the gas chambers to make people believe that the Nazis were monsters. As always in conspiracy theory, the more incredible the facts the more credible the conspiracy (Billig 1989).

The Holocaust denial had the advantage of flexibility. One need not go so far as to believe that it all was made up. One could also suggest that the cruelties were somewhat exaggerated. One does not have to believe that Zionism had invented the Holocaust, one could also believe that the Holocaust came in handy to the Zionist propaganda. One does not have to believe that the Nazis were innocent, one could just maintain the fault of the drama was not only theirs. There was the communist threat and the Jews must also have borne some of the responsibility.

At the end of the 1970s a new generation of Holocaust deniers presented themselves. Some of them came from the United States, where an Institute for Historical Review started translating the books of Paul Rassinier. In France, an anarcho-marxist publishing house, *La Vieille Taupe* (The Old Mole), was re-editing his books. A professor of the University of Lyon II, Robert Faurisson, became suddenly notorious because he maintained, in *Le Monde*, that no proof had ever been established for the existence of gas chambers in Auschwitz (see Vidal-Naquet 1981). In Canada, Ernst Zündel, who also denied the existence of gas chambers, found a consultant on the installation of electric chairs and gas chambers in the USA, Fred Leuchter, willing to testify that there were no traces of the Zyklon-B gas in the bricks of the Auschwitz gas chambers. In *The Leuchter Report: An Engineering Report on the Alleged Execution Gas Chambers at Auschwitz, Birkenau, and Majdanek, Poland* it was argued that the design and fabrication of these facilities made it impossible for them to have served as execution chambers (Lipstadt 1993). In Great Britain a prominent historian, David Irving, denied that Hitler bore any responsibility for the Holocaust.

This new generation of Holocaust deniers used the same arguments but followed a new discursive strategy. They concentrated on very specific—though not insignificant—detail of the extermination of Jews under the Nazi regime, such as the gas chambers in Auschwitz, using a juridical rather than a historical discourse. The presented their 'case' with the 'testimony' of 'technical experts' and tried to discredit the testimonies and eyewitnesses of the gas chambers. Their discourse was developed and facilitated because the Holocaust deniers were brought to court. Thus, during the trial of Ernst Zündel an eyewitness had to admit in a cross-examination that he had never actually *seen* a gassing. This demand for eyewitnesses was, of course, particularly cynical because those who had been inside the gas chambers were unable to testify. The author of *The Destruction of the European Jews*, Raul Hilberg, was accused of never having been in Auschwitz. Even though Zündel was convicted, his process and that of Faurisson in France, facilitated the argument of the Holocaust deniers for several reasons.

First, the form of a lawsuit established the artefact that there are two parties involved: those who believe in the Holocaust and those who doubt the historical truth of the Holocaust narrative. This structure of discussion favours the deniers in two ways. Not only can they present themselves as the underdog and the defenders of freedom of historical research, but also the form of a trial suggests that there are two different interpretations of Nazi history.

Secondly, the focus upon the (non) existence of gas chambers enabled the deniers to present these as a *pars pro toto*. If the gas chamber never existed then the Holocaust might not have existed. Leuchter testified that from a technical point of view 'it would have taken 68 years to gas 6 million people in Auschwitz-Birkenau', as if the Holocaust historians maintained that the 6 million Jews all died in the gas chambers of Auschwitz. Furthermore, the judicial form of its argumentation enabled the deniers to attack the discourse of the historians of the Holocaust without having to replace it with a counter-discourse that explains other occurrences of the Holocaust, like the transportation of Jews to the concentration camps and the fact the most of them did not return (See Authier-Revuz and Romeu 1984: 54).

Thirdly, the use of 'technical experts' suggests a degree of scientific proof that goes beyond the science of history. Holocaust deniers skilfully use the fact that scientific experts traditionally play such a central role in the definition of 'truth'. The have come up with 'chemical engineers' and other 'experts' who are willing to testify that the Zyklon-B gas could not have been used effectively in the buildings which were used as gas chambers. The arguments run from statements about chemical traces, to the suggestion that the gas chamber personnel would not have survived the operation of such poisonous gas. By concentrating on some technical details and neglecting all circumstantial evidence, the deniers falsely suggest that they have a point.

Finally, of course, the prohibition of the Holocaust denial meant that some intellectuals inevitably would come to support their case in defence of the freedom of expression. The most important of these intellectuals was Noam Chomsky, who defended Faurisson's right to deny the existence of the gas chambers and even wrote an article that was published as a preface to Faurisson's 1980 book. More recently, the French writer Michel Tournier compared the fate of Roger Garaudy to that of Salman Rushdie and concluded that the law against the Holocaust denial 'is a religious law that re-establishes the crime of blasphemy (. . .) that had fallen in disuse under Louis XIV' (*Tribune Juive* 16 October 1996).

These criticisms—to which one must add the opinion of historians like Pierre Vidal-Naquet: 'I have always been absolutely against a law that risks to lead us up to state truths and that turns zero intellectuals into martyrs' (*Le Monde* 4 May 1996)—notwithstanding, the denial of the Holocaust has become the subject of legislation. In France (1990), Austria (1992), Germany (1994), and Belgium (1995), new laws have been implemented or old legislation has been sharpened to punish the denial of the Holocaust (Verbeeck 1997). This is not to say that the denial of the Holocaust was not seen as an offence before. In Austria and France in particular, Holocaust deniers have been punished severely and even Le Pen was forced to pay indemnities to organizations representing the victims when, in September 1987, he cast doubt on the existence of gas chambers and called it 'a detail in history'. (Taguieff 1991: 240) The ex-communist philosopher Roger Garaudy went much further in his '*Les mythes fondateurs de la politique israellienne*' (1996). He maintained that the Nazi atrocities against the Jews have been systematically exploited and exaggerated by the Zionist movement. Garaudy denied the existence of gas chambers and maintained that the number of Jewish victims was 3.5 million rather than 6 million. Garaudy was found guilty of denying the Holocaust in February 1998 and had to pay 120,000 French Francs.

In 1992, the Belgian revisionist publisher S. Verbeke was sentenced for distributing publications in The Netherlands that denied the Holocaust, even though it was not considered a form of racism (*NRC-Handelsblad* 20 June 1994). Anti-Semitism is considered to be a greater danger for democracy than colonial racism or xenophobia. The desecration of Jewish graves in Carpentras (France) in 1990 has caused more public indignation and was more dangerous for the *Front National*—even though none of their members was directly implicated—than the murder of Ali Ibrahim by members of the *Front National* in

Marseille (February 1995) or the drowning of a Moroccan *sans-abri* during a *Front National* march in Paris in May 1995.

So far, the Holocaust denial has not been openly advocated by anti-immigrant parties and the Vlaams Blok has even voted in favour of the prohibition of the denial of the Holocaust in Belgian parliament. At the same time, members of the *Front National, Vlaams Blok* and CP'86 are distributing the revisionist literature for internal use. The Holocaust denial has helped to establish a party culture that has the characteristics of a 'counterculture'. It is cherished as a Grail truth among some militants of these parties.

Conclusion

Between 1945 and 1980, repression of extreme-right and racist parties has in most cases been based on anti-fascist legislation that was produced in the immediate post-war period. This legislation simply prohibited extreme-right and anti-Semitic propaganda. Outside neo-fascist and collaborationist circles there was very little protest against this restriction of freedom of expression. This was partly due to the conception of such expressions as 'anti-national', partly to the public trauma of the Holocaust. When, however, from 1980 onward, the traditional extreme-right could present itself as anti-immigrant parties, dissociated from the fascist tradition, it became more difficult to apply the anti-fascist legislation. The anti-immigrant parties were particularly successful in those countries with a historical tradition of extreme-right movements that have been occupied during the Second World War: Austria, Belgium, and France. Anti-immigrant parties were less successful in countries without such an extreme-right tradition, such as Great Britain, The Netherlands, and Denmark.

After the 1966 conclusion of the ICERD, anti-racist legislation has been implemented in all European countries, although it took Belgium and Italy nearly ten years to ratify and Belgium fifteen years to actually implement. Both in Italy and in Belgium fighting racial discrimination has, until recently, not been very high on the political agenda. The new legislation was predominantly aimed, or at least formulated, to prohibit racial *discrimination*. Whether this aim has been reached is difficult to judge because there are no systematic data on the occurrence of racial discrimination, neither do we have quantitative data on the number of court cases. There is a great need for reliable data if we want to evaluate the effectiveness of anti-discrimination laws. That they have been effective in creating awareness of the problem is beyond doubt. This chapter has focused on political racism, that is public incitement to racial discrimination and racial hatred, rather than acts of racial discrimination proper.

The anti-discrimination legislation seems to have been quite effective in fighting political racism. There are, however, certain limits to its application. We have shown that when the anti-discrimination laws have been applied to racist or anti-immigrant *propaganda* they tended to conflict with the democratic right of freedom of expression. This has caused some public debates about its conformity with the democratic process. Especially since 1995, legal repression of anti-immigrant parties has met with mounting opposition from intellectuals and politicians that have no connections with extreme-right circles. Especially in countries where anti-immigrant parties had substantial electoral support, like in Belgium, Austria, and France, debates on the legal repression of political racism have been heated. In France, the antagonism between the *Front National* and the remaining political parties was such that one may indeed speak of a ideological civil war, in which both parties wanted to destroy the other in the name of democracy. This was no better expressed than when the *Front National* campaigned in the local by-elections in Gardanne against the communist candidate who survived the first round, under the slogan 'La France ou la Mort' (National-Hebdo 639; 17–23 October 1996). In 1998 the *Front National*, which had retained its unity despite substantial ideological differences, suffered from a lethal internal fight between the traditional anti-establishment 'revolutionary' wing and those who wanted to participate in (local) government. It seems that legal repression finally had its destructive effect on the *Front National* as it had in other countries on anti-immigrant parties.[5]

The legal repression of extreme-right parties has shifted its ideological foundation from anti-fascism to anti-racism. In the process, the philosophical anchorage has changed. In the anti-fascist legislation, the underlying logic was that of a 'militant democracy' in which fascist propaganda was considered illegitimate because it was directed against democracy. In the present anti-racist legislation, however, the philosophical foundation is some form of human equality principle, which lies uneasily with the principle of freedom of expression.

There is, however, one notable exception. The prohibition of the Holocaust denial, which can be considered the most recent target of anti-racist legislation, is inscribed in the anti-fascist rather than in the anti-racist tradition. Yet, the legislation against the Holocaust denial also lies uneasily with the principle of freedom of expression. In this particular case it is, from a democratic point of view, even more delicate because revisionist historians claim freedom of scientific investigation, which is, of course, difficult to deny them. The fact that in some countries, notably in France and in Belgium, revisionist historiography has explicitly been prohibited shows how the history of the Second World War still dominates legal discourse.

The tendency, in increasingly multicultural societies, to fight racism and ethnic exclusion by legal means, leads to a painful paradox. As the Western European democracies become more multicultural, there seems more need for legal measures to protect ethnic minorities from racial discrimination. Yet by becoming more multicultural, a need for a more procedural form of democracy also becomes more pressing, since different cultural groups do not necessarily share a common history and also have fewer values in common. To fight ethnic exclusion and racial discrimination by legal means requires a societal consensus about the intrinsic equality of human beings. The principle of intrinsic equality, however, is a typical product of the Enlightenment tradition that may not be shared by non-European immigrants. And to prohibit revisionist history requires a societal consensus about a certain interpretation of European history, which is certainly not shared by all newcomers. Those immigrants that come from Arab countries especially tend to have a view on the relationship between the Holocaust and the foundation of Israel that is contrary to the official interpretation in Western European countries. Yet the prohibition of revisionist historiography is very much based on the official interpretation, as the converted Moslem Roger Garaudy has experienced. We live in a paradoxical world. To fight ethnic intolerance and racial discrimination seems to require a more substantial conception of democracy. Such a substantial conception of democracy, however, cannot, in a multicultural society, be based on popular consensus. Hence, the repression of racist and anti-immigrant propaganda tends to undermine the democratic consensus and to create a more élitist and paternalistic form of governance.

Yet, the same process of transnationalization that gave rise to multicultural societies also makes it more difficult to effectively *repress* racist propaganda. The electronic highway is very difficult to monitor let alone to censure: the Internet enables racist propaganda to travel fast. It becomes extraordinary difficult for governments to control these means of communication (see van Donselaar, Fanda, and Nelissen 1998). Also, different governments may have different conceptions of what should be tolerated. Not only has the USA a much more liberal conception of freedom of political expression, most Arab governments have a quite different view on what is racist, and especially what is anti-Semitic, propaganda. Again, the Garaudy affair serves as an example. Garaudy has been convicted in France for denying the Holocaust, yet in the Arab countries he is considered a hero. The Union of Arab journalists and the Union of Palestinian writers have supported Garaudy as a 'independent and courageous intellectual and freedom fighter' (Ghassan Abdallah as quoted in *Trouw* 28 February 1998). Such contradictory conceptions of what rights should be protected and what is considered as trespassing the law, makes it very difficult to implement antiracist laws without losing democratic legitimacy either at home or abroad. The Jordanian weekly 'The Star' called Garaudy a 'European Rushdie' and famous French novelist Michel Tournier used the same comparison. The problem has become even thornier because the French legislation prohibits not just the denial of the Holocaust but any denial of all crimes against humanity as defined by article 6 of the statute of the London Agreement of 8 August 1945 (Maussen 1997). A strict application of the *loi Gayssot* might make the recent contribution of Régis Debray (1999) to the debate about the war in Yugoslavia illegal, because Debray tends to deny the Serbian crimes against humanity. From this example it is clear that legislation that restricts freedom of expression by taking historical truth or falsity as the dividing line between legal and the illegal opinions can only function in a very specific historical setting. Globalization, international migration, and the lapse of time makes the punishment of opinions incompatible with democratic practice as it has always been with democratic theory.

Notes

*I want to thank Michael Banton and the editors of this book for their critical but helpful remarks on an earlier draft of this chapter.

1. The anti-racist advocates who maintain that the two fundamental rights—that of freedom of expression and that of being protected against racial discrimination—are in conflict, seem to confuse the right to be protected from racial discrimination by the authorities with the assumed right to be protected from any form of racial harassment. The latter can only be guaranteed up to a certain point, like whatsoever protection against any form of harassment.

2. In recent years some neo-republican countervoices can be heard in the USA who argue in favour of a more substantial 'Jeffersonian', conception of democracy (see Sandel 1996). These voices that plead for a 'public philosophy to defend democracy', however, are still very weak.

3. Interestingly enough, one of the founders of the Rote Armee Fraktion, Horst Mahler, was in 1999 one of the keynote speakers at the NPD party rally. (*Tageszeitung*, 23 April 1999).

4. This paragraph is based on a research note written by Susanne Olby on 'Legislation in Sweden against Racism and Fascism' as part of her MA Social Sciences at the University of Amsterdam.

5. Yet Ariane Chebel d'Appollonia, an expert on the extreme right in France, maintains that the extreme right has always been inclined to internal fission. Splitting up is thus the natural habitus of the extreme right in France (*Le Monde*, 25 January 1999).

References

AUBRY, MARTINE, and DUHAMEL, OLIVIER (1995), *Petit Dictionnaire pour lutter contre l'extrême droite* (Paris: Editions du Seuil).

AUTHIER-REVUZ, JACQUELINE, and ROMEU, LYDIA (1984), 'La place de l'autre dans un discours de falsification de l'histoire. A propos d'un texte niant le génocide juif sous le IIIe Reich', *Mots*, 8: 53–70.

BANTON, MICHAEL (1998), 'European Policy Report', *Journal of Ethnic and Migration Studies*, 24/1: 209–16.

BARDÈCHE, MAURICE (1948), *Nuremburg ou la Terre Promis* (Paris: Les Sept Couleurs).

BILLIG, MICHAEL (1989), 'The Extreme Right: Continuities in Anti-Semitic Conspiracy Theory in Post-war Europe', in Roger Eatwell and Noel O'Sullivan (eds.), *The Nature of the Right* (London: Pinter).

BONNAFOUS, SIMONE, and FIALLA, PIERRE (1992), 'Est-ce que dire la race en présuppose l'existence?', *Mots*, 33: 11–22.

BOVEN, THEO VAN (1997), *Nogmaals het IVUR*, LBR-Bulletin, (February).

BRAYARD, FLORENT (1996), *Comment l'idée vint à M. Rassinier. Naissance du révisionnisme* (Paris: Fayard).

CHIARINI, ROBERTO (1991), 'The "Moviemiento Sociale Italiano": A Historical Profile,' in Luciano Cheles, Ronnie Ferguson, and Michalina Vaughan (eds.), *Neo-fascism in Europe* (London and New York: Longman) 19–42.

CHOMSKY, NOAM (1980), 'Avant propos' in Robert Faurisson, *Mémoire en défense contre ceux qui m'accusent de falsifier l'histoire* (Paris: La Vieille Taupe).

COLIVER, SANDRA, BOYLE, KEVIN, and D'SOUZA, FRANCES (eds.) (1992), *Striking a Balance: Hate Speech, Freedom of Expression and Non-discrimination* (London and Colchester: International Centre against Censorship and Human Rights Centre, University of Essex).

COMAS, JUAN, et al. (1956), *The Race Question in Modern Science* (Paris: UNESCO).

CONWAY, M. (1993), *Collaboration in Belgium. Léon Degrelle and the Rexist Movement, 1940–1944* (New Haven, CT: Yale University Press).

COSTA-LASCOUX, JACQUELINE (1991), 'Des lois contre le racisme' in Pierre-André Taguieff (ed.), *Face au Racisme II. Analyses, hypothèses, perspectives* (Paris: Editions La Découverte).

CULLIN and KREISSLER, (1972), *L'Autriche Contemporaine* (Paris: Armand Colin).

DEBRAY, RÉGIS (1999), 'Lettre d'un voyageur au président de la République', *Le Monde*, 13 May.

DONSELAAR, JAAP VAN (1995), *De Staat Paraat. De bestrijding van extreem-rechts in West-Europa* (Amsterdam: Babylon/De Geus).

——FANDA, CLAUS, and NELISSEN, CARIEN (1998), *Monitor Racisme en Extreem Rechts. Tweede Rapportage. De Media* (Leiden: Leids Instituut voor Sociaal-Wetenschappelijk Onderzoek (LISWO)).

EATWELL, ROGER (1995), *Fascism: A History* (London: Chatto).

EINAUDI, JEAN-LUC (1991), *La Bataille de Paris* (Paris: Editions du Seuil).

European Commission (1997), *The European Institutions in the Fight Against Racism: Selected Texts* (Brussels: ECDGV).

FEINBERG, JOEL (1985), *Offense to others* (Oxford: Oxford University Press).

FENNEMA, MEINDERT (1997a), 'Het IVUR en de strijd tegen rassendiscriminatie', LBR-Bulletin, January: 14–17.

——(1997b), 'Extreem-rechts en de democratie', *Socialisme & Democratie*, 51–61.

——(1997c), 'Some conceptual issues and problems in the comparison of anti-immigrant parties in Western Europe', *Party Politics*, 3/4: 473–92.

——(1997d), 'Het recht of vrije meningsuiting tegenover het recht op bescherming tegen rassendiscriminatie', in Hans de Witte (ed.), *Bestrijding van racisme en rechts-extremisme* (Leuven/Amersfoort: ACCO).

——and MAUSSEN, MARCEL (2000), 'Dealing with Extremists in Public Discussion: Front National and Republican Front in France', *Journal of Political Philosophy*, 8/2: 179–202.

GALLHUBER, HEINRICH (1994), 'Rechtsextremismus und Strafrecht', in *Handbuch Österreichischen Rechtsextremismus* Herausgeber: Stiftung Dokumentationsarchiv des Österreichischen Widerstandes (Vienna: Denticke).

GARAUDY, ROGER (1996), *Les Mythes fondateurs de la politique israélienne* (Paris: La Vieille Taupe).

GEVERS, ANNE (1995) *Façades. Oostenrijkers en het oorlogsverleden* (Amsterdam: Spinhuis).

GORTAZAR ROTAECHE, CRISTINA J. (1998), 'Racial discrimination and the European Convention on Human Rights', *Journal of Ethnic and Migration Studies*, 24/1: 177–88.

HOFMANN, RAINER (1992), 'Incitement to national and racial hatred: the legal situation in Germany', in Sandra Colives, Kevin Boyle, and Frances D'Souza (eds.), *Striking a Balance: Hate Speech, Freedom of Expression and Non-Discrimination* (London: ICCHRC, University of Essex).

LAZARE, DANIEL (1998), 'America the Undemocratic', *New Left Review*, 232: 3–40.

LEOPOLD, PATRICIA M. (1977), 'Incitement to hatred—The history of a controversial criminal offence', *Public Law*, 389–405.

LERNER, NATAN (1980), *The U.N. Convention on the Elimination of all Forms of Racial Discrimination* (Alphen a.d. Rijn: Sijthoff en Noordhoff).

LIPSTADT, DEBORAH E. (1993), *Denying the Holocaust. The Growing Assault on Truth and Memory* (London: Penguin).

LOEWENSTEIN, KARL (1937), 'Militant democracy', *American Political Science Review*, 31: 417–32.

MACEWEN, MARTIN (1995), *Tackling Racism in Europe. An Examination of Anti-discrimination Law in Practice* (Oxford: Berg Press).

MARIS, CEES W. (1995), 'Wanftide, Tuftamara. Overvrijheid vanb meningsuiting en discriminatie', in Gerard A. I. Schuijt and Dirk Voorhoof (ed.), *Vrijheid van meningsuiting: Racisme en Revisionisme* (Gent: Academia Press).

MAUSSEN, MARCEL (1997), *La démocratie moderne et les règles du débat. Le cas du Front national en France*. Memoire de DEA (Paris: Institute d'Études Politiques).

MILL, JOHN STUART (1989), *On Liberty*, Stefan Collini (ed.) (Cambridge: Cambridge University Press).

MILZA, PIERRE (1987), *Facisme Française, Passé et Présent* (Paris: Flammarion).

MOÏSE, CLAUDE (1988), *Constitutions et Luttes de pouvoir en Haïti. Tome I* (Montreal: CIDIHCA).

MOTS (1992), 'Sans distinction de . . . race'. *Mots*, 33.

NOLTE, ERNST (1985), 'Between Myth and Revionism? The Third Reich in the Perspective of the 1980s', in H. W. Koch (ed.), *Aspects of the Third Reich* (Basingstoke: Macmillan).

——(1993), *Streitpunkte. Heutige und künftige kontroversen um den Nationalsozialismus* (Propyläen).

Pinol, Jean-Luc (1992), 'Le temps des droites?', in Jean-Francois Sirinelli (ed.), *Les droites françaises. De la Révolution à nos jours* (Paris: Gallimard), 507–662.

RASSINIER, PAUL (1949), *Passage de la Ligne, Du Vrai à l'humain* (Bourg: Editions Bressanes).

ROUSSO, HENRY (1990), *Le syndrome de Vichy de 1944 à nos jours* (Paris: Editions Du Seuil).

SANDEL, MICHAEL J. (1996), *Democracy's Discontent. America in Search of a Public Philosophy* (Cambridge, MA: The Belknap Press of Harvard University Press).

SCHUIJT, GERARD A. I., and VOORHOOF, DIRK (eds.) (1995), *Vrijheid van meningsuiting, racisme en revisionisme* (Gent: Academia Press).

SEIDLER, FRANZ W. (1995), *Die Kollaboration 1939–1945* (Munich/Berlin: Herbig Verlag).

SIDOTI, FRANCESCO (1992), 'The Extreme Right in Italy: Ideological Orphans and Countermobilization', in Paul Hainsworth (ed.), *The Extreme Right in Europe and the USA* (London: Pinter Publishers).

SOUDAIS, MICHEL (1996), *Le Front National en Face* (Paris: Flammarion).

STEIN, ERIC (1987), 'History against free speech: The new German law against the "Auschwitz"—and other—"Lies" ', *Michigan Law Review*, 85: 277–324.

TAGUIEFF, PIERRE-ANDRÉ (ed.) (1991), *Face au racisme I. Les moyens d'agir* (Paris: Editions La Découverte).

——(1992), 'Du racisme au mot 'race': comment les éliminer? Sur les premiers débats et les premières Déclarations de l'Unesco (1949–1951) conçernant la 'race' et le racisme', *Mots*, 33: 215–40.

VELAERS, JAN (1995), 'Recente ontwikkelingen inzake de beteugeling van racisme en revisionisme in Duitsland en Frankrijk', in Gerard A. I. Schuijt and Dirk Voorhoof (eds.), *Vrijheid van meningsuiting, racisme en revisionisme* (Gent: Academia Press).

VERBEECK, GEORGI (ed.) (1997), *De verdwenen gaskamers. De ontkenning van de Holocaust* (Leuven: Acco).

VIDAL NAQUET, PIERRE (1987), *Les Assassins de la Memoire* (Pairs: La Decourverte).

VOORHOOF, DIRK (1995), 'De wet tot bestraffing van het negationisme: een democratisch wapen?', *Perspectief*, 41: 39–46.

WOLLER, HANS (1991), 'Ausgebliebene Säuberung? Die Abrechnung mit dem Faschismus in Italien', in Klaus-Dietmar Henke and Hans Woller (eds.), *Politische Säuberung in Europa. Die Abrechnung mit Faschismus und Kollaboration nach dem Zweiten Weltkrieg* (Munich: Deutscher Taschenbuch Verlag).

7

Mobilization of Culture and the Reform of Citizenship Law: Germany and the United States

CHRISTIAN JOPPKE

This chapter is on the use of culture in contemporary citizenship debates. It differs from other chapters in this book in two respects. First, the focus is on élite mobilization, simply because the reform of citizenship law is mostly an élite affair, in which immigrants and minorities fare only peripherally, or not at all. Secondly, the focus is on the mobilization of culture, not of ethnic difference; however, national identities—as the form of culture that I will look at—form the context of ethnic mobilization and minority integration, and we cannot talk meaningfully about the latter without knowing something about the former. Including the United States in a book that is mostly about Europe provides a necessary comparative perspective, because, so I shall argue, American-style inclusive citizenship sets the norm that European states, including Germany, are bound to follow.

The concept of culture is used in the social sciences in at least two ways: as a sphere of society, set apart from other spheres like economy or polity, which is to be investigated as dependent variable; or as a tool to explain action and structure, where culture functions as independent variable. Regarding the latter one often speaks of cultural explanations, which are set in contrast to interest-based explanations.[1] However, the juxtaposition of 'ideas' and 'interests', classically formulated in Max Weber's sociology of religion, that drives the contemporary dispute between culturalist and rationalist approaches, is artificial and unhelpful. Consider, for instance, that ideas and interests cannot be meaningfully defined in separation from one another. 'Interests', separated from values and interpretive frames, that is, 'culture', would refer to physiological conditions or processes, like hunger, thirst, or lust, which are sociologically irrelevant. 'Ideas', abstracted from inclination and will, that is, 'interest', would refer to a being that is not subject to time constraints and scarcity, and thus likewise be no subject of sociology.

Ann Swidler (1986) has influentially tried to resolve the false dichotomy of ideas and interests in a pragmatist direction. In her view, cultures are not

Parsonian 'ultimate values' determining action; instead, cultures provide a 'tool kit' of symbols, stories, rituals, and world views that help individuals to solve concrete action problems. One may criticize this proposal for being one-sidedly instrumentalist, but it points in the right direction. Instead of artificially separating ideas and interests and outfitting each with its own ontology, it is more fruitful to relate both to different temporal aspects of action: 'idea' or cultural influence, then refers to the taken-for-granted assumptions that are not at the discretion of the actor, while 'interest' refers to those conditions that, from the point of view of the actor, are changeable. The underlying motive is borrowed from 'new institutionalism' (see Powell and DiMaggio 1991): action creates 'path-dependent' consequences, in the form of 'sunk costs' or the exclusion of alternative lines of action, which successively reduce the range of future action. At the same time, the line between the changeable and the non-changeable is not objectively given, but is itself the stake of social conflict. In the political field, for instance, one used to call 'right' a position that wishes to withdraw as much as possible from action, and to call 'left' a position that on the contrary wishes to make everything accessible to action—and which position one chooses, of course, is always a matter of 'interest'.[2]

Citizenship is an institution of modern societies that is commonly conceived of as not subject to interest conflict. This is because citizenship is closely linked with the collective identity of the nation, which binds individuals through ties of affection and loyalty. In this vein, Rogers Brubaker has influentially argued that citizenship law and politics in France and Germany are shaped by their 'cultural idiom' of nationhood, which makes the respective concept of citizenship resistant to change. In this view, Germany maintains its 'exclusive' concept of descent-based citizenship (jus sanguinis), because it is conditioned by the collective identity of a non-statal, ethnic nation. Conversely, France has kept to its 'inclusive' concept of territorially-based citizenship (jus soli), because it resonates with its Republican tradition of a state-constituted, civic nation. Brubaker concludes: 'The politics of citizenship . . . is first and foremost a politics of nationhood. As such, it is a *politics of identity*, not a *politics of interest*. It pivots more on self-understanding than on self-interest . . . The central question is not "who *gets* what?" but rather "who *is* what?"' (1992: 182).

This view is not so much wrong as incomplete. Modern western states are not only nation-states but also liberal states. As liberal states they have to adjust their citizenship law to the legitimate interests of non-citizen residents (see Rubio-Marin 1998). A critical turning-point in this regard was the guestworker migration of the post-war period, which has put pressure especially on the *jus sanguinis*-based citizenship regimes of continental European states. Until then, the ethnicization of citizenship, and the change from the feudal *jus soli* to the national-democratic *jus sanguinis*, had set a counterpoint to the domestic universalization of individual rights, which required a stronger demarcation from other states and their citizens (see Boes 1993). This applies also to France, which switched from feudal *jus soli* to the more modern *jus sanguinis* immediately after the Revolution, and reintroduced elements of *jus soli* in the mid-nineteenth century only for reasons of a 'just' military draft (Brubaker 1992: ch. 5). The labour migration of the post-war period—a period in which, in Western societies, the principle of ethno-nationalist exclusion was delegitimized because of the experience of Nazism—induced a reverse trend toward the re-territorialization of citizenship, in which the right of blood receded behind the right of territory. An expression of this, is that most European states today grant the right to citizenship to young second-generation immigrants (see Hansen 1998). This includes Germany, even before its fundamental reform of citizenship law in 1999.

Citizenship is not *per se* immune to interest conflict and once and for all determined by the collective identity of the nation. This picture is already wrong because national identities themselves are always subject to change. Instead, one can observe that, in response to post-war immigration, historically exclusive citizenship regimes have become increasingly inclusive, while inclusive regimes have proved resistant to the opposite demand for more exclusiveness. At least this is the view suggested by the following comparison between Germany and the United States. In both countries immigration has put pressure on the respective concepts of citizenship, but in opposite directions and with opposite results. In the United States, immigration—especially the illegal immigration of Mexicans—has raised demands for a more exclusive citizenship, but without success. In Germany, labour migration has occasioned the critique of an ethnically closed citizenship regime, and this with success. In both cases the defenders of the old citizenship have pointed to the cultural determination of their stance—understanding this as a call to non-action—but always in pursuit of an interest and with opposite outcomes.

The following comparison suggests conceiving of 'cultural idioms' (Brubaker) and collective identities not as fixed and conflict-transcending forces, but as stakes in social and political struggle, which are utilized by actors as 'tool kits' (Swidler) in the pursuit of their interests. The outcome of these struggles is uncertain, and can even contribute to the devaluation of certain traditions.

The Failed Attack on Inclusive Citizenship in the United States

American citizenship is 'thin citizenship' (Heller 1997: 26–7), easy to acquire if certain residence conditions are fulfilled, and conferring few privileges beyond those already granted to resident aliens. This is because, in a society that cherishes markets over the state and the open border over bounded community, entry and residence have always been more meaningful than citizenship. Accordingly, the American Constitution and legal order make personhood and residence, rather than citizenship, protected categories. A formal citizenship was only introduced with the 14th Amendment in 1868, with a limited purpose in mind: the enfranchisement of black slaves. Because of its elasticity and low acquisition threshold, American citizenship has not been modified since the country's reopening to mass immigration in the mid-1960s.

This, at least, is suggested by reading backwards the history of the failed attacks on inclusive American citizenship, because attacks there were, in two phases. Already since the mid-1980s, when the problem of illegal immigration became acute, there were intellectual and political attempts to revise the principle of *jus soli* citizenship, and to exclude from it the children of illegal immigrants. Since the mid-1990s, when the federal welfare cuts for legal immigrants caused an historically unprecedented naturalization wave, the voices for more restrictive naturalization rules have grown louder: those who wish to counteract the 'cheapening' of citizenship by its only 'instrumental' acquisition (Anon 1997). All such efforts for a more exclusive citizenship have failed. Among the many reasons for this, one sticks out: an exclusive, descent-based citizenship would contradict the liberal American creed.

The dual pillars of the US citizenship regime are a constitutionally guaranteed citizenship *jure soli* and statutory as-of-right naturalization if minimal residence and personal conditions are fulfilled. Both have been challenged in recent years for their overinclusiveness, but without success. While functional to the needs of an immigrant nation, *jus soli* citizenship in the US is only incidentally linked to immigration. Instead, the colonialists simply prolonged the English feudal common law tradition, according to which those born in the king's dominion were subjects of the king. *Jus soli* became constitutionally enshrined in the Citizenship Clause of the 14th Amendment of 1868, which for the first time established a national citizenship—and its priority over state citizenship—in order to trump the racially exclusive citizenship schemes of some Southern states and enfranchise the descendants of black slaves throughout the Union: 'All persons born or naturalized in the United States, and subject to the jurisdiction thereof, are citizens of the United States and of the State wherein they reside.' The resilience of racially neutral and inclusive *jus soli* citizenship is visible in the fact that it survived even in times of government-sanctioned racial exclusivism. For instance, in *United States v. Wong Kim Ark* (1898), the Supreme Court ruled that children born to Chinese alien parents in the United States were US citizens, even though their parents were not eligible to citizenship according to the racially exclusive naturalization laws of the time.

Almost a century later, the *jus soli* rule became attacked anew for indistinctly handing out the precious good of citizenship to the US-born children of illegal immigrant mothers, some of whom allegedly crossed the border from Mexico only to give birth on US territory, and to derive residence rights from this accidental fact.[3] Starting with the then Governor of California, Pete Wilson, a number of Republican Congressmen have repeatedly suggested a Constitutional amendment that would exclude the US born children of illegal immigrants from birthright citizenship.

The intellectual ground for the attack on unqualified *jus soli* was laid by two liberal East Coast scholars, who argued that ascriptive *jus soli* citizenship had always been a 'bastard concept' in the context of the American tradition of consent-based political community (Schuck and Smith, 1985). More precisely, Schuck and Smith interpreted the 'jurisdiction requirement' of the Citizenship Clause in a consensual, non-geographical sense, according to which the framers of the 14th amendment had not intended to indistinctly include all persons randomly present on the territory—such as the US born children of the diplomatic corps of foreign nations or the self-governing Indian tribes, who were originally excluded from citizenship under the 14th amendment. According to this consensual reinterpretation of the Citizenship Clause, Congress was free to exclude the children of illegal immigrants from birthright citizenship, even without a constitutional amendment. And, so argued Schuck and Smith, Congress should do so, in order to put American citizenship 'on a firm foundation of freely-willed membership' (ibid.: 140). Schuck and Smith's proposal was unorthodox thinking, because liberal values were invoked to make citizenship less inclusive. However, as its numerous liberal critics pointed out, consensual reasoning had also underpinned the Supreme Court's infamous Dred Scott decision of 1857, according to which free blacks born in the United States could not be 'citizens' because the framers of the Constitution had not considered them part of 'the people of the United States' at the time of the nation's founding, the overturning of which had been the whole point of the 14th amendment (Aleinikoff 1998: 8; Neuman 1996: ch. 9).

Among the flurry of restrictive citizenship and immigration proposals which circulated in the Republican-dominated Congress of the mid-1990s, the one to narrow the *jus soli* rule never gained momentum. The reasons for this are manifold. One cannot overlook, however, the cultural weight of the idea of inclusive, equal citizenship, for which the country had undergone a ferocious civil war in the mid-nineteenth century, and which has helped it to master the two massive immigration movements of the early and late twentieth century without major problems.

Since a constitutional amendment would not be reviewable by the Supreme Court, its opponents could not rely on straightforward legal reasoning. Instead, they had to show that it conflicted with the basic moral values that underpin the Constitution, and by implication, the American nation. This strategy is self-consciously pursued in an influential note published in the *Harvard Law Review*, which argued that the proposed citizenship amendment violated the principle of 'equality before the law', and thus 'one of the foundations upon which American society is built': 'If the government chooses to grant citizenship based on situs of birth, to deny citizenship to a child born in the United States, when the only factor that distinguishes her from the next child in the maternity ward is that her mother entered the country unlawfully, would offend the principle of equality' (Anon 1994: 1028). In addition to this moral objection, the opponents of amending the citizenship clause effectively raised a pragmatic objection: the denial of birthright citizenship would create a European-style 'hereditary caste of exploitable denizens' (Neuman 1996: 166). The reference to Europe, especially Germany's creation of a 'permanent class of the disadvantaged',[4] was a firm presence in the Congressional hearings over the proposed amendment, and a reform that would make the US more European could certainly not stir Congressional enthusiasm.

In contrast to the constitutionally anchored *jus soli* rule, the acquisition of citizenship through naturalization is ruled by simple statute, and it even counts as a prime function of judicially unreviewable 'plenary power' of the federal government over immigration matters. Accordingly, in contrast to *jus soli* citizenship, which was not dictated by immigration concerns, the US naturalization laws had always been centrally influenced by immigration concerns. The generally low threshold to naturalization reflects the needs of a country peopled by immigrants, who are set on a trajectory to citizenship from the start. At the same time, the mantle of plenary power allowed US naturalization law to be tainted by racial exclusivism over long periods. The first federal naturalization law in the late eighteenth century stipulated that only 'free white persons' could naturalize, a condition that was relaxed for blacks after the Civil War and for Asians after World War II, until the McCarran/Walter (Immigration and Nationality Act) of 1952 finally established racially-neutral naturalization rules (Neuman 1998: 8). Under the current rules, naturalization is a statutory right after five years of legal permanent residence, 'good moral character' displayed throughout this period, the passing of English language and civic knowledge tests which may be waived under certain conditions, and an oath expressing allegiance to the United States and renouncing all prior allegiances.

In response to the recent rush to citizenship and external political changes, the renunciation oath has become the subject of debate.[5] In principle, the need to renounce allegiance to any 'foreign prince, potentate, state, or sovereignty'— as is the awkward wording even today—means the rejection of dual citizenship. In reality, however, the US has always tolerated dual citizenship, also because it was forced to do so from early on, when the feudal-absolutist regimes of Europe kept their emigrating subjects in perpetual allegiance and did not recognize their adoption of US citizenship.[6] Over long periods, the toleration of dual citizenship was facilitated by extremely tight laws on the loss of citizenship. Well into the second half of the twentieth century, US citizens— naturalized and native-born—could lose their citizenship for naturalizing in a foreign state, marrying a foreigner, or voting in a foreign election. Only in 1967, in its *Afroyim v. Rusk* decision, which overruled the plaintiff's expatriation for having voted in the Israeli elections, did the Supreme Court establish that

Congress has no power to 'rob a citizen of his citizenship', unless he or she 'voluntarily relinquish(es)' US citizenship (Spiro 1997: 1451).

Ever since the government has lost its expatriation powers, dual citizenship appears in a less sanguine light. But only an external event catalyzed a reconsideration of dual citizenship. In 1998, Mexico introduced a constitutional amendment that allows its emigrants to keep their Mexican 'nationality' even after naturalizing abroad.[7] This reflects a general trend in immigrant-sending countries to relax their citizenship laws in the interest of retaining ties with their diasporas abroad.[8] Mexico's citizenship reform, which is bound to create a large number of US-Mexican dual citizens in the near future, has given new urgency to the old suspicion that Mexican immigrants are not assimilating like the other immigrant groups, and that they are not sufficiently loyal to their new country even after acquiring US citizenship. More concretely, the Mexican reform has stirred calls to give teeth to the naturalization oath, the renunciation component of which has so far never been enforced. However, even louder than the calls to tighten the oath, are those to abolish it altogether for 'postnational' reasons (see for example Spiro 1997). Chances are that the moderate centre will prevail, which proposes—like the 1990s Federal Commission for Immigration Reform—to 'modernize' the wording of the renunciation oath, or, in recognition of postnational sensibilities, to moderate the 'exclusive' loyalty requirement to a 'primary' loyalty requirement (Aleinikoff 1998: 38). That the advocates of exclusive citizenship have recently zeroed in on the naturalization oath, the role of which is rather marginal in the larger citizenship scheme, testifies to the resilience of inclusive citizenship in the United States.

The Successful Attack on Exclusive Citizenship in Germany

The German problematic of immigration and citizenship is diametrically opposed to the American one. Its baseline is a thick concept of citizenship, which is genealogical rather than territorial, and thus normally closed to nonnationals. Accordingly, post-war immigration has put huge pressure on ethnic citizenship, toward facilitating the acquisition of citizenship by long-settled and later-generation immigrants. In Germany, too, the defenders of the status quo have sought to mobilize the collective identity of the nation for their purposes, and, much more bluntly than in the American case, in the pursuit of electoral interests. But, in contrast to the United States, the defenders of the 'old' citizenship did not prevail in Germany. This shows that under the post-war hegemony of 'embedded liberalism' (Ruggie 1982), non-liberal national traditions have less chances of survival than liberal ones. As a commentator appropriately remarked, with its overdue reform of citizenship law Germany has finally entered the 'West European main road'.[9]

The *Reichs- und Staatsangehoerigkeitsgesetz* (citizenship law) of 1913, which was in force until 1999, had the original double purpose of excluding from the national citizenry the ethnically undesired Poles at the eastern flank of the German Reich, and of continuing to include in the citizenry Germany's overseas emigrants. This was achieved through its key provisions of citizenship by descent (*jus sanguinis*) and a discretionary naturalization that had to be always exceptional. The ethnic concept of nation, which stands behind exclusive citizenship, was in principle discredited by its racist aberration under Nazism. However, through the consolidation of communism in eastern Europe and the Soviet Union, which refused the right of self-determination to the eastern part of divided Germany and subjected ethnic Germans in the Eastern state territories to severe repressions, the concept of ethnic nation could survive at least indirectly. Accordingly, West Germany understood itself as a provisional state geared toward national reunification, and as homeland for the repressed and dispersed ethnic German diasporas in the Soviet empire. A vehicle of the unity mandate, which had constitutional status according to the preamble of the Basic Law, was the legal fiction that the German Reich of the pre-war period continued to exist in the incarnation of West Germany. And the construct of an all-German citizenship, heavily criticized in the times of '*détente*' but decisive for reunification after the collapse of East Germany (the GDR), was best maintained by simply prolonging the old *Reichs- und Staatsangehoerigkeitsgesetz* of 1913. For these reasons the West German citizenship regime was exclusive toward foreigners, and inclusive toward the citizens of the GDR and the ethnic Germans in the other states of the Soviet empire.[10] There certainly was no *logical* connection between excluding foreigners and including East Germans and ethnic Germans. However, it was the *empirical* connection made by the political élites of pre-unity Germany, for whom meddling with citizenship law meant meddling with the legal bridge to national unity.

Contrary to the views of some conservative legal scholars (for example Uhlitz 1986), the Basic Law nevertheless does not prescribe a nationalistic citizenship, but leaves the definition of citizenship to the political process. This is evident in Article 116(1) of the Basic Law, which defines as Germans the holders of German citizenship, and does not further specify how citizenship is to be determined. But the same article includes in its definition of Germans the expellees and refugees of German origins residing in the German Reich according to the borders of 1937, and their descendants. From the addendum 'and their descendants' some legal scholars have concluded that the Basic Law, at least indirectly, prescribes exclusive *jus sanguinis* citizenship (for example Ziemske 1994: 229). Considering that Article 116(1) was conceived of as only temporary device to cope with the consequences of the war, this has never been the dominant constitutional opinion. More widespread has been the view that the Basic Law's general conception of the Federal Republic as a provisional, incomplete nation-state commanded its closure toward foreigners, because the inclusion of the latter might undermine the social impulse for unification through changing the texture of the citizenry: 'Conceiving of the Federal Republic as a country of immigration with multiple national minorities would contradict the Basic Law's conception of a provisional state geared toward the recovery of national unity' (Hailbronner 1983: 2113).

Constitutionally prescribed or not, there has been a factual linkage between exclusive citizenship and the unresolved national question. Proof of this, is that precisely since reunification there has been a steady trend toward more inclusive citizenship. Once citizenship was divested from the national question, it could be seen as a tool of immigrant integration. Here Germany only followed a general trend across Western European countries, which have eased the access to citizenship in recent years in order to better integrate second- and third-generation immigrants (see Hansen 1998). The first step in this direction was the new Foreigner Law of 1990, which turned naturalization from the exception into the rule, lowered its costs significantly, and granted exceptions to the previously strict prohibition of dual citizenship. A second step occurred with the Asylum Compromise of 1992, which turned 'as a general rule' into 'as of right' naturalization. This removed the two pillars of the old Naturalization Rules: absolute state discretion and cultural assimilation as precondition for citizenship.

As a result of these changes, naturalization was already routinely available for long-settled foreigners in the early 1990s. This quickly showed in a strong increase of naturalization rates, the number of naturalizing Turks, for instance, increasing from about 2,000 in 1990 to more then 31,500 in 1995 (Freeman and Oegelman 1998: 776). Moreover, dual citizenship became widely tolerated in administrative practice, despite opposite political rhetoric, especially in conservative circles around the ruling party (CDU/CSU), which loudly denounced dual citizenship. About half of the discretionary naturalizations in 1993 entailed dual citizenship with the full knowledge of German state authorities. If one adds the effect of a new law in Turkey that allows its expatriated citizens to reacquire Turkish citizenship instantly, it is safe to assume that the vast majority of discretionary naturalizations in Germany today imply dual citizenship (Koslowski 1998: 744). As a result of little noticed legislative and administrative changes—the latter particularly in 'progressive' states with a high concentration of foreigners—only five years after national unification the old exclusive citizenship regime was practically undermined.[11]

However, as Rogers Brubaker (1992) has rightly seen, the politics of citizenship is identity politics, in which pragmatic considerations are often subordinate to deeply held views about the collective self: the nation. In the United States, this helped the defenders of a historically inclusive citizenship regime to withstand the pressure for more exclusive citizenship, which contradicted the American tradition. In Germany, there is the opposite constellation of identity considerations working against more inclusive citizenship. From

Germany's ethnocultural tradition of nationhood stems a special distrust of 'divided loyalties' that would result from handing out citizenship more easily. A leading opponent of citizenship reform in the CDU articulates the traditional view: 'Granting citizenship cannot be an instrument of integrating foreign residents. Instead, naturalization requires that the integration of the respective foreigner has already occurred. A foreigner who wants to acquire German citizenship must commit himself to our national community. Tolerating double citizenship would lead to the formation of permanent national minorities.'[12] Ethnocultural concerns were readily available for the opponents of a liberalized citizenship law, especially if such opposition promised to pay off electorally.

Despite the partial opening of citizenship through relaxed naturalization rules, by October 1998 there still were 7.3 million foreigners in Germany. Two-thirds of them had resided in the country for more than ten years, and thus were likely to stay; 20 per cent were even born in Germany; and 100,000 new 'foreign' births occurred each year—13 per cent of all births.[13] Further aggravated by a xenophobic groundswell since the early 1990s and alarming signs of social despair and failed integration among young 'foreigners' (see Heitmeyer *et al.* 1997), here was a clear problem that called for a solution. Because the space for administrative liberalization and small-step legislation had been exhausted by then, a furthergoing solution had to be political, and consist of a major overhaul of the outdated Wilhelminian citizenship law that locked out second- and third-generation immigrants through its *jus sanguinis* provisions. This meant that the administrative and incremental mode of citizenship reform, which had dominated so far, had to give way to 'big leap' legislation, which inevitably goes along with politicization and public scrutiny. A nominal majority in parliament for such legislation nevertheless existed already under the old conservative-liberal government; it was tried by repeated opposition bills, but could not be realized because of resistance from the Bavarian CSU and nationalistic sections in the CDU.

After the shattering defeat of the CDU/CSU in September 1998, this obstacle seemed gone. The new government of SPD and Greens promptly announced a new citizenship law. Hammered out as part of the coalition agreement, the reform proposal called for automatic *jus soli* citizenship if at least one parent was born in Germany or had lived there since the age of fourteen, and it would lower the residence minimum for as-of-right naturalization from fifteen to eight years.[14] Crucially, dual citizenship was to be officially accepted. As the government stressed, this was no philosophical acceptance of dual citizenship, but its pragmatic acceptance for the sake of immigrant integration. While being a complete rupture with Germany's ethnocultural citizenship and nationhood tradition, the envisaged reform was in line with the practice of Germany's European neighbours, such as Belgium, France, the United Kingdom, Ireland, Italy, The Netherlands, and Spain, all of which tolerated dual citizenship and had similar *jus soli* provisions (see Renner, 1993: 23f). Moreover, the reform would only put into law what had already been domestic administrative practice, in which dual citizenship was widely tolerated, not only regarding an increasing share of naturalizing foreigners, but regarding all naturalizing ethnic Germans and regarding children born either to binational parents in Germany, or to German parents in *jus soli* countries. When the new opposition in Parliament branded dual citizenship as a threat to the nation-state, there already were 2 million dual citizens in Germany. Dual citizenship was even partially sanctioned by the Constitutional Court, which ruled in 1974 that the interest of the state in reducing multiple nationality was not strong enough to deny a child the nationalities of both of its parents.[15]

Despite the widespread *de facto*, and partial *de jure*, toleration of dual citizenship, the CDU/CSU opposition parties decided to object to its official acceptance in form of an engineered social movement—a form of mobilization that was previously practiced only by the left and the Greens. The motivation was obvious: in the second half of the 1990s a 'foreigner friendly' reform, and one that touched upon the collective identity of the nation at that, had to meet public disapproval, not only in Germany; and here was a theme that could bring new popularity and agility to a badly battered and apathetic party. The CDU/CSU campaign broke an unwritten consensus among the political élites not only in Germany, but in all Western states, not to subject immigration-related issues to populist exploitation.[16] Since their votes in Parliament were not enough to block the reform, the people had to be mobilized. Urged by the Bavarian CSU, whose chairman Edmund Stoiber deemed the reform 'more dangerous' to Germany's domestic security than the terrorism of the Red Army Faction (RAF) in the 1970s and 1980s, the CDU agreed to mute its own liberal instincts and collect signatures against the 'double passport' or *Doppelpass*, as the Red-Green reform proposal became labelled in public discourse. The campaign proved immensely successful. A poll in early January 1999 found 52 per cent of respondents against it. The conservative opposition parties collected a total of five million signatures against dual citizenship. The campaign's biggest success was certainly the surprising defeat of SPD and the Greens in the state elections in Hesse in February 1999. This defeat must be attributed to the mighty societal groundswell against dual citizenship, because the CDU had made this the main theme of its election campaign. To avoid embarrassing fraternizing with the extremist right, one of whose leaders welcomed the signature campaign as 'something taken from the pages of our newspaper, the *Nationale Zeitung*',[17] the CDU tried to fashion its negative campaign as a positive campaign for 'integration and tolerance'.[18] This was at least a symbolic concession to the old liberal élite consensus on immigration, which the campaign itself had helped to destroy.

Before the turning-point of the Hesse elections the negative effect of the populist campaign on the envisaged citizenship reform was already readily visible. The first bill presented by the Interior Ministry in January 1999 stuck to the dual citizenship toleration of the coalition agreement, but it already carried the marks of the incipient signature drive: naturalization was to be contingent upon a written declaration of the applicant that he or she was loyal to the Constitution, tested German language competence, no welfare dependency or unemployment, and the (near-)absence of a criminal record.[19] This was remarkably tougher than the naturalization conditions then in place—with the exception of a lower residence requirement and the toleration of dual citizenship.

Dual citizenship became intolerable after the defeat of SPD and Greens in the Hesse elections, which removed their majority in the upper house of Parliament, the Bundesrat. Now any reform of citizenship law had to be agreeable to the Liberal Party (FDP), in order to pass the Bundesrat hurdle. The FDP had long been a champion of citizenship reform, but it was less sanguine about dual citizenship than the Greens, which had so far dictated the government approach. Its 'option model' (*Optionsmodell*) suggested a provisional *jus soli* citizenship for second-generation immigrants until the age of 23, by when the immigrant had to choose between abandoning the foreign citizenship or losing the German citizenship. Moreover, dual citizenship would not be available to naturalizing immigrants. This is the position eventually embraced by the government, and passed by both houses of Parliament in May 1999.

The *Optionsmodell* formally sticks to the old principle of avoiding dual citizenship, but it will factually increase the number of dual citizens in Germany. Since dual citizenship is inherently difficult to control, the reform is likely to be but a step in a furthergoing acceptance of dual citizenship in Germany. This has caused the opposition parties to reject the even more moderate option model, and thus to deprive themselves of the public image of the winner, which they were, after all, through forcing SPD and Greens to abandon their original proposal. However, what may be criticized as lack of tactical finesse, is still consistent in substantive regard. Because, once the smoke of campaigning has cleared, the rupture with Germany's exclusive citizenship and its underlying ethnic model of nationhood will stand out. *Jus soli* citizenship, which is totally foreign to the German tradition, is now the norm.

Culture and Citizenship

The case studies show that cultural motifs have strongly influenced the course and outcome of political debates about citizenship. However, it would be misleading to conceive of cultures in holistic terms as society-wide values and interpretive frames. Such a concept of culture, which was first developed in anthropology in view of isolated and static societies at the periphery of the state system, and then applied to modern societies by Talcott Parsons, is at odds with the complexity, hybridity, and multiplicity of cultural patterns in modern societies. Related to a particularly prominent cultural pattern in modern societies, the collective identity of the nation, there is not only one, but always competing, conceptions of the nation in each society. For instance, the dominant model of laicist Republicanism in France is countered by a strong Catholic-antisemitic concept of ethnic Frenchness, which became dominant for a moment in the Vichy regime and is kept alive today in Le Pen's National Front; The dominant American model of the political nation was eclipsed in the first half of the twentieth century by a countermodel of ethno-nativist Americanism, which excluded Blacks, Catholics, and Jews; and the model of ethnic nationhood commonly ascribed to Germany has found a strong competitor, after World War II, in a model of political nationhood whose strength is visible in the outcome of the citizenship debate. In light of this it would be wrong to conceive of national identities as fixed and holistic, embracing all members of society equally; instead I suggest conceiving of national identities as constituting 'fields' in a Bourdieuian sense, in which interested actors struggle for the implementation of their respective model of identity. However, when a model of identity prevails over its competitors and becomes institutionalized, it tends to shed its interest basis, and to take on the appearance of universality. Bourdieu has introduced the notion of 'doxa' to capture the power of dominant culture to appear as unconditional and interest-transcendent: 'The adherence expressed in the doxic relation to the social world is the absolute form of recognition of legitimacy through misrecognition of arbitrariness, since it is unaware of the very question of legitimacy, which arises from competition for legitimacy, and hence from conflict between groups claiming to possess it' (Bourdieu 1977: 168). Instead of reifying cultural patterns as holistic 'culture', it is the task of sociology to fold them back to agents and their interests.

The outcome of citizenship debates in Germany and the United States also shows that not 'anything goes' in the field of collective identities and the rules of membership. Michael Walzer (1983) has influentially argued that the admission of new members in a political community corresponds to an elementary right of national self-determination, and therefore cannot be subject to considerations of justice: justice is possible only within a political community, not beyond it. However, he adds that after the territorial admission of new members say, as labour migrants, their second admission into the political community as citizens must follow, if justice is to prevail. Germany's goodbye to ethnic citizenship shows the empirical relevance of Walzer's normative statement, at least in liberal states. In the post-war order, in which (American) liberalism has become hegemonic, national traditions that contradict liberal principles are not viable. This is the lesson to draw from the case of Germany, which for long was the most stubborn defender of an illiberal, ethnically closed citizenship regime.

In the literature on the changes of citizenship in Western Europe and North America during the 1980s and 1990s, one often finds the thesis of a countervailing convergence, according to which previously 'liberal' citizenship regimes have become more exclusive, whereas 'illiberal' regimes have become more inclusive (for example Feldblum 1998). This thesis is wrong. In western liberal states there has been either a territorial opening of ethnically closed citizenship regimes, or—as in the US case—a persistence of historically inclusive regimes. The few cases in which liberal regimes have become less liberal in some respects require a special, case-specific explanation—they are the exceptions that prove the rule (see Joppke 1999). This one-sided convergence toward inclusiveness is affirmed in an impressive comparison of 25 countries (Weil 1999).[20] According to Weil, convergence depends on three factors: stable borders, liberal-democratic values, and the transformation into a country of immigration. With a critical eye on Brubaker's 'cultural idiom' hypothesis, Weil concludes that there is 'no causal link between the dominant approach of national identity and nationality laws' (ibid.).

This conclusion goes too far. The US example suggests that there is a link between identity and citizenship law, and it has been consciously and successfully mobilized by the political and intellectual defenders of a liberal citizenship law against their opponents in the spectrum of the Republican Party. It is therefore more correct to conclude that closed citizenship regimes, conditioned by illiberal identities, are not viable in a world of liberal states. Instead of taking the German example as proof that there is no link between national identity and citizenship law, one can also read it as triumph of a new model of political nation over the old model of ethnic nation, which lost its last hold with the stabilization of borders after 1989. Conversely, this model of political nation, which was discursively long articulated in the notion of constitutional patriotism, has finally found its adequate legal membership basis in the new territory-based citizenship law. A new citizenship law thus can help create and stabilize a new national identity.

Notes

1. This trend is especially strong in political science and international relations, where culturalist approaches have recently challenged the dominant paradigm of rational choice. See, for instance, Katzenstein (1996) and Berman (1998).
2. This constellation may be changing in the era of so-called 'globalization': see Giddens (1994).
3. This alleged motivation resonates badly with harsh deportation practices in the United States, which do not shrink back from dividing families (see Neuman, 1998: 41f).

4. Quoted from the statement of Peter Schuck before the *Subcommittee on Immigration, Committee on the Judiciary, U.S. House of Representatives*, 13 December 1995, Washington, D.C. Schuck, who had delivered the intellectual ammunition for the amendment supporters, opposed the amendment, because—in the absence of effective controls of illegal immigration—it would 'transmogrify' an already large illegal population, and lead to 'a much larger, multi-generational, indeed permanent, alien underclass'.

5. After limiting practically all federal welfare programs to US citizens in the Welfare Reform Act of 1996, there has been a unique rush on citizenship: the number of new applicants increased from 543,353 in 1994 to 1,400,000 in 1997 (Aleinikoff, 1998: 16).

6. The UK, for instance, recognized US naturalization only in 1870.

7. After its amendment in 1998, the Mexican constitution now distinguishes between 'citizens' and 'nationals', the difference between both being the right to vote, which is reserved to citizens.

8. Another prominent example is Turkey.

9. E. Fuhr, 'Zu spät für Prinziplien', *Frankfurter Allgemeine Zeitung*, 25 November 1998, 1.

10. Here one must differentiate: East Germans were automatically German citizens according to the *Reichs- und Staatsangehoerigkeitsgesetz*; ethnic Germans in Eastern Europe and the Soviet Union had a statutory right to naturalize, which derived from Article 116(1) of the Basic Law.

11. In German 'co-operative' federalism, the *Länder* are in charge of naturalizing foreigners. This accounts for huge variation in naturalization rates due to different recognition practices in 'conservative' states like Bavaria and 'progressive' states like Berlin.

12. Erwin Marschewski (CDU), in *Information Sheet of the CDU/CSU Bundestagsfraktion* 10/93, 30 April 1993, 9.

13. 'Wer Deutscher werden will', *Die Zeit*, 8 October 1998, 8.

14. 'Yes, Hosgeldiniz is the word', *The Economist*, 31 October 1998, 31f.

15. This decision corrected an element of sex discrimination in the German citizenship law, according to which only German fathers in binational marriages could pass on German nationality to their legitimate children. Generally quoted for its declaration of dual nationality as an 'evil' (the so-called Uebel-doctrine), the Constitutional Court's 1974 decision equally meant that the interest of the individual in dual nationality outweighed the countervailing interest of the state in mono-nationality. See Kimminich (1995).

16. Gary Freeman (1995) has called it the 'anti-populist norm'.

17. Gerhard Frey, leader of the right-wing Deutsche Volks-Union (DVU), quoted in *Migration News Sheet*, February 1999.

18. 'Integration and Tolerance' is the title of a position paper of the CDU/CSU parliamentary group. It rejects dual citizenship, but supports state-supervised Muslim

education in Germany's public schools (*Frankfurter Allgemeine Zeitung*, 21 January 1999, 6).

19. 'Einbuergerungsbewerber muessen verfassungstreu sein', *Frankfurter Allgemeine Zeitung*, 13 January 1999, 1.

20. Weil's comparison includes all member states of the European Union, Australia, the USA, Canada, the Baltic States, Mexico, Russia, South Africa, and Israel.

References

ANON (1994), 'The Birthright Citizenship Amendment: A Threat to Equality', *Harvard Law Review*, 107: 1025–43.

——(1997), 'The Functionality of Citizenship', *Harvard Law Review*, 110: 1814–31.

ALEINIKOFF, ALEX (1998), *Between Principles and Politics: The Direction of U.S. Citizenship Policy* (Washington, DC: Carnegie Endowment for International Peace).

BERMAN, SHERI (1998), *The Social Democratic Moment: Ideas and Politics in the Making of Interwar Europe* (Cambridge, MA: Harvard University Press).

BOES, MATTHIAS (1993), 'Ethnisierung des Rechts? Staatsbuergerschaft in Deutschland, Frankreich, Grossbritannien und den USA', *Koelner Zeitschrift fuer Soziologie und Sozialpsychologie*, 45: 619–43.

BOURDIEU, PIERRE (1977), *Outline of a Theory of Practice* (New York, NY: Cambridge University Press).

BRUBAKER, ROGERS (1992), *Citizenship and Nationhood in France and Germany* (Cambridge, MA: Harvard University Press).

FELDBLUM, MIRIAM (1998), 'Reconfiguring Citizenship in Western Europe' in Christian Joppke (ed.), *Challenge to the Nation-State: Immigration in Western Europe and the United States* (Oxford: Oxford University Press).

FREEMAN, GARY (1995), 'Modes of Immigration Politics in Liberal Democratic States', *International Migration Review*, 29: 881–902.

——and OEGELMAN, NEDIM (1998), 'Homeland Citizenship Policies and the Status of Third Country Nationals in the EU', *Journal of Ethnic and Migration Studies*, 24: 769–88.

GIDDENS, ANTHONY (1994), *Beyond Left and Right* (Cambridge: Polity Press).

HAILBRONNER, KAY (1983), 'Auslaenderrecht und Verfassung', *Neue Juristische Wochenschrift*, 36: 2105–13.

HANSEN, RANDALL (1998), 'A European Citizenship or a Europe of Citizens?', *Journal of Ethnic and Migration Studies*, 24: 751–68.

HEITMEYER, WILHELM et al. (1997), *Verlockender Fundamentalismus* (Frankfurt on Main: Suhrkamp).

HELLER, THOMAS (1997), 'Modernity, Membership, and Multiculturalism', *Stanford Humanities Review*, 5: 2–69.

JOPPKE, CHRISTIAN (1999), 'How Immigration is Changing Citizenship', *Ethnic and Racial Studies*, 22/4: 629–52.

KATZENSTEIN, PETER (ed.) (1996), *The Culture of National Security: Norms and Identity in World Politics* (New York, NY: Columbia University Press).

KIMMINICH, OTTO (1995), 'The Conventions for the Prevention of Double Citizenship and their Meaning for Germany and Europe in an Era of Migration', *German Yearbook of International Law*, 38: 224–48.

KOSLOWSKI, REY (1998), 'European Migration Regimes: Emerging, Enlarging, and Deteriorating', *Journal of Ethnic and Migration Studies*, 24: 735–49.

NEUMAN, GERALD (1996), *Strangers to the Constitution* (Princeton, NY: Princeton University Press).

——(1998), *The Effects of Immigration on U.S. Nationality Law* (Manuscript).

POWELL, WALTER, and DIMAGGIO, PAUL (eds.) (1991), *The New Institutionalism in Organizational Analysis* (Chicago, IL: University of Chicago Press).

RENNER, GUENTER (1993), 'Verhinderung von Mehrstaatigkeit bei Erwerb und Verlust der Staatsangehoerigkeit', *Zeitschrift fuer Auslaenderrecht*, 1: 18–25.

RUBIO-MARIN, RUT (forthcoming), *Stranger in One's Own Home: The Inclusion of Immigrants as a Democratic Challenge* (Cambridge: Cambridge University Press).

RUGGIE, JOHN (1982), 'International Regimes, Transactions, and Change', *International Organizations*, 36: 379–415.

SCHUCK, PETER, and SMITH, ROGERS (1985), *Citizenship Without Consent* (New Haven, CT: Yale University Press).

SPIRO, PETER (1997), 'Dual Nationality and the Meaning of Citizenship', *Emory Law Journal*, 46: 1412–85.

SWIDLER, ANN (1986), 'Culture in Action', *American Sociological Review*, 51: 273–86.

UHLITZ, OTTO (1986), 'Deutsches Volk oder "Multikulturelle Gesellschaft"' *Recht und Politik*, 22: 143–52.

WALZER, MICHAEL (1983), *Spheres of Justice* (New York, NY: Basic Books).

WEIL, PATRICK (1999), *Access to Citizenship*, Paper presented at the conference, 'Citizenship: Comparisons and Perspectives', Carnegie Endowment for International Peace, Lisbon, Portugal, June 2–5.

ZIEMSKE, BURKHARDT (1994), 'Verfassungsrechtliche Garantien des Staatsangehoerigkeitsrechts', *Zeitschrift fuer Rechtspolitik*, 6: 229–32.

8

Conflict, Consensus, and Policy Outcomes: Immigration and Integration in Germany and The Netherlands*

DIETRICH THRÄNHARDT

The Comparison

Germans often look to The Netherlands as a model country for its integration policies. Dutch experts are frequently invited to Germany, and expected to tell the Germans how to deal with problems of immigration.[1] Indeed, it is fascinating that two countries so similar with respect to economic development, Protestant-Catholic composition, a 'Christian Democratic welfare state' (Schmidt 1996) and party systems composed of moderate centre-right and centre-left parties, have experienced politics of immigration looking so different.

The Netherlands, after some initial problems, smoothly agreed to a planned policy of voting rights for foreigners, anti-discrimination laws, security of residence after five years, and easy naturalization, with open opposition against this concept confined to small extremist parties at the very right that faded away after a few years. Some Dutch authors present multiculturalism as the showpiece of a society traditionally tolerant (Entzinger 1992: 69–82), with 'tolerance, non-discrimination and respect of diversity' as a 'most precious cultural asset',[2] in contrast to their neighbours.[3] In an official document, the Dutch government states that the policy of integration has been 'conspicuously successful', and 'the Netherlands is currently well ahead of all other European countries in a number of respects' (Lower House 1994: 17).

Germany, after a corporatist start, soon got into the heavy waters of political controversy, leading to a series of grand-style political conflicts about immigration, with the identification of immigration and specific immigrant groups as a grand issue between the Left and the Right. This conflict moved to the centre of attention after the end of the Cold War, and has repeatedly been a campaign issue, with the after-effect that in several waves of open xenophobia dozens of foreigners suffered arson attacks, beatings, and even killings, giving Germany an infamous reputation world-wide, and leading to a new point of German soul-searching.[4]

The comparison is puzzling, and gives rise to several questions: is the popular picture correct or should it be modified? Why are these developments so divergent? And what about the policy outcomes of such divergent political climates upon the social life, the economic situation, and the relations between immigrants and the indigenous population, or, as the Dutch would say, *Allochthones* and *Autochthones*? Let us, in a first step, look into the political history of immigration in the two countries.

Germany: Party Competition about the Immigration Issue

German immigration after World War II had three principal sources (for an overview see Bade 1987): Firstly, the expellees and refugees from former eastern Germany and the countries to the East. All in all, twelve million people were expelled to Germany in its reduced borders as decided at Yalta and Potsdam, and more than one million lost their lives during the expulsion. Ethnicity was the criterion for the transfer to Germany, and the people deported either held German citizenship or were considered Germans. The Basic Law of 1949 acknowledged a moral obligation to these Germans still in East European countries (Hinken 1998: 179–264), and the founding fathers and mothers provided in the Basic Law a right for the acceptance of ethnic Germans from communist countries who had made it to West Germany. In the refugee law, it was assumed that they were suffering persecution or its after-effects (*Vertreibungsdruck*). Consequently, this reception was discontinued in the early 1990s, except for the Germans from the C.I.S. countries who still are not allowed to move back to their pre-deportation homelands. At the same time, Germany began to accept Jews from the former Soviet Union as *Kontingentflüchtlinge* (quota refugees).

After some initial reluctance from regional parties, particularly the Bavarian Party and the CSU, against voting rights for the refugees, German public opinion was largely united about the moral grounds for freeing ethnic Germans from oppression which was conceived of as totalitarian, and particularly discriminatory against Germans.[5] Consequently, party competition inside Germany was limited to the question of whose policy would be more effective in freeing Germans from the realm of Communism. In the 1970s and 1980s this was an important argument for or against *détente* policies. Thus Chancellor Schmidt in 1976 at the Helsinki summit made a deal with Poland's Communist leader Gierek, offering Poland a soft (and lost) loan of one billion DM, against the promise to let 100,000 Germans go. Moreover, Germany paid 12,000 DM for every German from Ceauşescu's Romania.

Consensus also stood at the start of the second important influx of immigration: the recruitment of foreign workers from Mediterranean countries. The entrepreneurs' and the government's motives to recruit were the wish to balance the labour market, to prevent inflationary wage drifts, and to further growth. The trade unions, on the other hand, successfully demanded the complete equality of wages and working conditions under the German system of negotiated wage settlements, and subsequently tried hard to organize the foreign workers, in well reflected self-interest.[6] However, this tripartite consensus soon ran into trouble. As early as 1964, four years after the start of effective mass recruitment, Chancellor Erhard, who had promoted recruitments as a Minister of Economics, told the public that foreign workers would not be necessary if only every German would work one hour longer (Rist 1978: 125f). Thus he wanted to constrain the unions' campaign for the 40 hour week which went on under the motto that, on Saturday, fathers should 'belong' to their children (*'Samstags gehört Vati mir'*). On March 31, 1966, the conservative tabloid *Bild* had a headline asking if foreign workers were more industrious than Germans, angering German workers who organized a boycott campaign. One year later, the recruitment was stopped during the overheating crisis, and the numbers of foreigners decreased sharply.

The consensus to recruit was re-established in 1968. An 'uncontrolled expansion' (ibid.: 111) followed under the paradigm of growth, and in 1969 Economics Minister Karl Schiller even used the enhanced recruitment of guest-workers as an argument for the revaluation of the DM. Only just before the oil crisis of 1973, the recruitment was halted again. The number of foreign workers fell, many of them returning to their countries of origin, but this time the total number of foreigners remained stable at 3.5 million, as families were allowed to join the workers and children were born.

After some discussions about rotation programmes disguised as 'Swiss system', development aid, or re-migration, and separate schools or classes for foreign children in the southern states of Bavaria and Baden-Württemberg, the issue became national in 1982.[7] This was during the second oil crisis which caused a sharp rise of unemployment, up to two million in 1983, and was one of the core issues bringing the Schmidt government down and the Kohl government in. Whereas some right-wing CDU leaders were openly xenophobic, Kohl demanded the number of 'Turkish co-citizens to be reduced'.[8] *'Ausländerpolitik'* was proclaimed as one of four priorities in the official policy statement of the first Kohl government. Only half a year later, in the policy statement of the second Kohl government, it was hardly mentioned, and for some years it sank into oblivion except for a limited programme of return support and a long lasting controversy between the two smaller coalition partners, the liberals and the Bavarian CSU, concentrating on problems like the age of children who could join their families in Germany, but without much policy effect. At that time the public had come to believe—as could be documented in many polls—that the Social Democrats and the Liberals were 'soft' on immigration and foreigners, whereas the CDU and particularly the Bavarian CSU were 'hard' (IDA 1985).

It was the CSU that brought the issue back when they put it at the centre of their campaign for the 1986 Bavarian diet elections and the national elections of 1987. They needed a new confrontative issue, as their charismatic leader Strauss had dropped his expressive anti-Communism, regularly visited East Germany's Honecker and other Communist leaders, and had arranged a billion DM credit for the ailing East German economy. Rumours were going on about kickbacks from deals with East Germany. The CSU lost 3 per cent in that election but still retained a comfortable 56 per cent majority in Bavaria. At the European elections of 1989, CSU and CDU again stressed *Ausländer* as an issue. However, this time they received the worst result at a European election ever, and the extremist *Republikaner* were able to gain their first major victory as a result of the CDU/CSU's xenophobic campaign (see Thränhardt 1995: 321–43). For part of the electorate, it had become evident that they were talking about reducing the number of foreigners, but not acting. Due to Gorbachev's liquidation of the Soviet empire, the issue disappeared in 1990, and was overshadowed by reunification. However, it was brought back deliberately in 1991 when CDU/CSU started a campaign against the Germany's liberal asylum policies.

Asylum had an important symbolic place in the Basic Law but was traditionally conceived of as only for a small political élite. Since the early 1980s, however, seeking asylum had developed into a mass phenomenon, and Germany in 1992 counted 438,000 asylum requests: 52 per cent of all requests for West European countries. 40 per cent were from East Central Europe. This, then, was the third immigration stream into Germany. As long as the asylum seekers came from Communist countries, Germany had a strong pro-asylum consensus and the refugees were welcomed in an outspokenly hospitable way, the state even establishing and supporting cultural exile institutions like the Philharmonia Hungarica and Hungarian schools. Asylum only became a point of extreme controversy when, after the *putsch* in Chile, leftist refugees applied for asylum. They where accused by the CDU/CSU of constituting a Communist and subversive danger (Wolken 1988). This started a transposition of the immigration issue into Left–Right dimensions.

Not all immigrants but certain immigrant groups became the objects of negative attention. Whereas the anti-Italian feelings of the 1960s, uttered in jokes and slogans, were not overly politicized, every event since 1973 could be monitored on a Left–Right scale. The Christian Democrats campaigned against Chileans in the mid-1970s, against Turks after 1980, and against asylum seekers from 1986 on. The high point of xenophobia was in 1991/92 when the conservative government campaigned against the existing asylum laws, and forced the opposition to agree to the 'asylum compromise' on Nicholas Day 1992.

Looking back, Kanther, the Minister of the Interior, described this as producing 'heat degrees' (*Hitzegrade*) (Prantl 1994: 53) in the political camp, with the liberal Free Democrats arguing for a compromise. Individuals sceptical about the respective party line on both sides of society, felt it was necessary to bring about changes. Chancellor Kohl himself spoke of a 'state crisis'.

The campaigns were sometimes close to open racism, although the term 'race' is taboo in Germany after the Nazi experience. This taboo was once touched on by Bavaria's Edmund Stoiber, then the CSU's general secretary, and today its leader. He spoke of the danger of a *durchmischte und durchrasste Gesellschaft*, a society racially mixed, but backed down after a few days, accepting that the term 'race' should not be used.

Obviously, there are limits to xenophobia and racism in Germany, and this can be illustrated by looking at the political process which led to the new Jewish migration into Germany (Harris 1998: 105–47). Just before the anti-asylum campaign came to its height, the government agreed to accept Jewish migrants from the C.I.S. countries, giving in to the pressure from the Jewish Community in Germany, the Liberals and the opposition Social Democrats and Greens—but against explicit opposition from the Israeli government. The new policy which built upon an invitation to Soviet Jews by the last (democratic) East German government was achieved without public controversy, and includes broad state funding of the new immigration. In parliamentary debate in early 1991, all political parties unanimously welcomed the Russian Jews. Later, the Minister of the Interior Wolfgang Schäuble would add that he would be glad if as many Jews would live in Germany as in 1933.

In the competitive German political system, party conflict about migration has become an everyday experience. The last episode was the CDU/CSU's street campaign in early 1999 against the naturalization law of the red-green government, mobilizing the conservative are largely silent—with notable exceptions in liberal and religious CDU circles—thinking that critical statements would damage the party they belong to. This is even true for the Catholic bishops who can be proud of a pro-immigrant record but have a family feeling towards the Christian Democrats. The radical CDU approach against 'double citizenship' opened a new round of principled conflict.

Not only the Right, but also the Left have found their scapegoats. Whereas in the post-war years many local social Democratic party chapters in agricultural areas had been founded by refugees, and solid social democratic traditions from Bohemia or Silesia had been transferred to Bavaria or Lower Saxony, Willy Brandt's *Ostpolitik* produced a cleavage between the organized expellees and the Left. The Chairman of the exiled Silesians and SPD-Deputy Hupka, left the SPD and joined the CDU, and with generational turnover and *détente* enthusiasm the Left developed a distrust against the Germans from the East. The Green Party, some of whose representatives had a political past in Communist splinter groups, were even more sceptical, and at the same time cultivated a rather romantic relationship toward the *Ausländer*. Lafontaine, the eloquent SPD candidate of 1990, brought this to a point when he pronounced that a persecuted asylum seeker had a greater right to come to the country than a non-persecuted *Aussiedler* (Lafontaine 1990), and complained about '*Deutschtümelei*' (Germanishness).[9] From time to time, some leading SPD politicians have argued against the legitimacy of the ethnic Germans' claims of coming to Germany, as have some Left intellectuals. Ironically, one commentator wrote: 'If you beat my Ausländer, I shall beat your Aussiedler'.

This policy, however, was badly conceived in two respects: firstly, it alienated the *Aussiedler* even more. Since they had the right to vote, and the *Ausländer* not, the overall results of such statements were counterproductive. *Aussiedler* were the critical group who decided the elections of 1994 for Kohl's CDU who made, assisted by his *Aussiedlerbeauftragter* (Commissioner for Aussiedler) Waffenschmidt, a successful effort to woe them. Some *Aussiedler* saw Kohl as the Moses who helped them to get out of the empire of evil. Moreover, the public, even if resentful of taking in a great number of *Aussiedler*, was even more sceptical about great numbers of asylum seekers—although most people, whenever asked, were sympathetic with individuals and their suffering.

Even when the Kohl government denounced the Social Democrats about their statements critical of *Aussiedler*, they themselves changed the policy. Categories of applicants were removed, and social assistance programmes were cut severely. In 1991, an unofficial quota of about 220,000 was introduced, and made official in December 1992. Over the next years, this quota was reduced more and more through administrative measures, and came down to 103,000 in 1998. In 1997, the government implemented a test in the German language, thus severely reducing the numbers incoming.

In most elections from 1983 on, immigration and immigrants have been an important issue in favour of CDU and CSU—profiting from developments reported in the media and themselves stressing the issue and producing news. In the elections of 1998, the Social Democrats took great care to neutralize the issue. Chancellor-candidate Schröder made some well-publicized remarks about throwing criminal foreigners out of the country, and the party was careful not to be dragged into a controversy about the deportation of a 14 year old Turkish boy with an extremely criminal record which was spectacularly directed by political CSU entrepreneurs in Munich. Even in the elections of 1998 which were won so clearly by the SPD, the 'competence' for *Ausländer* and asylum was clearly attributed to the CDU/CSU (Fig. 8.1). The SPD's only chance of winning was to neutralize the issue. And the euphoria of the red-green coalition after its historic 1998 victory led to clumsy proclamations about dual citizenship and a disastrous defeat in the diet elections in Hesse after only a hundred days.

In the interaction from the late 1970s to the late 1990s, the highly competitive party system in Germany has produced a new cleavage in the society:

Which party has the best competence to solve the problems that I read to you:
the CDU/CSU or the SPD – or none of them ?

Problems of foreigners and asylum seekers

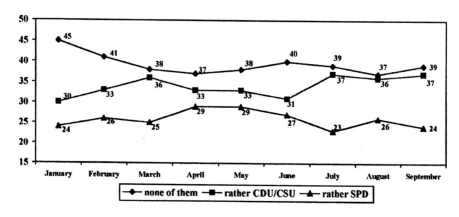

Social Justice

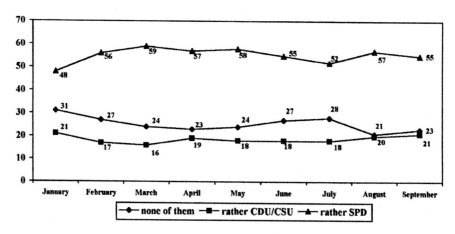

FIG. 8.1. Problem solving capacities of CDU/CSU and SPD, 1998

Notes: Rest—don't know/no statement, values in per cent. Basis: voting population in Germany

Source: EMNID

Aussiedler are conceived as conservative and in the realm of the Christian Democrats, *Ausländer* are an object of care for Leftists. Even naturalization is largely seen under these premises. Just before the elections, the CSU publicly warned that a red-green victory would lead to a regime change (*'eine andere Republik'*). Moreover, the CSU warned of the dangers of naturalizing 5.5 million foreigners, the 'creation of voters' and in the end an 'Islamic Republic Germany' (CSU 1998). The warning was based on a survey of the *Zentrum für Türkeistudien* about nine of ten naturalized Turks in Germany voting for 'Red' or 'Green', although as all other polls show less dramatic proportions, these figures do not seem particularly reliable.

The controversy of the early months of 1999 about naturalization and the collection of signatures on the streets against 'dual nationality' thus was not only a desperate attempt of CSU and CDU to create a new popular issue. In this, they were very successful, winning a surprise victory in Hesse against all predictions (Witte 1999: 15). It is also a fight for or against the creation of a new electorate. As in many other cases, the cleavage definition is strange:[10] the *Aussiedler*, largely working class, and state-oriented by socialization, are conceived as automatic followers of the centre-right; the *Ausländer*, many of them religious and the great majority not post-materialistic, are conceived as followers of the centre-left.[11] Political competition will, at least after some years, mitigate such politically created cleavages, if a large part of the foreign population gets the vote, and the integrative mechanisms of the German work and welfare society continue to operate.

The Netherlands: Élite Consensus Policies

The first post-war immigrants to The Netherlands came from the former colonies. Besides some 'whites' the majority of 280,000 was considered 'brown'—and in popular language even 'blue'—and can be termed post-colonial.[12] There were also a few thousand Chinese. By 1972 the numbers of this group had risen to half a million. One immigrant group, the Moluccans, who were aiming at creating an independent republic in their homeland, kept a special identity—today they number about 45,000. While they had traditionally provided soldiers for the Dutch colonial army in the East Indies, they were dismissed from the army upon arrival in The Netherlands, became stateless and lived in 'abominable conditions' (Jacobs 1998b: 105f), and were largely unemployed.[13] The Dutch trade unions successfully requested their exclusion from the labour market.[14] In the 1970s, young Moluccans were involved in a series of terrorist attacks, culminating in the spectacular hijacking of a train in 1974, to get attention for their complaints about unfair treatment, and thus made the public aware of their grievances.

A larger group of post-colonial migrants are the Surinamese who became Dutch citizens in 1954 as The Netherlands tried to do away with colonialism, and used this window of opportunity to migrate to The Netherlands before that status was taken away from them five years after independence in 1975 (Heijs 1995: 144). Living under Dutch dominance for centuries, they are well accustomed to the Dutch way of life even if they are identifiable because of physiognomic characterics. Some immigration continues from the Dutch Antilles which still belong to the kingdom. They only number 3,000–7,000 persons a year but get a lot of negative attention from the media and politicians and are considered 'black'.

Although The Netherlands began recruiting Mediterranean workers later than neighbouring countries, and proceeded more slowly, the first outbreak of violence had already occurred in 1961, in the textile cities of Enschede, Almelo, and Hengelo in the East of the country.[15] In 1972, fighting broke out between Turkish immigrants and indigenous people in the Afrikaanderwijk of Rotterdam. The city acted quickly and changed police routines as well as housing policies, trying to spread the immigrants over the city to avoid ghettos, and at the same enabling them to keep social ties and relations: the policy of 'concentrated deconcentration'.[16]

For the following argument it is important that it was not a kind of natural or traditional hospitality or tolerance that automatically made The Netherlands different from Germany. On the contrary, in the first years, integration in Germany seems to have been smoother. In particular, this is true if we compare the acceptance of foreign refugees: in the 1950s and 1960s, The Netherlands were hesitant with respect to refugees, and the number of refugees settling in the country was very limited. As late as 1985, Entzinger writes: 'Quite surprisingly, given the Dutch tradition in this field, the number of refugees accepted is very low in comparison with the number accepted by most other Western European countries' (Entzinger 1985: 55). However, the élite reaction was different. As early as 1961, the business paper NRC commented that the Twente riots were painful for the foreign workers, but that they also could become embarrassing for The Netherlands' image (Groenendijk 1990: 55). The newspaper expressed the fear of both the employers and the Dutch government that the publicity about the riots in the Italian and Spanish press would reduce opportunities for further recruitment in those countries.

The important reforms that The Netherlands introduced around 1980 were based on an élite consensus. It emerged during the debate about a total revision of the Dutch constitution, the challenge of the Moluccan train hijacking, the unexpectedly high immigration from Surinam before and after independence, and the uncertainty on how to deal with the foreign workers after the end of recruitment. The government requested a report by the Scientific Council on minority policies in 1979 which then led to a provisional White Paper in 1981 and the *Minderhedennota* in 1983 (WRR 1979). The concept consisted of four elements: stability of residence after five years, enlarged participation including easier naturalization and voting rights for foreigners in local elections, special programmes for underprivileged minorities, including special assistance for them to organize and represent the various groups, and the fight against racist discrimination. After lengthy discussions, the large parties found a compromise about these points (Jacobs 1998: 133). While the leftist parties were clearly more open and engaged for inclusive reforms, and were arguing for voting rights for foreigners on all levels, there were also powerful voices in the Christian Democratic and the Liberal parties for a reform.

The first prominent figure to argue for local voting rights for foreigners living in the country was the Christian Democrat *éminence grise* and former president of the European Court of Justice, A. Donner, who argued in an article that foreigners living in the country should have the right to vote.[17] His statement was taken up by the leftist coalition that ruled the country at that time (Jacobs 1998b: 103). It was particularly important that three consecutive ministers of the interior, one a Christian Democrat (CDA), one a Social Democrat (PvdA), and one a Liberal (VVD), spoke out in favour of the reforms (Groenendijk 1987: 23). There are indications that the centre-right parties agreed to local voting rights under the shock of the train incident mentioned earlier (Jacobs 1998a: 363). On certain points, however, a majority of CDA and VVD members in the indirectly elected First Chamber blocked reforms that seemed too far-reaching, as the principal openness for dual nationality, using the German law of that time as an argument (Jacobs 1998b: 136). Also, voting rights on all levels had been blocked in a package deal, in exchange for local voting rights (ibid.: 132ff). Parliament records also reveal deep scepticism by many deputies concerning the belongingness of the immigrants. In practice, however, even on these points, pragmatic compromises have been found. While foreigners, in principal, should give up their old nationality upon naturalization, an exception is made for 80 per cent of the potential candidates. In 1997, 57 per cent of the immigrants of Turkish origin held dual citizenship, even when the principal of dual nationality was not included in the law. This was done in a consensual process of including more and more categories. For the third generation, automatic nationality by birth had already been introduced in 1953 (Heijs 1995: 134f).

The whole process was not without difficulties and contradictions (Jacobs 1998a: 336; cf Groenendijk 1985: 38–52). On the whole, however, an attitude of pragmatic compromise became prevalent, with rising optimism about the possibility solving existing problems, and a sense of pride about The Netherlands as an open and tolerant country. In this sense, Kees Groenendijk argues that the educative effect of foreigners' voting rights in local elections have been more important than the effects on the foreigners (Groenendijk 1987: 25). This is illustrated by the fact that in 1998 all three larger parties had immigrants elected as members of Parliament, and ten of 150 members of Parliament (Tweede Kamer) have an immigrant background (Groenendijk 1999: 1)—Germany only has one 'red' and two 'green' deputies with a foreign background, along with many post-war expellees. After the PvdA had taken an active interest in immigrants, and put immigrant candidates on their lists, and local voting rights and naturalization had created an interesting new group of voters, the CDA and VVD also actively began to look for candidates and voters among the immigrants. Whereas in the first elections most immigrants voted for the Left, and in 1994, 60 per cent voted for the PvdA and the Greens, the general distribution of votes in 1998 mirrored that of the indigenous population more closely.

The integrative process included moments of deep symbolism, such as when Ruud Lubbers, then Prime Minister and leader of the CDA, visited Muslim mosques and Hindu communities during the campaign for the first local elections in which foreigners could participate. Surveys demonstrate that the majority of the population originally was not in favour of granting voting rights to foreigners. However, a change occurred after the experience of the foreigners' participation in local elections, and there is a majority in favour since that time (ibid.: 2). International football matches and the like, won by Dutch minority stars like Ruud Gullit also contain an integrative symbolism. Gullit was the captain of the national football team, and the relationship between 'black' and 'white' players was discussed publicly. This may be particularly impressive for aggressive young men who in many countries engage in violence against minority groups on the streets.

In the early 1990s, the discussion had taken a turn. Particularly, Frits Bolkestein, until recently the leader of the parliamentary party of the VVD—which is to the right of the CDA—warned publicly against giving in too much to the cultural peculiarities of immigrants, and argued that they should be expected to integrate much more into the Dutch way of life.[18] These remarks caused sensation and controversy, as they stood against the tradition of multiculturalism and legitimacy of difference that is so much a part of Dutch political culture in the tradition of pillarization (see Lijphart 1968). Bolkestein became popular with such remarks—and this was important in winning the elections of 1996—becoming the leader of Europe's most successful liberal party. Clearly, the ideological basis of these appeals and critiques was ethnocentric. Compared to campaigns in Germany, however, and even more to those of France and England, it was not only moralistic in the Dutch tradition but also more inclusive, at least in its wording. The message was that the immigrants should integrate, and that there should be less emphasis on cultural diversity. Moreover, reliance on welfare was evaluated very critically. This fitted into the remodeling of Dutch welfare in the 1990s and the attack on welfare dependency, although it was much more moderate than in some English speaking countries. Government programmes in the late 1990s became less multiculturalist and more integrative or assimilationist. The Dutch Scientific Council which had outlined a minority policy in 1979, opted for more 'social and economic integration' in 1989, thus using the central German catchword (WWR 1990). In Entzinger's words, the minority model was replaced by the integration model.[19]

In the 1990s, 'attitudes toward immigration and minority cultures appear to have become harsher—some would say more realistic—among certain segments of the population' (Entzinger 1994: 108). A particularly delicate turn of the public discourse occurred after the crash of an Israeli airplane in an Amsterdam suburb in 1992, killing hundreds of people. The awareness did not turn to the reasons for the accident, the poisonous goods on the plane—which have only been made public in 1998—but to the fact that many victims did not have a legal status but were undocumented aliens.

Policy Outputs: Social Attitudes and Socio-Economic Success Rates

Compared to other immigration countries, The Netherlands can be clearly proud of a tolerant political climate and a civilized style of political discussion. Dutch political leaders would not speak out against minorities as other European leaders, such as Strauss, Stoiber, Chirac, Giscard d'Estaing, and Thatcher have done. The Netherlands do not have a *Front National* or *Republikaner*, and the extremist Centre Party has faded away. It had important successes in some local elections, but not much in national ones. Moreover, open violence against minorities clearly seems to be less widespread than in other immigrant countries, and is not connected to competitive and noisy politics. For the well-being of the immigrants and their daily life, as well as for the quality of the political process, this is an important distinction.

After a consensus about the minority policy had been established and the extremist Centre Party had succeeded in having some deputies elected to Parliament, the leaders of the main political parties made a gentlemen's agreement to abstain from using immigration as an issue in electoral campaigns, and not win votes at the cost of immigrants. This agreement held for almost ten years, until Bolkestein broke it on 6 September 1991, interestingly not in a speech at home, but at a meeting of European liberal parties in Luzern.[20] In both the 1995 and 1999 elections to the Provincial Councils, VVD leaders openly and successfully made negative statements on immigrants. In 1999, the leader of the Partij van de Arbeid in Parliament tried to outdo them. However, the media were critical about these statements, and after the elections, the three politicians retreated from the statements they had made ten days earlier.[21] This is reminiscent of 'playing the race card' in other countries but it has much less become a part of Dutch political culture than in other countries, and is still detested in the public. Until now it seems largely to be confined to side elections, that is elections that are not seen as particularly important by both the politicians and the voters. For some politicians this is an opportunity to pep up their campaigns, and for some voters to vote for extreme parties without much fear for the consequences.

It is not surprising, then, that comparative measurement of blatant prejudice shows higher results in Germany than in The Netherlands: Germans express more open prejudice against Turks than their Dutch counterparts. Yet the analysis of subtle prejudice reveals an inverse trend: German subtle prejudice against Turks is lower than that of the Dutch (Pettigrew 1998: 84f). Pettigrew demonstrates that Dutch attitudes differ from that of their German, British, and French neighbours:

In normative terms, this unique pattern outlines the famed 'tolerance' of the Netherlands. There exists a stern Dutch norm against *blatant* prejudice. But *subtle* prejudice slips under the norm, unrecognized as prejudice. . . . Blatant prejudice is the traditional form; it is hot, close, and direct. The ten items that tap it involve open rejection based on presumed biological difference. Subtle prejudice is the modern form; it is cool, distant, and indirect. The ten items that measure it are not readily recognized as indicators of prejudice. They tap the perceived threat of the minority to traditional values, the exaggeration of cultural differences with the minority, and the absence of positive feelings towards them. . . . Both the blatantly and subtly prejudiced are less educated and older. They report less interest in politics but more pride in their nationality. They less often think of themselves as 'Europeans'. They are more politically conservative; but subtle prejudice is not, as some claim, simply a reflection of conservatism. The prejudiced also are more likely to have only ingroup friends. Finally, they reveal a strong sense of group, but not individual, relative deprivation. Thus, the prejudiced sense a group threat to 'people like themselves' from minorities, but not a sense of personal threat.   (Pettigrew 1998: 83–4).[22]

Pettigrew also mentions The Netherlands passing anti-discrimination legislation. However, he points to the inefficiency of such legislation, in the absence of powerful legal instruments like the American class actions (Pettigrew 1998: 90f). Comparing statistics on unemployment, the differences between immigrant groups and the indigenous population seem definitely worse than in Germany.

   This is particularly true for the young (see Table 8.1). For foreign women the unemployment figure was 24.3 per cent whereas it was only 8.2 per cent for indigenous women. In spite of the widely praised Dutch 'employment wonder' of the 1990s, the unemployment figure for non-EU women was the second highest among all EU countries in 1995 (Kiel and Werner 1998: Table 3.1). In contrast to the high occupation rates of Dutch women, immigrant women from non-EU countries had very low occupation rates in international comparison (ibid.: fig. 3.17). Ethnic minorities in The Netherlands also suffer particularly from long term unemployment (Werner 1997: 9). In 1996, Dutch statistics show an unemployment rate of 7 per cent among 'Europeans', 9 per cent among immigrants from the former Dutch East Indies, 16 per cent among Surinamese, 21 per cent among 'Mediterraneans', 25 per cent among Moroccans, 28 per cent among Antilleans/Arubans, and 36 per cent among Turks. Unemployment of the autochthonous Dutch decreased to 5.4 per cent in 1996, but was 'dramatic' at 19 per cent for the foreign born/foreign nationals (CBS).

TABLE 8.1. Unemployment in the indigenous and immigrant populations of West Germany and The Netherlands

Year	(West) Germany				Netherlands			
	Indigenous		Foreigners		Indigenous		Foreigners	
	all	<25	all	<25	all	<25	all	<25
1983	6.0	10.1	11.3	18.2	11.3	20.4	24.5	37.2
1984	6.3	9.8	11.3	17.1	—	—	—	—
1985	6.4	9.3	12.0	17.4	9.8	16.9	27.1	37.6
1986	6.1	7.3	12.0	14.8	—	—	—	—
1987	6.3	6.9	12.5	15.4	9.4	16.1	24.9	38.9
1988	5.9	6.4	10.9	12.7	8.8	13.6	25.9	31.7
1989	5.4	5.2	9.3	9.9	8.0	12.3	26.6	37.0
1990	4.5	4.3	8.7	7.5	7.0	10.2	24.7	31.6
1991	5.1	5.2	8.4	8.5	6.6	10.2	25.2	34.9
1992	6.1	5.5	9.2	10.4	5.1	7.7	16.5	16.0
1993	7.1	6.8	13.3	14.3	5.7	9.7	19.6	25.5
1994	8.1	7.7	15.5	17.1	6.5	10.7	22.5	25.9
1995	7.5	7.3	15.0	15.7	6.5	11.5	23.5	26.9

Source: Kiehl and Werner 1998, table 3.2 and 3.4; EUROSTAT.

CBS, the Dutch Statistical Office, noted that, '. . . the majority of the Turks and Moroccans between 15 and 64 years do not participate in the labour market, and of the remaining 44% (Turks), respectively 42% (Moroccans) one third to one quarter are registered as unemployed. . . . The employment growth is taking place largely outside the traditional immigrant categories' (CBS: 37f). Looking at the unemployment rates of Turks in The Netherlands, Germany, and France, Doomernijk finds particularly large discrepancies with the indigenous population in the Netherlands (1998: 68). For 1997, the Dutch government gives the unemployment figures as 5 per cent for the indigenous population, but 14 per cent for Surinamers, 20 per cent for Antillians / Arubans, 21 per cent for Turks, and 22 per cent for Moroccans (MBZK 1999: 23). Although unemployment has decreased for all groups from 1994 to 1997, the discrepancies have remained the same, and are higher than in other countries.

Moreover, the degree of separation of immigrants and non-immigrants in Dutch schools is rather high, due to the largely denominational structure of the Dutch school system. In the school year 1990–91, for example, 47 per cent of all Protestant schools did not have even one immigrant (*allochthon*) student.[23] Schools are openly labelled 'black' or 'white' which is quite uncommon on the European continent.[24] There is also a huge discrepancy between the school achievements of the children of indigenous and of immigrant origin: 8 per cent of the indigenous children left school without any qualification, as against this

TABLE 8.2. Minority children in secondary school systems, The Netherlands (%)

	1992–93	1994–95	1996–97	1997–98
Special schools (VSO)	14.7	17.4	18.8	19.0
Individual preparation schools for job training (IVBO)	19.0	19.6	20.0	22.1
Pre-vocational schools (VBO)	8.5	8.9	9.0	9.3
General secondary schools (AVO)	3.8	4.3	4.9	5.0

Source: Minderheidenbeleid (1999: 49).

figure rose to 35 per cent of the children of Turkish origin and 39 per cent of the children of Moroccan origin (Doomernik 1998: 65). Comparing the streams of the secondary schools, minority children disproportionately go to special schools for for underachieving children which do not offer ways into prestigious careers or middle class status. In comparison, the disadvantage of children of immigrant background in Germany, although clearly extant, is not as strong as in The Netherlands. Moreover, there are explicit discrepancies between the German *Länder*, and if the Dutch patterns can be compared at all, it is to the rather exclusive Bavarian school system.

Whereas the socioeconomic status of the immigrants from the Mediterranean countries—former recruitment countries, including Turkey—in Germany is comparable to that of the German working class—blue and white collar workers, population insured mandatorily—the situation of the same group in The Netherlands seems to be worse than that.[25] The same difference can be found with the performance in the educational system, with France showing a picture parallel to that of Germany (Doomernik 1998: 69).

In recent years, the International Labour Organization has undertaken interesting experiments in a number of countries whose labour agencies were prepared to co-operate. Persons of the same qualification, one group of indigenous and the other of immigrant origin, were sent to companies who were hiring personnel. The process was followed through the various stages, and the performance of the two groups was compared. Summarizing the data on The Netherlands, the authors conclude that 'discrimination has been proven to exist', and 'that the possibility of actually getting a job is almost zero for the Morroccan applicant' (Bovenkerk, Gras, and Ramsoedh 1995: 21, 52). From one stage to the next, more and more Moroccan testers were turned down, mostly in a polite way.

On the other hand, the analysis of the data on Germany does not show significant discrimination (Goldberg, Mourinho, and Kulke 1996: 47). It is likely from the data that there is discrimation in the banking and insurance sector, and with smaller companies. The figures for the various industries are, however, too small to become significant, and are balanced by other sectors, some with

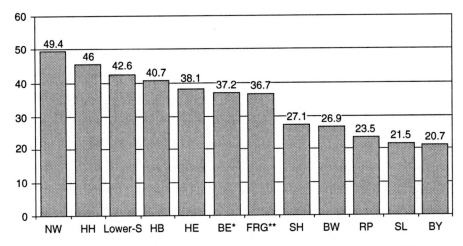

FIG. 8.2. Eligibility of foreign students for university study or technical school, 1996 (%)

Notes: * includes East Berlin; ** former West Germany

Sources: Statistisches Bundesamt, Fachserie 11, Reihe 1: Allgemeinbildende Schulen, 1996/97 school year, Weisbaden, 1997: 32–40. Own calculation

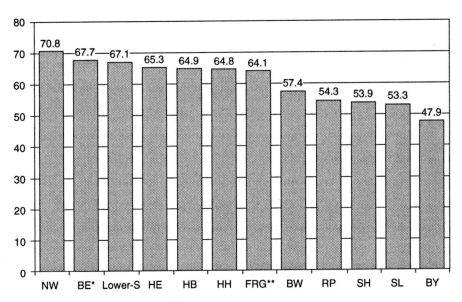

FIG. 8.3. Eligibility of all students for university study or technical school, 1996 (%)

Notes: * includes East Berlin; ** West Germany

Sources: Statistisches Bundesamt, Fachserie 11, Reihe 1: Allgemeinbildende Schulen, 1996/97 school year, Weisbaden, 1997: 32–40. Own calculation

negative discrimination rates. The comparative tests fit well into the pattern that has been discussed above.

As mentioned above, the lack of economic success of immigrants in the Netherlands has, in the late 1990s, been brought to the centre of political attention, reminiscent—although more civilized intone—of the American debates about the 'culture of poverty'. From quite a different ideological position, Jan Rath has described and denounced Dutch policies as *minorization*, the 'social construction of ethnic minorities' stressing the difference between the minorities and the majority in every aspect of life (Rath 1991). The theoretical approach was developed in parallel to the concept of *racialization* of British sociologist Robert Miles (Miles 1996). In a process of planned 'social engineering', the 'socio-cultural signifiers' and the dividing lines of the 'ethnic groups' are stressed, and in a steady process brought to the public's attention. The very existence and the symbolic acknowledgement of 'ethnic' organizations, modelled after the traditional Dutch *verzuiling* pattern that is fading away for the traditional 'pillars' of society—Catholics, Protestants, Liberals—a process that may be made easier with the construction of new groups. 'Ethnic' leaders are then co-opted into the political system, and function as a buffer between 'their' groups and the administration which has a strong influence on the process and can recognize and select the right representatives and organizations. Thus an 'ethnic minorities industry' (Rath 1991: 278)—a term invented in parallel to the British 'race relations industry'—is created, and this institutionalization is a living proof of the existence of the underlying dividing lines, a reification of a concept, shaping the minds of the people, and their way of acceptance. Rath notes, further, that 'Group specific (proto-)political institutions are products of minorization and express the idea that 'ethnic minorities' are not full members of the Dutch imagined community' (Rath 1991: 279). If they are not full members, they will be tolerated but not accepted into key positions or as equals. In contrast to the old *verzuiling* concept where the various pillars were kept largely separated but all held real power and compromised in Parliament, the new minorities depend on the good will of the indigenous population. In addition, minorities in the Dutch concept are acknowledged only when they are below average (*achterstand*). Only such groups are getting help to improve their situation while on the other hand their otherness is demonstrated. Thus a well-intentioned and carefully constructed policy may have some counterproductive results in the economic and social field.[26]

Foreigners in Germany had, up to 1999, rather low participation in the political field. Foreigners' councils (*Ausländerbeiräte*) that have been established in many cities and institutionalized in some *Länder* have not been very effective, and naturalization rates only began to rise substantially since 1994 (Hagedorn 1998, 1999). However, there is one outstanding institution that is only seldomly mentioned because it has old traditions only in Germany and

Austria: the works councils. In The Netherlands, it is a new institution, and foreigners have full voting rights. In contrast to general elections, foreigners have full voting rights and eligibility at these factory and company institutions. After a period of adjustment, including local strike movements taken by foreign workers, the trade unions put foreign nationality candidates on the lists for the elections, and every year more foreigners are elected, and some have become heads of the *Betriebsrat*. As this institution holds real power and the companies need the *Betriebsrat's* consent for working times, extra hours, the dismissal of workers, and a wide range of other measures, participation makes sense for both foreign and indigenous workers, and co-operation strengthens the workers' position. This construction has resulted in a productive situation. Even in times of dramatic political conflict, the working place has remained peaceful and the works councils co-operative.[27] Foreigners have thus been transformed into workers (*Arbeitnehmer*), but only in the workplace. A second institutional setting that is important for inclusionionary processes is the German apprentice system which in the late 1990s has been more and more extended to immigrant youths.

Conclusion

Comparing the two countries, we can explain how diverging political styles brought about diverging results. Beginning in the 1970s in both countries, mindful people were aware that recruitment had led to permanent immigration, and both governments commissioned reports. The recommendations of the German *Kühn Memorandum* of 1979 were in many ways comparable to those of the Dutch Scientific Council. In both countries there also was a broad range of people and institutions discussing immigration, and an active and caring interest by students, Christian groups, leftist activists, and many other citizens. Whereas, however, the Dutch political system worked smoothly to formulate and implement a policy consensus, in Germany *Ausländer* were taken hostage in bitter strife between the political parties and ideological camps, quite similar to the conflicts in Britain and in France in the same decades.

Instead of *playing the race card*, the Dutch political élite conceded voting rights and easy naturalization to immigrants, recruiting them as voters, and opening a *circulus virtuosus* in Hirschman's sense (Hirschman 1994: 203–18). Hirschman argues that the qualities of a liberal society do not rest in a given tradition or morality but that they are produced and transmitted through successful solutions of problems which then can be used as models and as an encouragement for the solution of further problems. Contrary to this, the Conservative parties in Germany—and in Britain and France—entered a *circulus vitiosus*, and were then repeating and varying the issue again and again

(Thränhardt 1995: 323–45).—although the phenomenon is less entrenched than the usual 'playing the race card' in the US.

Whereas the Dutch solution proved to be harmonious in the field of politics, and an immigrant élite was created and co-opted into the political and administrative system, the social and economic environment was not targeted successfully. The multicultural approach that was cultivated—sometimes not very coherently[28]—furthered the definition of the immigrants as being 'the other' and different from the indigenous population, even when the groups were labelled *Allochthones* and *Autochthones* in a scientific language. As an object of welfare policy, the immigrants at the same time were stereotyped as needy and underachieving, along with other *achterstand* groups.[29]

Germany was keeping and restructuring productive mechanisms for the integration of immigrants and particularly young immigrants into the economic system in the 1970s, in particular the apprentice system—which is especially important for the working classes and carries a certain public prestige—the inclusive works councils and trade unions, and integrative school policies in some *Länder*. In contrast, Dutch trade unions were less active or less successful in organizing immigrant workers. Moreover, early exclusionary decisions at the cost of post-colonial immigrants had far-reaching after-effects, as well as the post-colonial character of some migrations. In this context it is indicative that in spite of all elaborate efforts to 'educate' the population—a standard term in official documents—a language of 'black' and 'white' is used informally to define groups, schools and other places, and then given in official documents in quotation marks.

Closer comparison between the general and the focused programmes in the two countries could also enable us to evaluate how programme funding and policy implementation are related. To give one example: the 'policy' document proclaims in a high tone that the Randstadt cities shall be given 2 million guilders each over a period of three years for integration—which would be less than a guilder per capita in the cities of Amsterdam and Rotterdam (Lower House 1994: 34). On the other hand, the practice of doubling the teacher-per-student ratio for foreign born students in North Rhine Westphalia which has been the practice since the early 1980s—largely unnoticed from the public—can be calculated to cost two billion DM per year in that land—see the positive results in *Länder* comparison, Fig. 8.1. This might also be an example of the difference between long term policies that can translate into built-in structures over time, and short term programmes that always remain endangered and precarious just because of their limited time horizon—for clients as well as for the personnel.

Comparing The Netherlands and Germany, we can thus demonstrate that policy decisions make a difference and that they can start vicious or virtuous circles. At the same time, their outcomes can be traced to be specific and contingent, and not necessarily encompassing the whole system as such.

Notes

I am indebted to Kees Groenendijk and other Dutch collegues and friends for deepening my understanding about The Netherlands, developing the idea for this article after hearing his report on The Netherlands at the ZIF workshop on naturalization at Bielefeld in January 1999. He also read the manuscript and suggested corrections. I also want to thank Jim Hollifield and Daniela Ross who corrected the manuscript.

1. Leiprecht/Lutz mention six German educationists who argue that Germans should learn from The Netherlands. They also comment that some Dutch 'migration professionals' make minority policy 'a sort of immaterial Dutch export product' (Leiprecht and Lutz 1996: 239). The Netherlands are also positively compared to Belgium and Britain. An early example is Christopher Bagley (1973). See also the review on this book by John Rex (1973) who states that the Dutch have 'the most benign racial attitudes' and have 'managed business of immigration of coloured colonial workers far more successfully than has Britain'.
2. (Thijn 1997: 4). Thijn is a leading socialist politician.
3. In a comparison of the developments in Belgium and The Netherlands, Jacobs (1998) quotes many such evaluations by Dutch politicians and researchers. In his critical study of the parliamentary debates, however, he demonstrates a wide gap between the discourse of the left and the right in The Netherlands and argues that at certain points political compromise became possible (Jacobs 1998: 210–14).
4. There have been racist incidents and murders in The Netherlands too—however much less registered by world opinion and the media in both countries.
5. Consequently, high ranking members of the Communist nomenclatura were excluded from acceptance.
6. This organizational effort is an important difference in comparison to the situation in Switzerland where the unions took less interest in the foreign workers, leading to greater social distance. See Epple Schmitter (1979: 235).
7. Chancellor Schmidt at that time denounced 'the cynicist exploitation of a certain latent xenophobia by the Ministerpräsident in Stuttgart and in München' (Vorstand 1980: 50). For Baden-Württemberg see Meier-Braun (1979); for the education debate see Rist (1978: 206–22) on Bavaria.
8. Frankfurter Rundschau 203, 3 September 1992.
9. A more recent evaluation is Klaus Bade, *Ausländer, Aussiedler, Asyl. Eine Bestandsaufnahme* (Bade 1994: 161 ff.)
10. The original concept is from Lipset and Rokkan (1967).
11. In that sense, two politicians leaving the Berlin CDU because of the campaign reported about the ongoing discourse in the CDU as: 'The Turks don't vote for us anyway.' *In der Partei sagen sie immer: Die Türken wählen uns sowieso nicht* (SZ, 20 January1999).
12. For the categories see Thränhardt (1996: 33–8).
13. Jacobs reports than one group was housed in a former concentration camp.

14. Personal communication with Kees Groenendijk.
15. See Groenendijk (1990: 55–95). He describes the incidents, the different reactions of the mayors in the three cities and the resulting developments, gives an overview about other incidents, and discusses what these early incidents can teach us.
16. Kind information by the head of the Research Department of the Social Services in Rotterdam, Gerard Oude Engbering.
17. A. Donner, 'Nederlanders in het buitenland en het kiesrecht', cited in Jacobs (1998b: 103). For the development see Groenendijk (1987: 23).
18. For the text see Bolkestein (1991). Jabobs (1998a) argues that the change of public opinion began already in the late 1980s.
19. A summary of these points can be found in Entzinger (1994: 93–112). The emphasis of this article is in stark contrast to Entzinger's article of 1985.
20. Kees Groenendijk, letter to the author.
21. Kees Groenendijk, letter to the author. See also the Dutch press in late February/early March 1999, e.g. 'Dijkstal bepleit terugsturen van 23,000 Bosniërs', in NRC Handelsblad, 26 February 1999.
22. See also Pettigrew and Meertens (1996: 3–13). For American parallels see Pettigrew (1989) and Sears (1988); for the usefulness of the concepts 'blatant' and 'subtle' prejudice for Europe see Barker (1982), Bergmann and Erb (1986), and Essed (1990). See also Pettigrew (1998b), Meertens and Pettigrew (1997), and Pettigrew (1997).
23. Karsten (1995: 41), cited after Leiprech and Lutz (1996: 250); see also Doomernijk (1998: 60).
24. See for instance the first page of the social Democratic paper 'De Volkskrant' of 17 April 1999, carrying the title Kwaliteitsverschillen zwarte scholen groot (Large quality differences in black schools).
25. The German situation is interpreted on these lines in detail in Thränhardt et al. (1994). For more recent data see Mehrländer, Ascheberg, and Ueltzhöffer (1996).
26. For the policy, see e.g. Abell, Havelaar, and Dankoor (1997). In this sense, Portes and Rumbaut (1996: 136) agree with 'students of ethnic mobilization . . . that receiving nation-states play a crucial role in the rise of ethnicity through their defining and treating various groups differently'.
27. Günter Hinken is presently writing a doctoral thesis on foreigners' participation in the factory councils at Osnabrück Graduiertenkolleg.
28. This can be particularly observed in the official policy document 'Policy on the Integration of Ethnic Minorities' of 1993. Again and again, it speaks of a 'multicultural society' and the need for more cohesion and 'integration' without ever defining the borders of the concept. At the end there is talk of a need for 'redistribution of the vital social resources of employment and income, education and housing', but there are not concrete commitments' for any particular steps in that direction.

29. Sometimes this extends into scientific interpretation. In his comparative study on discrimation, Doomernik applauds critical German literature on discrimination in that country. However, he explains the much larger deficits in The Netherlands with a lack of 'cultural capital' at the side of the immigrants (Doomernik 1998: 65).

References

ABELL, J. P., HAVELAAR, A. E., and DANKOOR, M. M. (1997), *The Documentation and Evaluation of Anti-Discrimination Training Activies in the Netherlands* (Geneva, ILO: International Migration Papers 16).

BADE, KLAUS (1987), *Population, Labour and Migration in 19th and 20th century Germany* (Oxford: Berg).

——(1994), *Ausländer, Aussiedler, Asyl. Eine Bestandsaufnahme* (Munich: Beck).

BAGLEY, CHRISTOPHER (1973), *The Dutch Plural Society: a Comprehensive Study in Race Relations* (London: Oxford University Press).

BARKER, MARTIN (1982), *The New Racism: Conservative and the Ideology of the Tribe* (Frederick).

BERGMANN, WERNER, and ERB, RAINER (1986), 'Kommunikationslatenz. Moral und öffentliche Meinung', *Kölner Zeitschrift für Soziologie und Sozialpsychologie*, 223–46.

BOEHNING, WOLF R., and ZERS DE BEIJL, R. (1995), *The Integration of Migrant Workers in the Labour Market: Policies and Their Impact* (Geneva, ILO: International Migration Papers 8).

BOLKENSTEIN, FRITS (1991), 'Integratie van minderheden moet met lef worden angepakt', *De Volkskrant*, 12 September, 1991.

BOVENKERK, FRANK, GRAS, M. J. I., and RAMSOEDH, D. (1995), *Discrimination against Migrant Workers and Ethnic Minorities in Access to Employment in the Netherlands* (Geneva, ILO: International Migration Papers 4).

CSU (CHRISTIAN SOCIAL UNION) (1998), 'Ausländerwahlrecht schafft Mehrheit für Rot-Grün', *Frankfurter Allgemeine Zeitung*, 22 September, 1998.

DOOMERNIK, JEROEN (1998), *The Effectiveness of Integration Policies towards Immigrants and Their Descendents in France, Germany and The Netherlands* (Geneva, ILO: International Migration Papers 27).

ENTZINGER, HAN (1985), 'The Netherlands', in Tomas Hammar (ed.), *European Immigration Policy. A Comparative Study* (Cambridge).

——(1992), 'Einwanderung in den Niederlanden. Vom Multikulturalismus zur Integration', in Friedrich-Ebert-Stiftung (ed.) *Einwanderungsland Deutschland. Bisherige Ausländer- und Asylpolitik. Vergleich mit anderen Ländern* (Bonn: Friedrich-Ebert-Stiftung).

——(1994), 'Shifting Paradigms: An Appraisal of Immigration in the Netherlands', in Heinz Fassmann, and Rainer Münz (eds.) *European Migration in the Late Twentieth Century* (Aldershot: Edward Elgar).

EPPLE SCHMITTER, BARBARA (1979), *Immigration and Citizenship in West Germany and Switzerland*, Ph. D. Thesis, University of Chicago.

ESSED, PHILOMENA (1990), *Everyday Racism. Labour Market Discrimination against Foreign Workers in Germany* (Geneva, ILO).

GOLDBERG, ANDREAS, MOURINHO, DORA, and KULKE, URSULA (1996), *Labour Discrimination against Foreign Workers and Ethnic Minorities in Germany* (Geneva, ILO).

GROENENDIJK, KEES (1985), 'Minderheitenpolitik in den Niederlanden', in Dietrich Thränhardt (ed.), *Ausländerpolitik und Ausländerintegration in Belgien, den Niederlanden und der Bundesrepublik Deutschland* (Dusseldorf: Landeszentrale für Politische Bildung NRW).

——(1987), 'Vom Ausländer zum Mitbürger. Die symbolische und faktische Bedeutung des Wahlrechts für ausländische Immigranten', *Zeitschrift für Ausländerrecht und Ausländerpolitik*, 21–5.

——(1990), 'Verboden voor Tukkers, Reacties op rellen tussen Italianen, Spanjaarden und Twentenaren in 1961', in Frank Bovenkerk *et al.* (eds.), *Wetenschap en Partijdigheid. Opstellen voor André J. F. Köbben* (Assen/Maastricht: Van Gorcum).

——(1999), 'Ausländerwahlrecht und Einbürgerung in den Niederlanden: ein pragmatischer Kompromiss zur politischen Integration der Ausländer', in Ulrike Davy (ed.), *Einwanderung und politische Integration der ausländischen Wohnbevölkerung* (Baden-Baden: Nomos).

HAGEDORN, HEIKE (1998), 'Wer darf Mitglied werden? Einbürgerung in Deutschland und Frankreich', in Dietrich Thränhardt (ed.), *Einwanderung und Einbürgung in Deutschland. Yearbook Migration 1997/98* (Münster: LIT), 15–63.

——(1999), 'Falling Borders, Liberal Trends in German Naturalization Policy', Conference Paper 'Magnet Societies. Immigration in Postwar Germany and the United States', SMU Dallas, 1–2 March 1999, http://www,smu.edu/-tower/twrann.html.

HARRIS, PAUL (1998), 'Jewish Immigration to the New Germany. The Policy Making Process Leading to the Adoption of the 1991 Quota Refugee Law', in Dietrich Thränhardt (ed.), *Einwanderung und Einbürgerung in Deutschland* (Munster: LIT Verlag).

HEIJS, ERIC (1995), *Van vreemdeling tot Nederlander. De verlening van het Nederlanderschap ann vreemdelingen 1813–1992* (Amsterdam: Het Spinhuis).

HINKEN, GÜNTER (1998), 'Die Rolle der Staatsangehörigkeit bei der Konzeption des Grundgesetzes' in Dietrich Thränhardt (ed.), *Einwanderung und Einbürgerung in Deutschland* (Munster: LIT Verlag).

HIRSCHMAN, ALBERT O. (1994). 'Social Conflicts as Pillars of Democratic Society', *Political Theory*, 22: 203–18.

INSTITUT FÜR DEMOSKOPIE ALLENSBACH (IDA) (ed.) (1985), *Zwischen Toleranz und Besorgtheit. Einstellungen der deutschen Bevölkerung zu aktuellen Problemen der Ausländerpolitik* (Allensbach: IDA).

JACOBS, DIRK (1998a), 'Discourse, Politics and Policy: The Dutch Parliamentary Debate about Voting Rights for Foreign Residents', *International Migration Review*, 32: 350–73.

JACOBS, DIRK (1998b), *Nieuwkomers in de Politiek. Het parlementair debat omtrent kiesrecht voor vreemdelingen in Nederland en België (1970–1997)* (Gent: Academia Press).

KARSTEN, SJOERD (1995), 'Concentratie en segregatie in het Nederlandse basisonderwijs', *Pedagogisch Tijdschrift*, 20.

KIEHL, MELANIE, and WERNER, HEINZ (1998), 'Die Arbeitsmarktsituation von EU-Bürgern und Angehörigen von Drittstaaten in der EU', *IAB-Werkstattberichte*, 7.

LAFONTAINE, OSKAR (1990), 'Vorwort', in Karl A. Otto (ed.), *Westwärts—heimwärts? Aussiedlerpolitik zwischen 'Deutschtümelei' und 'Verfassungsauftrag'* (Bielefeld: AJZ).

LEIPRECHT, RUDOLF, and LUTZ, HELMA (1996), 'The Dutch Way: Mythos und Realität der interkulturellen Pädagogik in den Niederlanden' in Georg Auernheimer and Peter Gsettner (eds.), *Jahrbuch für Pädagogik* (Frankfurt / New York).

LIPSET, S. MARTIN, and ROKKAN STEIN, (1967), 'Cleavages, Structures, Party Systems, and Voter Alignments: An Introduction' in S. Martin Lipset and Rokkan Stein (eds.) *Party Systems and Voter Alignments: Cross National Perspectives* (New York, NY: Free Press).

LOWER HOUSE OF THE STATES GENERAL (1994), *Policy on the Integration of Ethnic Minorities*, The Hague, 11 April 1994. Doc. 23 684.

MEHRLÄNDER, URSULA, ASCHBERG, CARSTEN, and UELTZHÖFFER, JÖRG (1996), *Situation des ausländischen Arbeitnehmer und iher Familienanghörigen in der Bundesrepvblik Deutschand* (Bonn: Bundesministerium für Arbeit).

MEIER-BRAUN, KARL-HEINZ (1979), *Ausländerpolitik am Beispiel der baden-württembergischen Landesregierung* (Munich).

MILES, ROBERT (1996), 'Racism. The Evolution of the Debate about a Concept Changing Times' in Dietrich Thränhardt (ed.), *Europe. A New Immigration Continent. Policies and Politics in Comparative Perspective* (Munster: LIT).

MINISTERIE VAN BINNENLANDSE ZAKEN EN KONINKRIJKSRELATIES (MBZK) (1999), *Minderheidenbeleid 1999. Jaaroverzicht integratiebeleid Etnische Groepen 1999.* (The Hague: Tweede Kamer der Staaten-Generaal. Vergaderjaar 1998–1999, 26210).

PETTIGREW, THOMAS F. (1989), 'The nature of modern racism in the United States', Revue Internationale de Psychologie Sociale: 291–303.

——(1997), 'Generalized intergroup contact effects on prejudice', *Personality and Social Psychology Bulletin*, 173–85.

——(1998), 'Reactions toward the New Minorities of Western Europe', *Annual Review of Sociology*, 77–103.

——and MEERTENS RUND W. (1996), 'The verzuiling puzzle. Understanding Dutch intergroup relations', *Current Psychology*, 3–13.

PORTES, ALEJANDRO, and RUMBAUT, RUBÉN G. (1996), *Immigrant America. A Portrait.* (Berkeley, CA: University of California Press).

PRANTL, HERIBERT (1994), *Deutschland—leicht entflammbar* (Munich: Hanser).

RATH, JAN (1991), *Minorisering: de sociale constructie van 'etnische minderheden'* (Amsterdam).

REX, JOHN (1973), 'Dutch example', *New Society*, 10 May, 1973.

RIST, RAY C. (1978), *Guestworkers in Germany. The Prospects for Pluralism* (New York, NY: Praeger).

SCHMIDT, JOSEF (1996), *Wohlfahrtsverbände in modernen Wohlfahrtsstaaten. Soziale Dienste in historisch-vergleichender Perspektive* (Opladen: Westdeutscher Verlag).

Süddeutsche Zeitung 'Wahlrechtsreform ist Betrug an Deutschen', 219, 23 September.

THIJN, ED VAN, (1997), *Ons kostelijike cultuurbezit. Over tolerantie, non-discriminatie en diversiteit, Oratie* (Leiden: Rijksuniversiteit).

THRÄNHARDT, DIETRICH (1995), 'The Political Uses of Xenophobia in England, France and Germany', *Party Politics*, 321–43.

——(1996), *Europe—A New Immigration Continent. Policies and Politics in Comparative Perspective* (Munster: LIT).

——(1999), 'Germany's Immigration Policies and Politics' in Grete Brochmann and Tomas Hammar (eds.), *Mechanisms of Immigration Control: A Comparative Analysis of European Regulation Policies* (Oxford: Berg).

——DIEREGSWEILER, RENATE, FUNKE, MARTIN, and SANTEL, BERNARD (1994), Ausländerinnen und Ausländer in Nordrhein-Westfalen. Die Lebenslage der Menschen aus den ehemaligen Anwerbeländern und die Handlungsmöglichkeiten der Politik, Düsseldorf 1994 (Landessozialbericht Vol. 6).

VORSTAND DER SPD (ed.) (1980), *Wahlparteitag Essen, 9–10 June 1980. Protokoll* (Bonn: SPD).

WERNER, HEINZ (1993), *Integration ausländischer Arbeitnehmer in den Arbeitsmarkt. Deutschland, Frankreich, Niederlande, Schweden* (Geneva: Institut für Arbeitsmarkt und Berufs forschung).

WETENSCHAPPELIJKE RAAD FOR HET REGERINGSBELEID (WRR) (ed.) (1979), *Ethnic Minorities* (The Hague: WRR).

——(ed.) (1990), *Immigrant Minorities* (The Hague: WRR).

WITTE, JUTTA (1999), 'Hessen wählt: Keine Wendestimmung', *Das Parlament*, 5: 29 January.

WOLKEN, SIMONE (1988), *Das Grundrecht auf Asyl als Gegenstand der Innen- und Rechtspolitik der Bundesrepublik Deutschland* (Frankfurt: Lang).

III

Migrant and Xenophobic Challenges to Migration and Ethnic Relations Politics

9

Challenging the Liberal Nation-State? Postnationalism, Multiculturalism, and the Collective Claims-making of Migrants and Ethnic Minorities in Britain and Germany*

RUUD KOOPMANS and PAUL STATHAM

Introduction

If we are to believe the current *communis opinio* in political philosophy and sociology, the liberal nation-state as we know it is rapidly becoming endangered. While not yet extinct, it is at least in decline or seriously challenged. Two broad processes have been identified as driving this development (Habermas 1996). First, the nation-state's position as the predominant unit of social organization is being eroded from the outside by the forces of globalization, and the shift of the locus of power from the national to the supra- and transnational levels. Second, the nation-state's legitimacy, authority, and integrative capacities are being weakened from within by the increasing pluralization of modern societies. Moreover, the liberal, universalist values that support it are being challenged by claims for special group rights, or exemptions from duties, by a multitude of collective actors who emphasize their cultural difference from the rest of society. Although the normative evaluation of these real or supposed trends differs widely, immigration is invariably seen as one of the main driving forces behind both the external erosion of sovereignty and the internal cultural differentiation of liberal nation-states. For Western European societies, the presence of growing numbers of racially and culturally different migrants is perhaps the most concrete, tangible, and for some most provocative, way in which globalization and pluralization have become manifest features of modern life. This holds also for the traditional immigration countries such as the United States or Australia, which have only recently become the target of larger flows of non-European immigration.

Among scholars contributing to the contemporary debates on citizenship in the migration and ethnic relations field, collective claims-making by migrants and ethnic minorities are viewed as important social forces that actively contribute to, and shape these trends of globalization and pluralization. The collective mobilization of political demands by migrants is often seen as a driving force that is self-evidently carrying such general transformations forward. In this chapter, we do not intend to enter into the extensive debate on the normative and philosophical implications of such developments, nor, obviously, do we want to discuss pluralization and globalization in all their facets. Our specific interest lies with the way in which the claims-making of migrants, and ethnic minorities of migrant origin, affects and is shaped by the tendencies toward pluralization and globalization that supposedly challenge the liberal nation-state.[1] As the theoretical debate on this topic demonstrates, citizenship—the set of rights, duties, roles, and identities linking citizens to the nation-state—undoubtedly plays a crucial role.[2]

Three theoretical positions can be identified, two of which are directly linked to globalization and pluralization. First, some authors (Soysal 1994; Jacobson 1996) have argued that the postwar period has seen the rise of new forms of 'postnational' citizenship that have rendered national citizenship increasingly unimportant, and are based on the transnationalization of migrant communities and the growing role of supranational organizations and conventions that have strengthened the rights of migrants. A second branch of scholarship sees the increased cultural differentiation of nation-states that results from immigration leading to the development of a 'multicultural' citizenship, which gives special rights, recognition, and protection to minority groups and their cultures. How far such special group rights can be reconciled with the liberal basic values of Western nation-states is a highly contentious issue (Kymlicka 1995). And third, parallel to these highly resonant perspectives which emphasize new forms of citizenship that undermine traditional models of national citizenship, there is also a large number of studies that reaffirm the importance of national models of citizenship and that point out important cross-national differences in the modes of inclusion and exclusion of migrants and ethnic minorities (Brubaker 1992; Castles and Miller 1993).

Our aim in this chapter is to confront these three models of citizenship with data on the claims-making of migrants and ethnic minorities in Britain and Germany, two of the most important immigration countries in Europe, for the period 1990–95. Both have large populations of non-European migrants and significant Muslim communities, which makes them relevant cases from the multicultural perspective. As European Union (EU) members, both countries are exposed to the process of European integration, which is invariably referred to as a paradigmatic example in studies of globalization and postnationalism. However, Britain and Germany have very divergent traditions of national identity and citizenship, which also makes them interesting for comparing the impacts of different national models of citizenship.

In the following theoretical sections we first present and discuss the three theoretical approaches in more detail. After a brief discussion of the main features of the politics of migration and ethnic relations in Britain and Germany, we derive hypotheses from the three perspectives on citizenship, regarding the claims-making of migrants and ethnic minorities. We then confront these hypotheses with our data in order to assess the relative merits of the three models and to answer our central question: does the claims-making of migrant minorities constitute a challenge to the liberal nation-state, and if so, what is the nature of the challenge which it presents?

The Postnational Challenge

According to theorists of postnational citizenship, 'Transnational migration is steadily eroding the traditional basis of nation-state membership, namely citizenship. As rights have come to be predicated on residency, not citizen status, the distinction between "citizen" and "alien" has eroded' (Jacobson 1996: 8–9). The primary case in point are the guestworkers in Western Europe. Although originally recruited on a temporary basis during the period of labour shortages between the 1950s and early 1970s, the population of guestworkers and their descendants in Western Europe has continued to grow even after recruitment was formally terminated in the aftermath of the 1973 oil crisis (see for example, Baldwin-Edwards and Schain 1994). Contrary to the original rotation model, many guestworkers became permanent residents and brought over their spouses and children. However, most of them did not become citizens of their new countries of residence. One of the reasons for these low naturalization rates is certainly the fact that these 'denizens' (Hammar 1985) enjoy many of the same civil and social, though not political, rights as full citizens (Bauböck 1994). Postnationalists argue that these rights given to non-citizens derive from the fact that migrants have been able to sustain claims to residence and welfare rights with reference to universal rights of 'personhood' based in international human rights institutions and conventions. It is argued further that these have largely taken over the role of national citizenship as the main source of rights. This has led to a decoupling of identity and rights, the two main elements of citizenship: 'Rights increasingly assume universality, legal uniformity, and abstractness, and are defined at the global level. Identities, in contrast, still express particularity and are conceived of as territorially bounded. As an identity, national citizenship . . . still prevails. But in terms of its translation into rights and privileges, it is no longer a significant construction' (Soysal 1998: 208).

Postnationalists argue that the collective action of migrants plays an active role in the erosion and transcending of the frontiers of nation-states. The increasing speed and density of international communication and transport that are part of globalization have allowed migrants to maintain strong ties with their homelands. Migrant communities increasingly take on the character of transnationally linked diasporas and are well-equipped for taking advantage of the new opportunities of postnational citizenship (Lie 1995; Jacobson 1996; Shain and Sherman 1998). The conclusion Soysal (1998: 210–11) draws from these purported developments leaves no room for doubt regarding the fate of the nation-state, 'In a world within which rights, and identities as rights, derive their legitimacy from discourses of universalistic personhood, the limits of nationness, or of national citizenship, for that matter, become inventively irrelevant.'

Compelling as this view on postnationalism and the role of migrant minorities may be, it has not gone unchallenged. To begin with, a number of authors have pointed out that the transfer of authority to the supra- and transnational levels has not yet progressed to a level where it can seriously challenge the nation-state's prerogatives. More specifically, in migration and ethnic relations politics, the development of common EU policies and co-ordination of the national policies of members states has been highly restricted by the endurance of the different national policy frameworks and attachments to the 'public philosophies' that underpin them (Favell 1998: 245; see also Joppke 1997; Freeman 1998). Even those common policies that have been implemented hardly rank as the benign human rights type that postnationalists cherish. For example, the Schengen Accord, implemented in 1995, is oriented toward better-co-ordinated and stricter controls on unwanted immigration.[3]

In addition, the practical implications of international human and civil rights conventions on the rights of migrants have also been questioned. Thus, Goodwin-Gill, Jenny, and Perruchoud—representatives, respectively, of the United Nations High Commissioner for Refugees (UNHCR) and the Intergovernmental Committee for Migration in Geneva—conclude with regard to these treaties and conventions,

Their generality accommodates many shades of opinion, and what really counts is how the scheme of protection is worked out at the local level, particularly with regard to subsidiary rights and procedural guarantees. . . . Even under the European Convention on Human Rights the jurisprudence adopted . . . and the interpretation of 'civil rights' has sanctioned serious limitations upon non-nationals' entitlement to substantive and procedural due process. Deportation, termination of a residence permit, and the grant or refusal of entry, have all been found by the European Commission not to involve civil rights   (Goodwin-Gill, Jenny, and Perruchoud 1985: 566–8; see also Forbes 1995: 198, 207).

Existing empirical evidence is rather inconclusive regarding which of these contrasting views on the role of supranational and national contexts for the claims-making of migrants and ethnic minorities is closer to the truth.

Against the evidence brought forward for the continuing relevance of the nation-state as a frame of reference for migrant mobilization, postnationalists point to cases where migrants frame their claims in terms of universal human rights and have successfully appealed to supranational courts to prevent or overturn national incursions on their rights (see Soysal 1994, 1997 for examples). However, such evidence remains unsystematic and often does not go much beyond the discussion of a few, supposedly representative, examples.

The Multicultural Challenge

Theories on postnationalism are linked in two important ways to multicultural citizenship. First, postnationalists argue that international conventions providing for a right to one's own culture have greatly improved the opportunities for migrants and ethnic minorities to push for the recognition of their cultural difference by the nation-state. Second, if the postnational observation is correct, that ethnic communities increasingly take the form of transnational diasporas with strong ties to the homeland, then it follows that traditional models for integrating migrants through assimilation into the majority culture will no longer work (Kymlicka 1995: 9).

In the discussion of multiculturalism as a challenge to the liberal nation-state, it is not the nation-state's external sovereignty that is at stake, but its capacity to maintain social cohesion and the liberal conception of individual rights on which it rests. Again, the claims-making of ethnic minorities is seen as a central aspect of this challenge: 'Minorities and majorities increasingly clash over such issues as language rights, regional autonomy, political representation, education curriculum, land claims, immigration and naturalization policy, even national symbols, such as the choice of national anthem or public holidays. Finding morally defensible and politically viable answers to these issues is the greatest challenge facing democracies today' (Kymlicka 1995: 1). These problems are seen as arising from the fact that migrant minorities increasingly put forward demands for special group rights, and recognition and support for their cultural difference and identity by the state. Such claims are often seen as challenges to the very essence of liberal values, for instance, when Muslims demand the right to polygamy, the circumcision of females, or the banning of Salman Rushdie's *Satanic Verses* (Parekh 1996). In making such demands, migrant minorities challenge the conception of a unified, undifferentiated citizenship, a development that is viewed by supporters as a healthy and necessary antidote against the prevalent 'white' cultural hegemony (for example, Young 1998) or as a serious assault on the shared communal values and solidarity necessary for social cohesion and integration (for example, Schlesinger 1992).

We shall not dwell on the normative arguments made by these and many other participants in the debate, either for or against the granting of differential, multicultural citizenship rights to migrant minorities. Such questions are beyond the scope of this chapter. However, it seems to be an issue of consensus that, normatively justifiable or not, disquieting or not, claims for cultural group rights are central to the claims-making of present-day migrants and ethnic minorities. For opponents of further immigration, this is a result of the too strong cultural differences of recent, non-European migrants, which put strain on both the migrants' adaptive capabilities and the host society's integrative capacities. From the point of view of advocates of a multicultural citizenship, it reflects the fact that exclusion in modern societies is primarily a result of discrimination or biases against groups' cultural difference, and is no longer primarily a function of socioeconomic inequality and a lack of social and political citizenship rights.

Systematic empirical evidence that would allow us to ascertain the relative importance and nature of claims for cultural group rights both cross-nationally and compared to other types of claims is once more in scarce supply. Unfortunately, the high level of philosophical sophistication in the debate on multiculturalism is not matched at the empirical level. The claim that immigration and ethnic minority mobilization have led to pressures toward a differentiation of citizenship that is serious enough to potentially destabilize the liberal nation-state, remains at present no more than an assertion. The usual references to ethnic strife in Bosnia, Rwanda, or the former Soviet Union are quite irrelevant to the context of immigration in Western societies. Examples drawn from more relevant contexts are usually anecdotal and extremely repetitive between studies. Open a random book on ethnic minorities and multiculturalism and you have a fair chance of stumbling across the nth account of the French headscarf (*foulard*) and the British Rushdie affairs. To what extent such spectacular examples are representative for the wider claims-making of migrants and ethnic minorities remains unclear.[4]

National Citizenship Regimes for Incorporating Migrants

In the 1990s, comparative research refocused academic attention on the importance of citizenship rights for explaining the different national approaches in liberal democratic states for regulating immigration and the presence of foreign migrants. Not surprisingly with increasing European integration, these debates often see contemporary Western Europe as the empirical testing ground for hypotheses on why countries with ostensibly similar flows of immigration and numbers of immigrants continue to maintain different ways of attributing citizenship rights to non-nationals. An important stimulus to this lively debate on citizenship regimes and the immigration challenge to the nation-state is the work of Rogers Brubaker (1992).[5]

At a time when the rationale of EU integration calls for convergence, Brubaker points out that national regimes for incorporating non-nationals within a system of political and social rights remain, paradoxically, divergent. To explain the endurance of this national variance in citizenship regimes he draws attention to the cultural foundations of nation-states as ties that restrain and bind a community through nationhood. Brubaker's comparison of France and Germany shows that a state's legal definition for citizenship bears a distinct embedded cultural imprint of nationhood. He contrasts the *jus sanguinis* legal tradition for citizenship, where membership is acquired on the basis of ethnic descent, with *jus soli* where it is a territorial birth right. Whereas *jus sanguinis* is resistant to converts by enforcing social closure on the basis of the prescribed collective identity of national ethnicity, *jus soli* citizenship permits a contractual assimilation by an individual to nationhood, either by ritual conversion or automatically by birth. Brubaker's historical study defines Germany as a case of pure *jus sanguinis*, where citizenship rights are still based on ethnocultural belonging to nationhood. He sees France, on the other hand, as a country where citizenship is a mixture of *jus sanguinis* and *jus soli*, but where *jus soli* is strongly dominant and encoded in the Jacobin republican civic concept of nationhood.

Brubaker argues that these deeply embedded national self-definitions of citizenship continue to shape the divergent political responses of nation-states to migrants. He cites the persistently higher naturalization rates in France compared to Germany as empirical evidence that citizenship regimes are the best explanation for the national strategies that the two countries maintain for incorporating migrants.

Extending Brubaker's analyses, a number of scholars have analyzed the citizenship configurations of nation-states as the explanatory variable for responses to the challenge of incorporating ethnic difference.[6] A considerable degree of consensus exists on the 'types' of different citizenship regimes. Typically, these distinguish between two important dimensions of citizenship that can be seen to determine the degree and form of inclusiveness/exclusiveness of a national regime in relation to ethnic difference: first, the criteria for formal access to citizenship; and second, the cultural obligations that this access to citizenship entails. The first dimension relates to the distinction between an ethnocultural (*jus sanguinis*) and a civic territorial (*jus soli*) basis of criteria for attributing full citizenship, with the ethnocultural being the more 'closed' and civic territorial the more 'open' version. The second dimension relates to the distinction between assimilationism and cultural pluralism as the condition which a state places on attributing citizenship, with assimilationism being the more 'demanding' and cultural pluralism the more 'accepting'. By combining these dimensions one arrives at three ideal-type citizenship regimes that can be related to specific examples of European countries: the ethnocultural exclusionist, civic assimilationist, and the multicultural pluralist.

Within the Western European context, the ethnocultural exclusionist citizenship regime is best approached by Germany. Due to the absence of access to citizenship by territorial birth and relatively high hurdles to naturalization, foreign migrants find it difficult to obtain full citizenship rights and thereby join the national community.[7] In Germany, hundreds of thousands of German-born descendants of migrants are still officially 'foreigners' (Ausländer) without full political rights. Ethnic German immigrants (Aussiedler) newly arriving from Russia, on the other hand, receive full social and political rights on the basis of a hereditary link to the nation. By contrast, France has a civic-assimilationist regime, where the state offers easy access to full rights to migrants, but at the same time is loathe to accept cultural pluralism. In return for rights, migrants are expected to place allegiance to French republican values and political culture above allegiances to religious identity or ethnic belonging. French republicanism is a universalizing secular religion and ethnic collective organization has been officially accepted by the state only since 1981, which places restrictions on the form and strategic orientation of ethnic mobilization. Finally, multicultural-pluralist citizenship is represented in the European context by Britain, Sweden, and The Netherlands. Here, the state not only offers easy access to full social and political rights, but actually sponsors ethnic difference by recognizing immigrant groups as 'ethnic minorities' with their own cultural rights and privileges. For example, in The Netherlands, recognized ethnic communities have had the right to set up their own schools and to receive funding from the state.

The key question, of course, is whether these different national traditions have significant consequences for migrants. Brubaker's answer to this question is lucidly put. According to his formula, citizenship is less a system for attributing rights, and more a contested political field for redefining the symbolic boundary markers for a national identity: 'The politics of citizenship today is first and foremost politics of nationhood. . . . It pivots more on self-understanding than on self-interest. The "interests" informing the politics of citizenship are "ideal" rather than material. The central question is not "who gets what?" but "who is what?" ' (1994: 182). Here Brubaker correctly points out the importance of the signification process in structuring the relationship of migrants to the nation-state. This is well demonstrated by the different labels which national policies have applied to migrants: Ausländer (foreigners) in Germany; immigrés (immigrants) in France; etnische minderheden (ethnic minorities) in The Netherlands. However, Brubaker's emphasis on citizenship as primarily a politics of symbolic interaction obscures the real, material consequences that such ascribed identities may have. The different symbolic labels that nations attribute to migrants directly influence the distribution of material resources to them, and their potential for mobilizing challenges and participating within the political community of a society. It makes a difference whether one is a 'foreigner', an 'immigrant' or an 'ethnic minority'; these are not just symbols, but forms of social relationships that legitimate and facilitate certain types of participation in society, while delegitimating and negatively conditioning others. Similarly, racism and discrimination are not simply the drawing of a symbolic boundary marker, but actions that structure the life chances of those affected, leading to systematic—and material!—social disadvantage. Incorporating anti-racist and antidiscrimination legislation into citizenship rights, and enforcing them, does affect 'who gets what?' perhaps more centrally than 'who is what?' Contrary to Brubaker, there are important material interests at stake in citizenship rights. The resources of access to the political community, not least of which are voting rights, may indeed make a significant difference in the potential of migrant actors to mobilize and press their claims for social and political change.

However, surprisingly little systematic and comparative empirical work has been done to show how national political contexts impinge upon the collective actions and claims-making of migrants and ethnic minorities (Rex and Drury 1994). One of the very few comparative studies to empirically address the important question of political mobilization is Ireland's (1994) study of forms of political activism by migrants in France and Switzerland. Ireland uses the concept 'institutional channeling' for how different national forms of participatory mechanisms in which citizenship rights are fundamental, shape migrant political activism over time. He finds that similar migrant groups mobilize differently in the two countries, which makes institutional channeling a better explanation for mobilization forms than either ethnic origin or social class.

The perspectives that we have discussed in this section claim that different configurations of citizenship are embedded in national political and civic institutional frameworks, and that these have important consequences both for the incorporation of migrants and for political mobilization over ethnic difference. Before testing the relevance of these claims, it is necessary to give more contextual details on the two countries on which our empirical analysis focuses.

Comparing Britain and Germany: Similarities and Differences

Britain and Germany are well suited for testing hypotheses regarding the relevance of citizenship for the political claims-making of migrants and ethnic minorities. Taking the three different national citizenship regimes that we have discussed, they are opposite cases. Germany is a country with ethnocultural exclusionist citizenship, where non-ethnic German migrants are incorporated into the labour market, but where it is difficult for them to attain access to the political community. In contrast, Britain's citizenship model tends more toward the multicultural pluralist ideal-type, where most resident minorities have full equal social and political rights, while retaining much of their cultural difference from the majority society. To put at least some flesh on the bones of these schematic characterizations, we now look briefly at some contemporary aspects of the respective citizenship regimes, patterns and forms of immigration, as well as different policy approaches for integration.[8]

Historically, the countries have experienced broadly comparable patterns of immigration flows. Both sponsored large-scale foreign immigration due to labor shortages from the 1950s until the economic crisis in the early 1970s, when restrictive immigration controls were implemented and maintained. Many of the migrants in Germany came as a result of the 'guestworker' system for importing foreign labour. This produced an official policy that assumed that these 'guests' would one day return to their homelands, and so policies for integration were minimal. In contrast, many of the migrants to Britain were already subjects of the British Commonwealth and until 1971 they automatically received equal political and social rights.[9] Since 1965 race relations policies in the UK have officially taken measures to combat racism and discrimination and to promote social integration, thus acknowledging that political equality has not led to full equal treatment.

In 1995, the percentage of foreign migrants relative to total population amounted to 8.8 per cent in Germany compared to 3.4 per cent in Britain. The higher proportion of foreigners relative to nationals in Germany compared to Britain illustrates an important outcome of the different citizenship regimes. In Germany, most migrants are counted as foreigners, as there are higher restrictions placed on naturalization than in Britain—between 8 and 15 years' residence compared to 5 years—and dual citizenship is not a possibility. Between 1990 and 1995, the proportion of naturalizations per foreign population was higher in Britain than in Germany—between 2.0 and 3.4 per cent per annum compared to between 0.4 and 0.7 per cent (SOPEMI 1997). Moreover, the *jus sanguinis* restrictions in Germany are aptly demonstrated by the fact that in 1997 the number of 'foreigners' increased, despite conditions of negative net immigration. The net gain of new foreigners were born in Germany of migrant parentage. As a result of these differences, the percentage of foreigners in Britain grossly underestimates the size of the minority population. In fact, Britain and Germany have similar sizes of minority populations of migrant origin: estimates put the overall migrant population in Britain at about 8 per cent of the total population or about 4.5 million (Castles 1995: 300) compared to the 8.8 per cent or 7 million for Germany in 1995. This, of course, makes them suitable candidates for comparing the impact of citizenship configurations on migrant mobilization.

The countries of origin of the minority populations differ widely in the two countries. Today in Germany, the main foreigner groups are from Turkey—more than one-third—from the former Yugoslavia—one-quarter—and from

Italy, Greece, and Poland. In Britain, one-quarter of the 'ethnic minorities' are British-born African-Caribbeans and a half are South Asians. It should be pointed out, however, that both migrant populations contain ethnic and religious groups that may be taken as functional equivalents. For example, both the large Turkish community in Germany and the Pakistanis and Bangladeshis in Britain, who constitute about one-quarter of the minority population, are predominantly Muslim.

Nowadays, immigration to both countries is basically limited to family reunions and refugees, asylum seekers, or special cases.[10] An important exception to this rule in Germany are the immigrants of ethnic German origin (*Aussiedler*) who receive automatic full citizenship on arrival despite their distinct cultural difference in many cases. The collapse of Communism in the East has brought new flows of *Aussiedler*, totaling more than 2 million in the 1990s.

The major difference between the two countries is in the political strategies for integrating minority populations. These incorporation regimes reflect the two different traditions of citizenship to which these countries belong. As a result of their exclusion from formal citizenship, migrants and their organizations—under the label of 'foreigners'—play a marginal role in the German political process. In Britain, by contrast, migrant organization and political participation—under the label of 'ethnic or racial minorities'—is facilitated by the state, and a state-sponsored 'race relations' industry has emerged backed by antidiscrimination legislation, the authority of the Commission for Racial Equality, and local bodies which report and advise on practices for ensuring equal treatment, particularly in the labour market.[11] It is worth emphasizing that 'race' is a category that British political élites adopted when attempting to address the discrimination and disadvantage suffered by the minority population. This 'racialization' of policy measures in part reflected the fear of political élites that British race riots might escalate to the crisis point of those experienced in the United States. An outcome of this is that British policies were more tailored to the integration of African-Caribbeans under the generic umbrella term 'black' than the relatively later inflows of migrants from the Indian subcontinent, in particular Pakistan (Rex 1991). Race relations politics has been extended to Indians, Pakistanis, and Bangladeshis under the generic term 'Asian', which implies that groups with a self-identification that is non-racial, the prime example being groups with a Muslim identity, have been served relatively less well by the institutional apparatus (Modood 1988).

Another point worth making about the British case is that the constituency-based electoral system has provided the large concentrations of minority communities in specific towns and regions with a considerable resource base of voting power for influencing individual Members of Parliament, and has in turn led political parties to take up issues relating to ethnic minorities. At the local level of politics, minorities have also made a considerable impact in specific regions (see for example, Solomos and Back 1995).

By contrast, Germany has maintained a different policy approach in which migrants are excluded from political participation. Apart from the powerless and marginal foreigners' councils (*Ausländerbeiräte*) at the local level, foreigners in Germany have no institutionalized channels of access to the political process. The German state does not provide the kind of facilitation to migrant organizations that many of their British counterparts receive. There is no institutional focus for minority claims in the form of an official minority, racial equality, or antidiscrimination politics that might legitimate migrant demands and identify responsible authorities for their implementation. The official mantra—'Germany is not an immigration country'—therefore has real consequences for the opportunities for minority claims-making.

Data Retrieval

To investigate the political claims-making of migrants and ethnic minorities in Britain and Germany, we use data drawn from content analyses of daily newspapers in the two countries.[12] In contrast to many media content analyses, we are not primarily interested in the way in which the media frame events. On the contrary, our focus is on the news coverage of mobilization, public statements, and other forms of claims-making by non-media actors. Taking a cue from 'protest event analysis' in the study of social movements (Olzak 1989; Tarrow 1989; Rucht, Koopmans, and Neidhardt 1998), our units of analysis are not articles but individual instances of claims-making. Although we focus here on claims-making by migrant minorities, our larger data set includes the whole spectrum of claims-making acts related to immigration, minority integration, and xenophobia, irrespective of the actors involved. This includes civil society groups such as anti-racist and human rights organizations or labour unions, but also political parties and state actors, including the police, courts, legislatures, local and national governments, and supranational institutions. Instances of claims-making have been included irrespective of their form, and range from violent attacks on other groups, public demonstrations and legal action, to public statements.

Acts were included in the data if they involved demands, criticisms, or proposals related to the regulation or evaluation of immigration, minority integration, or xenophobia. Because of our special interest in minority claims-making, we included acts by resident ethnic minorities even if they were not related to these issues—provided, of course, that they involved some political claim. This in particular allowed us to include the claims-making of migrants related to the politics of their homelands.[13] Regarding territorial criteria we included acts in Britain and Germany,[14] respectively, even if they were made by foreign actors or addressed to foreign or supranational authorities, and also acts made outside Britain or Germany, but addressed to actors in these countries.[15]

Both types of acts were considered to be claims in the British or German public spheres.[16]

For the comparative analysis here, we use data drawn from every second issue (Monday, Wednesday, Friday) of the *Guardian* for Britain, and the *Frankfurter Rundschau* for Germany for the six-year period 1990–95.[17] These papers were chosen because they are of a comparable, moderately left-liberal political affiliation and because, compared to other national quality newspapers, they have the most encompassing coverage of the specific issues of interest. Of course, when using newspapers as a source one has to deal with the problem of selection, as not all events that occur receive coverage, and description bias, as events may get covered in a distorted way; for these issues see McCarthy, McPhail, and Smith (1996). We have tried to minimize the problem of description bias by explicitly basing the coding only on the factual coverage of statements and events in newspaper articles, and leaving out any comments and evaluations made by reporters or editors. In any case, quality newspapers have to protect their reputation and cannot afford to quote claims patently incorrectly. Since our interest here is in publicly visible claims-making, the problem of selection bias is less aggravating than in some other contexts, because acts of claims-making become relevant and potentially controversial only when they reach the public sphere.

However, it may be that our sources have specific biases that make the data drawn from them unrepresentative for the print-media landscape at large. To check for such biases, we have in each of the two countries drawn additional samples from other newspaper sources. In Germany, we coded two years of the right-wing tabloid *Bild Zeitung*, one year of the German-published edition of the Turkish daily *Hürriyet*, as well as four-month samples from three different local dailies. In Britain we have coded a cross-section of six national newspapers for the year 1995.[18] Comparisons among these sources confirm that our two main sources give relatively broad coverage to issues of immigration and ethnic relations. It is important to note that the sometimes large differences in coverage rates do not lead to very different distributions of acts on important variables. As an example we may take the *Frankfurter Rundschau* and the *Bild Zeitung*, which occupy diametrically opposed positions in the German print-media landscape, on both the Left/Right, and quality/tabloid dimensions. The number of reported claims in the domain of immigration and ethnic relations turns out to be 4.6 times higher in the *Rundschau* than in the *Bild Zeitung*. However, distributions across different issues, such as asylum, integration, or anti-racism, hardly differ among the two papers and neither does the representation of different actors in the coverage.[19] In as far as minor differences exist, they run in a direction that is helpful rather than harmful for our purposes. Thus, the *Bild Zeitung* has a somewhat stronger focus on national actors to the detriment of regional and local ones, and a somewhat weaker coverage of acts by minority actors—4.5 per cent vs. 6.8 per cent for the *Rundschau*. Our main source thus is somewhat less selective when it comes to covering the claims making of more marginal actors.

These similarities and minor differences concur with large differences in the evaluation of events, as is revealed by a comparison of editorials in both papers. Taking the issue of asylum, 70 per cent of *Bild Zeitung* editorials favored restrictions in the rights of asylum seekers, while 70 per cent of *Rundschau* editorials opposed such restrictions. However different these newspapers' political stances may have been, they had marginal effects on coverage. Of statements by other actors reported in the *Bild Zeitung* an average of 56 per cent were in favour of restrictions, against 48 per cent for the *Rundschau*. We may conclude, therefore, that our strategy of focusing on factual coverage and ignoring newspapers' framing and commenting of events, reduces biases that may effect the variables we are interested in to such an extent that we can safely conclude that our main sources give a representative picture of public claims-making on immigration and ethnic relations.[20]

Hypotheses

In the remainder of this chapter, we will use our data on migrant and ethnic minority claims-making to test the validity of the three theoretical views on the link between citizenship and migration. Although these perspectives are not as such theories of ethnic mobilization, minority claims-making figures centrally in theories of postnational and multicultural citizenship, both as a cause and as a consequence of shifts in the nature of citizenship away from the traditional unitary form of national citizenship. While the national citizenship model discusses ethnic mobilization less centrally, it also implies clear expectations about the nature of, and cross-national differences in ethnic minority claims-making. Thus, each of the three theoretical configurations of citizenship is associated with a particular pattern of minority claims-making.

As we have seen, migrants and ethnic minorities are seen by those who proclaim the advance of a postnationalist or multicultural citizenship as actors who, through their claims-making, make important contributions to these trends. Thus a high level of 'postnational' or 'multicultural' claims-making by migrants and minorities may be regarded as direct supportive evidence for these models. As indicators of postnational claims-making we will look at the prevalence of transnational collective identities and organizations, the degree to which claims are addressed at authorities beyond the nation-state, and the extent to which the substance of minority claims refers to supra- or transnational institutions and conventions. As indicators of multicultural claims-making we regard the degree to which minorities collectively identify themselves along cultural, and particularly religious, lines and the extent to which their claims-making focuses on extensions of cultural rights.

The three modes of citizenship can also be seen as political opportunity structures (McAdam 1982; Tarrow 1994; Kriesi *et al.* 1995) that shape the mobilization of migrants and minorities by facilitating some and constraining other forms of claims-making. Thus, the increased institutionalization of postnational and multicultural institutions, rights, and discourses implies increased opportunities for migrants and minorities for advancing postnational and multicultural claims of the kind indicated above. On the contrary, the national citizenship model implies that migrant and minority claims-making will be strongly affected by the opportunities and constraints for intervening in the public sphere set by the institutions, rights, and discourses that derive from nationally-specific modes of incorporation of migrants into the political community through citizenship. From these general expectations we can draw a number of concrete hypotheses relating to specific aspects of migrant and ethnic minority claims-making.

Hypothesis 1

At the most general level, the national citizenship model leads us to expect important differences in patterns of claims-making of migrant minorities between Germany and Britain as a result of the different ways in which migrants and minorities are incorporated into or excluded from the nation-state. The postnational citizenship model, by contrast, leads us to expect similarities between the two countries because of the fact that migrants' claims-making increasingly depends on the opportunities provided by universal human rights, which are defined and encoded at the supranational level and thus are not fundamentally different for minorities in Britain or in Germany. Although theories of multicultural citizenship are less explicit in this regard, they also lead us to expect cross-national similarities rather than differences. The affirmation of cultural difference by ethnic minorities and the concomitant rise of claims to differential citizenship rights are seen as trends affecting modern Western societies in general.[21]

Hypothesis 2.1

The type of minority actors involved in claims making may be distinguished along two dimensions of theoretical relevance: (2.1) the kind of collective identities they mobilize, and (2.2) the territorial scope of their organizations.

The first actor dimension refers to collective identities. The kind of collective identities that migrant minorities put forward in their claims-making are not self-evident, but signify specific constructions of the group's image of itself and its relation to the wider society, including other migrant groups. Moreover, identities and labels may be strategically used in such a way that the impact and legitimacy of claims is optimized. Since the multicultural model sees cultural difference as the primary source of minority claims making, we would expect cultural and religious forms of identification to dominate. The national citizenship model would again expect different outcomes in different national contexts, depending on which collective identities are sponsored and excluded, respectively, by the national model of migrant incorporation. In the British context, this leads to the expectation that migrants will primarily make claims on the basis of identification with one of the two officially recognized racial groups, 'blacks' and 'Asians'. To a lesser extent, British multiculturalism may also further claims-making on a cultural or religious basis. Homeland-based forms of identification should be relatively rare in Britain. In Germany, however, we would expect the collective identities of 'foreigners' to match precisely homeland-based categories, either through nationality such as the Turkish community in Berlin, homeland-based political affiliation such as the Turkish Communist Party, or homeland-based ethnic cleavages such as Kurdish nationalist groups.[22]

Hypothesis 2.2

Regarding the territorial scope of migrant organizations, postnationalism theories, which emphasize the transnationalization of ethnic communities, predict a significant involvement of actors that transcend the national context. These may be either international, such as the World Council of Roma and Sinti; Europewide, such as the European Association of Turkish Acadamics; homeland-based, such as the National Resistance Council of Iran,[23] or otherwise foreign-based, such as the American Jewish Committee. The national citizenship model, by contrast, does not see an important role for transnational actors. The involvement of homeland-based actors, however, would depend on the kind of national citizenship regime. In countries such as Germany, where immigrants continue to be defined as foreigners and have few opportunities to participate in German political life, we might expect migrants to remain strongly tied to their homelands, which might in turn strengthen the position of homeland-based organizations. In more inclusive countries such as Britain, where most migrants are citizens, and the state sponsors migrant and minority organizations that operate within the British political process, we might expect homeland-based organizations to play a relatively modest role.

Hypothesis 3

We can formulate hypotheses about the addressees of claims if we take into account the three perspectives on citizenship—postnational, multicultural, and national.[24] When looking at addressees, we can formulate hypotheses similar to those for the territorial scope of migrant organizations. Once more, the postnational model leads us to expect that, to an important extent, migrant minorities direct their claims at authorities that transcend national borders. These may be either international, such as the UNHCR, European, such as the European Parliament, or represent a foreign state, for example, the Turkish government. By contrast, from the national citizenship model we may draw the expectation that political authorities within the national polity are the most important addressees of claims. In Germany, we may in addition, expect a significant number of claims addressed at the authorities of migrants' homelands, linked to the persistence of homeland-based organizations and collective identities discussed above.

Hypothesis 4.1

Regarding the content of claims made by migrants and ethnic minorities, we ask a number of different questions. First, we look at the relative importance of migrant claims-making on immigration and ethnic relations, compared to migrant claims-making on homeland issues, and all claims-making on immigration and ethnic relations.

For the relation between migrants' claims-making on issues related to the countries of residence and of origin, respectively, the national citizenship model allows us to derive a clear expectation. We might expect the importance of homeland-related issues to depend on the degree to which migrants are symbolically included in the national political community and materially incorporated into the political process of their countries of residence. Thus, we expect a stronger emphasis on homeland issues in Germany, and a stronger orientation toward issues relating to integration into the host society in Britain. We shall interpret a strong and relatively similar representation of homeland issues in both countries as support for the postnational model. It is plausible to expect that the transnationalization of ethnic communities also leads them to retain a substantive interest in the politics of their homeland countries.

Hypothesis 4.2

Regarding the contribution of migrants to the overall claims-making on immigration and ethnic relations, both the postnational and multicultural model hypothesize a relatively important role for migrants and ethnic minorities. After all, their claims-making is supposed to be an active force in the emergence of new, postnational, or multicultural forms of citizenship that challenge the liberal nation-state. The national citizenship model would again say that it depends on the national context. In inclusive countries such as Britain, where minorities are citizens and their involvement in the political process is facilitated by the state, migrant and minority claims-making might be expected to be relatively important. Where migrants lack political rights and the state does not facilitate migrants' political organization and incorporation into the policy process, as in Germany, migrants might be expected to remain relatively marginal actors.

Hypothesis 4.3

Here we look at migrants' claims on immigration and ethnic relations in more detail. We first ask to what extent these claims are framed with reference to supranational, and transnational, or national institutions, rights, and conventions. Second, we look at the type of demands and particularly at the nature and relative importance of demands for cultural group rights.

With regard to the territorial scope of claims, we can draw a clear hypothesis from the postnational model. According to this perspective, the relativization of the nation-state occurs not only because foreign, transnational, and supranational actors intervene in national politics (hypothesis 2.2), and actors in the national polity directly address supranational or foreign authorities (hypothesis 3). At least as important as these direct forms of 'postnationalization' is the indirect form in which actors make claims on national authorities by referring to supranational institutions, conventions, and legislation. The postnational model predicts that such claims play an important role, while the national citizenship model would expect them to be relatively marginal compared to claims whose frame of reference remains within the national context.

Hypothesis 4.4

Finally, we look at the type of demands that minorities make with regard to immigration and ethnic relations. Here, only theories of multicultural citizenship allow us to formulate clear expectations. According to this perspective, demands for special group rights related to the recognition and protection of cultural differences are central to the claims-making of ethnic minorities. The national citizenship model does not allow us to say much about the relative importance of such claims compared to other types of claims. However, they may be expected to play a more important role in Britain than in Germany, because Britain officially sees itself as a 'multicultural society' with tolerance for cultural diversity as one of its constituent principles. Thus, opportunities for claims-making on the basis of cultural difference would seem to be more favourable in Britain than in Germany.

Findings

Starting with the type of actors involved in minority claims-making, Table 9.1 gives an overview of the type of collective identities that were expressed in claims-making by ethnic minorities and migrants (hypothesis 2.1). We distinguish four broad types of identities. First, migrants and minorities may identify themselves across ethnic and cultural boundaries on the basis of their common status as 'immigrants', (ethnic) 'minorities', or 'foreigners'. More specific status-group identifications include asylum seekers or the ethnic German immigrant category of *Aussiedler*. Second, minorities may identify, or be identified with a certain racial group, such as blacks or Asians. As a powerful cultural marker, religion can be a third possible basis for migrant and minority claims-making. Finally, migrants may identify themselves on the basis of their common national or ethnic descent. It is well worth noting that these possible types of identification overlap and are to an important degree in competition with each other. Whether immigrants from Bangladesh identify themselves as immigrants, as Bangladeshis, as Muslims, as Asians, or as blacks is a political outcome that may give us important information on the nature of the relationship between immigrants and the nation-state. As we have indicated in hypothesis 2.1, the multicultural model leads us to expect identification on the basis of cultural difference, whereas the national citizenship model predicts identification on the basis of national or ethnic origin in Germany, and on the basis of racial and cultural groups in Britain.

If we look first at the first and third columns of Table 9.1, we see that, indeed, identification with national or ethnic groups is much more frequent in Germany, with 83 per cent, than in Britain with only 19 per cent. It is interesting that, apart from some claims-making by Jewish religious groups, we find almost no claims making on a religious basis in Germany.[25] For a country with a Muslim population of several million it is particularly striking that there were only three instances of claims making by Muslim or Islamic groups: 0.4 per cent of the sample. While Muslim minorities in Germany enter the public sphere as Turks, Kurds, Bosnians, or Iranians, rather than as Muslims, we find the exact reverse pattern in Britain. While 24 per cent of claims-making originated in Muslim groups, only 1 and 4 per cent respectively, were made under the label of the two national groups, Pakistani and Bangladeshi, to which most British Muslims belong.

We find a similarly striking difference between Germany and Britain regarding the prominence of racial groups in claims-making. For obvious historical reasons related to the race politics of the Nazi period, race has never gained currency in post-war German political discourse and has no place in the state's aliens politics.[26] By contrast, race is a legitimate and regularly-used basis for claims-making in Britain, where 26 per cent of claims originated in black and another 9 per cent in Asian groups.[27]

An important objection that may be raised against these findings is that because they are based on media data they are likely to measure the ascription of identities by the majority society, which, interesting as it may be, is not necessarily the same as the self-identification of migrants and ethnic minorities. We therefore also present a second measure of collective identities—displayed

TABLE 9.1. Collective identities of actors in claims-making by migrants and ethnic minorities in Germany and Britain, 1990–1995 (%)

	Germany		Britain	
	all claims	named organizations	all claims	named organizations
Status groups	**14.1**	**8.0**	**19.1**	**0.0**
Foreigners	5.3	5.7	0.4	—
Asylum seekers	7.7	0.8	10.2	—
Immigrants	—	—	0.4	—
Minorities	0.3	0.5	8.1	—
Aussiedler	0.8	1.0	—	—
Racial groups	**0.1**	**0.0**	**37.7**	**34.2**
Blacks	0.1	—	26.3	34.2
Asians	—	—	9.3	—
African-Caribbeans	—	—	1.3	—
Black African	—	—	0.8	—
Religious groups	**3.3**	**6.4**	**24.6**	**47.4**
Religious Jewish	2.6	5.1	—	—
Muslim/Islamic	0.4	0.8	24.2	47.4
Other	0.3	0.5	0.4	—
National and ethnic groups	**82.5**	**85.6**	**18.6**	**18.4**
EU countries	0.5	0.3	0.4	1.3
Ex-Yugoslavs	1.7	1.5	0.4	—
Roma and Sinti/*Gypsies*	11.2	14.4	0.8	2.7
Secular (ethnic) Jewish	17.6	36.5	4.7	7.9
Other European	0.1	—	0.8	—
Turks	15.2	14.1	0.4	—
Kurds	32.9	20.1	0.8	—
Iranians	2.0	2.8	0.4	—
Pakistani	—	—	1.3	2.7
Bangladeshi	—	—	4.2	2.7
Indian	—	—	1.3	1.3
Sikhs	—	—	1.3	—
Other	0.8	1.1	1.8	—
Total	**100.0**	**100.0**	**100.0**	**100.0**
N =	757	389	236	76

Note: Chi-square (on the basis of main, bold-type groups for identities), for all claims: 491.17; p = 0.000; df = 3; for named organizations 259.17; p = 0.000; df = 3.

in Table 9.1, columns 2 and 4—which is based on the subsample of cases for which we had information on the full name of the organization that made the claim. This excludes cases in which the newspaper only gave a vague identification of the claim-makers—for example 'Turkish groups' demonstrating against racism—which leaves considerable room for the ascription of identities by journalists. Names of organizations, by contrast, are important vehicles for the self-presentation of groups toward both their constituency and the wider society, and therefore may be considered good indicators of the group's collective identity. For the German case, this different method does not lead to important changes. Asylum seekers almost completely disappear and the share of Jewish groups increases, but this is simply a result of the low degree of organization of the marginal group of asylum seekers, and the strong institutionalization of the state-sponsored Jewish community. Regarding theoretically more important findings, however, nothing changes: national origin becomes even more important as a basis for collective identities (86 per cent) and racial and religious identifications remain extremely marginal.

For Britain, the general pattern also remains much the same, but there are two significant, and probably interrelated, changes. First, unlike the category 'black', the racial category 'Asian' does not seem to be relevant for self-identification. In fact, we found no organizations at all which identified themselves as Asian. By contrast, the share of the religious category 'Muslim' almost doubles when we consider only named organizations. Since Asian and Muslim are alternative identifications for largely the same immigrant groups (Pakistanis and Bangledeshis), it may be the case that the difference between the results in columns 3 and 4 results from media bias, which—in line with the official categories of British race relations politics—describes self-identifying Muslim claimants as Asians. This fits other accounts of the problems British Muslims encounter in their claims-making on a race relations system that was modeled on African-Caribbean blacks and has difficulty incorporating Muslim immigrants from South Asia (see, for example, Modood 1988).

Overall, the comparative results provide strong support for the national citizenship model. Neither the postnational nor the multicultural model is able to explain why British minorities identify as racial or religious groups and their German counterparts identify on the basis of their homeland national or ethnic origin. Taken on their own, the British results are in line with what the multicultural model would lead us to expect, but the comparison with Germany shows that the strong mobilization of religious identities in the British context is not a general consequence of the presence of culturally different minorities, but depends on a facilitating political context, which stimulates claims-making on the basis of cultural identities. Where such an affirmation of multiculturalism by the state is lacking and immigrants are officially seen as citizens of another state, as in Germany, national origin becomes the overriding form in which migrants are identified and identify themselves.

One finding for Britain, however, is difficult to reconcile with the national citizenship model and supports the multicultural emphasis on cultural difference as an important source of migrant claims-making. Although the racial label 'Asian' is the officially sponsored identity for migrants from the Indian subcontinent, the Muslim identity of Pakistani and Bangladeshi immigrants is

TABLE 9.2. Territorial scope of organizations in claims-making by migrants and ethnic minorities in Germany and Britain, 1990–1995 (%)

	Germany	Britain
Supra/transnational	0.5	7.2
European	0.5	—
Foreign-based	0.3	1.2
Homeland-based	26.0	6.0
National	72.7	85.5
Total	100.0	100.0
N =	388	83

Note: Chi-square: 33.55; p = 0.000; df = 4.

much more powerful, especially in self-identification. Although the British variant of multiculturalism cannot be seen as a political environment hostile to the mobilization of cultural identities, British race relations politics certainly favors 'black' or 'Asian' over 'Muslim'. The dominance in migrant claims-making of 'Muslim' over 'Asian' therefore indicates that there are limits to the capacities of national modes of minority incorporation to shape migrant identities in their own image. And likewise it shows that there is at least some truth in the multicultural emphasis on cultural difference.

A second aspect of the actor dimension concerns the territorial scope of migrant and minority organizations (hypothesis 2.2). For those acts of claims-making for which an organization was explicitly mentioned, Table 9.2 shows whether these organizations were international, Europewide, homeland-based, or otherwise based in a foreign country, or whether their territorial scope remained confined to the German and British polities. Contrary to the hypothesis drawn from the postnational model, the territorial scope of the large majority of migrant and minority organizations does not reach beyond the boundaries of the nation-state: 73 per cent of all claims in Germany and as much as 86 per cent in Britain were made by national organizations of immigrants and minorities, based in, and limited to the German and British polities.[28] In contrast, international, European, and foreign migrant organizations played a marginal role in claims-making. In the light of all the talk about Europe, both in the postnational perspective and in the wider academic discussion, the most surprising finding is perhaps the virtual absence of European-level migrant organizations. In Britain we found no claims by such organizations at all; in Germany just two cases. This finding confirms the point of view of those authors who have pointed out that migrant organizations on the European level have remained relatively impotent actors, not least because migrant groups even from the same ethnic origins from different European countries often have widely diverging opinions about the aims and strategies of integration and anti-racism (see, for example, Favell 1998).

Of course, for those bent on looking for evidence of postnational trends, there were a few examples of the involvement of transnational organizations in claims-making. The data show, however, that such cases were the rare exception rather than the rule. The only—at least in Germany—significant form of organization that transcended national boundaries were organizations based in migrants' homelands, such as the Kurdish Workers' Party (PKK) or the Iranian People's Mojahedin. To the extent that they put forward claims aiming at the improvement of the situation of migrants from the respective homeland in Germany or Britain, such forms of migrant organization may still be interpreted as evidence of postnational tendencies. However, such cases were rare, too. Homeland-based groups were almost exclusively occupied with political issues relating to the politics of migrants' countries of origin: for example, Kurdish separatism, rivalry between Turkish extreme-right and left groups, or the opposition of Chinese exiles to the Communist regime in China. Far from constituting some kind of challenge to the nation-state, such forms of claims-making reflect the ongoing conflicts surrounding state-building and consolidation in many countries outside Western Europe and North America.

An additional weakness of the postnational model is that it has no answer to the question why homeland-based organizations play a much more important role in Germany than in Britain: 26 and 6 per cent, respectively. As we have indicated above, this result can be explained within the national citizenship model by the different ways in which migrants and minorities are included or excluded from the political community. As we saw in Table 9.1, the exclusive German model of ethnic citizenship, and the labelling of migrants and minorities by the state as foreigners, has led migrants in Germany to retain a collective identity based on the national and ethnic categories of their homelands. Such identifications, of course, benefit homeland-based groups, who, like the German state, continue to see migrants as citizens of their countries of origin who can be called upon to make a contribution to the political struggle in the homeland. By contrast, the British model facilitates migrant and minority organization within the national context, both because it actively facilitates such forms of organization through financial support and the opening of channels of access to the political process, and because it stimulates migrants to identify themselves as racial or cultural minorities within British society.

The postnational model does not stand or fall, however, by the transnational organization of collective action alone. One form in which postnational citizenship takes shape is when collective actors, whether themselves transnational or not, bypass national authorities and directly address institutions and authorities outside the nation-state (hypothesis 3). Our data contain several examples of claims-making along these lines. Thus, in 1994 a group of 200 German Kurds drove to French Strasbourg to offer a petition to the European

TABLE 9.3. Territorial scope of addressees of claims-making by migrants and ethnic minorities in Germany and Britain, 1990–1995 (%)

	Germany	Britain
Supra/transnational	1.1	2.2
European	1.1	0.7
Homeland governments	24.5	2.2
National authorities	73.3	95.0
Total	100.0	100.0
N =	351	141

Note: Chi-square: 34.60; p = 0.000; df = 3.

Parliament against the persecution of Kurds in Turkey. In another example, German Roma and Sinti groups appealed to the UNHCR to move against the German Government's plan to deport refugees from this ethnic group back to Romania. In Britain, there are two cases in which the International Islamic Front and the Supreme Council of British Muslims called upon the Allied Coalition during the 1991 Persian Gulf War to cease hostilities—but there is precious little else. While the postnational model suggests that these are typical examples of migrant claims making in the age of globalization, Table 9.3 makes clear that such postnational claims making was highly exceptional. Again, the most surprising finding may be the insignificance of the EU and its institutions as a target for migrant and minority demands: about 1 per cent of claims in both countries. With 2 per cent in Britain and 1 per cent in Germany, claims addressed to other supranational institutions were equally rare. By contrast, the nation-state was the target of 73 per cent of German and as much as 95 per cent of British minority claims-making. Once more, the only significant form of claims-making transcending national borders are claims addressed at the governments of migrants' homelands. Such cases are not of the type asking homeland governments to intervene with the German or British governments on behalf of migrant rights, which would still fit the postnational model. Almost exclusively they are related to political conflicts in the homeland. Finally, we note again that homeland-related claims are much more frequent in Germany than in Britain, which provides further support to the comparative arguments drawn from the national citizenship model discussed above.

Having discussed collective identities, organizations, and addressees, we now turn to the content of claims by migrants and minorities. Table 9.4, which shows the distribution of migrant and minority claims across main issue fields, adds further detail to the picture. Apart from immigration and asylum issues, which are roughly of the same importance in both countries, Britain and Germany provide a striking contrast. German minorities made claims on

TABLE 9.4. Main issue fields of claims-making by migrants and ethnic minorities in Germany and Britain, 1990–1995 (%)

	Germany	Britain
Immigration politics	1.5	5.9
Asylum politics	15.7	11.9
Minority integration politics	6.3	50.8
Anti-Racism/xenophobia	32.1	21.6
Inter-Ethnic conflict	0.9	3.8
Homeland politics	41.5	4.2
Other	2.0	1.8
Total	100.0	100.0
N =	757	236

Note: Chi-square: 319.50; p = 0.000; df = 6.

homeland issues ten times more often than their British counterparts: 42 per cent compared to 4 per cent. In Britain, 51 per cent of claims fall in the category of 'minority integration politics', by which we denote claims-making related to the integration, rights, and social position of resident minorities. By contrast, these make up only 6 per cent of German claims. The issue field of anti-racism, which includes claims-making against xenophobia and right-wing violence,[29] is somewhat, though not dramatically, more important in Germany: 32 per cent against 22 per cent. In line with the national citizenship model (hypothesis 4.1) we thus find that British minorities focus primarily on their integration and rights within British society, whereas the most important field of claims-making for their German counterparts refers to the political situation in migrants' homelands. In as far as German minorities make claims related to their position in Germany, these tend to be largely defensive: most of the anti-racist demands were protests against the wave of xenophobic violence that swept across Germany in this period, sometimes accompanied by the demand on German authorities to provide better protection against such attacks. Proactive demands for an extension of migrant and minority rights were, however, not very frequent in Germany, in stark contrast to Britain. We will return to this in more detail below.

For the moment, we would like to point to an interesting finding in the German case that emerges from a comparison of the percentage for homeland issues in Table 9.4 (42 per cent) and the percentage of claims addressed at homeland authorities in Table 9.3 (25 per cent). This difference is partly explained by claims for which no explicit addressee was mentioned. These were primarily attacks by Kurdish groups against Turkish targets in Germany, such as restaurants, banks, or travel agencies. Indirectly, such acts of violence of course also aimed at putting pressure on the Turkish government, but because this was not explicitly mentioned, they do not show up in Table 9.3. However, there also was a sizeable number of claims addressed at the German government, but related to homeland issues—6 per cent of all claims. For instance, Kurdish and Iranian groups accused the German government of supporting repression in their homelands by selling military equipment to the Turkish and Iranian regimes. In a way, such claims may be considered to be examples of transnational collective action, although of a rather different type than that which is assumed in the literature on postnational citizenship. While we found very few examples of migrants trying to mobilize supranational or homeland authorities to improve their position in the countries of immigration, we do find some support for transnational claims-making in the other direction; that is, attempting to mobilize host society authorities or using the relative political freedom in the host society against the homeland regime. The point is that there is little which is new or postnational about such forms of transnational claims-making by migrants, exiles, and political refugees. Just ask Karl Marx, Mikhail Bakunin, or the Ayatollah Khomeini.

Our main point regarding the greater importance of homeland-related organizations, addressees, and claims in the German context of an ethnic-exclusive model of migrant incorporation has now sufficiently been made. We will therefore now focus the remainder of our analysis exclusively on those claims related to immigration and ethnic relations in the host society. We first ask how important claims-making by migrants and ethnic minorities is in this respect, compared to the claims-making by actors based in the majority population of the host society, such as state and party actors, labour unions, churches, and other civil society groups.

Both the postnational and the multicultural perspectives strongly emphasize the active role of minority organizations in challenging immigration and minority politics (hypothesis 4.2). Table 9.5 shows, however, that minorities have been able to play such a role only in Britain. British ethnic minorities were responsible for 21 per cent of the total claims-making on immigration and ethnic relations, a higher percentage than was achieved, for instance, by the national Government (14 per cent) or by members of the national Parliament

TABLE 9.5. Share of ethnic minorities in all claims-making on immigration and ethnic relations in Germany and Britain, 1990–1995 (%)

	Germany	Britain
Migrants and ethnic minorities	6.8	20.7
Other actors	93.2	79.3
Total	100.0	100.0
N =	5,396	1,047

Note: Chi-square: 205.65; p = 0.000; df = 1.

(13 per cent). With 7 per cent of all claims, German minorities played a much less prominent role in the public debate on immigration and ethnic relations, which may have been about them, but was influenced by them not nearly to the same extent as in Britain. At the risk of becoming repetitive, we again have to conclude that the national citizenship model is best able to make sense of these striking cross-national differences. In Britain, ethnic minorities can challenge the official politics of ethnic relations because they command the political resources and are offered the opportunity to do so. Britain's race relations and antidiscrimination legislation and its self-proclaimed status as a 'multicultural society' constitute important discursive resources for minorities, who can challenge the British state by referring to its own aims and promises.

Finally, we focus our attention in closer detail on the contents of migrants' claims on immigration and ethnic relations. Although our earlier examinations of the model have not been very positive, we must still allow for the possibility of more indirect forms of postnational claims-making, which do not directly involve transnational actors either as claims-makers or as addressees. To be fair, it has to be said that in their more prudent formulations of the postnational thesis, authors such as Jacobson and Soysal acknowledge that the nation-state in many cases remains the forum through which postnational claims-making has to pass. In this view, national organizations may make claims on national governments, but frame their demands with reference to transnational or supranational actors, rights, and conventions (hypothesis 4.3). This may include calls on national governments to take action at the supranational level—for example to strive for a common European regulation of asylum procedures— or to respect international conventions such as the Geneva Convention on refugees. We also include in this category, claims that refer to the consequences that national policies and developments may have on the transnational level.

In Table 9.6 we show the territorial frame of reference of migrant claims-making. Even in this case, however, we find little support for the postnational

TABLE 9.6. Territorial frame of reference of minority claims-making on immigration and ethnic relations in Germany and Britain, 1990–1995 (%)

	Germany	Britain
Supra/transnational	1.0	1.4
European	0.2	—
Bilateral	0.2	2.3
National	98.6	94.4
Unclassifiable	—	1.9
Total	100.0	100.0
N =	421	213

Note: Chi-square: 15.77; p = 0.003; df = 4.

model, with 94 per cent of claims made in Britain being firmly locked within a national frame of reference, and as much as 99 per cent of those in Germany. Again Europe is surprisingly off the agenda in both countries. In fact the only example we found was a statement by German Roma and Sinti organizations calling on the German government to include the Romani language in the European Charter on Regional and Minority Languages. Other claims with a supra- or transnational dimension were also rare, both in Britain—three claims by organizations invoking the supranational authority of Islam—and in Germany with four claims by Jewish groups backing their claims for combating xenophobia and anti-Semitism by referring to the negative consequences that extreme-right tendencies in Germany might have for the country's image abroad and for foreign investments in the German economy. In Britain, we find five claims (2.3 per cent) with a bilateral dimension, including for instance a black Member of Parliament demanding reparations payments to British blacks and their homelands as a compensation for British involvement in slavery.[30] All in all, however, the results of Table 9.6 underline our previous findings that a few examples of claims-making beyond national boundaries exist, but that they are the exception rather than the rule and cannot in any way be considered a representative characteristic of minority claims-making. Given the fact that we have now given the postnational model three chances to prove its validity— with regard to actors, addressees, and the content and framing of claims—the clear conclusion to draw seems to be that from our data the postnational model of citizenship has little empirical underpinning, to the extent that it risks coming apart at the seams.

The last important feature of minority claims-making that we wish to examine concerns the type of rights that are demanded. This is particularly relevant for the multicultural citizenship thesis, which sees demands for special group rights related to the recognition and protection of cultural differences and cultural rights as central characteristics of minority claims-making (hypothesis 4.4). In Table 9.7 we present only those claims that are made in the field of ethnic relations—corresponding to the categories 'minority integration politics' and 'anti-racism/xenophobia' in Table 9.4—that make specific demands in terms of rights. The first point to make is that our findings give some credence to multicultural citizenship, as about half of the claims for rights in both countries are 'cultural', with most of these being group specific.[31] In the German case, by far the most important group demanding cultural rights—five of twelve cases—were Roma and Sinti (gypsies) demanding recognition as a national minority, with the same rights as the Danish and Sorbian—a Slavic people in the Czech-Polish border region—minorities. Since Roma and Sinti have been traveling through Germany and the rest of Europe for centuries, they occupy a different position from that of recent immigrants such as the Turks, and may therefore with some legitimacy claim the status of a national minority. In that sense, their important contribution to multicultural claims-making

TABLE 9.7. Claims by minority actors for rights in Germany and Britain, 1990–1995 (%)

	Germany	Britain
Citizenship Rights	11.5	—
Other Political and Civil Rights	26.9	11.5
Social and Economic Rights	3.8	20.5
Cultural Right	46.2	50.0
Anti-Discrimination Rights	—	15.4
Equal Rights Unspecified	11.5	2.6
Total	100.0	100.0
N =	26	78
Claims for rights as a % of all migrant claims-making on ethnic relations (i.e. immigration and asylum issues excluded)	8.9	42.4
N =	291	184

Notes: For the first part of Table 9.7, Chi-square: 22.58; p = 0.000; df = 5; for the second part Chi-square: 74.02; p = 0.000; df = 1.

in Germany confirms Kymlicka's (1995) point that national minorities have a stronger basis for claiming special cultural rights than ethnic groups of immigrant origin. Apart from this special case, more recent immigrants to Germany made very few claims to cultural rights, or, for that matter, to any rights at all. Claims for rights amounted to only 9 per cent of all minority claims-making on ethnic relations, the remaining 91 per cent being mainly defensive claims against discrimination and xenophobic violence—see also Table 9.4. The potential for societal disintegration as a result of culturally based demands seems thus very remote in the contemporary German context.

In contrast, we find more evidence to support the multicultural thesis in Britain. Here, the demands for specific group cultural rights were predominantly made by Muslims—23 of 37 cases—with others being under the self-definition of blacks, Jews, Rastafarians, African-Caribbeans, Indians, Pakistanis, and gypsies. These include examples of exactly the kind of cultural claims that are much discussed in the literature on multiculturalism. Thus the Muslim UK Action Front demands a cultural extension of British blasphemy law: in the words of its spokesperson: 'The case will point out the common ground between Christianity, Judaism and Islam. In many past blasphemy cases, protection was afforded to the Old Testament, which was essentially Judaism.'[32] We also have an example of a British headscarf case, where the activist states: 'There was nothing in the school rules about headscarves when we went there.

The rules were amended last year. We are not fanatics or fundamentalists. We just want the right to continue our education and practice our faith.' What is notable from these examples, which are not atypical, is that the demands are made for an extension of the existing British multiculturalism. In the first case, the Muslims want to be added onto the list of acknowledged religions in the same way that they claim an earlier wave of migrants, the Jews, were incorporated. Likewise the headscarf claims are demands made in an inclusive rather than an incommensurable way. We have very few examples of more fundamentalist Islamic demands that challenge rather than address the authority of the nation-state. One made by a group in relation to Rushdie was, 'Let us take him to Medina and let us stone him to death. Every Muslim should be prepared to cast the first stone.'

It seems therefore that apart from the odd exception, the majority of cultural demands are better explained by the national context of a state-sponsored multiculturalism that gives opportunities for framing demands in this way. This argument is backed up by the comparative finding that, in Britain than in Germany, there are many more demands for rights as a percentage of claims-making on ethnic relations 42 per cent compared to 9 per cent—and claims-making on ethnic relations is itself more important (Table 9.4). That Muslim identity has difficulty fitting in the British context may be explained by the fact that British discrimination legislation does not acknowledge the right to religious equality (except in Northern Ireland) and so Muslims are in real terms offered only the rhetoric and not the substance of equality in British multiculturalism. Indeed of the special group rights claimed by blacks, more were framed in terms of civil or social rights than as cultural rights, one example being the right of blacks to be tried by juries with black representation. This returns us once more to the point we have made several times about the impact of the racial configuration of the British citizenship model on claims-making.

Conclusions and Discussion

Our leading question in this article has been whether the claims-making of migrants and ethnic minorities fundamentally challenge the liberal nation-state, as is supposed in theories of postnational and multicultural citizenship. By making an overview of the results of our comparative analysis of claims-making by migrants and ethnic minorities in Britain and Germany in the 1990s, we find that the answer to this question must be negative. This is certainly the case with regard to the postnational model. Contrary to this perspective, which sees the nation-state as increasingly 'insignificant' and 'irrelevant' (Soysal 1998: 208, 211) the nation-state continues to be by far the most important frame of reference for the identities, organizations, and claims of ethnic minorities, and national authorities remain the almost exclusive addressees of the demands of these minorities. To be sure, some of migrant claims-making, especially in Germany, transcends national borders, but it does so in ways that are not post-national in any meaningful sense. These forms of claims-making simply take another nation-state not the host society, but the migrants' homeland, as their frame of reference. In some cases, such as that of the Kurds and the Kosovo Albanians in Germany, they even strive for the creation of new independent nation-states in their distant homeland. Such claims-making by political exiles is not a new phenomenon at all but has accompanied the nation-state since its formation.

By contrast, we found precious little evidence for the types of claims-making that are, according to the postnational model, typical for the modern migrant experience: transnational migrant organizations intervening in national politics, migrants addressing supranational institutions, minorities making demands on national governments in the name of international legal conventions and rights. None of these forms of postnational claims-making accounted for more than at most a small percentage of the claims making of migrants and minorities. While this holds for postnational claims-making generally, the almost complete absence of claims-making related to the EU is a particularly surprising finding, which suggests that European integration has not pro-gressed nearly as far as the rhetoric of both proponents and opponents of this project would have us believe. For the moment, Europe continues to be a co-ordinating committee for nation-states, laden with symbolism but with little autonomous power. Migrants in Europe seem to have understood this better than many social scientists, as have, by the way, European voters, the majority of whom do not even bother to vote for the Strasbourg puppet show called the European Parliament.

The last line of defense of postnationalists might be to argue that universal human rights declarations and conventions have been incorporated in the con-stitutions and legislation of liberal nation-states and that therefore even claims-making that remains fully confined to the nation-state may have a postnational dimension. This watered-down version of postnationalism implies a diffusion of universal human rights principles from the supranational to the national level, a claim that is not supported by historical evidence. Human rights appeared as 'self-evident truths' in national constitutions and bills of rights long before words such as 'supranational' or 'globalization' had been conceived. They are primary constituent principles of modern liberal nation-states, and are more of a basis for extending national citizenship than a pallbearer carry-ing it to an early grave.

Saskia Sassen (1998: 73) might have a point when she argues, in defense of the postnational position, that it is often easier to point at continuities than to detect new, emergent developments. But even if we see postnationalism merely as an incipient trend and not as a state of affairs, which is certainly not the position of bold postnationalists such as Jacobson and Soysal, we think the empirical evidence should at least produce significant indications of the dawning of such a new era. Of course it is no problem at all to find examples that fit the postnational model; we have mentioned some in this article. However, they are rare exceptions rather than the rule of migrant claims-making, and if they are indicative of a trend, it must be one that is at its earliest beginnings and remains for the moment more of a fiction than fact.

An additional weakness of the postnational model is that it stands empty-handed when it comes to explaining cross-national differences among liberal nation-states in reference to the claims-making of migrants and ethnic minorities.[33] As our comparison of Germany and Britain has shown, cross-national differences in this respect are striking. While British immigrants mobilize on the basis of their racial and cultural difference from the majority society, the identities of German minorities refer to the national and ethnic categories of their homelands. Whereas homeland issues play an important role in Germany, they are marginal in the claims-making of British minorities, who focus primarily on issues related to their rights and integration in British society. Insofar as German migrants focus on their position in Germany, their claims are primarily defensive and directed against overt xenophobia and racist violence. While such claims are not unimportant in Britain, too, we find in addition a sizeable number of proactive claims for extensions of minority rights. Finally, we have shown that ethnic minorities in Britain play a much more important role in the overall public discourse on migration and ethnic relations than do their German counterparts, who as foreigners are not only symbolically, but to an important extent also materially, excluded from the political community.

This brings us to theories that stress the continuing relevance of national models of citizenship for the incorporation of migrants and ethnic minorities. Within the European context, Germany and Britain represent in many respects diametrically opposed incorporation regimes, which we have labelled 'ethnocultural exclusionist' and 'multicultural pluralist', respectively. While the German model puts up important symbolic and material barriers to the acquisition of membership in the political community by foreign migrants, the British model provides for much easier access to citizenship, and in addition gives limited but still substantial recognition to their cultural difference. These liberal policies for resident migrants, it must be said, are coupled with immigration policies that make it in many respects more difficult for new migrants to enter the national territory than in the German case. Also in other respects, it is inappropriate to interpret German–British differences in a 'good guys versus bad guys' frame. The British model of migrant incorporation is to an important degree a consequence of its imperial, colonial past, and by way of several restrictive changes in citizenship legislation, subsequent British governments have done much to limit these consequences. By contrast, Germany has recently made an important step toward abandoning its ethnic conception of nationhood by way of a fundamental change in its citizenship legislation which came into force in 2000.

However, for the moment, Germany and Britain continue to embody two markedly different models of nationhood and migrant incorporation. The hypotheses we have drawn from these two models fit our evidence on minority claims-making remarkably well. Far from being insignificant, merely symbolic leftovers from a time when the nation-state still counted, national models of citizenship have important consequences for the identities, forms of organization, and types of claims of ethnic minorities. To an important extent, patterns of migrant claims-making mirror the way in which the nation-state in the two countries defines the relation between ethnic minorities and the political community. Germany sees immigrants as foreigners, and that is exactly the way in which German minorities behave: they organize and identify themselves on the basis of their national origin and are still, in spite of residing in Germany for several decades, preoccupied with the politics of their homelands. By contrast, the British multicultural state treats its immigrants as racial and cultural minorities within British society, and, again, that is pretty much how British migrants have come to see themselves: they mobilize as blacks or British Muslims and make claims on the British state for equal opportunity and multicultural rights.

In our theoretical discussion of national models of citizenship, we have identified a third ideal-typical model of citizenship, namely the assimilationist model, which in the European context is best represented by France. It will be an interesting question for further research to investigate whether a distinct pattern of migrant claims-making can be identified in France, which matches its particular model of migrant incorporation. On the basis of the findings reported here, we may hypothesize that such a French pattern of claims making will have certain similarities with our results for Britain. Because migrants have easy access to membership in the political community in France, too, we would expect them to have weak ties to their homelands' politics, as well. However, because of French pressures toward assimilation and the lack of recognition for ethnic and cultural difference, we would expect a different type of collective identity—more interethnic and based on the common status of immigrant— and different claims—equality and anti-racism, but not a strong focus on cultural rights—than in Britain.

Extending the analysis to include other countries would also allow us to arrive at more conclusive answers about the challenge of multicultural citizenship. The evidence from Britain and Germany is mixed. In Germany, we found little evidence of strong pressures from ethnic and cultural minorities for the recognition of cultural identities and special group rights on the basis of cultural difference. In Britain, however, we found a substantial number of such claims, mostly, though not exclusively, originating in Britain's Muslim community. At the very least, the lack of a significant number of such demands in

Germany, which also has a large Muslim population, shows that demands for multicultural rights are not a necessary consequence of the presence of a large population of non-European, culturally different migrants, but depend on the availability of political opportunities that legitimate and provide incentives for such claims-making. It may nevertheless be that the British experience shows where Germany will be going once it has liberalized its citizenship legislation and German minorities focus on their rights and position in Germany instead of on the politics of their homelands. That is certainly what opponents of such a liberalization fear. The French experience might again provide an interesting alternative here. Since France invites migrants into the political community on the basis of equality, but to the exclusion of cultural difference, it could follow that migrant claims for multicultural rights are not nearly as important in this country as in Britain. If that is the case, the multicultural challenge would not be an assault on the unity of the nation-state imposed on it by the pressures of cultural difference inherent to immigration, but a response to an opportunity structure willingly created by some, but not all nation-states. Far from being a mechanism to appease pressures arising inherently from immigration, state-sponsored models of multiculturalism may then turn out to stimulate such claims in the first place. And if indeed the multicultural appetite grows the more you eat, there may ultimately be something to the warnings against a self-sustaining fragmentation of the nation-state that opponents of multiculturalism fear.

However, even Britain does not as yet come close to such a scenario, and there is no indication that it will in the near future. Most demands by minorities in Britain seem to be made within the national configuration of citizenship. Even the special group demands for cultural rights that are predominantly made by Muslims are perhaps best explained by the resistance of race relations policies to the recognition of religious equality. British multiculturalism offers Muslims a racial equality that contradicts their self-definition as a religious group. However, with the exception of the relatively few examples of incommensurable claims of fundamentalist Islamic activists, most Muslim claims demand an extension of the classical understanding of political and social equality in citizenship, to include the recognition of religious equality. Given the appropriate 'cultural tools', British Muslims might be more likely to support than challenge the nation-state.

Although we are convinced that our analysis provides strong support for the importance of national models of citizenship and migrant incorporation, we do not want to conclude this article without having addressed a final caveat that may have been on some readers' lips for a while. There is an alternative explanation for the differences found between Britain and Germany that does not focus on national politics, but on the differences between individual migrant groups. As we have seen, Britain and Germany have drawn their immigrants from different countries and regions of the world. In Britain, the largest groups come from the Caribbean and the Indian subcontinent; in Germany by far the largest group of migrants come from Turkey. So perhaps the preoccupation of German claims-making with homeland issues is just a peculiarity of Turkish and Kurdish migrants, and the focus on cultural issues a typical characteristic of Muslims from Pakistan and Bangladesh. This is a rather atheoretical and primordialist explanation, but still cannot be discarded out of hand. The question remains, in our view, why Turkish Muslims would be so different from Pakistani Muslims. Conversely, it cannot be maintained that the Indian subcontinent has no equivalent of the Turkish-Kurdish conflict that could fuel homeland-related claims-making from this region in Britain. So the question is why Pakistani-Indian, Hindu-Sikh, and a myriad of other political conflicts on the Indian subcontinent do not to a significant degree translate into related claims-making by British minorities from these regions. While we consider these to be important arguments against the alternative interpretation, the ultimate test would of course be to compare the claims-making of migrants from the same region of origin in different countries of settlement. Because European immigration countries tend to have their own particular areas of migrant recruitment, this is easier said than done. Adding France to the comparison would not help much, for instance, because the most important French migrant groups come from the Maghreb countries and Portugal, which are marginal sources of immigration in both Britain and Germany. The Netherlands, however, would be a helpful case in this regard, because it has sizeable minorities from the Caribbean allowing a comparison with Britain, from Turkey which could be compared with German Turks, as well as from Morocco, and so comparable with France.

With our comparison of Britain and Germany, we have, to our knowledge, been the first to present a systematic empirical comparison of the claims-making of migrants and ethnic minorities in two of the most important immigration countries of Western Europe. Our interpretation of the striking differences between these two countries in the framework of national models of citizenship and migrant incorporation has shown what merits such an approach may have. However, as our concluding remarks indicate, many important questions regarding the relationship between nation-states, immigration, and minority claims-making remain. The challenge for further research therefore is to extend the kind of analysis we have presented here to include other countries and models of incorporation, both in Western Europe, and in the classical immigration countries of the New World.

Notes

*An earlier version of this chapter appeared in the *American Journal of Sociology* 105: 652–96, 1999. This study is part of a larger ongoing research project entitled

'Mobilization on Ethnic Relations, Citizenship and Immigration' (MERCI), which focuses not only on the mobilization of migrants and ethnic minorities, but encompasses political claims-making on issues related to immigration, minorities, and xenophobia, in five European countries. In addition to Germany and Britain, case studies are in progress for France and Switzerland—Marco Giugni and Florence Passy at the University of Geneva—and for The Netherlands—Thom Duyvené de Wit at the University of Amsterdam. The British data presented in this paper were collected with the assistance of a grant award from the British Economic and Social Research Council (R000236558) in co-operation with the Institute of Communications Studies at the University of Leeds. The German project has been funded by the Science Center Berlin (WZB). We would like to thank the anonymous reviewers of the *AJS* (*American Journal of Sociology*) as well as our colleagues at the Public Sphere and Social Movements Department at the WZB for their helpful comments on earlier versions of this paper. Christian Galonska provided valuable assistance with the data analyses.

1. This implies that we limit ourselves to ethnocultural minorities of migrant origin and exclude the problematic of so-called 'national minorities' such as the Basques, the Quebecois, or Native Americans. As Kymlicka (1995) has convincingly argued, such minorities pose a rather different, and in many ways much more serious, challenge to the liberal nation-state. For similar reasons, we think our results cannot be extrapolated to the situation of blacks in the United States. As descendants of involuntary migrants and forced labourers who have suffered centuries of systematic discrimination, the position of African-Americans is fundamentally different from the mostly voluntary migrants we deal with here.

2. It is important to note here that citizenship in this sense refers to much more than just the rules for acquisition of nationality. Speaking about citizenship in this narrow sense—denoted in German as *Staatsangehörigkeit*—would not even make sense in the British case for the period up to 1981, since strictly speaking there was no such thing as a British nationality before the implementation of the British Nationality Act. Apart from this formal, legal dimension, our notion of citizenship—similar to the connotation of *Staatsbürgerschaft* in German— includes embedded notions of the duties and rights of citizens that are not necessarily laid down in formal law, such as France's strong pressures toward cultural assimilation, as well as the more concrete policies of incorporation of immigrants that derive from such formal and informal notions of citizenship, such as Britain's facilitation of the participation of ethnic minority organizations in the political process in contrast to the marginal role reserved for foreigners' organizations in Germany.

3. Of course, with the 1992 Maastricht Treaty, the EU has implemented a form of European citizenship, which although still rudimentary, does include complete freedom of movement and residence within the European Union for citizens of member states. However, access to European citizenship is completely dependent on access to citizenship of one of the member states. It therefore does not infringe on the prerogatives of member states to define their own rules of citizenship acqui-

sition, nor does it alter the position of residents holding the citizenship of a non-member state.

4. Moreover, even these examples are not always well chosen. In the French *foulard* case, the overwhelming majority of public debate and attention was not created by the three schoolgirls who wore their headscarves in school, or by the Muslim organizations supporting them, but by French political leaders and intellectuals disagreeing about the nature of French republicanism and laicism.

5. There has been a growing body of important comparative research in this field. Other examples include Castles and Miller (1993), Cornelius, Martin, and Hollifield (1994), Ireland (1994), Kleger and D'Amato (1995), Kastoryano (1996), and Safran (1997).

6. Castles (1995), Smith and Blanc (1996) and Favell (1998) are examples of scholars who apply national configurations of citizenship to the incorporation of migrants; whereas Koopmans and Kriesi (1997) and Koopmans and Statham (1999b; 2000) apply a similar model by using national citizenship models as 'opportunity structures' for explaining the potential for mobilization over ethnic difference, extreme right, and anti-racist, respectively in different European countries.

7. Access to German citizenship has been made somewhat easier by legislative changes in 1990 and 1993. However, even after these changes, Germany continues to have one of the lowest naturalization rates in Europe (see Çinar 1994; Lederer 1997). In 1999, however, a proposal by the new government of Social Democrats and Greens has been passed in Parliament, which further lowers the barriers to naturalization and introduces a conditional form of *jus soli*, the condition being that children of migrant origin born in Germany have to give up their parent's nationality when they reach majority age in order to keep their German citizenship. The new policy, which came into force on January 1, 2000, implies a clear departure from the ethnic citizenship model.

8. Here we offer only a few background details of the country cases to assist interpretation of the data. More substantive contemporary overviews can be found in Solomos (1993), Layton-Henry (1994), Mason (1995), and Modood et al. (1997) for Britain, and Thränhardt (1992), and Bade (1994), Münz, Seifert, and Ulrich (1997) for Germany.

9. The Immigration Act of 1971 and the British Nationality Act of 1981 have made 'ancestry' by territorial birth, or patriality, within the UK a requirement for full citizenship, which in effect prioritizes the access of predominantly white subjects of the Old Commonwealth over the predominantly non-white subjects of the New Commonwealth.

10. The exception is EU citizens, who have the right to free movement and social rights within the member countries and receive local voting rights, too. Other special cases are nationally determined, such as the people of Indian origin resident in Hong Kong who were allowed to enter Britain prior to the end of the colonial rule in 1997.

11. For details on the history and implementation of British 'race relations', see Solomos (1993); for a comparison with Germany and the United States, see Joppke (1996).

12. More details on our approach and method appear in Koopmans and Statham (1999a).

13. This excludes acts of international terrorism that could not be plausibly interpreted as part of the claims-making of a particular resident ethnic community, such as most forms of Middle Eastern terrorism. Acts by terrorist groups were included, however, if they were significantly linked to a resident ethnic community, for example, the Kurdish PKK in Germany or the planting of a car bomb by Islamic fundamentalists outside the Israeli Embassy in Britain.

14. 'Britain' here does not refer to the whole of the United Kingdom, but to the main island; events in Northern Ireland were excluded. Moreover, because Scotland has its own press, our data include few Scottish events. If we talk about Britain, therefore, we are in fact mainly implying England and Wales which is where more than 90 per cent of the total population and an even larger percentage of ethnic minorities in Britain live.

15. Examples of this category include the open letter by the American Jewish Committee addressed to Chancellor Kohl expressing concern about xenophobia in Germany and the claim by a Nigerian government official that the Omibiyo Family Anti-Deportation Campaign was damaging his country's national image in Britain.

16. One may object that our focus on national public spheres introduces a bias in our results to the detriment of trans- and supranational actors. This would be true if there was such a thing as an international or European public sphere. In the absence of supranational media or transnational public debates of any importance, the public claims-making of supranational actors, or claims-making addressed to supranational actors, has to be mediated through national public spheres in order to be effective. At present the modest beginnings of an international public sphere in the form of television networks such as Cable News Network, or newspapers such as the now-defunct *European*, cannot compete in terms of audience or resonance with national media, not least because of the language factor, which may well prove to be an insurmountable barrier to the development of a transnational public sphere.

17. Data were coded from microfilm (Germany) and CD-ROM (Britain) versions of the newspapers by trained coding assistants on the basis of a standardized codebook. All articles in the home news section of the newspapers were checked for relevant acts: the search was not limited to articles containing certain key words. For the main variables in the analysis—actors, addressees, aims, etc.—open category lists were used, which allowed us to retain the detail of the original reports in the analysis. In addition, hard copies of the original articles were kept to allow us to go back to the original reports if information was needed that had not been captured by the variables and categories included in the codebook (codebooks are available from the authors on request). The use of very detailed open category

systems including hundreds of different actors and claims entails that conventional measures of intercoder reliability are not applicable to these variables. The categorizations used in this analysis are not based on coder decisions but are the result of aggregations of raw codes by the authors; for a similar two-stage procedure of content analysis, see Shapiro and Markoff (1998: chaps. 6, 11). Conventional reliability measures are, however, applicable to one important aspect of the coding process, namely the inclusion or exclusion of articles and claims from the newspaper source—we report results for intercoder reliability tests based only on the German case, since the British data were collected by one single coder and thus intercoder reliability is irrelevant here. In a first step, coders have to decide which newspaper articles contain any codable claims at all. This is a crucial step in the coding process because only these articles will be archived, and going back to the original source material for checks, corrections, and refinements will not be possible for any articles that are excluded at this stage. Comparing six coders regarding their inclusion or exclusion of articles, a reliability coefficient (Cronbach's alpha) of 0.95 was achieved. In a second step, coders have to identify claims, the final unit of analysis, in the selected articles. Often, articles contain several codable claims, which have to be identified and delimited from each other. This increases divergences among coders so that in the final instance we arrived at a reliability coefficient of 0.92 in our test. Unlike the lost information in the first step, coder unreliability in this second step of the coding process is reparable. For the present analyses, for example, we have checked many of the original source articles in order to improve our qualitative understanding of minority claims-making. In the process, we have found some coding errors and have been able to correct them.

18. Apart from the *Guardian*, these were *The Times*, the *Daily Express*, the *Daily Mirror*, the *Sun*, and the *Daily Mail*.

19. This becomes very clear if we compare actors with known political party affiliation. The distribution is strikingly similar in both papers, and, interestingly, closely matches the electoral strength of each of the parties.

20. A comparison of the *Rundschau* to the *Hürriyet* for the year 1995 produces similar results. As a mainstream newspaper with a readership drawn mainly from the majority culture, the *Rundschau* of course does not cover claims-making by ethnic minorities to the same extent as the *Hürriyet*, which caters specifically to the Turkish immigrant community. Indeed, the number of ethnic minority claims reported was about three times higher in the *Hürriyet*, with, of course, a heavy bias toward claims making by Turkish and Kurdish groups. Again, however, this difference in the quantity of coverage hardly affects the distributions among types of claims. As we will see further on, the most striking characteristic of German minority claims making is the predominance of homeland-related claims. The comparison with the *Hürriyet* shows that this result is not the product of a construction by German mainstream media, who would ignore claims-making by minorities for rights in Germany, and focus disproportionally on conflicts imported from migrants' homelands. For the year 1995, the percentages of homeland-related

claims in the two newspapers are very close: 67 per cent in the *Rundschau* and 60 per cent in the *Hürriyet*. Information on similar checks for biases in the British case, or for the comparison of national and local newspapers are available from the authors on request.

21. Significant cross-national variation could result, in this view, from differences in the composition of the migrant population, leading to different degrees of cultural difference between minorities and the majority society. However, since Britain and Germany have comparable numbers of non-European and Muslim minorities, we should not find large differences between these two countries.

22. All examples of organizations and claims given in this and the following section were drawn from our data.

23. As this example indicates, our definition of homeland-based includes exile organizations of opponents to the homeland regime.

24. By the term 'addressee' we refer to the authorities at whom minorities direct their demands, policy proposals, or criticisms. In other words, the addressee is the political actor that is called upon to act on behalf of the claim-makers or to refrain from acting against their interests.

25. In the case of Jews and Sikhs it is often difficult to tell whether the label used refers to ethnicity or to religion. Both in English and in German the same word, Jewish (*jüdisch*) is used to denote Jews both as a religious group and as an ethnic group. We have used the religious group category only if the name of an organization indicated a religious basis, such as the Synagogal Society Adass-Jisrael, while the ethnic category was used otherwise, for example the Central Council of Jews in Germany a secular organization that was responsible for the large majority of claims by Jews in Germany. This problem may have caused a minor underestimation of the religious component in the mobilization of Jews. For Sikhs we have only three cases, so the question does not have much practical relevance.

26. Even racism is usually not referred to in Germany as such, but as 'hostility against foreigners' (*Ausländerfeindlichkeit*).

27. Note that the label 'black' has two meanings in the British context, which our data do not allow us to disentangle. Black in the narrow sense of the word, as used in the state's race relations politics, refers to people of African-Caribbean and sometimes also of African origin. However, there is also a broader, political meaning of black, which refers to (non-European) ethnic minorities in general including Asians, and has become popular among radical minority and anti-racist groups.

28. The label 'national' here and in the remainder of this section refers to 'within the confines of the nation-state' and therefore includes the national, regional, and local levels of the polity.

29. Claims against institutional forms of discrimination, such as by the police or the judiciary, were included in the category of minority integration politics.

30. In addition, as Table 9.6 shows, there were four cases in Britain that were unclassifiable with regard to the territorial frame of reference of the claim. These were all made by Islamic groups whose claims consisted of asserting the importance of Islamic faith or the greatness of Allah, but without the contextual grounding that would enable their territorial categorization.

31. Demands for special group rights, that is, for a specific minority group, characterize most of the cases of cultural rights in both countries—10 of 12 in Germany; 37 of 39 in Britain. Most of the demands for rights in the other categories were claims for non-group-specific rights, such as equal citizenship and voting rights in Germany, and equal rights in the labour market in Britain. In total, 59 per cent of the demands for rights in Britain were for specific group rights, compared to 38 per cent of those in Germany.

32. Note that our method allows analysis of the strategic action of claims in relation to the qualitative detail of the 'speech' that is actually reported.

33. To the defense of Yasemin Soysal it must be noted that in *Limits of Citizenship* (1994) she acknowledges and presents important evidence on cross-national differences in migrant and minority mobilization in different European countries. To explain these differences she points, much along the lines of the argument here, at the different traditions and institutional arrangements of migrant incorporation in these countries. In that sense Soysal's empirical analyses, which point at the importance of national contexts, are strangely at odds with her main theoretical conclusions, which emphasize the irrelevance of national compared to postnational forms of citizenship.

References

BADE, KLAUS J. (1994), *Ausländer, Aussiedler, Asyl* (Munich: C.H. Beck).

BALDWIN-EDWARDS, MARTIN, and SCHAIN, MARTIN (eds.) (1994), *The Politics of Immigration in Western Europe* (London: Sage).

BAUBÖCK, RAINER (1994), *Transnational Citizenship. Membership and Rights in International Migration* (Aldershot: Edward Elgar).

BRUBAKER, ROGERS (1992), *Citizenship and Nationhood in France and Germany* (Cambridge, MA: Harvard University Press).

CASTLES, STEPHEN (1995), 'How Nation-States Respond to Immigration and Ethnic Diversity', *New Community*, 21/3: 293–308.

——and MARK MILLER (1993), *The age of migration. International population movements in the modern world* (London: Macmillian).

ÇINAR, DILEK (1994), *From Aliens to Citizens: A Comparative Analysis of Rules of Transition* (Vienna: Institut für höhere Studien).

CORNELIUS, WAYNE, MARTIN, PHILIP, and HOLLIFIELD, JAMES (eds.) (1994), *Controlling Immigration: A Global Perspective* (Stanford, CA: Stanford University Press).

FAVELL, ADRIAN (1998), *Philosophies of Integration. Immigration and the Idea of Citizenship in France and Britain* (Houndmills, Basingstoke: Macmillan).

FORBES, IAN (1995), 'Institutionalising Anti-Discrimination in Europe' in Alec G. Hargreaves and Jeremy Leaman (eds.), *Racism, Ethnicity and Politics in Contemporary Europe* (Aldershot: Edward Elgar).

FREEMAN, GARY P. (1998), 'The Decline of Sovereignty? Politics and Immigration Restriction in Liberal States', in Christian Joppke (ed.), *Challenge to the Nation-State. Immigration in Western Europe and the United States* (Oxford: Oxford University Press).

GOODWIN-GILL, G. S., JENNY, R. K., and PERRUCHOUD, R. (1985), 'Basic Humanitarian Principles Applicable to Non-Nationals', *International Migration Review*, 19/3: 556–69.

HABERMAS, JÜRGEN (1996), 'The European Nation-state—Its Achievements and Its Limits. On the Past and Future of Sovereignty and Citizenship' in Gopal Balakrishnan (ed.), *Mapping the Nation* (London: Verso).

HAMMAR, TOMAS (1985), 'Introduction' in Tomas Hammar (ed.), *European Immigration Policy* (New York, NY: Cambridge University Press).

IRELAND, PATRICK (1994), *The Policy Challenge of Ethnic Diversity. Immigrant Politics in France and Switzerland* (Cambridge, MA: Harvard University Press).

JACOBSON, DAVID (1996), *Rights across Borders. Immigration and the Decline of Citizenship* (Baltimore, MD: The Johns Hopkins University Press).

JOPPKE, CHRISTIAN (1996), 'Multiculturalism and Immigration: A Comparison of the United States, Germany, and Great Britain', *Theory and Society*, 25: 449–500.

——(1997), 'Asylum and State Sovereignty. A Comparison of the United States, Germany, and Britain', *Comparative Political Studies*, 30/3: 259–98.

KASTORYANO, RIVA (1996), *La France, l'Allemagne et leurs immigrés: Négocier l'identité* (Paris: Armand Colin).

KLEGER, HEINZ, and D'AMATO, GIANNI (1995), 'Staatsbürgerschaft und Einbürgerung—oder: Wer ist ein Bürger? Ein Vergleich zwischen Deutschland, Frankreich und der Schweiz', *Journal für Sozialforschung*, 35, 3/4: 259–99.

KOOPMANS, RUUD, and KRIESI, HANSPETER (1997), 'Citoyenneté, identité nationale et mobilisation de l'extrême droite. Une comparaison entre la France, l'Allemagne, les Pays-Bas et la Suisse' in Pierre Birnbaum (ed.), *Sociologie des nationalismes* (Paris: Presses Universitaires de France).

KOOPMANS, RUUD, and STATHAM, PAUL (1999a), 'Political claims analysis: integrating protest event and political discourse approaches', *Mobilization. The International Journal of Research and Theory about Social Movements, Protest and Collective Behavior*, 4/2: 203–22.

——(1999b), 'Ethnic and Civil Conceptions of Nationhood and the Differential Success of the Extreme Right in Germany and Italy' in Marco G. Guigni, Doug McAdam, and Charles Tilly (eds.), *How Social Movements Matter* (Minneapolis, MN: University of Minnesota Press), 225–51.

——(2000), 'Political Claims-making against Racism and Discrimination in Britain and Germany' in Jessika ter Wal and Maykel Verkuyten (eds.), *Comparative Perspectives on Racism* (Aldershot: Ashgate).

Kriesi, Hanspeter, Koopmans, Ruud, Duyvendak, Jan Willem, and Giugni, Marco G. (1995), *New Social Movements in Western Europe: A Comparative Analysis* (Minneapolis, MN: University of Minnesota Press).

Kymlicka, Will (1995), *Multicultural Citizenship. A Liberal Theory of Minority Rights* (Oxford: Clarendon).

Layton-Henry, Zig (1994), 'Britain: the would be zero immigration country' in Wayne Cornelius, Phillip Martin, and James Hollofield (eds.), *Controlling Immigration: A Global Perspective* (Stanford, CA: Stanford University Press).

Lederer, Harald W. (1997), *Migration und Integration in Zahlen* (Bamberg: Europäisches Forum für Migrationsstudien).

Lie, John (1995), 'From International Migration to Transnational Diaspora', *Contemporary Sociology*, 24: 303–6.

Marshall, Thomas H. (1950), *Citizenship and social class and other essays* (Cambridge: Cambridge University Press).

Mason, David (1995), *Race and Ethnicity in Modern Britain* (Oxford: Oxford University Press).

McAdam, Doug (1982), *Political Process and the Development of Black Insurgency, 1930–1970* (Chicago, IL: University of Chicago Press).

McCarthy, John D., McPhail, Clark, and Smith, Jackie (1996), 'Images of Protest: Dimensions of Selection Bias in Media Coverage of Washington Demonstrations, 1982, 1991', *American Sociological Review*, 61: 478–99.

Modood, Tariq (1988), ' "Black", Racial Equality and Asian Identity', *New Community*, 14/3: 379–404.

—— Berthoud, Richard, Lakey, Jane, Nazroo, James, Smith, Patten, Virdee, Satnam, and Beishon, Sharon (1997), *Ethnic Minorities in Britain. Diversity and Disadvantage* (London: Policy Studies Institute).

Münz, Rainer, Wolfgang Seifert, and Ralf Ulrich (1997), *Zuwanderung nach Deutschland. Strukturen, Wirkungen, Perspektiven* (Frankfurt: Campus).

Olzak, Susan (1989), 'Analysis of Events in Studies of Collective Action', *Annual Review of Sociology*, 15: 119–41.

Parekh, Bhikhu (1996), 'Minority Practices and Principles of Toleration', *International Migration Review*, 30/1: 251–84.

Rex, John (1991), *Ethnic Identity and Ethnic Mobilisation in Britain* Monographs in Ethnic Relations No. 5. (Warwick: Centre for Research in Ethnic Relations, University of Warwick).

—— and Beatrice Drury (eds.) (1994), *Ethnic Mobilisation in a Multi-Cultural Europe* (Aldershot: Avebury).

Rucht, Dieter, Koopmans, Ruud, and Neidhardt, Friedhelm (eds.) (1998), *Acts of Dissent. New Developments in the Study of Protest* (Berlin: Sigma).

Safran, William (1997), 'Citizenship and Nationality in Democratic Systems: Approaches to Defining and Acquiring Membership in the Political Community', *International Political Science Review*, 18/3: 313–35.

Sassen, Saskia (1998), 'The de facto Transnationalizing of Immigration Policy' in

Christian Joppke (ed.), *Challenge to the Nation-State. Immigration in Western Europe and the United States* (Oxford: Oxford University Press).

SCHLESINGER, ARTHUR D. (1992), *The Disuniting of America: Reflections on a Multicultural Society* (New York, NY: Norton).

SHAIN, YOSSI, and SHERMAN, MARTIN (1998), 'Dynamics of disintegration: Diaspora, secession and the paradox of nation-states', *Nations and Nationalism*, 4/3: 321–46.

SHAPIRO, GILBERT, and MARKOFF, JOHN (1998), *Revolutionary Demands. A Content Analysis of the Cahiers de Doléances of 1789* (Stanford, CA: Stanford University Press).

SMITH, DAVID M., and BLANC, MAURICE (1996), 'Citizenship, Nationality and Ethnic Minorities in Three European Nations', *International Journal of Urban and Regional Research*, 20/1: 66–82.

SOLOMOS, JOHN (1993), *Race and Racism in Contemporary Britain* (2nd ed.) (London: Macmillan).

——and LES BACK (1995), *Race, Politics and Social Change* (London/New York: Routledge).

SOPEMI (Système d'Observation Permanente des Migrations) (1997), *Trends in international migration. Continuous Reporting System on Migration. Annual Report 1996* (Paris: OECD).

SOYSAL, YASEMIN NUHOGLU (1994), *Limits of Citizenship. Migrants and Postnational Membership in Europe* (Chicago, IL: University of Chicago Press).

——(1997), 'Changing Parameters of Citizenship and Claims-Making: Organized Islam in European Public Spheres', *Theory and Society*, 26: 509–27.

——(1998), 'Toward a Postnational Model of Membership' in Gershon Shafir (ed.), *The Citizenship Debates. A Reader* (Minneapolis, MN: University of Minnesota Press).

TARROW, SIDNEY (1989), *Democracy and Disorder. Protest and Politics in Italy, 1965–1975* (Oxford: Clarendon).

——(1994), *Power in Movement. Social Movements, Collective Action and Politics* (Cambridge: Cambridge University Press).

THRÄNHARDT, DIETRICH (1992), 'Germany—An Undeclared Immigration Country' in Dietrich Thränhardt (ed.), *Europe—A New Immigration Continent. Policies and Politics since 1945 in Comparative Perspective* (Hamburg: Lit).

YOUNG, IRIS MARION (1998), 'Polity and Group Difference: A Critique of the Ideal of Universal Citizenship' in Gershon Shafir (ed.), *The Citizenship Debates. A Reader* (Minneapolis, MN: University of Minnesota Press).

10

Reaping What They Sow: Institutions and Immigrant Political Participation in Western Europe

PATRICK IRELAND

The tensions and conflicts associated with migration have forced themselves to the top of the political agenda across Europe. Europeans today live in societies that have become truly multicultural. Former immigrant and colonial labourers have become permanent residents with legitimate needs and demands on the host societies. How have immigrant-origin populations mobilized to have their demands met in Western European political systems, and why have they adopted the forms and strategies they have?[1] Have these marginal groups found meaningful, effective ways of participating in host-society politics? The political participation of such minorities is a complex process, involving many variables, and researchers are just now trying to provide cogent answers to these questions.

Europe experienced immigration before 1945, with migrants moving largely to a neighbouring country. Those people who did settle permanently in the receiving societies underwent a thorough, often painful process of individual assimilation. They adopted the languages and customs of their new country. The same was true of the Jews from Eastern and Central Europe and the refugees from religious persecution, civil wars, and revolutions who fled westward before World War II.

Post-war immigration into Europe has been a very different story. Immediately or shortly after 1945, rapid economic growth and shortages of workers across Western Europe spurred both private- and public-sector programmes for recruiting foreign labour. By the mid-1950s the in-migration involved workers from peripheral areas of Europe and developing countries, including overseas possessions and former colonies. For a long time, neither the foreign workers, their countries of origin, nor their 'hosts' saw their presence as permanent. Concerned primarily about meeting their industries' demand for cheap labour, European authorities implemented no coherent, co-ordinated policies for coping with the social and political effects of mass recruitment of migrant workers. The situation reached a critical turning point in the 1970s, when oil shocks precipitated a rapid economic deterioration in the labour-importing countries. Organized anti-immigrant reactions had developed, and ethnic relations soon soured. It became clear that an early return to the homeland was unlikely. All the host societies prohibited additional immigration during this period of rising unemployment. Their task became to integrate the variegated immigrant-origin communities that post-war migration had created and that have been growing more diverse and more stratified socioeconomically.

Immigrants' typical lack of formal political rights and other political resources at first led scholars and public officials alike to see foreign workers as largely unorganized and apolitical components of the economy. Political scientist Mark Miller was one of the first to challenge this 'quiescence thesis' (1981; 1982). In the years since, it has become apparent that immigrant-origin communities have not settled for a passive political role as the object of host-society policies and political discourse. The increasingly familial nature and slower turnover of their communities have reduced their willingness to accept their lot in the host societies. Even so, their participatory patterns have varied across the continent. In some places, for instance, immigrant organizations make reference to an ethnic community in their public pronouncements and informational literature. Elsewhere, discourse is formulated not in ethnic or community terms but in those of class, social work, human rights, or individual citizenship.

After a slow start, scholarship has now provided us with impressive amounts of data and valuable insights into the relationship between immigrants and politics in post-war Europe. A lot of this work has been descriptive or prescriptive, however. Analysts have supplied us with a trio of rather loose, tentative approaches to understanding such phenomena:

Class Theory. Scholars like Castles and Kosack (1974; 1985), Daniel Lawrence (1974), Ben Tahar (1979), Annie Phizacklea (1980), Robert Miles (1982; 1984), Miles and Phizacklea (1977), John Rex (1979; 1996), and Stephen Castles and his collaborators (1984; 1990) have argued that the immigrants' common class identity ultimately determines the nature of their participation. Here, capitalism's need for cheap labour has induced migration and has culminated in the creation of ethnic/racial sub-proletarians. Employers and the state have split the working class into foreign and autochthonous components, which makes it easier to impose on both, the costs of industrial reconstruction. Ethnicity and race have therefore become the modalities in which immigrants experience class relations in Western Europe. They represent a false consciousness that divides the working class and keeps it from taking collective action.

Neo-Marxists generally see all forms of immigrant political participation, especially anti-racist movements but also ethnic-based organizations, as part of a process whereby indigenous and foreign workers have been coming to realize and act on their common class interests. Host-society working-class movements—trade unions, left-wing political parties, and other associations—are both the arenas within which the desired proletarian solidarity occurs and a possible stimulus or a barrier to it. Since the origins of immigrant politics are seen in the structural tensions and contradictions of advanced capitalist society, such efforts to improve conditions and fight racism should be gradually converging in nature and objective in all the host societies. In the long run, ethnic politics should dissolve into the more fundamental politics of class conflict.

Ethnicity/Race Theory. Scholars like Robert Moore (1975), Nancy Foner (1979), John Rex and Sally Tomlinson (1979), Mark J. Miller (1981; 1982), Martin O. Heisler and Barbara Schmitter Heisler (1990), and Alain Touraine (1990) make an implicit or explicit assumption that the immigrants' ethnic identity is of fundamental importance and that ethnic politics will endure, at least for the foreseeable future. In some studies a multiethnic racial identity (Rex and Moore 1967; Rex and Tomlinson 1979; Ben-Tovin and Gabriel 1982; Banton 1985; Moulin 1985) or a common religious identity (Dumont 1986; Safran 1986; Balibar and Wallerstein 1988; Étienne 1989; see also Kramer 1993; An-Naim 1996; Huntington 1996) plays a comparably independent, durable role in determining the nature of immigrants' political mobilization.

In this optic, immigrants should organize and articulate their political interests along ethnic, racial, regional, or religious lines. Each group's own distinctive mode of political participation develops from group socialization processes and in response to discrimination and interaction with other groups (compare Barth 1969, with Spicer 1971) and should exhibit a unique participatory pattern. Most often, this is seen in combination with the effects of a 'homeland hangover', the persistence of patterns of participation that immigrants developed in their country of origin (Ireland 1994). Hence, the ethnicity theory predicts that immigrants of the same background in different host societies will adopt roughly similar forms of participation, a result even more likely in light of the similar socioeconomic conditions and levels of anti-immigrant sentiment that endured across Western Europe (see Ireland 1997). Such an approach has clear affinities with the identity politics fad, whereby people are mobilized not because of what they do, but in terms of who and what they are. Ethnic mobilization, like other forms, 'is seen solely as an expression of a way of life, divorced from economic and political conflicts' (Rex 1996: 196).

Institutional Channeling Theory. Researchers like Theodore Lowi (1964), Gaynor Cohen (1982), John L. P. Thompson (1983), Andrew Jakubowicz and his colleagues (1984), and Patrick Ireland (1989) have noted that certain kinds of immigration policies and administrative practices seem particularly likely to spark certain kinds of ethnic and immigrant group activity. Likewise highlighted has been the impact that policies and laws governing citizenship and naturalization have on the integration of immigrants and the nature of ethnic relations in modern industrial societies (Castles 1992; Brubaker 1989 and 1992; Soysal 1994). Building on these observations—which, important as they are, have been supported by largely impressionistic evidence—I constructed a two-country, four-city comparative study that ascribed immigrant behaviour to political opportunity structures (Ireland 1994), the legal and political institutions that have both shaped and limited the migrants' choice possibilities (Katznelson 1973: 42; see Esman 1985; Bousetta 1997a). Included herein are institutions like political parties, trade unions, and religious and humanitarian non-profit associations that can weaken or strengthen the effects of differences in resources. They act as institutional gatekeepers, controlling access to the avenues of political participation available to immigrants. My research has delineated the ways in which different frameworks and linking processes embedded in them, structure the participation of immigrant groups in Western Europe.

In this Chapter I will assess that participation–institution relationship in France, The Netherlands, Belgium, Germany, and Switzerland: countries at Europe's heart in which policy-makers have emphasized the incorporation of large, diverse immigrant-origin populations into the welfare state. In 1996, foreign resident population accounted for 9 per cent of all inhabitants of Belgium, over 6.3 per cent in France,[2] 8.9 per cent in Germany, and around 4.5 per cent in The Netherlands. Fully 19 per cent of Switzerland's population were not Swiss citizens then, the highest foreign share in Europe save for tiny Luxembourg and tinier Liechtenstein (SOPEMI 1998: 31–2). It must be noted that such official figures are partially an artifact produced by the different politics of citizenship and can leave out sizeable numbers of people of foreign origins who live in these countries, especially those like France and The Netherlands who have traditionally had generous legislation in this regard. This undercounting is 'even more true if we take into account that France and The Netherlands have taken [in] large numbers of immigrants from former colonies who were French or Dutch citizens by birth' (Koopmans and Kriesi 1997: 13–14).

These five countries have become home to different clusters of immigrant-origin communities, whose concentration has varied widely from city to city. The problems that they generate, both real and imagined, and the policies developed to address them, have therefore differed across regions and localities as much as across time and national boundaries. In an age of globalization, processes of identity redefinition and collective strategies depend increasingly on local-level realities; variations can sometimes be greater within countries than across them (Le Gales and Harding 1998). We definitely need more nuanced, empirical treatment than broad 'models of incorporation' can provide (compare Brubaker 1992; Castles and Miller 1993; Castles 1994; Soysal 1994).

Even at the national level, however, fruitful comparison is possible (compare Christian Joppke's contribution to Chapter 7 of this volume). Immigrants occupy similar class positions in France, The Netherlands, Belgium, Germany, and Switzerland, and these host societies have several national/ethnic communities in common, if not always of the same proportions, notably here: Italians, Spaniards, Turks, and Moroccans. Taking advantage of opportunities essentially to hold class and ethnic variables constant, within the context of varying national policy and institutional variables, one can gain meaningful insights into the degree to which each factor explains the observed participatory patterns. I will argue here that institutional forces—including immigrant integration policies, citizenship laws, and the actions of institutional gatekeepers—have determined what forms immigrant mobilization takes and, more than any intrinsically ethnic particularities or socio-professional status, along which lines immigrant mobilization occurs. Institutions, neither benign nor neutral, play a key role in instigating, perpetuating, and defusing ethnic, racial, and class conflict. They connect people to the state in particular ways, strengthening and weakening ethnic, class, and other collective identities in various places and at various times.

France

Since the Revolution, a largely Jacobin model of the nation-state has dominated France as a general paradigm. Under it, membership in the national community involves a voluntary commitment to the republic and its values. Religious, ethnic, linguistic, regional, and sub-cultural identities have been accepted but relegated to the private sphere. William Safran has observed that a 'legal reflection of this approach to the nation was the emphasis on jus soli, rather than descent from French ancestors, in the granting of French nationality' (1991: 221). Naturalization laws were designed 'to make Frenchmen out of foreigners' (Mauco 1932). Ensuring that often difficult and painful process was an array of important agents of assimilation, as described by Eugen Weber (1976): the army, industry, the French Communist Party (PCF), the trade unions, the Catholic church, and the centralized educational system.

Importing Diversity

After World War II, a demographic gap and the economic recovery meant that there were more jobs, particularly unskilled ones, than there were French workers to fill them. For the first time, France accepted the massive importation of an ever more diverse range of national groups: in addition to the Italians—most numerous as late as 1959—waves of Iberians, Serbs, North and sub-Saharan Africans, and Turks broke over each other in quick succession in the 1960s and early 1970s, more and more of them from rural, uneducated backgrounds. Generally speaking, the 'assimilation machines' of the pre-war period still functioned for post-war Southern Europeans. Yet the increasing ethnic, racial, and religious diversity posed a special challenge and soon overwhelmed them, even as modernization was undermining traditional authority structures like the Church and the family. Foreign workers were not returning to their homelands, nor were they assimilating into French society.

New labour immigration was banned a year after the 1973 oil crisis, and the Giscard administration vowed to absorb the immigrants already resident into French institutions and society. France had already created an ethnic minorities problem, however. *Ad hoc* post-war labour and housing policies, together with the sheer magnitude of the population movements, had produced stable immigrant communities. Governments' selective treatment of each had fostered collective, ethnic-based identities that were often lacking among arriving immigrants. The Jacobin ideal legitimated the wide provision of social benefits to foreign workers and their families, in the name of equal treatment. Steadily expanding and more inclusive, the French social welfare system reduced the emotional hold of the immigrants' homelands and their governments' organizational presence. The French Left, moreover, insisted that immigrant workers work within its movements. Powerful organizations like the Algerian Amicales and Southern European Catholic and Communist associations steadily lost their predominance. When upset, immigrants began to target French social policies: housing problems—the *SONACOTRA* rent strikes, 1975–1980—discrimination, and restrictive legislation and administrative procedures—the proposed Stoléru reform and Barre-Bonnet laws, 1979–1980—became the object of undeniably political protests (Ireland 1996).

The Opening from the Left

When François Mitterrand and the Socialists (PS) took the reins of power in 1981, they tinkered with the actual practice of assimilation. The new government implemented more liberal policies toward family reunification, strengthened the immigrants' protection against administrative abuses and deportation without due process, and streamlined the permit system. Committed advocates of cultural pluralism, the Socialists significantly increased immigrants' ability to organize on the basis of class, ethnicity, race, and even religion. With the law of October 9, 1981, 'foreign' associations became subject to the same conditions as French ones: a simple declaration to the Ministry of the Interior. Immigrants likewise won the right to act as administrators of their own and French associations and, like them, to receive public funding. Now, the Catholic Federation of Support Associations for Immigrant Workers (FASTI), the Protestant social action committee CIMADE, the pro-Communist Movement Against Racism and for Friendship Between Peoples (MRAP), and others had to compete with the immigrants' own associations for government subsidies (Verbunt 1985).

The new laws gave a fillip to immigrant associational activity. The number of associations skyrocketed and surpassed 4,200 by the mid-1980s. As diverse as the immigrant-origin communities themselves, they represented all possible currents. Some of them began to demand greater freedom of political expression and more respect for their national or regional ethnic group's cultural identity. Cross-ethnic co-operation and organization intensified.

The Younger Generations

At the same time, the sons and daughters of non-European workers, numbering well over a million by the early 1980s, were facing socioeconomic marginalization: most of them came to occupy the same menial occupational substratum as their parents, and unemployment rates have been high. Most second-generation immigrants have qualified for French citizenship either automatically or upon reaching age eighteen. With an undeniable claim on French society, then, their expectations and demands have diverged from those of the first generation. Their sense of identity and collective behavior have had less to do with their social-class status or ethnic origin, than with the web of local political, cultural, and economic relations in which they move. Most of them refuse to identify with the working class, angering the PCF and the trade unions. The task of assimilating and socializing these young people fell at first almost entirely to the public schools, which have held to their traditionally narrow republican ideology and have had problems absorbing those whose cultural backgrounds render them unable or unwilling to conform. Because of post-war policy choices, such people populate the cités and the concrete HLM (low-income housing) projects in France's industrial suburbs. There, the children of immigrant and French workers have lived and struggled together.

It was the suburban projects that witnessed the first collective initiatives by immigrant-origin youths. Limited opportunities for individual socioeconomic mobility, together with relatively easy access to French citizenship and full political rights, encouraged second- and third-generation immigrants to undertake group-based organization (see Huntington and Nelson 1976).[3] Whereas the first immigrant generation was shifting to more assimilative forms of participation by the early 1990s, members of the following generations favoured the unconventional 'weapons of the weak' that are often necessary and effective for outsider groups. Second-generation North Africans, nicknamed the Beurs, figured prominently in these movements, some of them violent—'Rock Against Police', 1980–1981—some non-violent and multiethnic—the March Against Racism and for Equality, 1983; Convergence, 1984; SOS-Racisme. Others focused primarily on the Beurs—the Paris–Bordeaux March, 1985; the Arab Youth of Lyon and its Suburbs (JALB)—or on that most assimilative of political activities, voter registration drives—France-Plus, Collectives for Civic Rights. Cultural activities like militant theatre groups, rock bands, and radio stations, government-subsidized since 1981, have likewise filled their need for expression (Ireland 1996).

Islam and the Lay State

Some have also made Islam the locus of political mobilization. Spiritual demands from an increasingly sedentary population combined with the new associational possibilities after 1981 to spur the construction of mosques, most of them Sunnite. Alongside them local Muslim cultural associations have intervened on members' behalf at social welfare offices, schools, police stations, and city hall. Islam has spread among foreign workers in the factories as well, and demands for Islamic prayer rooms there inspired immigrant-led strikes that hit Renault, Citroën, and Talbot automobile plants in several areas of France from summer 1981 to early 1983, then again in 1989–1990 (Benoît 1982; Lazzarato 1990).

In their overwhelming majority the second and third immigrant generations have not rejected the French political system or republican values. Nor has Muslim fundamentalism won large numbers of converts in France among those of North and sub-Saharan African or Turkish background. With their economic and social integration in France stalling, however, many of the younger generations have turned Islam into a mouthpiece and negotiating tool in a painful process of integration through protest. Official attempts to structure a 'Gallic' Islam—along the lines of the national 'consistories' that exist for France's Jews and Protestants—have met with very mixed results and have often only heightened tensions within the Muslim population (Lochon 1990).[4]

The Suburban Crisis

In the early 1980s, immigrants in France found themselves confronted by supporters of Jean-Marie Le Pen and his National Front, who fed on the atmosphere of social and economic crisis and found them convenient scapegoats. France's two-ballot, absolute-majority electoral system had long acted as a firebreak that kept the National Front out of French party politics. The situation changed significantly as a result of the decentralization programme pursued by the Socialists from 1981 through 1983. It was at the local level that the political struggle over immigration was most intense and that the *frontistes*, like the immigrants, were able to achieve their first political successes. President Mitterrand's decision to change the electoral system to one based on proportional representation for legislative elections in 1986 gave the National Front enough strength to constitute a parliamentary group. Its fortunes have fluctuated since then, but its status as a major political party in its own right has not waivered.

More repressive immigration policies came into effect during the period of cohabitation that followed the Right's victory in those 1986 legislative elections. There were more identification checks and expulsions of undocumented immigrants and refugees, especially non-Europeans. The new Interior Minister, Charles Pasqua, adopted a hard line and explicitly rejected multiculturalism. The government had to back down, even so, when confronted with opposition based on defence of France's tradition of inclusiveness and equality. In late 1986 and early 1987, student demonstrations forced the government to withdraw planned educational reforms—the Devaquet Plan. A few months later, it proposed a reform of the Nationality Code—the Chalandon Reform—that would have eliminated the automatic nature of second-generation immigrants' accession to French citizenship. When the same student groups started to take to the streets once again in opposition, Prime Minister Jacques Chirac quickly suspended the plan.

By 1988, the second immigrant generation accounted for 3 per cent of the total national electorate, more in some localities. In first-round balloting in that year's presidential election, François Mitterrand won the backing of nearly half of second-generation North Africans; between 80 and 84 per cent of them chose him over Chirac in the second round. Over 600 young people of North African, Asian, and Southern European stock figured on the candidate slates of all the mainstream parties in 1988, and in the 1989 municipal elections, over 300 second-generation immigrants won local-level office (Bouamama 1989). By this time, the PS had dropped its call for the 'right to difference' or 'droit à la différence', for a campaign in favour of 'living together' or 'vivre ensemble', emphasizing common ground instead of cultural diversity. The immigration challenge was merging inexorably with broader urban and social challenges, crossing traditional party lines and dividing the Left and Right alike between proponents of ethnic pluralism and defenders of the traditional, assimilationist Jacobin model. The wrenching effects on the French polity were clear during the famous 'headscarf' affair in autumn 1989. At issue has been the lay, Republican tradition, which many see embodied in and protected by the French educational system.

In the poor neighbourhoods, touted programs had failed to produce real changes. In autumn 1990, riots once again spread across France from the tinderbox of Lyon's suburbs. In the early 1980s, French officialdom had answered the angry protests of the second generation: first with police repression, and then with the institution of locally-based structures and subsidies that facilitated cultural and political expression. Those measures defused the revolt that was simmering in French cities and led hundreds of youngsters to work within the institutions of the host society. This reactive institutional tinkering had allowed the system to integrate the second-generation leadership, who became the organizers of the anti-racism movement, a 'beurgeoisie'. These new élites, many of them women, have acted as brokers between their generation and French society (Wihtol de Wenden 1990; Geisser 1997).

But the activists have lost touch with the bulk of immigrant-origin youth, whom socio-professional mobility still eludes. The agitators of the 'intifada of the suburbs' were the youngest and most marginalized of this cohort. They tend to see collective violence, albeit illegal, as their sole means of obtaining legitimate goals. Such disaffected suburban youths have developed 'parallel survival networks', an underground economy of petty delinquency and drugs organized around loose bands.

Meanwhile, the anti-racist movements, once so powerful in blunting the Right, are in a shambles. SOS-Racisme and France-Plus, which spearheaded the movement in the 1980s, no longer exercise much influence on the mass media. The immigrant-origin youths who participated in the violent demonstrations in spring 1994 against the government's proposal to introduce lower 'training' wages, resembled the anomic rioters of the early 1990s more than the friendly potes of the 1980s. Youths of North African origin have shown little confidence in associations representing them and their interests (Jazouli 1995). In the midst of the 'suburban crisis', a trend toward ethnic and multiethnic 'regrouping' by street and building has become noticeable; these are places where social disadvantages accumulate and over which an atmosphere of insecurity hangs (Bachmann and Le Guennec 1996).

Jacobinism Reborn

In response, the state has explicitly reaffirmed the traditional model of individual assimilation, defining and defending 'French values' and rejecting 'Anglo-Saxon ethnic pluralism' and the 'tribalism' that it allegedly generates (quoted in Ireland 1996: 42). Of course, today's ethnic conflicts are the logical consequence of a long process of settlement in French society and French officials' response to it. Jacobinism has been refashioned to take account of the new ethnic pluralism.

This remains true, despite the recent harshness of the immigration debate. When the Right crushed the divided Socialists in legislative elections in March 1993, Charles Pasqua became Interior Minister once again, and he brought with him another round of restrictive immigration policies and exclusionary rhetoric. Among the changes was a new requirement for immigrants born in France to make an express, formal request for French nationality between the ages of 16 and 21 and a tightening of the so-called double *jus soli* enjoyed by the French-born children of Algerians born before their country gained its independence in 1962 (Bruschi 1994). Yet at bottom, France has remained true to its universalistic, egalitarian republicanism: these and subsequent changes in the nationality law preserve *jus soli* (Hoffmann 1994: 14; SOPEMI 1998: 64).

Associations active among immigrant-origin communities have become fragmented and dispersed, but they remain a source of much spontaneous energy and creativity. Neighbourhood associations have been especially active, implicating the affected populations themselves in development projects such as 'C'est mon quartier' in 1995. In 1995–1996, conservative Prime Minister Alain Juppé faced a crisis when undocumented immigrants and asylum-seekers took refuge in churches and organized a March for Hope from Angoulême to Paris

(Coindé 1997). Then, early in 1997, Justice Minister Jean-Louis Debré introduced draconian immigration laws. An amendment requiring those lodging
foreigners to report their departure to city hall—'certificates of accommodation'—provoked a vast protest movement, launched by 59 filmmakers and critical of the Left as well as the Right. On February 27, 1997, over 100,000 people
marched through Paris in protest against the government's bill. Faced with such
a reaction, the government stepped down and retracted the more controversial
aspects of the bill (Waters 1998).

France's suburban turmoil roils on, as evidenced by riots in Toulouse,
Longwy, and Strasbourg at the close of 1998. Identities and conflicts seem to
be undergoing a 'territorialization' that is countered in some places, but not all,
by sometimes surprisingly resilient locally based organizational and institutional networks (Kastoryano 1996). Even then, Nathan Glazer's worry about
the United States might apply as well to France: 'To what do new immigrant
children assimilate? The conditions of life in big-city schools are so disordered,
the prevalence of violence so marked, the degree of school failure and of resistance to authority so great, that one can well fear that assimilation of new
immigrants may be to a dysfunctional America, the America of the lower
depths of the large urban centers' (Glazer 1995: 15).

The Netherlands

In contrast to France, The Netherlands is often cited as Europe's best example
of the multicultural model, along with Sweden (Castles and Miller 1998; Soysal
1994). The Dutch were relatively late getting into the labour-importing
game and have little heavy industry or coal mining. The consequence has been
fewer foreign residents overall but more non-Europeans than many places in
Europe. Over a quarter of those of foreign origin are Turks, and more than
a fifth, Moroccans. Fully 60 per cent of the minority population live in
the provinces of North and South Holland, home to just over a third of the
Dutch-stock population, most of them in the country's four largest cities:
Amsterdam, Rotterdam, The Hague, and Utrecht (Tesser, van Dugteren, and
Merens 1996).

Faced with such concentrated diversity, the Dutch have proved consistently
inclusive and have at times espoused a multicultural model, starting with a
version of it that jibed with their own 'pillarized' system. The result has
been more institutional participation and more ethnic-based mobilization
than in France, although not always of the type that Dutch policy-makers
intended. Sensitive to the risks of segregation and ghetto formation that
cultural pluralism brings, they have since adapted policies to local conditions
and have not hesitated to rejigger or jettison them when they have produced
unwanted effects. The recent trend away from ethnic-specific policies and

toward general policies to help all disadvantaged groups and neighbourhoods is explainable in this fashion.' Immigrant participatory patterns have responded in kind.

Toward an Ethnic Minorities Policy

The Dutch, who take great pride in seeing themselves as 'modern and enlightened' (Rath *et al.* 1996: 255), have demonstrated notable pragmatism and greater policy coherence than their neighbours. Even before they clearly defined a bundle of policies toward 'ethnic minorities', Dutch officials were responding to the 'givens' of post-war migration. Former colonials, Moluccans and Surinamese, and guestworkers (*gastarbeiders*) from the Mediterranean, at first received different treatment (Penninx, Schoorl, and van Praag 1994: 142–55). Meanwhile, temporary guestworkers, mostly Southern Europeans in the early 1960s, were first in the care of Catholic non-profit groups that received increasing levels of public support: from 40 per cent in 1964 to 100 per cent in 1975. When large numbers of non-Christians began to arrive later in the 1960s, the renamed Foundations for Assistance to Foreign Workers lost their Catholic character and became targeted at guestworkers alone and supplemented by the private sector. Nationally controlled social service provision ended for former colonials around the same time, taken over by new, government-subsidized foundations. Through a process of accretion, a well-equipped, well-financed, extensive subsystem of public, semi-public, and private organizations developed to deal with the housing, welfare, and recreational needs of the non-Dutch population.

This approach was entirely in keeping with the 'pillarization' (*verzuiling*) system that the Dutch institutionalized in the nineteenth century to manage their own diversity. Based on a vertical build-up of interest groups in all spheres of public life, this system has required co-operation among different confessional and secular groups (Lijphart 1975). The major cultural and religious communities—Christian Reformed, Catholic, and Secular/Liberal—have had their own associations, trade unions, political parties, schools, social work agencies, and broadcasting associations for radio and television. Many tasks that 'would have been carried out by the state, provincial or municipal bureaucracies in other countries were put in the hands of para- or quasi-governmental institutions in the Netherlands' (Toonen 1996: 615). Pillarization has been more complex than it appears, with significant regional differences and local variations. Differentiated and fragmented, the system has none the less facilitated social and political integration.

Not surprisingly, then, Dutch officials turned even more insistently to it when migration appeared to threaten that integration in the late 1970s. By that point, the social fallout of migration had become inescapable. The oil crisis of 1973 led to a halt in new labour recruitment, but it aggravated push factors in, and thus actually encouraged further emigration from' the Dutch Antilles, Aruba, and Surinam. Family reunification continued, too, peaking in 1979–1980. Ethnic communities were developing. Scuffles broke out between them and native Dutch in Rotterdam's Afrikaander neighbourhood in 1972 and in Schiedam in 1976. Some supporters of an independent Moluccan Republic resorted to terrorism, taking hostages, burning the Indonesian embassy, and hijacking trains in The Netherlands. Simultaneously, political mobilization against migrants was emerging: in the early 1970s, the Netherland's People's Union and, after 1980, the Centre Party (CP) gradually picked up strength. It won a seat in the second chamber of the national parliament in 1982 which it lost in 1986 but regained in 1989. In 1983, the CP won 9 per cent of the vote in Almere in a special election, and did well in elections to neighbourhood councils in Rotterdam the following year (Entzinger 1984).

The state responded by embracing an identity-based approach to integration. Pillarization meant that The Netherlands was far more prepared than neighbouring countries to see immigrant-origin people in terms of ethnic communities. The Scientific Council for Government Policy issued a report in 1979 in which it acknowledged that many immigrants were going to stay in The Netherlands and that the country had to learn how to cope. In 1983, the government presented a new ethnic minority policy in its *Minderhedennota*. It applied to 'those for whose presence the government feels a special responsibility (because of the colonial past or because they had been recruited by authorities) and who find themselves in a minority situation' (MBZ 1983: 12).[6] These ethnic minorities—including people from former Dutch colonies Surinamese, Moluccans/Indonesians, Antilleans/Arubans, foreign workers and their families mostly North Africans and Turks but also Cape Verdeans, Chinese, and Vietnamese, Sinti and Roma, refugees, caravan dwellers, recently naturalized members of these communities, and descendants of all of the above-mentioned groups down to the third generation if they regard themselves as non-indigenous—account for up to 15 per cent of the total resident population by some estimates (Penninx, Schoorl, and van Praag 1994: 1).

Citing the danger of isolation and the formation of 'foreigner colonies' (*vreemdelingenkolonies*) if these minorities shut themselves up in their own world, the government envisioned their 'emancipation' and gradual integration over two to three generations through state-supported participation in economic activities and vital sociopolitical institutions, and the encouragement of 'self-organization' (Voogt 1994). The ideal was a cohesive yet pluralistic society comprised of ethnically bounded but socially, culturally, and economically nested groups. To that end the Ministry of the Interior was now to offer grants-in-aid to finance minority programmes and associations and their administration at the local level. Consultative bodies at the national and local levels would give minorities a proportional say in policy-making, local authorities would stimulate the organization of associations whose frame of reference was the local situation of immigrants, and naturalization would be made easier (see Heijs 1995).

Immigrants' earlier mobilization, often by left-wing political and trade union activists opposed to homeland regimes, had centred around ideologically flavoured pronouncements about inequalities and injustice globally. Many Southern Europeans also maintained close links with Italian and Spanish Catholic Church organizations. During the 1980s, the new subsidies and other protections from Dutch officials spurred the development of immigrant associations with looser homeland ties as well. Turkish and Moroccan Muslims were particularly quick to organize, and sports and cultural organizations also multiplied (Layton-Henry 1990). So, too, did associations formed by second-generation migrants with their sights set squarely on a quest to develop collective forms of emancipation, in which they serve as the defenders of group interests and as social and cultural workers within Dutch society (Penninx, Schoorl, and van Praag 1994: 176–88). Several national, ethnic-based umbrella associations emerged to serve as a bridge to Dutch authorities. They never became very effective or representative, however, and mobilization strategies shifted more decidedly toward more nuanced and technical issues affecting integration at the local or even neighbourhood level. There, groups responding to Dutch expectations of ethnic communities ranged alongside those that did not.

Contemporaneously, resident non-citizens gained the right to vote in local elections. While they tended to turn out in lower numbers than native-stock Dutch, turnout varied by ethnic community and locality. Immigrant-origin candidates, not surprisingly, boosted participation rates, and their success rate improved over the years. The Labour Party (PvdA) received most of the minority vote, but the Greens and Christian Democrats also had their supporters. Ethnic-based parties have not been common, although in neighborhood elections in Rotterdam in 1984, a Turkish-Islamic party, Hakyol, did receive more than 40 per cent of Turkish voters' support (Böcker 1994). There has been great polarization within the Turkish community, the result of 'imported' regional, religious, and other differences into The Netherlands. The same has held for other groups, such as the Moroccans, two-thirds of whom are from the impoverished Rif (Buijs and Nelissen 1994).

Overall, there was a pronounced spurt in immigrant and ethnic mobilization orientated toward both the homelands and The Netherlands during the 1980s. Since other Western European countries witnessed a similar development, Dutch policies could not have been the only structuring factor. Still, compared to its neighbours, The Netherlands experienced noticeably more harmonious social relations in the 1980s, a period of economic stagnation and labour-market contraction.

Away From Multiculturalism

By the late 1980s, however, it was clear that marginalization was actually continuing despite the economic recovery underway by then. Unintentionally, linking the immigrant-origin communities to the welfare state had delinked them from Dutch society; to illustrate, a significant number of immigrants who had lived in the country for decades still did not speak Dutch (Nederlands Centrum Buitenlanders 1993). Some of the ethnic-based organizing stimulated by Dutch officialdom had had 'perverse' effects, leading to fragmentation and divisiveness that ran counter to express policy goals of minority socialization, integration, and emancipation (see Rath 1991). As a result, combating deprivation in disadvantaged areas came to supplant support for organizations and initiatives that cultivated ethnic identity and solidarity. Subsidies for social and cultural activities soon ebbed. There was freer play for market forces: rent subsidies replaced social housing, and the government initiated a public discussion over the merits of US-style enterprise zones. Equal access had become the desired end, to be attained by ensuring an equal legal status for minorities, and by improving the accessibility of public institutions to people from minority groups. If necessary, even so, officials could still undertake special measures aimed at such groups to remove stubborn obstacles to full participation (Tesser, van Dugteren, and Merens 1996).

Southern Europeans, it was agreed, had done well enough that they should no longer be the targets of such efforts (Lindo 1994). Their treatment in The Netherlands has increasingly come under the aegis of the European Union. Blending in without major incident into Dutch associational and political life, their own organizations already centreed on cultural and educational concerns that made them colourful buttresses of social harmony.

An emphasis on human capital enhancement and the 'non-discrimination principle', the introduction of a calculus of rewards and penalties—these are hallmarks of what has become known as the 'new Dutch model'. Whether taking advantage of new opportunities or out of desperation at a labour market where they still faced discrimination, ethnic entrepreneurs grew in number in the early 1990s to some 19,000 by 1992 (Kloosterman, van der Leun, and Rath 1997: 65–6). Although concerns were voiced in certain quarters that 'independent entrepreneurship' fed isolation and segregation, this development was generally welcomed as a sign that minorities could preserve their culture, identity, and internal solidarity and achieve economic success without having to assimilate or acculturate. Besides those who established their own businesses, those of the first immigrant generation who managed socioeconomic mobility largely did so as employees of the welfare state, performing 'ethnic functions' (Böcker 1994).

Searching for a Balance

Not everyone was tiptoeing happily through the tulips, however. The CP had split in two in the mid-1980s. Simmering resentment at all the socioeconomic changes and growth in the minority, and from 1988, refugee, population now revived its fortunes, and by the 1990s, anti-immigrant parties had elected council members in ten large cities. They turned Islam's presence in The Netherlands into a special bugbear (see Bolkestein 1997).

The Netherlands had long had contact with Islam through trading and in its colonies. Dutch officials entered into contact with Islamic organizations in the 1980s, both because of the growing prominence of such groups in the socio-cultural realm but also because of the belief that they could prove useful in the implementation of the minority policy. The government played a crucial role in setting up the Islamic Broadcasting Foundation, which received official recognition in 1985; a year later, imams were put on equal legal footing with preachers, priests, and rabbis (Shadid and Van Koningsveld 1996). Yet to Dutch officialdom's chagrin, occasionally extreme ethnic, regional, and political differences were reflected in the Islamic associations whose growth it had stimulated (Can and Can-Engin 1997). As Jan Rath and his collaborators have shown in their comparison between Rotterdam and Utrecht (1993), even in cities with similar immigrant-origin populations and run by the same political party, in this case the PvdA, the realities of local politics and networks could produce sharply contrasting Islamic associational profiles and cordial or hostile relations between Muslims and municipal officials.

The history of urban renovation in Rotterdam clearly shows how institutional changes can turn ethnic conflict into ethnic co-operation and collaboration (De Jong 1989). The city, which long subsidized the secular and often left-wing associations representing Southern European immigrant workers, encouraged them to form an umbrella organization, the Platform for Foreigners in the Mouth of the Rhine Area (Platform Buitenlanders Rijnmond). By 1988, it had successfully induced the creation of a 'representative body' of Islamic associations in Rotterdam, the multi-national Platform for Islamic Associations in Rotterdam (Stichting Platform Islamitische Organisaties Rotterdam). Overall, Dutch officials have attempted to steer the development of Islamic communities in a liberal and typically Dutch direction: away from orthodoxy and dogmatism, toward dialogue and integration. When not successful, policy-makers and administrators have attempted to delay Muslim initiatives (Landman 1996).

The controversy over Islam heated up markedly in the wake of the Gulf War and the Salman Rushdie affair. In response, policy-makers like former premier Ruud Lubbers and scholars like Arend Lijphart suggested that the erection of a fully-fledged Islamic pillar might assist the Muslims' emancipation without imperiling social peace. Others pointed out that such a suggestion was anachronistic, since secularization had been gnawing away at the existing pillars since the early 1960s. Convinced that there were enough churches in a secularizing Netherlands, the national government had stopped helping to fund their construction, including that of mosques, in 1983 (Vermeulen 1997: 120–1).

While such debate continued, the Minister of Home Affairs met with the National Islamic Council (ILC), a body established by a broad array of Islamic associations. Unhappily, the ILC quickly split into the Islamic Council of the Netherlands and the Netherlands Muslim Council, and formal consultations with the government ended. The Ministry has also made unsuccessful attempts to encourage secular and Islamic North African associations to collaborate. Advisory councils on immigrant policy at the national level, although organized along ethnic lines, have welcomed representatives of Islamic organizations. At the local level only Rotterdam has formulated a genuine policy for mosques which applies as well to Hindu temples.

When an El-Al 747 cargo plane destroyed a housing project in the shabby Bijlmermeer area of Amsterdam in 1992, many Dutch were shocked when it took so long to identify so many of the victims: they were undocumented and thus 'nameless' (Lucassen and Penninx 1994: 2). By later that year, the government's Commission on Non-Indigenous Students in the Classroom had issued a report, Cedars in the Garden, in which it called for a more nuanced strategy to combat disadvantage and to facilitate social integration (Commissie Allochtone Leerlingen in het Onderwijs 1992). Out of this and other analyses grew the Citizenship Program, through which the central government has envisioned a more standardized yet locally anchored 'mutual integration' policy. These projects, based on contracts with municipal officials, have tended to focus on the quality of life at the level of district (wijk) or neighbourhood (Van Zelm 1996). In 1996, the Integration Policy for Newcomers pushed the contract idea further when the government decided to require new immigrants to learn Dutch and set up local Offices for the Reception of Newcomers to implement the programme (Nekuee 1997).

The most recent policy responses have come under criticism for being 'hotchpotch', 'one-size-fits-all (stamppotbeleid) strategies that will not work for an immigrant-origin population that is increasingly diverse and differentiated by ethnicity and occupational category (Asscher 1996). True, almost one-third of Turkish and Moroccan residents have dual nationality, introduced in 1992,[7] and the country has nationalized by far the highest share of its resident foreign population—11 per cent in 1996—in Western Europe (Vermeulen 1997: 119). Some 140 candidates of immigrant origin, Turks and Moroccans being the most numerous, won office in March 1998 local elections, while far-right parties lost all but two of their 88 seats won in 1994 (Tillie 1994).

At the same time, other indicators do suggest worsening social and economic marginalization for a good number of minorities. Turks and, especially, Moroccans tend to face such problems most seriously and are disproportionately affected by discrimination, identity checks, and isolation from Dutch society (Buijs and Nelissen 1994). Its institutional openness has worked against the eruption of widespread social disorder and the development of bonafide social movements, even among the young (Holzhaus 1991; Distelbrink and Veenman 1994; Sunier 1996). The Dutch do, nonetheless, worry that poorer neighbour-hoods in their major urban conglomerations might come to resemble France's suburbs or even America's inner cities (Vandalisme/Jeugdcriminaliteit 1994). The emerging nexus of youth gang violence, the drug trade, and petty crime—known as 'the circuit'—has grown into an obsession. The 'delinquents' involved scoff at the notion of integration: they deride immigrant-origin police as 'Alibi Alis' (Coppes and Halsema 1991) and entrepreneurs as 'bounties': black on the outside (van buiten) but white on the inside (van binnen) (Angenent 1997: 96). Over the past two years, the uncovering of a network of Gray Wolves (nation-alist Turkish extremists) and Algerian Armed Islamic Group (GIA) activists, as well as the founding of several Islamic political parties, has added to the national angst. Overreacting, perhaps, officials from major cities like Rotterdam and Utrecht have even traveled to Los Angeles to learn how to deal with knif-ings and shootings.

Belgium

Wedged between France and The Netherlands, Belgium has responded to the evolution of the immigration challenge with policies and forms of immigrant mobilization that recall those in both of its neighbours. To understand Bel-gium one must keep in mind that two separate nations compete within it. The dawning realization that specific minority policies and more general anti-poverty measures are not mutually exclusive implies the partial coming together of Walloon and Flemish institutional and organizational patterns.

Belgium was the first area on the European continent to industrialize in the nineteenth century, and it drew in labour from neighbouring countries and from Southern Europe. That pattern repeated itself after World War II, as Italian and Spanish workers came to the mines and factories of French-speaking Wallonia. Belgium began to recruit North Africans, especially Moroc-cans, beginning in the 1960s. Turkish immigration began a few years later, taking place in three stages: at first into industrial Wallonia, then into Luxem-bourg and Brabant provinces to work in the mines and in construction, and, in the 1970s, into the big cities and Flanders for factory and low-level service sector jobs (Blaise and Martens 1992). That historical experience has made for a larger but more evenly distributed immigrant presence in Wallonia, with 11.35 per cent non-citizens in 1990, than in Flanders, with 4.26 per cent in 1990. Brussels also has a long tradition of relatively high immigration, and the influx has been very significant since 1960 (29 per cent). Large-scale migration into Flanders is more recent and more concentrated in big cities like Antwerp and Ghent. There are more Turks in Flanders, more Moroccans in the Brussels region, and more Southern Europeans in Wallonia and Brussels.

A Belated Policy Response

Until the late 1980s, immigration policy had rather restrained, modest goals: controlling entry and settlement in the kingdom, regulating access to the labour market, and determining the conditions to be met for the acquisition of Belgian nationality (Ducoli 1990). It was up to gatekeepers in the voluntary sector, especially Catholic institutions, to assist foreign workers and their families in trying to fit into Belgian society (Deslé 1992). Trade unions, albeit ideologically divided and decentralized, played an equally important integrating role. From 1946, the Catholic unions were active and effective in recruiting and incorporating Southern European workers, grouping them according to nationality. It took a long time and a mining disaster, on the other hand, for the Socialist unions to take a real interest. Leftists, strongest in Wallonia, organized multiethnic commissions by region and were characteristically slow to acknowledge ethnic differences.[8] Such telling differences notwithstanding, all trade unions were professing solidarity with foreign workers by the late 1970s and backing their claims to equal social, economic, and political rights (Martiniello 1990). Belgian and homeland activists in churches, trade unions, and welfare agencies long dominated all efforts involving immigrants, since until 1984, they themselves were not allowed to form their own associations or apply for public subsidies unless three-fifths of their members and contributors held Belgian nationality.

Replacing a similar institution dating from 1948, the Consultative Council on Immigration (CCI) was set up by the state in 1965 to 'create conditions permitting the integration and assimilation of the families of migrant workers into the Belgian community'. The CCI included representatives of more central ministries, regional economic councils, and provinces with many immigrant residents.[9] Provincial services with the same mission sprang up during this period in several Walloon cities, soon joined by local-level consultative commissions across Wallonia and in the Brussels region. To co-ordinate their efforts, the Liaison Committee for Immigrant Worker Organizations (CLOTI) brought together trade union representatives and immigrant workers' own organizations. Its reach extended into Flanders in the late 1960s, when that region began to welcome imported labour.

Belgium halted new immigration in 1974. Responsibility for 'welcoming' policy and labour market issues was eventually transferred to the regions, and the linguistic communities—which gained cultural autonomy in 1971—took over the other aspects. In the absence of clear-cut national policy, localities like Antwerp, Ghent, and Liège took the initiative and became known for their proactive stance. The Moureaux Low finally established an administrative statute for foreigners in 1980, but it was really the electoral breakthrough of the extreme-right later that decade that forced officialdom to respond. In a 1989 report, the government provided its definition of integration: assimilation where 'public order' demands it—that is, conformity with the penal and civil codes—the promotion of Belgian-style 'social insertion', and respect in other areas for 'cultural diversity'. In tandem with that agenda was the structural betterment of minorities in the labour and housing markets and in the educational and training systems. Visible in this grab bag of policy aims are elements of both the formerly dominant assimilationist, French-style republican and class-based socialist interpretations of integration typical of Wallonia, and the more identity-based, multicultural-friendly policy style found in Dutch-speaking Flanders (compare Grudzielski 1990, with Martiniello 1995).

Federalization

Not coincidentally, the federalization of Belgium was picking up speed in the late 1980s and early 1990s. Admissions and asylum policy, nationality law, voting rights, and most social welfare policies remained the under the purview of the Belgian federal state. Employment became a regional responsibility (Wallonia and Flanders); educational and cultural policies, that of the cultural communities (French-, Dutch-, and German-speaking). Muncipalities gained access to specially earmarked, supplemental funds to support their own initiatives.[10]

The strengthening of 'centrifugal forces' in the Belgian state can explain the 'differentiated political construction of ethnic categories of immigrant origin in Wallonia and Flanders' (Martiniello 1995: 132). In its own way Belgian decision-making is every bit as pragmatic as that in The Netherlands. Yet because it is imperative and difficult to balance cultural-linguistic and regional cleavages in Belgium, new policy arrangements tend to be added on top of or alongside existing ones. This has resulted in an incredibly complex, not to say baroque, institutional and administrative system that makes each new policy innovation a trickier proposition.[11]

Wallonia

Official political discourse in Wallonia has drawn on the French model of citizenship and national identity. Historically, there was also a type of Walloon ethnic nationalism alongside the dominant one. But the 'political dominance' of the notion of nation-state has long helped to 'impose a local version of assimilationism' (Martiniello 1995: 139). Flemings who arrived during the early days of Wallonia's industrialization either returned home or melted in with nary a trace. Many politicians of 'Flemish descent' are leaders in the modern Walloon socialist movement, and the Socialist Party remains dominant in the region. This history of assimilation, combined with the pervasiveness of socialist rhetoric, helps explain the relative neglect of the cultural and ethnic dimensions of immigration and racism in post-war Wallonia. Targeted policies for ethnic minorities and immigrants have long been taboo. Initiatives that affect them have been embedded in broader social policies aimed at eliminating inequities in employment, housing, health care, and the like (Rea 1993).

Few associations of Moroccans and others, as such, have existed in Wallonia, consequently, and it has been difficult for any groups to propose language courses in anything other than French. Continuing to reflect older patterns, Spanish and Italian organizations have maintained their connections with Belgian and homeland Catholic and labour movements. The organizational panoply has resembled that found in France, in short, although institutional channeling has nurtured homeland orientation longer in Belgium (Vandenbrande 1995b: 34–50).

A royal decree in 1979 created the Consultative Council for Immigrants in the French Community, which included representatives of the trade unions, employers organizations, provinces, the French Community, and the Regions of Wallonia and Brussels-Capital. It suffered from an absence of sustained contact with public authorities and insufficient institutional and logistical infrastructure. In 1988, the Community announced that it was embarking on a search for a coordinated policy aiming at the integration of young immigrants, embedded in a general policy fighting social marginalization. In reality, its approach was growing more decentralized and variegated, with regional centers popping up in the provinces of Liège, Namur, Hainaut, and Brussels-Capital. It was still condemning official use of the term 'ethnic minorities' in 1991, as it did not 'capture the reality of the immigrants' experience and situation' (Blaise and Martens 1992: 60).

Flanders

The Dutch Community, meanwhile, organized the Flemish Oversight Committee for Migration Development (VOCOM) in 1977 to co-ordinate its activities (Dossier 1978). Reflecting earlier Walloon-influenced Belgian assumptions, it first rejected a 'categorical' approach destined only for immigrants: that would only aggravate tensions between Belgians and immigrants. Soon, however, Flanders was moving toward a more targeted and multicultural model reminiscent of the one being tried out next door in The Netherlands. Despite now living in the more economically dynamic and politically powerful region of Belgium, Flemings have traditionally seen themselves as a minority within the country, which has made them sympathetic to ethnic-based approaches (Blommaert and Verscheuren 1992). Moreover, in heavily Catholic Flanders, notions of charity and subsidiarity combined to produce acceptance of a pluralistic model in which cultural identity was deemed both worthy of public support and a boon to integration.

In 1982, the Flemish executive body established the Flemish Council for Migrants (VHRM). With one-third of its members of foreign origin, the VHRM started making a large number of policy suggestions. Their impact remained modest due to limited means, limited competency, and a lack of recognition among the immigrant-origin communities. Even so, the VHRM did help inspire the establishment of regional and local integration centres, which could entail either adding services within the existing pubic administration or setting up a subsidized non-profit association—known by the acronym 'asbl' in Belgium. In education, housing, employment, and other policy sectors, Flanders was toeing the line followed in The Netherlands (see Zimmer 1996).

In 1990, the Flemish Center for the Integration of Migrants replaced the VOCOM, its ambitious mission being to focus on co-ordination and logistical and administrative support for regional, local, and neighborhood actions, the development of savoir-faire in integration policy and social assistance, the organization of informational and anti-racism campaigns, and last, but not least, the development of immigrant-origin leadership. Its General Assembly and administrative council are constituted one-third each by representatives of immigrant communities, institutions that assist immigrants, and social and cultural associations active in the general policy area of immigration.[12]

The immigrants' ethnic identities became an accepted element of the Flemish approach. The immigrants' 'democratic', ethnic-based self-organizations began to receive Community funding in 1992, as free to offer Arabic or Turkish classes as Dutch ones,[13] although local and neighbourhood integration centres had already been doing so for years. Ethnic-based immigrant associations—geared toward Belgium and the homelands—were spreading at all levels as a result.

Toward Policy Convergence or Paralysis

In both Wallonia and Flanders policy-makers have been well aware of the differences in the two regions' approaches to integration. The advantages and drawbacks of the 'French' and 'Dutch' models were the subjects of spirited debates. In the French Community it was becoming clear by the early 1990s that immigrant origin and ethnicity were markers of social marginalization that did not fade when global policies were put in place to fight poverty and exclusion. The Dutch Community was likewise realizing, as was The Netherlands, that group-specific policies could fuel tendencies toward social balkanization (Vandenbrande 1995a). Instructive in this regard has been the case of Brussels, where French and Dutch speakers live cheek by jowl and where there has thus been, of necessity, a greater balance between the two models since regional institutions came into being in the late 1980s. Some immigrant-origin organizations there are ethnically or religiously based, while others toe the social class line. Brussels has also demonstrated, unfortunately, that in the Belgian context such reforms tend to yield institutional complexity and fragmentation, higher costs, and the risk of duplicating efforts (Vandenbrande 1995b).

That Belgium as a whole faced a 'society problem' as much as an 'immigrant problem' was driven home by the rise of the ethnic-nationalist Flemish Bloc (*Vlaams Blok* or VB) in local elections in 1988 and the emergence of Walloon fellow-travellers, the National Front (*Front National* or FN) and Agir or 'Act' (Shu Yun 1990). Premier Wilfried Martens, then heading up his eighth government, created a national advisory institution, the Royal Commission for Immigrant Policy, to study the integration issue and to help the government define coherent, appropriate policies. In line with its advice, officials moved to promote the structural conditions enabling the participation of immigrants in the goals and activities of Belgian society, and added greater flexibility to the Belgian Nationality Code in 1991. Discussions opened over how to standardize the system of subsidies to autonomous immigrant associations, and how to encourage the development of Belgian-style national federations.

Upping the ante were Islam and young people of immigrant backgrounds. Belgium experienced a 'head scarf affair' along French lines in the late 1980s and early 1990s, and several Brussels neighbourhoods erupted into riots pitting police against North African-origin youths in 1991. Again as in France, Islamic references were prominent in the reproaches they leveled at Belgian society and the treatment they received from it.

Except for a couple of thousand North African miners who spilled over the French border into Wallonia in the 1920s and were largely ignored then and now, Belgium has not had the historical experience with Islam that The Netherlands has. Aping the Dutch, though, the Belgians have talked about setting up a Muslim 'pillar' along the lines of the Catholic/Flemish and Social Democratic/Walloon ones as a way to reduce tensions ('Pacificatie' 1992).

Islam does not have strong organizations in Belgium, however, nor has a common faith superseded national and ethnic differences. Belgium guarantees freedom of religion and the separation of church and state. Still, in the belief that religions serve social and moral needs and thereby promote general well-being, it also has a system of formal religious recognition that opens the door to many financial advantages: the payment of salaries and pensions of religious officials, grants for the purchase, renovation and upkeep of religious venues, tax concessions, exemption from postage, and full state funding for religious education in public schools. Once recognized, a faith's material resources are managed by a commission, instituted by law or royal decree, that also serves as a liaison body with the authorities.

Islam won official recognition in 1974. For a religion to activate its status and have access to the attendant benefits, however, it must put forth a representative executive body. Decades of conflict over Brussels' Islamic Cultural Centre, a Saudi-backed organization that has monopolized Muslims' contacts with public authorities since the early 1960s, left Islam without such an entity until just recently. In December 1998, elections were held to a fifty-one-member assembly that has, in turn, selected eleven representatives to sit on the Chief Organ of the Denomination (*Organe chef du culte*), subject to approval from the Ministry of the Interior.

The debate over Islam and Muslim youth has put the spotlight on social problems that plague Belgium's large cities: poverty, crime, poor public services, urban decay, the concentration of ills in certain neighbourhoods, and the widening gulf between rich and poor. Belgian officialdom responded with an attempt to control cultural diversity and make it compatible with the general stress on social harmony and equality. This perspective motivated the Royal Commission and its successor, the Centre for Equal Opportunity and the Fight against Racism. The Centre has striven to inject those elements in The Netherlands' policy mix that are applicable to Belgium in order to reduce the risks of social and political disruption arising from cultural diversity. Established by law in 1993, it is technically under the Prime Minister's aegis but is autonomous in practice (Blommaert and Verschueren 1993). It administers the Incentive Fund, financed from the national lottery to provide soft—one-time or limited-term—money for projects to foster integration, with the focus on the prevention of delinquency and social marginalization of youth, and the encouragement of intercultural activities.

Those represent true challenges. The VB, FN, and Agir attained the highest scores since their creation in the European elections of 1994. Unemployment has risen inexorably among immigrant-origin youth: in 1993, 45.5 per cent of Moroccan boys were jobless, 55.9 per cent of Moroccan girls, 42.1 per cent of Turkish boys, and 75.5 per cent of Turkish girls; but only 19 per cent of Belgian boys and 21.9 per cent of Belgian girls (Leman 1994: 72). Preoccupied with homeland language and culture, first-generation associations have had a relatively weak hold on immigrant-origin youths. Second-generation organizations have not been numerous, with most of their constituency refusing the 'young migrants' label and opting to work within Belgian youth movements if at all. French social movements have produced but a fainter echo in Wallonia and Brussels and have been much more likely to have Belgians in the starring roles (see Deschamps and Pauwels 1992).

On the other hand, Belgium has become all too familiar with the more dysfunctional forms of participation found in both France and The Netherlands. There was a fresh outbreak of riots in Molenbeek in the Brussels agglomeration in April 1995, and again in a number of neighbourhoods in Brussels, Liège, and outside Antwerp in November 1997. And although Belgium has no real youth gangs yet, less-organized crime 'webs' are active in many cities and involve young people of North African and, increasingly, Turkish origin (Bortolini 1996).

Belgium's policy-makers have not stopped responding gamely to such challenges. Federal officials have inched toward allowing third-country nationals civil service employment, as the Flemish government has already done. Naturalization laws moved closer to *jus soli* through modifications in 1984, 1991, and 1995 (Martiniello 1998). The issue of voting rights for non-EU citizens even remains an active issue in Belgium, partly owing to the deadlock over granting voting rights to EU citizens caused by Flemish fears that they will tip the balance toward French-speaking forces (Bortolini 1997).

Yet exactly such stalemates are becoming the norm. As the unbelievable institutional complexity of the country today hamstrings the state, political clans have been free to step into the breach and assure a share of the spoils for their clients. In the niches of this patron-client system, criminals find themselves free to operate (Wehrmann and Willeke 1998). The ongoing paedophilia scandal has brutally awakened Belgians to what has happened to their political system. Early in 1997, the discovery of the sexually molested corpse of a nine-year-old Moroccan girl, Loubna Ben Aïssa, reminded them of the immigrant communities who suffer from its pathologies as well (Bousetta 1997b).

Germany

Germany-bashing, always popular in academic circles, can seem particularly justifiable with respect to immigration: some seven million foreign residents notwithstanding, its leaders have steadfastly refused to accept that it has become a 'country of immigration' (*Einwanderungsland*). What's more, 'Germans have traditionally defined citizenship (*Staatsangehörigkeit*) in terms of jus sanguinis, that is, a Volkszugehörigkeit based on descent from German ancestors, and they have continued to perpetuate such a definition despite its racist overtones and despite the Nazi policies with which it came to be associated' (Safran 1995: 108). This Volk obsession sets limits on what policy-makers at any level can do to incorporate foreigners into German society. It is weaker in certain parts of the country, though: in the north some very forward-looking policies have emerged, and naturalization rates have been noticeably higher and less dependent on candidates' complete assimilation. There, resistance to multiculturalism, which traditionally reflected the prevalence of social democratic convictions, has melted in recent years, with the evolution in socialist thought and the rise of the Greens. Such recent developments notwithstanding, the lack of openings in Germany's organizational system and its ethnic-based self-identification have meant that German institutions have treated immigrants, even Southern Europeans, as clients. Outside of this control, they have been structured politically by groups operating along ethnic, religious, and regional lines that parallel those of the homeland to a greater degree than in the other countries figuring here so far.

Social Democracy

Germany's social market economy has been firmly rooted in the inclusion of individuals through social and economic rights. Precisely because of the persistent legacy of ethnic nationhood that makes accession to citizenship difficult, Germany's constitutional, administrative, and judicial systems have offered protection to foreigners (Kanstroom 1993: 160). Federal courts have consistently upheld non-citizens' civil and legal rights, and the Basic Law promises every resident the right to a life in keeping with human dignity, as well as the right to education and the development of one's capabilities. For fear of inviting segregationist tendencies, the explicit recognition and protection of ethnic minorities was left out (Oberndörfer 1994). At the same time, social institutions have exercised a powerful social control function that has shaped collective identities among those with and without a German passport, and has kept the latter in a clearly subordinate, dependent position within the German system.

After 1945, refugees from what had once been part of the Reich met most of the labour demands in a rebuilding Germany, although guestworkers (*Gastarbeiter*) also came up from Southern Europe. They tended to stay in the south, the closest and more advanced German region. When the post-war boom continued after the erection of the Berlin Wall in 1961, German employers and public officials looked more intently than before to the Mediterranean basin, particularly Turkey, to replace the lost inflow of labour from the east. By then, northern Germany was in direst need of workers. Even today, as a result, Turks constitute 43 per cent of the foreign population in Bremen, 38.7 per cent in Berlin, and 37 per cent in North-Rhine-Westphalia. By comparison, they account for only 27.5 per cent in Bavaria, five percentage points below the national average (Cohn-Bendit and Schmid 1993).

Initial misgivings about the influx of cheap labourers giving way to acceptance, German trade unions insisted that foreigners receive the same social and economic rights as 'native' workers, so as not to undercut their position. Guestworkers were by definition supposed to be temporary. Even when the 'rotation model' lost its appeal by the mid-1960s, the general assumption was that most of the foreigners would eventually return 'home'. Any who did not would blend without a trace into German society, just as the 'Ruhr Poles' and Italians of an earlier era had done (see Castles and Miller 1993). Success was to be measured first and foremost by improvements in labour-market and training/educational position. Entitlement to wide-ranging social benefits has meant that traditional political 'citizenship is not nearly as important to the day-to-day life of a foreigner in Germany as it might be elsewhere' (Kanstroom 1993: 184).

The social welfare system prevented the development of true 'foreigner colonies' or 'ghettos'. Guestworkers first lived in housing provided by employers, before they and their families entered Germany's social housing regime, which involves government intervention into the private market. Germany built few large projects like those surrounding French and Belgian cities, just a few in Hamburg and the Ruhrgebiet. Still, in most cities they ended up scattered across neighbourhoods next to Germans with similar socioeconomic characteristics (Blanc 1991).

A two-pronged strategy emerged toward education of guestworkers' children: integration into the German educational system—meaning German-language instruction—but given the inevitability of their departure, preparation for reintegration into the educational system of the country of origin, and thus supplementary instruction in the mother tongue. German states (Länder) are largely autonomous when it comes to education policy, and emphases and approaches differed. Generally, policies in the north shifted earlier and more insistently toward teaching German and targeting groups to address educational deficiencies, certainly after the official 'immigration stop' of 1973 (Vermeulen 1997).

Germany witnessed the same debate between 'minority rights' and 'worker' or 'human rights' that wracked neighbouring countries (Rittsteig 1996). Except for politically staged campaigns, however, these were not issues that engaged national politicians. They found the way blocked by the ethnically defined citizenship regime and by conservative reservations (Thränhardt 1988). Social experts and sub-national policy-makers were not as restrained: on the ground policy makes pragmatic adjustments, and ethnic groups and ethnic minority cultures have to be recognized in the development of social policy, particularly at the local level. Besides, in Germany there was always 'some tolerance of cultural diversity, since residents who [were] foreigners [were] encouraged to maintain their original cultures so that their eventual return might be facilitated' (Rex 1996: 51).

Despite official refusal to view guestworkers as ethnic minorities, therefore, social welfare work included an explicit targeted policy for foreigners (Ausländerarbeit). The inflexibility of the German bureaucracy instigated a turn toward three major quasi-public organizations, each of which took responsibility for specific nationalities: the Roman Catholic Caritas worked with Italians and Iberians; the Protestant Diakonisches Werk, with Greeks; and the secular, union-linked Arbeiterwohlfahrt, with people from Turkey. These associations were present and very active at the level of the municipalities.[14] Several Länder, as well as large cities, installed 'foreigners commissioners' to represent the immigrants' interests, just as the government in Bonn followed Berlin's lead and named a Federal Commissioner for the Interests of Foreigners in 1978.[15] With explicitly political participation illegitimate, debates shifted to educational and social policies toward immigrants, 'wars by proxy' that raged on the margins of the German neo-corporatist system (Boos-Nünning and Schwarz 1991: 2). In the workplace and out, German institutional gatekeepers advanced the interests of immigrants, who had little choice but to accept the role of 'helped' and thus controlled populations.

Responding to criticism of this paternalistic setup, a number of northern cities introduced Foreigners' Auxiliary Councils (*Ausländerbeiräte*), some of them chosen by immigrant associations or by a vote of resident aliens, to advise local authorities. These ersatz participatory structures have been organized along ethnic, that is, national, lines—Michael Bommes writes of 'forced self-ethnicization' (1993: 364). These bodies were justly criticized for not offering a true political voice. Turkish representatives often seemed to use them as an arena within which to carry out internecine conflicts rooted in the homeland. German supreme court justices in Karlsruhe, however, vetoed efforts by the (city-)state governments of Berlin, Hamburg, Lower Saxony, and Schleswig-Holstein to extend local voting rights to resident foreigners.

Immigrant associations, which had first appeared in the 1960s, increased markedly in number and in diversity as they and their communities sunk deeper roots in Germany. Labour movements, students, and trade unions opposed to homeland regimes were prominent from the beginning, followed by religious organizations—Christian, Greek Orthodox, and Muslim. Funding, albeit available only at the local level, helped foster the development of a social infrastructure reflecting in its richness and, to German eyes, chaotic ebullience those of the communities themselves (Özcan 1989; Schwarz 1992). Their focus never shifted to the host society as much as in France, The Netherlands, or even Belgium. In the 1980s, German-style 'umbrella' organizations were forming (*Dachverbände*), initially at the local and regional levels and eventually at the federal level, since it was the only way to win legitimacy in the eyes of German officialdom and have a hope of exercising any influence at all on the German policy-making system.[16]

By the close of the 1980s, educational and training deficiencies still affected foreign-worker children disproportionately, and foreigners still lived in shoddier housing than their German co-workers. But all things considered, Germans patted themselves on the back for having avoided the immigration-spawned social instability harrying their French and Belgian neighbours. Relatively speaking, structural indicators were positive for the country's millions of immigrant residents, over three-quarters of them from the Mediterranean basin. More than 70 per cent of them had lived in Germany for more than ten years, many for more than twenty, and almost 80 per cent of their children had been born there.

Unification

German unification has popped the integration illusion. The years following the fall of the wall saw an upsurge in anti-immigrant violence—Rostock, Mölln, Solingen—and legislation that tightened up asylum laws and made it easier to deport undesirable foreigners (Ireland 1997). It might be an exaggeration to accuse Chancellor Helmut Kohl's coalition of 'initiating a broad and aggressive campaign against refugees . . . , [giving] brutal gangs a pretext and legitimation to commit crimes and atrocities, feeling themselves as the heroes of the nation and the executors of the national will' (Thränhardt 1994: 20). But the federal government certainly did abandon any intentions of developing a more global and positive policy and turned almost exclusively toward the reforming the asylum law (Deponti 1999).

Policy-makers also failed to rally to the defence of the non-European immigrant-origin population.[17] In a unified Germany, nationalism has returned as a means to cope with reorganizational upheaval, economic crisis, and east-west reallocations (Bommes 1993). Reductions in social welfare benefits, the decentralization of social policy, and welfare 'chauvinism'—an unwillingness to share economic and social resources with immigrants—have contributed to mobilizing around ethnic boundaries (Faist 1994). Structural change in heavy industry has meant increased unemployment, particularly among foreign workers: almost 22 per cent of immigrants in the old Länder were unemployed in the mid-1990s, three times the native German rate (Norman 1998). The Zentrum für Türkeistudien in Essen points to one response to limited opportunities on the labour market: the burgeoning of Turkish, Greek, Iberian, Italian, and North African small businesses. There were already 150,000 'foreign entrepreneurs' (Ausländische Selbständige) in Germany by the mid-1990s.

As integrative forces in Germany's urban centres have weakened for the majority of them, young people of immigrant origin have been turning toward groups of similar ages and ethnic background. Analysis of MARPLAN Institute surveys measuring immigrants' concerns and fears confirms this growing isolation. Even among those resident in Germany for ten years or more, one-fifth have expressed worries about their residency status (Aufenthaltsstatus) in Germany (Thränhardt 1994: 226). Especially among the foreign workers' children and grandchildren—and especially among Turks and North Africans—bitterness, insecurity, and disappointment have been rife. They have begun to shun organizations and institutions that used to link their communities to German society. They have turned inward for protection, romanticizing traditional lifestyles and forging a new identity model with multiethnic and largely non-Western reference points.

Among Turks this 'self-ghettoization' has generated support for Dev Sol, the Gray Wolves, Milli Görüs (National World Vision) and other movements at both extremes of the political continuum.[18] Alevite and particularly Kurdish nationalism has led to attacks against Turkish institutions on German soil. In fact, there are dozens of distinct ethnic groups in Turkey that could be activated by multicultural policies and by transnational networks (Faist 1998). Already, ethnic-based political parties have sprung up, such as the Democratic Party of Germany (Demokratie Partei Deutschland) founded by naturalized Turks close to the government in Ankara in late 1995. Homeland-language televison and radio programmes have also flourished. Youth bands—right- and left-wing, anti-immigrant and anti-racist skinheads—roam downtrodden urban neighborhoods, their members taking part in robberies, murders, shakedowns, and angry confrontations with *Aussiedler* gangs and the police (see Farin and Seidel-Pielen 1991).

Others in cities from Hamburg to Nuremberg, from Berlin to Cologne, sing in rock bands of the unique despair of immigrant-origin young people, caught between Germany and the homeland. These 'Kanak-Kids' have contributed to a cultural flowering reminiscent of the Beur movement in France. Their unofficial spokesman, Feridun Zaimoglu, has become known as the 'Malcolm X of Germany's Turks'. When the Federal Commissioner for the Interests of Foreigners invited him to the official Multicultural Week, replete with Anatolian stepdance and Döner kebab, he asked: 'What does this shit have to do with my life?!' (Lottmann 1997). Thomas Schwarz draws on a range of scholarly studies in describing the potential for conflict among immigrant-origin youth (Schwarz 1992: 69–70; see Bade 1996). The German institutional setup still retains enough structuring power to hinder a true social movement or widespread rioting, but German authorities have not been able to structure 'minority communities' dependent on them and thus under their manipulation and control. Neither have the Turkish and other homeland governments seen the development of the lobbies of their nationals in Germany that they so desire (Kastoryano 1996).

Multiculturalism, German-Style

In church circles and on the political Left, arguments in favour of adopting a minorities policy along Dutch or Flemish lines have multiplied in Germany, despite lingering fears that it could lead to more tension and violence like that between the Kurds and the Turks (Stüwe 1996). The Social Democrats (SPD), reluctantly in the beginning, and the Greens, enthusiastically, have rallied to the ethnic-pluralist camp. They and other multicultural proponents have still had to contend with the refusal of German top-level officialdom to even accept that the country has become a multiethnic country of immigration.

What has often resulted is a sort of 'foreigner friendliness light': pleasant culinary contacts—what German city does not have an annual international food festival?—and expressions of solidarity that cost little and require no heavy lifting (Ulrich 1992). Multiculturalism has nevertheless made some inroads in the areas of social policy, social work, and education in northern Länder and a number of big German cities (Robertson-Wensauer 1993). Mirroring developments in The Netherlands and Flanders, indications that the immigrant-origin populations across Germany might be retreating into their own 'cocoons' have provoked a shift toward problem-specific instead of group-specific policies.[19]

Also as elsewhere, Islam has become an increasingly prominent source of agitation. In Germany the relationship between the state and religion is a matter for both the federal and Länder governments. They must be neutral and equal in their treatment of all faiths, but the state pays officials of recognized faiths, subsidizes the upkeep and restoration of church buildings, and collects taxes in the name of each religious community, that it then channels back to it. While a number of Islamic organizations have applied for public law status in the past, none has demonstrated that it is representative enough to speak for the entire faith. In the absence of a clear policy on mosques, the extent to which the needs and desires of Muslims are taken into account in urban planning depends on the city (Vermeulen 1997).

Kurdish terrorism has for a while had pride of place as immigration's biggest perceived danger to Germany. Islamic fundamentalism is now causing concern as well. Islamic lists have now outpolled traditionally dominant left-leaning ones among Turks and North Africans in municipal Ausländerbeiräte across Germany. Germany has just had its own 'head scarf affair': authorities in Baden-Württemberg have forbidden an Afghan-origin teacher to wear the hijab, because it is both a 'political symbol' and a 'symbol of cultural isolation' (Sommer 1998).

Campaigns against anti-foreigner violence have been slow in coming. After every high-profile incident, hundreds of thousands of Germans have taken to the streets carrying anti-hate banners and candles (lichterketten). Comprehensive policies have not followed.

Germany is nevertheless changing in small but potentially important ways. Slower than in France and The Netherlands, with their more inclusive naturalization laws, the immigrant-origin population has become a source of new members and activists for all of the mainstream German political parties, just as native-stock members are deserting them. Two per cent of the Berlin electorate is now comprised of naturalized foreigners, for example, and three people of Turkish origin now sit in the Bundestag ('Einfluss mit Immi-Grün' 1996). Naturalization became easier for the children of guestworkers in 1990, 1993, and 1994, although rates vary by Land and national background being higher for Europeans (SOPEMI 1998: 64).

Early in 1999, an ambitious proposal by the new SPD-led federal governing coalition to cut the length of residency required before German nationality could be granted, and to accept the notion of dual nationality, met with a fierce reaction and an impressive petition drive from the opposition Christian Democrats and Christian Social Union. At the end of the process, even so, the government 'succeeded in updating legislation dating from 1913 which has played an important role in shaping German attitudes towards foreigners and the integration of outsiders into its society' (Atkins 1999). The SPD latched onto a longstanding FDP proposal for an 'option model', a compromise position that allows the children of foreign workers to hold both German and their parents' nationality when one parent has lived in the country for at least eight years. They must decide on just one nationality by age 23. Only when it is impossible to renounce the nationality of another country will dual status be tolerated. General rules on granting citizenship have also been relaxed a little. Such reforms may seem paltry compared to developments in The Netherlands and Belgium. But they could herald further integration, with significant implications for immigrant political mobilization.

Switzerland

The German reforms can appear revolutionary when compared the policy stasis in Switzerland. Decentralized Switzerland, with twenty-six powerful cantons and half-cantons, is an exercise in extreme federalism, a loose, confederal arrangment that balances overlapping and crosscutting ethnic, religious, and geographic cleavages (see Lempen 1985). The highly developed Swiss practice of direct democracy—through the popular initiative, requiring 100,000 signatures collected over 18 months today, and the referendum on legislation, requiring 50,000 signatures, (see Ireland 1994)—means that politics thoroughly permeates Swiss society (Heller 1992). With little space between 'citizen' and 'sovereign', Switzerland has proven to be a club with very strict membership rules. As in Germany, immigrants have been treated as Swiss institutions' clients, but generally neglected ones, and their orientation toward the homeland has proved even more fixed than that of their counterparts living north of the Rhine River.

The Rotation Model

Immigration into Switzerland before World War II resembled that into other countries: movements were small, from neighbouring countries, and often temporary. German and Italian workers played a key role in Swiss industrialization and in founding the major trade unions and left-wing political parties (Castelnuovo-Frigesi 1978). The General Strike of 1918 shattered social tranquility and led to deportations. By 1931, the legislature had enacted the Federal Law of Abode and Settlement of Foreigners (ANAG), which remains in force with only minor modifications today. It confirmed that Switzerland would view its immigrants in a strictly economic light, creating a tiered permit system and instituting varying provisions for the entry and treatment of immigrants of different nationalities. The Swiss thereby created a highly differentiated hierarchy of foreigners. Policies explicitly balanced industries' needs with deep fears of Überfremdung ('Overforeignization') (Windisch, Jaeggi, and de Rham 1978). Citizenship has always flowed from the communal to the cantonal and federal levels, with naturalization a long, expensive, and difficult process. Based solely on *jus sanguinis*, it has always demanded the destruction of immigrants' former cultural identity (Thürer 1990).

Immigrants have been on equal legal footing with the Swiss only in the factories, in keeping with the Swiss view of them exclusively as workers. Still, they have been free to join Swiss political parties as well as trade unions; they could also form their own associations, circulate petitions for constitutional amendments, and participate in consultative structures that resonated with prevailing decision-making processes and helped preserve social order. By distinguishing between immigrants according to their socio-professional status and striving to maintain a 'rotation model', at the same time, restrictive Swiss labour policies made it less likely that immigrants would give up their focus on the homeland. Foreign political parties, trade unions, churches, and other voluntary associations maintained a separate organizational existence.

Switzerland has never spent more than a minimal amount on social welfare programmes, moreover, and severe, intentional discrimination has attended the immigrants' inclusion in what programmes have existed. Public and private welfare associations failed for years to take much interest in immigrants. They did not introduce any special services or training for them or particularly welcome immigrant members or administrators. The modesty of the Swiss social welfare response—indeed, the unresponsiveness of most major Swiss institutions—has had the important effect of encouraging sending-country governments and other organizations to step in to provide for their nationals' social, economic, and political needs. They established far more extensive networks of official and fraternal homeland organizations than elsewhere (Tschudi 1978; Schaller 1984; Tosato 1985). Given that high profile, the immigrants' political involvement with their homelands, for Italians and Spaniards as much as for more recent groups like Turks, proved more intense and persistent than in other countries, even Germany (see Schmitter Heisler 1983).

The Limits of Collective Immigrant Action

Such an emphasis on the foreign nature of the 'foreign workers' (*fremdarbeiter*) also affected their relationship with the Swiss labour movement. A neo-corporatist 'labour peace' between employers and employees has prevailed in the country since the 1930s, making strike activity a rare occurrence. Ambivalence toward immigrants on the part of the mainstream Swiss Left, with its great stake in the consensus, has robbed immigrants' participatory rights of much of their potential force (Wertenschlag 1980).

In the early 1970s, severe socioeconomic strains in several areas of Switzerland provoked a temporary break from characteristic participatory patterns, manifested in a rash of immigrant strike activity. Foreign workers' labour militancy in this period at first prompted sharply negative reactions from employers, public officials, and trade unions alike. Swiss officials prohibited new immigration, beefed up police forces and border controls, and reiterated their rights to expel non-citizens deemed threatening to the public order (Ireland 1994).

Simultaneously, however, they pledged to integrate the immigrants already resident in the country. In an attempt to defuse building xenophobic sentiment, the executive Federal Council had in 1970 established the Federal Consultative Commission for the Foreigners Problem (CFE/EKA), on which sat representatives of the federal government, the cantons, the churches, trade unions, political parties including xenophobic ones, and employers—but no immigrants. Federal, cantonal, and local authorities did respond to the immigrants' growing assertiveness by instituting more consultative structures that included them and were organized on the basis of national origin. Trade union rights expanded, and Swiss officials stepped up their efforts to maintain the immigrants' homeland ties.

Some left-wing political parties, solidarity groups, and trade unions awoke to the immigrants and their needs, but others did not. These gatekeepers thus split in two over immigration. Open hostility between clearly defined pro-immigrant and xenophobic camps, as opposed to the competition so useful to non-citizens in France and Belgium, often paralysed the Left. Owing to the decentralized structure of the Swiss Socialist Party and loosely confederated trade unions, debates over immigration shifted decidedly toward the cantonal and local levels.

In the final analysis, the immigrants' militancy in Switzerland was very limited and short-lived. The official nurturing of foreign workers' homeland-oriented participation steered pressures away from the Swiss political system more forcefully and longer than elsewhere. The appearance, if not the fact, of greater socioeconomic mobility in Switzerland—'exit' in Albert O. Hirschman's (1970) schema—was another critical factor in generating less confrontational participation or 'voice'—in fact, less collective immigrant political activity overall—than in other countries. The Swiss rotation model of immigration forced many out-of-work foreigners to return home countries. As their legal status and employment security advanced in tandem the longer they were able to stay in the country, the foreign workers who remained usually concentrated on individual advancement. The immigrants were thus not likely to stray from available participatory channels, nor did they forge a truly separate, collective identity, even if Swiss reality gradually, and of necessity, took on greater importance (Hoffmann-Nowotny 1973).

It was up to the immigrants' remaining allies to spearhead efforts to improve their lot. In 1974, the small Catholic Workers' Movement in German Switzerland drew up a 'Togetherness Initiative'. This carefully worded popular initiative would have eliminated the seasonal workers' statute and would have guaranteed the immigrants freedom of choice in employment, family reunification, equal social security coverage, and the right to renew their permits automatically. As for political rights, 'Togetherness' called diplomatically only for consulting the immigrants on all decisions concerning them (C. Farine 1981). With the Swiss Left divided over the initiative and the federal government opposed, it failed miserably at the polls in 1981: fully 84 per cent of voters and every canton disallowed the proposed constitutional amendment. Regrouping after the demise of 'Togetherness', local-level committees sought to mount a united progressive movement in the early 1980s. But participatory exhaustion had set in (Deike 1984). The string of defeats that the immigrants encountered wore down all but the most committed militants. Their political energies had dribbled away ineffectually along all of the participatory channels open to them.

Besides, xenophobes—National Action, the Republican Movement and the Democratic Party—were able to take advantage of the many points of access in the Swiss political system more successfully than disenfranchised immigrants and their usually divided allies. The xenophobic movement availed itself easily and quickly of Switzerland's vaunted instruments of direct democracy. A succession of proposed anti-immigrant federal initiatives in the 1970s and 1980s widened the splits rending the Swiss Left and sapped any remaining wherewithal it had to advance the immigrants' interests. Although permitted to circulate and campaign for petitions, the foreigners themselves could not vote on them. Thus they and their allies were at all levels battling opponents who, with more resources at their disposal, regularly defeated them. The breaking of the immigrants' political spirit was complete. They could only take some small solace in that the knife of direct democracy cut both ways: the xenophobes were unable to elect many candidates at any level. They split along the traditional fault lines of Swiss politics and certainly did not endanger the four-party centrist coalition in power since 1959.

Young People and Islam

The foreign workers' children proved even more docile than their parents. Immigrants and their progeny, as we have seen, faced a ladder of narrow functional and bilaterally determined distinctions that legitimated individual strategies for socio-professional advancement in their eyes. What's more, a 'forced' exit loomed as a very real threat during economic downturns. Enjoying no special access to Swiss citizenship, immigrant-origin youths remained no more than a social category, a group of individuals sharing recognized common traits, not a collective social actor. The political marginalization and passivity of this 'neither-nor' generation was nearly complete (Bolzman, Fibbi, and Garcia 1987). When youthful protests rocked Zurich in the early 1980s, immigrant workers were only one group among 'marginals' of all stripes whose daily problems served as themes. It was, in the end, an evanescent, postmaterialist outburst of rebels with a very eclectic cause (Kriesi 1982). The situation has not changed as the young immigrant-origin population has since stabilized and diversified (Piguet 1999).

Islam attained some public visibility with the settling in of immigrant communities starting in the mid-1970s and with the growth in the Turkish population and in the number of refugees from Africa, Asia, and the former Yugoslavia. Formal Islamic associations were rare, even so, and Muslims seemed to be following the participatory patterns set by Southern European migrants more than Muslims elsewhere in Europe. Homeland organizations retained their influence and reach (see Köppel 1982). Islam has grown into a *cause célèbre* of only modest proportions in Switzerland.

Of more immediate concern has been unemployment, insecurity, and the drug trade. Three to four times more non-citizens are out of work than are native Swiss. The Federal Office of Police announced that in 1997 the percentage of foreigners among those committing criminal acts had passed the 50 per cent mark for the first time, and the 'Letten Effect'—after the Zürich needle park—drew intense media attention to the drug trade and its alleged links with undocumented immigration (Mahnig 1998).

A Policy Impasse

Policy responses have been modest, with liberalizing and restricting ones balancing each other. A 1992 amendment to naturalization legislation allowed dual citizenship and facilitated the naturalization of the foreign spouses of citizens. A new anti-racism law came into effect in 1995. It had been approved in a referendum in September 1994, where it needed only a popular vote majority, but not one of the cantons, which it failed to secure. The Swiss Confederation has accepted one of Europe's largest intakes of political refugees, including, along with Germany, the lion's share of displaced Kosovo Albanians in 1999.

On other fronts, by comparison, official policy has tightened. Naturalizations have declined steadily in number since the mid-1980s and the defeat of the 'Togetherness' initiative: foreigners still have to be resident in the Confederation for twelve years and demonstrate that they have been sufficiently 'Swissified' to apply. An attempt by the federal government to ease naturalization procedures for second- and third-generation foreign residents in Switzerland was blocked by a 1994 referendum (Koopmans and Kriesi 1997: 23). At the end of that same year, almost 73 per cent of Swiss voters had approved a legislative revision that introduced 'coercive measures' to control undocumented migrants and refugees. While three Swiss nationals of African origin affiliated with the Socialist Party won office in local cantonal elections in 1996, proposals to grant or widen voting rights have been summarily rebuffed since 1990 in cantons Aargau, Basel-City, Bern, Fribourg, Geneva, Uri, Vaud, Zug, and Zurich.

The EKA/CFE, which remains the only institution at the federal level dealing with the integration of immigrants resident in Switzerland, has called for greater efforts on their behalf, concentrating on professional training, health, and intercultural and sports contacts, and for a legal basis for a policy of integration (Catacin 1996; SOPEMI 1998: 171). In August 1997, a commission of experts on migration insisted again on the issue (Commission d'Experts en Migration 1997). Parliament has dragged its feet, however. In March 1998, it voted with a solid majority of 87, for a law that gives the Confederation the possibility to subsidize the 'social insertion' of foreigners. Yet supporters were not able to achieve the absolute majority necessary to justify the added costs during a period of a 'brake on expenditures' (Mahnig 1998).

Responses have proved more numerous and effective at the cantonal and local levels. As of 1996, municipal integration projects have been underway in Zurich, Basel, and Bern (Mahnig 1998). Switzerland's strong tradition of communal and cantonal autonomy has meant that immigrants and their backers have aimed many of their political efforts at the sub-federal level. The patterns of immigrant politics have reflected the confluence of national and often highly divergent local institutional forces. In 'closed' cities, many immigrants have lapsed into inactivity or cultivated a regional identity that imposed less of a choice between Swiss and homeland identity (Bolzman, Fibbi, and Garcia 1987). Still others have turned to alternative points and levels of political access. They have spent their political capital participating in cantonal and federal petition drives and in the activities of immigrant associations in more vibrant neighbouring cities. Those additional institutional arenas have tended to drain away out-of-channel participation. In other areas, immigrants have enjoyed more political opportunities, even a limited local (Canton Neuchâtel) and even cantonal (Canton Jura) franchise. There, the political channeling process has generated high levels of institutional participation, based on a unique constellation of modes that blended class and ethnicity.[20]

Conclusion

Immigrants have built a very real political presence in all of the countries considered here. Just as they have been 'getting the Islam they deserve'—to paraphrase Rath and his colleagues (1996: 267)—so, too, are they reaping what they sow in terms of their immigrants' political mobilization. In each, institutions have channeled their energies in a variety of directions, with important and discrete consequences for the host-society polity. Integration policies, naturalization laws, and institutional gatekeepers have been neither benign nor neutral, shaping immigrant organizational life and social citizenship. Those of Southern European, North African, and Turkish origin in the five nations have adopted forms of participation resembling those adopted by other immigrants in the same host society more closely than those adopted by immigrants of the same national origin in another host society. The very content and focus of demands, as well as the terms in which they are formulated, have varied with the nature of the political opportunity structure.

Whether immigrant political mobilization has taken place along class, ethnic, or other lines has depended on such institutional factors. They have cultivated or defused ethnic conflict by encouraging or discouraging ethnic entrepreneurs who rally minorities or members of the majority in defense of collective interests (Richmond 1988; Esman 1977), and they have exercised control over minorities by selecting safe, generally older go-betweens and shaping social citizenship (Schierup and Alund 1990). Paradoxically, even compensatory policies that aim at reducing social inequalities can magnify the expression of cultural differences and the identification with those 'excluded from assimilation' (Kastoryano 1996: 210). Ethnic bonds, if not wholly invented by political leaders and intellectuals for purposes of social manipulation, are at the least linked to specific social and political projects (see Barth 1969). As Lawrence Fuchs (1990) has argued with reference to the United States, the promotion of minority art and culture can spur a rise in consciousness of their specificity and become a source of mobilization and pride. Subsidies for the creation of jobs or associations can intensify feelings of belonging to an ethnic group. The nature of government intervention at any level not only helps to define identities but can also effect changes in their content and their boundaries. Neither can the new ethnic assertiveness visible across the West be separated from minorities' experiences of exclusion or the inadequacy and reorganizing of existing services, which often leaves them with no option but to resort to ethnic-group-based self-help and community work (see Modood, Beishon, and Virdee 1994).

Class-based political organizing does not appear inevitable, either. Foreign workers in similar industrial sectors but in different institutional settings have often embraced strikingly divergent participatory strategies. Despite the emergence of an immigrant-origin middle/professional class, the bulk of the immigrant-origin population everywhere is still working class. Institutional ethnic and racial discrimination and the variable, intervening effects of the host-society labour movements have nonetheless worked against a unified class identity. Instead, Charles Sabel's 'ambiguities of class' are visible: institutional contexts seem to have produced durable variations among workers of different ethnic/national backgrounds in different localities and sectors (1982: 191–3). Trade unions and political parties in each country have linked together socio-economic, generational, gender, and contextually specific issues. The 'structural problems of advanced capitalism' may generate the potential for protest, as Sidney Tarrow has argued, but the forms it ultimately takes depends on the 'particular political institutions and opportunities of each country and social sector' (1989: 4).

Looking at the same immigrant groups in different host societies reveals some similarities, owing perhaps to homeland hangover but just as likely to institutionally determined levels of homeland government influence and to formal and informal networks. What's more, certain problems have been universal across host societies, such as the challenges posed by Islam—headscarves have caused a furor everywhere—and the second and third generations, and similar policies have sometimes been adopted. Lesson-drawing across borders has grown more common among policy-makers and immigrant activists alike. Similarly, scholars may debate to what degree European integration has induced transnational political action over immigration and asylum issues (see Favell and Geddes in Chapter 16 of this volume). Clearly, in any event, the rights that Southern Europeans have gained as a result, along with institutional discrimination between them and resident third-country nationals, have already affected the political mobilization of the former within the European Union, reducing the need for militancy and autonomous political organizations. The same holds true in Switzerland, which has been paralleling EU action on migration (see Ireland 1995).

Regardless, the differences in policies, institutional contexts, and immigrant participatory patterns in France, The Netherlands, Belgium, Germany, and Switzerland remain striking overall. In fact, with social and other policies undergoing decentralization across Europe in the late 1990s, local immigration history and political structure have, if anything, made for widening differences in the ethnic relations calculus within countries. Local-level comparison is needed to substantiate the cross-national findings here.

Notes

1. Since too much ink has already been spilled over the significance of the labels attached to the people at issue here, I will refer simply to 'immigrants' and 'immigrant-origin populations', except when use of another term might help illuminate policy differences or emphases in a particular context. My employing the terms 'second generation' and 'third generation' has no political or ideological connotations and simply follows common American usage (compare Hargreaves and Leaman 1995).
2. This figure is from the 1990 census and thus on the low side.
3. The same logic has dictated the political behaviour of people from France's overseas *departments*, most notably those from the West Indies (Guadeloupe and Martinique).
4. A case in point here is the Supreme Council of Mosques in France, set up recently by the directors of the grand mosques of Paris and Lyon with the support of the Algerian and Moroccan governments, to oppose the High Council of Muslims in France, chaired by the controversial Abderrahmane Dahmane.

5. Policies can be targeted at ethnic groups or at the immigrant populations more globally, or they can tackle social marginalization more generally. Underlying the adoption of policies in the latter instance are normally either liberal concerns for individual rights or a social democratic stress on the primacy of class incorporation. That distinction will be made in the analysis here.

6. In the Dutch context, minority status connotes a situation of residential segregation, cultural marginalization, and the accumulation of negative socioeconomic characteristics (Kaderadvies 1995).

7. As of 1997, even so, only nationals of countries that do not allow the loss of nationality in the acquistion of another (like Morocco) are eligible (SOPEMI 1998: 63).

8. Communists suffered under intense police repression in general, foreign ones even more so than native Belgians.

9. The CCI, later renamed the Consultative Council for Populations of Foreign Origin, concluded its mandate in 1991, although it continued to meet for several years thereafter.

10. Personal interview with Professor Andrea Rea, Université Libre de Bruxelles, Brussels, October 1997. Restrictions on foreign worker social participation gradually fell over the 1980s and through the 1990s, with changes often spurred by developments at the European level.

11. Personal interview with Johan Leman, Director, Center for Equal Opportunity and the Fight against Racism, Brussels, October 1997.

12. Funding comes from an overarching Flemish Fund for the Integration of the Disadvantaged, with 60 per cent of the money funnelled to the largest cities (Blaise and Martens 1992).

13. Personal interview with Johan Leman.

14. Personal interview with Erhard Heintze, Referent für Zuwanderungsangelegenheiten, Senat Bremens, November 1992.

15. Most policy-making power remained with the Ministry of the Interior, which consulted frequently with counterpart ministers of the *Länder*.

16. Comments made by Valentina Stefanski, University of Bremen, at the Centre for Social Policy Research, University of Bremen, Bremen, November 27, 1992.

17. The government did give special treatment to ethnic German resettlers (*Aussiedler*), all the same, and recognized Sorbs in Saxony—just as it had traditionally recognized the Danish minority in the northern state of Schleswig-Holstein (Vermeulen 1997).

18. Federal authorities have estimated that there are at least thirteen distinct extremist Islamic fundamentalist groups alone active in Germany, with around 26,000 militants (Verfassungsschutz 1995: 13).

19. Personal interview with Dr. Thomas Schwarz, Berliner Institut für Vergleichende Sozialforschung, November 1997.

20. Even Canton Neuchâtel with 56.2 per cent opposed failed in 1990 to allow foreigners to run for office in local elections. In June 1996, Canton Jura, with 52.6 per cent opposed, made the same decision.

References

ANGENENT, H. (1997), *Criminaliteit van allochtone jongeren* (Baarn: Uitgeverij Intro).

AN-NAIM, A. A. (1996), 'A New Islamic Politics', *Foreign Affairs*, 75/3: 122–6.

ASSCHER, B. (1996), 'Integratie minderheden moet anders', *Utrechts Nieuwsblad*, 3 Dec.: 9.

ASSHEUER, T. (1998), 'Was heisst hier deutsch?', *Die Zeit*, no. 30/16 July: 37.

ATKINS, R. (1999), 'Ambitious Plans for Reform Run into Trouble', *Finanical Times*, 1 June: V.

BACHMANN, C., and LE GUENNEC, N. (1996), *Violences urbaines* (Paris: Albin Michel).

BADE, K. J. (ed.) (1996), *Migration, Ethnizität, Konflikt* (Osnabruek: Universitätsverlag Rasch).

BALIBAR, É., and WALLERSTEIN, I. (1988), *Race, nation, classe: Les identités ambiguës* (Paris: La Découverte).

BANTON, M. (1985), *Promoting Racial Harmony* (Cambridge: Cambridge University Press).

BARTH, F. (ed.) (1969), *Ethnic Groups and Boundaries: The Social Organization of Cultural Difference* (London: Allen and Unwin).

BEN TAHAR, M. (1979), *Les arabes en France* (Rabat: Société Marocaine des Editions Réunies).

BENOÎT, F. (1982), *Le printemps de la dignité* (Paris: Editions Sociales).

BEN-TOVIN, G., and GABRIEL, J. (1982), 'The Politics of Race in Britain, 1962–79', in C. Husbands (ed.), *Race in Britain: Continuity and Change* (London: Hutchinson).

BERJONNEAU, J.-F. (1997), 'La contribution des églises', *Migrations-Société*, 9/50–51: 39–42.

BLAISE, P., and MARTENS, A. (1992), 'Des immigrés à intégrer', *Courrier Hebdomadaire*, 1358–9 (Brussels: Centre de Recherche et d'Information Socio-Politiques).

BLANC, M. (1991), 'Von heruntergekommenen Altenquartieren zu abgewerteten Sozial-wohnungen: Ethnische Minderheiten in Frankreich, Deutschland und dem Vereinigten Königreich', *Information zur Raumentwicklung*, 6–7: 447–57.

BLOMMAERT, J., and VERSCHEUREN, J. (1992), *Het Belgische migrantenbeleid* (Antwerp: International Pragmatics Association).

——— (1993), 'The Rhetoric of Tolerance, Or What Police Officers Are Taught about Migrants', *Journal of Intercultural Studies*, 14/1: 49–63.

BÖCKER, A. (1994), 'Op weg naar een beter bestaan: De ontwikkeling van de maatschap-pelijke positie van Turken in Nederland', in H. Vermeulen and R. Penninx, (eds.), *Het demokratisch ongeduld: De emancipatie en integratie van zes doelgroepen van het min-derhedenbeleid* (Amsterdam: Het Spinhuis).

BOLKESTEIN, F. (1997), *Moslim in de polder* (Amsterdam: Uitgeverij Contact).

BOLZMAN, C., FIBBI, R., and GARCIA, C. (1987), 'La deuxième génération d'immigrés en Suisse: catégorie ou acteur social?', *Revue européenne des migrations internationales*, 3/1–3: 55–71.

BOMMES, M. (1993), 'Ethnizität als praktische Organisationsressource', in M. Massarrat, B. Sommer, G. Széll, and H.-J. Wangel (eds.), *Die Dritte Welt und Wir: Bilanze und*

Perspektiven für Wissenschaft und Praxis (Freiburg: Informationszentrum Dritte Welt-Verlag).

BOMMES, M. (1995), 'Migration and Ethnicity in the National Welfare-State', in Marco Martiniello (ed.), *Migration, Citizenship, Ethni-National Identities in the European Union* (Aldershot: Avebury).

BOOS-NÜNNING, U., and SCHWARZ, T. (1991), *Traditions of Integration of Migrants in the Federal Republic of Germany* (Berlin: Berliner Institut für Vergleichende Sozialforschung).

BORTOLINI, M. (1996), 'La presse et les immigrés en Belgique en 1995', *Migrations-Société*, 8/44: 109–22.

——(1997), 'Le prix de l'oubli', *Écarts d'identité*, 81: 4–8.

BOUAMAMA, S. (1989), 'Élections municipales et immigration: essai de bilan', *Migrations-Société*, 1/3: 22–45.

BOUSETTA, H. (1997a), 'Citizenship and Political Participation in France and the Netherlands: Reflections on Two Local Cases', *New Community*, 23: 215–32.

——(1997b), 'The Voting Rights Issue in Belgium', *Merger*, 5/1: 12–15.

BOVENKERK, F. (1986), *Een eerlijke kans* (The Hague: Staatsuitgeverij).

——(1992), *Hedendaags kwaad: Criminologische opstellen* (Amsterdam: Meulenhoff).

——(1994), Een misdadige tweede generatie immigranten?', *Jeugd en Samenleving*, 11/4: 387–404.

BRETON, R. (1964), 'Institutional Completeness of Ethnic Communities and the Personal Relations of Immigrants', *American Journal of Sociology*, 70: 193–205.

BRUBAKER, W. R. (ed.), (1989), *Immigration and the Politics of Citizenship in Europe and America* (New York, NY: University Press of America).

——(1992), *Citizenship and Nationhood* (Cambridge, MA: Harvard University Press).

BRUSCHI, C. (1994), 'Moins de droits pour les étrangers en France', *Migrations-Société*, 6/31: 7–23.

BUIJS, F. J., and NELISSEN, C. (1994), 'Tussen continuïteit en verandering: Marokkanen in Nederland', in H. Vermeulen and R. Penninx (eds.), *Het demokratisch ongeduld: De emancipatie en integratie van zes doelgroepen van het minderhedenbeleid* (Amsterdam: Het Spinhuis).

CAN, H. (1992), 'Wir brauchen keine Alibiausländer', *Die Tageszeitung*, May 21: 45.

CAN, M., and CAN-ENGIN, H. (1997), *De zwarte tulp* (Utrecht: Uitgeverij Jan van Arkel).

CASTELNUOVO-FRIGESI, D. (1978), *La condition immigrée* (Lausanne: Éditions d'En-Bas).

CASTLES, S. (1992), 'The Australian Model of Immigration and Multiculturalism: Is It Applicable to Europe?', *International Migration Review*, 26/2: 549–67.

——(1994), 'Democracy and Multicultural Citizenship: Australian Debates and their Relevance for Western Europe', in Rainer Bauböck (ed.), *From Aliens to Citizens: Redefining the Status of Immigrants in Europe* (Aldershot: Avebury).

——and KOSACK, G. (1974), 'From Aliens to Citizens: Redefining the Status of Immigrants in Europe, How the Trade Unions Try to Control and Integrate Immigrant Workers in the German Federal Republic', *Race*, 15/4: 497–514.

————(1985), *Immigrant Workers and Class Structure in Western Europe*, (2nd ed.) (Oxford: Oxford University Press).

——and MILLER, M. J. (1993, 1998), *The Age of Migration* (New York, NY: The Guilford Press).

——*et al.* (1984), *Here for Good* (London: Pluto Press).

——COPE, B., KALANTZIS, M., and MORRISSEY, M. (1990), *Mistaken Identity: Multi-culturalism and the Demise of Nationalism in Australia*, (2nd ed.) (Sydney: Pluto Press).

CATACIN, S. (1996), 'Il federalismo integrativo: Qualche considerazione sulle modalità di integrazione degli immigranti in Svizzera', in Vittoria Cesari Lusso, *et al.*, *I come identità, integrazione interculturalità* (Zurich: Federazione Colonie Libere Italiane in Svizzera).

'C'est mon quartier' (1995), *Informations Sociales*, 45 (Paris: Caisse Nationale d'Allocations Familiales).

COHEN, G. (1982), 'Alliance and Conflict among Mexican Americans', *Ethnic and Racial Studies*, 5/2: 175–95.

COHN-BENDIT, D., and SCHMID, T. (1993), *Heimat Babylon* (Hamburg: Hoffmann und Campe Verlag).

COINDÉ, H. (1997), 'L'occupation de Saint-Bernard et l'asile dans l'eglise', *Migrations-Société*, 9/53: 81–85.

Commissariat Royal à la Politique des Immigrés (CRPI) (1993), *Rapport final: Desseins d'égalité* (Brussels: CRPI).

Commissie Allochtone Leerlingen in het Onderwijs (1992), *Ceders en de tuin* (Zoetermeer: Ministerie van Onderwijs en Wetenschappen).

Commission d'Experts en Migration (1997), *Une nouvelle conception de la politique en matière de migration* (Berne: Commission d'Experts en Migration).

Commission Fédérale des Étrangers (CFE) (1996), *Esquisse pour un concept d'intégration* (Berne: CFE).

COPPES, R. T., and HALSEMA, F. (1991), *Politie en allochtonen: preventie en conflicthantering, een plan van aanpak* (Utrecht: z.u.).

DE JONG, W. (1989), 'The Development of Inter-Ethnic Relations in an Old District of Rotterdam between 1970 and 1985', *Ethnic and Racial Studies*, 12/2: 256–77.

DEIKE, J. (1984), 'Y ahora, ?qué pasa con los extranjeros en Suiza?', *Être solidaires bulletin*, 21: 6–7.

DEPONTI, L. (1999), 'Politique d'immigration et droit de la nationalité en Allemagne', *Migrations-Société*, 11/6: 121–36.

DESCHAMPS, L., and PAUWELS, K. (eds.) (1992), *Eigen organisaties van migranten* (Brussels: Ministerie van de Vlaamse Gemeenschap).

DESLÉ, E. (1992), *Grenzen aan de racisme bestrijding* (Brussels: Vrije Universiteit Brussel, Interuniversitaire Attractiepool 37).

DISTELBRINK, M. J., and VEENMAN, J. (1994), *Hollandse nieuwe: allochtone jongeren in Nederland* (Utrecht: De Tijdstroom).

'Dossier opbouwwerk en migratie', (1978), *Bareel*, 1/3: 9–17.

Ducoli, B. (1990), *Note sur la politique d'immigration en Belgique* (Brussels: European Centre for Work and Society).

Dumont, G. F. (1986), *La France ridée* (Paris: Éditions Pluriel).

'Einfluss mit Immi-Grün', (1996), *Der Spiegel*, 27: 44.

Entzinger, H. B. (1984), *Het minderhedenbeleid; dilemma's voor de overheid in Nederland en zes andere immigratielanden in Europa* (Meppel/Amsterdam: Boom).

——(1991), 'Etnische minderheden, stedelijke armoede, gettovorming', in L. Brunt and J. Godschalk (eds.), *Armoede en gettovorming in Nederland*, Special issue of *Sociologische Gids*, 38/1.

——(1994), 'Shifting Paradigms: An Appraisal of Immigration in the Netherlands', in H. Fassmann and R. Münz, *European Migration in the Late Twentieth Century* (Aldershot: Elgar).

——(1996), 'Minderheden of medeburgers? Naar een nieuw integratieparadigma', in Henk Heeren, P. Vogel, and H. Werdmölder (eds.), *Etnische minderheden en wetenschappelijk onderzoek* (Amsterdam and Meppel: Uitgeverij Boom).

Esman, M. (ed.), (1977), *Ethnic Conflict in the Western World* (Ithaca, NY: Cornell University Press).

——(1985), 'Two Dimensions of Ethnic Politics', *Ethnic and Racial Studies*, 8/3: 438–40.

Étienne, B. (1989), *La France et l'islam* (Paris: Hachette).

Faist, T. (1994), 'Immigration, Integration, and the Ethnicization of Politics', *European Journal of Political Research*, 25: 439–59.

——(1998), International Migration and Transnational Social Spaces, Working Paper 9/98 (Bremen: Institut für Interkulturelle und Internationale Studien der Universität Bremen).

Farine, C. (1981), 'Votations sur les étrangers', *Tribune de Genève*, 31 March: 1ff.

Farin, K., and Seidel-Pielen, E. (1991), *Krieg in den Städten* (Berlin: Rotbuch Verlag).

Farine, P. (1998), 'Réactions suite aux propositions de M. Balladur sur la Préférence Nationale', *Migrations-Société*, 10/58-9: 131–5.

Fassmann, H., and Münz, R. (1994), *European Migration in the Late Twentieth Century* (Aldershot: Elgar).

Foner, N. (1979), 'West Indians in New York City and London', *International Migration Review*, 13/2: 284–97.

Fuchs, L. (1990), *The American Kaleidoscope* (Boston, MA: University Press of New England).

Gales, P. L., and Harding, A. (1998), 'Cities and States in Europe', *West European Politics*, 21/3: 120–45.

Geisser, V. (1997), *Ethnicité républicaine. Les élites d'origine maghrébine dans le systéme politique française* (Paris: Presses de la Fondation Nationale des Sciences Politiques).

Glazer, N. (1995), 'The Incorporation of Immigrants in the United States', International Migration Working Paper (Cambridge, MA: MIT Center for International Studies).

Grudzielski, S. (1990), *Immigrés et égalité des chances en Europe: Immigration et politiques sociales en Europe* (Brussels: European Centre for Work and Society).

HAOUARA, A. (1997), 'Du Luxembourg en général et des ses étrangers en particulier', *Migrations-Société*, 9/43: 127–32.

HARGREAVES, A. G., and LEAMAN, J. (1995), *Racism, Ethnicity and Politics in Contemporary Europe* (Aldershot: Edward Elgar).

HEIJS, E. (1995), *Van vreemdeling tot Nederlander* (Amsterdam: Het Spinhuis).

HEISLER, M. O., and SCHMITTER HEISLER, B. (1990), 'Citizenship: Old, New, and Changing', Paper Presented at the Workshop on Dominant National Cultures and Ethnic Identities, Free University of Berlin, June 11–14.

HELLER, D. (1992), 'Für eine qualitative Stärkung der direkten Demokratie', *Neue Zürcher Zeitung*, 24 July: 21.

HIRSCHMAN, A. O. (1970), *Exit, Voice, and Loyalty* (Cambridge, MA: Harvard University Press).

HOFFMANN, S. (1994), 'France: Keeping the Demons at Bay', *New York Review of Books*, 41/5: 14ff.

HOFFMANN-NOWOTNY, H.-J. (1973), *Soziologie des Fremdarbeiterproblems* (Stuttgart: Enke).

HOLZHAUS, I. (1991), *Een hoge prijs: Marokkaanse meisjes en jonge vrouwen in Nederland* (Amsterdam: De Balie).

HUNTINGTON, S. P. (1996), *The Clash of Civilizations and the Remaking of World Order* (New York, NY: Simon and Schuster).

——and NELSON, J. (1976), *No Easy Choice* (Cambridge, MA: Belknap Press of Harvard University Press).

IRELAND, P. (1989), 'The State and the Political Participation of the "New" Immigrants in France and the United States', *Revue française d'études américaines*, 41: 315–28.

——(1994), *The Policy Challenge of Ethnic Diversity* (Cambridge, MA: Harvard University Press).

——(1995), 'Migration, Free Movement, and Immigrant Integration in the European Union: A Bifurcated Policy Response', in S. Leibfried and P. Pierson (eds.), *European Social Policy: Between Fragmentation and Integration* (Washington, DC: Brookings Institution).

——(1996a), 'Asking for the Moon: Immigrant Political Participation in the European Community', in G. A. Kourvetaris and A. Moschonas, (eds.), *The Impact of European Integration* (Westport, CT: Praeger).

——(1996b), 'Vive le Jacobinisme: Les Étrangers and the Durability of the Assimilationist Model in France', *French Politics and Society*, 14/2: 33–46.

——(1997), 'Socialism, Unification Policy, and the Rise of Racism in Eastern Germany', *International Migration Review*, 31/119: 541–68.

JACOBS, D. (1998), *Nieuwkomers in de politiek: Het parlementair debat over kiesrecht voor vreemdelingen in Nederland en België* (Ghent: Academia Press).

JAKUBOWICZ, A., MORRISSEY, M., and PALSER, J. (1984), *Ethnicity, Class, and Social Welfare in Australia* (Sydney: Social Welfare Research Center, University of New South Wales).

JAZOULI, A. (1995), 'Les jeunes "Beurs" dans la société française', *Migrations-Société*, 7/38: 6–24.

KADERADVIES (1995), *Eenheid en verscheidenheid* (Amsterdam: Het Spinhuis for the Tijdelijke Wetenschappelijke Commissie Minderhedenbeleid).

KANSTROOM, D. (1993), 'Wer sind wir wieder? Laws of Asylum, Immigration, and Citizenship in the Struggle for the Soul of the New Germany', *Yale Journal of International Law*, 18/1: 155–210.

KASTORYANO, R. (1996), *La France, l'Allemagne et leurs immigrés* (Paris: Armand Colin).

KATZNELSON, I. (1973), *Black Men, White Cities* (London: Oxford University Press).

KLEINE-BROCKHOFF, T. (1997), 'Deutschland, deine Islamisten', *Die Zeit*, 26: 5.

KLOOSTERMAN, R., VAN DER LEUN, J., and RATH, J. (1997), *Over grenzen* (Amsterdam: Instituut voor Migratie- en Etnische Studies).

KOOPMANS, R., and KRIESI, H. (1997), 'Citizenship, National Identity, and the Mobilisation of the Extreme Right', Working Paper FS III 97–101 (Berlin: Wissenschaftszentrum Berlin für Sozialforschung).

KÖPPEL, U. (1982), *Immigration musulmane en Suisse* (Stuttgart: Comité International Catholique pour les migrations).

KRAMER, M. (1993), 'Islam and Democracy', *Commentary*, 95/1: 35–42.

KRIESI, H. (1982), *Die Zürcher Bewegung* (Frankfurt: Campus Verlag).

LANDMAN, N. (1992), *Van mat tot minaret* (Amsterdam: VU-uitgeverij).

——(1996), 'Islamitische organisatievorming in Nederland', in H. Heeren, P. Vogel, and H. Werdmölder (eds.), *Etnische minderheden en wetenschappelijk onderzoek* (Amsterdam and Meppel: Uitgeverij Boom).

LAWRENCE, D. (1974), *Black Migrants, White Natives* (Cambridge: Cambridge University Press).

LAYTON-HENRY, Z. (1990), 'Immigrant Associations', in Z. Layton-Henry (ed.), *The Political Rights of Migrant Workers in Western Europe* (London: Sage).

LAZZARATO, M. (1990), 'Peugeot 89', in *L'Europe multicommunautaire*, special issue of *Plein Droit* (Paris: Groupe d'Information et de Soutienaux Travailleurs Immigre's), 115–19.

LEMAN, J. (1994), *Kleur bekennen* (Tielt: Uitgeverij Lannoo).

LEMPEN, B. (1985), *Un modèle en crise: La Suisse* (Lausanne: Editions Payot).

LIJPHART, A. (1975), *The Politics of Accommodation: Pluralism and Democracy in the Netherlands* (Berkeley, CA: University of California Press).

LINDO, F. (1994), 'Het stille succes: De sociale stijging van Zuideuropese arbeidsmigranten in Nederland', in Hans Vermeulen and Rinus Penninx (eds.), *Het demokratisch ongeduld: De emancipatie en integratie van zes doelgroepen van het minderhedenbeleid* (Amsterdam: Het Spinhuis), 117–44.

LOCHON, C. (1990), 'Vers la création d'instances supérieures de l'Islam en France', *L'Afrique et l'Asie modernes*, 165 (Paris: CHEAM), 18–46.

LOTTMANN, J. (1997), 'Kanak Attack', *Die Zeit*, 47: 24.

LOWI, T. J. (1964), *At the Pleasure of the Mayor* (New York, NY: Free Press of Glencoe).

LUCASSEN, J., and KÖBBEN, A. (1992), *Het partiële gelijk: Controverses over het onderwijs in de eigen taal en cultuur en de rol daarbij van beleid en wetenschap (1951–1991)* (Amsterdam: Swets en Zeitlinger).

——and PENNINX, R. (1994), *Nieuwkomers, Nakomelingen, Nederlanders* (Amsterdam: Het Spinhuis).

MAHNIG, H. (1998), 'L'immigration en suisse en 1998', *Migrations-Société*, 10/58–9: 121–30.

MARTINIELLO, M. (1990), *Elites, leadership et pouvoir dans les communautés ethniques d'origine immigrée: le cas des Italiens en Belgique francophone*, Ph.D. thesis, European University Institute, Florence.

——(1991), 'Turbulences à Bruxelles', *Migrations-Société*, 3/18: 22–5.

——(1995), 'The National Question and the Political Construction of Immigrant Ethnic Communities in Belgium', in A. G. Hargreaves and J. Leaman, *Racism, Ethnicity, and Politics in Contemporary Europe* (Aldershot: Edward Elgar), 131–44.

——(1998), 'Les élus d'origine étrangère à Bruxelles: une nouvelle étape de la participation politique des populations d'origine immigrée', *Revue européenne des migrations internationales*, 14/2: 123–49.

MAUCO, G. (1932), *Les étrangers en France* (Paris: Armand Colin).

MILES, R. (1982), *Racism and Migrant Labour* (London: Routledge and Kegan Paul).

——(1984), *White Man's Country* (London: Pluto Press).

——and A. PHIZACKLEA (1977), 'Class, Race, Ethnicity, and Political Action', *Political Studies*, 25: 491–507.

MILLER, M. J. (1981), *Foreign Workers in Western Europe: An Emerging Political Force?* (New York, NY: Praeger).

——(1982), 'The Political Impact of Foreign Labour', *International Migration Review*, 16/1: 27–60.

Ministerievan Binnenlandse Zaken (MBZ) (1983), *Minderhedennota* (The Hague: Minister van Binnenlandse Zaken).

Ministerie van Sociale Zaken en Werkgelegenheid (1993), *Stichtingsakkoord over etnische minderheden in de praktijk; erste vervolgmeting*, (The Hague: MSZW/LTD).

MODOOD, T., BEISHON, S., and VIRDEE, S. (1994), *Changing Ethnic Identities* (London: Policy Studies Institute).

MOORE, R. (1975), *Racism and Black Resistance in Britain* (London: Pluto Press).

MOULIN, J.-P. (1985), *Enquête sur la France multiraciale* (Paris: Calmann-Lévy).

Nederlands Centrum Buitenlanders (NCB) (1993), *Het jaar van de omslag* (Utrecht: NCB).

NEKUEE, S. (1997), 'New in the Netherlands', *Merger*, 5/1: 20.

NORMAN, P. (1998), 'German Job Crisis Hits Turks Harder', *Financial Times*, 13 February: 2.

NRC Handelsblad (1992), 'Pacificatie is als model nog altijd relevant: Interview met Arend Lijphart', May 11: 2.

OBERNDÖRFER, D. (1994), 'Völkisches Denken', *Die Zeit*, 24: 12.

ÖZCAN, E. (1989), *Türkische Immigrantenorganisationen in der Bundesrepublik Deutschland* (Berlin: Hitit Verlag).

PARK, R. E. (1925), *The City* (Chicago, IL: University of Chicago Press).

PENNINX, R., SCHOORL, J., and VAN PRAAG, C. (1994), *The Impact of International Migration on Receiving Countries: The Case of the Netherlands* (The Hague: Netherlands Interdisciplinary Demographic Institute).

——*et al.* (1995), *Migratie, minderheden en beleid in de toekomst: Een trendstudie* (Amsterdam: Het Spinhuis).

PEROTTI, A. (1995), 'Des consultations populaires qui laissent beaucoup d'inquiétudes', *Migrations-Société*, 7/37: 99–113.

——(1998), 'Le débat sur la réforme du droit de la nationalité', *Migrations-Société*, 10/56: 105–119.

PHIZACKLEA, A. (1980), *Labour and Racism* (London: Routledge and Kegan Paul).

PIGUET, É. (1999), 'Les jeunes issus de l'immigration en Suisse', *Migrations-Société*, 11/62: 77–86.

PIVEN, F. F., and CLOWARD, R. A. (1979), *Poor People's Movements: Why They Succeed, how They Fail* (New York, NY: Vintage Books).

RATH, J. (1991), *Minorisering: De sociale constructie van etnische minderheden* (Amsterdam: Sua).

——(1997), 'A Game of Ethnic Musical Chairs?', Paper Presented at the Second International Cities Conference on Migrants and Minorities in European Cities, Université de Liège, November 6–8.

——GROENENDIJK, K., and PENNINX, R. (1993), 'De erkenning en institutionalisering van de Islam en België, Groot Britannië en Nederland', *Tijdschrift voor Sociologie*, 14/1: 53–76.

——PENNINX, R., GROENENDIJK, K., and MEIJER, A. (1996), *Nederland en zijn islam* (Amsterdam: Het Spinhuis).

REA, A. (1993), 'La politique d'intégration des populations d'origine étrangère', in M. Martiniello and M. Poncelet (eds.), *Migrations et minorités ethniques dans l'espace européen* (Brussels: De Boeck Université).

REX, J. (1979), 'Black Militancy and Class Conflict', in R. Miles and A. Phizacklea (eds.), *Racism and Political Action in Britain* (London: Routledge and Kegan Paul).

——(1996), *Ethnic Minorities in the Modern Nation State* (London: Macmillan Press).

——and MOORE, R. (1967), *Race, Community, and Conflict: A Study of Sparkbrook* (Oxford: Oxford University Press).

——and TOMLINSON, S. (1979), *Colonial Immigrants in a British City: A Class Analysis* (London: Routledge and Kegan Paul).

RICHMOND, A. H. (1988), *Immigration and Ethnic Conflict* (London: Macmillan).

RITTSTEIG, H. (1996), 'Minderheitenrechte oder Menschenrechte?', *Blätter für deutsche und internationale Politik*, 8: 993–1004.

ROBERTSON-WENSAUER, C. Y. (ed.) (1993), *Multikulturalität—Interkulturalität?* (Baden-Baden: NOMOS Verlag).

SABEL, C. (1982), *Work and Politics* (Cambridge: Cambridge University Press).

SAFRAN, W. (1986), 'Islamization in Western Europe: Political Consequences and Historical Parallels', *Annals*, 485: 99–112.

——(1991), 'State, Nation, National Identity, and Citizenship', *International Political Science Review*, 12/3: 219–38.

——(1995), 'Ethnicity and Citizenship: The Canadian Case—Conclusions', *Nationalism and Ethnic Politics*, 1/3: 107–11.

SCHALLER, V. (1984), 'Die CACEES', *Piazza*, 3: 8.

SCHIERUP, C.-U., and ÅLUND, A. (1990), *Paradoxes of Multi-culturalism* (Avebury: Aldershot).

SCHMITTER HEISLER, B. (1983), 'Immigrant Minorities in West Germany: Some Theoretical Concerns', *Ethnic and Racial Studies*, 6/3: 308–19.

SCHWARZ, T. (1992), *Zuwanderer im Netz des Wohlfahrtsstaats* (Berlin: Editions Parabolis).

SHADID, W. A. R., and van KONINGSVELD, P. S. (1996), 'Islampolitiek en islamonderzoek in Nederland', in H. Heeren, P. Vogel, and H. Werdmölder (eds.), *Etnische minderheden en wetenschappelijk onderzoek* (Amsterdam and Meppel: Uitgeverij Boom), 37–54.

SHU YUN, M. (1990), 'Ethnonationalism, Ethnic Nationalism, and Mini-nationalism', *Ethnic and Racial Studies*, 13/4: 527–41.

SOMMER, T. (1998), 'Der Kopf zählt, nicht das Tuch', *Die Zeit*, 30: 3.

SOPEMI Continuous Reporting System on Migration of the OECD (1998), *Trends in International Migration* (Paris: OECD).

SOYSAL, YASEMIN (1994), *The Limits of Citizenship* (Chicago, IL: University of Chicago Press).

SPICER, E. H. (1971), 'Persistent Cultural Systems', *Science*, November 19: 795–800.

STÜWE, G. (1996), 'Migranten in der Jugendhilfe', *Migration und Soziale Arbeit*, 3–4: 25–9.

SUNIER, T. (1996), *Islam in beweging: Turkse jongeren en islamitische organisaties* (Amsterdam: Het Spinhuis).

TARROW, S. (1989), *Democracy and Disorder* (Oxford: Clarendon Press).

TESSER, P. T. M., van DUGTEREN, F. A., and MERENS, A. (1996), *Rapportage Minderheden 1996* (Rijswijk: Sociaal en Cultureel Planbureau/The Hague: Vuga).

THÉVENAZ, J.-P. (1989), 'Quelques réflexions critiques', *Piazza*, 23: 14.

THOMPSON, J. L. P. (1983), 'The Plural Society Approach to Class and Ethnic Political Mobilization', *Ethnic and Racial Studies*, 6/2: 127–53.

THRÄNHARDT, D. (1988), 'Die Bunderepublik Deutschland—Ein unerklärtes Einwanderungsland', *Aus Politik und Zeitgeschichte*, 24: 3–13.

——(1994), *Landessozialbericht—Ausländerinnen und Ausländer in Nordrhein-Westfalen* (Munster: Institut für Politikwissenschaft der Westfälischen Wilhelmsuniversität).

THÜRER, D. (1990), 'Der politische Status der Ausländer in der Schweiz', *Zeitschrift für Ausländerrecht und Ausländerpolitik*, 1: 26–36.

TILLIE, J. (1994), *Kleurijk kiezen* (Utrecht: Nederlands Centrum Buitenlanders).

TOONEN, T. A. J. (1996), 'On the Administrative Condition of Politics', *West European Politics*, 19/3: 609–32.

TOSATO, O. (1985), 'Les communautés portugaises se manifestent', *Piazza*, 9: 8.

TOURAINE, A. (1990), 'Pour une France multiculturelle', *Libération*, 15 October: 8.

TSCHUDI, H. P. (1978), 'Social Security', in J. M. Luck *et al.*, *Modern Switzerland* (Palo Alto, CA: Society for the Promotion of Science and Scholarship).

TWCM (Tijdelijke Wetenschappelijke Commissie Minderhedenbeleid) (1996), *Bestrijding van vooroordeel, discriminatie en racisme* (Amsterdam: Het Spinhuis TWCM).

ULRICH, B. (1992), 'Immer mehr Feinde', *Kommune*, 2: 33–4, 43.

Vandalisme/Jeugdcriminaliteit (Infomap) (1994), (Apeldoorn: Bibliothek Apeldoorn).

VANDENBRANDE, K. (1995a), *Het Vlaams-Brussels migrantenbeleid* (Brussels: Vrije Universiteit Brussel, Interuniversitaire Attractiepool 37).

——(1995b), *Het Vlaams-Brussels migrantenbeleid bestaat niet* (Brussels: Vrije Universiteit Brussel, Interuniversitaire Attractiepool 37).

VERBUNT, G. (1985), 'Relations associations immigrés/associations de solidarité', in *Forum des associations* (Paris: Conseil des Associations d'Immigré's en France, May).

VERFASSUNGSSCHUTZ RHEINLAND-PFALZ (1995), *Islamistische Extremisten: Vom Gebet zum Gottesstaat* (Mainz: Ministerium des Innern und für Sport).

VERMEULEN, H. (1984), *Etnische groepen en grenzen: Surinamers, Chinezen en Turken* (Weesp: Het Wereld-venster).

——(ed.) (1997), *Immigration Policy for a Multicultural Society* (Brussels: Migration Policy Group), English version of H. Vermeulen, (ed.) (1997), *Immigrantenbeleid voor de multicultuele samenleving* (Amsterdam: Het Spinhuis).

——and PENNINX, R. (eds.) (1994), *Het demokratisch ongeduld: De emancipatie en integratie van zes doelgroepen van het minderhedenbeleid* (Amsterdam: Het Spinhuis).

VOOGT, P. W. (1994), *In de buurt: Participatie van migranten bij buurtsbeheer* (Rotterdam: Rotterdams Instituut Bewonersondersteuning).

WATERS, S. (1998), 'New Social Movement Politics in France: The Rise of Civic Forms of Mobilisation', *West European Politics*, 21/3: 170–86.

WEBER, E. (1976), *Peasants into Frenchmen* (Stanford, CA: Stanford University Press).

WEHRMANN, E. (1997), 'Ein Modell ist gefährdet', *Die Zeit*, 17: 5.

——and WILLEKE, S. (1998), 'Das Trauma von Belgien', *Die Zeit*, 9: 16.

WERTENSCHLAG, R. (1980), *Grundrechte der Ausländer in der Schweiz* (Basle: Universität Basel).

WIHTOL DE WENDEN, C. (1978), *Immigrés dans la cité* (Paris: La Documentation Française).

——(1990), 'Naissance d'une "beurgeoisie", *Migrations-Société*, 2/8: 9–16.

WINDISCH, U., JAEGGI, J.-M., and DE RHAM, G. (1978), *Xénophobie: logique de la pensée populaire?* (Lausanne: L'Age d'Homme).

ZELM, E. A. VAN (1996), *Sturen met twaalf kapiteins* (Rijswijk: Ministerie van Volksgezondheid, Welzijn en Sport).

ZIMMER, P. (1996), 'Le logement social à Bruxelles', *Courrier Hebdomadaire*, 1521–2.

11

Ethnic Minorities, Cities, and Institutions: a Comparison of the Modes of Management of Ethnic Diversity of a French and a British City*

ROMAIN GARBAYE

Introduction

In this chapter, I will seek to provide the basis for a more extensive research project aiming at understanding how Western European cities manage ethnic diversity arising from post-war immigration within the limits and resources of the institutional framework in which they operate. It is an attempt to bring the institutional approaches of ethnic conflict explored by Nordlinger (1972), Esman (1973), and Horowitz (1985), for instance, to the study of the politics of post-colonial minorities. The main thrust of these authors' argument has been that the élites of states that are faced with cross-cutting ethnic conflicts are able to maintain the stability of the system by using institutional arrangements as instruments. I seek to transpose this type of model to the urban politics of ethnic minorities in order to provide new understandings of the political processes underlying the responses of cities to ethnic cleavages on their terri-tories, ranging from urban regeneration programmes to anti-discrimination policies, institutionalisation, and symbolic recognition of ethnic groups.

I accept that the governments of cities in Western Europe are broadly autonomous, in that they have interests which are distinct from the interests of other actors, and particularly from those of local groups and local economic interests, on one side, and from those of the central state, on the other side. Furthermore, I accept that they are able to pursue these interests in relative independence from these actors: without being substantially constrained by local economic and social conditions, and without substantial interference by the national state (Gurr and King 1987). This does not entail, however, that the central state plays no role in local affairs; on the contrary, much of the discus-sion below will focus on the patterns of interaction between central and local state. But urban elected governments are considered as independent political actors; their general interest is to stay in power, and, to this end, to maintain law and order and to sustain continued electoral support for themselves.

In this perspective, the presence of a large ethnic minority populations within the territorial boundaries of local government has become a challenge to these objectives. Ethnic minorities of immigrant-worker origins have several distinctive characteristics. First, they have a very specific relation to space, because they have no claim to sovereignty on a part of the territory of the nation-state in which they live—contrarily to native minorities—and because they are overwhelmingly concentrated in specific areas of cities. Second, they mostly belong to the working class and vote in majority for left-wing parties, when they vote (Le Lohé 1998; Kelfaoui 1996). The conflict is thus not just an ethnic conflict but a combination of class and ethnic conflicts. What is important is that the presence of these minorities, and the reaction of native populations to this presence, does entail fundamental and specific challenges for cities. First, it breeds public disorder, both from second generation immigrants who express frustration at racial discrimination coupled with economic disadvantage, and from violent anti-immigrant movements. Second, it is often correlated with the development of anti-immigrant political movements which directly undermine electoral support for the mainstream political establishment, such as the *Front National* in France or the strong anti-immigrant movement which developed in the 1960s and 1970s in Britain around Enoch Powell, then the National Front. Third, ethnic groups often formulate specific policy demands: recognition of specific cultural needs, official policy against racial discrimination. These demands are often perceived by mainstream politicians, rightly or not, as potentially divisive for their electorate. All of these problems pose a serious threat to the goals of local authorities and arguably not to those of the central state (Le Gales 1995).

I argue that, in order to confront these challenges, local authorities devise 'strategies of management of ethnic conflict' (Esman 1973: 52) understood as the regulatory processes and practices that the local elected governments of cities use to minimize this challenge. I seek to understand how the strategy of management exercised by cities is influenced and shaped by their institutional framework. The institutional framework is understood here as a set of 'formal rules, compliance procedures, and standard operating practices that structure the relationship between individuals and various units of the polity and economy' (Hall 1986; following recent works that apply similar institutional approaches to the study of the politics of ethnic minorities, such as Kastoryano 1996; Brubaker 1992; Favell 1998; Guiraudon 1998, and, specifically on cities, Ireland 1994). I identify three elements that constitute the core of this framework for Western European cities: the relations between central and local government, the organization of political parties and of the party systems, and the organization of local government. This institutional framework plays an important role in shaping issues and the circumstances in which these issues appear on local political agendas. It also provides local authorities with a repertoire of instruments to operate different modes negotiation and conflict resolution. Finally, it also operates as a set of constraints that orients and limits their possibilities for action.

In this chapter, I sketch the outline of an application of this framework to a comparison of the cities of Birmingham in England and Lille in France. Britain and France are both old and centralized nation-states, which are very comparable in terms of post-colonial migration and in terms of social characteristics of ethnic minorities (Lapeyronnie 1993). Both cities are also similar in many respects. They are both old industrial cities that lie at the heart of large industrial urban areas, the West Midlands and the Nord-Pas de Calais. In both cases, post-colonial ethnic minorities—predominantly Pakistanis, Indians, and West-Indians in Birmingham, and Moroccans and Algerians in Lille—make up a sizeable part of the population of the city: 21.5 per cent in Birmingham, and around 15 per cent in Lille. These populations are overwhelmingly working-class populations with very high unemployment rates, especially among the young, with however some variations between groups. In both cities, there is also ample evidence of 'ethnic conflict' as defined above. In both cases, ethnic minorities are concentrated in particular areas of the city: the inner city areas in Birmingham, and the southern and peripherical parts of Lille. Within given neighbourhoods in these areas, they often comprise around half of the population. In both cities, there is clear evidence of widespread racial discrimination against minorities, and widespread awareness of this by the minorities. Both cities have suffered from important disturbances and riots in ethnic neighbourhoods. In both cities, immigrants are a significant electoral force, and are considered as such by the council and the Municipality, though much more so in Birmingham than in Lille. Finally, both cities have been controlled by the mainstream left for a long time: the Labour Party in Birmingham since 1983, and the Socialist Party in Lille, where the Mayor since 1973 has been Pierre Mauroy, who was also François Mitterrand's Prime Minister between 1981 and 1984. In a nutshell, the two cities are interesting for this comparison because they are both controlled by the moderate left and because they have comparable ratios of immigrant/native populations (following the criteria used by Browning, Marshall, and Tabb 1990).[1]

There are, however, two major differences which have to be taken into account. First, some social and cultural characteristics of the groups considered vary between the two cities: the Pakistanis in Birmingham have a much more traditional and institutionalized blend of Islam than the North Africans in Lille (Joly 1987), which leads them to formulate more policy demands and to keep a tighter control on their second generation than the North Africans. The socio-economic stratification of the groups in both cities is also different, because there are influential groups of Indian and Pakistani entrepreneurs in

Birmingham, who provide material resources for their community, while there are only a few successful Maghrebi entrepreneurs in the Lille area.[2]

Second, there is a time-period difference: post-war immigration started in the 1950s in Birmingham, and in the 1960s and 1970s in Lille, and the riots in Birmingham occurred suddenly and violently in the mid-1980s—three deaths during the Handsworth riots in 1985—while they took the form of numerous disturbances from the early 1990s onwards in Lille. While this time-lag probably plays a role in explaining the differences exposed below, it is necessary to look for additional factors, because political events related to ethnic minorities in Lille have not emulated those of Birmingham, even allowing for a gap of a decade.

Ethnic Alliance and 'Race-relations' in Birmingham, Political Exclusion and Republican Universalism in Lille

What are the strategies for managing ethnic conflict of these two local authorities? There is a broadly similar pattern of management in each city, characterized by a tension between conflicting aims. Both cities are confronted with claims by ethnic groups, consisting of policy demands such as for the funding of specific welfare and cultural needs, and demands for increased representation understood as an increase of the number of ethnic minority individuals serving as local councillors. Both wish to accede to these demands in order to maintain public order and satisfy the ethnic electorate; and both feel that the extent to which they can do this is limited because of the potential negative reactions from the wider electorate. Thus, both situations are characterized by an unstable and permanently renegotiated *modus vivendi* between the local power and ethnic interests. Both local authorities are also involved in the management of broadly comparable urban regeneration programmes funded by the central government, and designed to fund groups that promote economic development or perform various welfare tasks and services for urban communities—which are in practice very often minority groups, or, as is more commonly the case in France, groups whose members are predominantly from an ethnic minority.

Within this common mode of government, however, a fundamental divergence has been emerging since the early 1980s. During that period, the *modus vivendi* of the Birmingham City Council has been evolving towards a carefully considered alliance between the dominant Labour group and representatives of ethnic minorities. This alliance can be summarized as the following implicit deal: a relative inclusion of ethnic groups in the political process, and significant concessions to their interests, in exchange for electoral support, or absence of electoral challenge, and co-operation in maintaining law and order. The Labour group won control of the council in 1983, and it has remained in power since then, presently with a very comfortable majority. It has also increasingly included ethnic minority councillors, many in posts of prominent responsibility. The number of councillors who are from an ethnic minority background has jumped from just one to twenty-one, making the Asian population well represented—13.7 per cent of the councillors for 13.5 per cent of the population—and the Black population still under-represented—3.4 per cent of the councillors for 5.9 per cent of the population (Le Lohé 1998). They are all members of the ruling Labour group. In parallel to this, the council has continuously defended a pro-active policy in defence of specific ethnic minority interests in terms of racial discrimination and recognition of cultural difference. In 1984, the council created a department devoted to the fight against racial discrimination. After various changes of name and status over the years, it is at present an 'Equalities Unit', and also deals with women's rights and handicapped persons. One of the main roles of this structure is to encourage other services of the council—notably education, housing, and personnel—to work towards the elimination of racial discrimination in their sector. This type of anti-discrimination policy is not specific to Birmingham: it is carried out by most Labour authorities throughout Britain. And, compared to many other Labour local authorities, Birmingham is seen as moderate on the issue. Moreover, this policy is advocated to local authorities, though not imposed upon them as an obligation, by the third Race Relations Act passed by a Labour government in 1976. As a direct response to the 1985 Handsworth riots, there has also been a strong tendency to institutionalize ethnic groups and to incorporate them, to some extent, in the policy-making process of the City Council, through the creation of the Standing Consultative Forum, an umbrella organization that acts as a link between over 300 hundred organizations, grouped in nine ethnic sub-umbrella groups, and the departments of the council. According to most of the representatives of the ethnic groups involved, this structure has enabled them to obtain some demands, such as sponsoring by the council of the independence days of Pakistan and India or the construction of a community centre for the Bangladeshi community. The city has known only minor disturbances since 1985.

Because of these proactive policies, the Labour majority which controls the council has had to defend its commitment to ethnic minorities during electoral contests against a clearly opposed Conservative local press and against the local Liberal-Democrat and Conservative opposition. Both of these parties propose to abolish the Equalities Unit if they obtain power. The City Council's policy has also greatly encouraged the formulation of specific ethnic demands in terms of racial discrimination and cultural specificity from the part of all ethnic groups in the city, including the Irish, to the point that it now seems to view some of these demands as excessive and tries to play them down.

In Lille, on the contrary, there has been no evolution towards any kind of alliance comparable to the one in Birmingham, but, rather, a continued effort on the part of the Municipality to keep the issue out of the spotlights of electoral politics, and divide and weaken, or fund and control, ethnic groups, in order to neutralize potential electoral competition from them. Neither the ruling Socialist party headed by Mauroy, nor the local mainstream right-wing opposition is keen to push the issue to the forefront of electoral competition. The only ones to do so are the *Front National*, which reaches its highest scores in the southern part of the city where the population suffers from high unemployment and is ethnically mixed. In the 1989 and 1995 municipal elections respectively, one and two councillors of North African origin were elected, but they have remained powerless and have become unpopular with the North African community of the city. At the time of the 1995 election, the Municipality manipulated leaders of young, second generation immigrant groups to disrupt their plan to electorally challenge the Mayor, who was re-elected. It also puts forward a strong republican-assimilationist discourse, *de facto* refusing to recognize groups that are explicitly 'ethnic' or Muslim. Hence, there is only one oriental-style mosque tolerated by the Municipality in the city and the issue of racial discrimination is completely absent from the political agenda, to the extent that local groups of North-African youths, who feel extremely concerned by the issue, do not bother to mention it as one of their demands.

How can one account for these differences between the two cities in terms of institutional variables? There is first a fundamental and obvious factor, which is the difference in citizenship regimes. It is that ethnic minorities have enjoyed automatic voting rights upon entry into Britain and have used it to significant effect since the mid-1970s, especially at the local level.[3] During the 1980s and 1990s these ethnic minorities have been an important electoral support for the Labour party,[4] and have managed to elect several hundred councillors of ethnic minority background on local councils throughout the country. In France, first generation immigrants do not, as a rule, have the vote, and have traditionally played little role in French electoral politics.

However, the explanatory power of this variable must not be over-estimated because, since the early 1980s, the second generation in France has displayed some capacity for electoral mobilization. According to the data that is available, it seems that they have quite high registration and turn-out rates, and on the whole vote for the socialists, although this is not an absolute rule and is subject to local exceptions.[5] This second generation electorate, combined with those first generation immigrants who do have a vote, through naturalization or dual nationality, is considered as an important marginal electoral group for closely contested elections by the socialists in Lille.[6]

Explanations for the variation therefore need to be found with other institutional variables as well. In the rest of this chapter, I will focus on the relations between central and local government, the organization of political parties, the party systems, and the organization of local government in the two cities. The argument runs along the following lines: the issue of ethnic minorities has been politicized in a different way in each city. In Birmingham, it is a conventional political issue, which runs along the Labour/Conservative cleavage. In Lille, it *de facto* opposes both the conventional Left and the conventional Right to the *Front National*. Thus, it has been relatively easy for the Birmingham City Council to have an openly pro-minorities attitude. It has needed to have this attitude for two reasons: because the local institutional context has facilitated the emergence of a strong minorities lobby in Birmingham, and because of encouragements coming form the central polity and national political trends. The interest of Lille, on the contrary, has been to play down the issue to avoid confrontation with the *Front National*, which holds a quasi-monopoly over the issue. In order to effectively play down the issue, the Municipality has kept immigrants out of politics. It has been able to do so because the institutional context plays against the mobilization of ethnic minorities.

I will seek to show in the first section how the difference between the relations between central and local government is a powerful explanatory factor for the difference between the way the issue is shaped in the two cities. In the second section, I examine how political parties also contribute to shaping the issue, importantly by acting as a gateway into the system for minorities in Britain, and thus forcing the local authorities to be responsive to their demands. Finally, the third section proposes directions for exploring the role of the institutional structure of local government in acting both as a set of resources and constraints for local authorities in their efforts to control local communities, and as a window of opportunity for immigrants.

The Central-Local Relation

Both countries are similar in that they have highly centralized systems of government. However, the modes of centralization are very different. Here, I will focus mainly on two aspects of the central-local relation: the territorial organization of the welfare state, and the articulation of local and electoral competition. I will argue that these differences are the first step to understanding why the issue of minorities is high on local agendas on Britain, while it is not so prominent in French local arenas. In Birmingham, the ultimate outcome of this agenda-setting process has been the development of the issue of 'racial discrimination' and of the issue of the representation of ethnic minorities at the City Council. In Lille, it has been a persistent reluctance on the part of local élites to put any issue related to ethnic minorities on the political agenda.

The Territorial Organization of the Welfare State

In Britain, local authorities are traditionally seen as service deliverers as well as institutions of local democracy. In addition, the policy remits of the national and local levels of elected government are tightly separated, very much in a 'two layer cake' organization (Webman 1981), in spite of the trend since the mid-1980s which have seen an increasing number of attributions transferred to un-elected bodies, both at national and local levels—the so-called 'quangos' (Stoker 1988: 52). Local authorities are in charge of public (council) housing, social services which include many health services, and the education system— in spite of the 1988 Education Act which nationalized the curriculums: much of the decisions are still taken by Local Education Authorities (LEAs), which in the case of Birmingham is the City Council. These policy sectors are precisely the ones in which the issue of ethnic minorities is salient. First, because they are of concern to immigrant themselves, because many live in council housing—although this is very contrasted: the West-Indians in Birmingham live in Council Housing, but the Asians in Birmingham are mainly home-owners— are often strongly disadvantaged in the system of attribution of housing (Rex and Moore 1967; Rex and Tomlinson 1979) and often have demands regarding the school curriculums. In Birmingham, there was a long and successful negotiation in 1983 between the Education Department of the Council and a Muslim Liaison Committee, representing the main Muslim organizations of the city, on the issue of religious education. Second, because ethnic minorities are often perceived by local populations as the cause of the deterioration of these services. Finally, all of these issues appear particularly easily on the agendas of local authorities because post-colonial minorities are very concentrated in specific urban areas (Johnson 1990).

Because of this, the local arena in Britain has often been the arena where the issue arose first, well before it became a national issue. In fact, groups and institutions in Birmingham were sending signals to the central government as early as the late 1950s (Messina 1989; Hill and Issacharoff 1971), pointing to the strain put by immigration on the local housing availabilities. The fact that the areas concerned were services also created a climate favourable to the formulation of the issue in terms of improvement of service delivery for minorities.

In France, on the contrary, the Municipality is less a service deliverer to the local community than a means of representation of the local community in front of the central government. In addition, the distribution of competencies between central and local government is more along the lines of a 'marble cake' (Webman 1981). Of the aforementioned policy areas which are of direct interest to migrant workers, only the social services lie within the remit of an elected local authority, the *Conseil Général*, whose chief executive was the prefect until the decentralization laws of the early 1980s. The French equivalent of Council Housing is run by semi-public bodies, the *Offices des HLM*, which are often controlled by the municipalities, but which nonetheless maintain some autonomy over the allocation of homes. Thus, in Lille, there is one very large HLM, the SLE, which houses a third of the population of the city and most of its ethnic minorities, and takes all decisions single-handedly. When problems arise between groups of tenants and the HLM, it is dealt with between those two actors, and elected officials intervene in an individual, discrete, and very often clientelist manner. In addition, the central state was directly in charge of the housing of guestworkers during the large immigration wave of the 1960s through its own organizations, notably the foyers SONACOTRA. Finally, the education system is extremely centralized: local authorities deal almost exclusively with the construction and maintenance of buildings. When an 'Affaire du Foulard' (Headscarf Affair) arose in 1995 in a high school in Lille-Sud—a few Muslim female students refused to remove their headscarves, against the rules of the school—(Le Monde, 15 April 1995)—the conflict took place between the local branch of the Ministry of Education and Muslim groups.

Thus, municipalities do play an important role for certain issues, but more as brokers between individuals and administrations than as policy-makers. First, local elected officials can play an important role as intermediaries between their constituents and administrations in the resolution of individual pleas and conflicts. This is often the case for problems related to housing conditions, employment, and regularization of residence permits for those who are legally foreigners. Second, the Municipality plays a central role in the allocation of urban regeneration grants. In theory, it is jointly managed by the Region, the State via the 'sous-préfet à la ville' (sub-prefect in charge of urban policy), and the City. But in practice it is the Municipality, which has a real knowledge of the local community, which is able to push its favoured candidates. In addition, Mayors deliver construction permits, and they have long resisted the construction of outwardly oriental mosques, and, in all cases, they have to be courted by Muslim groups who wish to build religious centres.

Hence, the dominant picture in France is that of a blurred division of policy remits, with the issue of ethnic minorities cutting across different arenas. The main service providers, the education system and the social housing services, are out of the realm of representational politics. At the same time, elected officials may play a role on an individual basis as brokers between individual and administration. As a result, the French municipalities are not regarded as major arenas for political mobilization of minorities. In Britain, on the contrary, it is clear that the main local political actor, the local council, plays a major role as a provider of services that are of central interests to ethnic minorities, and thus is the focus of much attention and collective mobilization from ethnic minorities.

The Articulation of Local and National Electoral Competition

The different organization of local and national electoral competition is also a basic factor, along with the differences in the distribution of policy remits which I have just dealt with. In Britain, the political élites of each level of government are tightly separated from each other. Local politicians seldom attempt national careers. Conversely, local politics are less important preoccupations for national politicians than in the case of France. This is due to the fact that the most important prerequisite to get elected as Member of Parliament is to be selected by a local branch of one's party. In Birmingham, several constituencies have had prominent MPs, such as Roy Hattersley, the political architect of British race relations policy. Although he was concerned with issues of interest to his constituents, which included the race and immigration issue, he has never had to manage it as a local politician.

On the contrary, in France, affiliation to a party is indeed an important factor for the success of a national career, but at least as important is the local notoriety and popularity of a candidate, which can typically be attained through the exercise of local mandates, such as a seat at the *conseil général* or, most importantly, as mayor of a large community (Mabileau 1994). In fact, a candidate will often receive the support of both the local and national party, if they perceive him or her as popular in the constituency. Thus, French politics are mainly about building a local power base by controlling or being prominent in a Municipality or a *conseil général*—second lowest tier of elected government after the Municipality, corresponding to the territory of the *département*—in order to be able to compete for national parliamentary elections. Much of a politician's support is often derived from their ability to lobby for their constituents at the national level. This is made possible by the *cumul des mandats*, whereby the same person can cumulate local and national mandates. As a result, local politicians are often national politicians, and it is certainly the case of Lille's Mayor Pierre Mauroy, who is a historic figure of the Mitterrand era.

The Issue of Ethnic Minorities as it is Shaped by the Relation Between the Two Levels of Government

The two sets of differences outlined above have two consequences. First, the issue of ethnic minorities has been more salient in British local political arenas than in French ones from the late 1950s in Britain, and the 1960s in France, and it was always more likely to be understood as a problem of local and material allocation of resources in Britain. Second, when it became a national issue in Britain, national élites were able to depoliticize it nationally by making it predominantly a local issue.

The elements mentioned above make it very easy for national élites to get rid of an issue by 'sending it down to the local level', that is, by making it a policy issue for local authorities, who then have to deal with it, while Westminster can ignore it. This is precisely what British national élites have done with the issue of immigration and ethnic minorities since the mid-1960s, at times more than others, but always with great success. This has had two consequences. First, the issue has become even more salient at the local level, while it became much less so at the national level, with however some variations in time. Second, this shift of level has precipitated a shift from a formulation in terms of immigration to a formulation in terms of racial discrimination, and of relations between communities.

Racial riots in 1958 and anti-immigrant tendencies in the electorate in the early 1960s prompted the two main party élites in London to agree tacitly on a common policy line in order to remove the issue from electoral competition, and thus limit the potential damage to their domination of the political system. This consensual policy consisted in combining a gradual restriction of immigration from former colonies with policies designed to facilitate 'harmonious relations between communities' and a legislative framework to fight against racial discrimination (researched in detail by Katznelson 1973; Freeman 1979; Messina 1989; Saggar 1991; Layton-Henry 1992). A main inspiration for this policy was a group of liberal lawyers and black acitivists who sought to draw lessons from American policies (Bleich 1997). It also triggered the first of the various urban regeneration programmes funded by the central government that have taken place since then (summarized by Le Gales 1993).

A major aspect of these policies has been the devolution of responsibility for the development of the 'harmonious relations between communities' to local un-elected bodies, the Community Relations Councils. The second Wilson government passed a provision—'section 11', as it has been known since then—in the 1966 Local Government Act to make extra funds available for Local Authorities with a certain percentage of ethnic minorities within their boundaries. Then, in 1976, the third Race Relations Act—the two first ones dating back to 1965 and 1968—passed again by a Labour government with no real opposition from the Conservative opposition, explicitly gave local councils the responsibility for 'equality of opportunities' and 'good relations between people of different races'. Because of this, it has been argued convincingly that a major aspect of this continued consensual policy has been to send the issue down to 'low politics' in order to protect the national level from its destabilizing effects (see Saggar 1991; Messina 1989; but especially Bulpitt 1986). According to Bulpitt, this has continued unchanged during the 1980s, as an exception to the Thatcher governments' policies of reduction of the remit of local government, because it had proved an efficient strategy on that particular issue of immigration and race. This is one of the reasons why the Thatcher governments did little to prevent radical Labour local authorities from sponsoring ethnic groups and starting aggressive anti-racist and anti-discrimination policies. Another reason why the issue remained high on the agenda of local authorities is that the Labour/Conservative cleavage coincided with the local/central cleavage during the 1980s and until the 1997 general election, making local authorities the stronghold of race activists in front of a passive Conservative government. The Birmingham City Council was directly inspired by the example of radical cities such as the Greater London Council when it set up its first Committee on Racial Discrimination in 1983.

This policy of liberal consensus coupled with the devolution of the issue to the local level has had another far-reaching consequence: it has proved to be very efficient in wiping out extreme anti-immigrant votes, both nationally and electorally. On the whole, the Conservatives steered away from Enoch Powell, who was expelled from the shadow cabinet after his 'rivers of blood' speech in 1968.

In France, there have also been attempts by the state to localize the implementation of national policies in the early 1980s (Weil 1995: 409), and to engage in contractual policies with regions and cities to revitalize marginalized neighbourhoods which in effect contain a high proportion of immigrants, and to prevent violence from erupting again, as it did in suburbs of Lyon and Paris in 1981. In the 1970s, several communist municipalities outside Paris had overtly expressed concern about problems entailed by immigrant populations on their territory, and sometimes surfed on anti-immigrant feeling among their electorate (Schain 1993). However, since the 1983–1984 period, and in spite of these elements, the two levels of debate, local and national, have clearly been interlocked, and the formulation of the issue at the local level has followed the formulation of the issue in the national polity. The French national élite, confronted by a rising anti-immigrant vote in the 1980s—a similar problem to that faced by the British élite in the 1960s—responded similarly and depoliticized the issue in the sense that they perpetuated a tacit agreement over what policy should be implemented—attribution of a unique *Carte de Séjour* of ten years for all immigrants in 1984 coupled with the closing of the borders—which had slowly emerged from policy experimentations and errors in the 1970s.

However, the issue was not depoliticized in the sense that it was removed from the electoral debate, as has been the case in Britain (Weil 1995: 287–314). Both the Socialists and the right-wing parties attempted to play down the issue—for instance, it was not one of the main issues of the 1986 parliamentary elections—but it kept on reappearing in a prominent place on the national political agenda, because of the rapid rise of the *Front National's* electoral might from 1983 onwards (Schain 1993). Indeed, the issue has mostly been shaped by the Front National since then. Significantly, the Socialist Party has since then completely dropped its earlier plans to grant voting rights for all foreigners in local elections. This influenced the way the issue was constructed at the local level in three ways. First, the central élite never really managed to avoid the issue, and thus did not try to send it down to another level of government. Second, because of the inter-relatedness of the two levels of government, the continued politicization of the issue at the national level entailed a continued politicization in electoral elections. Third, the issue at the local level has been formulated in the same way that it has been formulated at the national level, namely in terms of immigration flows, and capacity of the country to absorb and incorporate extra-European immigrants. As at the national level, the agenda has been heavily influenced by the *Front National*, which polls very well in all local elections, as it does in national elections. Thus, in contrast to what happened in Britain, the debate at both levels of French politics has considered immigrants as objects of policy—are there too many? Is it possible to assimilate them and how should one go about assimilating them?—instead of citizens/consumers of policy, such as anti-discrimination policy and relations between communities (Crowley 1993: 627–8). As a result, there has been a continuing tendency in France to keep the immigrants out of politics.

Political Parties and the Local Politics of Minorities

The attitude of the parties towards the issue of post-colonial minorities, and the extent to which the parties can impose their attitude on the local authorities that they control, plays an important role in setting the agenda for minority participation. In this respect they play an important part in the construction of the issue at the local level which I have dealt with above. They are an especially relevant factor in the case of the issue of ethnic minorities because they can be a crucial springboard for the demand of increased representation on the part of the minorities.

Penetration of Ruling Parties by Minorities

Both parties have been deeply ambivalent regarding the issue of minorities, and particularly regarding their willingness to incorporate them. But, on the whole, they are also the ones which have been the most open in each country to the demands of ethnic movements.

However, the Labour party has been much more persistently so than the Socialist Party. Black and Asian activist movements have worked with the Labour party since the mid-1970s. From the early 1980s onwards, they have joined the Labour party in large numbers, especially in cities like Birmingham. Within the party, they have been confronted with important racial discrimination on the part of established circles of white local élites. The latter have often sponsored emerging local black figures in order to obtain the support of their community, arguably reproducing patterns of colonial rule; manœuvering to give them as little responsibilities as possible in exchange for their support. In particular, they have done this through the manipulation of the complex procedures of designation of the party candidates for local and national elections—for instance, the episode in the Birmingham constituency of Sparkbrook observed by Back and Solomos (1995).

However, what I wish to argue here is that it is precisely the existence of these formal procedures that has ultimately enabled minorities to get a foot in the door, to get elected in increasing numbers, and to play significant role in local party politics. Most visibly, the Pakistani communities have been able to take control of several inner-city party organizations during the 1990s because the procedures for the designation of candidates for local elections boil down to giving the choice to the members of the ward party, and because there are procedures of appeal to higher levels of the party in case of conflict over the choice of candidates—such conflicts are frequent in wards which have minorities activists. More generally, there have been possibilities for discussion of the issue in the Labour party.

First, ethnic minorities started mobilizing intensively at a time, the late 1970s and early 1980s, when leaders of the local right-wing of the Labour party such as Roy Jenkins and Roy Hattersley sought to build strong support among local Black community leaders because they were facing increasing competition from the left of the party (Back and Solomos 1995). At the beginning, this only brought support to 'community leaders' chosen for their capacity to supply electoral support without demanding changes in policy. However, this situation evolved rapidly during the 1980s with the emergence of a more ideological generation of black and sympathetic white, left-wing activists who managed to seize control of many ward party organizations from the right wing. This was helped by the fact that many Black and Asian activists had a strong left-wing culture, very often inspired by the political culture of their home countries or of their diasporas—Marxist Unionism with the influential Indian Workers' Association, the American politics of Black emancipation among African-Caribbean activists (Shukra 1998)—which gave them an ideological proximity with the Labour party. This, together with the liberality of the citizenship regime, whereby all immigrants all had full voting rights upon entry in Britain, enabled minority populations at the local level to become a constituency with real electoral leverage and specific policy demands focused on racial discrimination and cultural recognition.

This close association between the Labour party, and ethnic minorities' activists and politicians, is predominantly a local phenomenon. In addition, it contrasts with the situation in the Conservative party, where there are few representatives of minorities. This is correlated with the left/right polarization of the issue at the city level.

In the organization of the Socialist Party of Lille, by contrast, the procedure for the choice of candidates at local elections gives less power to the neighbourhood level, and the choice is usually consensually made in favour of the local notable or incumbent (Sawicki 1992: 6–11). This is typically the case in Mauroy's Lille. I argue here that this absence of institutionalized procedures reinforces the feeling of powerlessness and inaccessibility for outsider individuals, particularly North Africans in the deprived areas of the city who seek to join the party or access posts of responsibility within it. This is to the extent that some *secrétaires de section* (branch secretaries) have occasionally had to use their authority over their sections to make the incorporation of North African members possible. But, most of the time, North African potential members are discouraged at the outset.

This defiance is also strongly inspired by sorry memories of earlier co-operation of North African activists with the party that ended badly. There was a very strong wave of second generation North African mobilization in the early 1980s in France, which culminated in a demonstration of about 100,000 people in Paris in the autumn of 1983, protesting against racist violence by the police and demanding alternative modes of citizenship for immigrants. At that stage, the movement came under the influence of the Socialist Party, and in particular by supporters of the then president Mitterrand, who hoped to tap in on the electoral support of the young second generation immigrants. This led to the creation of *SOS Racisme* in 1985, followed a little later by *France Plus*, a rival organization sponsored by other groups within the party.[7] By the end of the decade, however, the decision was made by those same supporters of Mit-terrand to withdraw support, and the whole movement collapsed (Bouamama 1994). This was an illustration of the difficulty for new social movements to make themselves heard in the French political system without the support of one of the major parties (Duyvendak 1995).

In addition, both of these movements had been mainly national and media-driven, and dramatically failed to build permanent local support among urban North African communities (Poinsot 1993). In Lille, local North African and left-wing activists who were part of this movement are now hostile to the Municip-ality and are toying with the idea of forming an ethnic list for the elections.

Relation between Party and Local Authority

In Britain, local politics have been increasingly politicized since the 1950s, with the political parties within the Councils becoming the main arenas for decision-making. In the case of Labour-held authorities such as Birmingham, this is rein-forced by the traditional mode of relation between the party and councils, inherited from the Fabian conception of social reform. In this model, local councils are seen as instruments in the hands of the party to implement policy goals, notably to develop public services and welfare (Gyford and James 1983). This is still made possible by the fact that party groups are the effective holders of power within councils. Thus, in Birmingham, the local party has been markedly more influential on the attitude of the Council than in Lille. And, because the party was influenced by the presence of ethnic minorities members within its ranks, it pushed for the council to start anti-discrimination policies. In 1983, under the influence of mounting black mobilization, the District party organization produced a policy document entitled 'Birmingham Labour Party and Ethnic Minorities in Birmingham: Labour Party Politics and Multi-Ethnic Society in Modern Birmingham' (Back and Solomos 1995: 177). The then mod-erate Labour leadership of the Council had little choice but to follow these recommendations, although it was initially very reluctant to, because of a per-ceived hostility of the traditional white and blue collar working class vote. The local party has thus been an important factor in ensuring the development of anti-discrimination policy in Birmingham.

In the North of France, there has also been a long history of attempts by the Socialist Party to influence municipal policies (the *Socialisme Municipal*), of which Lille is an example. However, the party has not been able to influence the municipalities; on the contrary, it is the power structure of councils that have in the end shaped the local organization of the parties (Lefebvre 1999). In Lille, there is a structure, called the *Comité de Ville*, which is made of representatives of local sections, and is theoretically in charge of defining the party's policy recommendations for the city, and of selecting the leader of the list for the municipal election. In short, it has one fundamental role: choosing the next mayor of the city. But the Mayor, Pierre Mauroy, has been so dominant since his first election to the job in 1973 that this choice is mainly formal. Moreover, because of the way in which the issue of minorities is constructed, the party's main preoccupation regarding ethnic conflict is mainly to try and avoid mentioning any issue connected with immigration. This would probably highlight popular resentment against national economic and immigration policies in general—which the socialist party is largely viewed as responsible for—and comfort the position of total opposition and exclusion of immigrants of the *Front National*. Significantly, the *Comité de Ville* has a policy workshop on 'how to fight against the *Front National*', and none about immigration or ethnic minorities. This inertia on the part of the socialist party has a profound impact on the politics of the city; in the neighbouring town of Roubaix, where all political parties are weak, local ethnic groups manage to achieve high visibility in city politics.[8]

To sum up the difference, one could say that the Labour party regards the Birmingham City Council more as a means to implement policy change than does the Socialist Party in Lille. Conversely, the latter sees the Municipality more as a power-base than does the Labour party. This difference, combined with the might of the *Front National* in French local politics, helps explain why the Birmingham City Council is more prone to undertake policies in favour of ethnic minorities.

National Styles of Local Government and the Inclusion or Exclusion of Minorities in City Politics

The basic characteristics of the organization of local government in each country have two very different impacts on the strategies of the councils. Directly, because it gives them more or fewer instruments to reach their goals. Indirectly, because it gives immigrant groups more or fewer resources to push their demands and to get some of their representatives elected or accepted as legitimate interlocutors, who can then efficiently raise issues on the council's

agenda. In Birmingham, the overall result is that the organization of local government adds to the pressure on the Council to have a favourable attitude
towards minorities. In Lille, it gives the Council instruments to pursue its policy
of playing down the issue, by enabling it to keep minorities out of the arena
of electoral politics.

The basic unit of French elected government concentrates all the most
intense ingredients of majoritarian democracy, marginalizing minorities
(Mabileau 1994: 119–34); this is much less the case in Britain. Second, the modes
of local organization of national urban policy programmes tend to institutionalize local community groups in Birmingham, while they ignore them in
Lille. This encourages the formulation of collective claims around cultural and
discrimination issues in Birmingham, while it encourages the perpetuation of
patronage as the only mode of relation between ethnic minorities and the
council in Lille.

Local Representative Government and the Inclusion or Exclusion of Ethnic Minorities

A fundamental difference between the two cities is that the elected government
of Birmingham, the Birmingham City Council, covers a much larger area and
population than that of the Municipality of Lille. There are nearly 1 million
inhabitants in Birmingham, against only 170,000 in Lille, although it does lie at
the centre of a metropolitan area of 1.2 million people. This is due to the
extreme politico-institutional fragmentation of local authorities in France,
which is especially strong in the Lille metropolitan area, which is divided into
more than 80 communities, with only the three largest ones, Lille, Roubaix,
and Tourcoing, topping or nearing 100,000 people. This has a profound impact
on the difference between the two styles of local politics because it creates a
multitude of small political arenas in France, and a single large one in Birmingham. In the Lille area, the issue of ethnic minorities is diffused across the
several political arenas. For instance, because of the very high percentage of
North Africans and the weakness of traditional parties in Roubaix, issues
related to the North African minority are very salient, and North African
leaders of neighbourhood associations manage to exert leverage on city politics, and to have substantial representation. But, because of the political fragmentation of the area, this does not have any impact on the politics of Lille. In
fact, minority organizations in Roubaix perceive themselves as eminently
'Roubaisiennes', in the same way that the minority organizations in Lille perceive themselves as 'Lilloises', and there is no communication between the two.
There is also some degree of identification of minority groups to their ward
or to their area in Birmingham, but this does not result in a tight separation of
issues as it does in the Lille area, because the Birmingham City Council is the
only elected assembly that deals with all these wards or areas.

This difference also entails size effects. The Birmingham City Council has a very large bureaucratic organization which delivers services on a large scale. This in itself acts in favour of the rationalization of service delivery, of which setting targets in terms of racial equality is a part. In addition, the difference in the size of the political arenas also entails a difference in the size of local groups, which tend to be larger in Birmingham than in Lille, and reach the critical mass to be credible in front of the council or the European Social Fund (ESF) to run their own training and employment programmes.

The way electoral territories are organized also has far-reaching consequences. In Birmingham, the city is divided into 39 wards of around 20,000 inhabitants on average, which each elect one councillor every year, except every fourth year which remains 'fallow'. Because of this the inner city wards, where there are high concentrations of populations of ethnic minority background, often manage to elect ethnic minority councillors, especially those with high concentrations of Pakistani voters, such as Small Heath, Nechells, or Sparkhill. In Lille, the whole territory of the city acts as one single constituency for the municipal elections, thereby diluting the potential electoral power of North Africans. These reach concentrations of around 40 per cent in neighbourhoods in the south of the city, such as Lille-Sud Nouveau and Faubourg de Béthune, and could therefore exert significant leverage in a different system.

The structure of local government itself also plays a role. In France, the Municipality is by far the most important level of local government, and the idea of representation of the local community lies at its very heart. It is closely linked with the notion that the municipalities constitute the fundamental unit of the French representational system. Indeed, it is the only institution that has survived virtually unchanged since the revolution. It is seen as making local democracy possible, and as a very efficient way to stabilize the whole French political system, in the face of persistent disorder at the centre (Ashford 1982; Mabileau 1994). It has been able to play this role because of the ease with which local élites can access the central, governmental decision-making processes, particularly because of the *cumul des mandats* system, mentioned above. Because of this, the electoral politics of the Municipalities are considered by voters and politicians alike as the place of representation, and power, *par excellence* (Cordeiro 1996). For the insider, it is a gateway to considerable influence; equally important, it leaves outsiders with few resources. A closer look at its organization reveals that it concentrates power in the hands of a few leaders, essentially the mayor and his aides, and leaves out many actors, especially minority groups. It is also a symbolic stake for outsider groups, as getting elected as a *Conseiller Municipal* means entering the world of representational politics, as opposed to community and associational politics, to which ethnic minorities are usually confined (Cordeiro 1996).

The concentration of power in the hands of the Mayor is so intense that the system has sometimes been dubbed a 'presidential system' (Dion 1986: 3–43).

Elections take place every six years, with traditionally a relatively high turnout, on a single-constituency, proportional list basis. The *Conseil Municipal*, roughly the equivalent of the legislative branch of the Municipality, is always made up of at least 50 per cent of members from the majority list, the rest of the seat being distributed proportionally. The Mayor, usually the leader of the leading list, is elected on the first meeting of the newly elected council. Once elected, the Mayor becomes both the representative of the state in the city, and the executive branch of the Municipality for the next six years. Important decisions and the budget are voted by the council, but in practice the latter has only a role of approbation of the Mayor's decisions, thanks to the solid and stable majorities provided by the electoral system. The Mayor usually runs the city with the help of a cabinet of advisors, in the case of large cities. Mayors also delegates responsibilities to Adjoints—prominent members of the *Conseil Municipal* who were elected on the same list—but, these powers are only delegations and can be withdrawn at will by the Mayor in case of political disagreement: the Mayor thus keeps a very tight political control on the city. The administration is run by a *secrétaire general*, the equivalent of a chief executive in Britain, who usually works closely with the mayor and is associated with political decisions.

These basic characteristics have several far-reaching consequences. First, the long intervals between elections mean that, for the first three years, the Mayor has little interest in courting any interests other than those of his main constituency—in Lille, the white left-wing middle class and working class. Second, because there is virtually only one person with palpable power in the whole system, it is completely impossible, and unnecessary, to give some power to a representative of a group or minority of any kind. This is particularly problematic for minorities, because, as I have mentioned, one of their main goals is precisely political and institutional representation. It is extremely difficult to give a key role to a *conseiller* from a minority background—or to any outsider, for that matter—supposing one wants to. The few delegations go to senior politicians who are very close to the Mayor, and among whom are usually the candidates for Mayoral succession. Thus, the three *Conseillers Municipaux* of Maghrebi origin in Lille, of a total of fifty-six, are held by everyone, including themselves, to be 'tokens' given by the Mayor to the Maghrebi electorate when he assembled his list. Consequently, they are of little use at the *Mairie* (Town Hall), as indeed are most other *conseillers*, and are seen as 'traitors' by many young members of their community. As a result they lose all political influence. This also tended to be often the case in Birmingham when the first minority councillors started getting elected in the late 1970s and early 1980s, but it has largely changed since then, and their full incorporation in the decision-making processes of the City Council is now widely acknowledged.

By contrast, the organization of local political institutions in Britain offer many more opportunities for minorities attempting to participate and to formulate policy demands. First, local elections take place in three years out of four, which provides many opportunities for outsiders to run for election. In addition, the local elections work with a first-past-the-post system, which gives a decisive advantage to the majority group within one given ward, which in the inner city wards happen to be the ethnic 'minorities'.

In addition, the organization of the council itself makes it comparatively accessible for small outsider groups of councillors to participate fully in the decision-making process once they are elected. It can be broadly likened to a small 'parliamentary system': decisions are taken by various committees organized around policy sectors such as housing, personnel, or education, and made up of a mix of councillors reflecting the overall proportion of the different parties in the council. In Birmingham, the Labour group has a clear majority, and thus controls all the committees. Within the party, however, there are cleavages along policy issues. In contrast to the French system, the leading councillors do not dominate the council single-handedly; it is more often than not the ruling party as a whole that takes important decisions (Stoker 1988: 89). The policy of the council is thus determined by a game of fluid alliances between the leadership, elected by the group, and sub-groups. As a result, all councillors within a group have to be taken into account, and, even if a certain number of backbenchers will never mount significant opposition to the leadership, there are certain individual or groups which manage to impact on the leadership. In Birmingham, one of the longest serving Labour African-Caribbean councillors has co-operated with the leadership for the past fifteen years while always pushing for more radical and more extensive anti-discriminatory policies. In this way, he has been instrumental in shaping the council's policy. A young Asian councillor has recently been elected president of the Committee of the National Exhibition Centre, a highly important showcase for the economic development of the city. The twenty-one councillors of ethnic background, out of a total of 117, are always unanimous in supporting the anti-discriminatory policies, although they often have diverging positions on other issues.

The Control of the Local Community

In both cities, patronage is the prominent mode of relation between the council and the local ethnic minority groups, but this is especially the case in Lille, while some recognition of ethnic groups has taken place in Birmingham. I argue that this is due to the traditional importance of municipal patronage in Lille, and to the different organization and content of French and British urban regeneration programmes.

Local political actors in France who are not part of the representational system are particularly deprived of access to political power, while being increasingly dependent on elected bodies, and especially the Municipality for funding (Mabileau 1994: 135–48). The local community in France is organized overwhelmingly along the lines of a specific legal framework—the association as defined by the 1901 law on associations. This is broadly comparable to a charity in Britain: a non-profit organization dedicated to activities of general interest. Since the early 1980s, there has been a trend towards the strengthening of the control of associations by the municipalities, by controlling their source of funding. This is especially true in Lille, because of the long tradition of control of neighbourhood associations—including, say, sports clubs or brass bands—and clientelism between individual inhabitants of the city and adjoints of the Mayor which characterizes the socialist Municipality; other French cities often exercise less control. This is particularly visible in deprived areas of the city, where the concentration of populations of North African background is the highest. This mode of government has been able to perpetuate itself in the poor neighbourhoods of Lille in spite of a clear decline since the 1970s, which was due in large part to the sociological transformations of the population of the city, chiefly characterized by the decline of the working class population, which used to be the privileged clientele of the Municipality. What enabled to city to face these transformations was the appearance around the same period, the late 1970s, of nationally-funded urban regeneration programmes, the *Politique de la Ville* (Lojkine, Delacroix, and Mahieu 1978). The way these are organized in France reinforces the capacity of the Municipality for local control because it institutionalises the Municipality as the distributor of grants for the local groups. The city of Lille has been particularly efficient in exploiting these programmes because it has integrated them to an internal reorganization scheme started in 1977 which divides the city in neighbourhoods and attributes a permanent team of city officers and adjoints close to the Mayor—the *commissions de quartier*—for each of these neighbourhoods, in charge of monitoring the allocation of grants on their territory.

Most ethnic groups in Lille are associations, be it cultural or neighbourhood associations, tenant groups, or sports clubs for the younger, second generation. Many of these are funded jointly by the FAS (*Fonds d'Action Sociale*) and by the Municipality. Moreover, the groups of young, second generation immigrants are very often extremely dependent on Town Hall, because, as mentioned earlier, it is the latter which in effect controls the distribution of urban programme funding, and second generation groups are often within the remit of urban regeneration. In addition, the Municipality has considerable leverage with young community leaders because it deals with local sports centres, which are a hot issue in Lille-Sud, and because it can occasionally provide jobs at the council or other institutions to a mostly unemployed second generation immigrant population.

The *Politique de la Ville* thus acts as a convenient instrument reinforcing other instruments of control. It helps to ensure that local North African leaders, who are very influential among their peers in their respective neighbourhoods, contribute to maintaining law and order in the city. The Achilles heel of this form of patronage is that funding sports and providing occasional jobs is all the

Municipality can give. In addition, it only caters to bottom-line and short-term demands. As a result, the Municipality is caught in a perverse cycle whereby it entices clientelist demands that can only be addressed by giving more. Attempts to decrease funds by the council are usually met with the burning down of sports centres and of the offices of social workers by local youths, which happened several times in the 1990s, and which is precisely the opposite of the intended goal. In spite of this, there has been some scaling down of the funds allocated since the beginning of the 1990s, with much apprehension of possible violent reactions.

Another strategy is to divide and rule over groups which break out of the cycle of patronage and try to oppose to the council. When a group of young leaders, disgruntled because they had obtained less funding for their associations than previously, decided to join forces with controversial, older North African leaders who had been disappointed by the Socialist Party in the 1980s, to form a 100 per cent North-African list for the 1995 Municipal elections, the Municipality perceived this as a threat to the re-election of the Mayor, who was also being challenged by a serious candidate from the Right. In this context, ethnic minorities were perceived as an important marginal electorate. One of the leaders of the list was then offered a place, an eligible position on the socialist list, together with a job at Euralille, the new business centre which was then being built on the site of the new Eurostar station.

The present relationship between the Municipality and local groups is thus a combination of patronage, and division and exclusion of groups of young North Africans from local politics. The Municipality is therefore able to officially ignore the issue of ethnic minorities, and to put forward a republican-assimilationist discourse which presents ethnic issues as illegitimate, which fits well with its traditional socialist culture.

In Birmingham, traditional patterns of patronage have been functioning in similar ways (Back and Solomos 1995). However, other modes of relation between the Council and local groups have also appeared since the mid-1980s. First, the Handsworth riots of 1985, which were widely pictured in the national media as expressions of racial hatred against whites or between blacks and Asians—although their real motives had probably more to do with frustration in the face of cumulative economic and social disadvantage—shocked the city council and prompted a strong policy reaction in the form of the creation of a Standing Consultative Forum (SCF), an umbrella organization representative of ethnic groups. This has allowed these groups to gain some recognition and some access to the decision-makers of the Council.

Second, the various urban regeneration programmes that have followed each other since the early 1980s have acted less as instrument of control of the community in the hands of the Council, than was been the case in French cities. As stated by Le Gales (1993, 1995), it has not been in the fundamental interest of the British state, nor of the French state, to ensure that these programmes are efficient in reaching their goals. In the British case, however, the Thatcher governments have striven to reduce the role of local councils during the 1980s. They have done so by increasingly fragmenting the local British system, by transferring competencies from elected authorities to quasi-administrative bodies, or 'quangos'. In the field of urban regeneration, the attacks by central government on local authorities since the early 1980s have considerably limited the ability of the latter to control urban regeneration programmes. Since 1981, 'it has been a prerequisite of inner-city programme approval that local authorities should have consulted the private sector.' (Stoker 1988: 114). In addition, many programmes are increasingly managed by non-elected institutions. In this way, power is dispersed among many different players.

There is therefore a complex game for the control of financial resources by different local institutions trying to push their own interests. Elected local governments are only one type of actor among others, even if they do remain the most prominent ones. This attitude has softened since the launch of City Challenges programmes in 1991, which came back to a more traditional approach, but the latest developments have confirmed that the margin for action by local authorities remains clearly reduced. Since most of the governmental urban regeneration grants have been regrouped into the Single Regeneration Budget (SRB) in 1994, funds have been attributed to local authorities on a competitive basis, forcing councils who apply, to present programmes that fit as much as possible with the government's criteria of efficiency, though once the money has been distributed, it is still managed by the councils.

These developments have made the Birmingham City Council an important provider of funds, while relatively limiting its range for action. First, it has to work increasingly in partnerships with other institutions, such as the Solihull and Birmingham Training and Enterprise Council (TEC), which represents business interests, and the Health Authority. Second, in order to meet the SRB criteria, the Council has increasingly co-operated with groups from the voluntary sector which are often of ethnic minority background. For instance, one of the major policies of the Economic Development Department (EDD) is the creation of a network of twenty five 'Employment Resources Centres' scattered around the city, based in the premises of community organizations which can often be ethnic organizations such as the Islamic Resource Centre in Balsall Heath, or a Sikh temple in Handsworth. Through the institutionalization of these structured, long-lasting groups, the council delegates the management of the problem of youth to the community itself, while the Municipality in Lille places itself on the front line.

Finally, the emergence of the European Social Fund (ESF) as a major source of funding for local community groups is highly visible, with the creation of URBAN regeneration programmes. In order to maintain its ability to bid successfully for these European grants which it perceives as probably diminishing in the near future, the Council has adopted a 'Community Economic Development Framework' which proposes to rationalize its criteria of distribution of grants and encourage the participation of local groups in the elaboration of these criteria. It is hard to foresee the effects of this, but it does place new constraints on the use of funds by city officers and councillors. In Lille, the ESF is not involved directly, though it is in neighbouring areas of Roubaix and Tourcoing.

The Effect of the Councils' Policies on the Formulation of Claims by Local Ethnic Groups

The combination of clientelism, opposition to the emergence of strong local groups, and assimilationist discourse practised by the Municipality in Lille prevents specifically ethnic demands from emerging. It encourages the formulation of individual and limited demands about housing and employment, which the few existing youth organizations do proficiently, while strongly discouraging the generalization of such claims in terms of a collective problem, which would then lead to putting the issue of racial discrimination or recognition of racial difference on the agenda. Hence, although the perception of racial disadvantage is widely spread across the members of local community groups, the demand is never formulated, except in negotiations with an elected official for the employment of one youth or another at the Mairie or at the Communauté Urbaine. In addition, the only custom-built mosque of the city, in Lille-Sud, is only tolerated by the City Council, which does not grant it any funds nor include it in any urban regeneration programme. This is in spite of the fact that it is the largest mosque in the Lille area, seating 2000, and that it is clearly the largest and most institutionalized organization in this part of the city. This encourages the isolationist tendency of the Recteur, who has a mixed discourse about his relation with the council and French institutions in general, and whose involvement in Municipality-led activities in the neighbourhood is minimal.

In Birmingham, the creation of the Standing Consultative Forum (SCF) after the 1985 riots has clearly legitimized claims for the recognition of ethnic difference. As a result, an increasing number of groups have demanded to be recognized as ethnic minorities, such as the Chinese—with around 3000 people, only 0.3 per cent of the total population of the city—and more recently the Irish and the Yemeni. However, what was originally a strategy to appease claims, is now perceived as a problem by the Council because it has created inter-ethnic competition—the African-Carribean Community and the Pakistanis accuse each other of getting more favourable treatment by the Council—and accusations of corruption on all sides. As a result it is now disbanding the SCF and trying to promote a new discourse centred on the notion of transcommunity issues, such as better health, employment and housing policies for everyone, regardless of ethnic communities. The other fundamental concession made by the Council to minority interests, anti-discrimination policies, has on the contrary gained widespread currency and is commonly advocated in all local institutions.

Variables intrinsic to the ethnic communities also play a role in shaping claims. In Britain, ethnic groups are more likely to be recognized as inter-locutors than their French counterparts, because they have more financial and organizational resources from within their community, while the Muslim community in France has chronic organizational problems at both national and local levels (Boyer 1998). This is especially clear with the British Muslim community—predominantly of Pakistani origin—which has dense religious networks and receives funding from religious organizations and government. Birmingham, especially, has a very active Muslim community (Joly 1987). In addition, the traditional brand of Islam of the Pakistanis in Britain entails some degree of control of the second generation by the first generation through religious teaching and strong family structure, whereas North African Communities in France have been increasingly secularized, and the trend towards re-Islamization currently observed emanates from the younger members of the community alone. As a result, Muslim groups in Birmingham can more easily engage in constructive dialogues with the authorities and for-mulate claims related to cultural issues, than their North African counterparts in France.

Conclusion

In this chapter, I have sought to provide the bases of an explanation of the strategies of management of post-colonial ethnic conflict of the City Council of Birmingham and the Municipality of Lille. Each city has reacted very dif-ferently to the problems posed by electoral challenge from anti-immigrant forces and civil unrest. In Birmingham, since the early 1980s, there has been a *de facto* alliance between the ruling Labour group of the council and some ethnic minority groups. In addition, the Council has implemented proactive policies against racial discrimination and in favour of the participation of ethnic groups in the decision-making process of the Council. In Lille—dominated by the Socialist Mayor Pierre Mauroy since 1974—by contrast, there is no alliance with ethnic groups, which are kept out of the realm of conventional local pol-itics, and there are only limited efforts to implement policies addressing the issue of minorities.

I have argued that the differences between the two strategies stem, for a large part, from differences between the institutional frameworks in which the two cities operate. I have focused first on the relation between the cities and the central polity, which is characterized by a tight separation of 'low' and 'high' politics in Britain, and a strong inter-penetration of the two levels of government in France. This has made immigrant political mobilization at the grass roots level easier in Britain than in France. It has also facilitated a strategy of devolution of the issues of race and immigration to local level politics by British central élites in the 1960s, while it has raised the salience of the national issues of immigration control and nationality law at all levels of electoral competition in France, which has, in turn, encouraged the success of the *Front National* and kept immigrant groups out of the realm of conventional political participation.

Second, I have dealt with the structure of the party system and the internal organization of the parties. In Birmingham, there is a strategic openness towards minority groups on the part of the Labour party, because its local organization has made it more penetrable by ethnic minorities members at the local level. This in turn compels the Council to take the demands of minorities concerning, for example, racial discrimination or under-representation, into account. In Lille, the pervasive influence of the *Front National* on French politics, which discourages the Socialist party from striking an alliance with minorities, coupled with the failure of attempts made by the party to co-operate with ethnic minority political movements during the 1980s, encourage the Socialist party to avoid the issue.

Finally, I have argued that the organization of local government in the two countries—a more open 'parliamentary' style of government in British councils than in the French 'presidential' mode of government by the Mayors—facilitates the incorporation of ethnic minorities in the decision-making processes of the council in Birmingham, while it is unfavourable to outsider groups in France. This in turn makes it more difficult for the dominant political groups in the Birmingham City Council to ignore the demands of minorities, while it makes it relatively easier for the Mayor of Lille. This has greatly encouraged ethnic groups in Birmingham to put issues of racial discrimination and cultural recognition on their agenda, while it has entailed a continued self-limitation of claims by North Africans in Lille.

Notes

*The author is thankful for comments on this paper by David Goldey, Virginie Guiraudon, Randall Hansen, Desmond King, Alan Ware, Vincent Wright, and Rémi Lefebvre, and gratefully acknowledges the support of the Centre de Recherches Administratives, Politiques, et Sociales of the Université de Lille 2 in Lille, of the Department of European Studies of Aston University in Birmingham, and of the Philip Williams Fund of the Pôle Européen de Sciences Politiques, Institut d'Etudes Politiques de Paris.

1. It must also be noted that both cities are in many ways typical of both countries, but that they also have many specific features, especially the long-standing domina-

tion of the Socialist Party on the city politics of Lille, which requires caution when attempting to generalize from their case.

2. These differences no doubt have important roles to play in explaining many variations between the two cities and will be dealt with in later developments of the research. Here, I will limit myself to exploring institutionalist hypotheses.

3. In Britain, all persons from a post-colonial immigrant background have the vote, and they play an increasingly significant role in elections, especially at the local level, in spite of under-registration and of a lower turn-out rate than Britons of native, European descent (for a history of the British citizenship regime since 1948, see Layton-Henry 1992).

4. Though some sections of the 'Asian' electorate, mainly Indians and Pakistanis, vote Conservative. There are also local exceptions to the rule.

5. For details, see Kelfaoui (1996).

6. According to reports by members of the local North African community in Lille-Sud who are courted by members of Socialist lists during electoral campaigns; it is very difficult to obtain data on this from the town hall.

7. The major difference between the two was that SOS Racisme advocated the Droit à la Différence, a French version of cultural pluralism, while France Plus focused on campaigning for the participation of second generation immigrants in electoral politics.

8. Though this is also due to the fact that the proportion of North Africans is significantly higher in Roubaix than in Lille.

References

ANWAR, MUHAMMAD (1998), Ethnic Minorities and the British Electoral System. A Research Project (Coventry: Centre for Research in Ethnic Relations, University of Warwick and Operation Black Vote).

ASHFORD, DOUGLAS (1982), French Pragmatism and British Dogmatism, Central-Local Policy Making in the Welfare State (London: Allen and Unwin).

BACK, LES, and SOLOMOS, JOHN (1995), Race, Politics and Social Change (London: Routledge).

BLEICH, ERIK (1997), Changing the Natives: Anti-Discrimination Legislation in Britain and France. Paper prepared for the Centre d'Etude des Politiques de l'Immigration et de la Citoyenneté research workshop, Paris, April 2.

BOUAMAMA, SAID (1994), Dix Ans de Marches des Beurs, Chronique d'un Mouvement Avorté (Paris: EPI/Desclée de Brouwer).

BOUSETTA, HASSAN (1996), 'Citizenship and Political Participation in France and the Netherlands; Reflections on Two Local Cases', New Community, 23/3: 215–31.

BROWNING, RUFUS P., MARSHALL, DALE R., and TABB, DAVID H. (1990), Racial Politics in American Cities (2nd edn) (New York, NY: Longman).

BOYER, ALAIN (1998), L'Islam en France, Politique d'aujourdhui (Paris: Presses Universitaire de France).

BULPITT, JIM (1986), 'Continuity, Autonomy and Peripheralisation: The Anatomy of the Centre's Race Statecraft in England', in Zig Layton-Henry and Paul Rich (eds.), *Race, Government and Politics* (London: Macmillan).

BRUBAKER, ROGERS (1992), *Citizenship and Nationhood* (Cambridge, MA: Harvard University Press).

CORDEIRO, ALBANO (1996), 'Pratiques Associatives, Pratiques Citoyennes', *Hommes et Migrations*, March: 17–61.

CROWLEY, JOHN (1993), 'Paradoxes in the Politicisation of Race: A Comparison of the UK and France', *New Community*, 19/4: 627–43.

DION, STÉPHANE (1986), *La Politisation des Mairies* (Paris: Economica).

DUYVENDAK, JAN WILLEM (1995), *The Power of Politics: New Social Movements in France* (Oxford: Westview).

ESMAN, MILTON (1973), The Management of Ethnic Conflict, *Public Policy*, 21: 49–78.

FAVELL, ADRIAN (1998), *Philosophies of Integration: Immigration and the Idea of Citizenship in France and Britain* (Basingstoke: Macmillan).

FREEMAN, GARY (1979), *Immigrant Labor and Racial Conflict in Industrial Societies: The French and British Experience, 1945–1975* (Princeton, NJ: Princeton University Press).

GURR, TED, and KING, DESMOND (1987), *The State and the City* (London: Macmillan).

GYFORD, JOHN, and JAMES, MARIE (1983), *National Parties and Local Politics* (London: Allen and Unwin).

HALL, PETER (1986), *Governing the economy: the politics of state-intervention in Britain and France* (Cambridge: Polity Press).

HILL, MICHAEL, and ISSACHAROFF, RUTH (1971), *Community and Race Relations, a Study of Community Relations Committees in Britain* (London: Oxford University Press).

HOROWITZ, DANIEL (1985), *Ethnic groups in conflict* (Berkeley, CA: University of California Press).

IRELAND, PATRICK (1994), *The Policy Challenge of Ethnic Diversity* (Cambridge, MA: Harvard University Press).

JOHNSON, MARK (1990), 'Ressources Locales en Matière de Services de Protection Sociale pour les Minorités Ethniques en Grande-Bretagne'. Paper for the Colloque International Conference *L'Intégration des Minorités Immigrées en Europe* Paris, 8–9 October. (Paris: Agence pour le Développement des Relations Interculturelle).

JOLY, DANIELE (1987), *Making a Place for Islam in British Society: Muslims in Birmingham*, Research Paper in Ethnic Relations 4 (Coventry: Centre for Research in Ethnic Relations, University of Warwick).

JOPPKE, CHRISTIAN (1998), *Challenge to the Nation-State, Immigration in Western Europe and the United States* (Oxford: Oxford University Press).

KASTORYANO, RIVA (1996), *La France, l'Allemagne et leurs Immigrés: Négocier l'Identité* (Paris: Armand Colin/Masson).

KATZNELSON, IRA (1973), *Black Men, White Cities, Politics and Migrations in the United States, 1900–30, and Great-Britain, 1948–68* (Oxford: Oxford University Press).

KELFAOUI, SCHERAZADE (1996), 'Un Vote Maghrébin en France? Périls Géopolitiques en France', *Herodote*, 80/1: 130–55.

LAGROYE, JACQUES, and WRIGHT, VINCENT *Local Government in Britain and France, Problems and Prospects* (London: Allen and Unwin).

LAPEYRONNIE, DIDIER (1993), *L'Individu et les Minorités, la France et la Grande-Bretagne Face à Leurs Immigrés* (Paris: Presses Universitaires de France).

LAYTON-HENRI, ZIG (1992), *The politics of immigration: immigration, race, and 'race-relations' in post-war Britain* (Oxford: Blackwell).

LEFEBVRE, RÉMI (1999), *Le Socialisme des Beffrois, Etat des Lieux et Pistes de Recherches* (Lille: Actes des Journées de Recherche de l'IFRESI).

LE GALES, PATRICK (1993), 'L'Inner-City Policy en Grande-Bretagne', *Revue Française d'Administration Publique*, 71: 483–498.

——(1995), 'Politique de la Ville en France, Volontarisme et Ambiguite de L'Etat', *Sociologie du Travail*, 21: 249–75.

LE LOHÉ, MICHEL (1998), 'Ethnic Minority Participation and Representation in the British Electoral System', in Shamit Saggar (ed.), *Race and British Electoral Politics* (London: University College London).

LOJKINE, JEAN, DELACROIX, ROLAND, and MAHIEU, CHRISTIAN (1978), *Politique Urbaine et Pouvoir Local dans l'Agglomération Lilloise* (Lille: Centre de Recherches Administratives, Politiques et Sociales).

MABILEAU, ALBERT (1994), *Le Système Local en France* (2nd edn) (Paris: Montchréstien).

MESSINA, ANTHONY (1989), *Race and Party Competition* (Oxford: Oxford University Press).

POINSOT, MARIE (1993), 'Competition for Political Legitimacy at Local and National Levels Among Young North Africans in France', *New Community*, 20/1: 69–82.

NORDLINGER, ERIC (1972), *Conflict regulation in divided societies* (Cambridge, MA: Harvard University, Center for International Affairs).

REX, JOHN, and MOORE, ROBERT (1967), *Race, Community and Conflict: a Study of Sparkbrook* (London and New York, NY: Oxford University Press).

——and TOMLINSON, SALLY (1979), *Colonial Immigrants in a British City: A Class Analysis* (London: Routledge and Kegan Paul).

SAGGAR, SHAMIT (1991), *Race and Public Policy: A Study of Local Politics and Government* (Aldershot: Avebury).

SAWICKI, FRÉDÉRIC (1992), 'La Marge de Manœuvre des Candidats par Rapport aux Partis dans les Campagnes Electorales', *Pouvoirs*, 63: 5–16.

SCHAIN, MARTIN (1993), 'Policy-making and Defining Ethnic Minorities: the Case of Immigration in France', *New Community*, 20/1: 59–77.

SHUKRA, KALBIR (1998), *The Changing Patterns of Black Politics in Britain* (London: Pluto Press).

STOKER, GERRY (1988), *The Politics of Local Government* (London: Macmillan).

STUDLAR, DONLEY (1985), 'Race in British Politics', *Patterns of Prejudice*, 19/1: 3–16.

WEBMAN, GERRY (1981), 'Centralisation and Implementation, Urban Renewal in Great Britain and France', *Comparative Politics*: 127–48.

WEIL, PATRICK (1995), *La France et ses Etrangers* (Paris: Gallimard).

12

Major Anti-Minority Riots and National Legislative Campaigns Against Immigrants in Britain and Germany*

ROGER KARAPIN

Introduction

Opposition to ethnic minorities and to continued immigration has grown in many West European countries during the post-war period (see for example, Hammar 1985; Björgo and Witte 1993; Betz 1994; Cornelius, Martin, and Hollifield 1994; Witte 1996). Anti-immigrant or anti-minority responses have taken quite different forms, including legislative campaigns for immigration restrictions, violence against minorities, and voting for far-right parties. Even if anti-immigration politicians, the perpetrators of racist violence, and far-right political entrepreneurs are usually not consciously co-operating or competing with one another, their actions may reinforce or undermine each other. This chapter examines the relationship between two specific forms of anti-minority mobilization: popular rioting and national legislative campaigns. By an 'anti-minority riot', I mean intense physical violence, with an ethnic or racial motive, by a large number of people belonging to a dominant ethnic group against members of a minority group or their property;[1] by a 'national legislative campaign' against immigration, I mean a series of efforts by individual politicians, political parties, national interest groups, and/or local residents groups to change national laws or regulations in order to reduce foreign immigration rates.

These two forms of political participation are of interest because they both can gain space on the national political agenda and hence can help cause more restrictive immigration policies, especially if they reinforce each other. Large riots, unlike other forms of anti-minority violence, include an element of popular participation—by people seen as 'adults' or 'ordinary citizens'—which news media and politicians often interpret as indicating widespread dissatisfaction with relatively liberal immigration policies. Legislative campaigns might encourage anti-minority riots by signalling that some political élites support nativist sentiment, and that anti-minority actions could influence the outcome of the debate among élites. To the extent that riots and campaigns reinforce each other, West European polities might be vulnerable to an escalating dynamic of complementary mobilization; if they dampen or pre-empt each other, we could expect greater stability.

This chapter explores the relationship between anti-minority riots and immigration-control campaigns in Britain (1948–1966) and the Federal Republic of Germany (1989–1994).[2] These country-cases were chosen for three reasons. First, they both contain many examples of the two phenomena in question; unlike many liberal democracies, campaigns for immigration controls and popular rioting against immigrants overlapped in Britain and Germany during these periods. Hence this selection of cases is well-suited to examining any relationships between these two forms of mobilization.

Second, the two cases have important similarities with regard to mobilization against immigrants. Both began with unusually liberal immigration policies, experienced riots and immigration-control campaigns, and ultimately adopted more restrictive policies. In Britain, the right of all Commonwealth citizens to enter Britain freely was sharply restricted by the Commonwealth Immigrants Act of 1962, while in Germany the comparatively generous right to political asylum anchored in Article 16 of the Basic Law was seriously abridged by constitutional amendment in 1993. Although asylum seekers are not usually considered permanent immigrants, in Germany before 1993 their rights to judicial review enabled the bulk of them to remain in the country for periods of five to ten years (Münch 1993: 72); hence, for convenience in considering theoretical statements, German asylum seekers will be termed 'immigrants' in this chapter.

Third, there are important differences between the country-cases in terms of the nature of immigration, socioeconomic conditions, citizenship rights, and political institutions. Therefore, any factors which the country-cases none the less have in common are likely to have general relevance to anti-immigration mobilization in liberal democracies (Przeworski and Teune 1970: 34–9). Levels of immigration and unemployment were much lower in the British than in the German case—especially in eastern Germany after the communist era—and the types of immigrants differed greatly: laborers with jobs in Britain vs. asylum seekers mostly living from social assistance in Germany. Moreover, black immigrants to Britain enjoyed automatic citizenship and hence much more extensive civil rights than asylum seekers in Germany, who generally could not work or choose their places of residence. In the terms of this volume's chapter Britain's inclusive citizenship policies and lack of pressure for assimilation contrast sharply with Germany's exclusive approach to citizenship. Finally, these countries' political institutions differ sharply on several dimensions: state structure—centralized and unitary in Britain vs. decentralized federalism in

Germany; electoral system and government formation—majoritarian in Britain vs. proportional representation and coalition governments in Germany; and party system—stable, two-party in Britain in the 1960s vs. a multi-party system with the large parties declining in Germany in the 1980s and 1990s.

Theoretical Perspectives

Since theorizing about anti-minority riots and about anti-immigration campaigns is underdeveloped,[3] the most relevant sources of hypotheses are theories of social movements, collective violence, race riots, and immigration-control policies. These literatures provide good theoretical reasons to expect every possible relationship, or lack of a relationship, between anti-minority riots and anti-immigration campaigns.[4]

First, the political-opportunity theory of social movements suggests that anti-immigration campaigns encourage riots. In this view, when protest groups see increased opportunities to influence government actions, and decreased risks of repression, they become more likely to undertake disruptive, risky political activity.[5] Élite divisions indicate to potential perpetrators that rioting may be effective in producing restrictive policies, and may also signal to police and local authorities that it is politically less important to protect immigrants from attack. Second, however, another aspect of the same body of social-movement theory implies that campaigns would make riots less likely. The theory holds that the forms of political participation which are practiced are strongly influenced by the relative costs of alternative forms of participation (Smelser 1963; Tilly 1978: 101–15; Kitschelt 1986; Tarrow 1994: 19–20, 31; Kriesi et al. 1995; Tilly 1995: 367, 378, 381). Hence heightened campaigns for immigration control might channel participation into more conventional forms, such as lobbying and elections, and thus reduce the chances of riots.

Third, there are reasons to expect anti-minority riots to stimulate national anti-immigration campaigns. Theorists of social-movement outcomes argue that violence is often an effective form of political participation (Button 1978; Schumaker 1978; Gamson 1990), a finding confirmed by studies of immigration politics and of racist violence (Layton-Henry 1992; Björgo and Witte 1993; Witte 1996). In liberal democracies, politicians may use anti-minority riots as signals of the importance which the public attaches to immigration issues (Karapin 1999). Fourth, however, many analysts of immigration policy-making emphasize that political élites maintain a depoliticized consensus on liberal immigration policies (Freeman 1979, 1995a; Hammar 1985; Messina 1989). Hence, especially if élites believe in the political-opportunity theory, riots might make them even more reluctant to air their disagreements in public, for fear of encouraging more mobilization from below; if élites find it necessary to respond to riots, they would do so quietly, with policy changes which limit immigration.

Fifth, some political-process theories of social-movement development hold that the relationship between élite and challenger actions is different in different phases of a protest movement (McAdam 1982: 146; Tarrow 1989a: 21, 52–57, 338; Tarrow 1989b: 36, 51; Tarrow 1994: 96–8; Koopmans 1997: 14, 16). According to these theories, the outbreak of protest depends on favourable political opportunities provided by élites, but once major protests are under-way, reciprocal causation between any major protests and élite divisions is likely. This implies that legislative campaigns would tend to cause the first riots which occur in a protest movement, but that later riots would spur campaigns, as well as be affected by them.

By contrast, riots and campaigns may be caused independently of each other. The sixth set of hypotheses derives from theories of riots, which suggest that anti-minority rioting could be caused largely by local conditions, even in periods which lack broader national mobilization against immigrants. In previous work on riots in the former East Germany, I found that cultural conflicts, social movement organizations, and failures of state repression were important causes of riots (Karapin forthcoming). Theorists of ethnic relations have argued that cultural conflicts occur because a minority group's differences in appearance and customs produce an apprehensive, defensive reaction from native populations. Such reactions are especially likely where natives have little experience of interacting with ethnic strangers (Park 1950: 236–9; Husbands 1988: 706; Husbands 1989a; Willems et al. 1993, 173).[6] Different customs concerning matters such as noise, garbage, or sexual relations can become overlaid with inaccurate stereotypes and rumors, and hence give rise to local cultural conflicts. In cultural conflicts, the perpetrators of anti-minority violence are often motivated by the desire to express an identity, control a territory, or protect themselves from perceived physical threats (Björgo Chapter 14 of this volume). The magnitude of cultural conflicts often depend on quite specific local circumstances, such as housing practices, which affect the intensity of the cultural threats which ethnic minorities and native majorities perceive in each other.

The state's repression of violence and its facilitation of routine political activity normally prevent cultural conflicts from turning into large-scale violence, especially given the free-rider problem which confronts groups seeking to undertake collective action which has high individual costs (Olson 1965). However, if social-movement organizations opposed to minorities are available, they can use intra-organizational incentives to overcome the free-rider problem (Gamson 1990: 89–99) and thus help to escalate cultural conflicts into violence. Moreover, if police respond to violence with inaction or vacillation, major riots are possible (Smelser 1963: 262; Tilly 1978: 100–1; Turner and Killian 1972: 160–9; Keith 1993; Salert and Sprague 1980: 20–7). Further, a riot in one place can signal to other potential rioters that opportunities for low-risk or effective violence are available, especially when mass media transmit reports of riots (Brosius and Esser 1995; Koopmans 1997: Table 5).

Seventh, routine political mobilization for immigration control has been explained in terms of a variety of political institutions and processes which have no direct relation to anti-minority rioting, such as a fragmented national party system, electoral instabilities, and decisions by the national leaders of main-stream or far-right political parties (Hammar 1985; Messina 1989; Layton-Henry 1992; Brubaker 1995; Freeman 1995b; Perlmutter 1996a,b). Finally, some theories hold that riots and campaigns may both be caused independently but by similar factors: competition between dominant and subordinate ethnic groups for scarce resources due to increased immigration, unemployment, poverty, or housing shortages (Olivier 1991; Olzak 1992; Freeman 1995a; Perlmutter 1996b); and anti-immigration campaigns by state or local élites, which might create subnational opportunities for riots while exerting for national campaigns (Karapin 1999).

The following analysis tests the above hypotheses in a preliminary way by examining a relatively large number of cases: twelve riots and twelve peaks in legislative campaigns. The explanatory focus is on why anti-minority riots and anti-immigration campaigns happened when they did in these countries, and in the case of riots, in certain localities; I will not try to explain why certain kinds of people participated in them, such as young working-class males in riots.

Temporal Relationships between Anti-Minority Riots and Anti-Immigration Campaigns

Britain

Anti-immigration campaigns in Britain occurred in six main waves during 1948–1966. These campaigns can be traced by examining the public debates on immigration, as reported in national newspapers. Fig. 12.1 depicts these debates, drawing on the *Times Index* (London),[7] which covers major parliamentary debates and the statements of national politicians and interest groups in other settings; a debate peak is defined as twenty or more articles per twelve-month period. The first, small peak occurred in 1954–1955, when MPs, mainly Conservative backbenchers, began questioning Churchill's government and the first full-fledged parliamentary debate on immigration was held in November 1954. However, the first major calls for controls on New Commonwealth—'black', mainly Caribbean, Indian, and Pakistani—immigration did not occur until the next peak of campaigning, during a four-month period in autumn 1958. This campaign was led by long-time immigration-control advocate Cyril

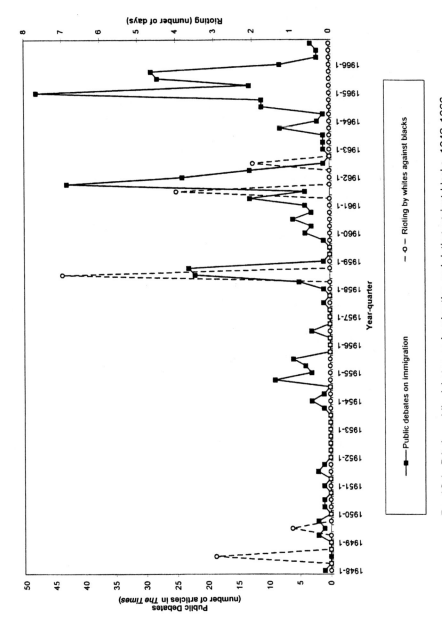

Fig. 12.1. Britain: public debates on immigration and rioting against blacks, 1948–1966

Osborne, aided by many members of the Conservative Party, and some Ministers in Harold Macmillan's Conservative government.

The third and fourth peaks came in 1960–1962, when Conservatives pushed for controls, and in April 1962, Parliament passed the Commonwealth Immigrants Act, which limited immigration from certain Commonwealth countries to those who could obtain work vouchers; this effectively cut annual immigration from about 90,000 at its 1960–1962 peak, to about 40,000 a year. Soon after taking power in 1964, the Labour party debated whether to accept the existing controls, with mobilization by proponents of immigration control in both major parties creating two more peaks in the debate. Ultimately, in 1965, Harold Wilson's Labour government decided to accept the 1962 Act, and it actually tightened controls further through regulations.

Since anti-minority violence varies greatly in intensity and scale, a minimum level of participation must be established in order to distinguish major popular riots from minor riots and other forms of anti-minority violence. Here I define a major anti-minority riot as a series of attacks on a group of ethnic-minority members by at least one hundred attackers and supporters during two or more twenty-four-hour periods within one week, or by at least five hundred attackers and supporters at one time.[8] For Britain, I identified six major anti-minority riots from academic accounts, which have extensively covered this period of black–white relations in Britain and which have been especially sensitive to inter-racial violence.[9] These six major riots occurred in two main periods (see Fig. 12.1 and Appendix Table 12A). Soon after the onset of West Indian immigration, major riots occurred in Liverpool (1948) and Deptford, London (1949). Later, major riots occurred in Notting Hill, London and Nottingham (1958), and in Middlesbrough (1961), and Dudley (1962), during a period which also included intense anti-immigration campaigning.[10]

TABLE 12A. Major riots by white natives against black immigrants in Britain, 1948–1966

Place	Date	Duration in days or nights	Number of white participants at peak (highest estimate or range of estimates)
Liverpool	31 July–2 Aug 1948	3	2,000
Deptford (London)	18 July 1949	1	1,000
Nottingham	23 Aug–6 Sept 1958	3	4,000
Notting Hill (London)	30 Aug–2 Sept 1958	4	800
Middlesbrough	19–23 Aug 1961	4	500
Dudley	1–2 Aug 1962	2	300

Sources: Refer to note 9.

Germany

Campaigns to restrict the right to asylum began in West Germany in 1978 and major national debates occurred in 1980, 1982, and 1986 (Meier-Braun 1980; Wolken 1988; Münch 1993; Perlmutter 1996b). However, the analysis here is limited to the period from 1989 to 1994, a period which included anti-minority riots. Fig. 12.2 shows a measure of anti-immigration campaigning, an estimate of the number of articles in the national, left-alternative daily newspaper *die tageszeitung* concerning a possible constitutional amendment of Article 16.[11]

The asylum debate largely pitted the Christian Democratic Union (CDU) and Christian Social Union (CSU) against the Social Democratic Party (SPD) concerning the question of constitutional amendment, and it reached six main peaks (defined as ten or more articles per month) during 1989–1994: in February 1989 in the wake of the surprising 7.5 per cent vote for the far-right Republikaner party in the West Berlin state elections; during the federal election campaign in August-October 1990 in which SPD leader Oskar Lafontaine supported restrictions; during September-November 1991 led by the CSU and CDU; in January-June 1992, with a peak in April when the issue was used successfully by far-right parties in the state elections in Baden-Württemberg and Schleswig-Holstein; from August 1992 to January 1993 when the CDU/CSU's campaign finally gained the support of SPD leaders; and briefly again in May 1993 when debate erupted once more within the SPD shortly before the passage of a constitutional amendment. The amendment helped reduce the number of applications for asylum from about 300,000 at the peak in 1990–1993, to about 100,000 a year since then.

For Germany, I identified major riots by searching *die tageszeitung* for large-scale attacks on foreigners between 1986 and 1997.[12] Applying the same definition as used for Britain, I identified six major anti-minority riots—against foreign labourers and asylum seekers—in this period, most of them during August-September 1992 and all in the new eastern states (see Fig. 12.2 and Appendix Table 12B).

Temporal Relationships

Examining the curves in Figs. 12.1 and 12.2 does not permit reaching conclusive findings. However, the temporal relationships between the major riots and legislative campaigns are marked by three patterns which suggest possible causal relationships.[13] First, in the early phase of anti-minority mobilization, riots occurred in the absence of intense legislative campaigns, and the former may have influenced the latter. In Britain, the first few years of the 1948–1957 period saw several riots at a time when immigration was not a national issue; in Germany from Spring 1989 through early Summer 1991, rioting broke out in one eastern city during a lull in the asylum debate. Second, during a middle

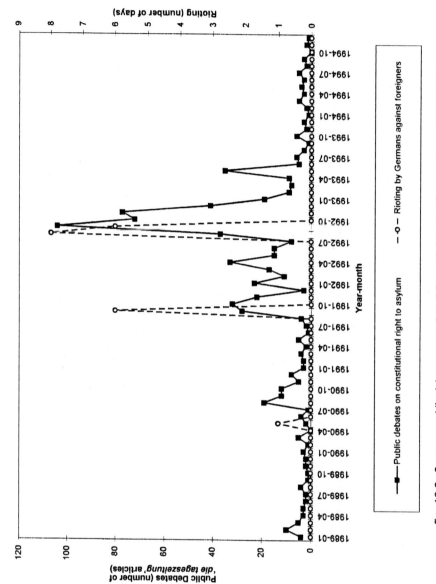

Fig. 12.2. Germany: public debates on asylum rights and rioting against foreigners, 1989–1994

TABLE 12B. Major riots by Germans against foreigners in Germany, 1989–1994

Place	Date	Duration in days or nights	Number of German participants at peak (highest estimate or range of estimates)
Hoyerswerda	1 May 1990	1	1,500
Hoyerswerda	18–22 Sept 1991	6	1,000
Rostock	22–26 Aug 1992	5	3,000
Cottbus	28–30 Aug 1992	3	200
Eisenhüttenstadt	5–6 Sept 1992	2	150
Quedlinburg	7–11 Sept 1992	4	300

Sources: *Sächsische Zeitung* Hoyerswerda, various issues October 1990 to September 1991; *die tageszeitung*, various issues, September 1986 to August 1997.

phase of mobilization, riots and campaigns overlapped and may have influenced each other. In Britain from 1958 to 1962, and Germany from September 1991 to September 1992, riots occurred just before, during, and just after intense legislative campaigns. Third, in the last phase, legislative campaigns were repeated in the absence of riots. Major debates surrounded Labour's official change in position in Britain (1964–1965) and the German parliament's passage of the constitutional amendment (May 1993), after which no major anti-minority riots have occurred to date in these countries. It seems that in this phase, something caused riots to cease, and legislative campaigns were driven by other factors.

Linkages between Riots and Campaigns in Britain

The 1948–1949 Riots

Severe rioting in several British cities in 1948 and 1949 occurred at the beginning of immigration from the West Indies, at a time when both government and opposition were almost completely silent in public on the issue of black immigration.[14] For example, during the first four post-war years (1946–1949), only four columns of Hansard showed mentions of immigration in the House of Commons, compared with one to two hundred columns a year at the peaks of the immigration-control debate in 1961–1962 and 1965 (Hansard, Vols. 429–752).[15] Yet in Liverpool in 1948, crowds ranging from two hundred to two thousand whites attacked black sailors in a cafe and a hostel on three nights, throwing bricks and stones (Richmond 1954: 102–3; Fryer 1984: 368–70). The next year in Deptford (London), up to one thousand whites besieged a hostel in which blacks lived and tried to break into it despite a police cordon; two black residents were seriously injured (Glass 1961: 128–9).

Given the absence of a national anti-immigration campaign, the causes of these riots must be sought elsewhere. The riots occurred soon after the sudden arrival in England of almost one thousand immigrants, mostly West Indians, on the *Empire Windrush* and several other ships in 1948 and 1949 (Pilkington 1988: 18–21, 33; Glass 1961: 5). Accounts of the immigrants' initial reception and of events in the riot areas suggest that the sudden immigration might have sparked local conflicts, culturally or economically based, which sometimes drew large crowds, depending on how local authorities reacted.

In Liverpool, a small increase in the black population coincided with an open conflict between black and white sailors over jobs on ships.[16] The National Union of Seamen was trying, largely successfully, to keep black sailors off British ships. In this context, with 60 per cent of Liverpool's black workforce unemployed (Fryer 1984: 368), Bank Holiday drinking and 'quarrels over women' may have been the pretext for an attempt to further harm blacks. The attackers were aided by the reactions of the police, who waited before intervening on the first night, and then acted mainly against the blacks and arrested few whites (Richmond 1954: 102–3; Fryer 1984: 368–70; *The Times*, 3 and 4 August 1948).

The Deptford case provides further evidence that police passivity or bias against blacks during black–white fighting contributed to the severity of rioting. In Deptford, police acted to protect blacks and were able to limit rioting to one night. After several nights of sporadic fighting between whites and blacks, police responded to a fight on Deptford Broadway by escorting the black men to the hostel in which they lived; police then tried to protect the hostel with a cordon of officers. This seems to have led to a parity of forces, as whites tried to break in and blacks fought back by throwing bottles and crockery; the conflict ended after only four hours.

The concentration of black immigrants in hostels seems to have greatly increased the risk of riots by making cultural conflicts more intense. Blacks faced significant discrimination in housing, and before 1950, about half of the black immigrants were housed in a relatively small number of hostels run by the central government's National Services Hostel Corporation. This housing practice concentrated the blacks and increased the scope of their everyday conflicts with hostel managers, who discriminated against blacks, and with white residents (Pilkington 1988: 20, 49–51). Blacks' concentration in hostels also made them more visible targets for attacks, and presented a greater potential threat to their attackers; fights between whites and blacks in or near hostels where a large number of blacks lived were likely to draw in large crowds of white attackers or sympathizers.

After 1950, blacks were less likely to be concentrated in this way, because policy in the hostels was changed by the Ministry of Labour and the Hostel

Corporation. Quotas were introduced, specifying a maximum of thirty blacks or 10 per cent of the total residents in each hostel; hostels in some areas were given lower quotas or allowed to keep blacks out altogether (Pilkington 1988: 50–1). Moreover, since many black immigrants who arrived in the first years of post-war black immigration found jobs and private housing, the much larger number who came in later years—108,000 between 1954 and 1957 alone—were more apt to join friends and family members in private housing. In the short run, the black population was deconcentrated, and this contributed to the absence of any major riots from 1950–1957, even though black immigration surged after 1953—see Fig. 12.3.

Although the 1948–1949 riots were noted in some Ministries and led to the housing-policy change noted above, the riots received relatively little public attention and triggered no national efforts to limit immigration. For example, in this period *The Times* carried only three riot stories, all on the Liverpool riots, which downplayed their racial character, the size of crowds, and the offensive nature of white actions. From 1948–1953, Hansard carried only seventeen columns on immigration policy, and most of these concerned a pro-immigration initiative launched by the Labour MP Anthony Wedgwood Benn in July 1951 (Hansard, Vol. 491, Cols. 805–14). The lack of national interest in black immigration is more easily understood if the small number of blacks in Britain is considered; by 1953, only about forty thousand West Indians, Indians, and Pakistanis lived in the country (Layton-Henry 1992: 10).

The 1954 Campaign

The first period of national anti-immigration campaigning in post-war Britain, peaking in autumn to winter 1954, centred on parliamentary questions and a parliamentary debate initiated by various Conservative MPs who lacked broader influence within the Conservative Party. Conceivably, this relatively small anti-immigration campaign was motivated by the minor riots which occurred at Camden Town (London) during two days in August 1954, but this is unlikely. Ruth Glass (1961: 129) observes that the Camden Town riots 'were not front-page news', and they were not reported at all in *The Times*. Similarly, in the main session of the parliamentary debate, on 5 November 1954, MPs did not mention or allude to rioting or other violence (Hansard: Vol. 532, Cols. 821–37).

Rather, a rising level of openly reported cultural conflicts probably signalled to MPs that 1954 was a good time to mount an anti-immigration campaign. That year saw sharp increases both in West Indian immigration and in reports of conflicts between white natives and blacks concerning discrimination in employment, housing, and dance halls, and both immigration and cultural

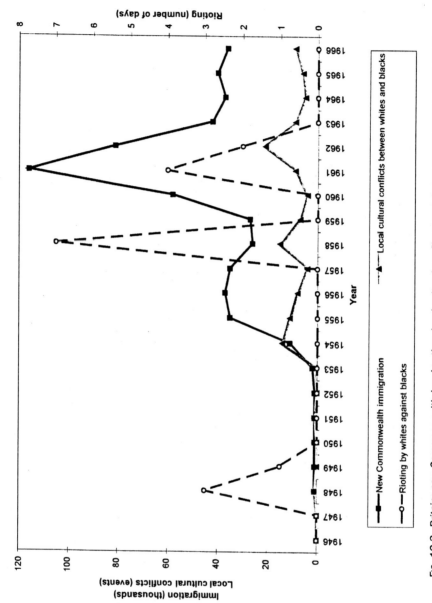

FIG. 12.3. Britain: new Commonwealth immigration, local cultural conflicts, and rioting against blacks, 1948–1966

conflicts continued at elevated levels until the mid-1960s—see Fig. 12.3).[17] As blacks began to seek entry to white occupations or establishments, whites responded with attempts to exclude them, and controversies sometimes erupted over whether 'colour bars', either tacit or official, should be adopted or upheld (Pilkington 1996: 173–4). These conflicts occurred in many cities, and therefore they would have indicated to national politicians that anti-immigration positions might gain broad support. Indeed, in the November 1954 debate, the MPs mainly discussed social tensions arising from overcrowded housing and sexual rivalries in dance halls (Hansard: Vol. 532, Cols. 821–37).

The 1958 Riots and Campaign

In contrast to the previous decade in Britain, anti-minority riots and anti-immigration campaigns reinforced each other in 1958. Violence began in Nottingham at the end of August, leading two MPs from that city to try to initiate an immigration-control campaign, which was followed immediately by much heavier violence, especially in Notting Hill (London). In Nottingham, crowds of 1,500, 4,000, and 150 whites gathered to menace West Indians on three consecutive Saturday nights from 23 August to 6 September, and several times the crowds hunted blacks or attacked blacks' houses (Glass 1961: 131–3; Wickenden 1958: 32–3). Much more serious rioting occurred in and near Notting Hill, where crowds ranging from two to eight hundred whites battled with West Indians, attacked their homes, and chanted anti-black slogans on four consecutive nights between 30 August and 2 September (Glass 1961: 137–40; Pilkington 1988: 113–24). In the two riot cities, over two hundred people were arrested, three-quarters of them white and almost all of them in London (Hiro 1973: 38, n. 4).

Although leading national politicians denounced the violence, the riots provided an opening for Britain's first major national immigration-control campaign of the post-war period. Some national politicians, mostly Conservatives, publicly claimed that immigration was responsible for the violence, and influential figures, such as the Conservative Secretary for Commonwealth Relations, for the first time joined the calls for restriction. The Conservative MP Cyril Osborne introduced a private member's bill calling for immigration controls, but the Conservative cabinet remained divided on the issue and the government decided not to take action on it before the next general election, in October 1959 (Layton-Henry 1992: 40, 74).

After the first night of rioting in Nottingham, anti-immigration statements by local political leaders and sensationalist news reporting attracted new participants and therefore helped increase the scope and duration of rioting during the next two weeks. But rioting began in Nottingham while the area was out of national attention, and the first large crowds assembled to attack blacks as a result of local factors. These included cultural conflicts, heightened by

material competition, the actions of Teddy Boys, and unpreparedness and passivity by police. These same factors were even more striking in Notting Hill,
where they contributed to even more severe violence.

As immigration increased in the mid-1950s, blacks faced housing discrimination and therefore became concentrated in a small number of neighborhoods and in the overcrowded, run-down houses where landlords were willing
to rent to them. This kind of segregation also concentrated residential conflicts
between blacks and their neighbours, as culturally based expectations clashed,
and made the riots of 1958–1962 more likely. Many white English people
objected to the habits of some black people, such as playing radios loudly late
at night, holding loud music parties, wearing fancy clothing, or 'whistling or
calling to each other from their houses' (Glass 1961: 102; Wickenden 1958: 26;
The Times, 27 August 1958). For their part, blacks often found the English to be
stiff, unfriendly, and prudish (Glass 1961: 104–8; Wickenden 1958: 20). The presence of large numbers of single black men,[18] a small number of whom organized white prostitution, brought sexual jealousies to the fore, leading to
conflicts at dance halls and black clubs; blacks sometimes used knives in fights,
or were rumored to have done so, and this was seen as despicable by English
working-class males (Pilkington 1996: 176; Wickenden 1958: 20–1, 32, 38; Glass
1961: 265). Competition for housing exacerbated these conflicts. The widespread discrimination facing blacks who sought housing permitted some landlords to get high rents from blacks, driving out white tenants who had enjoyed
low rents (Wickenden 1958: 16–18). By contrast, whites experienced relatively
little competition for jobs, despite rumors to the contrary (Glass 1961: 262, 264);
for example, the black unemployment rate in Nottingham was 14 per cent in
1958, while the rate for white workers was less than 1 per cent (Wickenden
1958: 9–10).

Social-movement organizations, both informal and formal, helped escalate
minor conflicts into larger riots in these two cities. By early Summer 1958,
active groups of Teddy Boys, young working-class males who dressed in Edwar-
dian style, began deliberately attacking blacks in Nottingham and Notting Hill
(Pilkington 1988: 101–2; The Times, 1 September 1958; Panayi 1996: 188). On
the first night of rioting in Nottingham, crowds gathered after blacks had
stabbed whites; police believed that the stabbings were in reprisal for attacks by
Teddy Boys in the previous weeks (The Times, 26 August 1958). Moreover,
Notting Hill and its surroundings had far-right organizations and activity,
including the headquarters of the White Defence League and many members
of the Union Movement led by the fascist, Oswald Mosley. Mosley's supporters held meetings on street corners in Notting Hill earlier in 1958, and during
the riots there, their leaflets and speeches urged whites to take action against
blacks (Pilkington 1988: 101–2, 117–18).

Finally, police failed to protect blacks, beginning in the weeks preceding the
riots and then during the riots themselves. In both riot areas, blacks reported

that police did not step in when Teds and others began attacking blacks earlier in the summer. The apparent leniency of the police would have emboldened potential white attackers, so that when sexual jealousies led to small fights, these petty disputes became pretexts for large crowds to gather and to menace and attack blacks. During the Notting Hill riots, the police were undermanned and sometimes gave in to the mobs' wishes. For example, even on the second night of rioting, there were still only ten police officers on duty, who were over-whelmed by the crowds and suffered injuries (Pilkington 1988: 112, 114–15). In Nottingham, by contrast, police intervened decisively on the first night of rioting and prevented large-scale attacks on blacks, and the crowds turned against the police instead.

The linkage between anti-immigration riots and campaigns was much tighter in this case than during the previous decade. The 1958 riots immedi-ately triggered an anti-immigration campaign, which in turn expanded rioters' apparent political opportunities and hence fuelled further rioting. On the Tuesday after the riots began in Nottingham, two MPs from that city, James Harrison (Labour) and J. K. Cordeaux (Conservative), came out in favour of controls on black immigration; Cordeaux travelled to London to meet with Cabinet members and was interviewed on a BBC news programme (*The Times*, 27 August 1958; Pilkington 1988: 110–11). These leaders' statements indirectly stirred further rioting by helping to keep press attention on 'race relations' in Nottingham and other potential trouble spots. Over the next week, the press speculated heavily about the activities of Teddy Boys and about where rioting might next develop, with Notting Hill widely reported as most likely (Pilkington 1988: 111–12). These press reports attracted large crowds from outside areas, including many sightseers and reporters, to the St. Ann's section of Nottingham by the next weekend (Glass 1961: 132; Wickenden 1958: 32–3), and may have contributed to the Notting Hill riots, too. In any case, it is likely that events in these two riot cities influenced each other via news reports.

Moreover, politicians, newspapers, and polling organizations often publicly linked the riots with the question of immigration control (for ex-ample, *The Times*, 28 August 1958). Pollsters asking questions specifically about riots and immigration controls made the linkage explicit. A Gallup poll taken a few days after the riots showed that over 90 per cent of the popu-lation had heard of the riots; another newspaper poll, cited in Parliament, found that almost 80 per cent favoured immigration controls (Layton-Henry 1992: 40, n. 51). In the parliamentary debate on 5 December 1958, Cyril Osborne alluded to the riots by using much more inflammatory language than he had earlier in the year in statements on the same question. At the start of his speech, Osborne said that 'this problem, like real dynamite, will not cease to be dangerous' and that 'an accidental spark could ignite the whole lot'; much of the ensuing debate concerned itself with Osborne's rhetoric (Hansard: Vol. 585, Cols. 1415–26; Vol. 596, Cols. 1552–97; quote at Col. 1552).

Riots and campaigns were more tightly linked in 1958 than in 1948 because of three factors. First, black immigration levels were higher than in the previous decade; the black population of Britain was near 200,000, compared with about 40,000 during 1948–1953. Second, cultural conflicts associated with immigration had been widespread, and widely reported, for four years prior to 1958—see Fig. 12.3. Both these considerations made an anti-immigration position seem more electorally viable or profitable than in 1949 or 1954. Third, the Notting Hill riots were much more extensive than any of the previous anti-black rioting, as they spread to several adjoining neighborhoods including Paddington and Kensal Rise, and occurred in tandem with the less serious, but equally heavily reported, Nottingham riots.

The 1961–1962 Riots and Campaign

The next period of anti-minority rioting and campaigning involved a reversal of the pre-1958 pattern, as campaigns encouraged riots more than vice versa. The national campaign for immigration control reached a relatively small peak in 1960–1961, when MPs raised the issue in Parliament, and became intense from November 1961 through to April 1962—see Fig. 12.1. The latter period was bracketed by the October 1961 Conservative Party conference, where immigration-control advocates were vocal; and the passage of the Commonwealth Immigrants Act in April the next year. The Middlesborough and Dudley riots were sandwiched around that campaign. In Middlesborough, crowds of up to 500 attacked shops owned by Pakistanis and 'Arabs' for four nights in August 1961 after an 'Arab' was arrested for murdering a local youth; twelve police were injured in subsequent fighting and fifty-five people were prosecuted (Panayi 1991: 143–5). In Dudley, crowds of 300 gathered to hunt blacks on at least two nights in late July and early August 1962; sixty were arrested (Reeves 1989: 44).

This chronology suggests that the Middlesborough riot may have contributed to the campaign for the Act, while the passage of the Act may have incited the Dudley riots. However, it is more likely that the Middlesborough riot was influenced by the national campaign for immigration control, which was rising during 1960 because of the success of local campaigns for immigration control, and that the riots had little independent effect on national politics.

In 1960–1961, national-level champions of immigration control such as Cyril Osborne and Norman Pannell were having no influence on Macmillan's government through meetings and little-noticed parliamentary debates, but their allies at the local level, especially in the Birmingham area, were creating an influential grassroots lobby. The Birmingham—later called the British—

Immigration Control Association formed, held mass meetings, organized at least 20,000 postcards to lobby local Conservative party organizations, and collected 55,000 petition signatures between October 1960 and November 1961, especially in spring and early summer 1961 (Foot 1965: 134–9, 201–3). Local activists' efforts led local Conservative party organizations to make thirty-nine resolutions in favour of immigration control at their national party's conference in October 1961, which tipped the balance toward immigration control within the party. At the conference, the Home Secretary, Richard Butler, voiced agreement with the local organizations' complaints, and three weeks later the government announced it would seek immigration controls.

These subnational anti-immigration campaigns were gradually making a mark on national politics before the Conservative conference in 1961, and thus contributed to a climate of racial hostility around Britain, which led to open conflicts in many places (Panayi 1991: 151). Hence the anti-immigration campaigns comprised one of several factors which probably triggered the Middlesbrough rioting. Other factors included a sharp increase in South Asian immigration during 1960–1961, a development which was in response to the growing threat of immigration control in Britain (Peach 1968), and a mild increase in unemployment after the government's austerity package in July 1961. Finally, the 1961 riot grew directly out of local cultural conflicts, namely the arrest of an Arab, who was later freed, for the stabbing death of a local white youth, which directly triggered the riots, and earlier conflicts between cafe owners and some of their patrons, which led to reprisals that created focal points for the rioting (Panayi 1991: 143, 148).

Although the Middlesbrough riots were widely reported as 'race riots' in the press, they seem to have had little influence on the national campaign for immigration control. In contrast to the period after the 1958 riots, no political figures with access to the national political stage used the Middlesbrough riots to call for immigration controls during the six weeks between the riots and the Conservative conference (Times Index, July–October 1961).

The intense campaign for the Commonwealth Immigrants Act may have sparked the Dudley riots of July 1962. The Act did not reduce the numbers of black immigrants living in Britain, since controls only reduced the rate of their increase, and deportations remained few. Rioters in the 1958 disturbances, through their actions and slogans, had already expressed a more extreme position than the control of further immigration: they wanted blacks living near them to be badly injured or killed, leave the neighbourhood, or be deported. Indeed, the passage of the Act in April 1962 seems to have encouraged neo-fascist demonstrations involving Oswald Mosley that spring and summer. In this context, the passage of the Act and then the far-right mobilization may have encouraged further rioting, by those who felt that violence at this time might lead to further government measures against blacks, such as repatriation.

Political opportunities created by subnational political leaders also may have encouraged the Dudley riots. In the neighbouring borough of Smethwick, local anti-black activists began publicity work in 1960 with the help of local conservatives. Minor 'racial disturbances' occurred on the Smethwick-Dudley border the same year, soon after a candidate for local city council had called for evicting blacks from city-owned housing, and more disturbances occurred in Smethwick in 1962 (Foot 1965: 31).

The Dudley riots had little effect on national politics, and were not even covered in *The Times*. For the first time since 1949, a major riot was not followed by an increase in the debate within the next few months. There are at least two reasons for the change in pattern. First, with the passage of the 1962 Act, the political opportunities for the anti-immigration forces had been exhausted for the time being. Second, police in the 1961–1962 riots had acted more quickly to control the disturbances. Moderately anti-black forces had been placated with legislation, and it seemed the militants could be kept in check with police measures.

The 1964–1965 Campaign

Although no major anti-black rioting occurred after 1962, two quite vigorous campaigns for immigration control occurred between September 1964 and December 1965—see Fig. 12.1. There were three principal reasons for these campaigns, all rooted in the national political process. First, some Conservatives, notably the Prime Minister Alec Douglas-Home and the Smethwick candidate Peter Griffiths, used the issue in the October 1964 general election campaign and remained on the offensive during the next session of parliament (Foot 1965: 165). Second, the success of Griffiths in winning a seat on a strongly anti-immigration platform despite the national electoral trend in favour of Labour created a sensation and led the Labour Party to reconsider its position. Third, and most important, Labour took power for the first time in thirteen years and had to confront the gap between its previous calls to rescind immigration controls and the fact that controls were in place and appeared to be popular. Ultimately, Labour responded by accepting the 1958 Act and reducing the number of work vouchers for black immigrants from 20,000 to 8,500 a year in 1965 (Messina 1989: 28–37; Foot 1965: 184).

Linkages between Riots and Campaigns in Germany

The 1990 Riot and Campaign

During the confused year between the collapse of the Honecker regime in East Germany and the effective date of the treaty which unified the eastern and western parts of the country, a brief but intense riot occurred in the eastern German town of Hoyerswerda. On 1 May 1990, between 150 and 200 German youths fought with fifty foreign labourers from Mozambique, and later a crowd estimated at 1,500 watched as the youths stoned the high-rise building in which the Mozambicans lived, breaking thirty windows (*Lausitzer Rundschau*, 5 May 1990; die *tageszeitung* (hereafter *taz*), 7 May 1990).

The causes of this brief riot lay not in anti-immigration campaigns, but rather in long-simmering cultural conflicts between Africans and Germans in Hoyerswerda, the sudden collapse of the East German state's repressive capacity in late 1989, and the activities of right-wing youth groups. The riot occurred during a long lull in the periodic campaigns against the right to asylum, which had subsided after a brief campaign in early 1989 and remained weak after the unification process began in November 1989—see Fig. 12.2. Conflicts between Germans and foreign workers in Hoyerswerda dated from at least the early 1980s, and had led to several stabbings. The cultural conflicts were heightened by the East German policy of discouraging contacts between Germans and foreigners outside their workplaces, and by the access of some foreign workers, such as Hungarians, to western currency, which piqued the envy of their German neighbours (Joedecke 1992; interviews with Martin Schmidt, Hoyerswerda, 31 July and 1 August 1997).

Cultural conflicts in Hoyerswerda were limited to a very small scale by the system of one-party rule and secret police, but after the communists were rejected in open elections in March 1990, the old system no longer functioned. In April, right-wing youths, who had a presence in Hoyerswerda already in the 1980s, began to openly insult Mozambican workers, leading police to respond to fights between German and Mozambican youths on fourteen occasions in April 1990. On May 1st, the traditional workers' holiday, German youths at a private party decided to attack Mozambicans at a nearby square; when the Africans armed themselves with clubs and retaliated, the riot began (*taz*, 7 May 1990).

Although the national debate on political asylum increased sharply in August 1990, it is unlikely that it was influenced by the 1990 Hoyerswerda riot. The riot gained virtually no press attention. The *Frankfurter Allgemeine Zeitung* failed to cover it at all, focusing instead on the left-wing riots in Kreuzberg on 1 May and the local elections in East Germany on 6 May. The riots in Hoyerswerda were so obscure that even die *tageszeitung*, a newspaper especially concerned with right-wing violence and with events in eastern Germany, covered it only five days later. Rather, the increase in the asylum debate in 1990 was due to national electoral politics. The debate was sparked by SPD leader Oskar Lafontaine's statement in late July that Article 16 needed to be changed in order to reduce the abuse of the asylum right—clearly a trial balloon in preparation for the Bundestag elections in December 1990 (*taz*, 1 August 1990).

The 1991 Riots and Campaign

By contrast, the September 1991 riots in Hoyerswerda were much more intense, multi-day events—see Appendix Table 12B. In important ways, they were similar to the 1958 British riots: the 1991 riots in Hoyerswerda were largely caused by the local political processing of cultural conflicts; they may have been made more intense by a national anti-asylum campaign which was beginning at this time; and they spurred additional anti-asylum campaigning by national politicians. The riots began when a large group of skinheads attacked several Vietnamese cigarette dealers and then, as German youths had done in 1990, attacked the apartment block where the Vietnamese lived along with Mozambican workers. Major riots continued for six days, the first three against the foreign workers and the last three largely against police who were guarding a hostel for asylum seekers on the other side of town; spectators numbered up to 1,000 (*Sächsische Zeitung* (Hoyerswerda edition; hereafter *SZH* and *taz*, 21 September 1991; Karapin 1997: 6–8); the attacks continued until both the foreign labourers and the asylum seekers were evacuated from Hoyerswerda.

The national anti-asylum campaign may have contributed to the riots, but probably was not an important cause of them. The rioting was preceded by a clear increase in the asylum debate in early August, as the Federal Interior Minister Wolfgang Schäuble (CDU) joined with CSU leaders in calling for a constitutional limitation on asylum, and the riots found resonance within the CDU and parts of the SPD, including Lafontaine. The Hoyerswerda rioters' calls for 'foreigners out!' overlapped with politicians' demands for effective measures to block asylum seekers from entering and remaining in Germany. A few neo-Nazis were active in Hoyerswerda, and radical right-wing skinheads led the attacks throughout the riots; they may have been attentive to national politics and encouraged by the latest anti-asylum campaign by the conservatives. Yet the national debate cannot explain the massive participation of Hoyerswerda residents. The asylum issue was much less important to the average eastern Germans than to western Germans; only 8 per cent of easterners found asylum seekers and foreigners to be an important issue in September 1991, compared with 60 per cent who mentioned unemployment, and between 15 and 20 per cent who were concerned with three other issues related to economic and social policies (Hennig 1991: 212).

Moreover, two circumstances suggest the 1991 riots grew out of local rather than national factors. First, the rioting began against foreign labourers rather than the asylum seekers living in Hoyerswerda, and the most serious violence and most active crowd participation was against the labourers (*Hoyerswerdaer Wochenblatt* and *Dresdner Morgenpost*, 20 September 1991; *Junge Welt* and *SZH*, 23 September 1991). Second, in Hoyerswerda, as we have seen, there was a history of cultural conflicts between Germans and Africans, and of fighting between German youth and the Mozambican workers, who sometimes defended themselves vigorously against German attacks. For example, besides the May 1990 riot, thirty German youths attacked a Mozambican hostel on the German national holiday in October 1990 (*Hoyerswerdaer Wochenblatt*, 5 October 1990; *Lausitzer Rundschau*, 10 October 1990).

Indeed, five local contextual factors are sufficient to explain why those conflicts grew into major riots in September 1991 (Karapin forthcoming). First, cultural conflicts between foreigners and Germans were extreme in this town, in part because the foreigners were concentrated in high-density apartment buildings with many German neighbours. Sexual jealousies and conflicts over issues such as garbage and reckless driving led to intense enmity and rumours. German neighbours frequently complained about noise from the Africans' parties, especially from an unusually loud farewell party which was held just two days before the riots began (*Hoyerswerdaer Wochenblatt*, 26 July 1991; *SZH*, 19 July, 29 August 1991; *Lausitzer Rundschau*, 29 August 1991).

Second, these conflicts were not adequately channelled into routine complaints to officials. Since Germans under the new system of democratically elected local government did not understand that they needed to make complaints to the Town Clerk's office, the Mozambicans' neighbours instead went to the police, who did not respond, and the neighbours became frustrated. By contrast, local politicians held a neighbourhood meeting to discuss complaints in the area around the asylum seekers hostel, on the other side of town. At the meeting, grievances were aired and some minor remedies were adopted (interview with Schmidt; *SZH*, 16 August 1991). Consequently, rioting in September began later and was less intense in that location than it was at the Mozambican labourers' residence (*SZH*, 18–24 September 1991).

Third, state repression failed dramatically in Hoyerswerda during 1991. Police tolerated a right-wing vigilante patrol group for many months, did little when a series of skinhead attacks on individual foreigners began a few weeks before the riots, and responded hesitantly and with inadequate personnel when the 1991 riots began. Local police in Hoyerswerda were under the authority of an Interior Minister (Rudolph Krause, CDU) who refused to protect foreigners, downplayed right-wing violence, and eventually quit his party to join the radical-right Republikaner party (*SZH*, 8, 28 June 1991, 19 July, 19, 21, 23 September 1991; *taz*, 23 September 1991). For their part, local elected officials were largely absent from the riot scene and did not implement a ban on public assemblies which the police commander requested.

Fourth, political opportunities increased at the local level during the several months before the riots. Police and local authorities began to act against foreigners, which may have led local skinheads to think that violence could be effective in driving the foreigners out of town (*SZH*, 6, 19 July, 29 August 1991). For example, police conducted a highly publicized raid against illegal

Vietnamese cigarette dealers on the Hoyerswerda marketplace in July; Vietnamese traders were the targets of the violence which sparked the September riots. Finally, a strong anti-foreigner organization was available in Hoyerswerda. The town had one of the largest and most active skinhead groups in the state of Saxony, with a tradition dating to the early 1980s, and a strength of between thirty and fifty youths in 1991 (SZH, 19–23 September 1991; interviews with Schmidt, with Bernd Wagner, Berlin, 14 August 1997, and with Friedhart Vogel, Hoyerswerda, 29 July 1997).

The effect of the 1991 riots on the campaign to amend Article 16 is as clear as the link between the 1958 riots and anti-immigration campaign in Britain. The Hoyerswerda riots were widely reported in the press and on television, with many reporters on the scene already by the third night of violence. The government's response to the riots was to use them to pressure the SPD on the asylum issue. While other politicians were condemning the violence, Federal Interior Minister Schäuble (CDU) took the opportunity to say, pointedly: 'Large parts of the population are concerned about the massive influx of asylum seekers. Federal and state politicians must therefore bring the asylum discussion to a speedy conclusion and eliminate the abuse of the asylum right' (Frankfurter Allgemeine Zeitung (hereafter FAZ), 24 September 1991, 1). While this debate was inconclusive, since the SPD's leaders remained ambivalent about providing the necessary votes for a constitutional amendment, the conservatives' campaign was massive and it set the stage for renewed legislative campaigns in 1992.

The 1992–1993 Riots and Campaigns

The Rostock riots of August 1992, the most severe in Germany, began with attacks on an asylum hostel in the Lichtenhagen neighbourhood on 22 August and continued over five nights. On the second night, 500 youths attacked the asylum hostel with stones and molotov cocktails while 3,000 people watched, chanted anti-foreigner slogans, and applauded; on the third night, youths stormed the hostel, and set it on fire (Ostsee Zeitung, 24–5 August 1992; taz, 25 August 1992).

More than for the 1991 Hoyerswerda riots, the evidence suggests that the national anti-asylum campaign helped to trigger the Rostock riots and to make them more intense. The riots occurred during a continuing campaign to amend the constitutional asylum right, led by the CDU and CSU, and gaining support from increasing numbers of SPD politicians. Although the debate subsided in July 1992, it picked up again in the first three weeks of August, as Bremen Mayor Klaus Wedemeier (SPD) came out in favour of changing Article 16 (taz, 31 July, 5 August 1992). However, the eastern press and eastern German population remained much less interested in the issue. Two eastern German newspapers examined carried no articles concerning proposed restrictions on asylum seekers during the two months prior to the Rostock riots.[19] When asked in an open-ended survey question, less than 10 per cent of the eastern German population considered the asylum and foreigners issue important from February to July 1992 (Kuechler 1994: 54).

None the less, Rostock was different from Hoyerswerda in two respects which indicate that the asylum campaign influenced the timing and extent of the Rostock riots. Rioting did not break out spontaneously from a conflict between German youths and foreigners, as at Hoyerswerda, but was planned by a politically organized group, which made anonymous phone calls to local newspapers announcing a demonstration and violence against the asylum hostel. Local police believed that even the first night of rioting was planned by groups outside Rostock (*Norddeutsche Neuste Nachrichten*, 19 August 1992; *taz*, 24 August 1992). Moreover, the skinheads in Rostock, which lies only several hours from the border to western Germany, were joined by many right-wing radicals from western German states already on the second night of rioting (*taz*, 25 August 1992), and a leading neo-Nazi from Hamburg was on the scene on the third night (*taz*, 25 August 1992). Western militants probably would have been attuned to the anti-asylum campaign in western Germany, where between 40 and 50 per cent of the population felt that asylum seekers or foreigners comprised an important problem during summer 1992 (Kuechler 1994: 54).

However, these factors cannot explain why 1,000–3,000 Rostock adults supported the skinheads on the first two days of the rioting, which made effective policing impossible since attackers disappeared into large crowds of sympathetic spectators. It is likely that the adults were motivated largely by local conditions, which were remarkably parallel to those at Hoyerswerda in 1991 (Karapin forthcoming). The Rostock riots were preceded and accompanied by cultural conflicts between Germans and foreigners, inadequate channels for the routine processing of conflicts, an apparent increase in opportunities to drive foreigners out of the city, large groups of locally organized skinheads, and police passivity in the face of violence.

Cultural conflicts occurred throughout Germany as the number of asylum applications shot up from 100,000 a year during 1988–1989 to an average of 300,000 a year during 1991–1993, and as state and local authorities forced asylum seekers to live in hostels scattered in many small and larger towns across Germany. The conflicts were mainly cultural rather than economic; asylum seekers posed little competitive threat for jobs or housing, since they were usually barred from employment and lived in group quarters in undesirable buildings. Hostile reactions from Germans were especially strong in eastern Germany, where about 20 per cent of new asylum seekers were distributed beginning early in 1991, and where the natives had gained little experience of living with foreigners under the East German government.

The conflicts in Rostock-Lichtenhagen were unusually intense, even by eastern German standards, for locally peculiar reasons. The hostel was the central hostel for incoming asylum seekers in the state of Mecklenburg-West Pomerania, and it was badly overcrowded for periods beginning in summer

1991. This forced up to 200 Romas and Sintis to live outdoors near the hostel (*Ostsee Zeitung*, 27 June 1991, 19 June 1992). The asylum seekers and their German neighbours came into conflict; the latter complained about defecation on the lawns, begging, and drinking, and these mundane complaints became mixed with wild rumours about the rape of German women and the torturing of animals. The hostel's neighbours repeatedly demanded that the hostel be moved out of their neighbourhood. However, their complaints were made individually to city officials rather than being processed in neighbourhood meetings, and no concessions were made to reduce the conflicts between the Roma and Sinti campers and the German population (*Norddeutsche Neuste Nachrichten*, 19 August 1992; *Ostsee Zeitung*, 22 August 1992).

There seemed to be some opportunity to drive the asylum seekers out of Lichtenhagen. Angered German residents found an ally in Peter Magdanz (SPD), the head of the city's Interior Department, who repeatedly referred to 'socially explosive material' around the hostel, and raised hopes that the hostel would be moved to a different neighbourhood by September. When residents had threatened to 'take matters into their own hands' earlier in the summer, this, together with Magdanz's public warnings, had prompted the city to move asylum seekers from the lawns into improvised shelters, which reduced the local conflicts for a time (*Ostsee Zeitung*, 25 June, 1, 14 July 1992; *Norddeutsche Neuste Nachrichten*, 19 August 1992).

Finally, police passivity contributed heavily to the Rostock riots. On the first night, despite the prior public announcement of trouble, only twenty police officers were on hand, and they were overwhelmed by the German youths who turned up to attack the hostel. The crucial lapse came on the third night, after the asylum seekers had been evacuated, when police retreated from guarding the hostel. This allowed seventy youths to set fire to the empty asylum hostel, along with adjacent apartments which housed Vietnamese workers; police waited two hours while the buildings burned and the foreign residents fled over the rooftops before they cleared the way for fire-fighters (*taz*, 25, 26 August 1992; Funke 1993: 128–45).

The Rostock riots, which were covered widely by press and television, provided major fuel for a renewed anti-asylum campaign by CDU and SPD politicians. The Interior Minister of Mecklenburg-West Pomerania, Kupfer (CDU), defended the police and called for 'clamping down on the uncontrolled inflow of asylum seekers' (*FAZ*, 25 August 1992). Two days later, CDU politicians pressured the SPD to begin negotiations within ten days or face a vote on a constitutional amendment in the Bundestag. The head of the Chancellor's office, Bohl, said that political action must occur within weeks because 'asylum seekers were overtaxing the residents of villages and towns, the police, and the housing resources of Germany' (*FAZ*, 27 August 1992).[20] Bohl rejected the SPD's demands for special police units to protect asylum seekers, on the grounds that it was pointless to 'cure symptoms' when the real problem was the legal right to asylum (*FAZ*, 27 August 1992). In the wake of such statements, the debate on asylum rights reached its highest peak yet in September–November 1992—see Fig. 12.2. This phase of the campaign created a major shift within the SPD, culminating in an emergency party meeting of the SPD in November which accepted the necessity of amending Article 16 (Braunthal 1994: 313–14).

In the weeks after Rostock, three major anti-foreigner riots occurred in eastern Germany. At Cottbus, between 150 and 200 youths attacked an asylum hostel, and were repulsed by police, on three nights beginning 28 August (*taz*, 31 August, 1 September 1992). In Eisenhüttenstadt, on two nights during the following weekend, 150 youths attacked a central asylum hostel housing 2,000 people with stones and molotov cocktails, while spectators applauded and police defended the building (*taz*, 7 September 1992). In Quedlinburg, up to 100 youths attacked the local asylum hostel with stones, fireworks, and molotov cocktails while crowds of up to 300 watched, beginning on 7 September 1992 (*taz*, 9–10, 12, 14 September 1992).

The clustering of these riots in the three weeks after the Rostock rioting strongly suggests there were triggered by political opportunities, which expanded for two reasons. First, the anti-asylum campaign reached a fever pitch in these weeks, as debate raged within the SPD. National politicians and news media argued that the violence and the debate would reinforce each other if the debate continued because the SPD, whose support was crucial for a restrictive constitutional amendment, did not give in. Second, the Rostock riots were a spectacular success for the right-wing youths of Rostock and their neo-Nazi supporters elsewhere in Germany. The evacuation of the asylum seekers and the burning out of the foreign workers were widely reported on television and in print, and led right-wing groups throughout Germany to celebrate and try to imitate the Rostock events.

The effects of the three post-Rostock riots are difficult to assess, since they occurred in the midst of the reaction to Rostock. The debate had increased sharply before the series of riots ended in mid-September, and the debate increased still more afterwards, suggesting that as with Rostock, the riots and debate drove each other. On the other hand, any impact they had on the asylum debate was dwarfed by the impact of the Rostock riots. The Cottbus, Eisenhüttenstadt, and Quedlinburg riots together received only about a quarter of the press attention which Rostock did, and they were much less likely to be mentioned in connection with the asylum debate during the next four months.

Conclusion

The British and German cases directly contradict the temporal hypothesis derived from political-opportunity theories; the first riots preceded the first major campaigns, rather than vice versa, and the largest campaigns did not trigger much major rioting. Indeed, the preceding analysis suggests that major riots and national campaigns have other important causes: cultural conflicts and subnational campaigns against immigration, for both riots and campaigns; weak state repression and social-movement organizations, for riots; and national electoral competition, for campaigns. These cases support several conclusions about the interaction of anti-minority riots and legislative campaigns against immigrants, which can be summarized in relation to three different phases of anti-minority movements.

First, when protest against immigration is emerging, riots have causes which are independent of national campaigns, and do not necessarily contribute to campaigns. In light of the preceding analyses, the most likely explanation for this pattern is that cultural conflicts are important causes of anti-minority riots. These conflicts are especially likely in the early phase of immigration by an ethnic minority, when native populations have recently first encountered the minority group and patterns of residential segregation and mixing have not been established (Husbands 1989a: 94–6; Panayi 1994: 275–6). This would explain why riots can occur when immigration is minor and anti-immigration campaigners have not yet found a broad audience; at such times, the élite consensus on a liberal immigration policy and a non-politicized discourse can hold. The British riots of 1948–1949 occurred after the arrival of only a few thousand blacks, and a riot occurred in Hoyerswerda in 1990 when the foreign population of eastern Germany was only about 1 per cent and political attention was directed toward other issues. Although immigration to East Germany by foreign labourers had begun in the late 1970s, the sudden introduction of civil liberties in 1990 was the missing element which allowed the previously suppressed cultural conflicts to be openly expressed. However, the above cases suggest that the mere existence of cultural conflicts is insufficient to cause rioting. Other important causes of popular riots in the early phase seem to include housing immigrants in hostels located in areas with little experience with foreigners, failing to provide routine forms of participation to process cultural conflicts, and inadequate policing.

The roles of cultural conflicts and routine participation channels can also explain why national campaigns to restrict asylum rights occurred in West Germany in the 1980s without triggering riots there. West Germans became gradually accustomed to foreigners after the gradual arrival of 'guestworkers' beginning in the early 1960s, and the conflicts between foreigners and their German neighbours in the 1980s and 1990s could be processed through a relatively robust system of local democratic politics. By contrast, the collapse of the communist system in East Germany liberated East German residents to pursue the cultural conflicts with foreigners which had been repressed for a decade, while also increasing cultural conflicts and reducing chances for channelling those conflicts into non-violent forms. The chaotic unification process led to the sudden redistribution of asylum seekers to localities in the eastern states, where ethnic strangers had not been integrated into society, and to a crisis of local political authority. During the first years after unification, local administrators were unprepared, channels for citizen participation unavailable, and policing inadequate in the eastern states (Ireland 1997: 555, 557; Karapin 2000).

Second, the importance of cultural conflicts can also help explain why anti-minority riots decline sharply after the first phases of ethnic relations: in the 'mature' phase of ethnic relations (Husbands 1989a), natives become more accustomed to the ethnic newcomers and feel less threatened. Britain has had no major anti-black riots since 1962 and no anti-black riots at all since 1965, while Germany has had none since 1992. Although other forms of anti-minority violence have become established in these countries, the small groups which carry out these attacks seem unable to mobilize large crowds of out-raged and fearful residents.

This thesis is also supported by the relations between cultural conflicts and legislative campaigns in Britain. Those relationships varied according to the phase of the overall anti-minority protest movement, in exactly the same way in which riots and campaigns are related. That is, local cultural conflicts slightly preceded the legislative campaign in winter 1954–1955, were simultaneous with the riots and campaigns in 1958 and 1961–1962, and were not much affected by the 1964–1965 debates—see Figs. 12.1 and 12.3. That said, the decline of riots in the mature phase of ethnic relations is probably also due to improved police responses to riots and more frequent anti-immigration campaigns led by established and far-right politicians, which channels anti-minority activity into more routine forms of participation.

Third, in the middle phase of an anti-immigration protest movement, riots and campaigns can affect each other. Riots can contribute to campaigns at this time because, in the context of other signals, riots become a sign that immigration issues are important to voters. A substantial share of the population supports tighter immigration controls in Britain and Germany (Kuechler 1994; Alber 1995). However, politicians are uncertain about how salient the issue is for voters, and mainstream politicians are reluctant to stir up the immigration issue unless it is very likely to make a difference in elections. The riots of the early phase are isolated instances and hence may not indicate a large enough electoral payoff. Only a few parliamentary constituencies in Britain were affected by black immigration before the late 1950s, and most anti-immigration candidates did poorly in the 1950s and 1960s (Karapin 1999). In Germany, few political élites anticipated that the first attacks on foreigners in the eastern part of the country in spring 1990 foreshadowed the major political problem which anti-foreigner rioting and other violence represented eighteen months later.

But when cultural conflicts between immigrants and natives became widespread, riots seemed to indicate widespread disaffection with liberal immigration policies. At such times, riots and campaigns can influence each other, as local conflicts are given new meaning by national events, and the perpetrators of violence may become inspired by the apparently increasing opportunities to influence government policy. The turning point in Britain occurred in 1958, when riots broke out after several years of widely reported cultural conflicts, and hence created a sense that riots or other major conflicts could happen in many places unless black immigration were checked; this impression was reinforced by the surge in immigration after 1959. The turning point in Germany is harder to pinpoint, but seems to have occurred sometime in the period from September 1991 to August 1992. The 1991–1992 riots in Germany occurred at a time when local government resistance to asylum seekers was rising along with reports of anti-foreigner violence.[21] In this context, the riots created fears of continued local unrest, especially after the Rostock riots, which forced even liberals in the SPD to join or give in to the conservative campaign against Article 16.

The potential for anti-minority riots and anti-immigration campaigns to reinforce each other during the middle phase of mobilization is troubling. It suggests that liberal immigration policies are vulnerable to xenophobic or racist movements which develop rapidly and are all the more effective for combining violent and routine methods. But the role of cultural conflicts suggests that anti-minority rioting can be made obsolete in liberal democracies. Where foreign and native ethnic groups are in contact with each other for long periods of time, there are chances to adjust expectations, dispel stereotypes, work out accommodations, and create routine channels for the remaining conflicts. In such settings, popular rioting, at least, may cease to be a viable part of the repertoire of anti-immigration movements.

Notes

*An earlier version of this chapter was presented at a conference on Citizenship, Immigration, and Xenophobia in Europe at the Science Center Berlin, 13–15 November 1997. I would like to thank Mathias Bös, Donatella della Porta, Klaus Eder, Christopher Husbands, Martin Schain, John Solomos, and other conference participants for their comments. In revising the paper, I benefited greatly from the detailed and thoughtful critique provided by Ruud Koopmans and Paul Statham. Of course, I remain responsible for any remaining faults. Research for this article was supported by Award Number 669559 from the Research Foundation, City University of New York.

1. Not considered here are incidents of violence committed by small numbers of people against ethnic minorities, which sometimes receive high levels of public attention, such as the arson attacks at Deptford (January 1981) in Britain, or at Mölln (November 1992) and Solingen (May 1993) in Germany.

2. More precisely, this country-case includes West Germany before November 1989, East and West Germany for the next eleven months, and unified Germany from October 1990.

3. Most theorizing on riots in liberal democracies concerns 'commodity riots' by minorities against property and police, rather than 'communal' riots, in which minorities are mainly victims (Janowitz 1969: 415–18); the anti-minority riots of this chapter are communal riots. For theorizing about anti-minority riots, see Husbands (1989a,b), and Willems *et al.* (1993); on anti-immigration campaigns, see Perlmutter (1996b), Money (1997), Koopmans (1997), and Karapin (1999).

4. For a more detailed review of this literature, see Karapin (1998: 3–6).

5. For the general approach, see Eisinger (1973), Tilly (1978), McAdam (1982), and Tarrow (1994); for applications to West European social movements and to anti-minority violence in Western Europe, see, for example, Kitschelt (1986), Kriesi *et al.* (1995), and Koopmans (1996).

6. This point is also made in an unpublished manuscript by Eckert and Willems (1994) 'Eskalationsmuster der Gewalt bei Ausländerfeindlichen Jugendlichen'.

7. This source was used because of its strong coverage of national politics and the convenience provided by its index. From the *Times Index*, I coded 383 references to articles which were based on statements by government spokesmen, party politicians, and established interest-group representatives on immigration policy, under 'Immigration' and 'Immigration Policy', or on blacks, under 'Coloured Persons'. The vast majority of these statements appear to have been calls for immigration control or reactions to such calls; proactive pro-immigration statements were usually filed under the separate heading 'Race Relations'. This measure of anti-immigration campaigning produced peaks broadly similar to those derived from a count from the index to Hansard, House of Commons Report (hereafter Hansard), which documents parliamentary statements only.

8. Additionally, for an event to count as a riot, crowds must have gathered in order to attack, or have moved to the site of attack, and they must have carried out significant violence against property or persons, such as smashing windows, throwing stones or firebombs, or beating people. An event in which a large crowd was present and witnessed an ethnically-motivated fight, for example at a soccer game or a street festival, or in which a crowd gathered and merely threatened significant violence, was not considered a major riot. Participants include attackers, supporters, and spectators from the dominant ethnic group; spectators are included in the analysis because they often provided passive support by encouraging perpetrators or shielding them from police. For multi-day riots, the number of days of rioting shown in the Tables and Figures include only the days in which at least one hundred participants were taking actions directed toward the minority group; attacks by similarly large crowds on police sometimes were included in the counts of rioting days, but only if they occurred at the end of a period of rioting in which the ethnic minority was attacked and at a time when the police were protecting the minority from further attacks. The anti-minority character of the

violence was inferred from rioters' statements and slogans, and ethnic divisions in the fighting.

9. The absence of many of these riots from national press accounts of this period, such as in *The Times*, suggests that either local newspapers or academic secondary sources would be required to accurately tabulate all major riots. Since surveying newspapers would be prohibitively expensive, and the academic accounts are rich sources, I chose to use the latter. For relatively broad histories, see Panayi (1996), Witte (1996), Layton-Henry (1992), and Holmes (1988); for more detailed accounts of riots, see Pilkington (1988), Fryer (1984), Richmond (1954), Glass (1961), Hiro (1973), Panayi (1991), Miles (1984), Pearson (1976), and Reeves (1989).

10. Several riots frequently mentioned in histories were not classified as major riots here, because available reports on their size and duration did not indicate numbers of participants large enough to meet the above criteria: Birmingham (May 1948 and August 1949); Camden Town, London (August 1954); Accrington (July 1964); and Wolverhampton (August 1965).

11. This newspaper was chosen because of its extensive coverage of the asylum issue and because it is the only national daily newspaper in Germany for which the editions covering the period in question are either indexed or available in machine-readable form. Articles were counted by using keyword searches on the 1997 CD-ROM edition of *die tageszeitung*; included was every article which mentioned 'asylum', the 'Basic Law', and at least one of the political parties represented in the Bundestag.

12. This source was richer than any set of academic accounts, and it can be thoroughly searched at low cost. I focused on larger-scale attacks by using keywords derived from reports of known riots, such as *Ausschreitung*, *Strassenschlacht*, *Randale*, *Schaulustige*, and *Menschenjagd*. This led me to examine 394 articles, which described nineteen attacks on foreigners involving at least one hundred German participants, as well as thirteen attacks of this size on other targets, mainly leftists and police.

13. Since all of the major riots in both countries occurred between May and September, when warmer weather brought many people outdoors for long periods, we should consider whether debate peaks were followed by riots during the next warm season, or vice versa.

14. Both Labour and Conservative governments, as well as parts of the trade unions, considered controls on black immigration from 1948–1957, but these discussions were deliberately held without attracting public attention (Solomos 1989; Miles and Phizacklea 1984; Bowling 1996).

15. Articles in *The Times* show a similar disproportion between the two periods. Although a very minor public discussion about immigration peaked in 1949 (see Fig. 12.1), even this concerned mainly the welfare of the new arrivals rather than immigration controls.

16. Yet it is unclear if increased grievances sparked the violence, since sources disagree about the state of the local labour market; Richmond (1954: 102) refers

to a peak in unemployment, while Hiro (1991: 38) states that plenty of jobs were available.

17. I identified 125 local cultural conflicts which received national attention from the *Times Index*, using the categories 'Coloured Persons' and 'Race Relations'. Included were all local actions which either were hostile toward blacks, such as colour bars, or were defenses against such hostile actions, such as protests against colour bars, and which did not use violence.

18. During the 1950s, before family immigration became more common, most black immigrants were single men or single women.

19. The Berlin-Brandenburg edition of the tabloid *BILD* and the Rostock-based *Ostsee Zeitung*.

20. The latter sentence is quoted from the newspaper's paraphrase of Bohl's statement.

21. As one indication, from July 1991 through to May 1993, the tabloid newspaper *BILD* presented forty-seven headlines for stories in which local government officials were critical of asylum seekers (from the author's analysis of 700 *BILD* headlines from May 1991 through December 1993; see also Willems *et al.* 1993: 214–17 and Benzler 1997: 242).

References

ALBER, JENS (1995), 'Zur Erklärung fremdenfeindlicher Gewalt in Deutschland,' in Ekkehard Mochmann and Uta Gerhardt (eds.), *Gewalt in Deutschland: Soziale Befunde und Deutungslinien* (Munich: Oldenbourg), 39–77.

BENZLER, SUSANNE (1997), 'Migranten in Wartestellung,' in Klaus Bade (ed.), *Fremde im Land: Zuwanderung und Eingliederung im Raum Niedersachsen seit dem Zweiten Weltkrieg.* (Osnabruck: Universitätsverlag Rasch), 213–48.

BETZ, HANS-GEORG (1994), *Radical Right-Wing Populism in Western Europe* (New York, NY: St. Martin's Press).

BJÖRGO, TORE, and WITTE, ROB (eds.) (1993), *Racist Violence in Europe* (New York, NY: St. Martin's Press).

BOWLING, BENJAMIN (1996), 'The Emergence of Violent Racism as a Public Issue in Britain, 1945–81,' in Panikos Panayi (ed.), *Racial Violence in Britain in the Nineteenth and Twentieth Centuries* (rev. ed) (New York, NY: Leicester University Press), 185–215.

BRAUNTHAL, GERARD (1994), *The German Social Democrats Since 1969* (2nd ed) (Boulder, CO: Westview Press).

BROSIUS, HANS-BERND, and ESSER, FRANK (1995), *Eskalation durch Berichterstattung?* (Opladen: Westdeutscher Verlag).

BRUBAKER, ROGERS (1995), 'Comments on Modes of Immigration Politics in Liberal Democratic States,' *International Migration Review*, 29/4: 903–8.

BUTTON, JAMES (1978), *Black Violence: The Political Impact of the 1960s Riots* (Princeton, NJ: Princeton University Press).

CORNELIUS, WAYNE A., MARTIN, PHILIP L., and HOLLIFIELD, JAMES F. (1994), 'Introduction,' in id. (eds.), *Controlling Immigration: A Global Perspective* (Stanford, CA: Stanford University Press), 3–41.

EISINGER, PETER (1973), 'The Conditions of Protest Behavior in American Cities,' *American Political Science Review*, 67: 11–28.

FOOT, PAUL (1965), *Immigration and Race in British Politics* (Baltimore, MD: Penguin).

FREEMAN, GARY (1979), *Immigrant Labor and Racial Conflict in Industrial Societies* (Princeton, NJ: Princeton University Press).

——(1995a), 'Modes of Immigration Politics in the Liberal Democratic States,' *International Migration Review*, 29/4: 881–902.

——(1995b), 'Rejoinder,' *International Migration Review*, 29/4: 909–13.

FRYER, PETER (1984), *Staying Power: The History of Black People in Britain* (London: Pluto Press).

FUNKE, HAJO (1993), *Brandstifter* (Gottingen: Lamuv).

GAMSON, WILLIAM (1990), *The Strategy of Social Protest* (2nd ed) (Homewood, IL: Dorsey Press).

GLASS, RUTH (1961), *London's Newcomers* (Cambridge, MA: Harvard University Press).

HAMMAR, TOMAS (ed.) (1985), *European Immigration Policy: A Comparative Study* (New York, NY: Cambridge University Press).

HANSARD (1946–1966), *The Parliamentary Debates: House of Commons Official Report*, 5th series. (London: HMSO), Vols. 429–752.

HENNIG, EIKE (1991), 'Deutschland von Rechts,' *Wochenschau für politische Erziehung, Sozial- und Gemeinschaftskunde*, 42/6: 211–39.

HIRO, DILIP (1973), *Black British, White British* (New York, NY: Monthly Review Press).

——(1991), *Black British, White British* (London: Grafton).

HOLMES, COLIN (1988), *John Bull's Island: Immigration and British Society, 1871–1971* (London: Macmillan).

HUSBANDS, CHRISTOPHER (1988), 'The Dynamics of Racial Exclusion and Expulsion,' *European Journal of Political Research*, 16: 701–20.

——(1989a), 'Racial Attacks: The persistence of racial vigilantism in British cities,' in Tony Kushner and Kenneth Lunn (eds.), *Traditions of Intolerance: Historical Perspectives on Fascism and Race Discourse in Britain* (Manchester: Manchester University Press), 91–115.

——(1989b), 'Is Anyone Listening?' *London Review of Books*, 11/4: 10–11.

IRELAND, PATRICK (1997), 'Socialism, Unification Policy, and the Rise of Racism in Eastern Germany,' *International Migration Review*, 31/3: 541–68.

JANOWITZ, MORRIS (1969), 'Patterns of Collective Racial Violence,' in Hugh Graham and Ted Gurr (eds.), *Violence in America* (New York, NY: Praeger), 412–43.

JOEDECKE, RAINER (1992), 'Willkommen in Hoyerswerda,' *Kursbuch*, 107: 69–108.

KARAPIN, ROGER (1997), 'Anti-Immigrant Riots in the Former East Germany: The Mischanneling of Political Participation'. Paper presented at the German Studies Association Conference, Bethesda, Maryland in September. Available from author.

——(1998), 'Racist Riots and Nonviolent National Political Campaigns Against Immigrants in Britain and Germany'. Paper presented at a conference on 'Citizenship, Immigration, and Xenophobia in Europe' at the Science Center Berlin in November 1997; revised version, October. Available from author.

——(1999), 'The Politics of Immigration Control in Britain and Germany: Subnational politicians and social movements', *Comparative Politics*, 31/4: 423–44.

——(forthcoming), 'Anti-Minority Riots in Eastern Germany: Cultural conflicts and mischanneled political participation', *Comparative Politics*.

KEITH, MICHAEL (1993), *Race, Riots, and Policing* (London: UCL Press).

KITSCHELT, HERBERT (1986), 'Political Opportunity Structures and Political Protest: Anti-nuclear movements in four democracies', *British Journal of Political Science*, 16/1: 57–85.

KOOPMANS, RUUD (1996), 'Explaining the Rise of Racist and Extreme-Right Violence in Western Europe', *European Journal of Political Research*, 30: 185–216.

——(1997), 'The Career of a Political Conflict: The asylum issue in Germany'. Paper presented at a conference on Inclusion and Exclusion, New School for Social Research, June.

KRIESI, HANSPETER, KOOPMANS, RUUD, DUYVENDAK, JAN WILLEM, and GIUGNI, MARCO G. (1995), *New Social Movements in Western Europe: A Comparative Analysis* (Minneapolis, MN: University of Minnesota Press).

KUECHLER, MANFRED (1994), 'Germans and "Others": Racism, xenophobia, or "legitimate conservatism"?', *German Politics*, 3/1: 47–74.

LAYTON-HENRY, ZIG (1992), *The Politics of Immigration* (Cambridge, MA: Blackwell).

McADAM, DOUG (1982), *Political Process and the Development of Black Insurgency, 1930–1970* (Chicago, IL: University of Chicago Press).

MEIER-BRAUN, KARL-HEINZ (1980), *Das Asylanten-Problem* (Frankfurt: Ullstein Verlag).

MESSINA, ANTHONY M. (1989), *Race and Party Competition in Britain* (Oxford: Clarendon Press).

MILES, ROBERT (1984), 'The Riots of 1958: Notes on the ideological construction of "race relations" as a political issue in Britain', *Immigrants and Minorities*, 3: 252–75.

——and PHIZACKLEA, ANNIE (1984), *White Man's Country* (London: Pluto Press).

MONEY, JEANNETTE (1997), 'No vacancy: The politics of immigration control in advanced industrial democracies', *International Organization*, 51: 685–720.

MÜNCH, URSULA (1993), *Asylpolitik in der Bundesrepublik Deutschland: Entwicklung und Alternativen* (2nd ed) (Opladen: Leske und Budrich).

OLIVIER, JOHAN L. (1991), 'State Repression and Collective Action in South Africa', *South African Journal of Sociology*, 22/4: 109–17.

OLSON, MANCUR (1965), *The Logic of Collective Action: Public Goods and the Theory of Groups* (Cambridge, MA: Harvard University Press).

OLZAK, SUSAN (1992), *The Dynamics of Ethnic Competition and Conflict* (Stanford, CA: Stanford University Press).

PANAYI, PANIKOS (1991), 'Middlesborough 1961: A British race riot of the 1960s?', *Social History*, 16: 139–53.

PANAYI, PANIKOS (1994), 'Racial Violence in the New Germany, 1990–93', *Contemporary European History*, 3/3: 265–87.

——(1996), 'Anti-Immigrant Violence in Nineteenth- and Twentieth-Century Britain,' in Panikos Panayi (ed.), *Racial Violence in Britain in the Nineteenth and Twentieth Centuries* (rev. ed) (New York, NY: Leicester University Press), 1–25.

PARK, ROBERT E. (1950), *Race and Culture* (Glencoe, IL: Free Press).

PEACH, CERI (1968), *West Indian Migration to Britain* (London: Oxford University Press).

PEARSON, GEOFF (1976), ' "Paki-Bashing" in a North-East Lancashire Cotton Town', in G. Mungham and Geoff Pearson (eds.), *Working-Class Youth Culture* (London: Routledge and Kegan Paul), 48–81.

PERLMUTTER, TED (1996a), 'Bringing Parties Back In: Comments on "Modes of Immigration Politics in Liberal Democratic Societies" ', *International Migration Review*, 30/1: 375–88.

——(1996b), 'The Political Asylum Debates in Germany, 1978–92: Polarizing politics in a moderate system?', unpublished paper, Center for European Studies, New York University, April.

PILKINGTON, EDWARD (1988), *Beyond the Mother Country* (London: I.B. Taurus).

——(1996), 'The West Indian Community and the Notting Hill Riots of 1958,' in Panikos Panayi (ed.), *Racial Violence in Britain in the Nineteenth and Twentieth Centuries* (rev. ed) (New York, NY: Leicester University Press), 171–84.

PRZEWORSKI, ADAM, and TEUNE, HENRY (1970), *The Logic of Comparative Social Inquiry* (New York, NY: John Wiley).

REEVES, FRANK (1989), *Race and Borough Politics* (Brookfield, VT: Avebury).

RICHMOND, ANTHONY (1954), *Colour Prejudice in Britain* (London: Routledge).

SALERT, BARBARA, and SPRAGUE, JOHN (1980), *The Dynamics of Riots* (Ann Arbor, MI: Inter-University Consortium for Political and Social Research.

SCHUMAKER, PAUL (1978), 'The Scope of Political Conflict and the Effectiveness of Constraints in Contemporary Urban Protest', *Sociological Quarterly*, 19: 168–84.

SMELSER, NEIL (1963), *The Theory of Collective Behavior* (New York, NY: Free Press).

SOLOMOS, JOHN (1989), *Race and Racism in Contemporary Britain* (London: Macmillan).

TARROW, SIDNEY (1989a), *Democracy and Disorder: Protest and Politics in Italy, 1965–75* (Oxford: Clarendon Press).

——(1989b), *Struggle, Politics, and Reform* (Ithaca, NY: Cornell University, Center for International Studies).

——(1994), *Power in Movement: Social Movements, Collective Action, and Politics* (New York, NY: Cambridge University Press).

TILLY, CHARLES (1978), *From Mobilization to Revolution* (New York, NY: Random House).

——(1995), *Popular Contention in Great Britain, 1758–1834* (Cambridge, MA: Harvard University Press).

TURNER, RALPH, and KILLIAN, LEWIS (1972), *Collective Behavior* (2nd ed) (Englewood Cliffs, NJ: Prentice-Hall).

WICKENDEN, JAMES (1958), *Colour in Britain* (London: Oxford University Press).

WILLEMS, HELMUT, ECKERT, ROLAND, WÜRTZ, STEFANIE, and STEINMETZ, LINDA (1993), *Fremdenfeindliche Gewalt: Einstellungen, Täter, Eskalationen* (Opladen: Leske und Budrich).

WITTE, ROB (1996), *Racist Violence and the State* (New York, NY: Longman).

WOLKEN, SIMONE (1988), *Das Grundrecht auf Asyl als Gegenstand der Innen- und Rechtspolitik der Bundesrepublik Deutschland* (Frankfurt: Peter Lang).

13

Ethnocentric Party Mobilization in Europe: the Importance of the Three-Dimensional Approach

ROGER EATWELL

Introduction

In recent years, a variety of ethnocentric parties have made notable electoral breakthroughs in Europe. Until recently the best known has been the *Front National* (FN), which in the late 1990s had the support of 15 per cent of French electors. In Italy, the ethno-regionalist *Lega Nord* (LN) has attracted more like 30 per cent in some areas; after losing support in the late 1990s, it has bounded back in the 2000 regional elections on a strongly anti-immigrant, anti-globalization programme. Most dramatically of all, in Austria, the Freedom Party (FPÖ) won 27 per cent of the national vote in the 1999 elections, again on a strongly ethnocentric programme; in early 2000, the FPÖ formed a new coalition government with the conservative Austrian People's Party. Other notable Western European parties which have achieved these levels of support nationally, or in significant localities, are the Norwegian Progress Party, with 15 per cent of the national vote in 1997, and the Flemish-Belgian *Vlaams Blok* (VB), which can poll approaching twice this in some areas.

It is important to stress at the outset that recent ethnocentric parties exhibit notable differences, both in terms of ideology and the socio-economic composition of their support. Indeed, major debates rage concerning typology. Can all these parties be lumped together under the label 'extreme right'—arguably the most common generic term among European academics? Are some better seen as 'radical right'—the more common generic term among Americans? Can some reasonably be termed 'neo-fascist'? Are most better subsumed under the less-loaded term, 'populist'? Do some constitute a 'new right' rather than a revival of old forms? And so on.

It is certainly wrong to think that all extreme-right parties are fundamentally racist/xenophobic parties in the sense that they overtly proclaim a racial hierarchy and/or a politics of racial hatred. Such views have been largely taboo outside the fringes since 1945—at least in parties' public, 'exoteric' appeals, as distinct from their internal, 'esoteric' discourse. The more sophisticated parties in Western Europe now tend to use a 'new racism' based on ideas of natural-ness, even democracy. Similarly, the more successful parties tend to stress the economic and social consequences of immigration rather than dealing in old stereotypes. Moreover, some post-Second World War extreme-right parties have not been founded primarily on issues relating to 'immigration'/'race'. A good example of this would be the neo-fascist Italian Social Movement (MSI), whose core ideology, after its creation in 1946, was a statist form of anti-com-munism. Conversely, the populist Progress parties in Norway and Denmark were founded during the early 1970s as anti-big state movements, little con-cerned with communism—initially, the foreign policy of the Danish party was based, not entirely facetiously, on recording the message 'We surrender' in Russian on the Foreign Ministry telephone answering machine.

Nevertheless, it is possible to identify a family of contemporary European parties—including the MSI's successor, the *Alleanza Nazionale* (AN), and the more recent manifestations of the Progress parties—which, with varying degrees of emphasis in their programmes, seek to mobilize support around some form of national/regional identity, accompanied by anti-ethnic minority sentiments, usually involving the advocacy of a complete, or large scale, repa-triation of 'immigrants'—a term which, in Western Europe, tends to be syn-onymous with non-white 'immigrants' including those who hold citizenship rights and/or have been born in the respective countries.

Rather than seeking to refine terminology/typology, this chapter attempts to explain why some of these ethnocentric parties gather far more electoral support than others.[1] More specifically, it seeks to explain why they can some-times make dramatic breakthroughs. The FN, for instance, was a marginal phe-nomenon throughout France during the first eight years of its existence, but it made a leap forward in local elections in the town of Dreux during 1982–3; by 1984 it was attracting 10 per cent of the national vote. In Britain, a country normally seen as immune to the extremist virus, the British National Party (BNP) emerged from obscurity during the first eight years of its existence to make notable gains in some London East End local elections, culminating in winning a Millwall council seat, during 1992–3. The same pattern of dramatic rise took place in Saxony-Anhalt in 1998, where the German People's Union (DVU)—essentially a West German party which had become electorally active during the 1980s, but which lacked any serious local organization in this 'East' German Länder—jumped to 13 per cent of the vote. It remains to be seen whether the German ethnocentric right can achieve the lasting implantation achieved by the FN, or whether its vote will collapse as quickly as that of the BNP—whose support fell from a local election highpoint of 13 per cent average of the poll in the very limited number of seats it contested in 1994, to 3 per cent by 1998.

In order to fully understand the rise, and sometimes rapid fall, of these parties, it is vital to distinguish between what I term 'macro', 'meso' and 'micro' approaches.[2]

1. The micro is essentially concerned with the individual and his/her basic motives for belief and behaviour.
2. The meso is concerned with local social organizations to which individuals belong, or through which they gain knowledge and norms, such as the family, school, or party.
3. The macro is concerned with the widest level of social organization, normally the state level, and considers the impact of factors such as national identity, specific institutions, or broad socioeconomic change.

It is important to stress that these three levels are in some ways heuristic and do not always lend themselves to clear operational rules. Nevertheless, the three levels point to the dangers of situating analyses primarily in one sphere.

The linking methodological argument is that what is needed analytically is an integrated analysis of these three dimensions, with an ultimate focus on the factors which make individuals receptive to the supply of messages conducive to ethnocentric party breakthrough. In the pages which follow I seek to demonstrate that most explanations have placed far too much emphasis on explaining take-off within primarily a single dimension and/or by assuming an almost mechanistic relationship between individual voting behaviour and socioeconomic structural conditions. Recently, an adaptation of Political Opportunity Structure (POS) approaches has offered more insights, including in some examples a focus on the supply-side aspect of extremist, and especially mainstream, party actions and discourse. However, even the best examples of this work contain notable weaknesses, especially an undue focus on the macro dimension.

It is impossible in the space of this chapter to set out a new theory, and it is vital to underline that no single approach can fully explain the complexity of all voting behaviour.[3] Nevertheless, the clear import of the following arguments is that much of the support for ethnocentric parties cannot be dismissed—as most commentators do—as some kind of essentially negative protest, although voters for such parties are unquestionably hostile to mainstream parties and sometimes even the political system.[4] Rather, there is a notable constituency open to the appeal of ethnocentric parties, especially their politics of identity— the way in which such parties seek to give people a sense of belonging, not least by demonizing who is the 'Other'. However, it needs a particular set of conditions to turn attitudes into action. Put very broadly, this requires a combination of three factors:

1. Rising legitimacy for the ethnocentric party—whilst some voters are attracted to parties precisely because they seem beyond the pale, this is not true in the main for the most successful ethnocentric parties like the FN.

2. A belief in personal efficacy—namely, ethnocentric parties can raise voters' sense of efficacy by making them feel less excluded from the mainstream agenda; they feel they can influence policy, including altering mainstream agendas.

3. Declining socioeconomic and/or socio-political system trust—this tends to be the necessary but not sufficient condition for take-off, though it is crucial to stress that the issue is one of perception rather than absolute levels of income, etc.

Theories of Ethnocentrism

A survey of recent theories of racism and xenophobia[5] holds that they can usefully be grouped into four main types: rational choice, functionalist, discourse analysis, and phenomenological.[6] The typology plays down some major approaches, for instance, classic psychological ones, and there are variations within each form of analysis. Nevertheless, it offers a useful starting point to provide a brief overview of the strengths and weaknesses of a variety of major approaches, underlining in particular the problems of moving directly from attitudes to voting behaviour.

Rational Choice

The most simple form of rational choice approach holds that recent racism is mainly a result of rivalry between migrant and indigenous people, especially in the labour market, though housing can be another area of competition.

The approach offers some insight into German developments in the 1990s. Racist violence was greatest in 1991–2, a time when a major wave of asylum seekers arrived—over 400,000 in 1992 alone. This was a time of rising unemployment in the old West Germany, and especially the new Länder, developments which led to serious doubts about the future. By 1998, the Allensbach Institute found that 59 per cent of East Germans thought that society was heading for a great crisis; 39 per cent of West Germans shared this view. Predictably, polls have shown a growing belief that there were too many foreigners in Germany. However, the relationship between the presence of immigrants and ethnocentric voting seems complex. In general, such parties have not done well in the 1990s. Moreover, there were significant numbers of Gastarbeiter (guestworkers) in (West) Germany during the 1970s and 1980s mini-recessions, but this did not produce either racist violence or voting for ethnocentric parties, although the mid-1960s mini-recession did witness the brief rise of the NPD. Indeed, the Republikaner Party made its breakthrough in European and state elections in the late 1980s, a time of relative economic prosperity and contentment.[7]

In Dreux, the proportion of foreigners rose from relatively low in the 1950s, to 21 per cent by 1982—an increase of over 50 per cent in some areas. This once prosperous small town was also struck by hard times, with unemployment in 1983 standing at 10 per cent, a departmental record.[8] However, a monograph on the rise of the FN in Dreux found that one of its key supporters was a butcher who made large sums of money supplying Arabs,[9] and it is misleading to see the FN's support as coming simply from those most affected by economic change. Moreover, only a short distance away, another town with a similar socioeconomic profile, Evreux, witnessed no significant FN activity at this time. It is worth adding that subsequently, whilst the FN has built notable support in economically-troubled groups—especially the less skilled working class and farmers—it enjoys a remarkable trans-class base.

The problems of the simple rational choice approach can also be seen by considering the case of Scandinavia. There is no doubt that ethnocentrism in the 1990s has added an important dimension to these parties' appeal. For example, in Norway in 1993, 42 per cent of Progress party voters considered immigration to be the most important issue, compared to 7 per cent for Conservative party supporters. In Sweden, New Democracy supporters mentioned immigration more than any other issue as the reason for their party choice. However, this tells us little or nothing about why the Swedish New Democracy party arrived on the scene well after the Danish and Norwegian Progress parties, and has in general been much less successful. This is especially perplexing as, in 1990, foreign residents accounted for 5.6 per cent of the population in Sweden, compared to 3.6 per cent in Denmark, and 3.4 per cent in Norway. Unemployment has also been higher in Sweden recently, and fears for the future greater, especially than in Norway, where oil-revenues bolster the economy.

However, these criticisms of the more economistic aspects of rational choice theory do not mean that we can dismiss ethnocentric voting as necessarily irrational. Recent work on the Belgian *Vlaams Blok* seems to undermine the claim that the extremist vote is simply a protest one, at least if protest is defined as essentially negative or almost random behaviour—interestingly, protest approaches rarely define 'protest'.[10] This work sees VB voting as rational in the sense that supporters voted for the party that was closest to their policy preferences, especially their anti-immigrant sentiments. They may have been protesting against existing élites, or the system, but there was an essential programmatic affinity. Interestingly, Green parties sometimes exhibit a similar balance of motives, though they are rarely portrayed as 'protest' parties. Nor should the affinity between ethnocentric parties and their voters be seen as necessarily based on a single issue. For instance, whilst French FN supporters exhibit strongly anti-immigrant views, those most hostile to immigrants also have a wider extreme right ideology.[11]

Functionalism

In the functionalist approach, the cultural differences of immigrants are made responsible for antagonism and conflicts. Those from Third World especially, are seen as incapable of assimilation, for example because of different religions, clannishness, etc. Socialization differences, including poor schooling, mean that the situation does not change notably with time, and ghettoization tends to take place.

The lack of any strong relationship between the size of national immigrant populations and ethnocentric voting has already been noted. However, the rise of such voting has at times followed periods of new immigration. For example, the two mini-peaks of the British NF in the 1970s followed the arrival of Ugandan and Malawian 'Asians', who had been expelled from their respective countries and who tended to concentrate in a limited number of areas in Britain.[12] In Austria, FPÖ support rose from just under 10 per cent in 1987 to almost 23 per cent by 1991. During this period Austria had seen rising immigration from ex-communist countries, and the FPÖ had highlighted the issue, linking it to housing and schooling. By the time of the 1991 elections, 40 per cent of Austrians identified immigration as a serious problem. However, in order to understand the rise of the FPÖ it is necessary to look at other factors, including its media-genic young leader, Jörg Haider. It is also necessary to look at the way the immigration issue was constructed by others, including the mainstream ÖVP, which in the capital ran under the slogan 'Vienna for the Viennese'.

The exact spatial relationship between the presence of immigrant communities and ethnocentric voting is also far from simple. In France, the NF vote correlates strongly with the number of immigrants at the departmental level, but only weakly at the commune level. This has led to so-called 'halo' or 'invasion' theories from noted commentators like Pascal Perrineau, which posit that ethnocentric voting is likely to be greatest in areas surrounding the main centres of immigrant communities, where there is fear of newcomers—whereas in the core immigration areas, ethnic communities have come more to terms with each other.[13] However, other studies have argued that ethnocentric voting has been strongest in areas of direct proximity with immigrants. Moreover, it is possible to find notable local examples of ethnocentric voting in France, Germany, and elsewhere where there are few immigrants.

A particularly controversial aspect of the functionalist approach is the way it seems to point to immigrants as the problem—a form of blaming the victims. Nevertheless, there are important issues of communal relations which need to be considered. One interesting question is why 'race' emerged on the local political agenda at different times in what socioeconomically appear to be comparable cases. Take Leicester and Manchester in Britain. Local opinion-makers in Manchester, like councillors and trade union leaders, played a far more active role in promoting understanding that in their counterparts in Leicester. Here too the local main newspaper often portrayed the NF in an uncritical light, and talked of 'immigrant invasions'.[14] Whereas Leicester became a centre of NF voting, Manchester largely remained immune from the virus. A higher level of integration, partly stemming from élite actions, also helps explain the much lower level of ethnocentric voting in Francophone Belgium compared to the Flemish speaking districts—though divisions within the Flemish FN, weak leadership, and its unitarian ideology are notable supply-side factors which must be added to any explanation of relative failure.

Far less research has been done on the sensitive issue of whether the specific activities of immigrant groups themselves might encourage ethnocentric voting. There are certainly some reasons in the East End of London to think they may have had an effect. For instance, the late 1980s witnessed growing identity movements, especially among Muslims, and a greater tendency to make demands on the local political system.[15] There was also a growing willingness to resist manifestations of white racism, which in some cases led to attacks on whites, though these were far less numerous than the wave of white intimidation and violence. Indeed, the BNP campaign which culminated in the Millwall victory was kick-started by a demonstration in 1991 against the killing of a white boy. However, it is clearly grossly wrong to place undue emphasis on this factor.

Discourse Theory

Discourse theory places emphasis on the way in which cultural distinctiveness and a sense of the 'Other' is constructed, especially in official and semi-official language and semiotics, and through policies such as immigration laws.

Discourse theory has been highly fashionable recently, and undoubtedly offers major insights into how reality is constructed and power legitimated. However, one major problem is that it can make it hard to understand the dynamics of ethnocentric party take-off. It seems better able to explain the pervasiveness of racist values than sudden changes in voting, and even here it can overstate such values, playing down the growth of multicultural sentiment. Discourse theory also tends to place too much emphasis on the official, playing down the ability of insurgent parties to help condition their own legitimacy.

The importance of discourse in the latter context can be seen by considering the work of Adorno and others on the 'authoritarian personality'—an archetypal example of the dominant tendency in academic psychology to believe that individuals like their views to be coherent. Such people are supposedly attracted to strong leaders, and to simple in-group/out-group ideologies. However, Michael Billig has stressed the 'dilemmatic' aspects of thought.[16] One of his key examples is racial prejudice. Billig argues that prejudice is a complex term, especially as recent research shows that many people now rarely talk about race in unambiguous ways, such as seeing blacks as inferior. This seems to point the importance of ethnocentric parties presenting their case carefully if they are to maximize their vote. Le Pen has frequently been labelled 'racist', and he has recently endorsed a hierarchical view of ethnic groups. However, in general, FN public discourse in the 1980s and 1990s sought to use a form of 'new racism' based on ideas of naturalness and democracy—'it's perfectly reasonable that most people in Paris do not want Halal killed meat on the school menu' etc.—It was almost certainly influenced in this area by the writings of a small number of intellectuals who made up the so-called 'Nouvelle Droite' after the 1960s.[17]

A further pointer to the potential impact of ethnocentric party discourse can be found in the research mentioned above on the *Vlaams Blok*. This found that most VB supporters were not characterized by low efficacy. Only a minority were in this category, although the association of extremism with low personal efficacy has been a commonplace in psychological theories of prejudice, which hold that people with low self-esteem create boundaries which reduce social categories to simple in-group versus out-group. The Belgian work does not explain why VB voters were not characterized by low efficacy. Possibly it was simply a reflection of recent electoral gains by the party, leading to a sense of likely influence. However, the fact that the VB addressed major concerns of voters, like immigration and crime, may have increased some people's belief that they were being listened to. Moreover, the VB highlighted issues which seem easy to understand, as opposed say, to serious discussion of managing the economy.

Another area where discourse sheds some light, relates to the extent to which true preferences remain hidden. Sudden electoral breakthrough may reflect changed preferences towards prioritizing the national/regional as the main form of self-identity. But it might indicate that views which had previously been hidden were now acted upon. For instance, in former communist countries there are often new élite norms which stress the values of democracy and the market. Most ordinary individuals will lack knowledge of the preference schedules of others and suppress values, such as radical nationalism, which they feel could produce hostile social reactions. However, cues that many others hold similar values could produce a sudden shift in behaviour. Charismatic leaders, are likely producers of such changes, especially if they can gain access to the media, which tends to like 'personalities'.

Phenomenology

This approach has made the discontinuities in social change the central object of enquiry, specifically trying to explain the recurrence of ethnocentric movements. On this view, hostility to foreigners has less to do with the activities of élites or the size of the ethnic minority population than with an overall crisis of the entire society. Intensive periods of modernization produce psychological strains, especially the rise of a sense of anomie. Racism is a form of boundary-drawings, which not only reinforces identity, but also provides a means of excluding some from welfare and other benefits.

Socio-economic changes like globalization and new technology feature prominently in the usual list of suspects stressed by noted extreme-right specialists like Hans-George Betz.[18] However, whether society has changed more in the forty years from 1958 than in the preceding forty years is a matter of debate. And how exactly does modernization lead to racism? It seems to point to the hypothesis that racism will be strongest among those most affected by change. But as has already been noted, this is a misleading view of the diverse support which some ethnocentric parties can attract.

Moreover, modernization has had little impact in terms of spawning major extreme-right parties in Central and Eastern Europe—in spite of major pockets of absolute and relative deprivation, even dramatically lower living standards for large groups. One major exception was the rise of Vladimir Zhirinovsky and his grossly-misnamed Liberal party in Russia during 1991–3. But other factors need stressing to explain his sudden breakthrough, such as extensive media coverage and Zhirinovsky's crude but catchy turn of phrase—including a male sexual imagery.[19] One hypothesis which may explain the relative weakness of right-wing extremist parties in Eastern Europe concerns expectations: people have hoped for better times in the near future as market reforms transform the economy. If this is the case, then the future may be ominous as the expectations of many have clearly been dashed. In other words, perceptions, especially of the future, may be more important than the current material and structural situation.

Social change, especially the breakdown of traditional socialization media such as religion and the family, offer a further form of modernization thesis. Social isolation could lead individuals to seek a new identity and to demonize outsiders. Individualization can also be hypothesized as producing a situation in which the social sanctions of milieus and neighbourhood have only a limited reach. There is certainly important empirical evidence for this approach. A major study by Nonna Mayer has shown that the factor most associated with Le Pen voting is social isolation. FN voters are also notably pessimistic economically, and place low trust in the main political institutions.[20] However, as will be argued below, it is a mistake to see ethnocentric voting simply in terms of anomie: indeed, such voting can take place where a sense of community is strong. Moreover, the anomie approach places far too much emphasis on socioeconomic as compared to political factors.

Political Opportunity Structure Approaches

Most of the approaches mentioned so far seek to explain the rise of ethnocentric values, rather than specifically to analyse electoral breakthrough. This lacuna is addressed in a much-acclaimed book by Herbert Kitschelt, who has sought to develop a specific model which explains why some West European 'radical right' parties have achieved far more success than others.[21]

Much of the recent literature on the value-change lying behind the ethnocentric Right adopts a reverse post-materialist conception of change. The theory of post-materialism was developed in the 1970s, especially by the American sociologist Ronald Inglehart. It holds that there is an increasing value-shift towards a non-materialist conception of the quality of life.[22] This culture-change has been thought to be especially strong among the educated young, and has been linked to the rise of issues such as women's liberation, and the formation of new movement like the Greens. 'New politics' theorists, like Piero Ignazi, have adapted this approach to argue that the move towards post-industrial society has further undermined mainstream parties because it has produced a mirror-image materialist and authoritarian response among a section of the electorate, especially blue collar males.[23] However, this approach has a variety of notable weaknesses, including the fact that many ethnocentric voters are not working class males and/or do not have strongly materialist values. Moreover, the relationship between affluence, post-material values, and the party system is complex: Germany, for instance, has a relatively strong Green Party but during most of the 1980s and 1990s extremism has been electorally weak; Norway has the reverse pattern.

Whilst Kitschelt accepts that there has been some pattern of value-change along post-material lines, he clearly realizes the error of moving directly from a structural account to changes in the party system. He therefore adds that for a 'radical right' party to make a breakthrough, two other crucial factors are required. Firstly, the mainstream parties need to cluster around the centre, or in some way open, what has been termed in New Social Movement theory, a favourable Political Opportunity Structure (POS).[24] Secondly, the insurgent parties need to adopt a winning programmatic formula which requires a break with classic statist fascism. Kitschelt's 'new radical right', epitomized by the French *Front National*, is defined by a programmatic combination of free market and socially authoritarian views, including ethnocentrism, and an electoral base centred on blue collar workers and small business. This is very different to 'welfare chauvinist' parties, like the BNP or German NPD. These combine support for the big state and authoritarianism with anti-immigrant views, and appeal mainly to a small section of the working class. They also tend to have clear links with the fascist tradition, which hinders them in two main ways. The presence of fascist coteries makes it difficult to break with the past and adopt the rational winning strategy;[25] moreover, they can be effectively tagged by opponents and/or the media with the 'fascist' label—a point under-stressed by Kitschelt. Kitschelt also identifies a third type of 'new radical right' party: the 'populist anti-statist' one, like the *Lega Nord* in Italy or FPÖ in Austria, which again tend to involve some form of ethnocentric conception of community, and hostility to immigrants. These can attract a relatively broad class base.

The idea of space seems a fertile one. A frequently-cited example of the effect of opening space for extremism is the centrist-Europeanist leadership of the British Conservative party after 1965—an opportunity subsequently closed when Margaret Thatcher began effectively to exploit anti-immigrant and nationalist sentiment in the late 1970s. Certainly it was during this period that the National Front (NF) showed signs of making notable gains on a platform based on compulsory repatriation of immigrants. The same point could be made about the Gaullists' move in the 1970s and early 1980s towards a more technocratic politics. Subsequently, the party began to pick up some of Le Pen's key themes, which meant direct programmatic competition for the FN, but this development simultaneously helped to legitimize FN concerns; other parties also helped in this process.[26] Indeed, it could be argued that legitimation is more important than space. For instance, Enoch Powell's much-publicized 'River of Blood' speech in 1968, predicting a future of racial violence in Britain, broke an élite consensus on 'immigration' matters, legitimating sentiments which previously had been largely hidden.

In Central and Eastern Europe, insurgent nationalists have often been squeezed by the way in which former communists, backed by an existing party organization, have been reborn as nationalists. In some countries, like Hungary, virtually all the parties are strongly ethno-nationalist, a factor which clearly limits the space for insurgents. Nevertheless, in 1998 the Hungarian Justice and Life party entered Parliament with fourteen deputies.[27] There has been a common assumption that the relative affluence of countries like Hungary protects them from extremism more than, say, economically-troubled Russia. Nevertheless, the process of restructuring is clearly producing many losers. Pressure within the less-skilled job market is also being increased by the tightening up of immigration into the European Union, which reduces opportunities for emigration and is likely to mean a growing number of immigrants remaining within countries like the Czech Republic and Hungary. In Hungary, the Prime Minister attributed the rising crime wave to immigrants, a comment exploited by the Justice and Life Party running into the 1998 elections, and which again points to legitimacy more than space as a key to take-off.

The tendency in some countries for all parties to have a nationalist dimension can be turned to advantage by an insurgent party, as the French case shows. In France all parties tend to be nationalist: even the communists campaigned after the war as the party of those who had gone to the firing squad in the Resistance; in the 1960s they campaigned on 'Buy French'; and in the early 1980s some local communists were anti-immigrant. Such a consensus can help legitimize a radical party in a way which has been far more difficult in (West) Germany, where nationalist discourse was virtually taboo from 1945 until the 1980s. Although it is impossible to prove a direct link, it is also worth noting that the Republikaner's electoral breakthroughs began in the late 1980s after a much-publicized debate about national identity—and more specifically the so-called *Historikerstreit*, which followed conservative historian, Ernst Nolte's, attempt to relativize the Holocaust by arguing that this was one of many forms of genocide, and that it needed understanding especially in the light of Soviet terror.

In 1997, a twist to the POS approach has been used by Ruud Koopmans, Hans-Peter Kriesi and Paul Statham, who talk of 'Discursive Opportunity Structures' (DOS).[28] This points to the way in which a language of exclusion is facilitated in some countries, especially by differing conceptions of citizenship. For instance, in Germany citizenship has remained based essentially on a conception of *jus sanguinis*, which excludes most immigrants, though not ethnic Germans returning from Eastern Europe. French citizenship since the Revolution has, in theory at least, been 'open' and based on *jus solis*, but it involves an assimilationist view of culture, which has tended to mean that Muslims especially are seen as incapable of becoming truly French. On the other hand, in Britain and The Netherlands, citizenship and views of identity have been multicultural. This has made it more difficult for ethnocentric parties in these countries to construct a legitimate discourse of exclusion. Clearly, this DOS approach points to an important supply-side factor, though it is weak on explaining the timing of electoral breakthroughs.

Early POS work on social movements often focused on institutional factors, and this produces further insights when applied to the Right. The British first-past-the-post election system is normally a barrier to insurgent voting—though in multi-party situations, it is possible to win on as low as 34 per cent of the vote, as Millwall showed in 1993. It also makes it less likely that mainstream parties will make a deal with insurgents. Another often neglected aspect of the first-past-the-post system is its effect on political entrepreneurs. It makes it less likely they will set up new parties, or cause splits in existing ones. On the other hand, the proportional list-system—introduced for the 1984 French European and 1986 legislative elections, when the FN made its first national election breakthroughs—tends to encourage a belief that votes are less likely to be wasted. Scandinavia offers another interesting example of the importance of electoral systems. In Sweden, an ethnocentric party emerged later and with less success, partly because of a higher threshold of entry into the system. Nevertheless, institutional factors alone cannot explain these differences. A lower level of politicization of debate within Sweden concerning entry into the European Union was another important factor, an issue which, in Norway and Denmark, heightened the saliency of conceptions of national identity and independence.

The issue of institutional facilitation or repression through policing and the law can be important too. A case can be made that the rapid development of violence in Germany during 1991–2 owed much to élite behaviour, including a failure to order the arrest perpetrators. Whilst this partly reflected local police inexperience at dealing with such matters, violence was politically useful to the government in terms of associating reform of the asylum laws with the

CDU/CSU. At the same time, the Republikaner, NPD, and DVU were harmed by association with the violence—though most was not carried out by members of these parties. The ability of the German Office for the Protection of the Constitution to brand a party 'radical' and especially 'extreme' right—as the Republikaner came to be labelled in the 1990s—can also send out powerful signals, especially to state employees.

Koopmans has argued that a POS model of violence, especially in the context of Germany during 1991–2, has far more explanatory power in terms of timing than a grievance model, which sees anomie among the socially marginal as encouraging attacks on foreigners and asylum seekers.[29] He also makes the important point that long-term institutional, as against specific situational repression—which can escalate violence—leads to lower extremist legitimacy. However, his attempt to relate the argument to voting seems debatable. He argues that, contrary to common assumptions but in line with POS expectations, violence tends to be high where extremist voting is low, and vice-versa. Problems with the reliability of both governmental and anti-fascist statistics on attacks, makes the issue difficult to fathom, but it is possible to find counter-examples to this thesis. Racial attacks in the East End of London apparently rose by 300 per cent in the nine months following the 1993 BNP victory; and Tower Hamlets, the main centre of BNP electoral activity, has the worst record for racial attacks in London.[30] Similarly, the DVU electoral breakthrough in Saxony-Anhalt in 1998 came at a time when attacks were increasing again in the old East Germany.

These elections in Millwall and Saxony-Anhalt point to fundamental weaknesses in Kitschelt's basic typology concerning which messages are necessary to be successful. His argument is further undermined by the fact that his archetypal 'new radical right' party, the FN, has, since its breakthrough, developed a relatively trans-class support, though it became more working class in the 1990s. Moreover, Kitschelt's analysis also fails to pick up the collectivist trend in its 1990s ideology. Together, these provide damning evidence for his own test of how to refute his central argument—namely, find a successful party which combines racism without a commitment to the free market.[31] Further problems for the typology come from Italy, where the *Alleanza Nazionale* made a leap forward in 1993–4 without using racism as a key part of its appeal—although anti-immigrant themes have become much more important to the AN than they were to the MSI (Italian Social Movement), partly a reflection of the growing numbers of immigrants from both Africa and the Balkans who now seek to stay in Italy. Moreover, whilst its economic policies were less statist than those of its predecessor, the MSI, it was certainly not a defender of *laissez faire* in the Anglo-American sense—contrary to the FN, it has subsequently moved more in this direction.[32]

Millwall and Saxony-Anhalt point to a further weakness in the basic POS approach: namely, the need to consider meso as well as macro party and institutional configurations. One important conclusion from adopting a meso perspective concerns the dangers of assuming that parties offer standardized 'products' to the electorate, rather than using a form of market segmentation or product differentiation.[33] In some cases, the insurgent parties are successful to the extent that they can tailor their messages to specific local clienteles— a point demonstrated very clearly by the FN in Dreux. Here, and more generally in the Centre Region during the early 1980s, the FN targeted diverse political families, including fundamentalist Catholics, monarchists, and ex- treme-right Republicans, though anti-immigrant views were a linking theme.[34]

This is easier in systems with strong notable or clientelistic traditions than in those like Britain, where politics became relatively 'nationalized' through organized parties and good communications at an early stage. In recent years more regional patterns have been emerging, but so far these have mainly bene- fited catch-all Welsh and Scottish nationalist parties, though an ethno-centric English backlash could be provoked by these developments. It is also easier in countries where there are long-standing sub-cultures, especially existing organ- ized groups, amenable to insurgent-right appeals, or which can be taken over by them. The latter point can be crucial to explaining the sudden growth of a party, though bringing together different groups can create self-destructive fac- tionalism and helps explain why such parties can fragment suddenly.

A further problem concerns the need to broaden the conception of the polit- ical system, both at the macro and meso levels, to include the media. Nation- ally, there seems little doubt that the *Alleanza Nazionale* breakthrough in Italy during 1993–4 was helped by extensive coverage from the Berlusconi media empire.[35] Less directly, the media have at times set an agenda favourable to eth- nocentric groups. For example, at the time of the 1992 Länd elections in Baden- Württemberg and Schleswig Holstein, the asylum issue was featured by *Bild* and other media sources: part of the Republikaner campaign involved simply copying *Bild* articles. In Baden-Württemberg, the Republikaner party went on to win 10.9 per cent of the vote, while the DVU captured 6.3 per cent in Schleswig. The localized media must also be considered. In Dreux, the *Echo Républicain* in the early 1980s helped set an agenda favourable to the FN. In Tower Hamlets in the early 1990s, the *East London Advertiser* and *Docklands Recorder* played a similar role by highlighting issues such as immigration and crime. Shortly before the election they gave publicity to a Labour canvas return which seemed to show that that the BNP was neck and neck with Labour, which almost certainly broadcast widely the possibility that the BNP vote not being 'wasted'—local Labour seems to have hoped to squeeze the vote of its Liberal rival by this tactic.

This focus on the media needs to encompass a theoretical perspective. Norm- ally, the media are perceived in terms of a causal relationship which runs from the media to the audience—though there are debates about how powerful this influence is. An interesting twist to the media power approach was developed in the 1960s and 1970s by the German opinion pollster, Elisabeth Noelle-Neumann, who talks of a 'spiral of silence' to describe the reluctance, partly conditioned by centre-left media, to express right-wing views.[36] However, at times it is more helpful to adopt an interactionist approach, where the audience can influence the media. Put another way, there is a dynamic in the racialization of politics which influences the media agenda, which in turn can influence audiences. Hamburg in 1997 would probably provide an interesting case-study, including local party behaviour, as there was a complex intermingling of rising racial tension and the media making crime and violence front page news. Interestingly, the DVU only just failed to cross the 5 per cent hurdle in the 1997 Hamburg elections, amid accusations of officials invalidating significant numbers of their votes, while the REP gathered 1.7 per cent.

The capacity of ethnocentric groups to distribute their own publicity must be considered too. Most parties, especially in the phase before they achieve notable electoral success, are poor. It should be noted that electoral success in some countries brings in state funding as well as greater contributions from supporters. A notable exception is the DVU, whose rich leader, Dr Gerhard Frey, runs a nationalist press and book club empire, and has at times spent considerable sums on campaigning. In the late 1980s, Frey is said to have spent approaching 20 million DM on door-to-door supplies of leaflets and other propaganda. Interestingly, this preceded notable DVU and Republikaner breakthroughs. He also spent large sums at the time of the 1998 breakthrough in Saxony-Anhalt. However, frequent DVU failure on other occasions underlines that money cannot guarantee success, even when the message is one that a notable minority wish to hear. In particular, people seem to repress their preferences when they think a party will fail to make an impact, and/or when espousing their true views will bring social sanctions.

Related to the last point—and another influence not fully considered by most POS approaches—it is important to study the activity of anti-racist groups. A powerful 'anti-fascist' campaign after the BNP's Millwall victory almost certainly helped de-legitimize the BNP in the eyes of many of its more decent supporters. This ad hoc anti-BNP movement encompassed a broad variety of groups, including white anti-racists, ethnic groups, unions, church leaders, and even local doctors who publicly condemned the BNP and racism. For the 1994 elections, both local newspapers called for an anti-BNP vote. It is especially important to stress the breadth of this campaign, as anti-racist fights run by the radical Left run the risk of backfiring. However, this does not apply within communist subcultures. Anti-'fascism' has been a major factor preventing the FN making greater inroads among communist working class voters in areas such as St Denis. Fascism was the historic 'Other' in communist propaganda, and older voters especially can find it difficult to embrace the FN for this reason. This has also been a problem in developing insurgent Right electoral support in the former East Germany, though other problems there include the perception of parties like the Republikaner as West German, and the presence of the former communist-based PDS as an alternative. Indeed, the latter has in many ways a similar appeal ideologically, including a holistic sense of community, hostility to capitalism, and a friend–enemy Manichaean world view.

A key channel of influence in anti-racist/fascist campaigns has been opinion leaders within social networks. Important work on the rise of the *Lega Nord* by Anna Bull shows the relevance of such relations to the wider issue of the breakthrough of ethnocentric parties.[37] Often whole families went over to the new *Lega*, with the young frequently influencing the old. Whereas the traditional academic view of socialization implies continuity, the youth-driven approach is consistent with radicalization. The *Lega's* ideological emphasis on activism, and the organization it quickly developed also probably helped take-off, especially as the organization was new and gave opportunities to the young.[38] Again, this points to important contextual reasons why votes can suddenly fluctuate. The emphasis on the role of opinion leaders and social networks further highlights the problems of anomie/mass society theory-based approaches. Sudden changes in electoral behaviour may well reflect the fact that in some ways the community has remained strong rather than broken down.

Indeed, it is probably more useful to hypothesize that on some occasions atomized groups, whose members lack cross-cutting cleavages, rather than atomized individuals can form the basis of sudden electoral take-off—though clearly this approach needs fleshing out with another hypothesis explaining what attracts people specifically to the ethnocentric right. Other work by Bull offers further insights into this process. She found in one northern Italian town she studied that racist views were especially strong among the young: 45 per cent of the 18–30 age group supported repatriation.[39] In part, this is explained by individual economic fears. But the localist ideology of the LN also exhibits a heightened sense of identity based on demonizing the 'Other', especially if it was not countered by strong communal pressures.

Conclusion

Clearly any understanding of ethnocentric party voting requires a broad-ranging consideration of micro, meso, and macro dimensions. The argument developed above suggests that the crucial focus of analysis should involve working back from the micro. However, this does not involve the methodological individualism of most rational choice theory: it sees individuals as embedded in wider contexts. The point is to identify the particular constellation of attitudes which leads to voting, and to work back from these to identify their wider causes.

It is impossible to develop a new theory within the confines of this chapter, but on the basis of the arguments presented above, my basic hypothesis is that:

insurgent group legitimacy + rising personal efficacy + declining system trust would increase extremist voting. Rational choice theorists often criticize concepts like legitimacy as vague, and they are certainly not easy to operationalize.[40] However, a purely rational choice approach fails to take account of preference formation, and the specific clustering of motivational forces which leads to changes in action.

Why should individuals, often coming from less privileged groups or suffering from relative economic and social decline, feel a sense of high efficacy, particularly a sudden increase in efficacy? A hypothesis in line with the above case-studies is that this can come from a variety of sources, but the parties' own resources are unquestionably important—both organizational and especially ideological/programmatic. The latter can give people a sense that they are not excluded by élite agendas: that they can change policy. Efficacy requires knowledge of how to act, and the belief that one has the strength and resources to act. There is considerable evidence that conscious membership of subcultures and of groups is important in developing a sense of efficacy.[41] Group identity and communication seems to increase voting.[42] Social isolation tends to produce low self respect, or apathetic alienation.

However, the above case studies also point towards the hypothesis that insurgent rightist parties need some form of legitimacy too, in order to make a major breakthrough. Put another way, they need a belief that they will appeal to a significant number of others, not just a fringe, and that the pursued goals are right, and achievable. In Germany the REP has been troubled by being tarred with the extremist brush; it also been rated lowly in terms of solving the main problem of the 1990s—rising unemployment. Undoubtedly some have voted for parties like the British NF in spite of believing them to be fascist, though without necessarily holding fascist views themselves—an example of protest voting in the irrational sense of the term. But the most successful parties in terms of vote maximization have tended to be those which can avoid acquiring the spoiled identity which comes from clear association with fascism, or racism of the traditional ideological type. The construction of legitimacy is a complex process, but clearly it cannot be achieved by the insurgent parties alone. It needs other factors, such as élite or media agenda-setting or linkages, to help.

Party legitimacy can also be helped indirectly by declining trust not just in mainstream politicians, but the system itself. Factors which can increase such sentiments include weak leadership, corruption, and especially economic failures. Clearly, recent developments such as globalization and increasing hyperchange in the job market have created insecurity, and undermined traditional party allegiances. Nevertheless, it is important not to overstate economic factors. A study carried out in St Denis by the leading French research institute into contemporary French politics, found that FN voters did not primarily discuss economic issues or welfare competition. It was more a case of seeing immigrants in 'us' versus 'them' terms.[43] Here the belief that élites had under-mined national identity—and the quest to rediscover identity—seems crucial. We have to be someone before we can be rational.

Notes

1. In this chapter, I follow the editors' convention of using 'extreme right' as the main generic term, and 'ethnocentric right' to point specifically to parties whose pro-gramme focuses especially on 'immigration'/'race'. For my own views on right-wing typology, see Part One of Eatwell, R. and O'Sullivan, N. (eds.), *The Nature of the Right* (London: Pinter, 1989); on fascism and populism see also Eatwell, R., 'On Defining the "Fascist Minimum": the Centrality of Ideology', *Journal of Political Ideologies*, 1/3 (1996).

2. See also Eatwell, R. (ed.), *European Political Cultures* (London: Routledge, 1997). NB the terms 'micro', 'meso', and 'macro', are used in varying ways by political sci-entists, with most adopting a binary micro–macro approach. Those who use the term 'meso' tend to employ it in notably different ways.

3. For more detail on the recent electoral performances of the extreme right, see the good surveys by Betz, H.-G. and Immerfall, S. (eds.), *The New Politics of the Right* (New York, NY: St. Martins, 1998); Hainsworth, P. (ed.), *The Politics of the Extreme Right* (London: Pinter, 1999); and Merkl, P. H. and Weinberg, L. (eds.), *The Revival of Right-Wing Extremism in the Nineties* (London: Frank Cass, 1997).

4. For a typical example of this interpretation, see the introduction by the noted his-torian of the French right, Rémond, R. in Mayer, N. and Perrineau, P. (eds.), *Le Front National à Découvert* (Paris: Presses de la Fondation Nationale des Sciences Politiques, 1989).

5. The terms 'racism' and 'xenophobia' are virtually synonyms in English; in many languages, especially German, the term 'racism' has been virtually taboo since the Nazi era and 'xenophobia' is the more commonly-used term.

6. Winner, A. 'Explaining Xenophobia and Racism: a Critical Review of Current Research Approaches', *Ethnic and Racial Studies*, 20/1 (1997).

7. On the pre-1990 extreme right see Stöss, R., *Politics against Democracy. Right-Wing Extremism in West Germany* (New York and Oxford: Berg, 1991); see also Eatwell, R., 'Towards a New Model of the Rise of Right-Wing Extremism', *German Politics*, 6/3 (1997).

8. Gaspard, F., *A Small Town in France* (Cambridge, MA: Harvard University Press, 1995), especially ix and 56.

9. Roy, J. P., *Le Front national en Région Centre, 1984–92* (Paris: L'Harmattan, 1993), 57.

10. Billiet, M. and de Witte, J. 'Attitudinal Dispositions to Vote for a "New" Extreme Right-wing Party: the Case of the "Vlaams Blok"', *European Journal of Political Research*, 27/2 (1995); Swyngedouw, M. and Billiet, J. 'Estimating the Relative Importance of the Different Motives for Voting for the Extreme Right in Belgium-

Flanders. The Use of Open-Ended Questions in Exit Polls'. Paper presented to the International Political Science Association World Congress, Seoul, 1997.

11. Mitra, S., 'The National Front in France—a Single Issue Movement?', *West European Politics*, 11/2 (1988), especially 62; Ivaldi, G., 'Conservatism, Revolution and Protest: a Case Study in the Political Cultures of the French National Front's Members and Sympathisers', *Electoral Studies*, 15/3 (1996).

12. For the best account of NF voting see Husbands, C. T., *Racial Exclusionism and the City* (London: Allen and Unwin, 1983).

13. Mayer and Perrineau, *Le Front National*.

14. Troyna, B., *Public Awareness and the Media: a Study of the Reporting of Race* (London: Commission for Racial Equality, 1981), especially 22–3, 51, 59–60.

15. Eade, J., 'Nationalism and the Quest for Authenticity: the Bangladeshis in Tower Hamlets', *New Community*, 16/4 (1990).

16. Billig, M. *et al.*, *Ideological Dilemmas* (London: Sage, 1988); see also Billig, M., *Banal Nationalism* (London: Sage, 1995).

17. See for instance, Taguieff, P. A., 'La stratégie culturelle de la nouvelle droite en France (1968–1983)', in Badinter, R. (ed.), *Vous avez dit fascismes?* (Paris: Montalba, 1984).

18. For example, Betz, H. G., *Radical Right-Wing Populism in Western Europe* (Basingstoke: Macmillan, 1994).

19. See Kartsev, V., *!Zhirinovsky!* (New York, NY: Columbia University Press, 1995).

20. Mayer, N., 'The National Front Vote and Right-Wing Extremism, 1988–1995', *Research on Democracy and Society*, 3/1 (1996), especially 203.

21. Kitschelt, H. (in collaboration with A. J. McGann), *The Radical Right in Western Europe: a Comparative Analysis* (Ann Arbor, MI: University of Michigan Press, 1995).

22. Inglehart, R., *The Silent Revolution* (Princeton, NJ: Princeton University Press, 1977).

23. Ignazi, P., 'The Silent Counter-Revolution. Hypotheses on the Emergence of Right-Wing Parties in Europe', *European Journal of Political Research*, 20/2 (1992).

24. Juan Linz had earlier stressed the importance of 'political space' to the rise of fascism: Linz, J., 'Some Notes towards a Comparative Study of Fascism in Sociological-Historical Perspective', in Laqueur, W. (ed.), *Fascism: a Reader's Guide* (Harmondsworth: Penguin, 1979).

25. For instance, BNP activist Michael Newland ('What's Wrong with the Right?', BNP WWW Homepage, June 1997) has noted that: 'The accusation of "populism", if any attempt is made to promote a modern nationalism, has long been used by the old guard to damn progress as a selling-out of the British cause, when it is nothing of the kind'; he added 'It must be repeated over and over again—the more moderate the language the more support it generates'.

26. Schain, M. A., 'The National Front in France and the Constitution of Political Legitimacy', *West European Politics*, 10/2 (1987); see also Thränhardt, D., 'The Political Uses of Xenophobia in England, France and Germany', *Party Politics*, 1/3 (1995).

27. On recent eastern European developments see Hunter, M., 'Nationalism Unleashed' and Mudde, C., 'The New Roots of Extremism', *Transitions*, 5/7 (1998).

28. For instance, Koopmans, R. and Kriesi, H., 'Citoyenneté, identité nationale et mobilisation de l'extrême droite', in Birnbaum, P. (ed.), *Sociologie des nationalismes* (Paris: Presses Universitaires de France, 1997); and Statham, P., 'The Political Construction of Immigration in Italy: Opportunities, Mobilisation and Outcomes', WZB Working Paper, FS III 98-102, 1998.

29. Koopmans, R., 'Explaining the Rise of Racist and Extreme Right Violence in Western Europe: Grievances or Opportunities?', *European Journal of Political Research*, 30/2 (1996); cf Willems, H., 'Development, Patterns and Causes of Violence against Foreigners in Germany: Social and Biographical Characteristics of Perpetrators and the Process of Escalation' in T. Bjørgo (ed.), *Terror from the Extreme Right* (London: Frank Cass, 1995).

30. *Searchlight*, September 1998, 7; Keith, M., 'Making the Street Visible: Placing Racial Violence in Context', *New Community*, 21/4: 552 (1995).

31. Kitschelt, *The Radical Right*, especially ix.

32. Ignazi, P., 'From Neo-Fascists to Post-Fascists? The Transformation of the MSI into the AN', *West European Politics*, 19/4 (1996); cf the more clear fascist, even violent, links of the MSI: see Ferraresi, F., *Threats to Democracy: the Radical Right in Italy after the War* (Princeton, NJ: Princeton University Press, 1996).

33. Cf the homogenous-rational choice approach of Jones, P. and Hudson, J., 'Why Do Political Parties (Political "Firms") Exist?', *Public Choice*, 94/1–2 (1998).

34. Roy, *Le Front National*.

35. Statham, P., 'Berlusconi, the Media and the New Right in Italy', *The Harvard International Journal of Press/Politics*, 1/1 (1996).

36. Noelle-Neumann, E., *Die Verletzte Nation* (Stuttgart: Deutsche Verlags-Anstalt, 1987).

37. Bull, A., 'An End to Collective Identities? Political Culture and Voting Behaviour in Sesto San Giovanni and Erba', *Modern Italy*, 1/2 (1996).

38. Gilbert, M., 'The Lega Nord and Italian Politics', *Political Quarterly*, 64/1 (1993).

39. Bull, A., *Social Identities and Political Culture in Italy. Continuity and Change* (Oxford: Berghahn, 1999).

40. Hechter, M., 'Rational Choice Theory and the Study of Race and Ethnic Relations', in Rex, J. and Mason, D. (eds.), *Theories of Race and Ethnic Relations* (Cambridge: Cambridge University Press, 1986), 272.

41. Andrews, M., *Lifetimes of Commitment* (Cambridge: Cambridge University Press, 1991), especially 29.

42. Schram, A. and Sonnemanns, J., 'Why People Vote: Experimental Evidence', *Journal of Economic Psychology*, 17/4 (1996).

43. Haegel, F., 'Xenophobic Expression in a Paris Suburb'. Paper presented to the 30th Anniversary Conference of *Patterns of Prejudice*, London, 1997.

14

Xenophobic Violence and Ethnic Conflict at the Local Level: Lessons from the Scandinavian Experience

TORE BJÖRGO

Introduction

Violent attacks against asylum seekers and labour migrants increasingly became considered a serious problem in Scandinavia during the late 1980s and early 1990s. Several local communities in Sweden and Norway in particular came into focus as strongholds for racist groups and their violent activities. However, these attacks gave rise to widely different interpretations. Some regarded the violence as expressions of racism and xenophobia, orchestrated by far-right organizations. Others saw the violence as a 'natural response' from locals who felt they are being swarmed by unwanted aliens, and that the violent outbursts indicated that the population's 'natural threshold' for assimilating foreigners has been exceeded. Still others considered the violent incidents as 'boyish tricks and drunken pranks', carried out by the usual local trouble-makers. Obviously, these divergent interpretations provided frameworks for highly different types of responses to the violence.

Common to most such interpretations is that they tend to be rather one-dimensional.[1] In this chapter, I will try to provide a multidimensional interpretation of the violence against foreigners, showing that both the violent actors, and those who respond to their violence, act on the basis of a mixture of motives and reasons.

Values at Stake in Interaction Related to Xenophobic Violence

Racist attacks do not only involve the perpetrators and their immediate victims. It may be seen as a complex system of diverse actors who respond to and influence the actions of other actors in a system of interaction. Even a simplified model of the involved actors and the relationships between them displays this complexity:

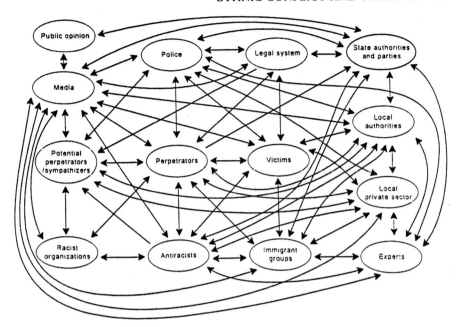

FIG. 14.1. Relations between actors involved in responding to racist violence

I am only slightly self-ironic when I call this spaghetti a 'simplified' model, because most of the actors depicted in the model represent institutions or groups which are complex sub-systems in themselves. However, I will not go into the details, but only use this to illustrate that many parties are involved in acting, interacting, and responding in relation to incidents of xenophobic violence. These actors struggle over different types of values. Which types of values are at stake?

I will identify and analyse six main 'value complexes' which the parties involved struggle over: ideology and immigration politics, identity, scarce resources, sexuality, territory, and security.

Immigration Politics and Ideology

The most obvious interpretation of anti-foreigner violence is that it has to do with immigration politics and ideology. Many of the perpetrators of violence against immigrants, asylum seekers, or their perceived allies claim to have committed the act because of opposition to the current immigration policy, or simply that they 'don't like foreigners'. Typically, they leave graffiti, symbols and slogans such as 'Foreigners out!', 'Norway for Norwegians', 'BSS' (Keep Sweden Swedish), WP (White Power), KKK, swastikas, and the like. In other cases, racist or xenophobic messages are conveyed through the act itself, or at least interpreted as such by others. Only a small but still a significant minority among the perpetrators hold explicit ideological ideas or are members of racist groups. However, in the context of police interrogation and court proceedings, perpetrators nevertheless tend to deny or play down such racist or xenophobic motives since it might be used against them as an aggravating circumstance, resulting in a stiffer sentence. On the other hand, anti-immigrant and racist organizations often praise such young violent perpetrators as good patriots and nationalists who want to defend their country and community against foreign intruders. However, these organizations usually express—at least officially—certain reservations about the form their desperate actions take.[2]

There are two main varieties of extreme right-wing movements in Scandinavia: First, anti-immigration groups with a radical nationalist or ethnocentric outlook, and second, groups with a neo-nazi or explicit racist ideology. Historical analogies and traditions play an important role for both, but they link themselves to two highly different, even opposed, historical and ideological traditions: the anti-German resistance movement of World War II, and traditions and discourse of anti-Semitism and National Socialism. However, in spite of the contrasting idiomatic content of their rhetoric, the fundamental structure is almost identical: the anti-immigration movement claim they are the new resistance movement, fighting against the Muslim invasion and the national traitors. Neo-Nazis assert to be the white, or Aryan, resistance movement, fighting the Zionist Occupation Government (ZOG) and the racial traitors. The first type of rhetoric is popular among anti-immigration activists in Norway and Denmark, especially among the older generation which experienced occupation by Nazi Germany. The overt Nazi and anti-Semitic rhetoric is more commonly voiced in Sweden. This is obviously related to the fact that Sweden was spared from Nazi occupation during the war. In Norway and Denmark, it is much harder to promote Nazism and patriotism as part of the same 'package' due to the historical experience of Nazi repression and local Nazis betraying their country by collaborating with the enemy. In Sweden, Nazism and patriotism do not in the same way appear as a contradiction in terms.[3]

Militant anti-racists tend to see the presence and actions of alleged racist and neo-Nazi groups as primarily a *political* threat 'which must be fought in the same way as the forces of the radical left fought the Nazis in the streets during the 1930s'.[4] More moderate 'mainstream' anti-racists may also be concerned with the legacy of Nazi Germany, but are usually more focused on human rights than ideological politics in a narrow sense. Immigrant and minority victims are also inclined to perceive acts of hostility against themselves from majority persons as expressions of racism.[5] However, they are usually less concerned with the alleged political threat of racism/Nazism than with the harassment, discrimination, and humiliation they experience from large sections of society on a daily basis.

The media also frequently emphasize the racist dimensions of violent acts against minorities. Especially when the police and other public institutions are slow to respond, some journalists see it as their role to make the public aware of the reality of racist violence, and to put pressure on those whose responsibility it is to act against it.[6] In this respect, they sometimes make important contributions to getting the problem onto the public agenda. However, journalists also sometimes tend to overdo the racism/Nazism dimension for a variety of reasons. When, during the wave of anti-foreigner violence in Germany in 1991–93, some commentators suggested that German society was relapsing back into the era of National Socialism, it was more than a mild exaggeration. Some apparently prefer a simple and snappy explanation and analogy rather than a more complex analysis. Sensationalist first-page exposés of clandestine neo-Nazi groups are often used to sell newspapers in rather obvious ways.

Other actors in the system, such as the police, local institutions, and politicians have often been hesitant to address possible racist or xenophobic dimensions of a violent incident. However, when racism finally gets onto the political agenda, moral and ideological values tend to play a prominent role in the responses: municipal or state-sponsored youth campaigns to promote tolerance and the 'multi-coloured society' and to fight racist attitudes, new legislation to define racist motivation as an aggravating circumstance in violent crimes, theme days in the schools on tolerance, racism, the Holocaust, etc. However, politicians may also choose to interpret racist violence against asylum seekers and immigrants as a symptom of widespread public resentment against the current immigration policy, and use such events as an occasion to make the policy more restrictive.[7]

However, although such acts of violence, and the responses to it, may be used to express ideological values regarding immigration politics, this racist dimension is frequently only on the surface. Both racist and anti-racist idioms may be used to express quite different values and interests.

Identity

Identity relates to how an individual or a group view themselves, and are viewed by others. Establishing and managing identities is an important concern for most people. To many perpetrators, their acts of violence against 'foreigners' are motivated more by a wish to impress their peers with a certain image of themselves, than by any political or ideological values. Many of these youths have a strong feeling of not being appreciated—neither by parents, whose expectations they cannot live up to, or who simply do not care, by teachers and classmates, by a labour market which does not need them, nor by society in general. However, there are many ways to establish an identity or make others take notice. In certain types of youth gangs and cliques, being one who dares to do what others merely talk about may give status and serve to build one's reputation and standing among one's peers. Frequently, violent attacks are the outcome of drinking parties where young men try to outdo each other in expressing hostility towards foreigners and suggestions about what ought to be done to them. Afterwards, perpetrators are often aware that they had such motives for carrying out the violent act, sometimes claiming that they were 'carried away'. However, they sometimes also express surprise that their actions changed their status in relation to the community around them, and not necessarily in ways they themselves perceived as all negative. From being known as a gang of petty criminal losers, they suddenly become *somebody*—dangerous Nazis and racists in the eyes of some, brave patriots and daredevils in the eyes of others. Donning a skinhead 'uniform' conveys an aggressive and violent image, and signals affiliation with a wider group of like-minded 'racists' who might be mobilized if the need arises. This gives some youths a feeling of being respected, or at least feared. Especially for those who in the past were looked down upon or even bullied, it is a remarkable change to see that their old tormentors suddenly give way to them, and even show deference. A former Swedish skinhead told:

When I was 14, I had been bullied a lot by class-mates and others. By coincidence, I got to know an older guy who was a skinhead. He was really cool, so I decided to become a skinhead myself, cutting off my hair, and donning a black Bomber jacket and Doc Martens boots. The next morning, I turned up at school in my new outfit. In the gate, I met one of my worst tormentors. When he saw me, he was stunned, pressing his back against the wall, with fear shining out of his eyes. I was stunned as well—by the powerful effect my new image had on him and others. Being that intimidating—to me, that was a great feeling!   (Interview on 19 June 1996 with the ex-skinhead P.K. (18))

Making media headlines, being courted by militant nationalist organizations, causing the initiation of local action plans, or just making things happen—all this may give marginalized young people a feeling of importance they have never experienced before. Finally they *are* something.

The identity dimension is also of vital importance to the victims. Being victimized by violence may in itself be an extremely traumatic experience. Becoming a target for harassment and violence just because of what the person is and cannot change—race, nationality and origin—may be even more devastating to one's self-esteem and identity. Even the so-called less serious forms of racial harassment, such as being 'given the finger', made faces at, refused access, discriminated against, receiving excrement by mail, or simply ignored and treated as a non-person, may systematically undermine a person's sense of dignity and humanity. It has been argued that in the long run, such daily experiences of contempt may be even more devastating to the individual than having one's bedroom window smashed or the family's car set on fire.[8] However, how people take it probably varies a lot. Some are not much bothered by gestures and discrimination, but are thoroughly shaken and stunned if they or their families are targeted for violence. On the other hand, more spectacular acts of violence are likely to elicit support and sympathy from neighbours and public institutions, whereas few bother to react against the more frequent 'minor' cases of hostility and contempt. The feeling of standing alone against hostile forces may also add to the feeling of victimization. If the direct victim of violence is identified as belonging to a wider group, such as inhabitants at a local asylum centre or a specific ethnic minority, that whole group will often be frightened and victimized. This is particularly the case if the direct victim was apparently targeted as an arbitrary representative of that group and not as a specific individual.

Since violence and victimization are so closely related to the identity, self-esteem, and honour of the direct perpetrators, the victims, and the peer groups to which they belong, victimized groups do sometimes carry out acts of revenge. This may be intended as a way to overcome their own feelings of humiliation and vulnerability, and to teach their adversaries a lesson. However, such retaliation may easily escalate into feuding and spirals of violence between native and immigrant youth gangs, or between 'racists' and 'anti-racists'.

Several so-called 'immigrant youth gangs' in Scandinavia had a strong anti-racist profile during their early stages of development. They considered their fights with rival 'white' gangs as a struggle against neo-Nazis and racists.[9] This became the core issue around which they mobilized members and support, and serving as legitimization for their own use of violence and weapons. Typically, many of these gangs go through a developmental process during which the group changes its purpose and patterns of action over time. Some of them eventually ended up as predominantly criminal groups.

A prime example of such a development was the so-called *Warriors*, an immigrant youth gang at the core of a network of similar gangs which emerged in Copenhagen during the late 1980s.[10] With their affiliated groups, the core gang of some twenty to forty members could mobilize close to 2000 supporters, according to the police. In the early stages of their development, they made a point of appearing as an anti-racist guard, armed with bats, knives, and guns. They were to a large extent established as a response to the violence and threats from the racist 'Green Jackets' (*Grønjakkerne*), a network of petty criminal White Power gangs, which were also focused around an original core group.[11] The Warriors beat up racists, singly or in large battles, and offered protection to immigrant-owned shops and kiosks vulnerable to racist attacks. Although many of the gang members even in this early period were widely involved in petty crime, they tried hard to maintain their image as anti-racist 'good-guys'. However, as the Green Jackets for various reasons fell apart and disappeared from the streets, partly but not solely by being displaced by the Warriors, graver forms of crime became more conspicuous among the Warriors. They were increasingly involved in robbery, burglary, and drug-pushing. A speciality they took over from the Green Jackets were the so-called 'gay robberies' (*bøsseran*).

One of the boys took his stand in a public park known as a meeting-place for homosexuals. When someone approached, he was assaulted by the decoy and his mates hiding in the bushes. The Warriors had learned from the Green Jackets that such gay victims of robbery rarely reported to the police.[12] When they assaulted people in the streets, often apparently at random, they usually claimed that the person in question had made a racist remark at them.

By the early 1990s, several of the older 'founding members' of the Warriors no longer took directly part in street violence and robberies. Instead they had their younger brothers and cousins to do the 'business', as they were generally below the minimum age for being charged with crimes. However, the older leaders enforced a tight control over criminal activities by the younger, including approving who may steal cars and who may drive them.

By the early 1990s the gangs hardly used the name Warriors anymore but rather a series of other names. Still, the structure of the network remained much the same. Police officers working closely with the Warriors and its descendants agree that resistance against racism was the main cause behind its emergence, and that this was the main issue at first. Simultaneously, however, it had always been important to the gang to be respected by evoking fear. Their weapons were not purely for protection but also a indispensable part of their image. They could frighten victims and witnesses into silence. The intimidating presence of the gangs have increasingly made ethnically-Danish youths cautious with not getting involved in conflicts with immigrant youths at school or in youth clubs, knowing that a 'punitive expedition' might quickly be mobilized against them. Thus, the fear the gangs caused and the power and dominance they had in the streets and schoolyards of Copenhagen became a useful resource when they gradually turned their attention from anti-racism to crimes for profit.[13]

Racist violence does not only affect the identities of the immediate perpetrators, victims, and their peer groups, but often also the local community in which such events take place. Spectacular incidents of racist violence or manifestations of racist activities attract the attention of the national news media. Recurring negative focus on a particular community as a place of xenophobic activity and violence may over time stigmatize the community as being a 'racist nest'. Even individual inhabitants interacting with outsiders frequently experience the stigma of being associated with their home community, and may feel obliged to defend their integrity by stating that 'Yes, I am from X, but I am certainly no racist!'. In Norway, Brumunddal was given this stigma during the early 1990s after a series of violent incidents, and fought a long and costly battle to solve the problem of racist violence and improve the community's image. In several other Norwegian communities with similar problems, mayors and the police frenetically denied that their community was 'another Brumunddal'. In Sweden, communities like Kode, Klippan, Vålberg, and Säffle—and for different reasons, Sjöbo—received the stigma of racism, with various degrees of damaging consequences. Stigmatized communities in Denmark are in most cases limited to specific quarters, such as Studsgårdsgade in Copenhagen during the 1980s, and the Folehaven quarter in Valby. In Germany, whole towns like Hoyerswerda, Rostock, and Mölln have become closely associated with violent racism in the minds of most outsiders, even internationally.[14]

The almost instinctive tendency of mayors, the police, and other locals to deny that a specific incident has any kinds of racist dimensions, or that there exists a problem of xenophobia in the community, is usually an attempt to avoid the stigmatization of the community. Their *intended* message is geared at preventing the event from being blown out of proportions. However, the message *received* by external audiences is often that community representatives are denying and belittling a real problem of racial violence which they rather ought to confront head-on. What may stigmatize local communities most severely is not the simple fact that racist violence has occurred, but the general perception that the community is not willing to address the problem and do something decisive about it—and thereby in practice condoning what happens.

However, identity management is also a concern for many of those who take an anti-racist stance. Public display of anti-racist attitudes, tolerance and support for immigrants and other minority groups, and contempt for groups and individuals who are identified as 'racists', may also be a way of presenting oneself in a favourable light, or even as better than certain others. This is part of the syndrome of what the Norwegian sociologist Ottar Brox calls 'the moral élite' and its struggle for the 'moral championship'. Actors may present themselves and their moral qualities through their liberal views on immigration and through condemnation of anything tasting of racism, and most effectively in contrast to others.[15] Just as members of xenophobic youth gangs sometimes try to outdo each other in expressing aggression against foreigners, the 'moral élite' has sometimes competed in doing the opposite, by expressing unreserved openness towards immigrants and asylum seekers. In several countries, these tendencies have effectively polarized the debate on immigration politics, making the more constructive and realistic middle ground, morally suspect.

A similar perspective can be applied to the relationship between youth groups at the local community level. The idioms of 'racism' and 'anti-racism' is sometimes a convenient way to express social differences and social contempt. In some communities characterized by strong class divisions, there is a tendency that 'nice' middle class youths—and working class youth with middle class aspirations—present themselves as 'anti-racists', in contrast to certain groups of marginalized working class youths who are known for their heavy drinking, rowdy behaviour, violence, and racism. These working class youths may use racist idioms to construct their identity by emphasizing values, behaviour, and style which contrast sharply with the dominant mainstream middle class culture represented by the 'nice kids' they hold in deep contempt. In one Norwegian community, young middle-class 'anti-racists' somewhat paradoxically labelled the working class youth gang of alleged racists as 'the minuses'—a form of devaluating other people one would hardly expect from true anti-racists.[16]

Scarce Resources

A struggle for the access to and distribution of scarce resources—money, jobs, housing, social services, leisure activities/facilities, etc.—lies behind much aggression and violence against immigrants and asylum seekers. In the general public debate, one of the main arguments for a more restrictive immigration and asylum policy, presented by the anti-immigration fringe and mainstream politicians alike, focuses on the economic costs involved in taking care of and integrating large numbers of immigrants. This argument has had considerable credibility in times of economic crisis, and when high unemployment gives immigrants limited opportunity for achieving self-sufficiency. There is, for instance, no doubt that the more than 80,000 asylum seekers arriving in economically depressed Sweden in 1992 represented a considerable financial burden to the country. Thus, it is argued, the resources spent on asylum seekers would be better spent on 'our own needy groups'. Countless stories circulate, some true, many not, of how demanding foreigners are given easy access to all kinds of social services, special grants, jobs, facilities, etc. Especially among relatively deprived and marginalized groups in society, such stories may easily evoke anger, bitterness, and jealousy. The claim that foreigners are given social goods they themselves have been denied, has been a recurring theme in many of the explanations young perpetrators of violence and harassment have given to the police and the media. Some marginalized youth groups even use (the threat of) violence against immigrants as leverage against local authorities to obtain goods they would not get otherwise. For instance, the Danish Green Jackets in the mid-1980s claimed that they harassed immigrants in their neighbourhood in order to catch the attention of the politicians for their demand to get their own apartments, and to chase away immigrants who occupied many of the flats in the neighbourhood. Some of the 'Green Jackets' actually got flats which became vacant after their immigrant occupants had been harassed to leave. And when the municipality provided them with premises for setting up their own club, the level of vandalism and violence in the neighbourhood dropped.[17]

Acts of arson or vandalism may have serious economic effects on victims as well. Immigrants who are in the process of establishing themselves with property and perhaps a small business of their own, are particularly vulnerable to vandalism and are often underinsured. If the window panes of the shop or apartment are smashed several times, they may be driven into bankruptcy—or even be driven out of town.

The economic dimensions of racist violence have also been important to some of the other actors in the community, especially the municipality and the business community. The realization that 'racism is bad for business' may explain why, in several cases, the local business community have been among the first actors to respond to racist violence and demand firm action against it. There are several ways in which racism and xenophobia may have negative economic consequences for businesses. Some companies are dependent upon maintaining good relationships with foreign customers and partners. Having visiting customers from Saudi Arabia, China, or Nigeria beaten up at restaurants or in the street may be damaging to business relations—especially if the million dollar contract is not yet signed. Many companies are also worried that they may have difficulties in recruiting highly skilled and highly demanded personnel to fill key positions if the local community becomes stigmatized as a racist nest. Who would like to move to, let us say, Hoyerswerda and have their children grow up in such an environment if you have other options? And the best people usually have. Thus, racist harassment can cost jobs, contracts, and key personnel. As a consequence, such developments will also affect the economy of the municipality, and thereby public services to the population.

On the other hand, racist violence may also, paradoxically, have some positive effects in terms of improved access to scarce resources for some of the actors involved. If, for instance, an emerging problem of racism and violence is defined by local authorities as being the result of marginalization or social deprivation, the youths in question will often be offered jobs, education, leisure time activities, or facilities, in order to provide positive alternatives to their destructive lifestyles. Critics argue that young racists thereby make profits from their negative behaviour. Municipalities and local police departments may also receive extra funds from the state to implement measures to fight racism and violence in the community. Anti-racist organizations, academic researchers, and other experts are also among those who might receive increased government grants when racist violence is placed on the political agenda.

However, in the struggle over scarce resources, there is one special form of 'scarity goods' which is more precious and emotionally charged than any other: the struggle over girls, sexual favours, and the procreation of children.

Sexuality

Both the racial ideologists and the nationalist anti-immigration lobby have placed a strong emphasis on controlling the sexual behaviour of women. To these movements, sexual relations between 'our' women and the 'strangers' constitute the original sin: the pollution and dilution of race and nation with foreign and inferior blood.[18] This is also a core issue in classical racist ideology and practice.[19] A main objective of both the so-called 'science' of racial hygiene of the inter-war period, Nazi Germany's Nuremberg Laws, and the South African Apartheid system was to prevent racial mixing and preserve racial purity. Among the more modern versions of racial revolutionary ideology, for instance as expressed in the ideological novel *The Turner Diaries*,[20] women are seen as holding the keys to the demise or survival of the white race. Neo-Nazis and other racial revolutionaries often describe the alleged glorification in the media—MTV in particular—of white women with black men, as part of a carefully planned Jewish plot to propagate racial mixing and the destruction of the white race.[21]

Nationalist anti-immigration groups and activists have also been highly concerned with women having sexual relations with 'foreign' men. In Norway and Denmark, in particular, the imagery of the 'the Germans' tarts'—that is, women having affairs with German soldiers during the war—is frequently evoked. In the propaganda of such groups, expressions like 'asylum mattress' and 'whores' are commonly used to describe these women. At the same time, male immigrants were frequently described as HIV-infected, sex-crazed animals only out to rape the local women.[22]

Behind these views there is a striking ambivalence about women as 'weak'. On the one hand, women may be seen as innocent and pure victims of foreign rapists, and therefore in need of protection from 'their own' males. On the other hand, women who enter liaisons with black men are considered morally weak because they are slaves to their own impure sexual lusts.[23]

It is difficult to evaluate whether ideological propaganda produced by organized groups has an impact on the general public or not. In some cases, it is obvious that the propaganda has had an effect on at least certain sections of the population. That notwithstanding, relations between local girls and 'foreign' men are also, almost literally, an explosive issue at the local community level. A large proportion of the violent attacks, confrontations, and fights—sometimes even knifings, shootings, and large-scale riots—begin as seemingly minor incidents involving jealousy and rivalry over girls. These incidents often take place at dance halls, bars, youth clubs or similar public arenas, and usually in connection with the consumption of alcohol. I have observed two main varieties of these triggering incidents: in the first type, a male 'foreigner' flirts with a girl who turns out to be a local man's girlfriend. The boyfriend then often reacts violently, especially if he suspects that his girlfriend is attracted to this exotic, cool, and often well-groomed male, or if the 'intruder' does not take the girl's 'no' for an answer. The second typical situation is that one or more 'foreign' men are out with their local girlfriends, and some of the local men react with anger and aggression against the girls and/or the 'foreign' men who allegedly take the local girls away from them. Being passed over, local boys may feel humiliated, and their masculinity threatened, by the experience that these girls consider the 'niggers' or the 'Arabs' more attractive, exciting, and possibly more virile than they are themselves.[24] Insulting comments against the girl or against the foreign rival often provoke a physical—often, but not necessarily, violent—response from the man who wants to defend her or his own honour and dignity. Then the fight is on. What distinguishes these incidents from ordinary rivalries over girls is that a similar quarrel between a local boy and someone from a neighbouring town does not usually have the same potential for escalation—at least not nowadays.[25] In contrast, when the rivals are foreign 'black' men, a large number of local boys frequently join in to 'teach the foreigners a lesson', sometimes ending up in an outright riot.[26] However, although such riots have racial dimensions, this does not mean that the participants are able to formulate any kind of racial ideological views. What is involved is more the gut feelings that the 'foreigners' are winners and they are losers in the struggle over girls and sexual favours. This experience is felt as a threat to the masculinity of the local boys.[27] And how can they better prove their masculinity than through a good fight?

Territory

In the rhetoric of both the nationalist anti-immigration lobby and the racial revolutionaries, the territorial dimension is at the core of their ideologies. As described earlier, the anti-immigration activists claim that the country is threatened by an on-going Muslim invasion. The arrival of thousands of labour migrants, asylum seekers and their families, is in reality part of a conspiracy to conquer Europe for Islam, they claim. In a few decades from now, they will have taken control of territory and the political system by means of a 'demographic time bomb', the argument goes.[28] The racial revolutionaries see immigration as part of a Jewish scheme to bring non-whites into our lands in order to destroy the white race through racial mixing. In their conception, the Zionist Occupation Government is already in control through their agents. In both ideological versions, a 'resistance struggle' is needed to fight back the invasion/occupation, ultimately involving the use of violence against both 'foreign invaders' and 'traitors'.

However, the territorial dimension is often highly important on the local level as well, without necessarily involving any ideology. When local youth gangs with xenophobic inclinations have carried out acts of violence against 'foreigners', the immediate cause has often been that they felt threatened because they believed these others were trying to take over their territory. The disputed territories may involve entire towns or quarters, or merely specific street-corners, pubs, or youth clubs.

Interestingly, this territorial dimension is also a core issue for other actors involved—although they may not always be aware of it! Radical anti-racist activists, with their slogan 'No Nazis in our streets!', sometimes use violent means to prevent racist groups from establishing themselves in certain areas. Sometimes this struggle has close similarities to rivalries between gangs fighting over turf. Several municipalities have declared their community as an 'Anti-racist Zone'. Increased patrolling from police and co-operating groups of adults as a response to violent confrontations and gangs fighting over turf, may also be seen as civil society's attempt to regain the territory from unruly youths.[29]

Security

To the immediate victims of racist violence, and the wider groups which feel threatened, security from further violence and harassment is a primary concern. When a spectacular act of violence attracts the attention of the media, the police, and the public, it is often only the climax in a long process of harassment and victimization directed against individuals and groups. Physically preventing the perpetrators from committing further attacks by arresting, prosecuting, and jailing those responsible, is of course the most effective measure. However, other responses may also strengthen the victimized groups' feeling of security. It is of great importance that neighbours, voluntary organizations, and local authorities show a determination to include exposed minorities in the community and take responsibility for their safety and well-being. Even if the police are not able to identify and arrest the perpetrators, the *attitude* displayed by the police towards the victims and the crime may have a strong impact on the victims' sense of security. In cases where the police in public statements swiftly brush aside the possibility of any racist or xenophobic dimensions—even when it is obvious—or try to play down the gravity of the incident(s), it may increase the feeling of insecurity among the victimized groups. If, on the contrary, the police display a willingness to explore possible xenophobic dimensions and take the victims' concerns seriously, it may even serve to subdue some of the negative effects of the post-traumatic stress disorder (PTSD) experienced by many victims of violence.

Even for perpetrators of xenophobic violence, their own feelings of fear and insecurity may have played an important role in the process leading up to their violent acts. Many of these perpetrators have in the past themselves been victims of threats and violence. Youths who have been bullied or violently attacked sometimes seek protection in gangs with a violent image. Racist skinhead gangs may offer the kind of collective protection and intimidating image they crave, even if their tormentors are 'native'. Individuals who have carried out extreme acts of violence against 'foreigners' have also in several cases personal histories of being victims of threats and violence from immigrant youth gangs. These experiences may have installed in them feelings of fear, anger, and hatred which were *generalized* towards dark-skinned young men as such. When a new and totally unrelated situation arose, their fear and hatred made them overreact in extreme ways, knifing or gunning their victims to death.[30]

Fear of crime from immigrants and minority groups is widespread among considerable sections of the population, sometimes based on what people themselves or persons close to them may have experienced, or more often, on rumours and media accounts emphasizing the ethnic origin of perpetrators of crimes. Criminality by immigrants, real or imagined, is in some cases applied as a legitimization of violence against immigrants and asylum seekers as such. The generalization of blame, guilt and punishment—from *some* specific 'foreigners' to 'foreigners' *as such*—is what gives this tendency a racist dimension.

Much of the violence from the more organized nationalist/Nazi youth groups is directed against anti-racists, particularly against the more militant variety. Although unprovoked attacks on anti-racists is a common pattern, some of the violence may also be seen as a response to violence and harassment from militant anti-racists. In most places, the anti-racist militants are numerically stronger than their counterparts, and are able to systematically harass—and sometimes even outright terrorize—local neo-Nazis and far-right activists, who feel that neither the police nor the media or any others care at all about their security from violence, and that they are left to protect themselves. Since they cannot usually match their enemies in street fights, they often arm themselves with guns, knives, and even use bombs. They compensate for their numerical weakness by using more powerful weapons than their adversaries. Thus, the spiral of violence between racist and anti-racist militants may easily end up with someone being killed.

The main task of the police is to maintain law and order, and thereby to prevent damage to life, limb, and property. The police are supposed to implement this duty in a non-discriminatory way—which means that it is their task to provide security not only for immigrants and anti-racists, but even for persons associated with racist and xenophobic groups. Thus, any person who is the victim of an act of violence has the right to protection, and to have his/her assailants brought to trial—without regard to ethnic origin or political conviction.[31]

One important objective of the police is to prevent violent clashes between racist and anti-racist militants by keeping the two sides separated. As a consequence, the police often end up in the thankless role of protecting racist and neo-Nazi demonstrations, meetings, and concerts against anti-racist protesters. In some cases, the police have even provided transportation and even loudspeaker equipment to racist groups in order to make the event run smoothly and without violent confrontations. This is a role the police themselves obviously find awkward and embarrassing, as it exposes them to heavy criticism and accusations from anti-racists, some politicians, and sections of the public. However, given their task of maintaining law and order, the only alternative for the police is to ban the meeting itself by ordering it dissolved, or by refusing to give prior permission for a public meeting. This might be done on the grounds that the event may represent a danger to public order. Until recently, the police in all the Scandinavian countries have been highly reluctant to use this provision. The right to freedom of expression has generally been given higher priority.

However, there are signs that in particular Scandinavian authorities are changing their policies by being more inclined to ban Nazi or 'nationalist' marches and concerts. Whereas Norwegian and Danish authorities sometimes withhold permits to stage such events by referring to dangers to the public order, Swedish authorities have also stopped White Power concerts and arrested participants by reference to the racist meanings of the songs, the slogans, and the signs. Recent changes in legislation and court practice in Sweden have explicitly defined *Sieg Heil*-salutes and certain Nazi symbols as forbidden according to laws against ethnic harassment and political uniforms.

Final Remarks

Although the present analysis is based on a Scandinavian study, the findings presented here are also likely to apply to other countries which have experienced anti-foreigner violence and similar forms of conflict. In fact, the identified values over which the involved parties struggle, are closely related to basic human needs—the needs for meaning, identity, subsistence, sex, territory, and security. Some of the actors try to fulfil these needs in rather peculiar and problematic ways, though, as is the case with those who turn to violence and racism.

'Racist' or 'xenophobic' violence is a highly complex form of interaction, which cannot be reduced merely to violence carried out for specific ideological or political motives. Racist expressions do not necessarily have a racist motivation. It is useful to make a distinction between racism as a form of expression, on the one hand, and racism as a driving force or motivation behind action, on the other. In some cases, both the mode of expression, and the motivation behind it, is racist. Obviously, responses from society should be strong and clear. However, many youths in particular tend to choose a racist form due to its expressive power and effectiveness in redefining social and inter-personal relations. Their motives for acting are often based on quite other concerns than a racist ideology or xenophobic attitudes. Nevertheless, the racist expression is real enough, and is usually experienced as such by the victims, to whom the deeper motivations of the offenders are irrelevant. Thus, even such forms of racist expression warrant firm reactions from the social surroundings, making clear that such racist acts are not acceptable.

Still, if we want to prevent groups of youths from turning to racist forms of action, it would also be wise to address the often very real concerns and needs which their violent behaviour is attempting to alleviate—albeit in harmful ways. Through creative preventive efforts, many of those needs could be fulfilled by opening up or providing some less destructive alternatives than the ones offered by militant racist groups and their violent modes of action.[32]

Notes

1. These observations are based on research made in connection with my doctoral dissertation at the University of Leiden, *Racist and Right-Wing Violence in Scandinavia: Patterns, Perpetrators, and Responses* (Oslo: Tano Aschehoug, 1997), where a more detailed version of the present argument is to be found in the conclusions chapter.

2. Cf. this author's interviews with FMI leader Arne Myrdal on 23 June and 12 August 1989, and numerous reports in the nationalist magazine *Fritt Forum/Norsk Blad*.

3. These discourses are analysed in more detail in Bjørgo (1997), Chapter 8, and in Bjørgo, Tore, 'Extreme Nationalism and Violent Discourses in Scandinavia: "The Resistance", "Traitors", and "Foreign Invaders"', in Tore Bjørgo (ed.), *Terror from the Extreme Right* (London: Frank Cass, 1995).

4. This is a common expression among AFA (Antifascist Action) activists in Scandinavia, formulated with minor variations in their magazines, fanzines, and newsletters. It has also been stated during numerous discussions between various radical anti-racist activists and the author.

5. Cf. Marianne Junger, 'Intergroup Bullying and Racial Harassment in the Netherlands', in *Sociology and Social Research*, 74/2 (1990), discussing this victim bias.

6. For further discussion and examples, cf. Bjørgo, Tore 'The Role of the Media in Racist Violence', in Tore Björgo and Rob Witte, *Racist Violence in Europe* (Basingstoke: Macmillan, 1993).

7. For a discussion on 'including' and 'excluding' forms of state responses, see Witte, Rob *Racist Violence and the State: A Comparative European Analysis* (Doctoral dissertation, University of Utrecht, 1995).

8. Cf. Bowling, Benjamin 'Racial Harassment and the Process of Victimisation: conceptual and methodological implications for the local crime survey', *British Journal of Criminology*, 33/2 (1993); Council of Europe, *Report on Racial Violence and Harassment in Europe* (prepared by Robin Oakley, Strasbourg, 1992); Høgmo, Asle 'Om den skjulte rasisme i en norsk småby', in Ottar Brox, *'De liker oss ikke': Den norske rasismens ytringsformer* (Oslo: TANO, 1996).

9. Lien, Inger-Lise, and Haaland, Thomas *Vold og gjengatferd. En pilotstudie av et ungdomsmiljø* (Oslo: NIBR/Ungdom Mot Vold, Report, 1998), 30–6, 63–4.

10. The following description is based on my interviews in 1991, and a follow-up in 1998, with youth workers, police officers, and other close observers of the gang scene in Copenhagen. For a journalistic account of this early 'anti-racist phase', see Jansen, Torsten, 'Krigerne', *Ekstrabladet* 14 August 1988.

11. For a description of the rise an fall of the Green Jackets, see Bjørgo (1997), 127–33.

12. These robberies are also described in Lars Villemoes well-informed article on the Green Jackets, 'Danmark er for danskerne', *Information* (31 May 1985).

13. The Pakistani 'Young Guns' gang in Oslo went through a remarkably similar development as the Warriors, although on a smaller scale. Cf. Lien and Haaland (1998), 30–6, 63–4.

14. For discussions on local communities as victims of stigmatization, see Carlsson, Yngve *Aksjonsplan Brumunddal—Gav den resultater?* (NIBR report 1995, No. 13), 48–55, 153–4; Wigerfelt, Anders, and Wigerfelt, Berit, 'Klippan—et stämplat samhälle'. Paper presented at the seminar 'Local Crime and Social Control—Fear and Anger', Lund, 15–16 September 1997.
15. Ottar Brox, *'Jeg er ikke rasist, men . . .' Hvordan får vi våre meninger om innvandrere og innvandring?* (Oslo: Gyldendal, 1991), in particular 44–88.
16. For a detailed study, see Eidheim, Frøydis, *Hva har skjedd i Brumunddal: Lokalsamfunnet i møte med de fremmede og seg selv* (Oslo: NIBR report, 1993, No. 20), particularly 50–3; see also Carlsson (1995: 66–73).
17. Interview with two former members of the 'Green Jackets', 4 June 1991.
18. Some racist groups take this concept of original sin literally: the so-called Christian Identity Movement in North America considers the Jews to be the offspring of Eve's illicit relation with the Satanic snake!
19. However, anthropologists will also point out that the sexual control of women is of critical concern to any social system based on the principle of patrilineal kinship. Paradoxically, with respect to their views on women, sexuality, honour, and purity, some neo-Nazis and anti-immigration activists have culturally more in common with some of the Middle Eastern and Asian immigrant groups they despise, than they have with the mainstream cultural values of their own society.
20. Andrew Macdonald (pen name for American Nazi ideologist William Pierce), *The Turner Diaries* (Hillsboro, WV: National Vanguard Books, 1980). In the futuristic novel's harrowing vision of 'the Day of the Rope', tens of thousands of female corpses were hanging from trees and lampposts, with placards in large block letters: 'I defiled my race'. They were white women married to or living with blacks, with Jews, or other non-white males (160–3).
21. For example, *Nordland* 4: 12–13, 16 (1995).
22. Cf. undated issue of Myrdal's propaganda flyer *Norge er vårt*, distributed in Arendal in 1988.
23. I owe this point to Nora Gotaas, *Farger i natten. Sosial kategorisering og stereotypisering i møtet mellom afrikanere og nordmenn på utesteder i Oslo* (Oslo: NIBR Report No. 19, 1996).
24. The White man's fearful image of the Black man as being sexually more virile, well-endowed, and attractive to White women than he is himself, has been a core theme in some versions of racism. This masculinity fear is also a central theme in the Black American novelist James Baldwin's writings.
25. In a not very distant past—during the 1950s or some places even up to the present—quarrels over girls with men from neighbouring communities did in fact frequently cause large-scale fights and riots in connection with dancing halls. In those days, when immigrants from abroad were an unknown phenomenon, xenophobia was often directed against people of a much closer origin.
26. One typical case happened in the small Norwegian town of Grimstad on 1 September 1996. Six African men and three Norwegian girlfriends were at a

discotheque when one of the Africans was pushed by a local man. When he asked why, he was hit in the face with a bottle. He hit back, and a fight followed, continuing at the street outside. Suddenly, almost 100 local youths started to chase the Africans and their girlfriends, throwing stones and shouting 'Kill the niggers!' and 'Nigger whores!'. The police and the Mayor nevertheless claimed that the incident was not racially motivated but only an ordinary gang fight over girls. *Agderposten* 2 and 3 September 1996; *Fedrelandsvennen* 3 September 1996.

27. When the Danish 'Green Jackets' complained that *'perkerne'* (the Turks) were stealing 'their' girls, a youth worker pointed out to them that they would probably improve their chances in the competition over girls dramatically if they started to wash and wear clean clothes . . . (from the author's interviews with youth worker René Johansen in 1991). Cf. Gotaas (1996) for further discussion.

28. Cf. *Nordmannen* No. 3 (Sept. 1995), p. 8.

29. Both the Swedish *'Farsan på stan'* ('Grand-dad in town') and the Norwegian *'Natteravn'* ('Night raven') projects are based on the observation that during weekend nights, urban streets are completely taken over by youths, often heavily intoxicated by alcohol. The idea is that an increased presence of sober adults may calm down the mood and prevent events from getting out of hand. The task of the adults is not to intervene if violent situations occur, but to report emerging conflicts to the police as soon as possible, and try to serve as a calming influence through their mere presence.

30. The first case (1989) involved a Polish man who after a very brief quarrel initiated by him, knifed down two Pakistani men who were out for a walk in the centre of Oslo with their Norwegian girlfriends. The second case (1995) involved a former UN soldier who felt threatened by an immigrant youth gang after a quarrel. He went home for a shotgun to threaten them off. When they came towards him, he fired, killing one and wounding another.

31. Recent legislation which defines 'racist motivation' as an aggravating circumstance may make it possible to judge an attack by a 'racist' against an immigrant, or possibly even an anti-racist, as a more serious crime than a similar attack in the opposite direction, carried out for 'anti-racist motives'. However, even 'anti-racist violence' may sometimes fall under provisions for aggravating circumstances, for example if it has been carried out by a group against an individual, or if it has the character of mistreatment, cf. the Norwegian Criminal Code, section 232, point 3.

32. For a discussion about what can be done to induce youths to disengage from racist groups and assist them through the process, see chapter 6, 'What happens to young people who join racist groups—and want to leave?', in Bjørgo (1997). That analysis has also provided the theoretical foundation for *Project Exit—Leaving Violent Groups*, an action plan adopted in Norway and Sweden. *Exit* organizes networks for parents with children in violent groups, educates professionals working with such youths such as teachers, police, and youth workers, and provides support directly to youths who want to disengage. See the following internet site: *http://home.powertech.no/vfb/exit.htm*

IV

A Transnationalization of Migration and Ethnic Relations Politics

15

Anti-racist Responses to European Integration

CATHIE LLOYD

Introduction

Since the early 1980s social and political movements have attempted to address an increasingly global agenda while also drawing their strength from local grassroots social protests. How effective can they be in the new circumstances? We have become accustomed to hearing from political analysts that the forces of what is widely known as globalization, coupled with social fragmentation, are reducing the capacity for democratic intervention in the issues which concern our lives.

In this chapter I examine the main characteristics of globalization and consider how they apply to the Europeanization of immigration controls. I then investigate to what extent anti-racists can mobilize and intervene in the international and European spaces of civil society about such crucial issues.

There is a great deal of disagreement about the characteristics and extent of globalization. I would agree with Hirst and Thompson (1996) who argue that it is neither a complete nor an entirely new process although we may be experiencing an accelerated phase which gives rise to the feeling that something radically different and new is taking place. For the purpose of this chapter I will emphasize three aspects of a limited concept of globalization. First, that due to the speeding up of communications it appears that events in different parts of the globe now act more immediately upon one another, 'the intensification of world-wide social relations which link distant localities in such a way that local happenings are shaped by events occurring many miles away and vice versa' (Giddens 1990: 64).

Second, that there is a greater economic interdependence, 'All economies are interrelated in one competitive marketplace, and everywhere the entire economy is engaged in the cruel games played on that stage . . . conventional physical boundaries begin to lose all meaning' (Dahrendorf 1995: 37). Commentators argue that 'the technological revolution has disaggregated the workforce' and capitalism has been given free rein across the globe, unconstrained by national state boundaries. According to Sivanandan, 'We are back to primitive accumulation, plunder on a world scale' (1995). Globalization may be interpreted as the most recent form taken by imperialism, giving rise to accentuated dependency and paternalism. Capitalism *'sans-frontières'* requires increasing flexibility and workers need to be prepared to accept and respond quickly to technological changes (Sivanandan 1995). The implications of globalization are for greater interdependence, but it also implies more inequality. Under certain circumstances, this growing inequality means that democracy may come under greater stress. One consequence may be a growth of racism and xenophobia.

Thirdly, some more pessimistic theorists emphasize that there are political effects in an ambience of disaggregation and fragmentation which demobilizes and disarms political struggles: for instance Zygmunt Bauman argues that 'life activities . . . tend to be fragmentary, episodic and inconsequential' (1994).

It is this political consequence which particularly concerns me in this chapter. Many theories of globalization see political demobilization as inevitable as multinational capital tends increasingly to control important aspects of the nation-state which may be forced to dance to the tune of multinational companies rather than listen to their electorates. It is a crisis of state power (Held 1991: 145), in which governments appear to be driven by impersonal forces, beyond the control of individuals, who respond by living in the present, avoiding broader strategic thinking. The nation-state, it is argued, loses its sovereignty, as governance is increasingly subject either to international agreement, regulation, or the intervention of other forces such as transnational companies. Prosperity, civil society, and democracy seem increasingly to be under threat (Dahrendorf 1995). Globalization threatens civil society because power leaves traditional political channels and decisions are taken away from national fora: politics becomes discredited. We can perhaps see the consequences in the many people who have fallen through the net of citizenship, in particular the homeless, or those so alienated from politics that they do not bother to register to vote.

Recent attacks on the welfare state throughout Europe also reflect this state of affairs. People are expected to uproot themselves from established communities to look for temporary, insecure work. All this change gives rise to growing feelings of personal insecurity without a unifying bond to help people resist. Ethnic minorities may be especially vulnerable as they are already excluded through racist processes of discrimination, and in many countries are towards the bottom of the class hierarchy. At the same time, declining and insecure social groups associate minorities and especially immigrants with the causes of their decline which gives rise to scapegoating, racism, and xenophobia.

There are further consequences for ethnic minorities in these processes. While the sovereignty of the nation-state may have been weakened, with key areas such as defence or economic policy passing out of its grasp, control over population movements is thought to remain one of the last spheres of unchallenged national sovereignty (Giddens 1990: 17–21; Held 1991: 16–17; Hirst and Thompson 1996: 181). As a result, immigration has been propelled to the centre of the political agenda in many countries. Globalization thus accentuates many of the tensions in society, which can encourage the growth of racism. Furthermore, as I shall argue later in discussing its paradoxes, globalization attacks some of the underlining ideas upon which anti-racism is rooted, notably that of universalism, while simultaneously standardizing social, political, economic, and cultural life. This may explain why people may feel the impact of events on a global scale, while also moving towards the embracing of local and particularist identities. Before turning to these questions, which affect mobilization, I shall next describe how some of the general processes noted above have operated within the European Union (EU). At one level the construction of the European Union is part of the process of globalization, at another it was formed to seek some control over some, especially economic, aspects of the changing world order. The new Europe provides both important constraints but also opportunities to influence policies on immigration control and racism (Held 1991: 151). I will begin by outlining some of the key characteristics by which the different institutions of the EU have operated in the sphere of immigration and frontier control, and then move on to consider responses to manifestations of racism within Europe.

The European Context

In the 1950s and 1960s immigration was largely structured by (ex-) colonial relationships. The metropolitan powers were obliged to recognize some rights and privileges for migrants from ex-colonies even though this varied from one country to another. Throughout the period 1960–1968, this relationship was being eroded. In the case of Britain it was chipped away by a series of immigration laws which culminated in the concept of *patriality* as the basis for citizenship. In the case of France, the important relationship with Algeria was transformed by the 1962 Evian Agreements, even though the *jus soli* principle mitigated the effects for people born in France until the Nationality code was changed in 1993.

Thus there were important changes in the realm of immigration already taking place by the 1970s. However, these processes have been speeded up by moves towards closer integration of the European Community and the formation of the European Union. In particular the Single European Act of 1986 (SEA) set up a target for the completion of the single market by the end of 1992. At the centre of this single market is the free movement of labour. This free movement is restricted to nationals of states of the European Union and 'third-country nationals' are excluded (Geddes 1995: 202). It has given rise to two parallel harmonizing movements on the part of member states, that of immigration and nationality law.

It is important here to note, in political and institutional terms, how these trans-European changes took place. The push towards tighter external frontier control and the harmonization of national policies has operated through informal inter-governmental structures. The SEA states that member-states could 'take such measures as they judge necessary for the purposes of controlling immigration from third countries' and that they should co-operate for this purpose (art 8a). This established that immigration remained the responsibility of national governments and was outside the remit of European Community institutions which might be more amenable to democratic pressure, such as the Parliament and the Commission (Geddes 1995: 206). This is connected to the desire of member-states to hold on to one of the last vestiges of their sovereignty, the control of population movements across their frontiers, although as we shall see, this idea of sovereignty is largely an illusion.

As the Single Market was being established, the subject of immigration control was discussed away from democratic fora. Interior Ministers placed the subject under the remit of informal inter-governmental structures such as the *ad hoc* group on immigration set up by a meeting of Interior Ministers in London in 1986. The Schengen agreement of 1985 was signed initially by France, Germany, and the Benelux countries to facilitate the free internal movement of labour, harmonize visa policies, and co-ordinate crime prevention. However their agreements have had a much wider impact, acting as a sort of trendsetter for the rest of Europe. The old Trevi group—established in 1975 to combat terrorism, then expanding its work to drug trafficking and international police and security co-operation—was taken within European structures in 1993. A new K4 Committee was set up, composed of senior Interior Ministry officials, which agreed to organize the computerized finger-printing of all asylum seekers through the Eurodoc scheme, to establish a new common definition of a 'refugee', and to discus the strengthening of expulsion procedures. The establishment of these agreements has rendered national sovereignty an illusion. Even countries which have deployed much rhetoric in publicly resisting the establishment of European competence in the area of immigration—such as the United Kingdom and Denmark—have changed their legislation and regulations in line with the rest of the EU.

Many of the measures introduced by different national governments in Europe, apparently as a result of internal debate, actually originated from these meetings. These unaccountable, secret structures served to further marginalize immigrants, as immigration was discussed alongside issues like national security, terrorism, and crime rather than human rights or economic development (Weil 1997). Since the fall of the Berlin Wall there have been several conferences to discuss how to control migration from the East and the South

(Vienna 1990; Berlin 1991; Budapest 1993). The borders of Eastern and South-ern Europe, along the Polish and Czech borders with Germany and around Melila—the Spanish enclave in Morocco—and the Italian coast, have been rein-forced with a strong military presence (Carr 1997). The Ford report to the Euro-pean Parliament (1992: 127–8) pointed out that by defining immigrants as a special kind of problem, associated with a threat to national security, European governments served to legitimize the racist discourses of the extreme right.

The Palma document (1990) (referred to by Ford 1992: 124) on the crossing of external frontiers specified that once a uniform visa, which would establish a common European frontier control, could be introduced by all European counties, there could be unchecked movement of third country nationals across national borders. The Dublin Convention (1990) introduced the 'one-stop' asylum procedure. Since then common legislation has been introduced throughout Europe: carriers laws establishing financial penalties for transport companies which carry illegal migrants, and a common visa requirement for people coming from certain countries—Britain, France, and Germany. There are new restrictions on the rights of dependants of primary migrants to claim social benefits or to work, and an increase in the power of the police to check identities in public places. Asylum seekers have been singled out for new control measures. All European countries have introduced new restrictions on the rights of asylum: in Germany article 16 of the Basic Law was amended in December 1992, to limit the number of asylum seekers entering the country. Similar constitutional amendment was enacted in France and an Asylum Act passed in Britain in 1996. Visa regulations have been tightened. In the middle of January 1997, the German government curbed the visa and residence rights of hundreds of thousands of foreign children who had been born and brought up in Germany, amid calls for 'national preference' in the giving of jobs (*Guardian*, 16 January 1997). These measures were echoed in most other Euro-pean countries. Throughout Europe, foreigners and asylum seekers are being denied access to welfare benefits as governments develop a distinction between different categories 'deserving' welfare.

The harmonization of immigration policy was speeded up in June 1991 at the instigation of Chancellor Kohl of Germany with agreement on three pri-ority areas: firstly, the harmonization of policies for entry for the purposes of family reunion, for employment, or on humanitarian grounds. Secondly, the establishment of common policies on illegal immigration and procedures for expulsion, and thirdly, policy harmonization on admitting third country nation-als who wish to work. Further priorities were agreed for asylum seekers through the Dublin Convention which harmonized rules on 'manifestly unfounded applications' on the principle of the first host country and the estab-lishment of the CIREA (Centre d'Information, de Recherche et d'Echange en Matière d'Asile) to share information about future asylum flows (Maesschlak 1997).

International conventions rather than supranational community law have thus made agreements on immigration and asylum policies. In terms of practice rather than rhetoric, it would seem that national governments are busily abandoning their independent control of immigration: one of the last redoubts of sovereignty. Since the mid-1980s there has been considerable reaction to these developments. At different levels and in different ways anti-racist movements have protested against these new restrictions and the undemocratic way in which they have been planned and introduced. Some protests have focused on immigration controls themselves, while others have concentrated on the need to alleviate the growth of racism which is seen as a by-product of this new Europe. But we need to specify what we mean by anti-racism and how anti-racists can influence policy.

Defining Anti-Racism

I would argue that we need to go beyond the commonly held concept of anti-racism as being solely oppositional, and to focus on how anti-racists organize, what they stand for and what they do (Lloyd 1998). This will involve understanding anti-racism both in terms of its institutional forms and its discourse.

At an institutional level we can understand anti-racism as a constellation of organizations (Heineman 1972) shifting between a series of linked pressure groups and a social movement. Anti-racism is expressed in varying forms in different European societies. Anti-racist organizations vary between relatively well endowed statutory bodies like the CRE Commission for Racial Equality to more informal organizations run by volunteers at the grassroots level, or a social movement. Within the category of more informal organizations, there are also two main subgroups: organized pressure groups, and the more reactive protest groups or social movement type organizations. It may be useful to think in terms of three levels: international, national, and local/ grassroots.

If we examine anti-racism as a set of practices and discourses, we are free to understand its main themes. I would define these broadly as opposition to discrimination, representation, solidarity and the hegemonic establishment of an anti-racist common sense indissociable from a wider agenda of social justice (Lloyd 1998). To date, the literature on anti-racism has focused on its oppositional features but there are also important aspects of anti-racism which affirms the need for a different way in which human beings can relate to one another, respect human rights and civil liberties (Feuchtwang 1990; Lloyd 1994). One important set of differences between anti-racist groups will be the relative weight which they place on the main themes.

Another important aspect is the basis of membership within anti-racist groups. Anti-racist organizations differ greatly both at national and European level. If we place these differences on a continuum between the two poles of universalism and particularism we can broadly categorize groups whose membership is based on their own status and those based on support for a more universalist programme (Neveu 1994: 103). I will return to this idea later in discussing the problems of anti-racist co-operation. Of course, empirical research reveals a much more complex picture over time, with the same organization articulating discourses based on different aspects at the same or different periods (Lloyd 1998). However, it is clear that anti-racists operate in an ambivalent field, caught between universalism and particularism: at one level they are appealing to the universal, arguing for human equality and the application of social justice. At the other, in the details of opposing discrimination, representing and practising solidarity towards certain groups of people, they are also working within a particularist agenda (Lloyd 1994). If we can understand this within the European context as a continuum, then we can begin to understand where different groups may fit in terms of their discourses and memberships.

Thus anti-racist mobilizations straddle two of the forms of mobilization defined by Koopmans and Statham (Chapter 2 in this volume): ethnic and anti-racist. Some aspects of anti-racist campaigning may comprise elements of ethnic mobilization, since ethnic minority group members and their organizations may play a leading role in defining the issues and in demonstrations, negotiations, and debates. In many ways the claims of anti-racists to legitimately represent a constituency depend on their endorsement. Groups from what Koopmans and Statham define as the 'dominant culture' may also be involved in anti-racist mobilization, but their action is dependent in important ways on the first, 'ethnic' form of mobilization. Importantly, different groups of people work together in many anti-racist groups, and for different reasons. In the next section I briefly examine how these tendencies are manifested at the transnational and international level before considering the national and grassroots sites of anti-racist activities.

Anti-Racism and Globalization

The paradoxical relationship between universalism and particularism is common to both globalization and anti-racism. As we have seen in the processes of globalization, increased consciousness of the international is accompanied by yearnings for the recognition of difference and identity (Held 1991: 149). We have also seen that the political aspects of globalization involve an apparent loss of control of key aspects of sovereignty by a nation-state, leading to a focus on the control of its own population and its borders. Under these conditions, power leaves traditional political channels leading to opaque areas of decision-making, which involves political demobilization and a loss of faith in the main political parties, a growth of social insecurity, and a paradoxical swing between universalizing and particularistic impulses.

Despite these limitations, theorists of globalization point to an increased awareness of an emerging international civil society, expressed through a growing number of transnational NGOs, such as Amnesty International or the International League for Human Rights, which collect and publish information about abusive behaviour in order to challenge offending states. These initiatives have been sustained by the validation of human rights conventions by the majority of governments so that 'The global spread of political democracy, with its roots in constitutionalism makes those persons within the territorial space controlled by the sovereign state increasingly aware of their political, moral and legal option to appeal to broader communities in the event of encroachment on their basic human rights' (Falk 1995: 164–5). The United Nations and other international development agencies also prioritize their relationships with NGOs.

The European Commission (DGV) is also attempting to stimulate a European civil society, acknowledging the need for voluntary and other representative organizations to have a role in a wide range of social issues at the European level (1997: 17). In March 1996 the European Forum on Social Policy brought together a range of organizations to develop 'mutual understanding about the respective roles, responsibilities, and capacities of the various actors in civil society in developing a strong civil dialogue, involving both social partners and NGOs' (EC 1997: 17).

The effort to build anti-racist co-operation is an example of the construction of this international civil society. At one level it may make sense to understand the developing consciousness of the European dimension of the problem of racism and of the existence of a common anti-racist agenda in terms of a pan-European social movement. At another level, anti-racists are faced with two broad and related problems. Firstly, how to gain access to the relevant power structures in order to make their case heard, and secondly how to work together.

The relatively few studies of anti-racism generally agree that it is a 'difficult issue' which is not easily accommodated within the policy-making process partly because its constituency is relatively powerless (Heineman 1972; Lloyd 1994, 1998; Stedward 1996). As a political movement anti-racism may be best understood as occupying different points on a continuum between well-organized, bureaucratic organizations, pressure groups, to protest or social movements which challenge dominant social practices and preconceptions.

Thus a central feature of anti-racism is its diversity. An assessment of its effectiveness as a constellation of pressure groups makes it clear that it does not fit neatly into any one category. For instance, anti-racist groups fall somewhere between sectional or representational, and promotional or universalist organizations (Finer 1958). Until we look at the overarching themes of anti-racist discourse it is not clear how anti-racists can be a clearly defined lobby. Most groups campaign on a variety of different issues: against unjust immigration controls, police harassment, welfare, education, or information gathering. Some offer legal services, all tend to vary according to the social and political context in which they operate. For instance, in the UK, the relatively well-funded statutory body, the Commission for Racial Equality, has affected the priorities of anti-racist organizations. In France, certain anti-racist associations, with tiny budgets, working with a largely voluntary legal advice service, are the main bodies responsible for the enforcement of the laws against racism.

The relationship between anti-racist organizations and policy-makers is not an easy one. While decision-makers may regard anti-racists as less than respectable or responsible, there may also be pressure from within the anti-racist movement to maintain a distance from the authorities. Both sides may be highly conscious of the disparity in terms of access to material resources and power. The nearer one approaches the social movement end of anti-racism, the more there is suspicion, antagonism, and distance towards authority. These attitudes are bound up with analyses of institutionally-entrenched racism. Anti-racist protest groups are torn between wanting to make a practical impact on policy and keeping faith with their grassroots. So there was a vitriolic debate in the UK during the debate of 1981 following the Brixton riots involving ethnic minorities about whether or not to co-operate with the Scarman inquiry or later, on the politics of accepting local authority grant aid.

Not all anti-racist groups are equally distant from centres of decision-making. In Britain, Race Equality Councils (RECs) are tied in to a structure funded by a mix of local authority and Home Office money through the CRE. In France, some organizations have received government grants: for instance *SOS-Racisme* and *France Plus* had a very comfortable relationship with the Socialist government during the 1980s. The main focus of these grants was major campaigns directed at young people which included lavishly produced 'rock' concerts and a national week of education against racism. These organizations both carried out important campaigns during this period to encourage young people from immigrant backgrounds to register to vote, like that in the late 1990s in the UK organized under the auspices of Charter 88. There are similar relationships between some anti-racist groups, political parties and churches in other European countries. This carries with it all the problems attendant on alliances or partnerships: in particular the risk of political manipulation and of co-option. Anti-racist groups' agendas may be distorted because funds may be available for one type of activity rather than another. Or they may become embroiled in political disputes which have little to do with their immediate concerns.

While groups may differ in their ability to benefit from subsidies and grants, another important factor of difference lies in the different resources at their disposal. While some groups may have few resources other than strongly motivated members, others such as the Joint Council for the Welfare of Immigrants (JCWI) in the UK or *Groupe d'Information et de Solidarité avec des Travailleurs Immigrés* (GISTI) in France, may have slender financial means, but benefit from supporters' professional activities based in law or social work. They are able to formulate demands in ways that policy-makers can understand and use. They form a sort of bridge between protest/social movement groups and policy-makers.

The other side of the equation of effective pressure is the attitude of decision-makers. The structures of the EU have been frequently criticized in terms of their opaqueness and emphasis on control measures rather than actions against racism. However, as I have already suggested, it is important to distinguish between aspects of the decision-making apparatus at the European level, and here the important difference is between the intergovernmental structures such as the Council of Ministers, and the European Commission and Parliament. Key individuals in both the latter institutions have sought to expand their roles in developing anti-racist initiatives.

Perhaps the most significant has come from the European Parliament in establishing that the rhetoric by which immigration controls are introduced and their content has helped to legitimize racism, and may partly account for the electoral success of the far right. Following the lack of response to the Evrigenis Report (1985), and the Ford report (1991), both to the European Parliament, emphasized the links between these controls, the growth of racist violence, and of electoral support for extreme-right political parties. Yet national governments resisted the idea that issues like racism and xenophobia should be covered by a European remit. The European Parliament called for European Community ratification of the European Convention on Human Rights and the Geneva Convention on refugees, and criticized the control of movements of third country nationals by unaccountable intergovernmental groups. However, its call for the establishment of a European body against racism on the lines of the CRE, and a European Resident's charter, was rejected by the Social Affairs Commissioner Vasso Papandreou who argued, in 1992, that the Commission had no influence over the criminal law of its members.

Papendreou's rebuff was in line with member-governments of the EU who have resisted the establishment of European policies against racism. This is despite their endorsement of international statements condemning racism, such as the European Convention on Human Rights or the preamble to the Social Charter which acknowledges the need to combat all forms of discrimination 'on the grounds of sex, colour, race, opinions and belief'. National provisions against racism vary considerably across Europe (Costa-Lascoux 1990; Geddes 1995: 211; MacEwen 1995). Faced with mounting evidence of the growth of the extreme right, and pressure from the European Parliament and the Commission, the Council of Ministers set up a Consultative Commission on Racism and Xenophobia in 1994. Chaired by Jean Kahn, President of the European Jewish Congress, the Consultative Commission was charged with 'making recommendations, geared as far as possible to national and local circumstances, on co-operation between governments and the various social bodies in favour of encouraging tolerance, understanding and harmony with foreigners' (Consultative Commission 1995: 2).

Some analysts think it was set up to 'bury' the issue, but despite the British Conservative Baroness Flather's dissenting minority report, the Kahn Commission concluded unequivocally in favour of amending the Treaty of Rome to cover racial discrimination. The European Parliament and Commission have taken up its proposals in their efforts to find ways of taking initiatives against racism and xenophobia at the European level.

At the forefront of such initiatives is the Starting Line Group which includes the CRE, the Churches Committee for Migrants in Europe, the Dutch National Bureau Against Racism, and the Commissioner for Foreign affairs of the Senate of Berlin, supported by over thirty national and European organizations. They all argue for unambiguous legal competence in the Treaty of Rome and a Community directive for the elimination of racial discrimination. The group organizes other NGOs and targets the Commission and political parties in the European Parliament. This is an important development in that it illustrates how groups can pool resources, expertise, and their access to decision-makers, through forming an 'advocacy coalition' (Kingdon 1984; Sabatier 1988; Stedward 1996: 225).

The unit on Freedom of Movement and Migration Policy DG(V) has recently taken a number of important anti-racist initiatives under the aegis of its social policy remit, through the White Paper on Social Policy (1994) which focused on racism, xenophobia, anti-semitism, and integration (Stedward 1996: 196). Several budget lines enabled DG(V) to offer financial assistance to NGOs intervening on issues involving migrants and on measures to combat racism, xenophobia, and anti-semitism. They can fund projects including educational packs, practitioner conferences, training sessions, and the establishment of the Migrants Forum (Stedward 1996: 196).

The idea of social exclusion is extremely malleable and can be applied to a broad set of issues. This is a tactic of finding a way round the denial of community competence against racism, and has been used to include racism and xenophobia in most of the main statements about social exclusion (Robbins et al. 1994). This rather unsatisfactory ramshackle approach was seriously disrupted in May 1998 by a ruling of the European Court of Justice to the effect that there was no legal basis for expenditure on a wide range of budget lines related to civil society and humanitarian actions. This temporary freeze has been unblocked, but it underlines the precarious and vulnerable nature of this expenditure, and has reinforced the campaign to establish a firm legal basis for these measures.

Leading Commission officials have also attempted to boost actions against racism through statements: in 1993 Leon Brittan spoke of the need to take every possible action against the growth of racism in Europe (*Guardian*, 22 January 1993). Similarly the Commissioner for Social Affairs and Immigration, Padraig Flynn has emphasized the need to balance control policies with measures for integration in a draft communication on asylum and immigration (*Guardian*, 28 January 1994) and Anita Gradin took a separate portfolio to co-ordinate Commission activity against racism, xenophobia, and anti-semitism. The European Year Against Racism was another symbolic high profile initiative, and according to Flynn, was intended to prepare public opinion for the revision of the Treaty of Rome to include racism and xenophobia.

Relatively well-organized groups who can exchange information and experiences and discuss common concerns at a professional level can take advantage of these political opportunities. Organizations which aim to disseminate information and legal advice can quite quickly identify practical and effective means of communication, often taking advantage of fast means of electronic data transmission—GISTI, JCWI, and United are good examples. Co-operation is less problematic when organizations work in similar ways. They may however experience some difficulty in maintaining their own priorities and activity agendas, especially when responding to domestic developments.

However, protest-oriented groups with fewer resources are more dependent on identifying opportunities through which they may gain access to policy-makers at exceptional moments. For instance, shortly after the election of the new government in France in June 1997, several anti-racist groups met those responsible for the drafting of the new legislation on immigration, nationality, and asylum, although this did not mean that the groups were satisfied with the legislative proposals. Other groups may take advantage of new technology to improve the reach and effectiveness of their communications, with the help of other organizations. So for instance the *sanspapiers* movement in Paris has a web-site and discussion list on which they make available the texts of the most recent ministerial circulars, and exchange advice and experience on the way in which the current regularization is taking place. This is a national example of how to maximize effective influence which is being applied at European and international level as through the 'United' information initiative in Amsterdam (funded by DGV).

Co-operation is a difficult issue for the more protest-oriented, reactive type of anti-racist group, which share many of the characteristics of social movements. They nearly all suffer from a lack of resources, a membership which identifies strongly, even emotionally, with the goals of the movement, which raises problems of representation, and a tendency to define themselves in terms of what they oppose rather than what they support. Let us examine these questions one by one.

Informal voluntary militant type of anti-racist groups or coalitions such as the British-based Assembly against Racism, the MRAX (Mouvement Contre le Racisme et la Xenophobie) in Belgium, the MRAP (Mouvement Contre le Racisme et pour L'Amitie entre les Peuples) in France and *Nero e non solo* in Italy have relatively few resources and rely heavily on small grants and members' contribution for their functioning. Anti-racist co-operation encounters the problem of the lack of available resources such as funds for travel to meetings, time and personnel, people with the necessary language skills: here European funding has helped. None the less these difficulties mean that organizations with meagre resources are at a disadvantage in competing for funding, co-operating with well-endowed partners, and insisting upon their priorities.

The second set of problems are around issues of identification and representation. One of the key aspects of social movements is the way in which people identify with the movement they support, especially when matters of one's identity are at stake. This is true for many anti-racists. Differences between groups' analyses of racism and anti-racism can lead to more intractable problems especially when they impinge strongly upon their identity as a group. As I suggested earlier, we may understand the different ways in which this is expressed in terms of a continuum between groups with a strongly universalist orientation through to those who are highly particularist. Co-operation between such groups is often difficult, with misunderstandings cropping up around fundamental issues such as the politics of representation and the priorities of anti-racist struggle.

An attempt to establish an anti-racist network for equality in Europe in 1991 foundered over these kinds of difficulties. There was a debate, led by the British based Anti Racist Alliance (ARA) and the Standing Conference on Racial Equality for Europe (SCORE) over the priority to be given to black leadership in the organization. This revealed very different analyses of the causes and extent of racism. It illustrated the uniqueness of the British analysis of anti-racism and of 'race relations' in Europe at the time. In the context of meetings between French and British anti-racist activists it became clear that the British had difficulties in accepting that there could be a situation where, according to Catherine Neveu, 'the dominant terminology is not a racialised one, . . . [and] groups most subjected to racism and discrimination are hardly [physically] distinguishable from the indigenous population' (1994: 99). While the British framed the debate in highly racialized terms, the French tended to think in what they saw as more 'universal' categories of equality and rights. Furthermore, it was argued that the black–white race relations paradigm was inadequate for explaining a situation where there are multiple sites of racism, for instance, against African migrant workers but also Yugoslavs, Chinese, Turks, and Muslims in general. This meant that there was different criteria for the establishment of anti-racist alliances: the British focusing on identity based on phenotype and ethnic identity, rather than experience and similar political economic and social position in forming anti-racist alliances, which tended to be the basis of other European groupings (Neveu 1994: 98).

These difficulties were also encapsulated in another attempt to form the Migrants Forum, a European Commission funded organization to represent all migrants. The term 'migrant' was unacceptable to ethnic minority citizens, who nevertheless wanted to be represented at European level. Protracted negotiations and debates simply drew attention to the British exception, where the experience of ethnic minority citizens has been that their access to political rights does not end racial discrimination. For the majority of 'migrants' in other European countries who enjoyed second class citizenship at best, the British case was hard to understand. Yet anti-racists in Britain were focusing largely on this very problem. 'Citizenship may open Europe's borders to black people and allow them free movement, but racism cannot tell one black from another, a citizen from an immigrant, an immigrant from a refugee and classes all third world people as immigrants and refugees and all immigrants and refugees as terrorists and drug dealers' (Sivanandan 1995).

It may be that the attempts to form a European anti-racist network raised an unnecessary problem. To the extent that anti-racists recognize a similar agenda, share parallel concerns and approaches to their work there may be no need to construct a formal set of anti-racist institutions at the European level. After all, informal co-operation has already given rise to spontaneous and joint demonstrations, as for instance in co-ordinating campaigns or opposing European meetings of the extreme right.

Most specialist anti-racist publications throughout Europe contain strikingly similar analyses: for instance there was a near universal adoption of the term 'Fortress Europe'. Anti-racists are well informed and there is considerable information about the extent of racism in different countries. One powerful view is that this may not be enough. During the European Year Against Racism there was a move by DGV to set up an Anti-racist Co-ordination Committee at the European level. This arises from its own need to have some sort of organized lobby to which the bureaucracy can relate. Anti-racists may be caught between two stools: the reluctance to co-operate among themselves if it involves compromising on dearly held positions, and the danger that the European bureaucracy may promote a structure with its own chosen groups and its own programme.

Conclusion

This chapter has focused on a set of issues with both general and specific implications. In general terms, I have addressed some of the problems of establishing democratic structures within civil society at a supranational level. The economic aspects of globalization may increase precariousness among migrants and ethnic minority populations. However, groups, providing they have the resources of course, can exploit the enhanced opportunities presented for rapid communications by means of the Internet and e-mail. I reject the idea that globalization has closed off means of intervention either within civil society or at the level of the nation-state. At the same time however, it does pose problems of scale in alliance building: just how structured should alliances be? Who should be driving the formation of alliances? How can we ensure that small, under-resourced organizations are not sidelined? The establishment of European policies and structures on migration and asylum have produced new problems and new interlocutors for anti-racists, whilst also opening up new opportunities for intervention. This chapter has examined some of the difficulties which under-resourced organizations may experience in responding to political opportunities at the transnational level. This is the specific focus, which addresses the theories of mobilization suggested in this volume. The specific and the general are tied together by the problem inherent in globalization, that while creating uniformity, it also stimulates particularist agendas, for example, identity politics, but also racism and extreme forms of nationalism. This is a difficult problem for anti-racists because they are not outside the dynamics they are trying to control.

Thus the factors which prevent anti-racists from responding to the opportunities for co-operation in the new Europe are inseparable from the political dynamics of globalization itself. Anti-racism is multifaceted and various. It cannot be wholly separated from ethnic mobilization because in some instances the two are closely intertwined, and depend on one another. If we separate out different levels of mobilization—European/national/civil society/grassroots—we can distinguish some of the factors which divide groups from one another. For instance, organizations vary in terms of their distance from policy makers. Groups with close relationships to centres of power benefit from funding and may find some of their priorities taken up by decision-makers. However, this may be at the expense of their credibility with the grassroots sections of the anti-racist movement who may suspect that their concerns are being diluted. This question of co-option is important for anti-racists because of the centrality of their claims to legitimately represent their constituency.

A central feature of the problem is its imbalance. It is widely accepted that decisions about immigration have been taken away from democratic fora and made behind closed doors. There is a widely perceived link between the harmonization of immigration and asylum controls and the rise of racism and xenophobia. These problems are out of proportion to the opportunities presented to anti-racists by the European Parliament and the European Commission. The opportunities also contain the danger that the anti-racist agenda could be co-opted by these powerful organizations and that groups could become dependant on European funding and lose touch with their grassroots support, which is a crucial resource.

Even if anti-racist organizations accept the need to form pan-European structures, they still face a number of problems. Racism takes a multiplicity of forms, depending on historical, political, social, cultural, and economic contexts: for similar reasons—not simply because it is a response to racism—anti-racism is also multifaceted. Serious study of anti-racism does reveal common themes: they all work with changing perceptions of discrimination, attempt to represent people who experience racism, and develop solidarity actions. Underpinning these themes is a wider social project about social justice, equality, and social cohesion. In different ways, at different moments, and in different contexts, anti-racists have sought to build consent for their ideas by promoting an anti-racist common sense, through broad campaigning, legislation, and through education.

If instead of focusing on the issues which divide them, anti-racists look at what they have in common, it may become clearer that some joint projects at European level may be possible. There are often as many difficult divisions between groups within, as between, countries. We know surprisingly little about these features of anti-racism in Europe, and this is an important theme for future research. There is a need for detailed study of the main organizations, and also of the way in which they co-operate with other groups in civil society like political parties, trade unions, and religious organizations. How do they co-operate within specific political campaigns, for example for the defence of public services and welfare?

A central issue is that of understanding alliances and how they work. My study of the way in which anti-racist groups have worked together within France has shown that, in spite of cultural and generational differences, a 'transversal' way of working was sometimes possible, based on recognition of common aims and respect for the positions of different participants. As a system of 'alliances', transversal collectives are unstable over a long period of time, but they also offer a more open, tolerant, and pluralist way for pressure groups and social movement type organizations to work together (Foucault 1977; Yuval-Davis 1997). This is the sort of loose, perhaps *ad hoc* co-operation which may be most effective at the European level, and suggests forms which global civil society may take in the future.

References

BAUMAN, Z. (1994), 'Deceiving the 20th Century', *New Statesman and Society*, 1: 24–5.
CARR, M. (1997), 'Policing the Frontier: Ceuta and Melilla', *Race and Class*, 39/1: 61–6.

CONSULTATIVE COMMISSION (1995), *Final Report of the Consultative Commission on Racism and Xenophobia* to the Permanent Representatives Committee (General Affairs Council 6906/1/95, April). Brussels: EU, DGV.

COSTA-LASCOUX, J. (1990), *Anti-discrimination in Belgium, France and The Netherlands*, Report to the Committee of Experts on Community Relations, (Strasbourg: Council of Europe, MG-CR).

DAHRENDORF, R. (1995), 'Preserving prosperity', *New Statesman and Society*, 15: 36–41.

EUROPEAN COMMISSION (1997), *Social Europe*, Progress report on the implementation of the medium-term Social Action Programme 1995–6. Brussels: EC DGV.

EUROPEAN PARLIAMENT (1985), *Committee of Inquiry into the Rise of Fascism and Racism in Europe* (Luxemburg: Office for Official Publications of the European Communities).

——(1993), *Report of the Committee on Civil Liberties and Internal Affairs on the Resurgence of Racism and Xenophobia in Europe and the Danger of Right Wing Extremist Violence* (PE 203.624/fin) (Luxemburg: Office for Official Publications of the European Community).

FALK, R. (1995), 'The world order between inter-state law and the law of humanity: the role of civil society institutions' in D. Archibugi and D. Held (eds.), *Cosmopolitan Democracy. An agenda for a new world order* (Cambridge: Polity).

FEUCHTWANG, S. (1990), 'Racism: Territoriality and Ethnocentricity' in A. X. Cambridge and S. Feuchtwang (eds.), *Antiracist Strategies* (Aldershot: Avebury).

FINER, S. (1958), *Anonymous Empire* (London: Pall Mall Press).

FORD, G. (1992), *Fascist Europe: The Rise of Racism and Xenophobia* (London: Pluto).

FOUCAULT, M. (1977), *Language, Counter-Memory, Practice—Selected Essays and Interviews* (Oxford: Blackwell).

GEDDES, A. (1995), 'Immigrants and ethnic minorities and the European Union's Democratic Deficit', *Journal of Common Market Studies*, 33/2: 197–218.

GIDDENS, A. (1990), *The consequences of modernity* (Cambridge: Polity).

GORDON, P. (1989), *Fortress Europe? The Meaning of 1992* (London: The Runymede Trust).

HEINEMAN, B. (1972), *The politics of the powerless* (London: Institute of Race Relations/ Oxford University Press).

HELD, D. (1991), 'Democracy, the nation-state and the global system', *Economy and Society*, 20/2: 138–72.

HIRST, P., and THOMSON, G. (1996), *Globalization in Question* (Cambridge: Polity).

KINGDON, J. W. (1984), *Agendas, Alternatives and Public Policies* (Boston, MA: Little Brown).

LLOYD, C. (1998), *Discourses of Antiracism in France* (Aldershot: Ashgate).

——(1994), 'Universalism and Difference: The crisis of anti-racism in the UK and France', in A. Rattansi and S. Westwood (eds.), *Racism, modernity and identity: On the Western Front* (Cambridge: Polity).

MacEWEN, M. (1995), *Tackling Racism in Europe* (Oxford: Berg).

MAESSCHLAK, A. (1997), 'Fermeture des Frontières', *Rapport CRIDA* (Paris: CRIDA).

NEVEU, C. (1994), 'Is "black" an exportable category to mainland Europe? Race and citizenship in a European context' in J. Rex and B. Drury (eds.), *Ethnic Mobilisation in a Multi-Cultural Europe* (Aldershot: Avebury).

SABATIER, P. A. (1988), 'An advocacy coalition framework of policy change and the role of policy-oriented learning therein', *Policy Sciences*, 21: 129–68.

SIVANANDAN, A. (1995), 'La trahison des clercs', *New Statesman and Society*, 14: 20–1.

STEDWARD, G. (1996), *Agendas, Arenas and Anti-Racism: An Exploration of Anti-racist Influence and British National and European Union Public Policy* Ph.D. thesis Department of Politics, University of Warwick.

YUVAL-DAVIS, N. (1997), *Gender and Nation* (London: Sage).

WEIL, P. (1997), *Pour Une Politique de l'Immigration Juste et Efficace* (Paris: Rapport au Première Ministre).

16

Immigration and European Integration: New Opportunities for Transnational Political Mobilization?

ADRIAN FAVELL and ANDREW GEDDES

Introduction

In this chapter we assess the extent to which EU responsibilities for free movement, immigration, and asylum lead to specifically transnational political action. For this to happen would be a novelty, because in the post-war period, control over immigration has been strictly the domain of nation-states, indeed a defining hallmark of national sovereignty: thus immigration policy has been a question struggled over predominantly at national level alone. Freer movement of persons is, however, a foundational tenet of European Union (EU) treaties, and in recent years the connection between free movement, on the one hand, and immigration and asylum, on the other, has led to the emergence of EU integration and co-operation in this field. The Amsterdam Treaty has now also created the scope for future EU level action against racist, ethnic, and religious based discrimination and raised questions about access to EU rights for legally resident non-EU nationals—'third country nationals' (TCNs), of whom there are around 11 million in the 15 member states. We pay close attention to new patterns of political action by pro-migrant organizations and to the motivations, calculations, and alliance-building strategies of EU level institutional actors. We illustrate how pro-integration alliances between lobby groups and EU institutions can develop, that seek European solutions to what have become the Europeanized issues of free movement, immigration, asylum, and which then lead to scope for new political opportunities. Our institutionalist approach means that we pay close attention to specification of the policy context in order to ascertain these associated political opportunities.

Scholars in migration, race, and ethnic studies have had problems accounting for the developing European dimension to immigration politics in western Europe. Everyone is aware that Europe matters because emerging institutions and policy engagements of the EU challenge and re-shape national approaches to immigration across the continent. But few studies specify the actual constraints and opportunities opened by the Europeanization of immigration politics. Migration, race, and ethnicity researchers appear unwilling, and perhaps unable, to explore the relation between new forms of political action and the institutional dynamics of European integration. Instead, an all-too familiar activist rhetoric has dominated and undermined academic studies of the effects of the EU on immigration issues: lamenting the building of 'fortress Europe', the inevitable 'exclusion' of ethnic and migrant minorities, and the inexorable progress of 'racist' or 'fascist' Europe; while the powers that EU institutions actually have, for either good or ill, are vastly exaggerated. Such rhetoric may be an effective strategy for protest by groups who feel marginalized by the EU institutions, but it is a misleading basis for analysing what is going on at this level. Mainstream EU scholars who might be able to temper these claims, meanwhile, have mostly overlooked the subject. The fact that immigration, asylum, and citizenship moved towards the top of the EU agenda as part of the Amsterdam Treaty of 1997 means that it is now highly apposite to explore opportunities for EU level political action.

We strip back the question to its essentials: asking what, if any, forms of action or mobilization can be associated with the emergence of immigration/asylum policy competencies and the institutionalization of a migration policy context (for more comprehensive studies along these lines, see Favell 1998c; Geddes 2000). We specify a two-stage approach to this question: first, specifying the institutional *context*, then specifying the *actual*, rather than imagined or normatively desirable, dynamics that it has induced because of the resultant opportunity structure. We pay particular attention to the construction of an emergent EU 'migrant inclusion' agenda that is structured by developing EU competencies that derive their potency from market making. This nascent agenda includes extended rights of free movement for TCNs, extended anti-discrimination provisions, and EU asylum procedures that accord with international standards. In other words, we explore the possibilities for transnational action specifically made possible by European integration. We examine the circumstances that present opportunities and/or impose constraints on *all* forms of mobilization connected to immigration policy at the European level. We contend that European integration should be conceptualized as a predominantly élite process which stimulates opportunities for élite forms of action, that privileges certain forms of political action and actors, that are found pursuing technocratic and judicial avenues to influence at the EU level.

Europeanization and Transnational Politics

Many studies of the EU commence with a rather hackneyed discussion of the respective roles of nation-states and EU institutions: is it the member-states controlling the scope and direction of European integration, or is the Commission the driving force of integration? The answer to this question is likely to be a rather uninteresting 'both, sometimes' (Putnam 1988). A more useful approach is to emphasize the importance of national level contexts and their EU level accommodation, but also to recognize that, in areas where policy competencies are established, the ability of member-states to control the scope, direction, and pace of European integration diminishes (Peterson 1995; Wincott 1995). Once commitments have been entered into by Treaty and turned into legislation that binds those member-states, then institutionalization creates potential for new patterns of political activity that address EU actors in a reconfigured European polity. In such circumstances member states are *key* actors, but not the *only* actors with the effect that state power becomes something to be explained rather than something viewed as causal or determining (Cox 1986).

Another key observation is that European integration creates an uneven, hybrid spread of powers arising from the combination of intergovernmental and supranational patterns of co-operation and integration. In turn, this is symptomatic of the tension in present-day European politics between state-centred power and authority, and new patterns of governance that do not take the state as their sole point of reference. In such circumstances, what we identify as 'transnational' action consists of political action or mobilization enabled outside of the existing opportunity structures of national level politics, as a direct or indirect result of decisions to integrate in particular policy sectors. Such transnational action is facilitated by the specifically élite and technocratic focus of policy-making in the EU, which seeks to incorporate a range of non-state and non-national actors as part of the process. Transnational action or mobilization can, therefore, be distinguished from the formal legal and institutional term 'supranational'; the latter refers to the formal structures of European politics, the former to actors and organizations within them. The effect is that the institutionalization of a range of policy competencies at supranational level means that to talk about 'transnationalism' in the EU context is to talk about understanding the specific sources of 'social power' enabled to specific people or organizations by European integration.

Given the highly intergovernmental nature of much European co-operation on immigration and asylum, it is plausible to start from the position that existing national institutions and patterns of interests alone define constraints and opportunities over policy-making in any new sector such as immigration. This could rule out space for new forms of transnational action to occur. That said, the very logic of using co-operative European fora in this way may create its own institutionalizing dynamic, regardless of the strictly national-interest based positions of national politicians and public officials. Co-operation on restrictive policy can still be a form of integration because routinization and elaboration of cross-national ties between the most nationalist public officials and politicians in the Brussels or Luxembourg context can lead to the Commission,

Parliament, and Court being drawn into these forms of European co-operation (Koslowski 1998). Immigration and asylum are far from being institutionalized at the EU level to the extent that free movement is, but new informal resources for other actors accrue from this incremental refocusing of activity. As we will see, the emergence of a pro-migrant NGO network in Brussels and Strasbourg is an example of this (Geddes 1998).

The stimulant for these new patterns of political activity are processes by which formal and informal resources associated with particular policy sectors begin, via their elaboration and discussion in the EU environment over time, to take more formalized meanings (Fligstein and Mara-Drita 1996; Wiener 1997). Processes of definition, redefinition, and elaboration of common interests become more than an intergovernmental process, and certain new relations can become routinized. A typical process of institutionalization has been the European Court's free movement and equal treatment logic. Thus by 'low' politics, such as legal rulings, jurisprudence and associated campaigning, funding, or directives, rather than the 'high' politics of intergovernmental treaties, or parliamentary business, actors are able to mobilize around and operationalize the new informal opportunities and pressures for their formal institutionalization in both low and high arenas. Typically, this results in lobbying activity directed towards the Commission as the privileged interlocutor in processes of elaboration of interests at EU level. It is important to view the Commission as a 'multi-organization' with internal conflicts of interest among even those committed to extend the remit of its powers away from the nation-state (Hooghe 1997). There is some convergence on 'Euro-norms' linked to the Commission's role as the putative engine of European integration—and associated socialisation processes—but the organization on the whole can be competitive across sectors: especially those that ambiguously fall across different DGs and institutional competencies, such as free movement, immigration, and asylum.

In circumstances where the establishment of supranational legal and political authority generates policy outcomes that extend and develop intergovernmental deals as a result of additional legislative activity and executive authority at the EU level, then EU institutions amount to more than a neutral repository of member-state policy preferences. The EU is more than a residual policy context subservient to national contexts. Initial intergovernmental deals between member-states can have a range of intended and unintended effect that could go beyond these intergovernmental deals because supranational institutions, particularly the Court and the Commission, acquire capacity to shape policy outcomes (Burley and Mattli 1993; Pierson 1996; Pollack 1997; Stone Sweet and Sandholtz 1998).

We can then ask what forms of political action or organization might we expect to thrive at the EU level? The technocratic corridors of power in Brussels have specifically encouraged specialized lobby groups and networks with well-located Brussels offices, and have privileged the co-option of experts and special interests into technical committees which can articulate interests very different to national governments (Mazey and Richardson 1993; Aspinwall and Greenwood 1997). European integration has also placed a premium on specific legal forms of action, capitalizing on the role of the ECJ as the most dynamic arm of supranational power (Slaughter, StoneSweet, and Weiler 1998). Although one or two commentators have been moved to see new forms of action at EU level as 'élite social movements' (Fligstein and Mara-Drita 1996)— and hence as the mobilization of a new euro-élite campaigning against the order of power and privilege of élites at national levels (Favell 1998c)— transnational mobilization would ordinarily be sought in more conventional social movements terms. That is, as a public demonstration or conflict strategy, 'in the streets' so to speak; as a public protest movement against existing political institutions and patterns of power. Classic social movement type approaches to mobilization put the focus of mobilization on the action of marginal and excluded groups to force representation in political systems which silence or fail to represent their voices. Some recent work has been done along these lines by EU scholars, in search of transnational social movements enabled or provoked by the Europeanization of European politics. However, the 'Europeanization of conflict' identified by Tarrow (1995, 1998) only really shows that 'Europe' can now be used in the media as an effective rhetorical source of blame for public policy failures, in the same way that national governments routinely blame 'Brussels' for their own policy failures or impotence in the face of globalization processes; not that it has convincingly inspired or enabled any cross-border European mobilizations against the power of nation-states.

To search for new forms of contentious politics, or new patterns of EU level migrant or ethnic minority mobilization within the 'contentious politics' frame is likely to be a fruitless exercise because Europeanization is wrongly construed as opening opportunities for social movement type mobilization. In its classic argument, social movements were associated with the rise of the modern state, and the steady accumulation of powers by central government and legal institutions. Social movements mobilized in the margins for inclusion, gaining rights and incorporation in return for acquiescence to the social regime—a logic of the kind made famous by T. H. Marshall's (1950) study of citizenship in Britain. Behind this logic, inevitably, lay a vision of nation-state building and the social integration of all sectors of society in a common national identity (Crowley 1998). The projection of a similar line of development—all too common in the many worried counterfactual reflections on European 'identity' or democracy, for example, the influential work of Weiler (1998)—is a misleading misrepresentation of the EU as an emergent 'state-like' thing on a par with national liberal democratic states. Its flawed teleological normative logic sees the movement of European politics as one towards more democratization and the emergence of a unified European public sphere, as the preliminary to the ultimate emergence of a (legitimate, democratic) European superstate. Empirically speaking, European integration upsets this 'teleological account' of modern nation-states and social change. Much of the recent reflection on the 'nature of the beast' has argued that European integration actually requires a new vocabulary of political analysis that is not entirely associated with the stable reference points of politics in the traditional national state, which locks us into a misleading replication of nationally bounded debates about representation, mobilization, and power (Schmitter 1996; Risse 1996). It might be more appropriate to think of the EU as a post-modern or regulatory rather than Westphalian state (Caporaso 1996; Majone 1996) where European integration opens 'fields' of action in a state of definition, which are not fully controlled by the intergovernmental actors that created them. Actors who successfully invest in the European level of action also try to pull up the drawbridge behind them, by defining themselves in relation to other specifically Euro-policy networks and insider contacts. They simultaneously try to extend the powers of the European field, in rivalry with the national level political actors, bureaucrats, lawyers and so on, who previously would have monopolized political activity in any given sector.

Looking for Transnational 'Ethnic Mobilization' in Europe

Few studies of supposedly transnational 'ethnic' mobilizations in Europe actually recognize these constraints in their discussions. The structuring role of institutions, and the interplay between these structures and actors at the EU level that defines policies and issues, is a key determining factor delimiting the range of migration-related political action enabled by European integration. So, although there has been a strong 'Europeanization' of ethnic and racial studies (for example, see King 1993; Wrench and Solomos 1993; Baldwin-Edwards and Schain 1994; Rex and Drury 1994; Miles and Thränhardt 1995; Cesarini and Fulbrook 1996; Modood and Werbner 1997) there has also been some distraction caused by the superficial normative rhetoric of European integration.

One problem with these approaches has been that the emptiness of 'European citizenship' provisions is routinely pointed to as an example of a 'democratic deficit', and the problem of legitimacy, that could be remedied by an improved 'recognition' of cultural and racial diversity (Martiniello 1994; Rex 1995; Brewin 1998; Kastoryano 1998a; Kostakopoulou 1998). The application of this strongly normative model of multicultural change to 'Europe' as a whole tends not to reflect the sources of legal, political, and social power opened up by European integration that are, in fact, closely associated with the requirements for constructing a single market and EMU. The hybrid, multi-levelled, and uneven institutional nature of the EU does, in fact, throw up new opportunities and constraints in places where the European integration process leads to a differentiation, and disintegration, of the political system, and new spaces of autonomous action for certain political groups in relation to specific sources of legal, political, and social power. The task is to be specific about what these sources are.

A second problem has been the misplaced location of the sources of social power and successful collective action—and hence the motor of social change—in the mobilization of 'difference'. That is, ethnic groups which have successfully pushed for improved recognition within the multicultural state— an often cited example being Islamic organizations in Europe—are said to have done so by mobilizing cultural, racial, or religious 'identity' as a collective force. This utilization of ethnic identities as explaining migrant mobilizations is flawed, because ethnicity may only be a successful mobilizing force under certain institutional conditions. Ireland (1994) identifies the importance of 'institutional channeling' of ostensibly ethnic mobilization. Similarly, Soysal (1994) stresses the importance of 'institutional repertoires' in countries of immigration. These institutionalist perspectives can usefully be applied to the EU level to explain how, why, and under what conditions new patterns of EU level political activity emerge. This political activity may or may not have an ethnic component. The task is to be specific about the institutional context that may or may not give meaning to ostensibly ethnic forms of political action. A very good example of this is the EU's Migrant's Forum, which, as shown later in this chapter, could be construed as an example of ethnic mobilization. In reality, however, it serves as an example of a standard form of EU level inter- est co-option, and accords with fairly standard EU level attempts to inculcate participation and consultation as a device for imparting an air of legitimacy to institutional processes.

In the one or two examples of studies that have explicitly looked for transna- tional ethnic mobilization in the new European context, both of the two errors identified above have been made. Kastoryano (1998b) reads an emerging transnational multicultural state into the European integration process, and connects it with a range of successful transnational 'ethnic' mobilizations that in fact have little grounding in actual European institutional developments. Here, a highly idealized, normative idea of an emergent 'European citizenship' is doing all the explanatory work; an idea of European citizenship that has little or no basis in the rather empty legal status of European citizenship which exists in European treaties. Meanwhile, in earlier, EU-focused studies by Soysal (1993) and Ireland (1991), the emerging European institutions and patterns of co- operation are misleadingly read as offering a fertile, preferential ground for new 'ethnic' based mobilizations, seeking to address claims to European level insti- tutions rather than traditional national ones. This overestimates what the EU, as an institutionalized 'state' power, can actually do, as well as wrongly inferring that it is naturally progressive in its leanings on immigrant or ethnic politics.

Successful transnational mobilization, such as Islamic protest movements across Europe (Blom 1999), Turkish political organizations (Amiraux 1998; Ögelman 1998), or new cultural identities based on transnational media (Hargreaves and Mahjoub 1997), in fact only have a coincidental connection with the European integration process. What none of these approaches reveals is anything specifically European about the emergent transnational opportunity structures they use, whether material or symbolic in kind. The emergence of the EU is indeed an example of a 'shift' in the post-World War II state system that has enabled new forms of post-national claims-making (Soysal 1994). But there are, after all, several other emergent 'supranational' institutions and institutional contexts that can be more plausibly pointed to as the ultimate sources of transnational empowerment beyond existing nation-state opportunity structures; none of these are specifically EU-related in nature. First, are shifts in the global political economy, opening new opportunities for transnational business and forms of organization (Sassen 1991; Portes 1997). Second, are shifts in the geo-political balance of world politics and international relations, such as the rise in prominence of Islam, and its increasing attraction as a pole of opposition to the hegemonic powers of the West (Ahmed 1992). Third, are shifts in international legal norms which, backed by universalistic international structures such as the UN, have provided new sources of justification for claims-making (Soysal 1997). These, indeed, may have some grounding in more diffuse 'universalistic' norms about personhood or equal rights of cultural difference, as claimed by some sociological institutionalists (Meyer et al. 1997; Boli and Thomas 1997).

The claim, then, that there was something specifically in the European integration process—either the formal institutions created or the new symbolic euro-ideas they give rise to—which has enabled some ethnic groups to mobilize transnationally, remains a theoretical assertion, not yet backed by any specific findings. Indeed, more recent work offers empirical refutation of such readings. A 1998 study shows that different ethnic groups in Italy and Spain have vastly different successes in organization in relation to supposed new European opportunities, which in fact depend on the help of go-between advocacy groups such as trades unions and the church (Danese 1998). Moreover, the organizational behaviour of different ethnic groups is still strongly structured by national political structures and/or the nature of local opportunities; and, despite a great deal of talk about new European opportunities, there is a clear underinvestment in the European level, or worse, the EU remains remote and uninteresting, indeed irrelevant, to these ethnic group's self-perceived interests. Other scholars show that, in empirical terms, Europe has not and does not yet really provide formal 'European' transnational sources of power for ethnic groups themselves (Guiraudon 1997, 1998; Koopmans and Statham, this volume). They find that the explanation of mobilization is invariably national in location, and most likely to do with party cleavages, the depoliticization of immigration politics by élites, and the structure of national level conflicts over the content and meaning of national citizenship.

In other words, to go out looking for ethnic transnational mobilization enabled by Europe is to put the cart a long way before the horse. There is little empirical evidence of it; and where opportunities exist for European-level political action, they are not necessarily salient for migrant and minority groups themselves. Transnationalism associated with the immigration issue at the European level still needs to be specified in terms of the actual structure of European institutions; and when it claims to be of an 'ethnic' nature, it should not always be taken at face value.

The Institutional Structure of EU Immigration Politics

A core component of our argument in this chapter is the requirement to closely specify the institutional context in order to understand new patterns of political activity that may emerge in relation to EU free movement, immigration, and asylum competencies. The risk is that such an approach lapses into Euro-jargon that is difficult for the non-EU specialist to untangle. We aim, therefore, to extract broader points about the relation between institutionalization of policy competencies and the development of new forms of transnational political action, and illustrate our points with examples of pro-migrant political activity at the EU level.

The components of a pro-migrant agenda at the EU level are closely related to EU market-making. The EU is an economic organization from which social and political competencies may arise, not *vice versa*. Free movement is a core component of market-making. Pro-migrant groups have sought to extend to legally resident third country nationals similar rights of free movement to those enjoyed by EU citizens. The EU's free movement framework has established a triangular relationship between EU citizens, the member-states, and EU institutions wherein individuals are empowered by being given access to EU institutions that constrain the competence and discretion of member states (Guild 1998). It is this relationship that distinguishes the EU from international organizations such as the Council of Europe that are not capable of creating such legal effects. Can this triangular relationship also be extended to third country nationals so that they too enjoy rights of free movement? Another key aspect of the agenda is the extension of anti-discrimination provisions to extend existing provisions from their coverage of nationality and gender based discrimination to also include racial-, ethnic-, and religious-based discrimination, irrespective of whether those discriminated against are EU citizens. The key issue here is equal treatment, enshrined in EC law by a 1976 directive. Key pro-migrant organizations in relation to these issues are the Starting Line Group and the EU Migrant's Forum. A further aspect of the agenda is the efforts made by groups such as Amnesty, the European Council on Refugees and Exiles, and Caritas to secure EU asylum provisions that accord with international standards.

The commitment to market-making and free movement has always been countered by a marked reluctance on the part of some member-states to countenance transfers to the European level of immigration and asylum responsibilities. Despite this, single market integration has drawn immigration and asylum closer to the evolving web of supranational interdependence because the creation of a single market defined by Article 8a of the Single European Act (1986) as 'an area without internal frontiers' means that immigration and asylum policy became matters of common concern. Attainment of freer movement for people has required 'compensating' immigration and asylum measures, but this requirement does not dictate the form that these measures will take—whether they will be supranational or intergovernmental or whether they are inside the formal treaty structure or, as was originally the case with the Schengen Agreement, outside it. Nevertheless, patterns of co-operation have led immigration and asylum to become Europeanized issues, even if by a less intentional backdoor route. Moreover, this development imparts fluidity to the nascent co-operative structures, which may offer opportunities for entrepreneurial actors interested in opening up new European level opportunities.

It would be wrong to characterize immigration and asylum co-operation as exclusively by-products of single market liberalization. Co-operation on aspects of immigration policy has also built upon the security co-operation between interior ministries and their officials, that developed in relation to customs from the late 1960s and developed into anti-terrorism/crime co-operation from the mid-1970s through the Trevi Group. Patterns of security co-operation are long established, and the structures for immigration and asylum co-operation have therefore drawn heavily from the model for co-operation established for internal security.

The recent history of evolving immigration and asylum policy can, then, be read in terms of these general structuring principles and tensions that are clearly evident in the Treaty of Amsterdam, which came into force on May 1 1999. The Amsterdam Treaty imports the Schengen arrangements into the Union and make provisions for the establishment of a new Treaty chapter dealing with free movement, immigration, and asylum. Free movement, immigration and asylum have been 'communitarized' in the sense that they have been brought into the main institutional framework of the Union and within the remit of the Commission and Court. Member-states have, though, maintained the machinery of intergovernmental co-operation that typified co-operation on these issues in the 1980s and 1990s.

Some observers have stressed that migration is mainly subsumed within a security paradigm, within which emphasis is placed on the development of the legislative apparatus technologies of cross-national population control (Bigo 1998; Huysmans 1995). But the Amsterdam Treaty's chapter on free movement, immigration, and asylum has established potential connections between free movement, market liberalization and immigration/asylum with implications for migrant inclusion.

Mobilizing for EU Level Migrant Inclusion

Following this brief overview of recent developments we can now examine who is able to successfully engage with these new opportunities for action, what forms of organization this action takes, what strategies are deployed, and how these groups seek to build alliances with EU institutions. As is now common in much POS based theory, we define the opportunity structure as a political and legal combination of 'material' resources—formalized resources of power or funding—and 'symbolic' ones—sources of normative and discursive power (see McAdam, McCarthy, and Zald 1996).

Most of the new forms of action associated with European integration in this sector are élite and technocratic in nature: this is an inescapable feature of the EU institutional context. Bottom-up mobilization and participation of all kinds are limited by the EU's lack of channels for democratic representation. It would, however, be wrong to conclude that this situation will automatically reinforce 'fortress Europe' tendencies that lead to migrant exclusion, because there are also tendencies of inclusion well established in the EU's institutionalized activities. In fact, the oft-cited argument that European integration has strengthened the fortress Europe tendency is weakened by the observation that pro-migrant groups at EU level tend to call for *more* not *less* integration. Extended supranational competencies are viewed as a potential progressive counterbalance to lowest common denominator Council decision-making, portrayed as focused on restrictive immigration policies and ever tougher asylum procedures.

In addition to the legal, political, and institutional context, 'Europe' also provides certain symbolic resources. On the 'security' side, the fortress Europe metaphor offers significant discursive resources to those seeking to accrue powers or mobilize opinion through immigration-related fears. That is, in the encouragement of a 'crisis' atmosphere over immigration and asylum—and the representation of such flows as a security threat—security focused officials and anti-immigration politicians can draw on a good deal of capital through promoting the idea that a fortress needs to be built to protect European welfare systems, or national models of democracy etc.

In other, more 'progressive' Europeanized circles, however, the idea of immigration is no less of a resource-stimulating area of policy activity. In some areas of European integration the 'regulatory' character of policy has always created scope for 'entrepreneurialism' by supranational level actors when legal and political competencies are established and a significant margin of autonomy for action has developed (Majone 1996). In such circumstances, the Commission can become a 'purposeful opportunist' (Cram 1996) emboldened by the material and symbolic resources associated with European integration to push new policy lines in different sectors. Particularly relevant in this respect are the resources associated with the quest for 'social inclusion'. The EU's social dimension has become more evident since the mid-1980s and has provided significant legal, political, and symbolic resources for EU institutions keen to promote a 'people's Europe'. So far, however, third country nationals have been largely excluded from this dimension because access to EU level entitlements has arisen from prior possession of the nationality of a member-state. From this perspective, a 'cure' for fortress Europe, the democratic deficit and social exclusion is *more* Europe—albeit often conceived as an unrealistic, counterfactual ideal of a democratic, multicultural, citizenship-grounded transnational polity. The underlying argument here, then, is not that the process of European integration *per se* is the problem; rather the problem is the actual form taken by immigration and asylum co-operation. The basic confusion in the anti-EU, pro-Europe argument may be intentional—it works in the same away as a national government's ability to generate symbolic resources by blaming the EU for its own impotence or failures—or it may indicate a basic ignorance of how the EU institutions in fact work, and how successful campaign groups do in fact get involved in the policy process. As long as people conceive of the EU in counterfactual normative terms that have little to do with the way the institutions actually work, they will keep making this mistake. Whatever is developed at the supranational level on immigration and asylum is more likely to arise because of an association with market-making and the commitment to free movement rather than from idealistic conceptions of European citizenship or multicultural democracy. The EU cannot be characterized as a social and political actor separate from its fundamental economic purposes. To characterize it as a social and political actor which can or should have an interest in promoting a transnational 'citizenship utopia', leads commentators and campaigners to project on to it problems and issues that it is simply not equipped to resolve.

That said, a growing awareness of the ways in which notions of social inclusion impinge on 'migrant inclusion' has informed the actions of EU institutions. Numerous DGs have now also opened activities relating to immigration and/or the position of minorities in Europe. DG5 (Employment and Social Affairs), DG10 (Information, Communication, and Culture) and DG12 (Science, Research, and Development), in particular, have been very active. Latterly, the Third Pillar Task Force and the Forward Studies Unit of the Secretariat have published reports on immigration policy, or tendered substantial sums of money for new research in this area. These entrepreneurial efforts have followed a familiar pattern of co-opting experts into the policy community—including academics, existing NGOs, public officials and so on—and some attempt at public awareness campaigning and localized activities such as multicultural activities associated with the European Cultural Capitals programme.

Moreover, because Brussels is a small world there are only a handful of people with direct responsibility within the Commission, and so strong personal contacts in Brussels can quickly lead to a prominent role in policy development circles. A small new 'field' is emerging of specialist policy campaigners—usually self-styled euro-NGOs—who have been able to monopolize European-level policy thinking, such as the production of reports or the organizing of conferences, through their well-located awareness of key contacts and specialized know-how needed to be effective in the Brussels environment (see Favell 1998c). Among those with a strong interest in immigration and migrants' rights are ECAS (European Citizenship Action Service) and the Migration Policy Group. Although organized as small-scale offices these organizations do provide an important port of access for wider nationally-based networks of activists and campaigners. Their achievements, though, are very far from substantiating the claimed existence of transnational ethnic mobilization in this policy sector. Rather they provide further evidence of the deployment of expert knowledge in an institutional environment that privileges technocratic avenues to influence.

A central focus of efforts to establish these measures was during the 1996/97 pre-Amsterdam Treaty intergovernmental conference, in which a whole plethora of campaign groups, with well-established insider positions, were able to push for new migrant and minority rights, alongside other well-heard 'citizenship' issues such as gender equality and the environment (Mazey and Richardson 1998). Pro-migrant organizations expressed some dissatisfaction with the outcome. The European Council on Refugees and Exiles characterized the establishment of a new chapter 4 of the EU Treaty that dealt with free movement, immigration, and asylum as a 'technical transfer' without the kinds of checks, in terms of Commission, European Court, and European Parliament powers, that they had called for. The new anti-discrimination provision was a cause of dissatisfaction too. It did not *forbid* discrimination on grounds of race, ethnicity, religion, age, disability, or sexual orientation. Rather, it empowered the Commission to bring forward proposals in these areas that needed then to be agreed to by unanimity among the member-states in the Council.

Pro-migrant groups have been keen to exploit new opportunities. They have sought extension of the provisions of the legal framework governing the single market to offer more extensive protection to migrants and their descendants. In 1998, the Starting Line Group (SLG) brought forward a draft directive on the rights of third country nationals that would have had the effect of creating a 'resident's charter': after three years legal residence third country nationals would acquire the same rights of free movement as EU citizens (SLG 1998). The SLG's proposals actually drew from a very specific resource, the 1964 association agreement between Turkey and the EU, which extends established rights to Turks resident in an EU member-state. The SLG posed the question that if such rights were extended to Turks then why couldn't they be open to all third country nationals? The SLG was not ploughing a lone furrow. The Commission's draft convention on the rights of third country nationals also indicated a willingness at Commission level to promote developments in this area as the post-Amsterdam allocation of responsibilities for free movement, immigration, and asylum plays itself out (CEC 1997).

The Starting Line Group also brought forward new proposals for anti-discrimination legislation. The original rationale had been the 1976 equal treatment directive, which sought to guarantee gender equality. In the wake of Amsterdam's new anti-discrimination provisions, the SLG brought forward proposals that would protect people—whether citizens of a member states or not—from discrimination when exercising rights associated with European integration. The major impediment to developments in the areas of extended residence rights and anti-discrimination is the requirement for unanimity in the Council and the diverse and patchy frameworks of anti-discrimination legislation in EU member states that render problematic intergovernmental agreement on supranational action (European Parliament 1998).

In the area of asylum too, there has been rapid development of lobbying activity during the 1990s. The intention is not so much to include asylum seekers—who by definition are not migrants with an intention to settle permanently—but to include the EU's asylum provisions within the scope of EU law with jurisdiction for the European Court. The hope is that the Court will be a progressive guarantor of asylum rights in an era when the international standards laid down in the post-war period appear threatened by move towards systems of 'temporary protection' (ECRE 1997a, 1997b, 1997c).

Clearly, it is difficult to categorize any of this worthy activity as ethnic mobilization. The one direct attempt by the Commission to create an ethnic 'forum' for direct representation within the European institutions—the European Union Migrants' Forum—has fared much less happily. A large amount of money was invested by DG5 in creating this consultative body drawn from national-level associations in order to give migrants and minorities a voice at the European level. The EUMF's early years were, however, dogged by inter-ethnic conflict over the goals and strategy of the Forum, a financial scandal amongst the executive, and an overwhelming sense of the operation as a well-meaning but ineffective sounding box, in which a few migrant élites got to voice their anger at well-funded conferences, but without it leading to any direct impact in the policy process. Similar things might be said about the European Year Against Racism of 1997, in which a large range of funding was spent unevenly on local projects often monopolized by go-between groups and immigrant entrepreneurs, with a weak claim to be representative of migrant and minority interests on the whole. As with many other areas of EU intervention, good intentions are hampered by corrupt and uneven implementation at the national and local levels. Very little grassroots activity has been directly inspired by the EU's material or symbolic resources, and it remains an area of policy firmly monopolized by the élite gatekeepers working in the shadow of the Commission; much to the anger, for example, of other local Brussels-based Belgian campaign groups and migrants associations, who are most conscious of being excluded from the benefits flowing to other parts of the city.

Given, as we have argued, that market-making is a key force underpinning arguments for more inclusionary tendencies in migration policy, it is surprising to note the absence in the past, of any significant business-led pressures for expansion in this policy sector. The fact that transnational corporations have always been active in Brussels makes this all the more surprising. Further down the line, then, there is still the possibility that the dynamics of the European labour market and business interests—as they did in the post-war boom years and the age of the guestworker—will start to have the clout within the EU agenda to push for more open immigration policies. This is a major point of difference between Europe and the US/NAFTA, where a sizeable right wing pro-immigration lobby has always pushed for open borders and the import of cheap labour from Mexico and elsewhere (Freeman 1995). Perhaps on smaller, local level there is evidence for this: such as the Berlin labour market influencing new, pragmatic bilateral agreements between Germany and Poland; or seasonal labour needs in Spain or Italy pushing regularization efforts by their respective governments. The involvement of transnational business interests in this way could indeed provide a decisive shift in the balance of powers in immigration policy, moving away from the intergovernmental to supranational level. To incorporate an awareness of the underlying structural labour market factors in determining population movements, would also be a significant step towards a more rational European immigration policy; a policy which at present is so hamstrung between opposite but complementary ideological arguments about inviolable national interests and sovereignty on the one hand, and a transnational, multicultural Euro-idealism, on the other.

Conclusion: Europeanization Versus Globalization

The Europeanization of immigration politics in Europe brings with it a fundamental challenge to one of the defining characteristics of the European nation-state: its powers of self-definition and authority over a territorially bounded population (Joppke 1998). The powers of the state—and the institutions of law, democracy, welfare it sustains—were centralized through this exclusive process of identity formation. Immigration and the integration of newcomers in the post-war period has previously followed this pattern in most European nations (Brubaker 1992; Favell 1998a). All of the above is thrown into question by the establishment of supranational powers and jurisdiction over immigration questions at the EU level.

We have argued that, empirically, it makes sense to look for a distinct European 'transnational opportunity structure' in the immigration policy sector, only where specific channels and sources of empowerment have begun to be *institutionalized*. These are limited, and as yet exclusive to organized élite groups putting the accent on technocratic and judicial channels of campaigning. These efforts may indeed contribute to challenging European nation-states' control over immigration, and to national models of migrant inclusion, but they cannot be said to contribute to better democracy or citizenship-style inclusion for migrants and minorities in Europe. In fact, they can be said to be positively damaging to the value of national citizenship as it is understood at the national level, because new 'postnational' rights, such as those based on residence, will render national citizenship less meaningful, less identity forming, more instrumental, and more incidental for migrants. If, however, the response to this is to move back towards an idea of European citizenship premised on naturalization and incorporation, control over new populations would be returned back to the nation-state, and thus the European integration process that had opened up 'new opportunities' would be reversed in favour of the old Marshallian option which can see nothing beyond national identity formation as the background to social change (see Hansen 1998; Weil 1996). Indeed, at the point at which it stands, the current, empty, nation-state-derived idea of EU citizenship only reinforces this older idea of national membership and belonging.

Within the strictly delimited picture of EU integration we have offered, what kind of transnational opportunities remain for a true migrant- or minority-led mobilization? The symbolic resources provided by the emergent idea of Europe should perhaps prove the most fertile source. However, 'transnational claims-making' is as yet more backed up by other more obvious 'transnational structures' than the limited European context. Indeed, were the Europeanization of immigration and asylum to be fully institutionalized at the supranational level, it would probably prove directly damaging to the kinds of universalistic, global values powering visions of post-national membership: European-bounded rights and membership is not same thing as human rights or a world community.

The question, of course, remains as to how far the supranationalizing tendency will be institutionalized at the European level with consequent effects for migrant inclusion. If they are to develop then, rights for third country nationals are likely to be associated with the logic of free movement and its connection with market-making. If this space were to be opened, it would provide a strong impetus to transnational communities interested in rights derived from residency in two or more countries, particularly if these rights are linked to the growing acceptance of dual citizenship (Freeman and Ögelman 1998). There is a very anti-Marshallian kind of idea at work here: the idea that certain rights might be given to resident workers of the European free market, unconditional on nationality, belonging, moral investment in the nation, or even nation-state welfare contributions (Bommes and Geddes 2000). These are interesting possibilities for those ethnic groups most able to organize themselves transnationally, and whose support networks and business networks in any case stretch across their nations of residence and back and forth to their homeland. Were these opportunities to develop, they may well open up a form of symbolic legitimation of action not at all grounded in the old equality and justice-based logic of inclusion and incorporation, that has been at the heart of most classic social movements style campaigning.

What this underlines ultimately, is that European integration is a particular type of internationalizing process: the institution-building process of a specifically *regional* cross-national co-operative entity. European integration is the political supranationalization of sovereignty, over certain political powers and a specifically European 'geographical' space, and over an uneven range of policy sectors and law, that is both responding to *globalizing* transnational processes and associated powers—particularly those led by international capital—while, at the same time, creating new political and legal institutions which formalize the possibility of transnational action of a specifically delimited European kind. The essentially ambiguous dynamic of the European integration process lies here: in that it is caused by globalization, an attempt to harness globalization, and in some sense a campaign against globalization. This also leaves the EU in a paradoxical relation with other forms of transnationalism, such as the global environment or human rights movements. As a regional entity— between nation-state and united nations—European institutions and Europeanization often cut across and/or contradict these universalising movements and the universalistic norms they are built on: for example, those often said to be behind progressive changes by IR scholars in the idealist tradition (e.g. Klotz 1995).

This last point may pose severe difficulties for NGOs and other idealist-based social movements who ground their *raison d'être* in universal ethical norms of this kind. Europeanization in the end leads to a rather different form of transnational action and legitimation. To date, most progressive minded campaigning on immigration issues in Europe has grounded its arguments in ethical norms, that are either based on a logic of citizenship grounded in nation-state incorporation—and therefore not transnational at all—or on a logic of universal personhood which is global, and not connected to the specific European context. Our argument suggests that both of these strategies are ineffective and poorly suited for seizing the dynamics of European integration. Campaigners would do much better to push for a rational immigration policy that seeks to reconnect policy with the labour market mechanisms and market-building needs that are actually a primary cause of migration flows. Were this to happen—were, in other words, Europeanization genuinely be seen to truly enable claims-making in virtue of being a non-national resident worker of a European common market—the possibility of membership beyond the nation-state may still turn out to true. But an extraordinary European development such as this, would also entail that the transnational rights of non-nationals in Europe are established at the expense of the most distant, global 'ethical' norms and values that have been hitherto seen as the grounding for effective transnational social and political action.

References

AHMED, AKBAR (1992), *Postmodernism and Islam: Predicament and Promise* (London: Routledge).

AMIRAUX, VALERIE (1998), 'Transnationalism as a resource for Turkish Islamic associations in Germany'. Paper presented to the European Forum on International Migrations, European University Institute, Florence, 5 March.

ASPINWALL, MARK, and GREENWOOD, JUSTIN (eds.) (1997), *Collective Action in the European Union: Interests and the New Politics of Associability* (London: Routledge).

BALDWIN-EDWARDS, MARTIN, and SCHAIN, MARTIN (1994), *The Politics of Immigration in Western Europe* (London: Cass).

BIGO, DIDIER (1998), 'Europe passoire et Europe forteresse: la sécuritisation/humanitarisation de l'immigration', in Andrea Rea (ed.), *Immigration et racisme en Europe* (Brussels: Editions Complexe).

BLOM, AMÉLIE (1999), 'Is there such a thing as transnational belonging?', in Andrew Geddes and Adrian Favell (eds.), *The Politics of Belonging: Migrants and Minorities in Contemporary Europe* (Aldershot: Ashgate).

BOLI, JOHN, and THOMAS, GEORGE (1997), 'World culture in the world polity: a century of international non-governmental organization', *American Sociological Review*, 62/2: 171–90.

BOMMES, MICHAEL, and GEDDES, ANDREW (2000), *Immigration and the Welfare State in Contemporary Europe* (London: Routledge).

BREWIN, CHRISTOPHER (1997), 'Society as a kind of community: communitarian voting with equal rights for individuals in the European Union' in Tariq Modood and Pnina Werbner (eds.), *The Politics of Multiculturlism in the New Europe* (London: Zed Books).

BRUBAKER, ROGERS (1992), *Citizenship and Nationhood in France and Germany* (Cambridge, MA: Harvard University Press).

BURLEY, ANNE-MARIE, and MATTLI, WALTER (1993), 'Europe before the court: a political theory of legal integration', *International Organization*, 47/1: 41–76.

CAPORASO, JAMES (1996), 'The European Union and forms of state: Westphalian, regulatory or post-modern?', *Journal of Common Market Studies*, 34/1: 29–52.

CEC (1997), *Proposal for a Decision on Establishing a Convention on Rules for the Admission of Third Country Nationals to the Member States of the European Union*, COM (97) 387 final (Brussels: OOPEU).

CESARINI, DAVID, and FULBROOK, MARY (eds.) (1996), *Citizenship, Nationality and Migration in Europe* (London: Routledge).

COX, ROBERT (1986), *Production, Power and World Order: Social Forces in the Making of History* (New York, NY: Columbia University Press).

CRAM, LAURA (1996), 'Integration theory and the study of the European policy process', in Jeremy Richardson (ed.), *European Union: Power and Policy-Making* (London: Routledge).

CROWLEY, JOHN (1998), 'The national dimension in T. H. Marshall', *Citizenship Studies*, 2/2.

DANESE, GAIA (1998), 'The European transnational collective action of migrants: the case of Italy and Spain', in Favell (1998b: 715–33).

ECRE (1997a), *Position on the Functioning of the Treaty on European Union in Relation to Asylum Policy* (Brussels: ECRE).

——(1997b), *Analysis of the Treaty of Amsterdam in so far as it Relates to Asylum Policy* (Brussels: ECRE).

——(1997c), *Comments from ECRE on the Proposal of the European Commission Concerning Temporary Protection of Displaced Persons* (Brussels: ECRE).

EUROPEAN PARLIAMENT (1998), *EU Anti-Discrimination Policy: From Equal Opportunities Between Men and Women to Combating Racism*, European Parliament Directorate General for Research, Public Liberties Series Working Document, LIBE 102 EN (Brussels: European Parliament).

FAVELL, ADRIAN (1998a), *Philosophies of Integration: Immigration and the Idea of Citizenship in France and Britain* (London: Macmillan; New York, NY: St.Martin's Press).

——(ed.) (1998b), 'The European Union: Immigration, Asylum and Citizenship', *Journal of Ethnic and Migration Studies*, 24/4 (sp. edn.).

——(1998c), 'The Europeanisation of immigration politics', in *European Integration online Papers (EIoP)*, 2/10, http://eiop.or.at/eiop/texte/1998-010.htm.

FLIGSTEIN, NEIL, and MARA-DRITA, IONA (1996), 'How to make a market: reflections on the attempt to create a single market in the European Union', *American Journal of Sociology*, 102/1: 1–33.

——and McNICHOL, JASON (1998), 'The institutional terrain of the EU', in Alec Stone Sweet and Wayne Sandholtz (eds.), *European Integration and Supranational Governance* (Oxford: Oxford University Press).

FREEMAN, GARY (1995), 'Modes of immigration politics in liberal democratic societies', *International Migration Review*, 29/4: 881–913.

——and ÖGELMAN, NEDIM (1998), 'Homeland citizenship policies and the status of third country nationals in the European Union' in Favell (1998b: 769–880).

GEDDES, ANDREW (1998), 'The representation of "migrants" interests' in the EU' in Favell (1998b).

GEDDES, ANDREW (2000), *European Integration and Immigration: Towards Fortress Europe?* (Manchester: Manchester University Press).

GUILD, ELSPETH (1998), 'Competence, discretion and third country nationals: the EU's legal struggle with migration' in Favell (1998b: 613–26).

GUIRAUDON, VIRGINIE (1997), *Policy Change Behind Gilded Doors: Explaining the Evolution of Aliens' Rights in Contemporary Western Europe*, Ph. D. Harvard University, Department of Government.

——(1998), 'Third country nationals and European law: obstacles to rights' expansions', in Favell (1998b: 657–74).

HANSEN, RANDALL (1998), 'A European citizenship or a Europe of citizens?' in Favell (1998b: 751–68).

HARGREAVES, ALEC and MAHJOUB, DALILA (1997), 'Satellite television viewing among ethnic minorities in France', *European Journal of Communication*, 1214.

HIX, SIMON (1998), 'The study of the European Union II: the "new governance" agenda and its rival', *Journal of European Public Policy*, 5/1: 38–65.

HOOGHE, LIESBET (1997), 'Serving "Europe": Political orientations of senior commission officials', *European on-line Integration Papers*, http://eiop.or.at./eiop/texte/1997-008a.htm.

HUYSMANS, JEFF (1995), 'Migrants as a security problem: dangers of "securitizing" societal issues', in Robert Miles and Dietrich Thränhardt (eds.), *Migration and European Integration* (London: Pinter).

IRELAND, PATRICK (1991), 'Facing the true "fortress Europe": immigrants and politics in the EC', *Journal of Common Market Studies*, 24/5: 457–80.

——(1994), *The Policy Challenge of Ethnic Diversity* (Cambridge, MA: Harvard University Press).

JOPPKE, CHRISTIAN (ed.) (1998), *Challenge to the Nation-State: Immigration in Western Europe and North America* (Oxford: Oxford University Press).

——(1999), *Immigration and the Nation-State: The United States, Germany, and Great Britain* (Oxford: Oxford University Press).

KASTORYANO, RIVA (ed.) (1998a), *Quelle identité pour l'Europe? Le multiculturalisme à l'épreuve* (Paris: Presses de Sciences Politiques).

——(1998b), 'Transnational participation and citizenship: immigrants inside the European Union', *Transnational Communities on-line working paper series* WPTC-98-12, http://www.transcomm.oxford.ac.uk.

KING, RUSSELL (ed.) (1993), *Mass Migration in Europe: the Legacy and the Future* (London: Wiley).

KLOTZ, AUDIE (1995), *Norms in International Relations: The Struggle Against Apartheid* (Ithaca, NY: Cornell University Press).

KOSLOWSKI, REY (1998), 'European migration regimes: emerging, enlarging and deteriorating', in Favell (1998b: 735–50).

KOSTAKOPOULOU, THEODORA (1998), 'European citizenship and immigration after Amsterdam: openings, silences, paradoxes', in Favell (1998c).

MAJONE, GIANDOMENICO (ed.) (1996), *Regulating Europe* (London: Routledge).

MARSHALL, THOMAS H. (1950), *Citizenship and Social Class* (London: Pluto).

MARTINIELLO, MARCO (ed.) (1994), 'Citizenship of the European Union: a critical view', in Rainer Bauböck (ed.), *From Aliens to Citizens* (Aldershot: Avebury).

MAZEY, SONIA, and RICHARDSON, JEREMY (eds.) (1993), *Lobbying in the European Community* (Oxford: Oxford University Press).

————(1998), 'Agenda setting, lobbying and the 1996 IGC', in Geoff Edwards and Alfred Pijpers, *The Politics of European Treaty Reform: The 1996 IGC Negotiations and Beyond* (London: Pinter).

MCADAM, DOUG, MCCARTHY, JOHN, and ZALD, MAYER (eds.) (1996), *Comparative Perspectives on Social Movements: Political Opportunities, Mobilizing Structures and Cultural Framings* (Cambridge: Cambridge University Press).

MEYER, JOHN, BOLI, JOHN, THOMAS, GEORGE, and RAMIREZ, FRANCO (1997), 'World society and the nation state', *American Journal of Sociology*, 103: 144–81.

MILES, ROBERT, and THRÄNHARDT, DIETRICH (eds.) (1995), *Migration and European Integration* (London: Pinter).

MODOOD, TARIQ, and WERBNER, PNINA (eds.) (1997), *The Politics of Multiculturalism in the New Europe* (London: Zed Books).

ÖGELMAN, NEDIM (1998), 'Identity, organizations and the transnational political opportunity structure of Turkish-origin inhabitants of Germany'. Paper presented at the 11th International Conference of Europeanists. Baltimore, 26 February to 1 March.

PETERSON, JOHN (1995), 'Decision-making in the European Union: towards a framework for analysis', *Journal of European Public Policy*, 2/1: 69–93.

PIERSON, PAUL (1996), 'The path to European integration: an historical institutionalist analysis', *Comparative Political Studies*, 29/2: 123–63.

POLLACK, MARK (1997), 'Delegation, agency and agenda setting in the European Community', *International Organisation*, 51/1: 99–134.

PORTES, ALEJANDRO (1997), 'Immigration theory for a new century: some problems and opportunities', *International Migration Review*, 31/4: 799–825.

PUTNAM, ROBERT (1988), 'Diplomacy and domestic politics', *International Organization*, 42/3.

REX, JOHN (1995), 'Ethnic minorities and the nation state: The political sociology of multicultural societies', *Social Identities*, 1/1.

——and DRURY, BEATRICE (eds.) (1994), *Ethnic Mobilisation in a Multi-Cultural Europe* (Aldershot: Avebury).

RISSE, THOMAS (ed.) (1996), 'Exploring the nature of the beast: international relations theory and comparative policy analysis meet the European Union', *Journal of Common Market Studies*, 34/1: 53–80.

SASSEN, SASKIA (1991), *The Global City* (Princeton, NJ: Princeton University Press).

SCHMITTER, PHILIPPE (1996), 'Imagining the future of the Euro-polity with the help of new concepts' in Gary Marks, Fritz Scharpf, Philippe Schmitter and Wolfgang Streeck (eds.), *Multi-level Governance in the Emerging European Polity* (London: Sage).

SLAUGHTER, ANNE-MARIE, STONE SWEET, ALEC, and WEILER, JOSEPH (1998), *The European Court and the National Courts: Legal Challenge in its Local Context* (Oxford: Hart).

SOYSAL, YASEMIN (1993), 'Immigration and the emerging European polity', in Svein Anderson and Kjell Eliassen, *Making Policy in Europe: The Europification of National Policy Making* (London: Sage).

——(1994), *Limits of Citizenship. Migrants and Postnational Membership in Europe* (Chicago, IL: University of Chicago Press).

——(1997), 'Changing parameters of citizenship and claims-making: organized Islam in European public spheres', *Theory and Society*, 26/4: 509–27.

Starting Line Group (SLG) (1998), *Proposals for Legislative Measures to Combat Racism and the Promotion of Equal Rights* (Brussels: Starting Line Group).

STONE SWEET, ALEC, and SANDHOLTZ, WAYNE (eds.) (1998), *European Integration and Supranational Governance* (Oxford: Oxford University Press).

TARROW, SIDNEY (1995), 'The Europeanisation of conflict: reflections from a social movements perspective', *West European Politics*, 18/2: 223–51.

——(1998), *Power in Movement* (2nd ed) (Cambridge: Cambridge University Press).

WEIL, PATRICK (1996), 'Nationalities and citizenships: the lessons of the French experience for Germany and Europe', in David Cesarini and Mary Fulbrook (eds.), *Citizenship, Nationality and Migration in Europe* (London: Routledge).

WEILER, JOSEPH (1998), *The Constitution of Europe* (Cambridge: Cambridge University Press).

WIENER, ANTJE (1997), *European Citizenship Practice: Building Institutions of a Non-State* (Boulder, CO: Westview).

WINCOTT, DANIEL (1995), 'Institutional interaction and European integration: towards an everyday critique of liberal intergovernmentalism', *Journal of Common Market Studies*, 33/4: 597–609.

WRENCH, JOHN, and SOLOMOS, JOHN (eds.) (1993), *Racism and Migration in Western Europe* (Oxford: Berg).

Index

Europeanization 9, 18, 41, 389, 408, 411–12, 416, 421
European Migrants' Forum 43, 399, 402, 413, 416, 421
European Monitoring Centre for Racism and Xenophobia 133–4
European Monetary Union (EMU) 412
European Parliament 43, 132, 205, 219, 392, 399, 403, 410, 419
 Committee of Inquiry into the Rise of Racism and Fascism in Europe (1986) 132, 398
 Ford report (1991) 132, 393, 398
European Union, 391
 anti-racist legislation 132, 391, 393, 398–9, 407, 410, 415, 419–20
 as an addressee of migrant demands 212, 417–21
 CIREA Centre d'Information, de Recherche et d'Échange en Matière d'Asile 393
 Consultative Committee on Racism and Xenophobia 398–9
 convergence or divergence in immigration policies 13, 392
 democratic deficit 412
 DG5 Employment and Social Affairs 418
 DG10 Information, Communication, and Culture 418
 DG12 Science, Research, and Development 418
 dual citizenship 423
 Dublin Convention (1990) 41, 393
 Eurodoc Scheme 392
 European Citizenship Action Service 419
 European Cultural Capitals Programme 419
 European Forum on Social Policy (1996) 396
 external border controls 41, 393; see also Fortress Europe
 Forward Studies Unit of the Secretariat 418
 freedom of movement (labour) 391, 407, 410, 415, 422
 Freedom of Movement and Migration Policy Unit (DG5) 399
 funding NGOs 399
 immigration policies 1, 8–9, 13, 358, 389, 391–2, 400, 408, 415–17, 422–3

 intergovernmental co-operation 401, 416
 Maastricht Treaty (Treaty on European Union, 1992) 41, 61, 133
 Migration Policy Group 419
 Palma Document (1990) 393
 rights of entry 46
 representation of migrant and minority organizations 43, 419
 rights of third-country nationals 41, 271, 392, 407–8, 415, 418–19, 422
 Schengen Treaty (1985) 41, 192, 392, 416
 Single European Act (1986) 391, 416
 Social Charter 398
 social inclusion 418
 Third Pillar Task Force 418
 Treaty of Amsterdam (1997) 407, 416–17
 Treaty of Rome 399
 White Paper on Social Policy 399
European Year Against Racism (1997) 133, 400, 402, 420
extreme right 79, 119–141, 393
 communication, media, internet 140, 353–4, 361–2, 364, 372
 concept of 348, 351–2
 electoral breakthroughts/opportunities 7, 34, 348–67
 movements 32, 90, 329, 370
 political parties 1, 16, 23, 30, 34, 36, 67, 138, 348–67
 voting 7–8, 16, 58, 69, 139, 173, 294, 319, 348–50, 354–7, 360–4
 see also new right; repression; xenophobia

family reunification and formation 40
Fascism 16, 71, 120
Faurisson, Robert 126, 135
Favell, Adrian 9, 17, 31, 70
Federal Commission for Immigration Reform (United States) 151
Federal Consultative Commission for the Foreigners Problem (CFE/EKA, Switzerland) 266, 268
Féderation d'Action Nationale et Européenne (FANE) 128
Fennema, Meindert 4, 7
Flather, Baroness 399
Flemish Centre for the Integration of Migrants (Belgium) 254
Flemish Council for Migrants (VHRM, Belgium) 254
Flemish Front National 354

Printed in the United States
23797LVS00001B/27-42

9 780198 295617